TERRORISM IN PERSPECTIVE

Dedicated to

Helen L. Griset
and
Aubrey Anne Harlan

TERRORISM IN PERSPECTIVE

Pamala L. Griset
University of Central Florida

Sue Mahan
University of Central Florida at Daytona Beach

SAGE Publications
International Educational and Professional Publisher
Thousand Oaks ▪ London ▪ New Delhi

For information:

Sage Publications, Inc.
2455 Teller Road
Thousand Oaks, California 91320
E-mail: order@sagepub.com

Sage Publications Ltd.
6 Bonhill Street
London EC2A 4PU
United Kingdom

Sage Publications India Pvt. Ltd.
M-32 Market
Greater Kailash I
New Delhi 110 048 India

Printed in the United States of America

Library of Congress Cataloging-in-Publication Data

Terrorism in perspective / [edited] by Pamala Griset and Sue Mahan.
      p. cm.
Includes bibliographical references and index.
ISBN 0-7619-2752-2 © — ISBN 0-7619-2404-3 (P)
  1. Terrorism. I. Griset, Pamala L., 1946- II. Mahan, Sue.
HV6431 .T4667 2003
303.6′25—dc21

                        2002012736

04 10 9 8 7 6 5 4 3 2

Acquiring Editor:	Jerry Westby
Editorial Assistant:	Vonessa Vondera
Production Editor:	Diana E. Axelsen
Copy Editor:	A. J. Sobczak
Typesetter:	C&M Digitals (P) Ltd
Indexer:	Mary Mortensen
Cover Designer:	Michelle Lee

Contents

Acknowledgments ix

Introduction xi
    What Is Terrorism? xiii
    Chapter Outline xiv
    Video Notes xvi
    References xvi

1. History of Terrorism **1**
    Early Justifications for Terrorism 1
    Religious Terrorism: Guy Fawkes and the Gunpowder Plot 2
    State-Sponsored Terrorism: The French Revolution 4
    Political Terrorism: Anarchists and Propaganda by Deed 6
        Political Terrorism of the Russian Narodnaya Volya 7
    Terrorism and Nationalism: The Philosophy of the Bomb 8
        Nationalism Makes Latin America a Hotbed of Terrorism 9
        The Urban Guerrilla 9
    Lessons Learned From History 10
    Highlights of Reprinted Articles 10
    Exploring the History of Terrorism Further 12
    Video Notes 12
    References 12

    FEAR AND TREMBLING: TERRORISM
      IN THREE RELIGIOUS TRADITIONS 15
        David C. Rapoport

    THE ENDLESS NATURE OF TERRORISM 38
        Jeffrey D. Simon

2. International Terrorism **45**
    Terrorism Around the World 46
    State-Sponsored Terrorism 48
    Religious Fanaticism: An Old Trend and a New Threat 49
    A Few Famous Terrorists 49
        Che Guevara 50
        Carlos the Jackal 51

Osama bin Laden	52
Pan Am Flight 103	54
Highlights of Reprinted Articles	55
Exploring International Terrorism Further	56
Video Notes	56
References	56

TERRORISM, CRIME, AND TRANSFORMATION   59
Chris Dishman

SOMEBODY ELSE'S CIVIL WAR   73
Michael Scott Doran

3. Homegrown Terrorism in the United States   **85**

State-Sponsored Terrorism	86
Leftist Class Struggles	87
Anarchists/Ecoterrorists	88
Racial Supremacy	89
Religious Extremists	91
The New Century	92
Highlights of Reprinted Articles	92
Exploring Homegrown Terrorism Further	93
Video Notes	93
References	94

POLITICAL ESCHATOLOGY: A THEOLOGY
OF ANTIGOVERNMENT EXTREMISM   97
Jonathan R. White

FIGHTING TERRORISM AS IF WOMEN MATTERED: ANTI-ABORTION
VIOLENCE AS UNCONSTRUCTED TERRORISM   111
Philip Jenkins

4. Reporting Terrorism   **129**

Media, Law, and Terrorism	129
Irresponsible Reporting	131
Interfering in State Operations Against Terrorism	131
Cooperating With Terrorists or With Government Control	133
Selling Terrorism: Commercial and Political	
Interests in Media Reports	134
Making Martyrs: Terrorists and the Death Penalty	135
Highlights of Reprinted Articles	138
Exploring Media and Terrorism Further	139
Video Notes	139
References	139

TERRORISM, THE MEDIA, AND THE GOVERNMENT:
PERSPECTIVES, TRENDS, AND OPTIONS FOR POLICYMAKERS   143
Raphael F. Perl

TERRORISM AND CENSORSHIP: THE MEDIA IN CHAINS   150
Terry Anderson

5. Women as Terrorists   **157**
    Roles and Activities for Female Terrorists   158
        Sympathizers   158
        Spies   159
        Warriors   159
        Dominant Forces   159
    Two Exceptional Terrorist Groups   161
        The RAF in Germany   161
        The Sendero Luminoso in Peru   161
    Two Female Terrorists   162
        Ulrike Meinhof   162
        Augusta La Torre Guzman   162
    Ideology and Female Terrorists   163
    Highlights of Reprinted Articles   164
    Exploring Women as Terrorists Further   165
    Video Notes   165
    References   165

    TOKEN TERRORIST: THE DEMON LOVER'S WOMAN   167
        Robin Morgan

    MAFIOSI AND TERRORISTS: ITALIAN WOMEN
      IN VIOLENT ORGANIZATIONS   182
        Alison Jamieson

6. Conventional Terrorist Tactics   **191**
    Children at War   192
    Conventional Tactics Becoming More Deadly   194
    Leaderless Resistance   195
    Guidebooks of Terror Tactics   196
    The Basics   197
        Assassinations   197
        Hijacking   198
        Kidnapping and Hostage Taking   200
        Bombing   201
    Highlights of Reprinted Articles   201
    Exploring Conventional Terrorist Tactics Further   202
    Video Notes   203
    References   203

    THE BOMBING OF OMAGH, 15 AUGUST 1998:
    THE BOMBERS, THEIR TACTICS, STRATEGY,
    AND PURPOSE BEHIND THE INCIDENT   207
        James Dingley

    SUICIDE TERRORISM: A GLOBAL THREAT   220
        Rohan Gunaratna

7. Unconventional Terrorist Tactics   **227**
    The 21st Century Arsenal   228
        Chemical Weapons   228
        Biological Weapons   229
        Nuclear Weapons   229

    Cyberterrorism 230
   How Real Is the Threat? 230
    A Misguided Response to the Threat? 231
   Aum Shinrikyo: A Terrorist Cult 232
    Shoko Asahara: A Chaotic Leader 232
    From Bizarre to Dangerous 232
    The Attack 234
    The Aftermath 234
   Highlights of Reprinted Articles 235
   Exploring Unconventional Terrorist Tactics Further 236
   Video Notes 236
   References 236

WEAPONS OF MASS DESTRUCTION 239
   Walter Laqueur

CYBERHATE: A LEGAL AND HISTORICAL ANALYSIS OF EXTREMISTS'
USE OF COMPUTER NETWORKS IN AMERICA 254
   Brian Levin

8. Counterterrorism **277**
   Counterterrorism and U.S. Foreign Policy 277
    A Global Perspective on Transnational Terrorism 278
    International Responses to Terrorism 279
    International Cooperation and the Use of Military Forces 280
    The High Cost of Retaliation 281
   Domestic Counterterrorism Policy 282
    Legislating Against Terrorism 282
    Controversial Detentions and Racial Profiling 285
    Military Tribunals 286
    Three Infamous Cases from the U.S. History of Counterterrorism 288
   Highlights of Reprinted Articles 290
   Exploring Counterterrorism Further 291
   Video Notes 292
   References 292

LESSONS AND FUTURES 295
   Paul R. Pillar

A CAUTIONARY TALE FOR A NEW AGE OF SURVEILLANCE 303
   Jeffrey Rosen

Appendix A: Locations of Worldwide Terrorist Activity (Maps 1-8) 313

Appendix B: Background Information on Terrorist Groups 323
   U.S. Department of State
   Background Information on Designated Foreign
    Terrorist Organizations 323
   Background Information on Other Terrorist Groups 346

Appendix C: Video Notes 363

Index 365

About the Authors 387

About the Contributors 389

ACKNOWLEDGMENTS

Jackie Connelly and Bonnie Marsh provided invaluable assistance during all phases of this project. A million thanks would not be enough to express our gratitude.

Today there is no longer a choice between violence and nonviolence. It is either nonviolence or nonexistence. I feel that we've got to look at this total thing anew and recognize that we must live together. That the whole world now it is one—not only geographically but it has to become one in terms of brotherly concern. Whether we live in America or Asia or Africa we are all tied in a single garment of destiny and whatever affects one directly, affects [all] indirectly.

—Dr. Martin Luther King, Jr.

INTRODUCTION

This is not the end. It is not even the beginning of the end. But it is, perhaps, the end of the beginning.

—Winston Churchill

September 11, 2001, began with an ordinary morning, but the day quickly turned into one of unfathomable destruction. The most devastating terrorist attack ever waged against the United States began shortly before 8:45 a.m., as hijackers crashed an American Airlines plane into the north tower of the World Trade Center in lower Manhattan. A few minutes later, with smoke billowing from the damaged tower, and just as the enormity of the disaster was starting to sink in for stunned observers and television viewers, a United Airlines plane slammed into the south tower. In less than an hour, one of the 110-story towers collapsed, followed shortly by the other. The 25-year-old glass and steel complex, which symbolized New York City's position as the economic center of the world, crumbled into a mountain of debris, ash, and death.

At about 9:30 a.m., another American Airlines plane smashed into the Pentagon, the five-sided headquarters of the American military. One side of the building collapsed as smoke rose over the Potomac River. About half an hour later, another United Airlines plane crashed outside Pittsburgh, apparently headed for the White House or Capitol Hill.

Comparisons were quickly made to another day that lives in infamy in the American psyche: December 7, 1941, when 183 Japanese warplanes bombed United States Navy forces in Hawaii's Pearl Harbor. Nearly 2,400 were killed and more than 1,100 wounded in that early morning sneak attack.

The death toll in the September 11, 2001, attack was much higher. The initial estimates were more than 6,000 lives lost; but by September 2002, these estimates were reduced to around 3,000, according to the *New York Times*. President George W. Bush compared the attack to one on "freedom itself" and vowed that the nation's "freedom will be defended."

For years, experts had warned government officials that the United States was vulnerable to a terrorist assault with unconventional weapons of mass destruction, especially chemical and biological weapons. But on September 11, conventional weapons yielded unconventional results, as hijacked airplanes were transformed into weapons of mass destruction.

Internationally known as symbols of U.S. financial power, the two towers of the World Trade Center burn before collapsing.

"Here is New York," Image #6327 by Limarie Cabrera. Reprinted with permission.

In the immediate aftermath of the attacks, the United States came to a virtual standstill. Public facilities were evacuated and top government officials were whisked away to undisclosed locations. Guards armed with sophisticated weapons patrolled the nation's capitol, and military aircraft secured the skies. The Federal Aviation Administration closed airports nationwide. Bus and railroad service was suspended in the Northeast.

Security was tightened at all U.S.-Canada border crossings. Financial markets were shut down, including the New York Stock Exchange, the Nasdaq stock market, and the Chicago Board of Trade. The United Nations was evacuated, General Motors sent Detroit employees home, and Chicago's Sears Tower closed. New York City's mayoral primary election was postponed, as were all major league baseball games and Broadway shows. In Florida, Walt Disney World closed its theme parks and the Kennedy Space Center shut down.

Federal law enforcement authorities quickly identified Osama bin Laden, a Saudi Arabian millionaire living in Afghanistan, as the terrorists' mastermind and financier. Bin Laden had supported the U.S.-backed Afghan warriors in their fight with the Soviet Union in the 1980s, but he turned against the United States after the 1991 Gulf War, when it ousted Iraq from Kuwait. The United States had desecrated sacred Saudi land when it based its soldiers on Saudi soil, bin Laden said, and he called on Muslims worldwide to join in a holy war against the United States. Since then, bin Laden has been suspected of masterminding and financing several terrorist attacks on U.S. citizens, including the 1993 bombing of the World Trade Center, the shooting of U.S. troops in Somalia in the same year, the 1996 bombing of the Khobar military complex in Saudi Arabia, the nearly simultaneous explosion of car bombs outside the United States embassies in Kenya and Tanzania in 1998, and the attack on the Navy destroyer USS *Cole* in Yemen in 2000.

The subsequent and ongoing military and political responses by the United States and its allies to the September 11 attacks are changing the world in many as yet unknown ways. Regardless of the number of victories won in the current "war," history teaches that terrorism is endemic to the human condition and cannot be eliminated by diligent application of the "right" strategies. Terrorism is not a disease that can be wiped out, but it can, perhaps, be managed and confined, at least temporarily (Pillar, 2001).

WHAT IS TERRORISM?

Global terrorism today, like terrorism of earlier eras, defies simple explanations. Terrorism remains difficult to define because "there is not one but many different terrorisms" (Laqueur, 1999, p. 46). The distinction is often blurry between terrorism, guerrilla warfare, conventional warfare, and criminal activity. Terrorist tactics are used frequently during wars, and the tactics used by violent criminals may be indistinguishable from those used by terrorists. Repressive regimes call those who struggle against them terrorists, but those who struggle to topple the regimes call themselves freedom fighters.

The term *terrorism* has a negative connotation. People and organizations are degraded when labeled as terrorists, and political or religious movements can lose followers and funding as a result of the label. Citizens, even those in a democracy, may be more apt to accept repressive government actions if they are presented in terms of counterterrorism.

The term *terrorism* is often used interchangeably with the term *terror*, causing further definitional confusion. Many activities, from wars to rampages by youth gangs to writing science fiction, are meant to strike terror into the enemy (or reader). In this context, the scope of potential definitions is endless.

More than a hundred definitions of terrorism exist (Laqueur, 1999, p. 5). For example, Jenkins (1984, quoted in White, 1998) defined terrorism as the use or threatened use of force to achieve political ends. Laqueur (1987, p. 72) added to Jenkins's definition by including the requirement of targeting innocent people. The Federal Bureau of Investigation defines terrorism on its Web site as "the unlawful use of force or violence against persons or property to intimidate or coerce a Government, the civilian population, or any segment thereof, in furtherance of political or social objectives."

Some definitions specifically include religious motivations; others include hate, millenarian, and apocalyptic groups. Several definitions refer only to non-state actors, whereas others include state-sponsored terrorism. Terrorism by groups is an essential part of several definitions, but some definitions include terrorism by individual actors.

The difficulty in defining terrorism is not new. Cooper (2001, p. 881) notes that "there has never been, since the topic began to command serious attention, some golden age in which terrorism was easy to define." The meaning of terrorism is embedded in a person's or nation's philosophy. Thus, the determination of the "right" definition of terrorism is subjective.

Rather that trying to reach an agreement on the definition of terrorism, Cooper (2001, p. 887) argues that we "can no longer afford the fiction that one person's terrorist may yet be another's freedom fighter. Fighting for freedom may well be his or her purpose, but if the mission is undertaken through the employment of terrorist means, a terrorist he or she must remain."

This book seeks to avoid the definitional quagmire by using a broad-based conceptual scheme that focuses on acts of terrorism and their relationship to culture, religion, history, politics, economics, and ideology. State-sponsored terrorism, subnational and transnational terrorism, homegrown terrorism, and individual and group terrorism all are considered, as are the media's role in terrorism reports, female terrorists, conventional and unconventional terrorist tactics, and counterterrorism strategies and laws. Terrorism is viewed comprehensively, and the reader is afforded a panorama of historical, contemporary, and futuristic positions.

Chapter Outline

Terrorism in Perspective combines original thematic overview essays with the best of the existing literature on terrorism. Each of the eight chapters is divided into two parts. The first part is an overview of the issues, actors, and actions relevant to the specific topic under discussion. The second part presents two previously published articles or chapters culled from a wide variety of popular, academic, and governmental sources. The selected articles deepen understanding of terrorism by focusing more intently on specific themes.

Chapter 1 links contemporary terrorism to the endless conflicts of history that will remain part of the human experience as long as the conditions that breed it—ethnic and class conflicts, religious fanaticism, extreme ideologies, and ancient hatreds—remain. Terrorists have altered the course of history time and again, putting their indelible mark on many of the colossal events of the past. The chapter highlights a few of them, including Guy Fawkes and the religiously motivated Gunpowder Plot, the French Revolution, the growth of anarchism and the philosophy of "propaganda by deed," the Russian Narodnaya Volya, the nationalist movement in India, and the Latin American urban guerrilla movement. The first article selected compares three ancient terrorist organizations: the Jewish Zealots who died defending Masada in the first century A.D.; the Hashashin (Arabic for "hashish-eaters"), known also as the Brotherhood of Assassins, active in Persia from the 11th through 13th centuries, who believed killing was their holy mission, much as some of today's Islam extremists have launched a jihad with religious blessing (*fatwa*); and the Hindu Thugs of the 13th through 19th centuries. The second article overviews the early experience of the United States with foreign and homegrown terrorism. Topics include the exploits of the Barbary Pirates, the assassination of President William McKinley, and the labor unrest inspired by the Molly Maguires.

Chapter 2 discusses international terrorism in the age of globalization. The presentation covers four continents: Africa, Asia, Europe, and South America. History, ideology, religion, and economics are important everywhere, and the world's terrorists are animated by a variety of causes. The regional analysis focuses on state-sponsored terrorism, long-standing ethnic conflicts, separatist movements, and class struggles. Among the infamous terrorists discussed are Che Guevara, Carlos the Jackal, and Osama bin Laden. An overview is presented of the worldwide implications of the 1988 bombing of Pan Am flight 103 over Lockerbie, Scotland. The first article selected for this chapter analyzes the synergistic relationship between terrorism and organized crime as well as discussing how the economic allure of the illegal drug and arms trade often blurs the distinction between terrorism and organized crime. The second article discusses the religious and political motivations of Osama bin Laden and his al-Qaeda followers. The author argues that the United States has been dragged into somebody else's civil war.

Homegrown terrorism is the topic of Chapter 3. Our nation's experience with terrorism from within is placed in historical and contemporary perspectives. The ideological far left, the socialists and communists of the 1960s and 1970s, including the Weather Underground and the Symbionese Liberation Army, were replaced in the 1980s and 1990s with an untold number of right-wing groups, including antigovernmental extremists, hate groups, and Christian fanatics. The first article covers the relationship between religion and racist violence. The author examines the factors that must be present to form a theology of hate. Anti-abortion terrorism is the subject of the second article on homegrown terrorism. The article discusses the impact of definitions on how terrorism is treated, as well as examining the dependence of news organizations and academics on official sources of information.

Chapter 4 analyzes the organic relationship between the media and terrorism. Former British Prime Minister Margaret Thatcher called the media the oxygen of terrorism, and the chapter explores the critical issues in the complex, symbiotic relationship between terrorism and the media. The articles explore various forms of media involvement, from journalism and reporting to participation. The author presents lessons to be learned from the positive and negative consequences of media involvement in terrorist situations and makes recommendations for more appropriate use of the media. The first article summarizes the relationship between the media and terrorists by looking at what each wants from the other. The second article is based on the firsthand experiences and insights of Terry Anderson, an American journalist kidnapped in Lebanon in 1985 by a group of Iranian-inspired terrorists.

Women, by design, are not represented in decision-making positions in most terrorist organizations, but they have played a vital role in many causes. Chapter 5 discusses the history of female involvement in social conflict and the types of roles female terrorists are assigned. Case studies are presented of women who dominate terrorist groups, particularly Ulrike Meinhof of the German Red Army Faction and Augusta La Torre Guzman of the Peruvian Shining Path. The first article argues that most female terrorists are attracted to causes because of their attachment to their lovers or husbands, not because they want to achieve political benefits for women. The second article compares the Italian women of the terrorist Red Brigade with women in the Mafia. The common element of violence links the two groups and provides the basis for the analysis.

Chapter 6 discusses conventional terrorist tactics: assassinations, hijackings, kidnappings, and bombings. As the events of September 11, 2001, vividly demonstrated, traditional tactics, which are still the popular first choice for terrorists, can have devastating results. The chapter also discusses the tactic of leaderless resistance as well as the use of children in terrorist campaigns. The first article discusses the background and history of the Irish Republican Army (IRA) conflict in Northern Ireland, then follows with an in-depth analysis of the tactics involved in an actual bombing. The threat posed by suicide terrorism is spreading around the globe. The second article in this chapter discusses the growing need for preventive and reactive tactics to deal with suicide bombers.

Unconventional terrorist tactics are the subject of Chapter 7. The chapter discusses the history and potential impacts of weapons of mass destruction, such as chemical, biological, and nuclear weapons, as well as outlining the threats posed by cyberterrorism. The recent anthrax attacks in the United States demonstrate that traditional constraints against the use of unconventional weapons may be lifting. The chapter discusses the only non-state terrorist organization that is known to have tried to use these weapons on a large scale: Aum Shinrikyo, the Japanese apocalyptic and millenarian cult controlled by a messianic and highly eccentric leader that launched a sarin gas attack on Tokyo's subways. The first article presents a brief history of chemical, biological, and nuclear weapons as well as highlighting the careers of some famous "mad scientists" and their efforts at mass destruction. The second article focuses on the use of the Internet by right-wing and left-wing homegrown terrorists. The article also analyzes the implications of Supreme Court decisions on free speech in cyberspace.

The final chapter discusses counterterrorism from the perspectives of foreign affairs and domestic policy. Terrorist acts against the United States are placed in a global perspective, as are the events and alliances that occurred in the wake of the September 11 attacks. As the only remaining superpower, the United States has evoked hatred and retaliation in some parts of the world. The chapter discusses the so-called "clash of civilizations," which some observers believe will define international relations in the future. It also highlights issues concerning the role of the United Nations, as well as other international alliances, in counterterrorism. The second section of this chapter is framed in terms of U.S. civil liberties, with special focus on four issues: antiterrorism legislation, including the USA PATRIOT Act (2001); the detentions of Arabs and Muslims that occurred after September 11; the use of military tribunals to try terrorists; and infamous counterterrorism operations from U.S. history that some consider to have been overly zealous. The first article makes recommendations for conducting foreign affairs in a manner that promotes U.S. counterterrorism policy. The final article discusses biometrics and Great Britain's use of surveillance cameras to fight terrorism.

VIDEO NOTES

State-sponsored terrorism is depicted vividly and validly in *The Killing Fields* (Warner Bros., 1984, 142 min.).

REFERENCES

Cooper, H.H.A. (2001). The problem of definition revisited. *American Behavioral Scientist, 44,* 881-893.

Laqueur, Walter. (1987). *The age of terrorism.* Boston: Little, Brown, and Company.

Laqueur, Walter. (1999). *The new terrorism: Fanaticism and the arms of mass destruction.* New York: Oxford University Press.

Pillar, Paul R. (2001). *Terrorism and U.S. foreign policy.* Washington, DC: Brookings Institution.

USA PATRIOT Act of 2001. Uniting and Strengthening America by Providing Appropriate Tools Required to Intercept and Obstruct Terrorism Act, Pub. L. No. 107-56 (2001).

White, Jonathan R. (1998). Terrorism: An introduction. Belmont, CA: Wadsworth.

1

History of Terrorism

History is a relentless master. It has no present, only the past rushing into the future. To try to hold fast is to be swept aside.

—John Fitzgerald Kennedy

To study the history of terrorism is to study the history of human civilization. From the murder of Julius Caesar in 44 B.C. to the atrocious airplane attacks of September 11, 2001, terrorists have been the cause of many of the monumental events of human experience. Terrorism has been part of the history of virtually every country in the world, and its causes have varied widely over time and place.

This chapter links the terrorist act with the terrorist philosophy by highlighting a few of the major moments and people in the history of terrorism. The discussion analyzes how social, economic, political, and religious conditions have given rise to terrorism over the centuries.

By dagger or dynamite, by bullet or bomb, terrorists have sought to achieve their goals through whatever technologies were available to them. The technology of mass destruction is now, at least potentially, part of the terrorists' arsenal. Yet, despite changes in its manifestations, modern terrorism is similar in many ways to terrorism of earlier eras. Many of the concerns that motivate today's terrorists have existed over the entire span of human history. Many of the terrorist organizations of the 21st century are inspired by events that occurred hundreds, even thousands, of years ago. Contemporary terrorist groups often justify their actions in terms of theoretical arguments that were popular in much earlier eras. It is this connection between past and present that makes understanding the history of terrorism so fundamental to understanding modern terrorism.

Early Justifications for Terrorism

The concept of terrorism is closely linked to the great theoretical debates of history. Since antiquity, philosophers have asked whether, and under what conditions, it is permissible to kill a political opponent. Some early Greeks, for example, glorified the killing of a tyrant (tyrannicide).

To many of history's great thinkers, violent resistance to a despotic ruler was not a crime: it was a civic duty. The Greek philosopher Aristotle (384-322 B.C.) presented

1

several examples of assassinated tyrants who deserved their fate. Aristotle argued that there

> are two chief motives which induce men to attack tyrannies—hatred and contempt. Hatred of tyrants is inevitable, and contempt is also a frequent cause of their destruction. Thus we see that most of those who have acquired, have retained their power, but those who have inherited, have lost it, almost at once; for living in luxurious ease, they have become contemptible, and offer many opportunities to their assailants. Anger, too, must be included under hatred, and produces the same effects. It is oftentimes even more ready to strike—the angry are more impetuous in making an attack, for they do not listen to reason. And men are very apt to give way to their passions when they are insulted. (*Politics*, Book V, as quoted in Laqueur, 1978, pp. 12-13)

Those who killed tyrants were often seen as heroes, as was Brutus, the assassin of the Roman emperor Julius Caesar. Cicero, although not part of the assassination plot, justified the killing when he wrote that

> there can be no such thing as fellowship with tyrants, nothing but bitter feud is possible. . . . For, as we amputate a limb in which the blood and the vital spirit have ceased to circulate, because it injures the rest of the body, so monsters, who, under human guise, conceal the cruelty and ferocity of a wild beast, should be severed from the common body of humanity. (*De Officiis*, as quoted in Laqueur, 1978, p. 16)

The terrorist attack on Julius Caesar has remained a potent symbol spanning the centuries. Political leaders have everywhere been the targets of terrorists. When, in 1865, John Wilkes Booth jumped onto the stage at the Ford Theatre shouting "sic semper tyrannis" ("thus always to tyrants"), the despot he felt justified in killing was Abraham Lincoln, president of the United States (Poland, 1988, p. 180).

The Jewish Zealots of the first century, also known as the Sicarii, constituted one of the earliest large-scale terrorist organizations. Their goal was to prevent Roman rule over Judea (now Israel). They died for their efforts in a mass suicide at Masada in 20 A.D., but not before they had incited an insurrection of the populace against the Roman occupation of Judea.

RELIGIOUS TERRORISM: GUY FAWKES AND THE GUNPOWDER PLOT

Another religiously inspired terrorist group, whose best-known member was Guy Fawkes, was much less successful. Many people have heard of Guy Fawkes—in Great Britain, there is a holiday named for him—but most people don't know that he was caught red-handed in 1605 trying to blow up London's Palace of Westminster (see, e.g., Fraser, 1996; Haynes, 1994; Nicholls, 1991).

Fawkes and about a dozen other conspirators hoped to kill King James I and all the government officials who would be attending the opening day of Parliament. The plot (known as the Gunpowder or Papacy Plot) was foiled after the king was shown an anonymous letter warning a brother-in-law of one of the co-conspirators to stay away from Parliament on opening day. On November 5, 1605, the king's officials captured Fawkes, who was guarding the gunpowder. The others fled, but they were soon tracked down. The terrorists were dragged through the streets of London and then brutally drawn and quartered by galloping horses before the crowds at Westminster.

Guy Fawkes and his fellow plotters wanted to install the Pope as head of England. Their attempt in 1605 to blow up the British Parliament and kill King James I failed; they were viciously drawn and quartered in front of jeering crowds for their "holy" terrorism.

The Scrap Album (www.scrapalbum.com). Reprinted with permission from M. Warrington.

Like many terrorists throughout history, Fawkes and his colleagues justified their actions in terms of religion. Like other instances of "holy terror," the Gunpowder Plot was deeply rooted in events that had occurred long before. In 1529, King Henry VIII was obsessed with producing a male heir and maintaining his dynasty. He asked Pope Clement VII for an annulment from his marriage to Catherine of Aragon to marry Anne Boleyn, but the pope refused. The king retaliated by separating from the Roman Catholic Church and forming the Church of England, with himself as its head. The king accomplished the break from Rome with the help of Parliament, which passed a variety of laws giving the king power over religious affairs.

The king's chancellor, Thomas Cromwell, confiscated Catholic Church property and closed the monasteries. When Elizabeth I came to power in 1558, Catholics were driven underground. After 1563, all her subjects were required to swear an oath attesting that Elizabeth was the Supreme Governor of the Church. Catholics who refused to submit to the Church of England were known as recusants.

Guy Fawkes, who used the alias John Johnson, was among those recusants, many of whom were aristocrats, who wanted to instigate a counterreformation and install the Roman pope as head of England. Fawkes and his co-conspirators incorrectly believed that Catholics in England would rise up against the government after the bombing of

Parliament. Like many other terrorists throughout history, Fawkes grossly misjudged the mood of others of his religion, most of whom were content to keep their religious practices secret and swear obedience to the monarch in public. Today, Guy Fawkes Day is celebrated each November 5 with bonfires, fireworks, and burning of effigies of Fawkes, all in honor of the failure of the conspirators to blow Parliament and James I sky high.

STATE-SPONSORED TERRORISM: THE FRENCH REVOLUTION

Religious impulses have not been the only driving force behind terrorism. The Enlightenment, an intellectual movement of the 18th century, challenged the divine right of kings, arguing against a society of privilege and in favor of a political system that recognized the equality of men. The squalid conditions that defined the lives of most people stood in stark contrast to the extravagant wealth of the aristocrats. Terrorists of the 18th and 19th centuries fought against the system of amazing riches for a few and hard work and depravation for all others.

Not only have hereditary rulers and their representatives been targeted for assassination by terrorists who reject the existing government, but in addition revolutionary governments have themselves turned on their citizens, launching terrorist attacks of breathtaking cruelty and slaughtering untold numbers of civilians. It was through such state-sponsored evil that the word "terrorism" entered our lexicon.

On July 14, 1789, a French mob attacked the Bastille prison in Paris, massacring the soldiers stationed there. The rioters later walked through the streets carrying the heads of the prison commandant and several of the guards on pikes. The mob was supported by a group of radical revolutionaries, who soon gained control of the government. In October of the same year, the radicals forced King Louis XVI and the royal family to move from Versailles to Paris; later, the king unsuccessfully tried to flee. He ultimately was tried by the revolutionary court and, on January 21, 1793, was executed.

Immediately after the execution of the king, the Committee of Public Safety and the Revolutionary Tribunal were established under the leadership of Maximilien Robespierre, and the *regime de la terreur* began. From May 1793 to July 1794, the new government sponsored widespread surveillance of all strata of society, searching for possible enemies of the revolution (see, e.g., Blanning, 1998; Hunt, 1998; Lefebvre, 1962).

Robespierre and his followers depicted themselves as saviors of the people and portrayed terrorism as the solution to internal anarchy and external invasion by other European monarchs. Arrests were made on the flimsiest evidence, and people were expelled from the country, imprisoned, and executed, all in the name of the revolutionary cause.

Scholars disagree about how many people fell victim to state-sponsored terrorism in France. Estimates of the number of executions range from 17,000 (Anderson & Sloan, 1995, p. xxiii) to 40,000 (Hoffman, 1998, p. 16). Between 300,000 and 500,000 people were arrested, and up to 200,000 may have died in prison as the result of either starvation or brutal treatment (Crenshaw & Pimlott, 1997, p. 48). In Lyon, 700 people were sentenced to death by the revolutionaries and gunned down by cannons in the village square. In Nantes, boats holding thousands of prisoners were sunk in the Loire river (Crenshaw & Pimlott, 1997, pp. 46, 48).

Like modern terrorists, the French revolutionaries took advantage of technological advances. Doctor Joseph Guillotine, the inventor of a new execution technology, saw himself as a humanitarian. His machine was intended to make capital punishment less

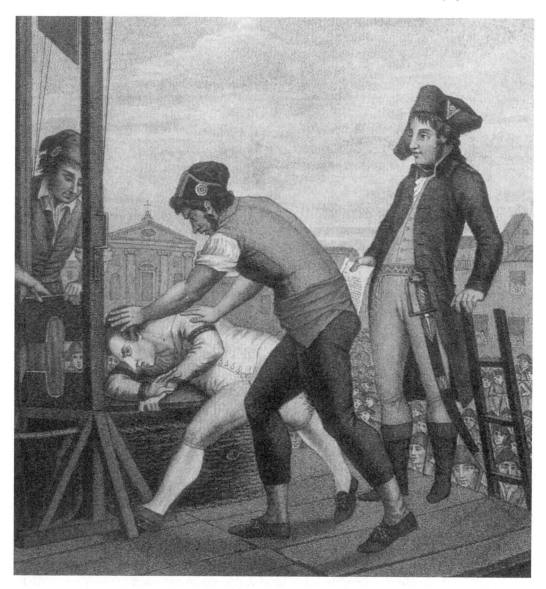

An engraving of the beheading of Maximilien Robespierre, whose state-sponsored *regime de la terreur* took the lives of thousands of French men, women, and children.

Reprinted with permission from ARTEHISTORIA.COM.

painful to the victim. Dr. Guillotine's idea for a "merciful killing machine" was the perfect fit for France's ruthless state-sponsored terrorism.

The end came for Robespierre when he announced in the summer of 1794 that he had a new list of enemies of the state. Fearing that their names might be on the list, a conspiracy of deputies staged a coup d'état, and Robespierre was assassinated. The so-called White Terror followed, with victims of the reign of terror attacking the former terrorists. Not until Napoleon Bonaparte came to power 1799 was the counter-revolution crushed.

In his youth, Robespierre was opposed to violence and cast himself as a humanitarian, yet he is remembered in history as a prototype for brutal dictators such as Adolf

Hitler of Germany, Benito Mussolini of Italy, Joseph Stalin of Russia, and Pol Pot of Cambodia.

POLITICAL TERRORISM: ANARCHISTS AND PROPAGANDA BY DEED

Hereditary rulers and their representatives all over the world have often been the targets of anarchists, who rejected all ruling authority. Most anarchists simply gave speeches and handed out leaflets, a few published newspapers, but some became terrorists. As was true for revolutionaries, their acts of terrorism had philosophical justifications.

In 1849, a German radical, Karl Heinzen, published *Der Mord* (Murder), which has been called "the most important ideological statement of early terrorism" (Laqueur, 1978, p. 47). Heinzen justified political murder in terms of its positive impact on history:

> We must call a spade a spade. The truth must out, whether it seems amiable or terrible, whether it is dressed in the white of peace or the red of war. Let us then be frank and honest, let us tear away the veil and spell out in plain speech what the lesson is which is now being illustrated every day before our eyes in the form of actions and threats, blood and torture, cannons and gallows by both princes and freedom-fighters . . . ; to wit, that murder is the principal agent of historical progress. (Heinzen, 1849, quoted in Laqueur, 1978, p. 53)

In a chilling prelude to Hitler's Nazi era, Heinzen justified terrorism on a massive scale: "If you have to blow up half a continent and pour out a sea of blood in order to destroy the party of the barbarians, have no scruples or conscience" (Laqueur, 1987, p. 28). Heinzen foresaw the importance of technology to terrorism, and he even suggested that prizes be given to researchers who developed better explosives and poisons (Laqueur, 1977, p. 27).

John Most, whose newspaper *Freiheit* was published in London, was a strident supporter of terrorism. The September 13, 1884, issue of his newspaper contained his "Advice for Terrorists," in which he asked "What is the purpose of the anarchists' threats—an eye for an eye, a tooth for a tooth—if they are not followed up by action?" He advised fellow anarchists to get money for their operations any way they could, and he chastised anyone who complained about ruthless methods.

> No one who considers the deed itself to be right can take offense at the manner in which the funds for it are acquired. . . . So let us hear no more of this idiotic talk of "moral indignation" as "robbery" and "theft"; from the mouths of socialists, this sort of blathering is really the most stupid nonsense possible. (Most, 1884, as quoted in Laqueur, 1978, p. 101)

Later, Most published a book with the following subtitle: *A Handbook of Instruction Regarding the Use and Manufacture of Nitroglycerine, Dynamite, Gun Cotton, Fulminating Mercury, Bombs, Arson, Poisons, etc.* (Vetter & Perlstein, 1991, p. 32). Again, terrorists made use of technological and scientific advances. Today's cyberterrorism is no exception to this historical pattern.

Carlo Pisacane, an Italian anarchist, is credited with developing the concept that would become known as "propaganda by the deed" (Hoffman, 1998; Laqueur, 1977). Pisacane argued that the masses were too exhausted at the end of their long working day to read leaflets and listen to speeches; only violent actions could catch their attention: "The propaganda of the idea is a chimera. Ideas result from deeds, not the latter from the former, and the people will not be free when they are educated, but educated when they are free" (as quoted in Hoffman, 1998, p. 16). The phrase "propaganda by deed" was coined around 1886 by Paul Brousse, a French anarchist (Stafford, 1971).

Political Terrorism of the Russian Narodnaya Volya

One of the early anarchistic theorists, the Russian Michael Bakunin, published a manifesto in 1848 calling on the Russian people to revolt against the tsar and attack state officials (Vetter & Perlstein, 1991). His advice was taken by one of the most successful, if short-lived, terrorist groups in history: the Narodnaya Volya.

A secret society of about 500 members, the Narodnaya Volya existed from 1878 to 1881. It is credited as being the first group to put into practice Pisacane's "propaganda by deed." Unlike the state-sponsored terrorists in the French Revolution, who jailed and killed thousands of their countrymen, the Russian terrorists targeted only high-level officials. The Narodnaya Volya counted on the tsar's regime toppling.

> If ten or fifteen pillars of the establishment were killed at one and the same time, the government would panic and would lose its freedom of action. At the same time, the masses would wake up. (Laqueur, 1977, p. 34)

Land distribution was at the heart of the struggle in Russia. In 1861, Tsar Alexander II abolished serfdom and lifted strict government controls over freedom of speech and assembly. These progressive actions were influenced by the ideas of the European Enlightenment, but they would prove to be the tsar's undoing and lead eventually to his assassination.

The newly freed serfs expected to be given the land that they had always tended, plus additional land, but the rich landowners had other ideas. Former serfs were forced to pay high prices for small parcels of land. Some of the Russian aristocracy rebelled against their own class and made quick use of the new freedoms of expression to criticize the tsar for the continued enslavement of the lower classes.

The Narodnaya Volya terrorist group was guided by the famous booklet *Catechism of the Revolutionist* by Sergey Nechaev (1869), which taught that the true revolutionary must always be prepared to face torture or death, and he must give up love, friendship, and gratitude in the single-minded pursuit of his mission. The *Catechism* discusses the principles guiding the true revolutionary. The revolutionary has

> only one science, the science of destruction. To this end, and this end alone, he will study mechanics, physics, chemistry, and perhaps medicine. To this end he will study day and night the living science: people, their characters and circumstances and all the features of the present social order at all possible levels. His sole and constant object is the immediate destruction of this vile order. . . . For him, everything is moral which assists the triumph of revolution. Immoral and criminal is everything which stands in its way. (quoted in Laqueur, 1978, pp. 68-69)

Believing that the tsar's regime was evil and that society could not advance until it was overthrown, the Narodnaya Volya assassinated prominent officials in the tsar's government, including police chiefs, government agency heads, members of the royal family, and the tsar himself. More than a quarter of the Narodnaya Volya were women (Vetter & Perlstein, 1991, p. 106). One, Vera Zasulich, committed the group's first terrorist act when she tried to assassinate the governor-general of St. Petersburg in July 1877. Another, Vera Figne, was part of the group's last terrorist attack—the murder of the tsar.

Hoffman (1998) tells the story of the tsar's end.

> Four volunteers were given four bombs each and employed along the alternate routes followed by the Tsar's cortege. As two of the bomber assassins stood in wait on the same street, the sleighs carrying the Tsar and his Cossack escort approached the first terrorist, who hurled his bomb at the passing sleigh, missing it by inches. The whole entourage came to a halt as soldiers seized the hapless culprit and the Tsar descended from his sleigh to check on a bystander wounded by the explosion. "Thank God, I am safe," the Tsar reportedly declared—just as the second bomber emerged from the crowd and detonated his weapon, killing both himself and his target. (pp. 18-19)

The end of the Narodnaya Volya came quickly, as its members were caught and hanged. Yet, the seeds planted by this group ultimately led to the Bolshevik Revolution of 1917, which ushered in the communist era. In London, at the first meeting of the International Congress of Anarchists, shortly after the tsar's murder, the activities of the Narodnaya Volya were warmly endorsed (Laqueur, 1977, p. 51).

TERRORISM AND NATIONALISM: THE PHILOSOPHY OF THE BOMB

The Russian terrorists pioneered the systematic use of bombs to destroy their enemies, but it was not until half a century later that Indian terrorist Bhagwati Charan illegally distributed a manifesto titled *The Philosophy of the Bomb* (Laqueur, 1978, p. 137).

Nationalism and the desire for independence was at the heart of the social, economic, political, and religious struggle in India. British rule over India began in 1857, and isolated instances of terrorism occurred from the beginning (Laqueur, 1977). In 1947, massive nonviolent resistance to colonial rule led the British to withdraw, and India became independent (see, e.g., Chandra, 1989; Farwell, 1991; French, 1998; Ramakrishnan, 1994).

Indians opposed to British rule split over tactics. On one side, Mahatma Gandhi and his followers advocated nonviolent resistance to colonial rule. Noncooperation and peaceful civil disobedience were their favored tactics; Gandhi explicitly rejected terrorism. Gandhi wanted Hindus and Muslims to unite against the British, and he wanted the religious strife that had long characterized the subcontinent of Asia to cease.

Bhagwati Charan and his colleagues in the Hindustan Socialist Republican Association (HSRA) took the opposite tack. Their manifesto reasoned that terrorism

> instills fear in the hearts of the oppressors, it brings hope of revenge and redemption to the oppressed masses. It gives courage and self confidence to the wavering, it shatters the spell of the subject race in the eyes of the world, because it is the most convincing proof of a nation's hunger for freedom. . . . It is a pity that Gandhi does not understand and will not understand revolutionary psychology. . . . To think a revolutionary will give up his ideals if public support and appreciation are withdrawn from him is the highest folly. . . . A revolutionary is the last person on the earth to submit to bullying. . . . There is not a crime that Britain has not committed in India. Deliberate misrule has reduced us to paupers, has bled us white. As a race and as a people we stand dishonored and outraged. . . . We shall have our revenge, a people's righteous revenge on the tyrant. (Charan, 1930, excerpted in Laqueur, 1978, pp. 137-140)

Bhagwati Charan not only preached violence but also practiced it. He died when a bomb exploded in his hands (*Bhagwati Charan*, 2000).

Although the HSRA tried to blow up a train, shot a police officer, and threw bombs from the public gallery in the Legislative Assembly, Gandhi's nonviolent resistance movement was much more effective than terrorist attacks in convincing the British to leave India (Laqueur, 1977). Gandhi's dream for fellowship between Hindus and Muslims was shattered, however, when independence in 1947 was followed by terrible violence between the two sects and the partition of the country into Muslim Pakistan and Hindu India.

Nationalism Makes Latin America a Hotbed of Terrorism

In Latin America as well, terrorism was tied to colonial rule and the desire for self-determination; resistance to the Spanish conquistadors dates from the 16th century. The link between terrorism, guerrilla warfare, conventional warfare, and criminal activity is particularly murky in Latin America, where state-sponsored terrorism and brutal military repression have been widespread. During the Cold War with Russia, Latin American dictators were tolerated, even feted, by the United States in the name of anticommunism, providing further justifications for terrorists (see, e.g., Halperin, 1976; Rosenberg, 1991; Tarazona-Sevillano, 1990).

Both Western and Eastern philosophers heavily influenced the growth of terrorist thought in Latin America. Germany's Karl Marx, Russia's Vladimir Lenin, and China's Mao Zedong were carefully studied by Fidel Castro and Che Guevara, who launched the Cuban Revolution of 1959; by Abimael Guzman, the founder of Peru's Shining Path, which has been called one of the world's "most elusive, secretive, and brutal guerrilla organizations" (Tarazona-Sevillano, 1990, p. xv); and by Carlos Marighella, the Brazilian author of the *Manual of the Urban Guerrilla* and the leader of the terrorist organization Action for National Liberation (ALN).

The Urban Guerrilla

Mao Zedong began his revolution in the Chinese countryside, but Carlos Marighella thought that urban terrorism should be the first stage of the revolution. From March 1968, through November 1969, the ALN robbed more than 100 banks, blew up military installations, attacked prisons and freed inmates, bombed the buildings of U.S. companies, and kidnapped important people, including an American ambassador (Marighella, 1985, p. 25).

The *Manual of the Urban Guerrilla* is "the most widely read, translated, and studied urban terrorist manual in modern history" (Marighella, 1985, p. 15). It has been the official guidebook of many terrorist organizations, including the Italian Red Brigade, the German Red Army Faction, and the Irish Republican Army.

The *Manual of the Urban Guerrilla* lays out the nitty-gritty of terrorism. It states that terrorists should be in good physical shape so they can withstand the rigors of their chosen craft. They must study chemistry and mechanics, and

> dynamite must be well understood. The use of incendiary bombs, of smoke bombs, and other types is indispensable prior knowledge. To know how to make and repair arms, prepare Molotov cocktails, grenades, mines, homemade destructive devices, how to blow up bridges, tear up and put out of service rails and sleepers, these are requisites in the technical preparation of the urban guerilla that can never be considered unimportant. (Marighella, 1969, as excerpted in Laqueur, 1978, p. 163)

Marighella advocated "a scorched-earth strategy, the sabotage of transport and oil pipelines, and the destruction of food supplies" (Laqueur, 1977, p. 185). Urban terrorism would create a crisis atmosphere, he argued, causing the government to overreact and repress ordinary people, who would then join the revolution and overthrow the government. Like Guy Fawkes and other terrorists throughout the centuries, Marighella overestimated the will of the people to join in the struggle to topple the government. After he was lured into a trap and killed in a police ambush in 1969, the ALN was crushed.

LESSONS LEARNED FROM HISTORY

Walter Laqueur observes that terrorism has taken so many forms that "[a]ny explanation that attempts to account for all its many manifestations is bound to be either exceedingly vague or altogether wrong" (1977, p. 133). No theory has emerged from political science, criminal justice, economics, philosophy, or any other discipline to satisfactorily explain terrorism.

From all corners of the earth, terrorism has been carried out by ideologues on the left and the right, by wealthy aristocrats and poverty-stricken farmers, and by men and women, although the former significantly outnumber the latter. The ends sought by terrorists have varied enormously. Some terrorists hoped to overthrow the government so they could assume power, and autocratic and democratic regimes alike have served as terrorists' targets. Liberating their country from colonial rule has motivated some terrorists, and nationalist and separatist movements have flourished in many places. Religion has been a driving force for some terrorist organizations, whereas others have struck blows against secular leaders or wealthy industrialists. Terrorism often has been directed against governments, but it also has been used by governments to frighten the populace, eliminate perceived enemies, and quell dissent. Terrorist organizations have ranged in size from just a handful of members to many thousands, and many of history's most memorable terrorist acts have been committed by lone individuals without the help or knowledge of any organization.

Thus, terrorism is a complex phenomenon that varies from country to country and from one era to another. The best way to understand terrorism is to examine the social, economic, political, and religious conditions and philosophies existing at a particular time and place.

HIGHLIGHTS OF REPRINTED ARTICLES

The two readings that follow, concerning the history of terrorism, were selected to provide two different types of analysis: comparative and specific. The comparative article by David Rapoport focuses on three manifestations of religious terrorism in different time periods and countries. The specific article by Jeffrey Simon highlights some of the major moments in the history of terrorism in the United States.

David C. Rapoport. (1984). "Fear and Trembling: Terrorism in Three Religious Traditions." *American Political Science Review, 78*(3), 658-677.

Rapoport's article focuses on the Jewish Zealots-Sicarii of the first century, the Islamic Assassins of the 11th through 13th centuries, and the Hindu Thugs of the 13th through 19th centuries. Longer lasting and, in that sense, more successful than modern terrorist groups, these three early versions of groups advocating "holy terror" are revealing for what they teach us about contemporary terrorism.

Table 1.1   "Holy Terror": Comparisons of Three Terrorist Organizations

	Thugs	*Assassins*	*Zealots-Sicarii*
Religion	Hinduism	Islam	Judaism
Country of origin	India	Persia (Middle East)	Judea (Israel)
Years of duration	600+ (13th-19th centuries)	200+ (11th-13th centuries)	25+ (1st century)
Method of attack	Noose	Dagger	Sword
Primary victims	Travelers on remote roads	Political elites in public places	Prominent Jews, especially priests, in public places; Greeks and Roman rulers
Intended audience	Kali, God of Terror—avoided publicity	God and Islamic world—sought publicity	God and Jews in Judea and Roman occupiers—sought publicity
Objective	Human sacrifices to the god Kali (victims' suffering pleases Kali)	Purify/spread Islam (political conquest for religious purposes)	Mass insurrection against Roman rulers (national liberation)
Contemporary parallels	Religious fanatics and cults that shun publicity	Middle Eastern martyrs (*fidayeen*) for Islam	Movements to overthrow colonial rulers in South America and Asia

Rapoport disputes the myth that terrorism has increased as technology has advanced. Terrorists have always had weapons, transportation, and communication—no matter how rudimental. From the sword of the Zealots-Sicarii to the dagger of Assassins to the silk scarf noose of the Thugs, terrorists have used whatever technology was available. Rapoport thus concludes that "the critical variable cannot be technology; rather, the purpose and organizations of particular groups and the vulnerabilities of particular societies to them are decisive factors" (p. 659) in understanding terrorism. Rapoport thus echoes the theme used throughout this book, that understanding the culture, religion, politics, economics, and ideology of a country and its people is the best way to comprehend the phenomena of terrorism.

Table 1.1 compares key features of these three ancient terrorist organizations. Their objectives were in many ways similar to those of contemporary terrorists. The parallels between past and present will be revisited in subsequent chapters.

Jeffrey D. Simon. (1994). *The Terrorist Trap: America's Experience With Terrorism.* Bloomington: Indiana University Press.

The excerpt from Simon's book provides a fascinating overview of the early history of the U.S. experience with transnational and homegrown terrorism. The excerpt begins with the 18th-century exploits of the Barbary pirates, who, on behalf of the governments of Morocco, Algiers, Tunis, and Tripoli, terrorized American vessels on the high seas. The pirates took Americans as hostages and demanded high ransom payments, leading in 1795 to the first arms-for-hostage deal in U.S. history. The excerpt also features the activities of anarchists in the United States, including the assassination of President William McKinley in 1901, the labor unrest inspired by the Molly Maguires, and the bombing of the *Los Angeles Times* building in 1910. It ends with World War II and the emergence of a new age of terrorism.

EXPLORING THE HISTORY OF TERRORISM FURTHER

- Several chronologies of terrorism are available on the Web. One site, maintained by the historian for the U.S. Department of State, briefly discusses the major terrorist events between 1961 and 2001. Its Web address is http://usinfo.state.gov/topical/pol/terror/01103131.htm
- The history of anarchism, along with pictures some of the world's most remembered anarchists, including Michael Bakunin, Peter Kropotkin, and Emma Goldman, can be found at http://dwardmac.pitzer.edu/anarchist_archives/index.html
- Definitions of terrorism vary with the worldview of the definer. Several online articles weigh in on the definitional debate, including one that pictorially distinguishes between terrorism and guerrilla warfare. Its Web address is www.ict.org.il/articles/define.htm
- The United States is labeled as among the worst terrorist states in history by a privately maintained Web site whose chronology begins in the early 1600s with the "American genocide" of the Native people of America and Africa. Other examples include U.S. intervention in the Philippines from 1945 to 1953, in China from 1945 to 1951, and in Guatemala from 1953 to the present. The site address is http://free.freespeech.org/americanstateterrorism/ChronologyofTerror.html

VIDEO NOTES

Many historical films about regional and class conflicts might be useful for envisioning the present global situation. For example, the history of the Irish Republican Army is portrayed in *Michael Collins* (Warner Bros., 1996, 132 min.).

REFERENCES

Anderson, Sean, & Sloan, Stephen. (1995). *Historical dictionary of terrorism*. Metuchen, NJ: Scarecrow Press.
Bhagwati Charan (1907/8-1930). (2000). Retrieved June 3, 2002, from www.webwallas.com/characbhagwati.htm
Blanning, T.C.W. (1998). *The French Revolution: Class war or culture clash?* New York: St. Martin's.
Chandra, Bipan. (1989). *India's struggle for independence*. Columbia, MO: South Asia Books.
Crenshaw, Martha, & Pimlott, John. (Eds.). (1997). *Encyclopedia of world terrorism*. Armonk, NY: M. E. Sharpe.
Farwell, Byron. (1991). *Armies of the raj: From the mutiny to independence, 1858-1947*. New York: W. W. Norton and Company.
Fraser, Antonia. (1996). *Faith and treason: The story of the Gunpowder Plot*. Garden City, NY: Doubleday.
French, Patrick. (1998). *India's journey to independence and division*. North Pomfret, VT: Trafalgar Square Books.
Halperin, Ernst. (1976). *Terrorism in Latin America*. Beverly Hills, CA: Sage.
Haynes, Alan. (1994). *The Gunpowder Plot: Faith in rebellion*. Stroud, England: A. Sutton.
Hoffman, Bruce. (1998). *Inside terrorism*. New York: Columbia University Press.
Hunt, Jocelyn. (1998). *The French Revolution*: New York: Routledge.
Laqueur, Walter. (1977). *Terrorism*. Boston: Little, Brown, and Company.
Laqueur, Walter. (1978). *The terrorist reader: A historical anthology*. Philadelphia: Temple University Press.

Laqueur, Walter. (1987). *The age of terrorism.* Boston: Little, Brown, and Company.

Lefebvre, Georges. (Trans.). (1962). *The French Revolution* (Elizabeth M. Evans, Trans.). New York: Columbia University Press.

Marighella, Carlos. (1985). *Manual of the urban guerrilla.* Chapel Hill, NC: Documentary Publications.

Nicholls, Mark. (1991). *Investigating the Gunpowder Plot.* New York: Manchester University Press.

Poland, James M. (1988). *Understanding terrorism: Groups, strategies, and responses.* Englewood Cliffs, NJ: Prentice Hall.

Ramakrishnan, Padma. (1994). *Gandhi and Indian independence.* Columbia, MO: South Asia Books.

Rapoport, David C. (1984). Fear and trembling: Terrorism in three religious traditions. *American Political Science Review, 78*(3), 658-677.

Rosenberg, Tina. (1991). *Children of Cain: Violence and the violent in Latin America.* New York: Penguin.

Simon, Jeffrey D. (1994). *The terrorist trap: America's experience with terrorism.* Bloomington: Indiana University Press.

Stafford, David. (1971). *From anarchist to reformist: A study of the political activities of Paul Brousse within the First International and the French Socialist Movement 1870-90.* Toronto: University of Toronto Press.

Tarazona-Sevillano, Gabriela. (1990). *Sendero Luminoso and the threat of narcoterrorism.* New York: Praeger.

Vetter, Harold J., & Perlstein, Gary R. (1991). *Perspectives on terrorism.* Belmont, CA: Wadsworth.

FEAR AND TREMBLING: TERRORISM IN THREE RELIGIOUS TRADITIONS

DAVID C. RAPOPORT

As the first comparative study of religious terror groups, the article provides detailed analyses of the different doctrines and methods of the three best-known groups: the Thugs, Assassins, and Zealots-Sicarii. Despite a primitive technology, each developed much more durable and destructive organizations than has any modern secular group.

The differences among the groups reflect the distinguishing characteristics of their respective originating religious communities: Hinduism, Islam, and Judaism. The distinctive characteristics of religious terror are discussed, and relationships between religious and secular forms of terror are suggested.

In 1933 The *Encyclopaedia of the Social Sciences* published fascinating, useful articles on assassination (Lerner) and terrorism (Hardman), which ended on a strange note, namely that the phenomena, which had reached an exceptionally high point at the turn of the century, were declining so much that the subjects would remain interesting only to antiquarians. Future events would be determined by classes and masses, because modern technology had made our world so complex that we had become increasingly *invulnerable* to determined actions by individuals or small groups. Terrorist activity became extensive again after World War II, not in Europe and America, as was the case earlier, but in western colonial territories, particularly in the Palestine Mandate, Cyprus, Malaya, Kenya, Vietnam, and Algeria. But the second edition of the *Encyclopedia*, which was published in 1968, ignored both subjects; perhaps the editors believed the prophecies in the earlier edition!

Academics returned to the subject when terrorist activity revived again in the center of the western world. The flow of articles and books began in the 1970s, and that flow continues to increase every year. A journal entitled *Terrorism* has been established, and many universities offer courses on the subject. As they did 50 years ago, political scientists dominate the field, and in some respects the conventional wisdom governing terrorist studies has not changed: the technological, not the political, environment is normally seen as the decisive determining condition for terrorist activity. Many contemporary studies begin, for example,

I wish to thank members of the UCLA Political Theory Colloquium for useful comments. Special acknowledgments should be given to Blair Campbell, Cornelia Cyss-Wittenstein, Ibrahim Karawan, and Fernando Lopez. P. J. Vatikiotis and Ismail Poonawala read the section on the Assassins closely. Although I did not take all their suggestions, they corrected glaring errors. I also appreciated the constructive suggestions of two anonymous *APSR* reviewers.

by stating that although terrorism has always been a feature of social existence, it became "significant" for the first time in the 1960s when it "increased in frequency" and took on "novel dimensions" as an international or transnational activity, creating in the process a new "mode of conflict."[1] The most common explanation for this "new mode of conflict" is that now we are experiencing the cumulative impacts of specific developments in modern technology. Individuals and tiny groups have capacities that they previously lacked. Weapons are cheaper, more destructive, easier to obtain and to conceal. "The technological quantum jumps from the arrow to the revolver and from the gun to the Molotov Cocktail" (Hacker, 1976, p. ix). Modern communications and transport allow hitherto insignificant persons to coordinate activity quickly over vast spaces. Finally, by giving unusual events extensive coverage, the mass media complete the picture. "You can't be a revolutionary without a color TV: it's as necessary as a gun" (Rubin, 1970, p. 108). [. . .]

Although one can never be sure of what is meant by the term "modern terrorism," the characterizations normally focus on increases in the number of incidents or amounts of damage and on the fact that assaults transcend state borders. Because early experiences are insignificant in these respects, they are deemed irrelevant. One purpose of this article is to show that this view is simply wrong and that the past can provide materials for useful comparisons.

I shall do this by a detailed analysis of three groups: the Thugs, the Assassins, and the Zealots-Sicarii.[2] I have chosen them for several reasons. They are the examples most often cited to illustrate the ancient lineage of terrorism, but they are not discussed in our literature. We cite them because they are so well known elsewhere; no other early terror group has received as much attention. Ironically, although the words thug, assassin, and zealot have even become part of our vocabulary (often to describe terrorists), and most educated persons can identify the groups, they have never been compared.[3]

The cases are inherently interesting and peculiarly instructive. Each group was much more durable and much more destructive than any modern one has been; operating on an international stage, they had great social effects too.

Yet the noose, the dagger, and the sword were the principal weapons they employed, travel was by horse or foot, and the most effective means of communication was by word of mouth. Although a relatively simple and common technology prevailed, each example displayed strikingly different characteristics. The critical variable, therefore, cannot be technology: rather, the purpose and organization of particular groups and the vulnerabilities of particular societies to them are decisive factors. Although the point may be more easily seen in these cases, it must be relevant, I shall argue, in our world too.

Furthermore, the three cases illustrate a kind of terror nowhere adequately analyzed in our theoretical literature, terror designated here as holy or sacred (cf. Laqueur, 1977; Price, 1977; Rapoport, 1971, 1977, 1982a; Thornton, 1964; Walter, 1969). Before the nineteenth century, religion provided the only acceptable justifications for terror, and the differences between sacred and modern expressions (differences of nature, not scale) raise questions about the appropriateness of contemporary definitions. The holy terrorist believes that only a transcendent purpose which fulfills the meaning of the universe can justify terror, and that the deity reveals at some early moment in time both the end and means and may even participate in the process as well. We see terrorists as free to seek different political ends in this world by whatever means of terror they consider most appropriate. This trait characterizes modern terrorism since its inception in the activities of Russian anarchists more than a century ago, and it is found also in many modern terrorist organizations in our century which have had important religious dimensions, i.e., the IRA, EOKA (Cyprus), the FLN (Algeria), and the Irgun (Israel). Sacred terror, on the other hand, never disappeared altogether, and there are signs that it is reviving in new and unusual forms.

As instances of sacred terror, the Thugs, the Assassins, and the Zealots-Sicarii seem remarkably different from each other, and hence they provide some orientation to the range of possibilities associated with the concept. On the other hand, each closely resembles other deviant groups within the same parent religion, Hinduism, Islam, and Judaism, and the three kinds of deviant groups reflect or distort themes distinctive to their particular major religion.[4] In the last respect, what seems to be distinctive about modern terrorists, their belief that terror can be organized rationally, represents or distorts a major theme peculiar to our own culture: a disposition to believe that any activity can be made rational.

I shall begin with a detailed analysis of the cases and in an extended conclusion draw out some implications and comparisons. My concern is largely with methods and doctrines, not the social basis of group activity. The order of the presentation (Thugs, Assassins, and Zealots-Sicarii) is designed to carry the reader from situations where only religious ends are served to one where the political purpose seems, but in fact is not, altogether dominant. The order also illustrates an irony, namely that there can be an inverse relationship between proximity in time and distance from us in spirit. Although extinguished in the nineteenth century, the Thugs seem wholly bizarre because they lacked a political purpose, and we invariably treat terror as though it could only serve one. The Assassins, who gave up terror in the thirteenth century, are comprehensible because their ends and methods remind us of nineteenth-century anarchists who originated modern rebel terror and were themselves conscious of affinities. But it is the Zealots-Sicarii, destroyed in the first century, who appear almost as our true contemporaries because they seem to have purposes and methods that we can fully understand. By means of provocation they were successful in generating a mass insurrection, an aim of most modern terrorists, but one that has probably never been achieved. The purpose of the Zealots-Sicarii, it seems, was to secure national liberation inter alia. The striking resemblances between their activities and those of terrorists with whom we are familiar will put us in a better position to conclude by elaborating the differences already suggested between holy and modern terror.

Thugs

"Terror," Kropotkin wrote, is "propaganda by the deed." We are inclined to think of it as a crime for the sake of publicity. When a bomb explodes, people take notice; the event attracts more attention than a thousand speeches or pictures. If the terror is sustained, more and more people will become interested, wondering why the atrocities occurred and whether the cause seems plausible. Hence virtually all modern conceptions of terrorism assume that the perpetrators only mean to harm their victims incidentally. The principal object is the public, whose consciousness will be aroused by the outrage.

For the holy terrorist, the primary audience is the deity, and depending upon his particular religious conception, it is even conceivable that he does not need or want to have the public witness his deed. The Thugs are our most interesting and instructive case in this respect. They intend their victims to experience terror and to express it visibly for the pleasure of Kali, the Hindu goddess of terror and destruction. Thugs strove to avoid publicity, and although fear of Thugs was widespread, that was the unintended result of their acts. Having no cause that they wanted others to appreciate, they did things that seem incongruous with our conception of how "good" terrorists should behave.

Indeed, one may ask, were the Thugs really terrorists? They are normally identified as such in the academic literature (DeQuincey, 1877; Freedman, 1982; Gupta, 1959; Laqueur, 1977; Lewis, 1967). As persons consciously committing atrocities, acts that go beyond the accepted norms and immunities that regulate violence, they were, according to one established definition, clearly terrorists.[5] Their deceit, unusual weapon (a noose), and practice of dismembering corpses (thereby preventing cremation or proper burial) made Thug violence outrageous by Hindu standards, or, for that matter, by those of any other culture. Cults of this sort may not exist anymore, but as the case of the Zebra Killers or the Fruit of Islam in San Francisco in 1975 demonstrates, the religious purposes of a group may prescribe murders that the public is not meant to notice.[6] A city was terrorized for months, but no one claimed responsibility. It is doubtful whether any American terrorist group produced as much panic as this one did, although terror may not have been its purpose.[7]

No one knows exactly when the Thugs (often called Phansigars or stranglers) first appeared.

Few now believe that the ancient Sagartians, whom Herodotus (VII, 85) describes as stranglers serving in the Persian army, are the people whom the British encountered in India some 2500 years later.[8] But there is evidence that Thugs existed in the seventh century, and almost all scholars agree that they were vigorous in the thirteenth, which means that the group persisted for at least six hundred years.[9] By our standards, the durability of the Thugs is enormous; the IRA, now in its sixth decade, is by far the oldest modern terrorist group.

There are few estimates of the number of people killed by the Thugs. Sleeman (1933) offers a conservative figure of one million for the last three centuries of their history.[10] This figure seems too large, but half that number may be warranted, and that, indeed, is an astonishing figure, especially when one remembers that during the life of modern terrorist organizations, the deaths they cause rarely exceed several hundred, and it would be difficult to find one group that is directly responsible for more than ten thousand deaths.[11] The Thugs murdered more than any known terrorist group, partly because they lasted so much longer. Their impact on Indian economic life must have been enormous, although there is no way to calculate it. If the significance of a terrorist group is to be understood by these measures, the Thugs should be reckoned the most important ever known. The paradox is that, unlike most terrorist groups, they did not or could not threaten society for the simple reason that their doctrine made them attack individuals rather than institutions.

The reinterpretation of a cardinal Hindu myth and theme provided the Thugs with their peculiar purpose and method. Orthodox Hindus believed that in early times a gigantic monster devoured humans as soon as they were created. Kali (also known as Bhavani, Devi, and Durga) killed the monster with her sword, but from each drop of its blood another demon sprang up, and as she killed each one, the spilled blood continued to generate new demons. The orthodox maintained that Kali solved the problem of the multiplying demons by licking the blood from their wounds. But the Thugs believed that Kali sought assistance by making two men from her sweat who were given handkerchiefs from her garment in order to strangle the demons, that is, kill them without shedding a drop of blood. Upon completing their mission, they were commanded to keep the handkerchiefs for their descendants.

In Hindu mythology Kali has many dimensions. She represents the energy of the universe, which means, as the legend suggests, that she both sustains and destroys life. She is also the goddess of time, who presides over endless cycles in which both essential aspects of the life process are carried out. The Thug understood that he was obliged to supply the blood that Kali, his creator, required to keep the world in equilibrium. His responsibility was to keep himself alive as long as possible so that he could keep killing, and it has been estimated that each Thug participated in three murders annually: one claimed to have helped strangle 931 persons.[12] No one retired until he was physically unable to participate in expeditions. The logic of the cycle or balance required the brotherhood to keep its numbers relatively constant. New recruits came largely from the children of Thugs, and the deficiencies were made up by outsiders. The children were initiated into the tradition early by a carefully calculated gradual process—a circumstance that contributed to their resoluteness. Adult Thugs never seemed to experience revulsion, but sometimes the young did; invariably the cases involved those who witnessed events before they were supposed to. Drugs were used rarely, and then only among the young.

For obscure religious reasons Thugs attacked only travellers, and although they confiscated the property of their victims, material gain was not their principal concern, as indicated by their custom of "distinguish(ing) their most important exploits" not by the property gained but "by the number who were killed, the Sixty Soul Affair . . . the Sacrifice of Forty" (Russell & Hira, 1916, vol. 4, p. 567). The legend of their origin also shows murder to be the Thugs' main business, murder in which the death agony was deliberately prolonged to give Kali ample time to enjoy the terror expressed by the victims. It was forbidden to take property without killing and burying its owner first. The Thugs judged the ordinary thief as morally unfit.[13] When religious omens were favorable, many without property were murdered. Similarly, unfavorable omens protected rich travellers.

Although murder was the Thugs' main object, they needed loot—enormous quantities of it—to pay princes who provided their expeditions with international sanctuaries. Without those sanctuaries the brotherhood would not have persisted for such a long time. As we have learned again and again in the contemporary world, when international sanctuaries are provided, relations between states are exacerbated constantly. After numerous frustrating experiences, British authorities decided that appropriate cooperation from neighboring native states was not forthcoming. Nor did recourse to doctrines of hot pursuit prove adequate (Sleeman, 1836, p. 48).[14] Ultimately, the international law governing piracy was utilized, enabling British officials to seize and punish Thugs wherever they were found. The cost was a more massive violation of the rights of independent states, culminating in a direct expansion of imperial jurisdictions, the result that critics of the policy feared most.

A striking feature of Thug operations was that virtually all activity was hemmed in by self-imposed restraints. From the moment he joined an annual sacred expedition until it was disbanded, a Thug was governed by innumerable rules, laid down by Kali, that specified victims, methods of attack, divisions of labor, disposal of corpses, distribution of booty, and training of new members. In a sense, there were no choices to be made because in dubious circumstances Kali manifested her views through omens.

British observers were impressed with the extraordinary "rationality" of the rules established. "Whatever the true source may be, (the system) is beyond all doubt the work of a man of genius, no ordinary man could have fenced and regulated it with so elaborate a code of rules—rules which the Thugs seem to believe are of divine origin, but in each of which we can trace a shrewd practical purpose" (Sleeman, 1839, p. 31).[15] "Ridiculous as their superstitions must appear . . . they serve the most important purposes of cementing the union of the gang, of kindling courage, and confidence; and by an appeal to religious texts deemed infallible of imparting to their atrocities the semblance of divine sanction" (A religion of murder, 1901,

p. 512). "The precautions they take, the artifices they practice, the mode of destroying their victims, calculated at once to preclude any possibility of rescue or escape—of witnesses of the deed—of noises or cries for help—of effusion of blood and, in general of trades of murder. These circumstances conspire to throw a veil of darkness over their atrocities" (Sherwood, 1820, p. 263).

The list of persons immune from attack—women, vagabonds, lepers, the blind, the mutilated, and members of certain artisan crafts (all considered descendants of Kali, like the Thugs themselves)—suggests, perhaps, that the cult may once have had a political purpose. Nonetheless, there can be no politics without publicity.

Whatever purpose these rules were designed to serve, they could not be altered even when the life of the brotherhood was at stake, because they were perceived to be divine ordinances. Europeans, for example, were immune from attack—a prohibition that virtually enabled Thugs to escape attention. When the Thugs were discovered, the same rule kept them from retaliating directly against the small, relatively unprotected group of British administrators who ultimately exterminated them.[16] Their commitment to rules produced another unanticipated consequence: in the nineteenth century when some of its members became increasingly concerned with loot, the brotherhood became lax. This gave the British a unique opportunity to persuade older, more tradition-bound members that the ancient Thug belief that Kali would destroy the order when its members no longer served her required them now to help their goddess by becoming informers.

To us, a Thug is a brute, ruffian, or cut-throat, but the word originally signified deceiver, and the abilities of Thugs to deceive distinguish them radically from other related Hindu criminal associations, which also worshipped Kali but "exercised their (criminal) profession *without* disguise."[17] Thugs literally lived two very different sorts of lives, which continually amazed the British. For the greater portion of the year (sometimes 11 out of 12 months), Thugs were models of propriety, known for their industry, temperance, generosity, kindliness, and trustworthiness. British officers who unwittingly had employed them as guardians for their children lavishly praised the reliability of Thugs who had strangled hundreds of victims. An extraordinary capacity for deception was a cardinal feature of Thug tactics too. Long journeys in India always involved great hazards, requiring parties large enough to repel attacks by marauders. Groups of Thugs disguised as travellers, sometimes numbering as many as 60 persons, were often successful in persuading legitimate travellers to join forces, thereby increasing the security of all. In some cases, the intimate congenial associations would last months before the opportunity to strike occurred. (Strangling is a difficult art and requires exceptional conditions.) Usually, close contacts of this sort create bonds between people which make cold-blooded murder difficult. In fact, the striking way in which intimacy can transform relationships between potential murderers and their victims in our own day has stimulated academics to invent a new concept—the Stockholm syndrome (Lang, 1974). But the Thugs seemed indifferent to the emotions that make such transformations possible, testifying that pity or remorse never prevented them from acting. Nonetheless, their victims were never abused. The early judicial records and interviews do not provide a single case of wanton cruelty: the victims were sacrifices, the property of Kali, and, as in all religions, the best sacrifices are those offered without blemish.[18] "A Thug considers the persons murdered precisely in the light of victims offered up to the Goddess, and he remembers them, as a Priest of Jupiter remembered the oxen and as a Priest of Saturn the children sacrificed upon the altars" (Sleeman, 1836, p. 8).

Thugs believed that death actually benefited the victim, who would surely enter paradise, whereas Thugs who failed to comply with Kali's commands would become impotent, and their families would become either extinct or experience many misfortunes. British observers admired the cheerfulness of convicted Thugs about to be hanged, sublimely confident that they would be admitted to paradise.[19] Thugs spoke also of the personal pleasure that their particular methods generated. "Do you ever feel remorse for murdering in cold blood, and after the pretense of friendship, those whom you have beguiled into a false sense of security?" a British interrogator asked. "Certainly not. Are you yourself not a hunter of big game, and do you not enjoy the thrill of the stalk, the pitting of your cunning against that of an animal, and are you not pleased at seeing it dead at your feet? So it is with the Thug, who indeed regards the stalking of men as a higher form of sport. For you *sahib* have but the instincts of wild beasts to overcome, whereas the Thug has to subdue the suspicions and fear of intelligent men . . . often heavily guarded, and familiar with the knowledge that the roads are dangerous. Game for our hunting is defended from all points save those of flattering and cunning. Cannot you imagine the pleasure of overcoming such protection during days of travel in their company, the joy in seeing suspicion change to friendship until that wonderful moment arrives. . . . Remorse, sahib? Never! Joy and elation often" (Sleeman, 1839, pp. 3-4).

ASSASSINS

The Assassins (known also as Ismailis-Nizari) survived two centuries (1090-1275). Unlike the Thugs they had political objectives; their purpose was to fulfill or purify Islam, a community whose political and religious institutions were inseparable.[20] Although by Thug standards they inflicted few casualties and wrought negligible economic damage, the Assassins seriously threatened the governments of several states, especially those of the Turkish Seljuk Empire in Persia and Syria.

As Weber (1955, p. 2) pointed out, Islam has always been preeminently dedicated to delivering a moral message aimed at transforming social existence in *this* world. Terror in Islam, therefore, has an extra dimension not present in Hinduism. The Thugs were concerned with three parties (the assailant, his victim, and a deity), but the Assassins reached out to a fourth one as well, a public or a moral community whose sympathies could be aroused by deeds that evoked attention. They did not need mass media to reach interested audiences, because their prominent victims were murdered in venerated sites and royal courts, usually on holy days when many witnesses would be present.

To be noticed is one thing, to be understood is another, and when the object of a situation is to arouse a public, those threatened will try to place their own interpretations on the terrorist's message. Their opportunities to do so will be maximized if the assailant breaks down, or even if he tries to evade arrest. The doctrine of the Assassins seems constructed to prevent both possibilities. One who intends his act to be a public spectacle is unlikely to escape in any case. The Assassins prepared the assailant for this circumstance by preventing him from even entertaining the idea that he might survive. His weapon, which "was always a dagger, never poison, never a missile," seems designed to make certain that he would be captured or killed. He "usually made no attempt to escape; there is even a suggestion that to survive a mission was shameful. The words of a twelfth-century western author are revealing: "When, therefore, any of them have chosen to *die* in this way . . . he himself [i.e., the Chief] hands them knives which are, so to speak, 'consecrated'" (Lewis, 1967, p. 127).

Martyrdom, the voluntary acceptance of death in order to "demonstrate the . . . truth" to man, is a central, perhaps critical, method of message-giving religions, used both to dispel the doubts of believers and to aid proselytizing efforts. One cannot understand the Assassins without emphasizing the deeply embedded Muslim admiration for martyrs, particularly for those who die attempting to kill Islam's enemies. Assassin education clearly prepared assailants to seek martyrdom. The word used to designate the assailants—*fidayeen* (consecrated or dedicated ones)—indicates that they (like the victims of the Thugs) were considered religious sacrifices who freed themselves from the guilt of all sins and thereby gained "entry into paradise" (Kohlberg, 1976, p. 72).[21]

The Hindu image of history as an endless series of cycles makes Thuggee conceivable. Message-oriented religions are inclined to assume a unilinear view of history that may be fulfilled when all humans hear and accept the message. Because this aspiration is frustrated, these religions periodically produce millenarian movements predicated on the belief that an existing hypocritical religious establishment has so corrupted their original message that only extraordinary action can renew the community's faith.

Islamic millenarian movements are largely associated with the Shia (the minority), who believe that eventually a *Mahdi* (Messiah or Rightly Guided One) would emerge to lead a holy war (*jihad*) against the orthodox establishment to cleanse Islam. In the various Jewish and Christian messianic images violence may or may not appear, but "an *essential* part of the Mahdist theory regards the *jihad* in the sense of an armed revolutionary struggle, as the method whereby a perfected social order *must* be brought into being" (Hodgkin, 1977, p. 307; see also Kohlberg, 1976; MacEoin, 1982; Tyan, 1960). The believer's obligation is to keep his faith intact until the *Mahdi* summons him. To protect a believer among hostile Muslims until the moment arrives, the Shia permit pious dissimulation, *taqiyya*. The pure are allowed to conceal their beliefs for much the same reason that we condone deception during war. Should an opportunity materialize, the Shia must "use their tongues," or preach their faith openly; but not until the *Mahdi* arrives are they allowed to "draw the sword" (MacEoin, 1982, p. 121).

The Assassins apparently interpreted the injunction prohibiting swords against other Muslims to mean that the true believer could use other weapons, or perhaps even that he should do so in order to expedite the arrival of the *Mahdi*. In this respect, they resemble earlier Islamic millenarian groups, which always attached a ritual significance to particular weapons. Some eighth-century cults strangled their victims, and one clubbed them to death with wooden cudgels (Friedlaender, 1907, 1909; Watt, 1973, p. 48). In each case the weapon chosen precluded escape and invited martyrdom.

The Assassins originated from the more active Shia elements who "used their tongues," organizing missionaries or summoners to persuade fellow Muslims with respect to the true meaning of their faith. Although their roots were in Persia, many were educated in Egyptian missionary schools. When the capabilities of the Shia (Ismaili) state in Egypt to promote millenarian doctrines waned, the founder of the Assassins declared his independence, seized several impregnable mountain fortresses, and made them hospitable to all sorts of refugees. Here the Assassins developed a distinctive systematic Gnostic theology which promised a messianic fulfillment of history in a harmonious anarchic condition in which law would be abolished and human nature perfected.

Like the Thugs, the Assassins moved across state lines constantly. But the differences are important. The Thugs found it easy to make arrangements with princes who would protect them for profit and upon condition that they operate abroad. But the Assassins, aiming to reconstitute Islam into a single community again, were compelled by their doctrine to organize an international conspiracy that could not be planted in an existing Islamic state. Therefore, they had to establish their own state: a league of scattered mountain fortresses or city-states (Hodgson, 1955, p. 99).

For the first time in history, perhaps, a state found its principal raison d'etre in organizing international terror. The state provided means for the creation of an efficient enduring organization that could and did recover from numerous setbacks. The earlier millenarian sodalities were too scattered, their bases were too accessible, and their consequent insignificance often made them unable to achieve even the acknowledgment of historians, which alone could make them known to us. Isolation gave the Assassins both the space and the time required to create a quasi-monastic form of life and to train leaders, missionaries, and *fidayeen*. When their popular support in urban centers evaporated after 50 years, the Assassins survived for still another century and a half and would have persisted much longer had not Mongol and Arab armies destroyed their state (Hodgson, 1955, p. 115).

To facilitate their work they organized an extensive network of supporting cells in sympathetic urban centers. Often key persons in the establishment provided internal access, support the Assassins gained through conversion, bribery, and intimidation. Since orthodox Muslims understood the importance of internal support, the Assassins manipulated apprehensions by implicating enemies as accomplices— a maneuver that multiplied suspicions and confusion.

A successful assassination policy depended upon establishing the purpose of a murder as a measure necessary to protect missionaries. Thus, one professional soldier likens the *fidayeen* to armed naval escorts, which never engage the enemy unless the convoy itself is attacked (Tugwell, 1979, p. 62). Victims were orthodox religious or political leaders who refused to heed warnings, and therefore provoked an attack by being scornful of the New Preaching, by attempting to prevent it from being heard, and by acting in ways that demonstrated complicity in Islam's corruption.

Assassin legends, like those of any millenarian group, are revealing. A most remarkable one concerned the victim-*fidayeen* relationship. Normally the movement placed a youthful member in the service of a high official. Through devotion and skill over the years he would gain his master's trust, and then, at the appropriate time, the faithful servant would plunge a dagger into his master's back. So preternatural did this immunity from personal or ordinary feelings seem to orthodox Muslims that they described the group as "hashish eaters" (*hashashin*), the source of our term assassin. (Although there is no evidence that drugs were used, the ability to use the doctrine of *taqiyya* and the fact that training began in childhood may help explain *fidayeen* behavior.) The legend is significant, too, for what it demonstrates about public responses. Everywhere Assassins inspired awe. Those favorably disposed to their cause would find such dedication admirable, whereas opponents would see it as hateful, repulsive, and inhuman fanaticism. Less obvious but much more interesting, perhaps, as a clue to responses of neutrals, is the transformation that the meaning of the term assassin underwent in medieval Europe, where initially it signified devotion and later meant one who killed by treachery (Lewis, 1967, p. 3).

The potential utility of an assassination policy is obvious. Dramatically staged assassinations draw immense attention to a cause. In the Muslim context too, the basis of power was manifestly personal. "When a Sultan died his troops were automatically dispersed. When an Amir died his lands were in disorder" (Hodgson, 1955, p. 84). When conceived as an alternative to war, assassinations can seem moral too. The assassin may be discriminating; he can strike the great and guilty, leaving the masses who are largely innocent untouched.

The problems created by an assassination policy become clear only in time. A series of assassinations must provoke immense social antagonism in the normal course of events; popular identification with some leaders will exist and assassinations themselves entail treachery. "There can be good faith even in war but not in unannounced murder. Though Muslims . . . commonly . . . used an assassination as an expedient, the adoption of . . . a regular and admitted (assassination) policy horrified them and has horrified men ever since" (Hodgson, 1955, p. 84). A similar logic moved Immanuel Kant (1948, p. 6) to describe belligerents who employ assassins as criminals; such a breach of faith intensifies hatred and diminishes the possibility of achieving a peace settlement before one party exterminates the other.[22]

As one might expect, the orthodox often responded by indiscriminately slaughtering those deemed sympathetic to the *fidayeen* (Hodgson, 1955, pp. 76-77, 111-113). The Assassins, however, reacted with remarkable restraint, eschewing numerous opportunities to reply in kind. Acts of urban terrorism occurred, the quarters of the orthodox were firebombed, but so infrequent were these incidents that one can only conclude that the rebels believed that another assassination was the only legitimate response to atrocities provoked by assassination.[23] The political consequence of this restraint was clear; after forty years, support for the Assassins among urban elements disappeared, and the massacres ceased (Hodgson, 1955, p. 115).

The commitment to a single, stylized form of attack is puzzling. Most of the Assassins' early millenarian predecessors found assassination attractive too, but other forms of terror were known.[24] More than any other millenarian group, the Assassins had resources to use other tactics and much to lose by failing to do so. Still, Assassin armies only protected their bases and raided caravans for booty, for it seems that Assassin doctrine made assassination and war mutually exclusive alternatives. The pattern is quite conspicuous during one of those strange periods in the movement's history when, for tactical reasons, it decided to become an orthodox community. "Instead of dispatching murderers to kill officers and divines, Hasan III sent armies to conquer provinces and cities; and by building mosques and bathhouses in the villages completed the transformation of his domain from a lair of assassins to a respectable kingdom, linked by ties of matrimonial alliance to his neighbors" (Hodgson, 1955, pp. 217-239; Lewis, 1967, p. 80). Assassin encounters with Christians also reflected the view that the dagger was reserved for those who betrayed the faith and the sword for persons who had never accepted it. When the Assassins first met invading Crusaders in Syria during the early twelfth century, they used their armies, not their *fidayeen* (Lewis, 1967, p. 108).

The peculiar reluctance to modify their tactics or to use their resources more efficiently probably had its origins, as the doctrines of all millenarian groups do, in reinterpretations of major precedents in the parent religion. To the millenarian, those precedents explain the religion's original success, and the abandonment of those precedents explains why there has been a failure to realize its promise. The life of Mohammed probably prescribed the model for Assassin strategy. The group began, for example, by withdrawing to primitive places of refuge (*dar al-hijra*), a decision that "was a deliberate imitation of that archetype from Mohammed's own career," who fled to remote but more receptive Medina when he failed to convert his own people in Mecca. "Medina was the first *dar al-hijra* of Islam, the first place of refuge—whence to return in triumph to the unbelieving lands from which one had to flee persecuted" (Hodgson, 1955, pp. 79-80). Islam's calendar dates from this event, and the pattern of withdrawing in order to begin again became one that millenarian elements in Islam normally followed and in fact do still, as recent studies of Muslim terrorist groups in Egypt show (Hodgkin, 1977; Ibrahim, 1980).

Mohammed's unusual employment of military forces and assassins while in Medina seems particularly instructive.[25] Initially, the army had only two tasks, to defend the community against attacks and to raid caravans for booty. Simultaneously, he permitted (authorized?) assassinations of prominent persons within or on the fringes of Islam, "hypocrites" (*munafikun*) who had "provoked" attacks by displaying contempt for some aspect of Mohammed's teachings. Their deaths released hitherto latent sympathies for Islam among their followers.[26] The process of purifying, or consolidating the original nucleus of the faith, seemed to be the precondition of expansion. When Mohammed decided the community was ready to become universal, the army was given its first offensive role and assassinations ceased!

Other aspects of the assassination pattern may have seemed suggestive too. The assassins' deeds were means to compensate or atone for deficiencies in ardor. The ability to overcome normal inhibitions or personal attachments to the victim was a significant measure of commitment. In every case, for example, assassin and victim were kinsmen, and no stronger bond was known then.[27] The victims were not likely to defend themselves (e.g., they might be asleep or be women or old men), and they were often engaged in activities likely to evoke the assailant's compassion (e.g., they were playing with children or making love). As known associates of Mohammed, the assassins could only gain access to their victims by denying their faith or denouncing the Messenger of Allah.

A major difference between the earlier assassins and the later *fidayeen* is that one group returned to Mohammed for judgment, whereas the other actively sought martyrdom. In explaining this difference, remember that the origin of the *fidayeen* is in the Shia and Ismaili sects. Those groups link themselves to Ali and Husain, whom they consider Mohammed's true heirs. Ali and Husain were themselves both martyred after authorizing assassinations, and their martyrdoms became as central to their followers as Christ's passion is to Christians.

We do not have the primary sources to determine how the Assassins actually justified their tactics, but we know they saw themselves as engaged in a struggle to purify Islam and made extraordinary efforts to demonstrate that they acted defensively. The *fidayeen* put themselves in situations in which intimate bonds or personal feelings would be violated in order to demonstrate conviction. Assassin armies had one purpose in the *hijra*; later, they were likely to have another. The precedents were well known to anyone familiar with Mohammed's life and with the lives of figures most central to the Shia. Can there be justifications more compelling for believers than those that derive directly from the founders of their faith?

ZEALOTS-SICARII[28]

There are resemblances between the Assassins and the Zealots-Sicarii. Both were inspired by messianic hopes to seek maximum publicity. Both interpreted important events in the founding period of their religion as precedents for their tactics and to mean also that those who died in this struggle secured their places in paradise. Like the Assassins, the Sicarii (daggermen) were identified with a particular weapon, and both rebellions had an international character. Nonetheless, the differences between the two, which derive from variations in the content of their respective messianic and founding myths, are even more striking.

The Zealots-Sicarii survived for approximately 25 years, a brief existence by the standards of the Assassins, but their immediate and long-run influence was enormous. Holy terrorists are normally concerned with members of their own religious culture, but the Jews were also interested in generating a mass uprising against the large Greek population that lived in Judea and against the Romans who governed them both. The revolt proved disastrous and led to the destruction of the Temple, the desolation of the land, and the mass suicide at Masada. Moreover, Zealot-Sicarii activities inspired two more popular uprisings against Rome in successive generations, which resulted in the extermination of the large Jewish centers in Egypt and Cyprus, the virtual depopulation of Judea, and the final tragedy—the Exile itself, which exercised a traumatic impact on Jewish consciousness and became the central feature of Jewish experience for the next two thousand years, altering virtually every institution in Jewish life. It would be difficult to find terrorist activity in any historical period which influenced the life of a community more decisively.

The impact of the Jewish terrorists obviously stems from their ability to generate popular insurrections, an unusual capacity among religious terrorists which makes them particularly interesting to us because ever since the Russian Anarchists first created the doctrine of modern terror, the development of a *levée-en-masse* by means of provocation tactics has been the principal aim of most groups. Very few have succeeded, and none has had as much success as the Zealots-Sicarii did. Why were they so peculiar?

The nature of their messianic doctrines simultaneously suggested the object of terror and permitted methods necessary to achieve it. Jewish apocalyptic prophecies visualize the signs of the imminence of the messiah as a series of massive catastrophes involving whose populations, "the upsetting of all moral order to the point of dissolving the laws of nature" (Scholem, 1971, p. 12). This vision saturated Judaism for a generation preceding the genesis of Zealot-Sicarii activity, creating a state of feverish expectancy. "Almost every event was seized upon . . . to discover how and in what way it represented a Sign of the Times and threw light on the approach of the End of the Days. The whole condition of the Jewish people was psychologically abnormal. The strongest tales and imaginings could find ready credence" (Schonfield, 1965, p. 19). New messianic pretenders flourished everywhere, because so many people believed that the signs indicating a messianic intervention were quite conspicuous: Judea was occupied by an alien military power, and prominent Jews were acquiescing in "the desecration of God's name" or accepting the culture of the conqueror.

In all apocalyptic visions God determines the date of the redemption. Still, these visions often contain some conception that humans can speed the process. Prayer, repentance, and martyrdom are the most common methods. When these do not produce results and a period of unimaginable woe is perceived as the precondition of paradise, it will only be a matter of time before believers will act to force history, or bring about that precondition. Jewish terrorist activity appeared to have two purposes: to make oppression so intolerable that insurrection was inevitable, and, subsequently, to frustrate every attempt to reconcile the respective parties.

The names Zealot and Sicarii both derive from a much earlier model in Jewish history, Phineas, a high priest in the days of Moses. His zeal or righteous indignation averted a plague that afflicted Israel when the community tolerated acts of apostasy and "whoring with Moabite women." Taking the law into his own hands, he killed a tribal chief and his concubine who flaunted their contempt for God in a sacred site. Phineas is the only Biblical hero to receive a reward directly from God (*Numbers* 25:11). In purifying the community, his action prepared the way for the Holy War (*herem*) which God commanded Israel to wage against the Canaanites for the possession of the Promised Land. The Bible repeatedly refers to the terror that the *herem* was supposed to produce and to Israel's obligation to destroy all persons with their property who remain in the land, lest they become snares or corrupting influences. The word *herem*, it should be noted, designates a sacred sphere where ordinary standards do not apply, and in a military context, a *herem* is war without limits.[29]

The name Sicarii comes from the daggers (*sica*) used when the group first made its appearance. Rabbinic commentary indicates that Phineas used the head of his spear as a dagger, and the Sicarii normally assassinated prominent Jews, especially priests, who in their opinion had succumbed to Hellenistic culture. As in Phineas's case, these acts were also efforts to create a state of war readiness, and, more specifically, to intimidate priests who were anxious to avoid war with Rome and whose opposition could prevent it from materializing.

The Sicarii committed murders in broad daylight in the heart of Jerusalem. The holy days were their special seasons when they would mingle with the crowd carrying short daggers concealed under their clothing with which they stabbed their enemies. Thus, when they fell, the murderers joined in cries of indignation, and through this plausible behavior, were never discovered. The first assassinated was Jonathan, the high-priest. After his death there were numerous daily murders. The panic created was more alarming than the calamity itself; everyone, as on the battlefield, hourly expected death. Men kept watch at a distance on their enemies and would not trust even their friends when they approached (Josephus, 1926a, vol. 2, pp. 254-257).

Although their name reminds us of Phineas's weapon, his spirit and purpose were more decisive influences. Unlike the *fidayeen*, the Sicarii did not limit themselves to assassinations. They engaged military forces openly, often slaughtering their prisoners. They took hostages to pressure the priests and terrorized wealthy Jewish landowners in the hopes of compelling a land redistribution according to Biblical traditions. The Zealots illustrate the point even more clearly. Their Hebrew name signified the righteous indignation that Phineas personified, but they rarely plotted assassinations, and their principal antagonists were non-Jews who dwelled in the land. Phineas was also known for his audacity, which Zealot-Sicarii assaults often reflect. (It is not without interest that rage and audacity are qualities most admired and cultivated by modern terrorists.) Their atrocities occurred on the most holy days to exploit the potential for publicity therein, and, more important, to demonstrate that not even the most sacred occasions could provide immunity. Note, for example, Josephus's description of how the Sicarii massacred a Roman garrison, after it had secured a covenant (the most inviolable pledge Jews could make) that guaranteed the troops safe passage.

> When they had laid down their arms, the rebels massacred them; the Romans neither resisting, nor suing for mercy, but merely appealing with loud cries to the covenant! . . . The whole city was a scene of dejection, and among the moderates there was not one who was not racked with the thought that he should personally have to suffer for the rebels' crime. For to add to its heinousness the massacre took place on the Sabbath, a day on which from religious scruples Jews abstain from even the most innocent acts (Josephus, 1926a, vol. 2, p. 451).

The massacre electrified the Greeks, who constituted a significant portion of the population in Judea and were the local source of Roman recruitment. Jews in numerous cities were massacred, and everywhere the Greeks were repaid in kind. The action and the response illustrate vividly some salient differences between Muslim and Jewish terrorists. *Fidayeen* terror was an auxiliary weapon designed to protect their missions where the main work of the movement was done, converting the population to a particular messianic doctrine. Patient and deliberate, the Assassins acted as though they expected to absorb the Muslim world piecemeal. The Zealots and the Sicarii saw themselves not as the propagators of a doctrine but as revolutionary catalysts who moved men by force of their audacious action, exploiting mass expectations that a cataclysmic messianic deliverance was imminent.

To generate a mass uprising quickly and to sustain constantly increasing polarizing pressures, the Zealots-Sicarii developed an array of tactics unusual by Thug and Assassin standards. Participants (despite their contrary intentions) were pulled into an ever-escalating struggle by shock tactics which manipulated their fear, outrage, sympathy, and guilt. Sometimes these emotional affects were provoked by terrorist atrocities which went beyond the consensual norms governing violence; at other times they were produced by provoking the enemy into committing atrocities against his will.

Thugs and Assassin tactics always remained the same, but in the different phases of the Jewish uprising, striking changes occurred which seemed designed for specific contexts. The rebellion began with passive resistance in the cities. This tactic, of which the Jewish example may be the earliest recorded by historians, merits comment, for in our world (e.g., Cyprus and Northern Ireland), passive resistance has often appeared as an initial step in conflicts which later matured into full-scale terrorist campaigns.[30] Our experience has been that many who would have shrunk from violence, let alone terror, often embrace passive resistance as a legitimate method to rectify grievances, without understanding how the ensuing drama may intensify and broaden commitments by simultaneously exciting hopes and fanning smoldering hostilities.

In the Jewish case, before antagonisms had been sufficiently developed and when Roman military strength still seemed irresistible, passive resistance might have been the only illegal form of action that many Jews would willingly undertake. Initially, the confrontations involved Jewish claims, sometimes never before made, for respect due to their sacred symbols, and governments learned that, willy-nilly, they had backed, or been backed, into situations in which they either had to tolerate flagrant contempt for the law or commit actions that seemed to threaten the Jewish religion, the only concern that could unite all Jews. More often than one might expect, the Romans retreated in the face of this novel form of resistance. They admired the Jews' displays of courage, restraint, and intensity, and they learned how difficult and dangerous it was to break up demonstrations that included women and children (Josephus, 1926a, vol. 2, pp. 169, 195; 1926b, vol. 18, pp. 55, 269). They feared a rebellion that could engulf the eastern portion of the Empire, which was at least one-fifth Jewish and contained a significant class of Jewish sympathizers (*sebomenoi*, God-fearers) whose influence seemed to reach members of Rome's ruling circles.

The possibility that the conflict could become an international one troubled Rome. Judea was on the frontier next to Parthia, the last remaining major power in the ancient world. Parthia had intervened in earlier conflicts. Even if Parthia wanted to avoid involvement, she might find it difficult to do so because her Jewish population was large, and one Parthian client state had a Jewish dynasty that bore a special hatred for Rome. Parthian Jews were important figures in the early stage of the rebellion. The great annual pilgrimages of Parthian Jews to Jerusalem and the massive flow of wealth they contributed to maintain the Temple gave evidence of the strength of their tie to Judea, a bond that a modern historian compares to that which knitted American Jews to those in Palestine during the uprising against Britain.

For some time before the rebellion, Rome kept expanding the unusual exemptions given Jews, and the uprising was fueled partly by rising expectations. But Rome's anxiety to avoid a serious conflict simply made her more vulnerable to tactics calculated to produce outrage. Her restraint encouraged reckless behavior and weakened the case of Jewish moderates who argued that although Rome might be conciliatory, she was wholly determined to remain in Judea.

Large passive demonstrations against authority tend to produce violence unless both sides have discipline and foresight. When some on either side prefer violence, or when passive resistance is viewed not as an end in itself, but

as a tactic that can be discarded when other tactics seem more productive, explosions will occur. Whatever the particular reason in this case, demonstrators soon became abusive, and bands of rock-throwing youths broke off from the crowds. When Roman troops (trying to be inconspicuous by discarding military dress and exchanging swords for wooden staves) were attacked, Roman discipline dissolved. The crowds panicked, and hundreds of innocent bystanders were trampled to death in Jerusalem's narrow streets. This pattern kept repeating itself, and the atrocities seemed especially horrifying because they normally occurred on holy days when Jerusalem was crowded with pilgrims, many of whom were killed while attending religious services. The massive outrage generated by Roman atrocities and the assassination campaign against the moderates finally intimidated reluctant priests into refusing to allow Roman sacrifices at the Temple. Rome viewed that act as a rejection of her sovereignty or as a declaration of war, and this gave the militants a plausible case that the war was indeed a *herem*.

When the war finally occurred, many on both sides hoped to conclude it quickly with a political settlement. These hopes were given a severe jolt early after the first military engagement. When the tiny Roman garrison in Jerusalem, which had laid down its arms for a covenant of safe passage, was massacred, a pattern of reprisal and counter-reprisal spread throughout the eastern portion of the Empire. Roman troops ran amuck. Yet when military discipline was finally restored, the Roman campaign quite unexpectedly was restrained. Military advantages were not pressed, as hope persisted that the olive branch offered would be seized. Understanding that most Jews wanted peace, Rome believed that the atrocities of Jew against Jew would eventually destroy the popular tolerance requisite for all terrorist movements. A significant Jewish desertion rate, including many important personalities, kept Roman hopes alive for negotiating a peace without strenuous military efforts. But various Jewish atrocities, which culminated in the cold-blooded murder of Roman peace envoys, led to the conclusion that only total war was feasible (Josephus, 1926a, vol. 2, p. 526).

Zealot-Sicarii strategy seemed admirably designed to provoke a massive uprising. Consecutive atrocities continually narrowed prospects for a political, or mutually agreeable, solution, serving to destroy the credibility of moderates on both sides while steadily expanding the conflict, which enlisted new participants. But no master hand can be detected in this process, and one can see it as an irrational process. Jewish terrorists reflect a bewildering assortment of forces. Several Zealot and at least two Sicarii organizations existed, and many other groups participated, but only a few can be identified. Then, as now, the effect of multiplicity was to encourage each element toward even more heinous atrocities, in order to prove the superiority of its commitments, and in time the groups decimated each other. As these extraordinary actions unfolded, the participating groups, like so many of their modern counterparts, found it necessary to make even more fantastic claims about their enemies and even more radical promises about the social reconstruction that would result from their victory. Ferrero's comment on the dynamics of the French Reign of Terror seems quite pertinent. "The Jacobins did not spill all that blood because they believed in popular sovereignty as a religious truth; rather they tried to believe in popular sovereignty as a religious truth because their fear made them spill all that blood" (1972, p. 100; cf. Josephus, 1926b, vol. 18, p. 269).

To focus on popular insurrection as the principal object, however, is to misconstrue the Zealot-Sicarii view. Insurrection was only a sign of messianic intervention, and because they were concerned with a divine audience, they did things that no one preoccupied with a human audience alone would dream of doing. The decision of Zealot leaders to burn the food supply of their own forces during Jerusalem's long siege becomes intelligible only if one believes that He might see it as proof that the faithful had placed all their trust in Him. God, therefore, would have no choice; was He not bound by His promise to rescue the righteous remnant? Because many thought God would be moved by their sufferings, the most profound disaster often created new hopes. When the Temple was burning (and the war irretrievably lost), a messianic impostor persuaded six thousand new

recruits that the fire signified that the time for deliverance had finally arrived. Compared to the Thugs and Assassins, the Zealots-Sicarii seem free to choose their tactics, but how can one be free to follow an impossible goal?

CONCLUSION

These cases provide materials to broaden the study of comparative terrorism. Each contains parallels worth pondering, and the three together illustrate the uniqueness of sacred terror and thus provide a perspective for viewing modern terror and a glimpse of the latter's special properties.[31]

Our obliviousness to holy terror rests on a misconception that the distinction between it and the modern form is one of scale, not of nature or kind. A most conspicuous expression of this misconception is the conventional wisdom that terrorist operations require modern technology to be significant. There are relationships between changes in technology and changes in terrorist activity, but they have not been seriously studied. More important, every society has weapon, transport and communication facilities, and the clear meaning of our cases is that the decisive variables for understanding differences among the forms terror may take are a group's purpose, organization, methods, and above all the public's response to that group's activities.

This conclusion should shape our treatment of the dynamics of modern terrorism. There is no authoritative history of modern terrorism that traces its development from its inception more than a century ago. When that history is written, the cyclical character of modern terror will be conspicuous, and those cycles will be related not so much to technological changes as to significant political watersheds which excited the hopes of potential terrorists and increased the vulnerability of society to their claims. The upsurge in the 1960s, for example, would be related to Vietnam just as the activities immediately after World War II would appear as an aspect of the decline in the legitimacy of Western colonial empires. Since doctrine, rather than technology, is the ultimate source of terror, the analysis of modern forms must begin with the French, rather than the Industrial Revolution.

When the assumption concerning technology is abandoned, early cases seem more valuable as a source for appropriate parallels. We have already suggested a number of potentially instructive instances. For example, the Zealot-Sicarii case may be the only instance of a successful strategy that actually produced a mass insurrection—the announced objective of modern revolutionary terror. It illuminates predicaments inherent in this strategy while exposing aspects of societies especially vulnerable to it. It is worth noting that the problems illustrated by this particular experience concerned Menachem Begin greatly, because his strategy as the leader of the Irgun in the uprising against Britain was in part conceived to avoid "mistakes" made by the Zealots-Sicarii (Rapoport, 1982b, pp. 31-33).

The international context provides another parallel. It played a crucial role in sustaining the terror. The Thugs and Assassins had valuable foreign sanctuaries. Favorable, albeit different, international climates of opinion helped all three groups. In each case there was cooperation among terrorists from different countries; in one instance a state was actually directing an international terrorist organization, and in another there existed the threat of potential military intervention by an outside power. The problems posed and the constraints involved provide useful points of comparison with modern experiences. The difficulties in dealing with terrorists who have foreign sanctuaries and the ways in which those difficulties may exacerbate international relations are familiar. Rome's vulnerability to terror tactics reminds one of Western colonial empires after World War II, but the ultimate reason for the different outcomes was that Rome never doubted her right to rule. Britain's ability to exterminate the Thugs quickly in the nineteenth century was to a large extent the consequence of a favorable British and an indifferent international opinion. Perhaps the doubt expressed in the 1930s by a student of the Thugs that Britain could not have acted as decisively to deal with the same problem a century later was unwarranted, but the concern reflected a very different political environment, one that is even more deeply rooted today.[32]

How should we characterize sacred terror? Obviously there are enormous variations in its expressions which extend to purposes, methods, responses, and differences that derive from the ingenuity of the individual terror cult which in turn is limited by boundaries established by the original religion. In an odd, interesting way, the terrorist as a deviant highlights unique features of the parent religion that distinguish it from other religions, e.g., concepts of the relation of the divine to history and to social structure.

Because Hinduism provides no grounds for believing that the world can be transformed, the Thugs could neither perceive themselves nor could they be perceived as rebels. In imagining themselves obligated to keep the world in balance, they were part of the established order, though obviously not in it. In Islam and Judaism, the potentialities for radical attacks on institutions are inherent in the ambiguity of unfulfilled divine promises, which no existing establishment can reconcile fully with its own dominance. Because the promises are known to every member of the religious community, the Islamic or Jewish terrorist has a human audience not present in Hinduism. To reach this audience Islamic and Jewish terrorists must become visible and must either conquer all or be extinguished. There can be no such imperative with respect to the Thugs, as the extraordinarily long life of the order suggests. Initially the British were very reluctant to suppress the Thugs because they believed that it would be dangerous to disturb the local and foreign interests embedded in Thug activity. The decisive impetus was a rekindling of evangelical feeling in Victorian England which struck out at the world slave trade and was outraged by accounts of three ancient Hindu practices: infanticide, immolation of widows, and Thuggee. Under Hindu administration, Thuggee would have survived much longer.

If a particular religion creates boundaries for its terrorists, it follows that similarities within traditions will be as striking as differences among traditions. In the Hindu world, an ancient species of criminal tribes, all of which worshipped Kali, persisted. Each performed a particular criminal vocation, was committed to a special way of achieving it, and believed that its actions were legitimate by Hindu standards. The

Thugs were unique among those tribes in not professing their practices openly; perhaps they could not have been able to survive the outrage and horror provoked by them. The Assassins' situation is more straightforward; they were the latest and most successful Muslim millenarian assassination cult and the only one that established a state, the mechanism required for thorough organization. The Assassins consummated a millenarian tradition of terror, but the Zealots-Sicarii appeared to have initiated one, which ended after three disastrous massive revolts in as many generations. Holy terrorists normally victimize members of the parent religion, but the Jews attacked non-Jews too, those who resided in the land. The concern with the land as the site of the messianic experience may be a distinguishing feature of Jewish terror. The conception of a war without limits in which large military forces are engaged probably had its roots in the extraordinary Holy War (*herem*), which, according to the Bible, God Himself authorized in the original conquest of Canaan. The belief that assimilation impeded messianic deliverance and that all members of the community were culpable gave Jewish terror a character that seemed indiscriminate, certainly by the standards of the Assassins, who held leaders responsible.

Sacred terrorists find their rationale in the past, either in divine instructions transmitted long ago or in interpretations of precedents from founding periods of the parent religions. Their struggles are sanctified with respect to purpose and with respect to means; this is why their violence must have unique characteristics. The very idea of the holy entails contrast with the profane, the normal, or the natural. The noose of the Thug and the dagger of the Assassin illustrate the point. It is difficult, in fact, to avoid feeling that the act of terror is holy just because one is acting against his natural impulses. The immunities of Assassins and Thugs to natural feelings (i.e., the Stockholm syndrome) astonished observers. But, unlike terrorists we are familiar with, they began training for their tasks as children. Our sources provide no information on the personal stress that the methods of the Jewish terrorists might have created for them, but perhaps it is relevant that the Bible relates instance after instance of individuals, including

King Saul himself, who violate commands for indiscriminate destruction in the original *herem* to conquer Canaan.

Religion normally embodies ritual, and it does seem natural that rules prescribe every detail of Hindu and Islamic terror. As observers of the Thugs pointed out, those rules may have been rationally designed to resolve perennial practical problems, thus helping the groups to endure and become more effective. Still, divinely authorized rules cannot be altered even when they become destructive. So conspicuous were the Assassins' political concerns that an eminent historian has described them as the first to use "political terror" in a "planned systematic fashion" (Lewis, 1967, p. 269); but their religious mandate kept them committed to the same tactics even when they proved politically counterproductive. Jewish terror appears unique, being thoroughly antinomian and embracing a large variety of activities. The success in provoking insurrection and the freedom regarding means suggest that political considerations were paramount. But since their ultimate concern was to create *the* catastrophe that would compel God to redeem the righteous remnant, in the end they, like the Thugs and Assassins, continued to act in manifestly self-destructive ways.

The transcendent source of holy terror is its most critical distinguishing characteristic; the deity is perceived as being directly involved in the determination of ends and means. Holy terror never disappeared, and it seems to be reviving in new forms especially in, but not exclusive to, the Middle East. Still, modern terror, which began initially in the activities of *Narodnaya Volya*, a nineteenth-century Russian organization, now is much more common. The modern terrorist serves political ends to be achieved by human efforts alone, and he, not God, chooses the most appropriate ends and means. It is also true that modern terrorist organizations (especially the most durable and effective ones) are often associated with religious groups, for religion can be a major factor of ethnic identity. Although the IRA attracts Catholics and repels Protestants, its object is political, and no member believes that God participates in the struggle. The FLN in Algeria stressed its Muslim character, and EOKA in Cyprus was affiliated with the Greek Orthodox church, but the tactics in both cases were designed to appeal to various domestic and international audiences.

When the members of *Narodnaya Volya*, the first modern rebel terrorists, began their activities, they seemed to be engaged in a kind of sacred ritual. More specifically, they remind one of the Assassins. Highly ranked officials who symbolized the system and bore some responsibilities for its injustices were the victims, and the assailant hoped to attract moral sympathy through his own suffering, specifically by his willingness to accept death in a public trial where he could indict the system. Even his weapon—a hand-thrown bomb—suggests the *fidayeen*'s dagger because it forced face-to-face encounters virtually precluding escape, which persuaded many observers that his will to die was more compelling than his desire to kill (Ivianski, 1982). But, unlike the Assassins, the possibility of other terror tactics was visualized early by their contemporaries, and their initial patterns were soon discarded.

Modern terrorism has two unique, dominant features. Organizations and tactics are constantly modified, presumably to enhance effectiveness and terror is used for very different ends, ranging from those of anarchists with millenarian visions to anti-colonialists, to individuals who simply want to call attention to a particular situation that they find offensive. The early forms of sacred terror cannot be characterized this way. The ends are predetermined, and no real evidence exists that the participants learn to alter their behavior from others within their own tradition, let alone from those outside it.[33] Modern terrorists take their lessons from anyone, and in an important sense they constitute a single tradition which reflects and caricatures a much-observed tendency in our world to subject all activities to efficiency tests. Over the decades the tendency has been to choose methods that minimize the terrorist's risks; the targets, accordingly, are, increasingly, defenseless victims who have less and less value as symbols or less and less responsibility for any condition that the terrorists say they want to alter. The question is whether one can place a premium on reducing the assailant's risk without undermining his potential impact. The problem did not exist for the sacred terrorist, which may be one reason why he was so effective.

The desire to make terror "rational" dominated the first modern terrorist text, Nechaev's *Revolutionary Catechism*, produced before the birth of *Narodnaya Volya*. "The revolutionary (terrorist) . . . knows only one science: the science of destruction. For this reason, and only for this reason, he will study mechanics, chemistry, and perhaps medicine. But all day and night he studies the living science of peoples, their characteristics and circumstances, and all the phenomena of the present social order. The object is the same. The prompt destruction of this filthy order" (1971, p. 71). Nechaev's work is simply an exercise in technique, suggesting devices for provoking governments to savage their peoples until the latter can bear it no longer. It has had numerous successors, the latest and most notorious being Marighella's *Minimanual of the Urban Guerrilla*.

Although the disposition to apply standards of expediency distinguishes modern from holy terror, the presence of this disposition itself cannot mean that modern terrorists are rational. Some ends in principle may be impossible to achieve, like those of the anarchist; others may be so ill-considered that no means can be made rational—the situation, it seems, of the Baader Meinhoff group and the Italian Red Brigades. Sometimes, under the guise of expediency, the safety of the terrorist might become the prime concern. More fundamentally, the very idea of a rational or expedient terror may be contradictory, since by definition terror entails extranormal violence, and as such, is almost guaranteed to evoke wild and uncontrollable emotions. Indeed, the people attracted to it may be so intrigued by the experience of perpetrating terror that everything else is incidental.

NOTES

1. "Terrorism is an activity that has probably characterized modern civilization from its inception. In the past decade, however, terrorist activity has increased in frequency and has taken on novel dimensions. For example, incidents are being employed more as a means of political expression and are becoming characterized by a transnational element" (Sandler, Tshirhart, & Cauley, 1983, p. 36). The phrase "new mode of conflict" was coined by Jenkins (1975). See also Mickolus (1980, Introduction) and Hacker (1976, Preface). As is often the case with

conventional wisdom, the view is expressed without elaboration in the first paragraph or preface. To Gurr (1979, p. 23), the "conventional wisdom (concerning terrorism) is a fantasy accepted as an ominous political reality by (virtually) everyone." Cf. Rapoport (1982a, Introduction).

2. I do not distinguish Zealots from Sicarii, although they are distinctly different groups, as Smith (1971) demonstrates. The Sicarii terrorized mostly Jews, whereas the Zealots were more concerned with Romans and Greeks. But for our purposes this is not a critical distinction. A more extensive discussion of the Jewish uprising appears in Rapoport (1982b). Horsley (1979a) is the only other essay I know which discusses the Jewish activity as terrorist activity.

3. The cases are so well known and interesting that Thomas DeQuincey (1877), a nineteenth-century Romantic writer and the first student of comparative terrorism, pointed out the importance of comparing them. DeQuincey himself concentrates on the Sicarii in various essays. Lewis (1967, chap. 6) compares the three briefly.

4. It would be useful to extend the analysis by treating Christian terror, but the materials are not as conveniently available. No single Christian terror group has caught the public imagination in a way that is comparable to those I have chosen. Unlike those groups discussed here, the numerous millenarian sects using terror in the late medieval period did not rely on hit-and-disappear tactics. Their terror was a sort of state terror; the sects organized their communities openly, taking full control of a territory, instituting gruesome purges to obliterate all traces of the old order, and organizing large armies, which waged holy wars periodically sweeping over the countryside and devastating, burning, and massacring everything and everyone in their paths. The military pattern reminds one of the Crusades, an unlimited or total war launched by the Papacy (Cohn, 1961; cf. Rapoport & Alexander, 1982), in which seven essays discuss relationships between sacred and modern justifications, focusing largely on Christian traditions.

5. Although the Thugs may do what they do because they know that ordinary Hindus regard such actions as terrifying and horrible, they want victims only to experience terror. The earliest contemporary discussions of terrorism emphasized the extranormal character of its violence as the distinguishing feature, but the importance of that distinction has been largely lost. Compare Thornton (1964), Walter (1969), Rapoport (1977), and Price (1977). Since terror is extranormal violence, it is likely to flow initially from a doctrine, and it tends to be a historical rather than a universal phenomenon. In recent years our definitions generally treat terror and violence as synonyms. (See, for example, Russell, 1979, p. 4.) Since violence is a universal phenomenon, it is not surprising that there is a tendency for those who do not distinguish between violence and terror to treat differences in the latter as largely differences in scale. Hostile

sources compiled the materials for all three groups, which poses important questions of reliability. Specific footnotes for each case treat these problems, although obviously only historians of each period can assess the documents adequately. The pictures drawn for each group differ so dramatically that at the very least they represent archetypes of specific religious traditions.

6. When early twentieth-century Hindu terrorist groups used Kali to justify their activities, secrecy was shunned because they had a political purpose, the independence of India (Pal, 1932).

Because terror can give the perpetrator joy, it can be undertaken for its own sake. An example might be the Tylenol killer in the fall of 1982, who laced capsules with arsenic, terrorizing the American public and drug industry in the process. Publicity would be important in this case of terror for terror's sake only if the terrorist desired an audience too.

7. The experience is described in a reasonably accurate, overly gruesome bestseller (Clark, 1979). The group apparently believed that a race war would develop from its efforts, and perhaps at this point it would become visible.

8. Primary sources on the Thugs are extensive. Numerous archival and published government materials exist for virtually every year from 1826 to 1904, the latter being the termination date of the special Indian institution created to deal with Thuggee and related problems, the Thag and Dakaiti Department. By 1850 Thug activity itself ceased almost entirely. Pfirrmann (1970) is the only person who has examined all the primary source materials. His conclusions are substantially those offered by W. H. Sleeman, the remarkable officer who made the Thugs an issue in British politics, contrived the specials methods used to destroy them, and proved to be a perceptive sociologist of religion. Sleeman's six published books (1836, 1839, 1940, 1893, 1858, and 1849) are listed in order of their pertinence. Two useful nineteenth-century secondary accounts based on Sleeman are Hutton (1847) and Thornton (1837). The best twentieth-century books published before Pfirrmann are Sleeman (1933) and Bruce (1968).

The Thugs have captured literary imaginations. Meadows Taylor, a British officer with Sleeman, wrote a bestselling novel (1839) which was reprinted several times. Wilkie Collins's novel, *The Moonstone*, has gone through eleven editions at least, and John Masters (1952) has provided the latest fictional account.

9. The thirteenth-century writings of Jalalu-d din Firoz Khilji, Sultan of Delhi, refer to the banishment of a thousand persons generally identified as Thugs. But before their demise, not much was known about them. Afterward, the thoroughness of British officials, trial records, and police informants provided much material. Although the information was compiled by British police administrators and the Thugs were denied public trials, legal counsel, and the right to question witnesses, the picture developed

from this information was accepted completely for more than a century. Recently, it was challenged by Gupta (1959) and Gordon (1969), who believe that the group developed only when the British arrived. Gupta provides no evidence for this view, and Pfirrmann is justified in simply brushing it aside as a polemic. Gordon's thesis seems more substantial and depends on allegations of inconsistencies in the primary sources. His essay was published too late for Pfirrmann to evaluate, but I found that the inconsistencies cited come largely from Gordon's tendency to take quotations out of context, which may explain why he did not develop this thesis in subsequent writings and why it has been ignored by others.

10. The estimate is incorporated in J. L. Sleeman's title (1933). Every estimate flounders because we don't know the age of the organization or its size in various periods. It is generally assumed that the number remained constant because the group was largely hereditary. In my view, the administrative chaos that prevailed in the wake of the Moghul Empire's collapse when the British arrived gave the brotherhood unusual opportunities for new victims and swelled its ranks, which suggests that Sleeman's "conservative estimate" represents a maximum, not a minimum, one.

11. When terrorist activities are part of a larger military struggle (i.e., Vietnam and Algeria), we have no reliable statistics on the terror alone. In situations when terror alone prevails (e.g., Cyprus, Aden, Northern Ireland) the casualties terrorists inflict rarely exceed three figures.

12. "Bhowanee is happy and most so in proportion to the blood that is shed. . . . Blood is her food. . . . She thirsts for blood!" (Sleeman, 1836, p. 36). The estimates made by various British officials are compiled in a review article which also provides a list of 20 leading Thugs who murdered 5120 persons, an average of 256 each (A religion of murder, 1901)!

13. "There are many thieves in my village but I would not go with them. My father Assa used to counsel me against the thieves saying—do not join them, they take money without thugging. Go with Thugs. If I had a (farthing) by Thuggee, I would take it, but never by theft" (Pfirrmann, 1970, p. 70). Another on-the-spot observer, Sir John Malcolm (1823, vol. 2, p. 187), suggested that robbery was the prime concern, "their victims . . . are always selected for having property. . . ." But the evidence seems to be clearly against him.

14. To allay Hindu anxieties concerning Thug reprisals, the British waived many rights of the defendants. Individuals could be convicted simply for being members of the group and then would be interned for the rest of their lives on grounds that they perceived Thuggee as a religious obligation and would always continue to do so. Thomas Macauley probably drew up the legislation. The rationale is explained by Hervey (1892, vol. 2, pp. 443-45 and Appendixes E and F). In World War II Gillie (1944)

contended that the principles should be revived to dispose of Nazi leaders, and to some extent they were embodied at Nuremberg.

15. No serious argument has been made that the Thugs ever had a political purpose. Russell and Hira (1916) conclude that the immunities were probably linked with Hindu concepts of luck and impurities, although the immunities may have represented tribes from which Thugs originated or disguises Thugs often assumed.

16. Thirty to forty Europeans normally participated in these operations against some 10,000 Thugs. A few assassination attempts against officials occurred, but the assailants lost their nerve, so pervasive must have been the taboo. As far as we know, the Thugs murdered only one or two European travellers.

17. "So far from shrinking at the appellation, when one of them is asked who he is, he will coolly answer that he is a robber" (Hutton, 1961, p. 127).

18. The prolongation of the death agony (the only exception?) was required by Thug doctrine.

19. Apparently the major anxiety of Thugs was that they might be hung by a person of a lower caste (Spry, 1837, vol. 2, chap. 5).

20. For the convenience of readers unfamiliar with Islamic references, I shall refer to the Nazari by their more familiar name, Assassins. When I refer to sympathetic elements, I have in mind the Shia and especially the Ismaili, the groups from which the Assassins originated. Orthodox Muslims are Sunni.

Few Assassin documents have survived, and our picture of the sect is reconstructed mostly from bitterly hostile orthodox chroniclers who obviously could not pierce the veil of secrecy, even if they had wanted to do so. Poonawala (1977) provides the most recent bibliography of sources and secondary works. Many items are annotated. The difficulties of the contemporary historian are aptly described in Hodgson (1955, pp. 22-32). Universally recognized as the best source, Hodgson's work was later sharpened (1968). My analysis is based largely on these accounts and on Lewis (1940, 1967).

21. The reference is to Shia doctrine, but it applies equally to the Assassins.

22. "A state ought not during war to countenance such hostilities as would make mutual confidence in a subsequent peace impossible such as employing assassins, poisoners, breaches of capitulation, secret instigations to treachery and rebellion in the hostile state . . . (for there must be) some kind of confidence in the disposition of the enemy even in the midst of war, or otherwise . . . the hostilities will pass into a war of extermination. . . . Such a war and . . . all means which lead to it, must be absolutely forbidden" (Cf. Vattel, I, 19, 233).

23. The sect, of course, was the subject of many allegations, but it was never charged with instigating counter-atrocities against groups or individuals. The sober Sunni view was that the Nizari wanted "to destroy Islam but not necessarily any . . . Muslims" (Hodgson, 1955, p. 123).

24. The Azraqites apparently practiced indiscriminate slaughter, arguing that every member of a family of unbelievers was an unbeliever (Watt, 1973, p. 22).

25. The initial assassination, that of Asma bent Marwan, was occasioned by Mohammed's question, "Will no one ride me of (her)?" Henry II encouraged his knights in the same way when he grumbled about Becket. But how different the results were! Becket was martyred, the knights were punished, and the English king did penance. For a discussion of Greco-Roman and Christian attitudes toward assassination, see Rapoport (1971, chap. 1).

Six assassinations are discussed by Rodinson (1971, chap. 5). They are also described by Watt (1956), but because Watt's references are scattered throughout the text and fewer details are provided, it is more difficult to perceive patterns.

26. In the Koran, the term hypocrite (*munafikun*) refers to those whose fidelity and zeal Mohammed could not rely upon, persons "in whose hearts there is sickness, weakness, and doubt . . . who had joined Islam perhaps reluctantly . . . usually members of the aristocracy" (Buhl, 1913). Most of those assassinated were Jews, but Mohammed's "Constitution of Medina" clearly indicates that his original community included Jews, and initially he intended to bring Islam as close as possible to Judaism. When that policy failed, the assassinations were an essential aspect of the struggle to separate the two religious bodies and to gain converts out of the Jewish tribes. The process is illustrated in the aftermath of the first assassination, that of a Jewish poetess by 'Umayr, her kinsman: "'Umayr returned to his own clan, which was in a great uproar. Decide what is to be done with me, but do not keep me waiting! No one moved. . . . That was the day when Islam first showed its power over the Banu Katma. 'Umayr had been the first among them to become a Muslim. On the day the daughter of Marwan was killed, the men of the Banu Khatma were converted because of what they saw of the power of Islam" (Ibn Hisham quoted by Rodinson, 1971, p. 171).

27. Margoliouth (1923, p. 116) notes that Muslim initially meant "traitor, one who handed over his kinsmen or friends to their enemies," and that "Mohammed . . . displayed great ingenuity" in transforming its meaning into "one who handed over his own person to God." The new religion, he believes, could not survive without challenging the kin bond; and "Islam, as appears from the most authorized traditions, had the effect of making men anxious . . . to signalize their faith by parricide or fratricide" (p. 265). The traditional or orthodox interpretations of these incidents is that the assailants, shamed by their kinsmen's behavior, acted on their own initiative.

28. No terrorist campaign before the nineteenth century is better known, and virtually all our information comes from Josephus Flavius, a Jewish commander who later became a Roman supporter and portrays the Zealots and *Sicarii* as provoking the popular uprising when no irreconcilable issues divided Roman and Jew. How reliable is Josephus? Historians have always disagreed. He has been seen as a "mere Roman apologist," and the accounts he challenges have vanished. His description, like those of all ancient historians, wildly exaggerates statistics and contains inconsistencies which serve explicit didactic purposes. Still, moderns increasingly find him credible, except on particular matters where good reason to mistrust him exists. When his sources can be checked, he "remains fairly close to the original. Even when he modifies the source to suit a certain aim, he still reproduces the essence of the story. More important, he does not engage in the free invention of episodes . . . like other (ancient) authors. . ." (Cohen, 1979, p. 233). All other extant sources, Roman and Jewish materials alike, are more hostile to the rebels than Josephus himself was. Although some say "that Josephus' good faith as a historian cannot be seriously questioned" (Shutt, 1961, p. 123), most agree that despite other concerns he truly had "an interest as a historian in the course of events themselves" (Bide, 1979, p. 201).

The second issue is which of Josephus' different and contradictory assessments or motives is most credible? I have followed the modern tendency in playing down the criminal and personal motives Josephus gives to the rebels in order to emphasize their religious and political concerns. And I have taken seriously his frequently repeated contention, which some scholars question, that the terrorists forced their will on reluctant parties. The process of polarizing a society by exploiting latent hostilities through shock tactics was not understood well by the nineteenth- and early twentieth-century commentators on Josephus who knew of no terror campaigns with which to compare the revolt. More recent scolars display less skepticism on this point. My earlier study (1982b) is a step-by-step analysis of the dynamic presupposed by Josephus' account, and the description above is based upon that essay.

The literature on the revolt is quite extensive. The following articles (in addition to those cited above) were particularly helpful: Applebaum (1971), Betz et al. (1974), Borg (1971), Farmer (1956), Grant (1973), Hengel (1961), Horsley (1979b), Kingdom (1970, 1971), Kohler (1905), Roth (1959), Smallwood (1976), Stern (1973), Thackeray (1967), and Zeitlin (1967).

29. For a convenient discussion of the *herem* and its revival by the Zealots-Sicarii as reflected in the Dead Sea Scrolls, see de Vaux (1972, pp. 258-267). The later conception had new elements: the war would be a war to end all wars, it would involve all men, and the enemy was under Satan's influence.

30. Rapoport (1982b, pp. 36-37) discusses relaitonships between the process described here and modern campaign experiences. For a general discussion of passive resistance and terrorism, see Thornton (1946, p. 75.)

31. A third reason for studying sacred terror is that there are direct links between some of its concepts and those that animate modern forms (Dugard, 1982).

32. In 1933, J. L. Sleeman wrote, "it is of interest to speculate as to what the procedure would be today were such an organization of murder to be discovered in India, and imagination runs riot at the long vista of Royal Commissions, Blue, Red, and White Books, Geneva Conferences and the political capital which would be made of it, the procrastination and the delay, tying the hands of those on the spot, and the world propaganda which would ensue. . . . Thuggee could shelter behind disunited party government" (p. 103).

33. The Crusades are the major exception, for they were inspired by the *herem* and undertaken to regain the Holy Land in order to initiate a messianic era.

REFERENCES

A religion of murder. *Quarterly Review*, 1901, *194*, 506-513.

Applebaum, S. The Zealots: the case for revaluation. *Journal of Roman Studies*, 1971, *61*, 155-170.

Betz, O., Haacker, K., & Hengel, M. *Josephus-Studien*. Gottingen: Vanderhoeck and Ruprecht, 1974.

Bilde, P. The causes of the Jewish War according to Josephus. *Journal for the Study of Judaism*, 1979, *10*, 179-202.

Borg, M. The currency of the term "Zealot." *Journal of Theological Studies*, 1971, *22*, 504-513.

Buhl, Fr Munafikun. *Encyclopedia of Islam*. London: Luzac, 1913.

Bruce, C. *The Stranglers*. London: Longmans, 1968.

Clark, H. *Zebra*. New York: Merek, 1979.

Cohen, S. J. D. *Josephus in Galilee and Rome*. Leiden: Brill, 1979.

Cohn, N. *The pursuit of the millennium: revolutionary messianism in medieval and reformation Europe and its bearing on modern totalitarian movements*. New York: Harper Torchbooks, 1961.

Collins, W. *The moonstone*. London: Tinsley, 1868.

DeQuincey, T. Supplementary paper on murder considered as one of the fine arts. In *Works*. Boston: Houghton Mifflin, 1877.

Dugard, J. International terrorism and the Just War. In D. C. Rapoport & Y. Alexander (Eds.). *The morality of terrorism: religions and secular justifications*. New York: Pergamon, 1982.

Farmer, W. R. *Maccabees, Zealots, and Josephus*. New York: Columbia University Press, 1956.

Ferrero, G. *The principles of power*. New York: Arno, 1972.

Freedman, L. Z. Why does terrorism terrorize? In D.C. Rapoport & Y. Alexander (Eds.). *The rationalization of terrorism*. Frederick, Md.: University Publications of America, 1982.

Friedlaender, I. The heterodoxies of the Shi-ites in the presentation of Ibh Hazm. *Journal of the American Oriental Society*, 1907, *28*, 1-80, *29*, 1-183.

Gillie, D. R. Justice and Thugs. *The Spectator*. 1944, *172*, 567-568.

Gordon, S. N. Scarf and sword: Thugs, marauders and state formation in 18th century Malwa. *Indian Journal of Economic and Social History*, 1969, *6*, 403-429.

Grant J. *The Jews in the Roman world*. London: Wiedenfeld, 1973.

Gupta, H. A critical study of the Thugs and their activities. *Journal of Indian History*, 1959, *38*, 167-176.

Gurr, T. Some characteristics of terrorism. In M. Stohl (Ed.). *The politics of terrorism*. New York: Dekker, 1979.

Hacker, F. *Crusaders, criminals, and crazies*. New York: Norton, 1976.

Hardman, J. *Terrorism. Encyclopedia of the Social Sciences*. New York: Macmillan, 1933.

Hengel, M. *Die Zeloten*. Leiden: Brill, 1961.

Herodotus. *Persian Wars*.

Hervey, J. *Some records of crime*. London: Sampson Low, 1892.

Hodgkin, T. Mahdism, Messianism and Marxism in the African setting. In P. Gurkind & P. Waterman (Eds.). *African social studies: A radical reader*. New York: 1977.

Hodgson, M. G. S. The Ismaili state. In W. B. Fisher (Ed.), *The Cambridge history of Iran*. Cambridge: Cambridge University Press, 1968.

Hodgson, M. G. S. *The order of Assassins*. The Hague: Mouton, 1955.

Horsley, R. A. Josephus and the bandits. *Journal for the Study of Judaism*, 1979, *10*, 38-63. (b)

Horsley, R. A. The Sicarii; ancient Jewish "terrorists." *Journal of Religion*, 1979, *59*, 435-458. (a)

Hutton, J. *A popular account of the Thugs and Dakoits*. London: W. H. Allen, 1857.

Hutton, J. H. *Caste in India*. Oxford: Clarendon Press, 1961.

Ibrahim, S. Anatomy of Egypt's militant Islamic groups. *International Journal of Middle Eastern Studies*, 1980, *12*, 423-453.

Ivianski, Z. The moral issue: some aspects of individual terror. In D. C. Rapoport & Y. Alexander (Eds.), *The morality of terrorism: religious and secular justifications*. New York: Pergamon, 1982.

Jenkins, B. *International terrorism: a new mode of conflict*. Los Angeles: Crescent, 1975.

Josephus. The Jewish War. In *Works*. Loeb Classical Library. London: Heinemann, 1926 (a).

Josephus. Antiquities of the Jews. In *Works*. Loeb Classical Library. London: Heinemann, 1926 (b).

Kant, I. *Perpetual peace*. M. Smith (Trans.). New York: Liberal Arts, 1948.

Kingdom, H. Origin of the Zealots. *New Testament Studies*, 1971, *79*, 74-61.

Kingdom, H. Who were the Zealots? *New Testament Studies*, 1970, *17*, 68-72.

Kohlberg, R. The development of the Imami Shii doctrine of Jihad. *Deutschen Morgenlandischen Gesellschaft Zeitschrift*, 1976, *126*, 64-82.

Kohler, K. Zealots. *The Jewish Encyclopedia*. New York: Funk & Wagnalls, 1905.

Lang, D. A reporter at large: the bank drama (Swedish hostages). *The New Yorker*, 1974, *50*(40), 56-126.

Laqueur, W. *Terrorism*. Boston: Little Brown, 1977.

Lerner, M. Assassination. *Encyclopedia of the Social Sciences*. New York: Macmillan, 1933.

Lewis, B. *The Assassins: a radical sect in Islam*. London: Nicholson and Weidenfeld, 1967.

Lewis, B. *Origins of Islamism*. Cambridge: Cambridge University Press, 1940.

MacEoin, D. The Babi concept of the Holy War. *Religion*, 1982, *122*, 93-129.

Malcolm, J., Sir. *A memoir of Central India*. London: Kingsbury, Parbury and Allen, 1823.

Marighella, C. *For the liberation of Brazil*. Harmondsworth: Penguin, 1972.

Margoliouth, D. S. *Mohammed and the rise of Islam*. London: G. P. Putnam, 1923.

Masters, J. *The deceivers*. New York: Viking, 1952.

Mickolus, E. F. *Transnational terrorism: a chronology of events*. Westport, Conn.: Greenwood, 1980.

Nechaev, S. The revolutionary catechism. In D. C. Rapoport, *Assasination and terrorism*. Toronto: Canadian Broadcasting Corp., 1972.

Pal, B. *Memoirs of my life and times*. Calcutta: Modern Book Agency, 1932.

Pfirrmann, G. *Religioser character und organisatin der Thag-Brueberschaften*. Tuebingen: Ph.D. dissertation, 1970.

Poonawala, K. *Bibliography of Ismaili literature*. Malibu, Calif.: Undena, 1977.

Price, H., Jr. The strategy and tactics of revolutionary terrorism. *Comparative Studies in Society and History*, 1977, *19*, 52-65.

Rapoport, D. C. Introduction. Religious terror. In D. Canadian Broadcasting Corp. 1971.

Rapoport, D. C. The politics of atrocity. In Y. Alexander & S. Finger (Eds.), *Terrorism: Interdisciplinary perspectives*. New York: John Jay, 1977.

Rapoport, D. C. Introduction. Religious terror. In D. C. Rapoport & Y. Alexander, *The morality of terrorism: religious and secular justifica*tions. New York: Pergamon, 1982. (a)

Rapoport, D. C. Terror and the messiah; an ancient experience and modern parallels. In D. C. Rapoport & Y. Alexander (Eds.), *The morality of terrorism: Religious and secular justifications*. New York: Pergamon, 1982. (b)

Rapoport, D. C. & Alexander, Y. (Eds.). *The morality of terrorism: Religious and secular justifications*. New York: Pergamon Press, 1982.

Rodinson, M. *Mohammed*. London: Penguin, 1971.

Roth, C. The Zealots and the war of 66-70. *Journal of Semitic Studies*, 1959, *4*, 332-334.

Rubin, J. *Do it*. New York: Simon and Schuster, 1970.

Russell, C. A., Banker, L. J., & Miller, B. H. Outinventing the terrorist. In Y. Alexander, D. Carlton, and P. Wilkinson (Eds.), *Terrorism: theory and practice*. Boulder, Colo.: Westview, 1979.

Russell, R. V., & Hira, L. *The tribes and castes of the Central Provinces of India*. London: Macmillan, 1916.

Sandler, T., Tshirhart, J. T., & Cauley, J. A theoretical analysis of transnational terrorism. *American Political Science Review*, 1983, *77*, 36-54.

Scholem, G. *The messianic idea in Judaism*. New York: Schocken, 1971.

Schonfeld, J. *The Passover plot*. New York: Geis, 1965.

Sherwood, R. On the murderers called P'hansigars. *Asiatic Researchers*, 1820, *13*, 250-281.

Shutt, R. J. H. *Studies in Josephus*. London: S.P.C.K. 1961.

Sleeman, J. L. *Thugs; or a million murders*. London S. Low and Marston, 1933.

Sleeman, W. H. *Ramaseeana*. Calcutta: Huttman, 1836.

Sleeman, W. H. *The Thugs or Phansigars of India*. Philadelphia: Carey and Hart, 1839.

Sleeman, W. H. *Report on the depredations committed by the Thug gangs of Upper and Central India*. Calcutta: Huttman, 1940.

Sleeman, W. H. *A journey through the kingdom of Oudh in 1849-50*. London: Bentley, 1858.

Sleeman, W. H. *Rambles and recollections of an Indian official*. V. A. Smith (Ed.). Westminster: Constable, 1893.

Smallwood, E. J. *The Jews under Roman rule*. Leiden: Brill, 1976.

Smith, M. Zealots and Sicarii: their origins and relations. *Harvard Theological Review*, 1971, *64*, 1-19.

Spry, H. *Modern India*. London: Whitaker, 1837.

Stern, J. Zealots. *Encyclopedia Judaica Yearbook*. New York: Macmillan, 1973.

Taylor, M. *Confessions of a Thug*. London: R. Bentley, 1839.

Taylor, M. *The story of my life*. London: Oxford University Press, 1920.

Thackeray, H. St. J. *Josephus, the man and the historian*. New York repr. Ktva, 1967.

Thornton, E. *Illustrations and practices of the Thugs*. London: W. H. Allen, 1837.

Thornton, T. P. Terror as a weapon of political agitation. In H. Eckstein (Ed.), *Internal War*. New York: Free Press, 1964.

Tugwell, M. *Revolutionary propaganda and possible counter-measures*. Kings College, University of London: Ph.D. dissertation, 1979.

Tyan, E. *Djihad, Encyclopedia of Islam*. Leiden: Brill, 1960.

Vattel, E. *The law of nations.* London: Newbery, 1760.

de Vaux, R. *Ancient Israel.* New York: McGraw-Hill, 1972.

Walter, E. V. *Terror and resistance: a study of political violence.* New York: Oxford University Press, 1969.

Watt, M. W. *The formative period of Islamic thought.* Edinburgh: University Press, 1973.

Watt, M. W. *Mohammed at Medina.* Oxford: Clarendon Press, 1956.

Weber, M. *The Sociology of religion.* E. Fischoff (Ed.). London: Methuen, 1955.

Zeitlin, S. The Sicarii and the Zealots. *Jewish Quarterly Review,* 1967, *57,* 251-270.

THE ENDLESS NATURE OF TERRORISM

JEFFREY D. SIMON

At about the same time that the French people were experiencing terrorism carried out by their own government, the United States was forced to deal with another form of terrorism that originated from abroad: hostage taking. The founding fathers were thus faced with a problem that would become all too familiar to U.S. leaders more than two centuries later.

The image many people have of pirates is a mysterious band of adventurers stalking the high seas, boarding ships, taking gold and other valuables, then vanishing into the night. And that has been a major aspect of piracy throughout the centuries. But the Barbary Coast states—Morocco, Algiers, Tunis, and Tripoli—perfected the art of piracy into a profitable and integral part of their foreign policy. They became the first state-sponsors of terrorism, utilizing pirates to target foreign vessels in the Mediterranean and Atlantic and taking hostages as a way of obtaining large sums of ransom payments from the victims' governments. Payments to the various rulers of the Barbary states, who were known as deys (Algiers), beys (Tunis), bashaws (Tripoli), and emperors (Morocco), were also made on a regular basis to prevent ships from being seized. But these extortion payments, which many governments felt were cheaper than the risk of losing their ships, still did not ensure that their ships would not be seized.

When the United States won its independence from Britain, it had to fend for itself against the activities of the Barbary states.

Thomas Jefferson, sent to Paris in 1785 to negotiate treaties for the United States, became increasingly frustrated with the ability of the Barbary states to attack U.S. vessels and take American citizens as hostages. For Jefferson, the sight of a weak America being plagued by piracy was difficult to accept. In a correspondence to Nathanael Greene, Jefferson wrote of being torn between "indignation and impotence." Although he realized that continual ransom payments would only encourage further acts of terrorism and that a military response would be preferable, Jefferson had very few options. The United States was a weak military power in the late eighteenth century; not even a navy was available to respond to the Barbary attacks. The frustration of not being able to retaliate against the Barbary states, themselves not major powers, convinced Jefferson of the need to build a strong navy. Even before such a force could be built, Jefferson still hoped for a military response. He was convinced that John Paul Jones "with half a dozen frigates would totally destroy their commerce . . . by constant cruising and cutting them to pieces piecemeal."[17]

In this first U.S. debate over how to respond to terrorism, Jefferson did not have much support for his advocacy of a strong American response. John Adams argued that the United States should continue paying tribute since he believed that was a wiser economic policy than spending the much larger sums of money needed to build a navy. He also argued that the U.S. would not be able to significantly harm the Barbary states since they had no commerce upon which retaliatory strikes could be directed. The U.S. Congress was also initially against the idea of building a navy in the 1780s, and instead instructed Jefferson to continue to make payments to the Barbary states. In fact, an amount of money—not to exceed $80,000—was set aside for this very purpose. Yet over a ten-year period, the United States ended up paying more than $2 million as ships continued to be seized and American hostages taken. Between 1776 and 1816, several hundred Americans were taken captive by the terrorist states. Their treatment was usually harsh; after being captured, they were placed in chains and put into prisons infested with disease. Most of the hostages were also forced to perform hard labor.[18]

Much like the hostages in Lebanon in the 1980s, the Barbary hostages appealed to the American public and government to come to their aid. "Remember us, your unfortunate brethren, late members of the family of freedom, now doomed to perpetual confinement," wrote one hostage to U.S. ministers in 1792. "Pray, earnestly pray, that our grievous calamities may have a gracious end. . . . We ask you in the name of your Father in heaven, to have compassion on our miseries. . . . Lift up your voices like a trumpet; cry aloud in the cause of humanity. . . ."[19]

The plight of the hostages was not forgotten by the American people. The "incarceration of over four hundred and fifty citizens drawn from all parts of the Atlantic seaboard could not, and did not, fail to excite commiseration throughout the land."[20] Even when the number of hostages was only eleven, their fate was still a major concern of the government. President Washington presented a report on the hostages to Congress on December 30, 1790, and Congress referred the matter to a committee, which eventually recommended that a naval force be built as soon as public finances would permit. Congress, though, did not act immediately on this recommendation.

Jefferson was particularly affected by the sufferings of the hostages and tried all that he could to win their release. Ironically, one strategy he pursued resulted in the hostages actually accusing him of not caring about their fate. In 1787, he became convinced that the more attention the U.S. gave to the Barbary states, the more likely it would be that additional hostages would be taken and that those already in captivity would not be released. He decided that ignoring the issue might reduce the price that Algiers was demanding for the hostages' freedom. He left the false impression with the dey that the United States no longer intended to pay ransom and was not preoccupied with the hostage issue. This only resulted in the hostages blaming him for their prolonged captivity.[21]

The Barbary states were experts at playing the hostage game. They continued to up the ante for the release of American hostages, even setting prices for different types of hostages. A master required $6,000, a mate $4,000, and a sailor $1,500. Passengers on ships had a $4,000 price tag. These figures constantly changed as the Barbary leaders reneged on promises and kept the U.S. and other countries continually guessing what their next demands would be. Negotiations would be held with the different Barbary states, hopes would be raised that the hostages would be freed, only to have complications arise. The U.S. even tried using the services of a religious sect, the Mathurins, whose mission was to aid countries in negotiations with the Barbary states. The Mathurins, who were officially known as the Order of the Holy Trinity and Redemption of Captives, was founded in 1199 in Paris by the Church of St. Mathurin. For centuries its members devoted their lives to helping the victims of the Barbary pirates by raising ransom for their release and setting up missions and hospitals in the Barbary states.

Jefferson met with the general of the religious order in 1787, hoping he could resolve America's hostage crisis. Although he was eager to help, nothing came of these efforts as delays and complications, including the continual raising of ransom demands by the dey, arose before anything could be accomplished. The Mathurins were ultimately dissolved along with other religious orders during the French Revolution.[22]

The United States was also frustrated in its efforts to gain international cooperation in neutralizing the Barbary threat. Since the pirate states were themselves weak military powers, they would have been no match for any concerted effort by more powerful European nations, who also were victimized by the pirates. Yet this period in world history was characterized by escalating economic warfare among nations and "the very advantages gained by one country from the depredations on the commerce of another would have made co-operation . . . difficult." Or as a popular phrase of the time illustrated, "if there were no Algiers, it would be worth England's while to build one." [23]

The desire to resolve the Barbary problem led to the first arms-for-hostages deal in U.S. history. In 1795, the U.S. secured a peace treaty with the dey of Algiers that included a cash payment, annual tributes, and naval arms and frigates that eventually totaled almost $1 million. While this led to the release of a hundred hostages, it encouraged the other Barbary states to increase their demands upon the United States. It also did not prevent Algiers from taking more hostages in later years. The U.S. agent in Algiers, Joel Barlow, described one of the deys in terms that could easily apply to some contemporary state-sponsors of terrorism. According to Barlow, Hasan Pasha, who ruled from 1791 to 1798, was "a man of a most ungovernable temper, passionate, changeable, and unjust to such a degree that there is no calculating his policy from one moment to the next." [24]

The United States was finally able by 1816 to significantly reduce the Barbary threat through a combination of factors. These included the emergence of a U.S. Navy that was used in wars with Tripoli and Algiers, Barbary wars with other European countries, and internal problems within the Barbary states themselves. Ironically, the first U.S. military operation against a state-sponsor of terrorism took place against Tripoli—"the least considerable of the Barbary States," according to Jefferson—[25]just as the most decisive U.S. military strike against a state-sponsor in the 1980s would be the bombing of Libya's capital, Tripoli. During this war—which began during Jefferson's first year as president in 1801 when the bashaw, or ruler, cut down the flagstaff of the American consul's residence after the United States refused to pay an increased ransom for hostages—Stephen Decatur and a small raiding party burned the frigate *Philadelphia*. The ship had been seized in 1803 when it ran aground in the harbor of Tripoli and was used by the Tripolitans to

increase their demands for ransom. Although the sabotage of the *Philadelphia* in 1804 was a dramatic act that received widespread approval in the United States and made a hero out of Decatur, it was not decisive in the war, which ended when the bashaw of Tripoli faced mounting domestic problems. But in terrorism and counterterrorism, the symbolic act can be as important as actual decisive events. For the United States, the war with Tripoli and the burning of the *Philadelphia* indicated that after years of capitulation to state-sponsors of terrorism, the United States would fight back.

That the terrorist threat did not end due to any specific U.S. response was among the early lessons on terrorism that the Barbary experience held for the United States. Many of the traits about terrorism that would haunt U.S. policy-makers in later years were evident during this first U.S. experience with state-sponsored terrorism. These included the continual taking of hostages, the raising of false hopes for their release, the constantly increasing ransom demands, frustration in not being able to completely eliminate the threat, debates over military responses, and difficulty in acquiring international cooperation. The emotional grasp that hostages can have on presidents and the public was also evident during this period, as was the ability of terrorists to play upon human compassion and fears.

[. . .]

For most of the nineteenth and early twentieth centuries, the major form of terrorism confronting the United States came from within the country rather than outside. These were primarily incidents of domestic violence associated with the anarchists and labor movements. One anarchist, Leon Czolgosz, assassinated President William McKinley in 1901, which led to Teddy Roosevelt becoming president. Czolgosz was tried, sentenced, and executed within two months of the terrorist act. Other anarchists emigrated to the United States in the hope of launching a revolution against capitalism. Jonathan Most—known as the anarchist without a country after being expelled from his native Germany and Austria, and imprisoned in Britain—arrived in the United States in 1882 and embarked on a speaking tour to rally the masses. He published a pamphlet that set forth specific instructions in the making of bombs, fuses, and poisons. He also included in his book details on how to place explosives for maximum effect in such public gathering places as churches and ballrooms.[46]

But violence for the sake of violence did not take hold in the United States, and the anarchist movement failed to achieve its goal of uprisings and revolution. The labor movement, on the other hand, waged a long and successful struggle for better working conditions and more pay. Terrorist-related incidents were a part of labor-management conflicts and were perpetrated by both sides. Strikers were killed by company-hired guards, vigilante committees, and soldiers, while factory and mine operators and foremen were murdered by individual workers. In one case, violence in the Pennsylvania coal mines in the 1860s and 1870s led to rumors that an Irish terrorist group, the Molly Maguires, was on the rampage. The name originated in an Irish folk story about the widow Molly Maguire, who after being evicted from her farm in Ireland fought back against landlords and government officials with the aid of young Irishmen. The Molly Maguires in the Pennsylvania coal mines were believed to be connected with an Irish fraternal society, the Ancient Order of Hibernians.

Franklin Gowen, the president of the Philadelphia and Reading Railroad and its subsidiary, the Philadelphia and Reading Coal and Iron Company, decided to exploit public fears about terrorism by linking the Molly Maguires with organized labor and thus crush the emerging labor movement. Gowen hired the Pinkerton detective agency in 1873 to infiltrate the Mollies and gather evidence for their arrests. In a letter from Alan Pinkerton to one of his superintendents, he compares the Molly Maguires to the Thugs of India and calls for tough action against them:

> The M.M.'s are a species of Thugs. You have probably read of them in India. Their religion taught them to murder, to mark out their victims, and their plans by which they were to strike, and not to divulge anything even if they were brought to the stake. So it is with the M.M.'s. They are bound to stick by their oath, and to carry out their revenge. He, who they think does a wrong, is

marked out, and he must die. It is impossible to believe that a jury in the mining districts would not give a verdict of guilty against the M.M.'s should they be brought to trial but I believe that some one on the jury would hang on, and get the guilty men to escape. The only way then to pursue that I can see is, to . . . get up a vigilence committee. It will not do to get many men, but let him [one of Pinkerton's men] get those who are prepared to take fearful revenge on the M.M.'s. I think it would open the eyes of all the people and then the M.M.'s would meet with their just deserts. It is awful to see men doomed to death, it is horrible. Now there is but one thing to be done, and that is, get up an organization if possible, and when ready for action pounce upon the M.M.'s when they meet and are in full blast, take the fearful responsibility and disperse.[47]

But Pinkerton did not need to use any vigilantes against the Molly Maguires. By the end of the summer of 1875, his undercover agent, James McParland, had spent two years with the Mollies in the Pennsylvania coal mines and produced enough names, dates, and places of various murders to bring several Irish miners to trial. These trials, however, were not very fair, as some defense witnesses were charged with perjury and immediately arrested and put in jail after testifying, thereby intimidating others from coming forth for the defense. Furthermore, McParland's testimony, which was the heart of the state's case, was suspect and corroborated only by disreputable individuals who received immunity from prosecution for their crimes by testifying for the state. But all of this did not matter to Gowen, who was a brilliant orator, businessman, and prosecutor and knew how to play upon public fears about violence and terrorism. He told the jury during one of the trials that if the Molly Maguires were destroyed, then "we can stand up before the whole country and say: 'Now all are safe in this country; come here, with your money; come here with your families and make this country your residence; help us to build up this people and you will be safe.'"[48]

The Mollies were convicted and sentenced to death, with ten members hanged on June 21, 1877, and nine more hanged within the next two years. To this day there is still debate among historians whether the Molly Maguires were in fact an organized group of terrorists or instead just an exaggerated threat fostered by Gowen for his own purposes. Gowen continued to use the threat of brandishing labor militants as Molly Maguires to crush any fledgling union. "It was sufficient to hang a man to declare him a Molly Maguire," Gowen once boasted.[49]

Meanwhile, terrorist-related violence continued to characterize labor-management struggles throughout the country. Among the more notable incidents was the Haymarket Square riot in Chicago on May 4, 1886, where a bomb was tossed into a column of policemen, killing seven officers. The police had been trying to break up a protest by thousands of people who were upset with the police for firing into a crowd of striking workers the day before at the McCormick harvester plant. But it was not until the early part of the twentieth century that the impact that a single terrorist bomb can have upon the American public was clearly demonstrated.

A long period of union-management disputes and strikes at the *Los Angeles Times* culminated with the dynamiting of the *Times* building on October 1, 1910. The bombing shocked the nation, as twenty-one non-union workers were killed and an estimated $500,000 in damages resulted. "Los Angeles seemed to be in a state of panic," wrote William Burns, the country's most famous detective, who would be hired by the city of Los Angeles and *Times* owner Harrison Otis to track down the bombers. "Another earthquake would not have created such fear as the citizens were experiencing. An earthquake is an act of nature, but what was going on in Los Angeles was the act of a cunning, heartless, ruthless enemy of society."[50] Two other bombs were discovered that same day: one at the home of Otis and another at the home of the secretary of the Merchants and Manufacturers' Association. Police were able to remove the bomb at Otis's home to an open area where it exploded harmlessly, while the second bomb failed to explode due to a weak battery.

Otis vented his anger with an editorial in his newspaper that called the bombers "anarchist scum," "cowardly murderers," and "midnight assassins . . . whose hands are dripping with the innocent blood of your victims. . . ." He lamented about "the wails of poor widows

and the cries of fatherless children" and was relentless in trying to pin the bombing on organized labor. When John J. McNamara, the secretary-treasurer of the International Association of Bridge and Structural Iron Workers, and his younger brother James were arrested in Indiana the following April by Burns and police detectives and brought back to Los Angeles to stand trial for the *Times* bombing, Otis could only rejoice with a headline that implied that no trial was really necessary: "The Dynamiters of the Times Building Caught. Crime Traced Directly to High Union Labor Officials."[51]

Clarence Darrow, one of the country's most famous lawyers, was retained to defend the McNamara brothers, but as evidence against them mounted, the two brothers confessed to the crime in order to escape the death penalty. James B. McNamara admitted placing a suitcase with sixteen sticks of dynamite and a timing device in the *Times* building the night before the explosion, while John J. McNamara confessed to being an accessory to that bombing as well as to one at the anti-union Llewellyn Iron Works plant in Los Angeles. James McNamara was sentenced to life imprisonment while John McNamara was sentenced to fifteen years. The McNamaras' confessions were a blow to the labor movement since union leaders and workers throughout the country had rallied to their defense and argued that the brothers were being framed by big business as a way to destroy labor.

The bombing led to a congressional inquiry as lawmakers became concerned that the United States might be facing a new wave of violence if striking workers increasingly turned to the use of dynamite in their disputes with management. Darrow was called to testify and was urged by the committee to repudiate and condemn the McNamaras' bombing. He refused, and in his testimony implied that political terrorism was a justifiable act. "There was no element [in the bombing] that goes to make up what the world calls a criminal act, which is an act coupled with a selfish criminal motive," Darrow told the lawmakers. James B. McNamara "did not do it for malice. He was a union man in a great industrial struggle running over the years. He believed in it and believed it was necessary to the welfare of his class; . . . in his mind he thought he was serving his class, and taking his life in his hands without reward. Now, if anyone can condemn him for it, they reason differently from myself. . . . I can not."[52]

Many Americans, though, did condemn the McNamaras in particular and the labor movement in general for the violence. One historian noted that the bombing and its aftermath "stopped the Los Angeles labor movement dead." But a foreign journalist traveling through the United States to cover the story observed that while many newspaper editors, reporters, and the American public were opposed to the bombing, they "seemed, nevertheless, to feel that there were deep evils in the country which were in a sense responsible [for it]."[53] An examination of the causes of violence in labor-management relations was conducted by the president-appointed United States Industrial Commission. While the commission focused initially on the McNamara case, it also studied the plight of workers in America and "played an important role in educating public opinion about the realities of the labor-capital conflict."[54]

The dynamiting of the *Times* building served the same purpose as many contemporary terrorist actions: to bring public attention to a particular cause, whether it be workers' rights, territorial demands, or ethnic and religious grievances, through a spectacular violent act. While the short-term effect is negative public reactions or official government crackdowns, the long-term benefit can be the raising of a nation's consciousness on the issue that propelled the terrorists into action in the first place.

Technological innovations in weaponry played a key role in the labor and anarchist violence of the late nineteenth and early twentieth centuries. It provided militants with dynamite, a new weapon to use against government, military, and big business. Dynamite was invented in 1867 by Swedish chemist Alfred Nobel, who intended it for peaceful purposes and was dismayed to see it used for violence. He left millions of dollars in his will to establish the annual Nobel prizes, including the Nobel Peace Prize. But dynamite was hailed by anarchists who believed that "in providing such a powerful but easily concealed weapon, science was thought to have given a decisive advantage to revolutionary forces."[55] For labor militants, the existence of dynamite meant that a new tactic could be used against management efforts to break up the unions. The International Association of Bridge and Structural Iron Workers—the McNamara brothers' union—decided in 1906 that traditional labor tactics of strikes and protests were failing to prevent U.S. Steel and other companies from imposing the open-shop at various plants. They therefore turned to dynamite, and between 1906 and 1911 was responsible [*sic*] for more than one hundred explosions at bridges, factories, and plants across the country.[56] Thirty-eight members of the union were ultimately convicted of these crimes, which resulted mostly in minor property damage and no casualties until the bombing of the *Times* building.

[. . .]

Domestic violence and related terrorist incidents in the United States continued in various forms through the first half of the twentieth century. But it would not be until after World War II that a new age of terrorism truly began to emerge.

NOTES

Only those notes from the original material that correspond to text excerpted here are reproduced. The original note numbering has been preserved.

17. Dumas Malone, *Jefferson and the Rights of Man* (Boston: Little Brown, 1951), pp. 27-28. For a discussion of U.S. policy toward the Barbary states, see Ray W. Irwin, *The Diplomatic Relations of the United States with the Barbary Powers, 1776-1816* (Chapel Hill: University of North Carolina Press, 1931); Samuel Flagg Bemis, ed., *The American Secretaries of State and Their Diplomacy*, vol. 2 (New York: Knopf, 1928); Richard Hofstadter, William Miller, Daniel Aaron, *The American Republic*, vol. 1: *To 1865* (Englewood Cliffs, New Jersey: Prentice-Hall, 1959).

18. Irwin, *Diplomatic Relations*, pp. 9-10.

19. A. B. C. Whipple, *To the Shores of Tripoli: The Birth of the U.S. Navy and Marines* (New York: Morrow, 1991), p. 41.

20. Irwin, *Diplomatic Relations*, p. 204.

21. Malone, *Jefferson and the Rights of Man*, p. 32; Irwin, *Diplomatic Relations*, p. 45.

22. Irwin, *Diplomatic Relations*, pp. 11, 44-46, 70; Malone, *Jefferson and the Rights of Man*, pp. 28, 31-32; Gardner W. Allen, *Our Navy and the Barbary*

Corsairs (Hamden, Connecticut: Archon Books, 1965 [first published in 1905]), pp. 2, 41-42.

23. Irwin, *Diplomatic Relations*, p. 17; Malone, *Jefferson and the Rights of Man*, p. 31.

24. Irwin, *Diplomatic Relations*, p. 55.

25. Thomas Jefferson, *Public and Private Papers* (New York: Vintage Books/Library of America, 1990), p. 176.

46. Parry, *Terrorism: From Robespierre to Arafat*, pp. 95-96.

47. Wayne G. Broehl, Jr., *The Molly Maguires* (Cambridge, Massachusetts: Harvard University Press, 1964), pp. 247-48.

48. Philip S. Foner, *History of the Labor Movement in the United States*, vol. 1: *From Colonial Times to the Founding of the American Federation of Labor* (New York: International Publishers, 1947), p. 461.

49. Sidney Lens, *The Labor Wars: From the Molly Maguires to the Sitdowns* (New York: Doubleday, 1973), p. 27.

50. William Burns, *The Masked War* (New York: Doran, 1913), p. 44. Reprinted as part of Mass Violence in America series, Robert M. Fogelson and Richard E. Rubenstein, eds. (New York: Arno Press and The New York Times, 1969).

51. Foner, *History of the Labor Movement in the United States*, vol. 5: *The AFL in the Progressive Era, 1910-1915* (New York: International Publishers, 1980), p. 13.

52. Page Smith, *America Enters the World*, vol. 7: *A People's History of the Progressive Era and World War I* (New York: McGraw-Hill, 1985), pp. 252-60. Darrow was later indicted for bribing two jurors in the McNamara trial. He was acquitted in one case, but there was a hung jury in the other case. The prosecutor did not file charges again against Darrow. For an excellent account of Darrow's bribery trial and the trial of the McNamara brothers, see Geoffrey Cowan, *The People v. Clarence Darrow: The Bribery Trial of America's Greatest Lawyer* (New York: Times Books/Random House, 1993).

53. Ibid., pp. 258-60.

54. Foner, *History of the Labor Movement*, vol. 5, p. 31.

55. Crenshaw, "The Logic of Terrorism: Terrorist Behavior as a Product of Strategic Choice," in Walter Reich, ed., *Origins of Terrorism: Psychologies, Ideologies, Theologies, States of Mind* (New York: Cambridge University Press and Woodrow Wilson International Center for Scholars, 1990), p. 15.

56. Foner, *History of the Labor Movement*, vol. 5, p. 8.

2

INTERNATIONAL TERRORISM

An eye for an eye only leads to more blindness.

—Margaret Atwood

The attacks of September 11, 2001, were the most ghastly acts of transnational terrorism in history. Yet, as is true for other terrorists' strikes throughout the ages, understanding the atrocities of September 11 requires knowledge of the social, economic, political, and religious conditions from which terrorism arises.

As in earlier eras, advances in communication, transportation, and weaponry are exploited by today's terrorists. Contemporary terrorists have a vast and terrifying array of choices, but they also face a new enemy: the forces of globalization.

Our world has become more unified, and evidence of interconnections are everywhere. Commerce and technology have brought the people of our planet together in ways previously unimaginable. The Internet has penetrated into remote corners of the planet, and new discoveries in digital and optical technologies are likely to drive human beings even closer together. McDonald's sells hamburgers in Beijing, and American music and videos can be heard and seen in remote corners of the world. Free-trade agreements make national borders more porous; someday, they may make them obsolete.

Falling stock markets in Tokyo devastate investors in Chicago. The International Monetary Fund intervenes in the economies of many underdeveloped countries because of global interdependence and the push for prosperity. International peace and stability are invaluable in this new world order. Problems and their solutions are no longer isolated geographically.

Terrorism is at odds with civilization's march toward globalization. Terrorists often focus on separatism and pitting one religious, ethnic, or social group against another. Terrorism generally is not about coming together as a unified whole; it is about breaking apart into smaller, antagonistic units. Some terrorists would like to impose their religion or political ideology on the whole world, but their tactics are brute force, not the international collaboration that is the hallmark of globalization.

Barber (1992) captures this phenomenon when he notes that the "planet is falling precipitately apart AND coming reluctantly together at the very same moment" (p. 53). He labels this division as "Jihad" versus "McWorld." *Jihad*, which means "struggle" in Arabic, can be applied to either the internal struggle against evil or the external struggle against the perceived enemies of Islam. It is the latter meaning that has been invoked by many contemporary terrorists, who are on a collision course with the forces of globalization.

The effects of globalization were quickly evident after the September 11, 2001, assaults on the United States. The day after the attacks, the North Atlantic Treaty Organization (NATO), founded in 1949 and comprising 19 member states, invoked, for the first time, Article 5 of the Washington Treaty, which declares that an armed attack on one member was an attack against all of them. Other nations around the world joined in condemning the terrorists and demonstrating solidarity with the United States. Many Muslim leaders in Africa and Asia expressed sympathy with the United States, noting that the Koran and Islamic teachings prohibit the slaughter of innocents.

The international display of unity in the immediate aftermath of the attacks does not diminish the reality that, in many spots around the globe, the United States and Western nations are despised. Anti-American sentiment is particularly virulent in portions of southwestern Asia and northern Africa, an area known as the Middle East, although the sentiment exists elsewhere. Poverty, authoritarian governments, and U.S. intervention in the area have provided fertile ground for the growth of religious extremists and denunciations of the United States as the "Great Satan."

TERRORISM AROUND THE WORLD

Although the outcome of the clash between "Jihad" and "McWorld" is unknown, it is clear that terrorism continues to exist in virtually every region of the globe. No one knows the true number of foreign terrorist groups. The United States Department of State (2000) identified 42 foreign terrorist groups. A list for the Terrorism Research Center (2000), compiled by the Dudley Knox Library Naval Postgraduate School, named 85 foreign terrorist groups. Precise counts are difficult, in part, because terrorist organizations are dynamic; change is therefore endemic to the phenomenon. Some terrorist organizations splinter into subgroups, and others disband and reassemble with new names.

Being labeled as a terrorist organization carries political repercussions. Every 2 years, the U.S. secretary of state publishes a list of active foreign terrorist groups. These are divided into two categories—Foreign Terrorist Organizations (FTOs), which are terrorist organizations that meet the criteria of the Antiterrorism and Effective Death Penalty Act of 1996, and Other Terrorist Groups (OTGs), which do not meet the criteria of the Act. In the secretary of state's 2001 report (U.S. Department of State, 2002), released in April 2002, 33 groups were designated as FTOs and another 28 were identified as OTGs. The report, which is reproduced in Appendix B of this volume, notes the specific terrorist activities attributed to each group.

The legal and fiscal consequences of being designated an FTO are severe. It is a crime to donate money or otherwise assist an FTO, even if the funds are to be used for charitable purposes. Medicine and religious materials are excluded from the ban. Some FTOs have used charitable donations to provide sorely needed basic social services, such as hospitals and schools. Nevertheless, U.S. citizens are prohibited from contributing to these organizations on the premise that charitable donations make it easier for the groups to recruit supporters. In addition, members of FTOs are denied visas and barred from the United States. Financial institutions are required to block any funds intended for FTOs.

The identification of an FTO is inherently political. By definition, FTOs threaten the security of U.S. citizens or endanger the national defense, foreign relations, or economic interests of the United States. A few highlights of FTOs from the U.S. secretary of state's list follow.

1. *Europe*
   - The Basque Fatherland and Liberty (ETA) group, founded in 1959, aims to create an independent state in northern Spain comprising the seven Basque provinces.
   - Issued during the Easter Rising of 1916, the *Proclamation of the Republic*, which declared Ireland independent from England, is considered to be the founding document of the Irish Republican Army (IRA). The Easter Rising was crushed and its leaders were executed, but the struggle for independence continued. Today, the IRA is the terrorist wing of Sinn Fein, the Northern Ireland political organization trying to unite Ireland and expel British forces. In 1999, for the first time, the IRA was identified as an OTG, not an FTO, because of its willingness to enforce a cease-fire and participate in the peace process in Northern Ireland.
   - Established in 1974, the Kurdistan Worker's Party (PKK) wants to create an independent Kurdish state in southeastern Turkey. Its leader, Chairman Abdullah Ocalan, was captured and sentenced to death in 1999.

2. *South America*
   - The Revolutionary Armed Forces of Colombia (FARC), established in 1964, is believed to be responsible for atrocities claiming untold numbers of innocent victims.
   - Begun in 1965 by Jesuit priests influenced by Fidel Castro and Che Guevara, the National Liberation Army (ELN) engages in widespread kidnapping for ransom and wages an insurgent war against the Colombian government.
   - Peru's Tupac Amaru Revolutionary Movement (MRTA), founded in 1983, is most famous for its 1996 assault on the Japanese ambassador's residence in Lima, where 72 *BookClub* hostages were held for more than 4 months. No new terrorist activities have been attributed to MRTA since Peruvian armed forces rescued all but one of the hostages and killed most of the group's leaders.
   - Sendero Luminoso (Shining Path), founded in the late 1960s and based on a communist ideology, is believed responsible for roughly 30,000 deaths. Leaders of the group were the focus of massive counterterrorism operations by the Peruvian government.

3. *Asia*
   - Aum Shinrikyo (Aum), founded in 1987 by Shoko Asahara, is a Japanese doomsday cult responsible for releasing sarin nerve gas on several Tokyo subway trains in 1995, killing 12 and injuring thousands.
   - During its heyday in the 1970s, the Japanese Red Army (JRA), which is devoted to overthrowing the Japanese monarchy and fostering world revolution, conducted terrorist attacks around the world, including the massacre in 1972 at Lod Airport in Israel and the hijacking of two Japanese airlines. Fusako Shigenobu, one of the founders and leaders, had been on the run for 30 years when she was captured in Japan in 2000.
   - Liberation Tigers of Tamil Eelam (LTTE), founded in 1976, engages in assassinations and bombings to promote its goal of creating an independent Tamil state in Sri Lanka. LTTE is known outside Sri Lanka for the suicide bomb attack that killed India's Prime Minister Rajiv Gandhi in 1991.

4. *Middle East and Africa*
   - For the first time, the 1999 report added al-Qaeda, meaning the "Base," the organization led by Saudi millionaire Osama bin Laden, to the list of FTOs.
   - Abu Nidal Organization (ANO) split from the Palestine Liberation Organization (PLO) in 1974 and launched an international campaign of terrorism, carrying out attacks in 20 countries against the United States, Britain, Israel, and various Arab countries.

- Hamas (Islamic Resistance Movement) was formed in 1987 with the goal of establishing an Islamic state and expelling Israelis. Located primarily in the Gaza Strip and West Bank, Hamas has gained widespread support from Arabs throughout the region.
- Hizbollah (Party of God; also called Islamic Jihad) seeks to create an Iranian-style Islamic republic in Lebanon. It is believed responsible for the bombings of the U.S. embassy and U.S. Marine barracks in Beirut in 1983, as well as for the kidnapping of Western hostages in Lebanon in the 1980s.

STATE-SPONSORED TERRORISM

A traditional view of terrorism is that it pits an individual or an organization against a sovereign state. Another type of terrorism, however, presents perhaps an even greater threat: the secret use of terrorism by a sovereign state.

State-sponsored terrorism is as old as the history of military conflict. States may opt to use terrorism instead of conventional armies for many reasons. Modern warfare is extraordinarily expensive and is likely to provoke counterattack. States can sponsor terrorism covertly, allowing the state to deny its role as an aggressor and avoid retaliation. The relationship between the patron state and the terrorist organization can be mutually beneficial: Terrorists obtain the sponsorship necessary to maintain and expand their struggle, and the state obtains a potent weapon against its enemies.

State-sponsored terrorism takes many forms. At one extreme, a government can establish its own brutal death squads, whose sole purpose is to advance the interest of the state. At the other extreme, a state can simply provide a safe haven for terrorists, allowing them to operate without restrictions. Some states that sponsor terrorism take a middle path by assisting terrorists financially and refusing to extradite them to face criminal charges in another state. Government funds can be channeled to terrorists directly or indirectly through social, cultural, or charitable associations, many of which "serve as front organizations for groups that engage in terrorism" (Paz, 2000, p. 4).

The U.S. secretary of state is authorized to identify state sponsors of terrorism. The primary threat to the United States and its allies is reported to come from South Asia and the Middle East. Seven states were designated as state sponsors of terrorism in 2000: Iran, Iraq, Syria, Libya, North Korea, Cuba, and Sudan. Economic and political sanctions accompany the designation. The sanctions are intended to force state sponsors of terrorism to "renounce the use of terrorism, end support to terrorists, and bring terrorists to justice for past crimes" (United States Department of State, 2000, p. 1).

The seven state sponsors of terrorism are believed to have engaged in a variety of activities. For example, Iran supports numerous terrorist groups in its effort to undermine the process of procuring peace in the Middle East between the Palestinians and Israel. Iraq provides bases and support for Palestinians and Iranian terrorists. Syria provides a safe haven and funds for several terrorist training camps. Libya has refused to pay compensation for the bombing of Pan Am Flight 103 over Lockerbie, Scotland, in 1988, although in 1999 it finally surrendered for trial the two Libyans accused of the bombing. North Korea harbors hijackers of a Japanese airliner in the 1970s. Cuba harbors U.S. fugitives from justice. Sudan serves as a meeting place and training hub for several terrorist groups.

The sanctions experienced by a country as a result of the U.S. designation of state sponsor of terrorism are significant, and they have contributed to famine, economic stagnation, and other deprivations for the citizens of some sanctioned states.

The concept of a list of state sponsors of terrorism breaths life into the hackneyed expression that "one man's terrorist is another man's freedom fighter." The countries on the U.S. list no doubt have their own list of terrorist states, and the United States is likely at the top of many of them.

For example, Chileans would be justified in considering the U.S. intervention in their country in the 1970s as terrorism. According to documents declassified in 2000 and released by the National Security Archives, the United States tried to overthrow the government of Chile and its democratically elected Marxist president, Dr. Salvador Allende, in the early 1970s (National Security Archive, 2000). President Richard M. Nixon ordered the Central Intelligence Agency (CIA) to mount a covert terrorist operation to keep Allende from taking office. When that failed, the CIA tried to undermine Allende's rule. It eventually succeeded when the Chilean military seized power under General Augusto Pinochet, who ruled until 1990. Pinochet's death squads murdered more than 3,000 people, and government forces jailed and tortured thousands more. The definition of terrorism thus depends on the experience of the definer.

RELIGIOUS FANATICISM: AN OLD TREND AND A NEW THREAT

"Holy Terror" was practiced in earlier centuries by groups such as the Jewish Zealots, the Assassins, and the Thugs, and contemporary observers are particularly concerned about the growth of religious fanaticism. According to Laqueur (1999), the new terrorism is different from the old,

> aiming not at clearly defined political demands but at the destruction of society and the elimination of large sections of the population. In its most extreme form, this new terrorism intends to liquidate all of what it deems to be "satanic forces," which may include the majority of a country or of mankind, as a precondition for the growth of another, better, and in any case different breed of human. In its maddest, most extreme form it may aim at the destruction of all life on earth, as the ultimate punishment for mankind's crimes. (p. 81)

Half of the organizations designated by the U.S. secretary of state in 2001 as FTOs are in the Middle East and Africa. Some of these groups are dedicated to replacing secular society with strict Islamic law and rejecting all Western influences. Of particular concern is the spread of Islamist terrorist activity to Eastern Europe and central and southern Asia. Terrorism in Kosovo, Chechnya, Uzbekistan, Afghanistan, Kashmir, Indonesia, and the Philippines has been associated with radical interpretations of Islam that elevate terrorism to a religious duty (Paz, 2000).

Many Americans and Europeans equate Islam with terrorism, but this is incorrect and unfortunate. Most Muslims, even most fundamentalists, are not terrorists. Instead, they have overwhelmingly been the victims of violent conflicts. Hundreds of thousands of Muslims were killed in the war between Iran and Iraq, and the civil wars in Afghanistan and Algeria led to similarly horrific numbers of casualties. Noncombatant Muslims have suffered untold losses in the war between Chechnya and Russia, in the turmoil in Indonesia, and throughout much of Africa and the Middle East. Terrorism has destroyed the lives of many Muslims and non-Muslims throughout the world.

A FEW FAMOUS TERRORISTS

The above discussion focused on terrorist groups and their sponsors. The discussion now shifts to the terrorists themselves. Hundreds of thousands of human beings have

A billboard in Cuba pays tribute to the revolutionary leader Che Guevara.

Copyright © 2002 by Tim Page/CORBIS. Reprinted with permission.

filled this role, but a few names stand out in history. The following discussion highlights the careers of three of them: Che Guevara, Carlos the Jackal, and Osama bin Laden.

Che Guevara

Che Guevara is a pop-political legend whose romantic photograph, taken in 1960 at a funeral for dead seamen in Cuba, today adorns murals and posters, Internet Web sites, and CD covers all over the world. Although he died in 1967, Guevara remains a potent symbol for the disaffected everywhere. His image represents freedom and is the epitome of youthful rebellion against authority. A Marxist revolutionary, a philosopher, a poet, and a warrior, Guevara is remembered not as a terrorist but for his deep convictions, for living his dream and dying for his ideals. Philosopher Jean-Paul Sartre called Guevara "the most complete human being of our age" (Che Guevara Information Archive, 2001).

Guevara influenced the structure of violent revolution throughout Latin America. Revolution, he maintained, should begin in the countryside, and indiscriminate urban terrorism should serve as a supplementary form of revolt (Laqueur, 1977, p. 180). He authored three books—*Guerrilla Warfare* (1961), *Man and Socialism in Cuba* (1967), and *Reminiscences of the Cuban Revolutionary War* (1968)—read by left-wing radicals around the world.

Ernesto "Che" Guevara was born in 1928 into a middle-class family in Rosario, Argentina. He earned a medical degree from the University of Buenos Aires in 1953, but his interests turned from medicine to helping the poor and challenging authority through revolution. He participated in riots against the Argentine dictator Juan Perón. He worked in a leper colony and joined the pro-Communist regime of Jacobo Arbenz Guzmán in Guatemala. When Arbenz was overthrown in 1954, Guevara fled to Mexico, where he met Fidel Castro and other Cuban rebels (White, 1998, p. 56). He later fought in Castro's guerrilla war against Cuban dictator Fulgencio Bautista, becoming a chief strategist and respected guerrilla fighter. When Castro assumed power, Guevara served as president of the national bank and later as minister of industry, traveled widely to communist countries, and even addressed the United Nations on behalf of Cuba.

Guevara wanted to export the Cuban experience to other countries. Convinced that peasant-based revolution was the only remedy for Latin America's poverty and social inequities, Guevara, who may have fallen out of favor with Castro, left Cuba and became a revolutionary leader in Bolivia. He believed that acts of terrorism would create an environment of fear ripe for revolution. According to Vetter and Perlstein (1991), Guevara "resorted to terrorizing Bolivian village leaders and elders in a deliberate program of mutilation and assassination when he found himself unable to influence the peasants to support his revolution" (p. 45). Guevara was captured and executed by the Bolivian army in 1967. Today, the circumstances of his activities in Bolivia and his capture, killing, and burial are still the subject of intense public interest around the world, and some have suggested that the U.S. CIA was involved in his death. (For more on Guevara, see, for example, Anderson, 1998; Camejo, 1972; Castaneda, 1997; Harris, 1970; and Hodges, 1977.)

Carlos the Jackal

Che Guevara is remembered as a romantic figure, but Carlos the Jackal's legend is shrouded in mystery (Follain, 2000). Frequently blamed for crimes he did not commit, including the killing of 11 Israeli athletes at the 1972 Olympics in Munich, Carlos collaborated with terrorists in Japan, Germany, Spain, and Italy. He was particularly well known for his activities on behalf of Arab terrorists seeking to drive Israel out of Palestine. He lived freely under the protection of Communist-bloc countries (Laqueur, 1999, p. 164) and is believed to have worked for Libya's Colonel Muammar al-Qaddafi, Iraq's Saddam Hussein, and Cuba's Fidel Castro. When finally arrested in Sudan in 1994, Carlos the Jackal was 44 years old and until shortly before that time had been living in Syria with his wife, Magdalena Kopp, a former member of the German Baader-Meinhoff terrorist group.

Separating the myth from the reality of Carlos is not easy, in part because he spread false stories about himself, used multiple disguises, and changed his name and passport frequently. He was dubbed "the Jackal" after the sinister assassin in a Frederick Forsyth novel. A wanted poster showing his wide, unemotional face in dark glasses became a symbol for left-leaning terrorist movements around the globe.

A Venezuelan whose real name is Ilich Ramirez Sanchez, Carlos was born in 1949 and named by his Marxist father after Russian leader Vladimir Ilich Ulyanov, or Lenin, as he was better known. His brothers were named Lenin and Vladimir. As a youth, Carlos joined the Venezuelan Communist Youth in their violent demonstrations against the ruling government. Later, he attended Moscow's Lumumba University, a training center for future leaders of the Soviet Union's expansion into underdeveloped countries. There he met Palestinian students and came to admire the teachings of George Habash, the leader of the Popular Front for the Liberation of Palestine (PFLP). After the PFLP hijacked several airlines, Carlos left Russia for the Middle East and began his terrorist career in earnest (Bellamy, 2000).

Carlos's most notorious terrorist act was the kidnapping of 11 oil ministers at an OPEC (Organization of Petroleum Exporting Countries) meeting in Vienna in December 1975. Three people died in the takeover, and Carlos and his fellow terrorists, along with several hostages, were flown to Algeria and released, reportedly with a big payoff from an undisclosed Arab state. Carlos was also a suspect in several bombings and grenade attacks, and he publicly admitted to a 1973 assassination attempt on British millionaire Edward Sieff, a Jewish businessman and owner of the Marks and Spencer stores in London. He was convicted in absentia in France in 1992 and was sentenced to life imprisonment for the 1975 murder of two French intelligence agents who wanted to question him about attacks on Israeli El Al planes at Orly Airport in Paris. In the shootout with the police, Carlos also killed a fellow terrorist and PFLP member whom he suspected of being an informer.

Carlos seemed to drop out of sight during the late 1980s, and reports circulated of his death, although other reports had him living in Mexico, Colombia, and Syria. The collapse of the Soviet Union may have left him with few sponsors, and he was eventually betrayed by the Sudanese police. After being arrested and flown to France, he was convicted in 1997 and sentenced to life imprisonment.

At his trial, Carlos said he was a "professional revolutionary." After hearing the guilty verdict against him, he raised his fist and shouted "viva la revolución." In prison, Carlos went on a hunger strike to protest being held in solitary confinement but ended it at the request of his father. Several excellent biographies of this "superterrorist" have been written (see, for example, Dobson, 1977; Follain, 2000; Smith, 1977; and Yallop, 1993).

Osama bin Laden

Osama bin Laden is the best-known contemporary terrorist. Born in Saudi Arabia around 1957 to a father of Yemeni origin and a Syrian mother, bin Laden grew up fabulously wealthy. His father, Mohammed bin Laden, had many wives and more than 50 children. Having been favored with royal patronage and awarded the contract to rebuild, among other things, the mosques in the holy cities of Mecca and Medina, Mohammed bin Laden became a billionaire.

At Abdul Aziz University in Jedda, Saudi Arabia, the young Osama was introduced to the wider world of Islamic politics. The 1979 Soviet invasion of Afghanistan was a turning point for him. He began to use his wealth and organizational skills to help train thousands of young Arabs and Muslims to fight in the Afghan resistance, which was supported by the United States.

After the Soviet Union withdrew from Afghanistan, bin Laden returned to Saudi Arabia and founded an organization to assist veterans of the Afghan war. In 1990, when Iraqi forces invaded Kuwait, the United States was allowed to station its troops in Saudi Arabia. This outraged bin Laden, who saw it as a sacrilege that nonbelievers should occupy the birthplace of Islam. When bin Laden turned against the Saudi government, it expelled him from the country. He moved to the Sudan, where he continued training recruits in terrorist tactics.

Bin Laden subsequently returned to Afghanistan, where he was given sanctuary under the protection of the Taliban, the fundamentalist Islamic movement that came to power in 1996. The Taliban arose out of the chaos produced at the end of the Cold War. When the Soviets withdrew from Afghanistan in the late 1980s, the United States also left, leaving Afghanistan devastated. Into this vacuum marched the Taliban (Rashid, 2001).

Bin Laden, with the help of the Taliban, jeopardized the stability of south and central Asia and Africa by training radical Arabs and Muslims in the tools of terrorism. Students from all over the region have studied in Afghanistan, and thousands are determined to carry out Taliban-style Islamic revolutions in their homelands.

Bin Laden is a hero to radical Muslim youth throughout the Middle East and Africa (Bodansky, 1999), and his organization oversees a loosely tied network of local cells that operate independently of each another.

A glimpse into bin Laden's mind was provided by a 1998 interview with an ABC news correspondent.

It is hard for one to understand if the person does not understand Islam. . . . Allah is the one who created us and blessed us with this religion, and orders us to carry out the holy struggle "jihad" to raise the word of Allah above the words of the unbelievers. . . . It does not worry us what the Americans think. What worries us is pleasing Allah. The Americans impose themselves on everyone who believes in his religion and his rights. They accuse our children in Palestine of being terrorists. Those children that have no weapons and have not even reached maturity. At the same time they defend a country with its airplanes and tanks, and the state of the Jews, that has a policy to destroy the future of these children. . . . Each action will solicit a similar reaction. We must use such punishment to keep your evil away from Muslims, Muslim children and women. American history does not distinguish between civilians and military, and not even women and children. They are the ones who used the bombs against Nagasaki. Can these bombs distinguish between infants and military? America does not have a religion that will prevent it from destroying all people. (as quoted in Miller, 1998)

Osama bin Laden, the Saudi Arabian leader of Al-Qaeda, as shown on the FBI's Most Wanted Terrorist poster.

Photo provided courtesy of the Federal Bureau of Investigation.

In addition to the attacks on September 11, 2001, bin Laden's al-Qaeda organization has been held responsible for the bombings at the Khobar Towers housing complex in Saudi Arabia that killed 19 U.S. servicemen; the nearly simultaneous blasts on the U.S. embassies in Nairobi and Tanzania, which left more than 300 people dead; and the 1993 truck bomb attack on the World Trade Center in New York.

Bin Laden is also suspected of being involved in the bombing of the destroyer USS *Cole*, which was attacked as it refueled in the Yemen port of Aden on October 12, 2000. The attack killed 17 Navy sailors and wounded dozens more. A motorized skiff, carrying explosives and two suicide bombers, tore a ragged hole in the *Cole*, which is the length of a football field and equipped with long-range cruise missiles.

In 2001, a Federal District Court in Manhattan began hearing testimony in the case of the Kenya Embassy bombing. A top deputy to bin Laden, Jama Ahmed Al-Fadl, was caught stealing money from al-Qaeda. Fearing retaliation from bin Laden, he became an informer for the United States and entered the witness protection program. Al-Fadl testified against the four defendants at the embassy bombing trial and provided details of bin Laden's terrorist organization. He described a thoroughly modern organization that used international companies and social relief agencies as fronts; communicated by fax, coded letters, and satellite phones; and trained recruits in the use of sophisticated weapons.

Al-Fadl testified that the American embassies were chosen for terrorist attacks because bin Laden was angry about U.S. intervention in the civil war in Somalia. Regardless of the truthfulness of the informer's claim, the embassy bombings did not go unpunished. Shortly after the bombings, the United States launched cruise missile attacks on what was believed to be bin Laden's camp in Afghanistan. Again, attack and counterattack are the familiar pattern. (For more on bin Laden, see Bodansky, 1999; Engelberg, 2001; Huband, 1999; and Reeve, 1999.)

The lives of Che Guevara, Carlos the Jackal, and Osama bin Laden illustrate some of the variations in the lives of famous terrorists. The following discussion is more limited still, focusing on only one terrorist event, but it is one that had worldwide implications: the bombing of Pan Am Flight 103.

PAN AM FLIGHT 103

On December 21, 1988, liquid fire and twisted metal fell from the skies over the tiny village of Lockerbie, Scotland, after the explosion of Pan Am Flight 103. All 259 passengers and crew were killed, including 189 Americans, along with 11 people on the ground. The explosion of Pan Am Flight 103, en route from London to New York, exemplified the political nature of international terrorism (see, for example, Emerson & Duffy, 1990; U.S. Congress, 1991; and Wallace, 2001).

In 1991, two Libyan intelligence agents were charged with the bombing, and the government of Colonel Muammar al-Qaddafi was widely believed to have been involved. When al-Qaddafi refused to surrender the suspects for trial, the United Nations Security Council imposed sanctions on Libya in 1992. The UN resolution banned all airline flights to and from Libya, prohibited sales of weapons and aircraft to Libya, forced drastic reductions in oil sales, and limited Libyan diplomatic presence in foreign capitals. The economic and political sanctions were designed to pressure al-Qaddafi to turn over the two suspects. In 1999, 11 years after the downing of Flight 103, he complied, and the suspects were handed over to a special Scottish court in the Netherlands. The United Nations suspended the sanctions against Libya, but the United States did not.

On January 31, 2001, Abdelbaset Ali Mohmed al-Megrahi was found guilty of arranging for the bomb, hidden in a Toshiba radio-cassette player inside a brown Samsonite suitcase, to be loaded onto the flight. No witnesses saw the suitcase placed on board the plane, but the Lockerbie prosecutors were able to link al-Megrahi to the bomb-making materials. He was sentenced to life imprisonment and must serve a minimum of 20 years before parole eligibility.

His codefendant, Al Amin Khalifa Fhimah, the station manager for Libyan airlines in Malta, was acquitted because the court found no convincing evidence that he knowingly helped put the suitcase in the international baggage system. He returned to a hero's welcome in Libya. In an internationally broadcasted ceremony, Colonel al-Qaddafi rallied against the guilty verdict and objected to the way the entire case had been handled, with particularly vitriolic comments reserved for the United States.

Libya was then considered by the West to be one of the most vigorous state sponsors of international terrorism during the 1970s and 1980s. Colonel al-Qaddafi, who came to power in a coup d'état in 1969, wanted "to spearhead an Arab-Islamic revolution in which he saw himself not only as the chief ideologist (by virtue of his little 'Green Book') but also as chief strategist" (Laqueur, 1999, p. 168). Thousands of foreign terrorists were trained in Libya, including Carlos the Jackal, who was believed to be on al-Qaddafi's payroll.

Attack and counterattack were building blocks of the Pan Am terrorist attack. The Libyan government was believed by the United States to have arranged terrorist attacks in airports in Vienna and Rome, as well as the 1986 bombing of the La Belle Discotheque in West Berlin, in which two American servicemen were killed. In retaliation, the

United States launched an air strike, dubbed El Dorado Canyon, against the Libyan capital, Tripoli. Among the casualties was the daughter of Colonel al-Qaddafi.

President George H. W. Bush responded to the Lockerbie verdict by vowing to continue the U.S. sanctions and calling for the Libyan government to pay compensation to the families of the victims. At the welcome home ceremony for the Libyan acquitted of the bombing, al-Qaddafi likewise demanded compensation. He wanted the United States to pay for the bombings on Tripoli.

The events surrounding the bombing of Pan Am Flight 103 illustrate how one terrorist event had repercussions around the globe. The September 11, 2001, attacks on the United States were consistent with this pattern of transnational terrorism with worldwide ramifications.

HIGHLIGHTS OF REPRINTED ARTICLES

The two readings that follow were selected to illustrate two aspects of international terrorism not discussed above. The first discusses the interconnections between terrorism and narcotics trafficking and other crimes. The second focuses on the religious and political motivations underlying the September 11 attacks.

Chris Dishman. (2001). "Terrorism, Crime, and Transformation." *Studies in Conflict & Terrorism, 24*(3), 43-58.

Chris Dishman analyzes the popular image of terrorists and members of organized crime groups, especially drug traffickers, working closely together. Filling their coffers with proceeds from lucrative narcotics and smuggling operations enables terrorists not only to enhance their conventional arsenals but also to purchase expensive ingredients needed to manufacture sophisticated and destructive weapons. Strong evidence, however, suggests that terrorists and criminals are unlikely to forge lasting bonds.

In this article, Dishman argues that the different goals of the two groups make long-term cooperation unlikely. Terrorists, by definition, engage in violence to promote political or religious aims. Terrorists' public pronouncements are full of political rhetoric, and they see themselves as serving noble causes. Terrorists' targets are often symbolic and chosen to attract the widest possible attention.

Transnational Criminal Organizations (TCO), on the other hand, aim to make as much money as possible, and their use of violence generally is limited to people or institutions that threaten their profit-making operations. TCOs are much less likely than terrorists to want public notice, and they are unlikely to purposely seek massive casualties from their attacks. Dishman uses examples from all over the globe to show the limits of collaboration between terrorists and criminals.

Michael Scott Doran. (2002). "Somebody Else's Civil War." *Foreign Affairs, 81*(3), 22-42.

Michael Scott Doran provides a glimpse into the religious motivations of Osama bin Laden and his al-Qaeda followers. According to Doran, bin Laden had "no intention of defeating America. War with the United States was not a goal in and of itself but rather an instrument designed to help his brand of extremist Islam survive and flourish among the believers. Americans, in short, have been drawn into somebody else's civil war" (p. 23).

Bin Laden's primary target was the *umma*, or universal Islamic community, Doran argues. He expected the United States "to use its military might like a cartoon character trying to kill a fly with a shotgun" (p. 23). The savagery of the American reaction would outrage Muslims everywhere, and they would rise up against those governments allied with the West. The revolution within the Muslim world was to center in the Arab lands, especially in Saudi Arabia.

Doran notes that, aside from insisting on the implementation of the *shari'a*, the strict Islamic law, Arab and Muslim extremists have offered little assistance to the poor people in their countries. Doran concludes that the United States should help Arab and Muslim nations to realize that their own interests and those of the United States coincide "so that demagogues like bin Laden cannot aspire to speak in the name of the entire umma" (2002, p. 41).

EXPLORING INTERNATIONAL TERRORISM FURTHER

- Many FTOs and OTGs have their own Internet sites, although they are unlikely to identify themselves as terrorists. The Web site of the Liberation Tigers of Tamil Eelam (LTTE) (www.eelam.com) declares that the "Tamil people of the island of Ceylon (now called Sri Lanka) constitute a distinct nation. They form a social entity, with their own history, traditions, culture, language and traditional homeland. The Tamil people call their nation Tamil Eelam."
- A Web site about Hamas (www.palestine-info.com/hamas) includes a "Glory Record" of Palestinian militants who were "martyred" in attacks on Israelis.
- Sinn Fein, the political wing of the IRA, has been a key participant in the peace process, yet it remains committed to a united Ireland free from British rule. Its Web site is www.//sinnfein.ie
- A variety of bibliographies on international terrorism are available online. The Dudley Knox Library at the Naval Post Graduate School in Monterey, California, has one divided by subject and region at web.nps.navy.mil/~library/terrorism.htm

VIDEO NOTES

Background about international terrorism is explained often in documentaries about the Central Intelligence Agency. One noted exploration of the U.S. role in the "blowback" of transnational terrorism is titled *C.I.A.: America's Secret Warriors* (Discovery Channel, 1997, 2 vols., 50 min. each).

REFERENCES

Anderson, Jon Lee. (1998). *Che Guevara: A revolutionary life*. New York: Grove Press.
Antiterrorism and Effective Death Penalty Act, Pub. L. No. 104-132 (2001).
Barber, Benjamin R. (1992). Jihad vs. McWorld. *Atlantic Monthly, 269*(3), 53-65.
Bellamy, Patrick. (2000). *Carlos the Jackal: Trail of terror.* Retrieved June 4, 2002, from www.crimelibrary.com/terrorists/carlos/text.htm
Bodansky, Yossef. (1999). *Bin Laden: The man who declared war on America*. Rocklin, CA: Prima Publishing.
Camejo, P. (1972). *Guevara's guerilla strategy*. New York: Pathfinder Press.
Castaneda, Jorge G. (1997). *Companero: The life and death of Che Guevara*. New York: Knopf.
Che Guevara Information Archive. (2001). Retrieved June 4, 2002, from www.geocities.com/Hollywood/8702/che.html.
Dishman, Chris. (2001). Terrorism, crime, and transformation. *Studies in Conflict & Terrorism, 24*(3), 43-58.

Dobson, Christopher. (1977). *The Carlos complex: A study in terror*. New York: Putnam.

Doran, Michael. (2002). Somebody else's civil war. *Foreign Affairs, 81*(3), 22-42.

Emerson, Steven A., & Del Sesto, Cristina. (1991). *Terrorists: The inside story of the highest ranking Iraqi terrorist ever to defect to the West*. New York: Villard.

Emerson, Steven, & Duffy, Brian. (1990). *The fall of Pan Am 103: Inside the Lockerbie investigation*. New York: Putnam.

Engelberg, Stephen. (2001, January 14). One man and a global web of violence [Electronic version]. Retrieved June 4, 2002, from *The New York Times on the Web*, www.library. cornell.edu/colldev/mideast/jihdbnl.htm

Follain, John. (2000). *Jackal: The complete story of the legendary terrorist, Carlos the Jackal*. New York: Arcade Publishing.

Guevara, Che. (1961). *Guerrilla warfare*. New York: Monthly Review Press.

Guevara, Che. (1967). *Man and socialism in Cuba*. Havana: Book Institute.

Guevara, Che. (1968). *Reminiscences of the Cuban Revolutionary War*. New York: Monthly Review Press.

Harris, R. (1970). *Death of a revolutionary: Che Guevara's Last Mission*. New York: Norton.

Hodges, Donald C. (Ed.). (1977). *The legacy of Che Guevara: A documentary study*. London: Thames and Hudson.

Huband, Mark. (1999). *Warriors of the prophet: The struggle for Islam*. Boulder, CO: Westview.

Laqueur, Walter. (1977). *Terrorism*. Boston: Little, Brown, and Company.

Laqueur, Walter. (1999). *The new terrorism: Fanaticism and the arms of mass destruction*. New York: Oxford University Press.

Miller, John. (1998, May 28). An exclusive interview with Osama bin Laden: Talking with terror's banker. Retrieved January 5, 2001, from www.abcnews.go.com/sections/world/ dailynews/terror_980609.html

National Security Archive. (2000). *Chile: 16,000 U.S. secret documents declassified* [Press release]. Washington, DC: National Security Archive.

Paz, Reuven. (2000, September). *Targeting terrorist financing in the Middle East*. Paper presented at the International Conference on Countering Terrorism through Enhanced International Cooperation, Mont Blanc, Italy. Retrieved June 4, 2002, from www.ict. org.il/articles/articledet.cfm?articleid=137

Rashid, Ahmed. (2001). *Taliban: Militant Islam, oil and fundamentalism in Central Asia*. New Haven, CT: Yale University Press.

Reeve, Simon. (1999). *The new Jackals: Ramzi Yousef, Osama bin Laden and the future of terrorism*. Boston: Northeastern University Press.

Smith, Colin. (1977). *Carlos: Portrait of a terrorist*. New York: Holt, Rinehart and Winston.

Terrorism Research Center. (2000). *Terrorist group profiles*. Retrieved June 4, 2002, from www.terrorism.com/terrorism/Groups2.shtml

U.S. Congress. (1991, December 18). *Drug Enforcement Administration's alleged connection to the Pan Am Flight 103 disaster*. Hearing before the Government Information, Justice, and Agriculture Subcommittee of the Committee on Government Operations, House of Representatives, 101st Congress, 2nd Session. Washington, DC: Government Printing Office.

U.S. Department of State. (2000). *Patterns of global terrorism: 1999*. Washington, DC: Department of State.

U.S. Department of State. (2002). *Patterns of global terrorism: 2001*. Washington, DC: Department of State.

Vetter, Harold J., & Perlstein, Gary R. (1991). *Perspectives on terrorism*. Belmont, CA: Wadsworth.

Wallace, Rodney. (2001). *Lockerbie: The story and the lessons*. Westport, CT: Praeger.

White, Jonathan R. (1998). *Terrorism: An introduction*. Belmont, CA: Wadsworth.

Yallop, David A. (1993). *Tracking the Jackal: The search for Carlos, the world's most wanted man*. New York: Random House.

TERRORISM, CRIME, AND TRANSFORMATION

Chris Dishman

This article argues that some of today's terrorist groups have transformed into transnational criminal organizations (TCOs) who are more interested in profits than politics. This dynamic has important implications for policymakers as some traditional, politically motivated terrorist groups further profit-minded agencies under a political banner. The author argues that there are different degrees of transformation; some terrorists commit criminal acts to support political operations, while others view profit-driven criminal acts as their end game. The article further argues that unlike some observers suggest, TCOs and terrorist groups will not cooperate with each other to advance aims and interests, instead utilizing their "in-house" capabilities to undertake criminal or political acts.

The relative decline of state supported terrorism in this decade has led many scholars to believe that terrorist groups will increasingly engage in drug trafficking and other illicit activities to acquire money and material. Some suggest that criminality has overtaken certain politically motivated guerrilla groups, making negotiation near to impossible. Others point to the lurid possibilities of a terrorist cooperating with a transnational criminal organization (TCO)[1] to acquire ingredients for a chemical, biological, radiological, or nuclear (CBRN) weapon that could potentially be used against U.S. citizens.

Examples of guerrilla groups committing nonviolent criminal activities dot the headlines of world papers. During the Kosovo conflict, reports surfaced that the Kosovo Liberation Army (KLA) trafficked heroin in order to raise money for its operations. The Revolutionary Armed Forces of Colombia (FARC), the country's largest guerrilla group, draws much of its revenue from involvement in the narcotics trade. Some evidence indicates that guerrilla groups in Spain, Sri Lanka, Turkey, and Lebanon also engage in drug trafficking and other crimes to raise funds for their violent activities.

These headlines have prompted many scholars to suggest that terrorists and transnational criminal organizations are creating strategic partnerships to boost profits or enhance military capabilities. This theme paints an ominous picture of a future where TCOs and terrorists work hand in hand to destabilize society and further criminal ends.

In fact, little evidence suggests that Mafia groups and terrorists are interested in pursuing collaborative arrangements with each other to traffic contraband or commit other violent acts. The differing aims and motivations of a profit-minded Mafia group, and a revolutionary-driven

The author would like to thank Alison Kiernan, Kelly Lieberman, and Ken Myers for their valuable insight into this project. Address correspondence to Chris Dishman, 1230 N. Scott Street, Apt. 202, Arlington, VA 22209, USA.

terrorist group, hobble any attempts at collaboration. Witness the activities of the Russian Mafia or Mexico's Zapatista National Liberation Army (EZLN)—both notable examples of a political and criminal group unwilling to engage in any activity that crosses their ideological fence, be it profit or politics. The Russian Mafia and the EZLN have shied away from potentially vibrant collaborative relationships with political or criminal entities (respectively) in large part because their aims and motivations differ with that of their potential collaborators, both choosing instead to remain on an authentic political or criminal course.

Some terrorist and guerrilla groups, however, have strayed from their political agenda and engaged in organized crime as a means to generate revenue for their war effort. In some instances, criminal activity has become much more than a means to purchase "one more gun," arguably emerging as the overriding motivation of the group. By most accounts, guerrilla groups in Colombia and Burma[2]—among others— appear disinterested in giving up their illicit activities in favor of a position at the bargaining table. Driven by a mix of profit and politics, these groups often maintain a public veneer that can be quite different from their underlying motivations. These "transformed" guerrilla groups have not sought partnerships with national or global Mafia syndicates, even though their profit-driven goals would suggest otherwise.

The disinterest of TCOs and guerrillas to forge lasting alliances is a pattern supported by the limited number of examples where cooperation between the two groups has actually occurred. It is important to highlight these cases, however, because they shed light on why cooperation between terrorists and TCOs is usually episodic and impermanent, and they support the conclusion that cooperation between the two will not be forthcoming. Two contemporary examples of collaboration in Chechnya and Kosovo, however, do partially challenge this conclusion, but while insightful, these cases will likely prove to be the exception rather than the rule. The pattern of concern for the future then, will not be cooperation among TCOs and terrorists, but rather, the *transformation* of

revolutionary aims where financial well being co-exists or overrides traditional political motivations.

AIMS AND MOTIVATIONS OF POLITICAL AND CRIMINAL GROUPS

The aims and motivations of TCOs and terrorists are what set revolutionaries and Mafiosos apart and make collaboration between the two entities difficult. A useful starting point for understanding these different motives lies with an examination of the definition of terrorism itself—which scholars and policymakers have long debated.[3]

Defining acts as terrorism attempts to set them apart from other horrid criminal acts. In his latest book, noted terrorist expert Bruce Hoffman illuminates what he considers the most widely accepted components of terrorism: it is ineluctably political in aims and motives; it is violent or at least threatens violence; it is designed to have far-reaching psychological repercussions beyond the immediate victim or target; and it is conducted by an organization or conspiratorial cell structure and perpetrated by a subnational group or non-state entity.[4] In this respect, violent actions committed by TCOs are not defined as terrorism, primarily because they lack the traditional political component. As Hoffman states, "the terrorist is fundamentally an altruist: he believes he is serving a 'good' cause designed to achieve a greater good for a wider constituency . . . the criminal, by comparison, serves no cause at all, just his own personal aggrandizement and material satiation."[5]

This definitional analysis highlights the fundamental difference between a TCO and a terrorist-guerrilla group: TCOs aim, by and large, to preserve a status quo beneficial to their illegal, profit-making activities, while terrorists and guerrillas aim to overthrow the government or, at the least, gain an independent territory or seat at the political table. This historical distinction between the two is still evident today; TCOs generally do not seek to overthrow or dent the state in an attempt to gain political attention.[6] There are no calls for a separate homeland, a different form of government, or a fast track into the political system from TCO leaders. TCO leaders do not support radical political change through violence, nor do they use their strong financial foundations to mount political campaigns.

The motivations of a terrorist or criminal syndicate shape the way each uses violence. TCOs usually attack only those who seek either directly or indirectly to disrupt or illuminate their profit-making operations. They use selective and calibrated violence to destroy competitors or threaten counternarcotic authorities. As such, a violent attack directed by a TCO is intended for a specific "anti-constituency" rather than a national or international audience, and it is not laced with political rhetoric. Their targets usually include journalists, judges, politicians, revolutionary groups, and of course, competing criminal organizations. Medellin's attacks in the late 1980s and early 1990s were illustrative of this selective violence: over 500 policemen and 40 judges were killed by narcotics-related violence.[7] Terrorists, in contrast, target symbolic structures like companies, train stations, airports, planes, apartment buildings, and other government and commercial landmarks, seeking to attract national and international attention to an enduring cause through indiscriminate[8] violence. Even terrorists whose aims are not traditionally political, such as religious fundamentalists, still seek to alter society in some radical way. The result is that terrorists, more often than not, aim to kill significant numbers of people and do not refine and limit their attacks to the same degree as TCOs. The increasing lethality of terrorism in the 1990s also highlights that terrorists and TCOs use violence differently, as TCO leaders have shown little interest in fomenting mass-casualty attacks.

The different ways that TCOs and terrorists use violence to achieve their ends is a key indicator as to why the two entities have not cooperated in the past. A TCO kingpin is not interested in blowing up a city block, much like a terrorist bent on maximizing national and international publicity is unlikely to kidnap and murder inconspicuously. But isn't it possible that TCO leaders and terrorists could set aside these operational differences to collaborate in ways that are beneficial to both groups?

STAYING TRUE TO THE POLITICAL OR CRIMINAL COURSE

The ways that TCOs and terrorists use violence is a symptom of an important underlying phenomenon—political and criminal groups maintain different ends and means. This factor has inhibited cooperation in the past and will likely poison efforts at long-term collaboration in the future. Simply put, drug barons and revolutionary leaders do not walk on the same path to success. Terrorists may commit kidnappings or extort local businesses, but their fundamental goal remains to shape or alter the political landscape in some manner. TCOs may also employ terrorism as a tactical weapon, but their end game is to avoid prosecution and make money. In short, the collision between political and financial aims of TCOs and terrorist organizations erects significant barriers to collaboration.

TCOs and terrorists, more often than not, view each other with suspicion. TCO kingpins are hesitant to collaborate with a terrorist group because they believe that the relationship will bring unwanted pressure from a government more interested in political subversion than illegal crimes. More generally, TCOs are unwilling to engage in any criminal or collaborative activity that would bring *predictably* suffocating pressure from the government. By the same token, terrorist groups are reluctant to cooperate with narcotics syndicates, cognizant that any involvement in drug trafficking—and especially enduring cooperation with a narcotics syndicate—would fuel state campaigns aiming to poison the terrorists' image by portraying them as drug traffickers and thieves. They also understand that state authorities will paint insurgents as drug traffickers to appeal to the large anti-drug resource pool in the United States.[9]

Organizations that are cognizant of these considerations are usually ones that have stayed on a straight and visible criminal or political course, unwilling to blend their activities by getting involved in political matters, or vice versa, using organized crime to generate revenue. These rigid political and criminal forces highlight the fundamental barriers to cooperation that are evident with all TCOs and terrorists—even those who do not avoid criminal or political activities. Two noteworthy examples—the Russian Mafia and the EZLN in Mexico—are model illustrations of a criminal or political group that has little desire to cooperate with any political (in the case of the Russian Mafia) or profit-minded (as in the case of the EZLN) entities. They provide a useful example of subversive groups who intentionally avoid risky partnerships that could potentially jeopardize their ultimate aims.

Russia

The apprehensiveness of transnational criminal leaders to cooperate with terrorists or [sic] is evident in the former Soviet Union, where national security experts and analysts have kept a close eye on Russian organized criminal groups. Observers are fearful that the Russian Mafia will use its entrenched networks to move CBRN material out of Russia and into the hands of terrorists or hostile states. Thus far, however, little evidence suggests that the Russian Mafia is willing to smuggle CBRN materials. Russian organized criminals are well placed to transport nuclear ingredients: they have made substantial inroads into the Russian military; they have corrupted a number of high level Russian officials; and they maintain smuggling networks that would be well suited for obtaining, transporting, and selling CBRN materials. Nevertheless, as a recent report noted, there have only been a handful of nuclear material smuggling incidents in the former Soviet Union and none of these have involved organized crime.[10] Most of these cases involved local Russian gangs rather than organized criminal groups.

Russia's criminal syndicates are unwilling to get involved in the CBRN market because they are satisfied with the money raised by their role in "krysha" arrangements, where Russian companies pay a percentage of their profits to the Mafia to protect their businesses. This low-risk, profit-making activity infuses a stable and regular amount of money into Mafia accounts with little risk of government interference. Russian criminal kingpins provide a wide range of services including debt collection, co-opting law enforcement, physical security, banking privileges, assistance with customs clearances, and protection from other racketeers.[11] On the other hand, involvement in acquiring, smuggling, and selling CBRN materials would likely bring a powerful response from Russian authorities, and as such, most Mafia groups are reluctant to become involved. Moreover, nuclear trafficking is a capricious, high-risk endeavor, and the supply-side nature of the market makes finding a buyer a risky and difficult proposition.[12] As one observer questioned, "Why drag across multiple frontiers kilograms of uranium that require years of reworking and enrichment and then spend months looking for a potential buyer? Why not just ship non-ferrous metals out of the country or make millions from banking manipulations and ruble-dollar exchange transactions?"[13]

Mexico

The same phenomenon is evidenced to a lesser extent in Mexico, where the EZLN has not approached Mexican cartels in pursuit of collaborative arrangements.[14] Like the Russian Mafia in the CBRN market, the EZLN is well positioned to transport or cultivate drugs. The remote and rugged territory in the Mexican state of Chiapas would provide a prime location to conceal the cultivation or transportation of narcotics, and one could envision arrangements being worked out with the Tijuana and Juarez cartels to transit drugs. They have chosen not to do so, however, primarily for the reason mentioned earlier; simply put, the EZLN's predominant goal is not to make money, but to gain legitimacy as a relevant political force in Mexico. The Tijuana and Juarez cartels are also reluctant to establish alliances with the EZLN or any political revolutionaries, fearful of the government's reprisal toward a drug cartel wedded to a revolutionary group.

The EZLN has shied away from drug trafficking at least in part so they will not fuel the Mexican government's campaign to receive more counternarcotics funding from the United States, which the government would in turn utilize to clamp down on the EZLN. Also, involvement in the narcotics trade would likely erode the EZLN's foreign support, which provides crucial *licit* financial and political capital. EZLN solicits most of its donations from foreign sympathizers through its web site, music concerts, and other means.[15]

The unwillingness of the EZLN to exploit a potentially lucrative relationship with Mexican drug cartels is a useful example in understanding the barriers inhibiting cooperation among TCOs and terrorists (or in this case guerrillas). The Russian Mafia is also an insightful example that illuminates TCO motivations for not cooperating with politically motivated subversive groups. Unlike these examples, however, both of which have refrained from engaging in any overtly political (Russian Mafia) or organized criminal (EZLN) behavior—some political radicals have in fact turned to organized crime as a means to raise monies for their operations. These groups do not share the same concerns of the EZLN or Russian Mafia, who were fearful that involvement in an activity outside their normal realm of operations—stealing and transporting CBRN ingredients, or growing or refining marijuana, cocaine, or heroin—would stoke a strong response from federal authorities. This in turn raises the question: Have these "crossover" groups looked for potential collaborators to participate in their new, nontraditional criminal endeavors?

TRANSFORMING ORGANIZATIONS (A SPECTRUM)

Political radicals that turn to organized crime to generate revenue ostensibly retain paramount political objectives, and as such, ill-gotten monies serve only as a means to effectively reach their political ends. They claim to still hang their political banner high, even though much of their organization is transformed to undertake profit-minded activities. This transformation—or mutation—changes the way that guerrillas and terrorists operate, as significant amounts of the group's energies and resources are directed at committing profit-driven criminal acts. Though less notably, this mutation can also occur within a criminal group that decides to depart from its traditional use of selective violence to employ mass, indiscriminate violence—more like a terrorist group than a TCO. These transformations are usually sparked by changing circumstances, which in the minds of terrorist and TCO leaders, necessitate an operational transition: a political group whose

traditional sources of funding have evaporated, or a criminal group employing terrorism—in its tactical sense—to force government leniency and negotiation.

There are different degrees of transformation. If one considers a linear spectrum, at the left end sit groups like the EZLN and Russian Mafia who have not transformed any of their organization and remain politically or criminally "authentic." These groups might at times involve themselves in a nontraditional activity, such as the Russian Mafia funding a political campaign, but these activities are sparse and only serve to further their "end game." At the other extreme (the right end), transformation has occurred to such a degree that the ultimate aims and motivations of the organization have actually changed. In these cases, the groups no longer retain the defining points that had hitherto made them a political or criminal group. It is possible they still may maintain a public façade, supported by rhetoric and statements, but underneath, they have transformed into a different type of group with a different end game. The best example of this phenomenon exists in Burma, where many traditional insurgent groups have given up all prospects of a political solution and focused solely on generating revenue by cultivating and processing drugs.

One would suspect that organizations sitting on the middle-right end on the transformation spectrum (who participate to a significant degree in criminality or politics) would seek collaborative arrangements to flatten the steep learning curve when undertaking nontraditional operations. The reality, however, is that the learning curve is in fact not that steep; both TCOs and terrorists already maintain organizations that are capable, to some extent, of engaging in terrorism and organized criminal activities. Most TCOs already possess extensive arsenals and bomb-making capabilities, while most guerrilla groups maintain active contacts in the criminal underworld. These contacts are often involved in a range of criminal activity and can facilitate a smooth transition to organized crime for a guerrilla group. This "inhouse" capability obviates the need for terrorists to appeal to criminal organizations to foster profit-minded business relationships. In essence, a political or criminal organization would rather *mutate* their own structure and organization to take on a nontraditional, financial, or political role, rather than cooperate with groups who are already effective in those activities. A number of examples support this observation, and it is important to examine them in turn.

The Irish Republican Army

Following a crackdown on the IRA's fundraising efforts in the United States in the early 1970s, the IRA was forced to find new sources of revenue. Rather than seek collaborative partnerships with Irish criminals and gangs, the IRA used its own members to commit crimes normally associated with ethnic mobs. These included smuggling livestock and cars, running protection and extortion rackets, managing underground brothels, and engaging in contractor fraud. The IRA even entered the transportation market by purchasing a number of cabs and buses. Much like an organized criminal group, they threatened the competition until there was none and subsequently monopolized the market. Citybus, Belfast's bus service, was gradually forced to retire more than 300 buses, costing the city $15 million.[16] The cab companies claimed to have over $1.5 million in assets.[17]

The IRA's transition to organized crime in Ireland was the group's next logical step following the evaporation of crucial North American financial support. While they had been involved in microcriminal activity before, never had the group invested so much of its resources in committing Mafia-like criminal acts. But their contacts (and manpower) inside and outside Ireland paved the way for the group to become successfully involved in organized crime and as such, they did not seek alliances or relationships with TCOs at home or abroad—content to keep all operations "in-house."

The IRA is a prime example of a mutated terrorist group who invested significant energies into committing profit-driven criminal acts. To most observers the IRA's political objectives were still paramount, and the group could be dealt with accordingly. (As such, the IRA would best be placed in the middle of the transformation spectrum.) Many insurgent groups, however, have stepped so deeply into organized crime that the aims and motivation of the group's leaders are, at the very least, up for debate. In many of these cases, the transformation of the group's operations has occurred to such a degree that the underlying aims and motivations of the group's leaders may have also changed—even though their rhetoric continues to espouse their traditional political goals.

NARCO-GUERRILLAS

Many insurgents view narcotics as a fertile and risk-free source of revenue. Often dubbed "narco-guerrillas," these groups participate to differing degrees in the drug industry; some tax drug producers and provide safe havens for cultivators, while others prefer a more "hands on" approach, using their own manpower to refine and smuggle narcotics. Typically, guerrillas are involved in what one author coined the "upstream" phase of drug trafficking, which refers to the initial cultivation stage of drug production—the least profitable leg of the industry.[18] The historic record for guerrilla involvement in the narcotics trade is extensive.

In the early 1980s, many insurgents participated in the lucrative drug market emerging in Western Europe. During this time, guerrilla involvement in narcotics trafficking peaked, and many groups reportedly harnessed ill-gotten funds from the drug trade.[19] In the late 1990s this involvement began to diminish considerably. *Sendero Luminoso*, one of the most active drug-ensconced guerrilla groups, has largely been stamped out by the Peruvian government, and many of the aforementioned Colombian groups (except of course FARC) have either been incorporated into the political system or have chosen other illegal routes to make money. Some evidence indicates that the Basque Homeland and Freedom movement (ETA) continues to smuggle drugs, but not on a scale close to its 1980s involvement. The Liberation Tigers of Tamil Eelam (LTTE) has also been accused of smuggling narcotics, although the evidence for this allegation is sparse, and the movement appears to have largely distanced itself from the narcotics activities of the 1980s.[20]

While many of today's insurgent groups avoid involvement in drug trafficking, others do not. Burmese insurgents—most notably the

United Wa State Army—continue to actively cultivate, refine, and traffic opium and heroin out of the Golden Triangle (the border between Burma, Thailand, Laos), and some have even moved into the methamphetamine market.[21] The FARC is still profiting from Colombia's lucrative drug market, and the Turkish government claims that the Kurdistan Worker's Party (PKK) is heavily involved in drug trafficking, although Western analysts have difficulty pinpointing specific evidence.[22] Israeli and U.S. sources indicate that the Hizbullah receives money for protecting laboratories involved in the manufacture of heroin and cocaine.[23] It is alleged that the Taliban receives money derived from Afghanistan's position as supplier of two-thirds of the world's opium.

This list of "narco-guerrilla" examples highlights that guerrillas and terrorist leaders are unwilling to cooperate with TCO kingpins because they do not want to be associated with people they consider to be greedy, profit-seeking entrepreneurs. Politically motivated subversive groups believe that their cause is noble and just, and that they are pursuing an altruistic drive for the betterment of society. Revolutionaries frown upon suggestions that they are just "common criminals."

This attitude is evident in Colombia, where guerrillas have historically maintained antagonistic relations with Colombian drug barons. FARC leaders are unwilling to cooperate with Colombian drug cartels fearful of being branded common criminals and further clouding the purpose and clarity of their revolution. Additionally, one of the foremost aims of the FARC—the demand for pervasive land reform in Colombia—collided with the interests of Medellin and Cali leaders, who, during the 1980s and 1990s, purchased over one-twelfth of Colombia's land.[24] The FARC and other revolutionary groups raid the ranches and kidnap family members of Colombia's richest traffickers. This conflict of interest has prevented any meaningful collaboration between the FARC and Colombian narcotics syndicates. This pattern of non-cooperation (and indeed animosity) between the FARC and Colombian drug cartels highlights the underlying reasons why other criminal and political groups are not likely to collaborate. Even though the FARC,

IRA, and other insurgent groups are steeped in criminality, by and large, most of them are still unwilling to work with organized, ethnic Mafias to lower risk and maximize profit.

TCOs Will Also Transform, But Not Cooperate

The examples of the IRA, and other narcotics-involved guerrilla and terrorist groups, highlight that politically motivated entities are unlikely to cooperate with TCOs when engaging in a non-traditional, profit-driven criminal activity. In the same vein, with a few exceptions, criminal syndicates have not tapped the resources of guerrilla or terrorist groups when committing mass casualty violent acts. TCOs have at times embarked on terrorist-like campaigns of violence, departing from their traditional use of select violence aimed towards their "anti-constituency." TCOs have employed terrorism (in a loose sense) when they felt the survival of their organizations was threatened, and they used it as a last resort to force the government to negotiate terms beneficial to criminal leaders. Like revolutionary groups, TCO leaders have not felt compelled to cooperate with terrorist groups to gain bomb-making expertise and material, intelligence, or tactics—instead they have chosen to mutate their own organizations to adapt to changing realities. While examples of criminal groups adapting terrorist-like strategies of violence are sparse, there are a few notable illustrations that again highlight that criminal syndicates—much like the aforementioned guerrilla and terrorist groups—are unlikely to build strategic relationships with any politically driven movement.

The Medellin Cartel

A good illustration of a TCO that for a period of time could have been mistaken for a terrorist group is the Medellin cartel in the early 1980s. During this time, Medellin leaders launched a brutal and indiscriminate campaign of violence on Colombian leaders and citizens. A group called the "Extraditables"—a collection of drug traffickers opposed to a sweeping crackdown by the Colombian government—declared total war on Colombia and its citizens.[25] A communiqué issued by the Extraditables illustrated their desire to attack a wide range of targets:

> We declare total and absolute war on the government, the industrial and political oligarchy, the journalists who have attacked and outraged us, the judges who have sold themselves to the government, high court extraditing judges and presidential and sectorial (social, business and labor) associations, and all who have persecuted and attacked us.[26]

This campaign of violence was far more formidable than attacks unleashed by the FARC and the National Liberation Army (ELN) around the same period. Targets ranged from shopping malls, theaters, airports, newspapers, banks, and liquor stores—turning Medellin and Bogota into virtual battlegrounds. In one incident, a bomb blew up a commercial airliner, killing 119 people, while in another, a gunman opened fire in an international airport. Both of these attacks mimicked the operations of a terrorist group (like the Japanese Red Army, who also sprayed bullets in an airport) more than any drug cartel. Medellin also utilized a traditional terrorist weapon, exploding over 400 bombs from August 1989 to July 1990 and killing 1,000 Colombians.[27]

The terrorist-like violence conducted by the Medellin cartel was not without precedent. The Sicilian Cosa Nostra, one of three notable Italian criminal groups, assassinated a number of Italian officials following a crackdown on its operations from 1979 to 1983. This ensuing period of violence resulted in the deaths of a number of top Italian political and judicial representatives including the Christian Democratic Party secretary, the chief examining magistrate of Palermo, the President of the Sicilian region, and many others. One author noted that these attacks were considerably more violent than those of the Italian Red Brigades during the same period.[28]

In both of these cases, the Medellin cartel between 1989 and 1993 and the Sicilian Mafia between 1979 and 1983, a criminal organization launched a brutal campaign of violence against Colombian and Italian societies—much like their terrorist counterparts (the FARC and the Italian Red Brigades). Rather than create an alliance with these groups, however, the Medellin cartel and the Sicilian Cosa Nostra employed their campaigns of mass violence without the help of the FARC or the Red Brigades. (As we will see later, the Naples Camorra, another Italian mafia group, did seek a short-term alliance with the Red Brigades, but it was not to tap its expertise or create a pan-criminal/political organization.)

Since the evidence indicates that TCOs, terrorists, and guerrillas are more likely to transform their own organizations rather than cooperate with each other, what are the problems associated with transformation?

DON'T JUDGE A GUERILLA BY ITS COVER

This extensive list of examples supports the conclusion that both terrorists (IRA) and guerrillas (FARC) who participate in illicit activities outside their traditional political or criminal spectrums, choose to transform their own organizations to perform these operations rather than cooperate with local or international Mafias. These groups, which are positioned on the middle-right end of the transformation spectrum (due to their heavy involvement in organized crime), have not sought criminal-political alliances because they continue to remain distrustful of each other—unwilling and unlikely to tap each other's expertise. The in-house adaptation by these groups of each other's "core competencies" (for example, a TCO's experience in smuggling drugs or a guerrilla group's ability to commit terrorism) should remain a pattern for coming years.

Nevertheless, this pattern of non-cooperation is likely to be accompanied by a more concerning development. Groups that have undergone a virtual "sea change" in their operations (sitting at the far right end of the spectrum) pose a number of significant problems for policymakers. Most notably, the extensive participation of subversive political movements in the narcotics trade clouds a clear view of the underlying aims and motivations of many of today's guerrilla groups. In some cases, it is arguable that financial gain has become the overriding motivation, rather than simply a means to support a political agenda. A profit-minded group will not wish to seek a negotiated settlement, determined to prolong the very war that affords it a profit. The Shan United Army in Burma is a good illustration of a group with once legitimate political goals that has transformed into a *de facto* drug enterprise. Its organized participation in the heroin and methamphetamine trade goes well beyond merely supporting the political banner for the movement.[29] The FARC has also become so reliant on an influx of drug money[30] that it is arguable whether any political solution would compel its leader, Manuel Marulanda, and a majority of its members to use the ballot box instead of armed attacks. This poses tough questions for the Colombian government: What if Marulanda and the FARC have become more interested in money than politics, and are committed to continuing the FARC's lucrative involvement in the drug trade regardless of government concessions? Does Marulanda still aim to reform Colombia's political process and its social programs, or is he more concerned about prolonging the civil war that has afforded his group so much profit?

Perhaps more importantly, guerrilla groups like the FARC who are steeped in criminality are able to significantly sharpen the military edge of their organizations. The battlefield successes of the FARC stem from its sizable war chest, which grows annually anywhere from $100 to 500 million.[31] This money is harnessed from the FARC's participation in drug trafficking; FARC soldiers collect "war taxes" from coca cultivators, refiners, and traffickers. In turn, FARC provides a virtual shield from anti-drug authorities in the Caqueta and Putumayo provinces in southern Colombia. The money grossed from these activities funds the purchase of sophisticated weapons and high-tech communications equipment including encryption and voice scrambling technology.[32] Perhaps most importantly, illicit funds are channeled to FARC soldiers who are paid reportedly twice as much as Colombian army conscripts.[33]

The transformation of the FARC is a pattern likely to be followed in the future by political radicals; ones who lack key financial support begin to believe that they cannot win their war, or simply lose interest in their traditional goals. They will perhaps turn their formidable assets

towards committing profit-driven criminal acts, transforming into a criminal enterprise with a political façade. This mutative process is the key pattern that should be on the radar screen for future analysts and policymakers. Nevertheless, this article would be remiss not to acknowledge and examine the cases where terrorist and TCO groups have in fact cooperated. Criminal groups have at times sought material and expertise from terrorists, while terrorists have in rare circumstances sought partnerships with Mafias. These few examples, however, further support the conclusion that political and criminal groups will not cooperate with each other: in each instance the relationships proved short-term and unsustainable.

Two especially noteworthy examples in Chechnya and Kosovo, however, do partially challenge this idea that criminals and political radicals will not develop alliances; in these cases, cooperation between a Mafia and a guerrilla group occurred to an unprecedented degree. Nevertheless, for reasons that will be noted later, it is likely that these examples will prove unique and will serve as the exception rather than the rule.

TRIAL EFFORTS AT TCO AND TERRORIST COLLABORATION: A HISTORY OF FAILURE

Organized crime expert Phil Williams accurately details two cooperative modalities between profit-minded groups. These categorizations provide a useful construct for examining collaborative possibilities between terrorists and TCOs.

> Strategic alliances have several qualities that set them apart from other linkages (among TCOs). They are long-term, involve operational linkages, are based on some kind of formal or tacit agreement, and are underpinned by mutual expectations of continued cooperation. At the other end of the spectrum are one-off arrangements or spot deals in which criminal organizations come together for a specific transaction without any notion that the relationship will become more enduring.[34]

These constructs define two types of linkages between organized criminal groups—strategic and tactical (one-spot). Strategic alliances between TCOs are created for a number of reasons including: the desire of a TCO to enter a new market, the need for a specialized service, or more generally, as a means to reduce the risk of a TCO's illegal operations.[35] Conversely, a tactical relationship involves the same types of exchanges, but for a shorter timeframe and without complementary long-term goals. Often enough, the aims and motivations of competing criminal enterprises are not complementary, and as such, alliances between TCOs remain short-term linkages.

In much the same way, terrorist groups and TCOs rarely cooperate on a long-term basis, due to their greatly differing views on what constitutes success. Most of the evidence of TCO/terrorist cooperation has consisted of what Dr. Williams called "one-spot" linkages, and did not evolve into longer-term alliances. In these instances, a terrorist or TCO was using another for a one-time service or function. Colombian police reports indicated, for example, that Pablo Escobar hired ELN guerrillas to plant car bombs in 1993 because of Medellin's limited ability to commit terrorist acts.[36] Medellin's war against Colombia also led to the explosion of 1,100 pounds of dynamite in front of the Department of Administrative Security building in Bogota, and some reports indicate that this bomb was planted on behalf of the cartel by a Spanish terrorist with ties to the Basque Fatherland and Liberty group.[37] More recently, Colombian police report that an alliance has developed between Carlos Castano, the leader of Colombia's largest paramilitary group, and La Terraza, an urban-based organized criminal group, formed from the remnants of the Medellin cartel and some of Escobar's former rivals. La Terraza allegedly kills human rights activists at the behest of Castano, since his organization lacks the intelligence necessary to plan and execute high profile, urban kidnappings and murders.[38]

In another illustration of short-term TCO/terrorist cooperation in the early 1980s, the Italian Red Brigades attempted to establish an alliance with the Naples Camorra, Italy's most organized mainland criminal group. In a five-page statement issued in 1982, the Red Brigades offered to help the Camorra spread organized crime. The statement applauded the efforts of the Camorra to extort small business owners and championed its traditional aims:

> The indications of this new type of fight come also from Secondigliano and Sant Antonio D'Abate (communities near Naples), where the proletariat is putting restrictions on tradesmen, who for a long time have been trying to exterminate the extra-legal worker.[39]

The Red Brigades claimed credit in the slaying of a Naples police chief who had arrested the close friends and relatives of a jailed Camorra godfather. Several months later the Red Brigades failed in an attempt to stage a massive escape from a Naples prison that housed many Camorra members.[40] In another example of this alliance, a senior politician from the Christian Democratic party was kidnapped in 1981 by the Italian Red Brigades, and a Camorra godfather acted as an intermediary during negotiations between the authorities and the terrorist group. In the end, the Camorra pocketed a sizable $1 million commission, and allegedly as part of the deal, the Camorra agreed to assassinate a number of people designated by the Red Brigades.[41]

The Red Brigades sought this alliance because the organization had been seriously crippled by Italian authorities in the early 1980s. In the end, the fate of the alliance was accurately forecasted by an antiterrorism police official at the time: "We don't think any such alliance will work because, while they have a common enemy in the police and the establishment, their aims and ideological beliefs are so vastly different . . . the Camorra and the Red Brigades possibly can cooperate on practical matters, like plotting to get rid of a judge, but their alliance at best would be superficial and short-lived because neither of them would want to compromise the group's secrets."[42]

This official accurately portrays the obstacles of long-term cooperation between a criminal and political subversive group. The barriers to cooperation between the Camorra and Red Brigades—namely their different views of what constitutes success—are also evident with TCOs and guerrillas in other countries including Mexico, Russia, and Colombia. In Italy, the

Camorra and Red Brigades were able to exchange services for a brief period of time in contractual or one-spot arrangements, but this relationship did not evolve into a longer-term alliance. In sum, cooperation between the Mafia and terrorist groups—as evidenced by these examples—was episodic and impermanent, illuminating a pattern of non-cooperation between TCOs and terrorists that should continue well into the future. Unlike the EZLN and Russian Mafia mentioned earlier, these groups actually sought cooperative relationships that eventually degenerated and proved that sustaining cooperation between a criminal and political group is a difficult route to take.

DOES THE FUTURE POINT TO DIFFERENT POSSIBILITIES?

There are contemporary examples, however, that at first glance challenge the aforementioned conclusions. In both Chechnya and Kosovo, criminal and political groups created vibrant partnerships that outlasted many of the previous collaborative attempts. In both cases, the Kosovo Liberation Army and Chechen guerrillas accumulated significant amounts of money and material from collaborative relationships with the Albanian and Chechen Mafias, respectively. It is important to examine these examples, and understand what factors were in place that allowed these relationships to flourish.

Chechnya

Perhaps the most notable example of a strategic linkage that developed between a political and criminal subversive group is that of the Moscow-based Chechen Mafia and Grozny-based Chechen guerrillas. The Russian incursion into Chechnya to root out Chechen rebels was complemented by a total crackdown on Moscow-based Chechen criminal groups. The Kremlin, fearful of the Chechen rebels' threat of terrorism and the possibility of a "fifth column," ordered Russia's anti-crime police to crackdown on the Chechens' criminal operations within Russia and arrest the syndicates' kingpins.[43]

According to the Russian Interior Ministry, the Chechen Mafia sent large amounts of money to Chechen rebels. Even more alarming, although it is hard to determine the extent of the Mafia's participation, Russian authorities allege that Chechen rebels were responsible for the spate of apartment bombings in Moscow and two other cities that killed 300 people last September. If Chechen guerrillas were in fact responsible, one could speculate that the Mafia would have been well suited to provide safe havens, intelligence, and supplies for the terrorists. It is also a possibility—although no evidence supports this—that the Mafia could have committed the attacks themselves at the behest of guerrilla leader Shamil Basayev.[44]

It is important to note that the aims of these two groups did not initially overlap. Basayev's determination to ignite a larger Islamic uprising in Dagestan was clearly not on the minds of Chechen gangsters grossing large profits in Moscow. The views of the Chechen Mafia changed, however, as Russia began an extensive crackdown on Chechen criminal activities.

Kosovo

Enduring cooperation between two separate groups—one criminal and the other political—has also occurred in Kosovo, where the KLA maintained a strategic alliance with Albanian criminal syndicates before and during the Kosovo crisis. After the demise of the Berisha government in Albania in 1997, the ensuing disorder allowed Albanian organized criminal groups to secure their hold on heroin trafficking through the Balkan route—a well traveled smuggler's corridor that transports an estimated $400 billion worth of narcotics per year.[45] At roughly the same time, the KLA emerged as an organized guerrilla force seeking an independent state from Serbia. Members of the KLA's political wing, the Kosovo National Front (KNF), manned a drug cartel centered in Pristina that collaborated with the Albanian Mafia to smuggle heroin. The close ties between the three groups—the KNF, the KLA, and the Albanian Mafia—provided a well-oiled arrangement; the profits from the Pristina cartel, estimated to be in the "high tens of millions,"[46] were funneled to the KLA, where they were used primarily to buy weapons, often in "drugs for arms" arrangements.

CONCLUSION

At first glance, the pattern of cooperation modeled by Chechen and Kosovar guerillas points to some alarming possibilities for the future. A political group—empowered by a criminal alliance—could gain weapons, money, intelligence, explosives, and other wartime goods and services. A pan-criminal-political alliance would be a force multiplier for radicals, sharpening their military edge and making it difficult for legitimate governments to combat them.

Fears that these types of arrangements will flourish, however, will likely prove unfounded. The Chechen guerrillas were fortunate—in their eyes—to have a sympathetic, ethnically similar Mafia group who was willing to donate funds to support Basayev's cause. Since the Chechen Mafia is based largely in Moscow, they—unlike most criminal groups—were not worried about the instability hundreds of miles to their South, which would not affect their Moscow operations. They also most likely realized that a Chechen state under Russian control would not be as lax regarding border control, since the Mafia often used Chechnya as a route for smuggling goods out of Russia. This set of circumstances is unlikely to be replicated elsewhere, and perhaps more importantly, the relationship was not quite the "force multiplier" that one might suspect. Chechen guerrillas were not as well armed as other guerrillas bands (like the Shining Path and FARC) who committed criminal acts using their own manpower and *without* the help of any local or international Mafia groups.

Nevertheless, such headlines prompt some observers to contend that the patterns of criminal-political collaboration are already in force today, and that the global development of these linkages has already reached epidemic proportions. In the words of one expert, "a grand shift is occurring that few people have noticed . . . international drug traffickers and international terrorists are in a hedonistic marriage of design . . . these groups are now linked at the hip, and they are extremely wealthy."[47] This observer further stated that in the absence of Soviet funding, terrorist organizations are more often turning to drug trafficking to make money.

The reality of this threat, however, is much less sensational and grandiose. A diagnosis based on the historical record suggests that future cooperation between TCOs and terrorists is unlikely. As this article has shown, the differing aims and motivations of the two make it unlikely that political and criminal groups will cooperate with each other in long-term, strategic alliances. If cooperation does occur, it will most likely be short-term linkages of convenience, and even these will be limited and spotty.

Instead, analysts should be cognizant of a transformation of political motivations and ends. Criminal motives, spread deep and wide throughout a terrorist group, will transform the aims and motivations of its leaders. Terrorists and guerrilla groups who view their cause as futile, might turn their formidable assets towards crime—all the while under a bogus political banner. Other groups might turn to organized crime if their *raison d'être* evaporates in the face of negotiation or peace.

This transformation is more likely to occur than any strategic partnerships between TCOs and terrorists. The evaporation of Soviet and other state sources of funding are unlikely to spur insurgents to become involved in narcotics since many continue to distance themselves from drug trafficking, even though their coffers have not been filled by Soviet funds for years. And perhaps more telling, the guerrilla/drug nexus was strongest in the early 1980s, a time when state sponsorship for terrorism reached epidemic heights.

Clearly there are dangerous potentialities when guerrillas generate money through drug trafficking—as evidenced with the FARC—and this issue should be addressed accordingly. But alarming prognostications about a "grand shift" where terrorists and criminals operate hand in hand will likely prove unfounded.

NOTES

1. Transnational Criminal Organizations (TCOs) are best defined as "contemporary organizations (which) are adaptable, sophisticated, extremely opportunistic, and immersed in a full range of illegal and legal activities . . . they have expanded their activities to a quasi-corporate level where they are active in large scale insurance fraud, the depletion of

natural resources, environmental crime, migrant smuggling, and bank fraud . . . they are not afraid to work globally in any country where legal and bureaucratic loopholes allow them to take advantage of the system." See Canadian Security Intelligence Service, "Transnational Criminal Activity" November 1998.

2. Officially known as the Union of Myanmar, but referred to here as Burma.

3. For the purposes of this article, guerrillas and terrorists will be used interchangeably (as politically motivated groups). This does not mean that there are not important differences, however. In particular, terrorists are unwilling or unable to occupy large chunks of land. As a result, guerrillas are more likely than terrorists to exercise direct control over a population. Finally, terrorists avoid direct confrontation with military forces, while guerrillas usually focus attacks on military and police outposts or convoys as evidenced in Colombia, Sri Lanka, and other locales.

4. Bruce Hoffman, *Inside Terrorism* (Columbia University Press, 1998), p. 43.

5. Ibid, p. 43.

6. Nowhere is this more evident than in Colombia, where recent evidence indicates that new criminal syndicates appear to have learned from the mistakes of Cali and Medellin leaders before them. A recent sting uncovered a technologically sophisticated and active drug network that purposely avoids the political limelight, does not commit large-scale acts of violence, and utilizes sophisticated communications technology. See *The Washington Post*, "Colombian Drug Cartels Exploit Tech Advantage," 15 November 1999.

7. Patrick Clawson and Rensselaer Lee, *The Andean Cocaine Industry* (New York: St. Martin's Press, 1996), p. 51.

8. It is important to note that the word "indiscriminately" is used loosely here. Politically motivated terrorists have traditionally tried to confine their attacks to certain groups, fearful of alienating their supporters and sparking a strong government response. On the other hand, religious and apocalyptic terrorists are more likely to commit mass, indiscriminate attacks aiming to kill a large number of people since they are not trying to garner national or international support.

9. It is important to note that there are two sides to this coin. Some guerrillas clearly do not care about their international image or what measures the state authorities may take to crack down on them.

10. This is not to say that there are not networks that will procure and smuggle materials out of Russia, but as Rensselaer Lee notes in a recent book, these groups do not maintain the characteristics of an organized criminal group. See Rensselaer Lee, *Smuggling Armageddon* (New York: St. Martin's Press, 1998), pp. 140-141.

11. Global Organized Crime Project, *Russian Organized Crime*, Project by Center for Strategic and International Studies, 1997, p. 29.

12. Lee (op. cit.), pp. 140-141.

13. Ibid, p. 63.

14. Despite allegations by the Mexican government that the EZLN is involved in drug trafficking, most experts agree that they are not. See *The San Diego Union-Tribune*, "Mexico's Drug-War Effort Gets Poor Grade," 24 May 1996.

15. *The Scotsman*, "Rebel Yell: The Zapatista National Liberation Army Has Garnered World Support Via the Web for its Fight Against the Mexican Government," 6 July 1999.

16. The IRA's "black cabs" (since they were painted black) were favored by locals due to their reasonable rates. See James Adams, *The Financing of Terrorism* (New York: Simon and Schuster, 1986), p. 173.

17. Ibid.

18. See Clawson and Lee (op. cit.).

19. Some of these include the April 19th Movement (Colombia), FARC (Colombia), Popular Liberation Army (Colombia), Sendero Luminoso (Peru), Burmese Communist Party (Burma), Kachin Independence Organization (Burma), *mujahedin* guerrillas (Afghanistan), Tamil Tigers (Sri Lanka), Armenian Secret Army for the Liberation of Armenia (Armenia), Kurdish separatists (Turkey), and the Basque Fatherland and Freedom Group (Spain). For a more extensive discussion on guerrillas and drug trafficking in the 1980s, see Mark Steinitz, "Insurgents, Terrorists, and the Drug Trade," *The Washington Quarterly*, 1985.

20. In 1996, a European Commission envoy to South Asia claimed that "there is some indication of the Mafia backing the LTTE." The envoy has reason to be suspicious. The vibrant LTTE networks, which smuggle arms from Cambodia to Thailand, would be well suited for trafficking drugs as well. The official provided little evidence, however, and if the LTTE was involved in drug trafficking, it is hard to conceive how none of its members have been arrested in recent years on narcotics-related charges. Moreover, the LTTE still continues to receive sizable sums from its widespread diaspora, which by some estimations reaches $2-3 million each month. Estimations of diaspora contributions does [*sic*] vary. See *Jane's Intelligence Review*, "Cash for Carnage: Funding the Modern Terrorist," 1 May 1998. Another source reports that 60 percent of a total $2 million a month revenue comes from abroad. See *Asiaweek*, "How a Secret Global Network Keeps Sri Lanka's Tamil Organization Up and Killing," 26 July 1996.

21. *AgenceFrance Presse*, "Burmese Drug Production on Rise Despite Accords with Rebels," 24 November 1996. Also see *Jane's Intelligence Review*, "Burma, the Country that Won't Kick the Habit," 1 March 1998.

22. See *San Diego Union-Tribune*, 6 July 1996. In one state-wide operation, authorities arrested 551 members of the PKK on drug charges. See Ankara Anatolia, "Security Directorate on 'Terrorist' Ties to Drug Deals," 20 May 1998.

23. *The Jerusalem Post*, "US May Hit Hizbullah Drug Trade," 17 June 1997. Also see *International Narcotics Control Strategy Report*, U.S. Department of State, 1996.

24. Rachel Ehrenfeld, *NarcoTerrorism* (New York: Basic Books, 1990), p. 91.

25. The group vowed to set off 5.5 tons of dynamite in residential areas of the capital for every drug trafficker extradited to the United States.

26. "Drug Lords Vow War on Colombia," *Los Angeles Times*, 25 August 1989.

27. "The Drug War: Who Won?" *Orange County Register*, 21 July 1991.

28. Alison Jamieson, "Terrorism and Drug Trafficking in the 1990s," 23 March 1995, p. 47.

29. Other groups known to be involved include the Kokang, Shan, and remnants of Khun Sa's Mong Tai Army—the leader of which turned himself into [*sic*] the government.

30. Some estimates indicate 50 percent of their money comes from drugs.

31. Federal News Service, 6 August 1999. Prepared testimony of General Barry R. McCaffrey, Director, Office of National Drug Control Policy Before the House Committee on Government Reform, Criminal Justice, Drug Policy and Human Resources Subcommittee. Subject, "The Evolving Drug Threat in Colombia and Other South American Source Zone Nations."

32. Interestingly, FARC's most popular weapon is the gas tank mortar, first designed and used by the IRA. This weapon, made from common gas tanks, can shoot roughly 2000 meters and is powerful enough to destroy bunkers. They have also purchased AK-47 assault rifles, Dragunov sniper rifles, explosives, hand grenades, ammunition, and rocket-propelled grenades. See *Jane's Intelligence Review*, "FARC's innovative artillery," 1 December 1999.

33. Federal News Service, August 6, 1999. Prepared testimony of General Barry R. McCaffrey, Director, Office of National Drug Control Policy Before the House Committee on Government Reform, Criminal Justice, Drug Policy and Human Resources Subcommittee. Subject, "The Evolving Drug Threat in Colombia and Other South American Source Zone Nations."

34. Prepared testimony of Dr. Phil Williams before the House International Relations Committee, 31 January 1996.

35. Phil Williams, *Washington Quarterly*, "Transnational Criminal Organizations: Strategic Alliances," Winter 1995.

36. Clawson and Lee (op. cit.), p. 53.

37. Ibid.

38. The recent kidnapping of a Colombian senator provided the first concrete evidence of this alliance. See *Los Angeles Times*, "A Chilling Crime Network Rears its Head in Colombia," 16 March 2000.

39. *United Press International*, "Red Brigades Praises Camorra," 19 July 1982.

40. *Associated Press*, 5 October 1982.

41. Adams (op. cit.), pp. 187-188. A parliamentary report confirmed that the Red Brigades and the Camorra had agreed to cooperate in the killing of a number of police magistrates and police officials.

42. *Associated Press*, "Police Say Red Brigades Alliance with Organized Crime Won't Work," 20 July 1982.

43. *Moscow News*, "Pre-Election War in the Caucasus," 18 August 1999.

44. *Insight on the News*, "Russia Hammers Chechnya," 29 November 1999.

45. Interpol statistic cited in *The San Francisco Chronicle*, "KLA Linked to the Enormous Heroin Trade," 5 May 1999.

46. As one would expect, estimates vary. See *The Washington Times*, "KLA Buys Arms with Illicit Funds," 4 June 1999.

47. See *Armed Forces Journal*, "The Enemy Next Door," March 2000.

SOMEBODY ELSE'S CIVIL WAR

MICHAEL SCOTT DORAN

Call it a city on four legs heading for murder. . . . New York is a woman holding, according to history, a rag called liberty with one hand and strangling the earth with the other.

—Adonis [Ali Ahmed Said], "The Funeral of New York," 1971

In the weeks after the attacks of September 11, Americans repeatedly asked, "Why do they hate us?" To understand what happened, however, another question may be even more pertinent: "Why do they want to provoke us?"

David Fromkin suggested the answer in *Foreign Affairs* back in 1975. "Terrorism," he noted, "is violence used in order to create fear; but it is aimed at creating fear in order that the fear, in turn, will lead somebody else—not the terrorist—to embark on some quite different program of action that will accomplish whatever it is that the terrorist really desires." When a terrorist kills, the goal is not murder itself but something else—for example, a police crackdown that will create a rift between government and society that the terrorist can then exploit for revolutionary purposes. Osama bin Laden sought—and has received—an international military crackdown, one he wants to exploit for his particular brand of revolution.

Bin Laden produced a piece of high political theater he hoped would reach the audience that concerned him the most: the *umma*, or universal Islamic community. The script was obvious: America, cast as the villain, was supposed to use its military might like a cartoon character trying to kill a fly with a shotgun. The media would see to it that any use of force against the civilian population of Afghanistan was broadcast around the world, and the *umma* would find it shocking how Americans nonchalantly caused Muslims to suffer and die. The ensuing outrage would open a chasm between state and society in the Middle East, and the governments allied with the West—many of which are repressive, corrupt, and illegitimate—would find themselves adrift. It was to provoke such an outcome that bin Laden broadcast his statement following the start of the military campaign on October 7, in which he said, among other things, that the Americans and the British "have divided the entire world into two regions—one of faith, where there is no hypocrisy, and another of infidelity, from which we hope God will protect us."

Polarizing the Islamic world between the *umma* and the regimes allied with the United States would help achieve bin Laden's primary goal: furthering the cause of Islamic revolution within the Muslim world itself, in the Arab lands especially and in Saudi Arabia above all. He had no intention of defeating America. War with the United States was not a goal in and of itself but rather an instrument designed to help his brand of extremist Islam survive and flourish among the believers. Americans, in short, have been drawn into somebody else's civil war.

Washington had no choice but to take up the gauntlet, but it is not altogether clear that

From "Somebody Else's Civil War," Doran, *Foreign Affairs, 81*(3), 22–42. Copyright © 2002 by the Council on Foreign Relations, Inc. Reprinted by permission.

Americans understand fully this war's true dimensions. The response to bin Laden cannot be left to soldiers and police alone. He has embroiled the United States in an intra-Muslim ideological battle, a struggle for hearts and minds in which al Qaeda had already scored a number of victories—as the reluctance of America's Middle Eastern allies to offer public support for the campaign against it demonstrated. The first step toward weakening the hold of bin Laden's ideology, therefore, must be to comprehend the symbolic universe into which he has dragged us.

AMERICA, THE HUBAL OF THE AGE

Bin Laden's October 7 statement offers a crucial window onto his conceptual world and repays careful attention. In it he states, "Hypocrisy stood behind the leader of global idolatry, behind the Hubal of the age—namely, America and its supporters." Because the symbolism is obscure to most Americans, this sentence was widely mistranslated in the press, but bin Laden's Muslim audience understood it immediately.

In the early seventh century, when the Prophet Muhammad began to preach Islam to the pagan Arab tribes in Mecca, Hubal was a stone idol that stood in the Kaaba—a structure that Abraham, according to Islamic tradition, originally built on orders from God as a sanctuary of Islam. In the years between Abraham and Muhammad, the tradition runs, the Arabs fell away from true belief and began to worship idols, with Hubal the most powerful of many. When bin Laden calls America "the Hubal of the age," he suggests that it is the primary focus of idol worship and that it is polluting the Kaaba, a symbol of Islamic purity. His imagery has a double resonance: it portrays American culture as a font of idolatry while rejecting the American military presence on the Arabian peninsula (which is, by his definition, the holy land of Islam, a place barred to infidels).

Muhammad's prophecy called the Arabs of Mecca back to their monotheistic birthright. The return to true belief, however, was not an easy one, because the reigning Meccan oligarchy persecuted the early Muslims. By calling for the destruction of Hubal, the Prophet's message threatened to undermine the special position that Mecca enjoyed in Arabia as a pagan shrine city. With much of their livelihood at stake, the oligarchs punished Muhammad's followers and conspired to kill him. The Muslims therefore fled from Mecca to Medina, where they established the *umma* as a political and religious community. They went on to fight and win a war against Mecca that ended with the destruction of Hubal and the spread of true Islam around the world.

Before the Prophet could achieve this success, however, he encountered the *Munafiqun*, the Hypocrites of Medina. Muhammad's acceptance of leadership over the Medinese reduced the power of a number of local tribal leaders. These men outwardly accepted Islam in order to protect their worldly status, but in their hearts they bore malice toward both the Prophet and his message. Among other misdeeds, the treacherous *Munafiqun* abandoned Muhammad on the battlefield at a moment when he was already woefully outnumbered. The Hypocrites were apostates who accepted true belief but then rejected it, and as such they were regarded as worse than the infidels who had never embraced Islam to begin with. Islam can understand just how difficult it is for a pagan to leave behind all the beliefs and personal connections that he or she once held dear; it is less forgiving of those who accept the truth and then subvert it.

In bin Laden's imagery, the leaders of the Arab and Islamic worlds today are Hypocrites, idol worshippers cowering behind America, the Hubal of the age. His sword jabs simultaneously at the United States and the governments allied with it. His attack was designed to force those governments to choose: You are either with the idol-worshiping enemies of God or you are with the true believers.

The al Qaeda organization grew out of an Islamic religious movement called the Salafiyya—a name derived from *al-Salaf al-Salih*, "the venerable forefathers," which refers to the generation of the Prophet Muhammad and his companions. Salafis regard the Islam that most Muslims practice today as polluted by idolatry; they seek to reform the religion by emulating the first generation of Muslims, whose pristine society they consider to have best reflected God's wishes for humans. The

Salafiyya is not a unified movement, and it expresses itself in many forms, most of which do not approach the extremism of Osama bin Laden or the Taliban. The Wahhabi ideology of the Saudi state, for example, and the religious doctrines of the Muslim Brotherhood in Egypt and a host of voluntary religious organizations around the Islamic world are all Salafi. These diverse movements share the belief that Muslims have deviated from God's plan and that matters can be returned to their proper state by emulating the Prophet.

Like any other major religious figure, Muhammad left behind a legacy that his followers have channeled in different directions. An extremist current in the Salafiyya places great emphasis on jihad, or holy war. Among other things, the Prophet Muhammad fought in mortal combat against idolatry, and some of his followers today choose to accord this aspect of his career primary importance. The devoted members of al Qaeda display an unsettling willingness to martyr themselves because they feel that, like the Prophet, they are locked in a life-or-death struggle with the forces of unbelief that threaten from all sides. They consider themselves an island of true believers surrounded by a sea of iniquity and think the future of religion itself, and therefore the world, depends on them and their battle against idol worship.

In almost every Sunni Muslim country the Salafiyya has spawned Islamist political movements working to compel the state to apply the *shari`a*—that is, Islamic law. Extremist Salafis believe that strict application of the *shari`a* is necessary to ensure that Muslims walk on the path of the Prophet. The more extremist the party, the more insistent and violent the demand that the state must apply the *shari`a* exclusively. In the view of extremist Salafis, the *shari`a* is God's thunderous commandment to Muslims, and failure to adopt it constitutes idolatry. By removing God from the realm of law, a domain that He has clearly claimed for Himself alone, human legislation amounts to worshiping a pagan deity. Thus it was on the basis of failure to apply the *shari`a* that extremists branded Egyptian President Anwar al-Sadat an apostate and then killed him. His assassins came from a group often known as Egyptian Islamic Jihad, the remnants of which have in recent years merged with al Qaeda. In fact, investigators believe that Egyptian Islamic Jihad's leaders, Ayman al-Zawahiri and Muhammad Atef (who was killed in the U.S. air campaign), masterminded the attacks of September 11. In his 1996 "Declaration of War against the Americans," bin Laden showed that he and his Egyptian associates are cut from the same cloth. Just as Zawahiri and Atef considered the current regime of Hosni Mubarak in Egypt to be a nest of apostates, so bin Laden considered the Saudi monarchy (its Wahhabi doctrines notwithstanding) to have renounced Islam. According to bin Laden, his king adopted "polytheism," which bin Laden defined as the acceptance of "laws fabricated by men . . . permitting that which God has forbidden." It is the height of human arrogance and irreligion to "share with God in His sole right of sovereignty and making the law."

Extremist Salafis, therefore, regard modern Western civilization as a font of evil, spreading idolatry around the globe in the form of secularism. Since the United States is the strongest Western nation, the main purveyor of pop culture, and the power most involved in the political and economic affairs of the Islamic world, it receives particularly harsh criticism. Only the apostate Middle Eastern regimes themselves fall under harsher condemnation.

It is worth remembering, in this regard, that the rise of Islam represents a miraculous case of the triumph of human will. With little more than their beliefs to gird them, the Prophet Muhammad and a small number of devoted followers started a movement that brought the most powerful empires of their day crashing to the ground. On September 11, the attackers undoubtedly imagined themselves to be retracing the Prophet's steps. As they boarded the planes with the intention of destroying the Pentagon and the World Trade Center, they recited battle prayers that contained the line "All of their equipment, and gates, and technology will not prevent [you from achieving your aim], nor harm [you] except by God's will." The hijackers' imaginations certainly needed nothing more than this sparse line to remind them that, as they attacked America, they rode right behind Muhammad, who in his day had unleashed forces that, shortly after his death, destroyed the Persian Empire and crippled Byzantium—the two superpowers of the age.

AMERICA, LAND OF THE CRUSADERS

When thinking about the world today and their place in it, the extremist Salafis do not reflect only on the story of the foundation of Islam. They also scour more than a millennium of Islamic history in search of parallels to the present predicament. In his "Declaration of War," for instance, bin Laden states that the stationing of American forces on the soil of the Arabian peninsula constitutes the greatest aggression committed against the Muslims since the death of the Prophet in AD 632.

To put this claim in perspective, it is worth remembering that in the last 1,300 years Muslims have suffered a number of significant defeats, including but not limited to the destruction of the Abbasid caliphate by the Mongols, an episode of which bin Laden is well aware. In 1258 the ruthless Mongol leader Hulegu sacked Baghdad, killed the caliph, and massacred hundreds of thousands of inhabitants, stacking their skulls, as legend has it, in a pyramid outside the city walls. Whatever one thinks about U.S. policy toward Iraq, few in America would argue that the use of Saudi bases to enforce the sanctions against Saddam Hussein's regime constitutes a world-historical event on a par with the Mongol invasion of the Middle East. Before September 11, one might have been tempted to pass off as nationalist hyperbole bin Laden's assumption that U.S. policy represents the pinnacle of human evil. Now we know he is deadly serious.

The magnitude of the attacks on New York and Washington make it clear that al Qaeda does indeed believe itself to be fighting a war to save the *umma* from Satan, represented by secular Western culture. Extreme though they may be, these views extend far beyond al Qaeda's immediate followers in Afghanistan. Even a quick glance at the Islamist press in Arabic demonstrates that many Muslims who do not belong to bin Laden's terrorist network consider the United States to be on a moral par with Genghis Khan. Take, for instance, Muhammad Abbas, an Egyptian Islamist who wrote the following in the newspaper *Al Shaab* on September 21:

Look! There is the master of democracy whom they have so often sanctified but who causes criminal, barbaric, bloody oppression that abandons the moral standards of even the most savage empires in history. In my last column I listed for readers the five million killed (may God receive them as martyrs) because of the crimes committed by this American civilization that America leads. These five million were killed in the last few decades alone.

Similar feelings led another *Al Shaab* columnist that day, Khalid al-Sharif, to describe the shock and delight that he felt while watching the World Trade Center crumbling:

Look at that! America, master of the world, is crashing down. Look at that! The Satan who rules the world, east and west, is burning. Look at that! The sponsor of terrorism is itself seared by its fire.

The fanatics of al Qaeda see the world in black and white and advance a particularly narrow view of Islam. This makes them a tiny minority among Muslims. But the basic categories of their thought flow directly from the mainstream of the Salafiyya, a perspective that has enjoyed a wide hearing over the last 50 years. Familiarity thus ensures bin Laden's ideas a sympathetic reception in many quarters.

In Salafi writings, the United States emerges as the senior member of a "Zionist-Crusader alliance" dedicated to subjugating Muslims, killing them, and, most important, destroying Islam. A careful reading reveals that this alliance represents more than just close relations between the United States and Israel today. The international cooperation between Washington and Jerusalem is but one nefarious manifestation of a greater evil of almost cosmic proportions. Thus in his "Declaration of War" bin Laden lists 10 or 12 world hot spots where Muslims have recently died (including Bosnia, Chechnya, and Lebanon) and attributes all of these deaths to a conspiracy led by the United States, even though Americans actually played no role in pulling the trigger. And thus, in another document, "Jihad Against Jews and Crusaders," bin Laden describes U.S. policies toward the Middle East as "a clear declaration of war on God, His messenger, and Muslims."

As strange as it may sound to an American audience, the idea that the United States has taken an oath of enmity toward God has deep roots in the Salafi tradition. It has been around for more than 50 years and has reached a wide public through the works of, among others, Sayyid Qutb, the most important Salafi thinker of the last half-century and a popular author in the Muslim world even today, nearly 40 years after his death. A sample passage taken from his writings in the early 1950s illustrates the point. Addressing the reasons why the Western powers had failed to support Muslims against their enemies in Pakistan, Palestine, and elsewhere, Qutb canvassed a number of common explanations such as Jewish financial influence and British imperial trickery but concluded,

> All of these opinions overlook one vital element in the question . . . the Crusader spirit that runs in the blood of all Occidentals. It is this that colors all their thinking, which is responsible for their imperialistic fear of the spirit of Islam and for their efforts to crush the strength of Islam. For the instincts and the interests of all Occidentals are bound up together in the crushing of that strength. This is the common factor that links together communist Russia and capitalist America. We do not forget the role of international Zionism in plotting against Islam and in pooling the forces of the Crusader imperialists and communist materialists alike. This is nothing other than a continuation of the role played by the Jews since the migration of the Prophet to Medina and the rise of the Islamic state.

Sayyid Qutb, Osama bin Laden, and the entire extremist Salafiyya see Western civilization, in all periods and in all guises, as innately hostile to Muslims and to Islam itself. The West and Islam are locked in a prolonged conflict. Islam will eventually triumph, of course, but only after enduring great hardship. Contemporary history, defined as it is by Western domination, constitutes the darkest era in the entire history of Islam.

America and the Mongol Threat

When attempting to come to grips with the nature of the threat the modern West poses,

extremist Salafis fall back on the writings of Ibn Taymiyya for guidance. A towering figure in the history of Islamic thought, he was born in Damascus in the thirteenth century, when Syria stood under the threat of invasion from the Mongols. Modern radicals find him attractive because he too faced the threat of a rival civilization. Ibn Taymiyya the firebrand exhorted his fellow Muslims to fight the Mongol foe, while Ibn Taymiyya the intellectual guided his community through the problems Muslims face when their social order falls under the shadow of non-Muslim power. It is only natural that bin Laden himself looks to such a master in order to legitimate his policies. Using Ibn Taymiyya to target America, however, marks an interesting turning point in the history of the radical Salafiyya.

Bin Laden's "Declaration of War" uses the logic of Ibn Taymiyya to persuade others in the Salafiyya to abandon old tactics for new ones. The first reference to him arises in connection with a discussion of the "Zionist-Crusader alliance," which according to bin Laden has been jailing and killing radical preachers—men such as Sheikh Omar Abdel Rahman, in prison for plotting a series of bombings in New York City following the 1993 bombing of the World Trade Center. Bin Laden argues that the "iniquitous Crusader movement under the leadership of the U.S.A." fears these preachers because they will successfully rally the Islamic community against the West, just as Ibn Taymiyya did against the Mongols in his day. Having identified the United States as a threat to Islam equivalent to the Mongols, bin Laden then discusses what to do about it. Ibn Taymiyya provides the answer: "To fight in the defense of religion and belief is a collective duty; there is no other duty after belief than fighting the enemy who is corrupting the life and the religion." The next most important thing after accepting the word of God, in other words, is fighting for it.

By calling on the *umma* to fight the Americans as if they were the Mongols, bin Laden and his Egyptian lieutenants have taken the extremist Salafiyya down a radically new path. Militants have long identified the West as a pernicious evil on a par with the Mongols, but they have traditionally targeted the internal enemy, the Hypocrites and apostates, rather than Hubal itself. Aware that he is shifting the focus considerably, bin Laden quotes Ibn Taymiyya at length to establish the basic point that "people of Islam should join forces and support each other to get rid of the main infidel," even if that means that the true believers will be forced to fight alongside Muslims of dubious piety. In the grand scheme of things, he argues, God often uses the base motives of impious Muslims as a means of advancing the cause of religion. In effect, bin Laden calls upon his fellow Islamist radicals to postpone the Islamic revolution, to stop fighting Hypocrites and apostates: "An internal war is a great mistake, no matter what reasons there are for it," because discord among Muslims will only serve the United States and its goal of destroying Islam.

The shift of focus from the domestic enemy to the foreign power is all the more striking given the merger of al Qaeda and Egyptian Islamic Jihad. The latter's decision to kill Sadat in 1981 arose directly from the principle that the cause of Islam would be served by targeting lax Muslim leaders rather than by fighting foreigners, and here, too, Ibn Taymiyya provided the key doctrine. In his day Muslims often found themselves living under Mongol rulers who had absorbed Islam in one form or another. Ibn Taymiyya argued that such rulers—who outwardly pretended to be Muslims but who secretly followed non-Islamic, Mongol practices—must be considered infidels. Moreover, he claimed, by having accepted Islam but having also failed to observe key precepts of the religion, they had in effect committed apostasy and thereby written their own death sentences. In general, Islam prohibits fighting fellow Muslims and strongly restricts the right to rebel against the ruler; Ibn Taymiyya's doctrines, therefore, were crucial in the development of a modern Sunni Islamic revolutionary theory.

Egyptian Islamic Jihad views leaders such as Sadat as apostates. Although they may outwardly display signs of piety, they do not actually have Islam in their hearts, as their failure to enforce the *shari'a* proves. This non-Islamic behavior demonstrates that such leaders actually serve the secular West, precisely as an earlier generation of outwardly Muslim rulers had served the Mongols, and as the Hypocrites had served idolatry. Islamic Jihad explained itself back in the mid-1980s in a long, lucid statement titled "The Neglected Duty." Not a political manifesto like bin Laden's tracts, it is a sustained and learned argument that targets the serious believer rather than the angry, malleable crowd. Unlike bin Laden's holy war, moreover, Islamic Jihad's doctrine, though violent, fits clearly in the mainstream of Salafi consciousness, which historically has been concerned much more with the state of the Muslims themselves than with relations between Islam and the outside world. The decision to target America, therefore, raises the question of whether, during the 1990s, Egyptian Islamic Jihad changed its ideology entirely. Did its leaders decide that the foreign enemy was in fact the real enemy? Or was the 1993 bombing in New York tactical rather than strategic?

The answer would seem to be the latter. Bin Laden's "Declaration of War" itself testifies to the tactical nature of his campaign against America. Unlike "The Neglected Duty," which presents a focused argument, the "Declaration of War" meanders from topic to topic, contradicting itself along the way. On the one hand, it calls for unity in the face of external aggression and demands an end to internecine warfare; on the other, it calls in essence for revolution in Saudi Arabia. By presenting a litany of claims against the Saudi ruling family and by discussing the politics of Saudi Arabia at length and in minute detail, bin Laden protests too much: he reveals that he has not, in fact, set aside the internal war among the believers. Moreover, he also reveals that the ideological basis for that internal war has not changed. The members of the Saudi elite, like Sadat, have committed apostasy. Like the Hypocrites of Medina, they serve the forces of irreligion in order to harm the devotees of the Prophet and his message:

> You know more than anybody else about the size, intention, and the danger of the presence of the U.S. military bases in the area. The [Saudi] regime betrayed the *umma* and joined the infidels, assisting them . . . against the Muslims. It is well known that this is one of the ten "voiders" of Islam, deeds of de-Islamization. By opening the Arabian Peninsula to the crusaders, the regime disobeyed and acted against what has been enjoined by the messenger of God.

Osama bin Laden undoubtedly believes that Americans are Crusader-Zionists, that they threaten his people even more than did the Mongols—in short, that they are the enemies of God Himself. But he also sees them as obstacles to his plans for his native land. The "Declaration of War" provides yet more testimony to the old saw that ultimately all politics is local.

THE FAILURE OF POLITICAL ISLAM

If the attacks on the United States represented a change in radical Salafi tactics, then one must wonder what prompted bin Laden and Zawahiri to make that change. The answer is that the attacks were a response to the failure of extremist movements in the Muslim world in recent years, which have generally proved incapable of taking power (Sudan and Afghanistan being the major exceptions). In the last two decades, several violent groups have challenged regimes such as those in Egypt, Syria, and Algeria, but in every case the government has managed to crush, co-opt, or marginalize the radicals. In the words of the "Declaration of War,"

> the Zionist-Crusader alliance moves quickly to contain and abort any "corrective movement" appearing in Islamic countries. Different means and methods are used to achieve their target. Sometimes officials from the Ministry of the Interior, who are also graduates of the colleges of the *shari'a*, are [unleashed] to mislead and confuse the nation and the *umma* . . . and to circulate false information about the movement, wasting the energy of the nation in discussing minor issues and ignoring the main one that is the unification of people under the divine law of Allah.

Given that in Egypt, Algeria, and elsewhere regimes have resorted to extreme violence to protect themselves, it is striking that bin Laden emphasizes here not the brutality but rather the counterpropaganda designed to divide and rule. Consciously or not, he has put his finger on a serious problem for the extremist Salafis: the limitations of their political and economic theories.

Apart from insisting on the implementation of the *shari'a*, demanding social justice, and turning the *umma* into the only legitimate political community, radical Salafis have precious little to offer in response to the mundane problems that people and governments face in the modern world. Extremist Islam is profoundly effective in mounting a protest movement: it can produce a cadre of activists whose devotion to the cause knows no bounds, it can galvanize people to fight against oppression. But it has serious difficulties when it comes to producing institutions and programs that can command the attention of diverse groups in society over the long haul. Its success relies mainly on the support of true believers, but they tend to fragment in disputes over doctrine, leadership, and agenda.

The limitations of extremist Salafi political theory and its divisive tendencies come to light clearly if one compares the goals of al Qaeda with those of the Palestinian terrorist group Hamas, whose suicide bombers have also been in the headlines recently. The ideology of Hamas also evolved out of the Egyptian extremist Salafiyya milieu, and it shares with al Qaeda a paranoid view of the world: the *umma* and true Islam are threatened with extinction by the spread of Western secularism, the policies of the Crusading West, and oppression by the Zionists. Both Hamas and al Qaeda believe that the faithful must obliterate Israel. But looking more closely at Hamas and its agenda, one can see that it parts company with al Qaeda in many significant ways. This is because Hamas operates in the midst of nationalistic Palestinians, a majority of whom fervently desire, among other things, an end to the Israeli occupation and the establishment of a Palestinian state in part of historic Palestine.

The nationalist outlook of Hamas' public presents the organization with a number of thorny problems. Nationalism, according to the extremist Salafiyya, constitutes *shirk*—that is, polytheism or idolatry. If politics and religion are not distinct categories, as extremist Salafis argue, then political life must be centered around God and God's law. Sovereignty belongs not to the nation but to God alone, and the only legitimate political community is the *umma*. Pride in one's ethnic group is tolerable only so long as it does not divide the community of believers, who form an indivisible unit thanks to the sovereignty of the *shari'a*. One day, extremist Salafis believe, political boundaries will be erased and all Muslims will live in one polity devoted to God's will. At the moment, however, the priority is not to erase boundaries but to raise up the *shari'a* and abolish secular law. Nationalism is idolatry because it divides the *umma* and replaces a *shari'a*-centered consciousness with ethnic pride.

If Hamas were actually to denounce secular Palestinian nationalists as apostates, however, it would immediately consign itself to political irrelevance. To skirt this problem, the organization has developed an elaborate view of Islamic history that in effect elevates the Palestinian national struggle to a position of paramount importance for the *umma* as a whole. This allows Hamas activists to function in the day-to-day political world as fellow travelers with the nationalists. Thus one of the fascinating aspects of Palestinian extremist Salafiyya is a dog that hasn't barked: in contrast to its sibling movements in neighboring countries, Hamas has refrained from labeling the secular leaders in the Palestinian Authority as apostates. Even at the height of Yasir Arafat's crackdown against Hamas, the movement never openly branded him as an idolater.

Like al Qaeda, Hamas argues that a conspiracy between Zionism and the West has dedicated itself to destroying Islam, but for obvious reasons it magnifies the role of Zionism in the alliance. The Hamas Covenant, for example, sees Zionism as, among other things, a force determining many of the greatest historical developments of the modern period:

[Zionists] were behind the French Revolution, the communist revolution. . . . They were behind World War I, when they were able to destroy the Islamic caliphate [i.e., the Ottoman Empire]. . . . They obtained the Balfour Declaration [favoring establishment of a Jewish homeland in Palestine], [and] formed the League of Nations, through which they could rule the world. They were behind World War II, through which they made huge financial gains by trading in armaments, and paved the way for the establishment of their state. It was they who instigated the replacement of the League of Nations with the United Nations and the Security Council. . . . There is no war going on anywhere, without [them] having their finger in it.

Do a number of intelligent and educated people actually believe this? Yes, because they must; their self-understanding hinges on it. Since their political struggle must be for the greater good of the *umma* and of Islam as a whole, their enemy must be much more than just one part of the Jewish people with designs on one sliver of Muslim territory. The enemy must be the embodiment of an evil that transcends time and place.

Although the sanctity of Jerusalem works in Hamas' favor, in Islam Jerusalem does not enjoy the status of Mecca and Medina and is only a city, not an entire country. To reconcile its political and religious concerns, therefore, Hamas must inflate the significance of Palestine in Islamic history: "The present Zionist onslaught," the covenant says, "has also been preceded by Crusading raids from the West and other Tatar [Mongol] raids from the East." The references here are to Saladin, the Muslim leader who defeated the Crusaders in Palestine at the battle of Hattin in 1187, and to the Muslim armies that defeated the Mongols at another Palestinian site called Ayn Jalut in 1260. On this basis Hamas argues that Palestine has always been the bulwark against the enemies of Islam; the *umma*, therefore, must rally behind the Palestinians to destroy Israel, which represents the third massive onslaught against the true religion since the death of the Prophet.

Despite the similarities in their perspectives, therefore, al Qaeda and Hamas have quite different agendas. Al Qaeda justifies its political goals on the basis of the holiness of Mecca and Medina and on the claim that the presence of U.S. forces in Arabia constitutes the greatest aggression that the Muslims have ever endured. Hamas sees its own struggle against Israel as the first duty of the *umma*. The two organizations undoubtedly share enough in common to facilitate political cooperation on many issues, but at some point their agendas diverge radically, a divergence that stems from the different priorities inherent in their respective Saudi and Palestinian backgrounds.

The differences between al Qaeda and Hamas demonstrate how local conditions can mold the universal components of Salafi consciousness into distinct world views. They display the creativity of radical Islamists in addressing a practical problem similar to that faced by communists in the early twentieth century: how to build a universal political movement that can nevertheless function effectively at the local level. This explains why, when one looks at the political map of the extremist Salafiyya, one finds a large number of organizations all of which insist that they stand for the same principles. They do, in fact, all insist on the implementation of the *shari'a*, but the specific social and political forces fueling that insistence differ greatly from place to place. They all march to the beat of God's drummer, but the marchers tend to wander off in different directions.

The new tactic of targeting America is designed to overcome precisely this weakness of political Islam. Bin Laden succeeded in attacking Hubal, the universal enemy: he identified the only target that all of the Salafiyya submovements around the world can claim equally as their own, thereby reflecting and reinforcing the collective belief that the *umma* actually is the political community. He and his colleagues adopted this strategy not from choice but from desperation, a desperation born of the fact that in recent years the extremist Salafis had been defeated politically almost everywhere in the Arab and Muslim world. The new tactic, by tapping into the deepest emotions of the political community, smacks of brilliance, and—much to America's chagrin—will undoubtedly give political Islam a renewed burst of energy.

Explaining the Echo

The decision to target the United States allows al Qaeda to play the role of a radical "Salafi International." It resonates beyond the small community of committed extremists, however, reaching not just moderate Salafis but, in addition, a broad range of disaffected citizens experiencing poverty, oppression, and powerlessness across the Muslim world. This broader resonance of what appears to us as such a wild and hateful message is the dimension of the problem that Americans find most difficult to understand.

One reason for the welcoming echo is the extent to which Salafi political movements, while failing to capture state power, have nevertheless succeeded in capturing much cultural ground in Muslim countries. Many authoritarian regimes (such as Mubarak's Egypt) have cut a deal with the extremists: in return for an end to assassinations, the regime acquiesces in some of the demands regarding implementation of the *shari'a*. In addition, it permits the extremist groups to run networks of social welfare organizations that often deliver services more efficiently than does a state sector riddled with corruption and marred by decay. This powerful cultural presence of the Salafis across the Islamic world means not only that their direct ranks have grown but also that their symbolism is more familiar than ever among a wider public.

But the attack on America also resonates deeply among secular groups in many countries. The immediate response in the secular Arab press, for example, fell broadly into three categories. A minority denounced the attacks forcefully and unconditionally, another minority attributed them to the Israelis or to American extremists like Timothy McVeigh, and a significant majority responded with a version of "Yes, but"—yes, the terrorist attacks against you were wrong, but you must understand that your own policies in the Middle East have for years sown the seeds of this kind of violence.

This rationalization amounts to a political protest against the perceived role of the United States in the Middle East. Arab and Islamic commentators, and a number of prominent analysts of the Middle East in this country, point in particular to U.S. enforcement of the sanctions on Iraq and U.S. support for Israel in its struggle against Palestinian nationalism. Both of these issues certainly cause outrage, and if the United States were to effect the removal of Israeli settlements from the West Bank and alleviate the suffering of the Iraqi people, some of that outrage would certainly subside. But although a change in those policies would dampen some of bin Laden's appeal, it would not solve the problem of the broader anger and despair that he taps, because the sources of those feelings lie beyond the realm of day-to-day diplomacy.

Indeed, secular political discourse in the Islamic world in general and the Arab world in particular bears a striking resemblance to the Salafi interpretation of international affairs, especially insofar as both speak in terms of Western conspiracies. The secular press does not make reference to Crusaders and Mongols but rather to a string of "broken promises" dating back to World War I, when the European powers divided up the Ottoman Empire to suit their own interests. They planted Israel in the midst of the Middle East, so the analysis goes, in order to drive a wedge between Arab states, and the United States continues to support Israel for the same purpose. Bin Laden played to this sentiment in his October 7 statement when he said,

> What the United States tastes today is a very small thing compared to what we have tasted for tens of years. Our nation has been tasting this humiliation and contempt for more than eighty years. Its sons are being killed, its blood is being shed, its holy places are being attacked, and it is not being ruled according to what God has decreed.

For 80 years—that is, since the destruction of the Ottoman Empire—the Arabs and the Muslims have been humiliated. Although they do not share bin Laden's millenarian agenda, when secular commentators point to Palestine and Iraq today they do not see just two difficult political problems; they see what they consider the true intentions of the West unmasked.

Arab commentators often explain, for instance, that Saddam Hussein and Washington are actually allies. They ridicule the notion that the United States tried to depose the dictator. After all, it is said, the first Bush administration had the forces in place to remove the Baath Party and had called on the Iraqi populace to rise up against the tyrant. When the people actually rose, however, the Americans watched from the sidelines as the regime brutally suppressed them. Clearly, therefore, what the United States really wanted was to divide and rule the Arabs in order to secure easy access to Persian Gulf oil—a task that also involves propping up corrupt monarchies in Kuwait and Saudi Arabia. Keeping Saddam on a leash was the easiest way to ensure that Iran could not block the project.

Needless to say, this world view is problematic. Since World War I, Arab societies have been deeply divided among themselves along ethnic, social, religious, and political lines. Regardless of what the dominant Arab discourse regarding broken promises has to say, most of these divisions were not created by the West. The European powers and the United States have sometimes worked to divide the Arabs, sometimes to unify them. Mostly they have pursued their own interests, as have all the other actors involved. Bin Laden is a participant in a profoundly serious civil war over Arab and Muslim identity in the modern world. The United States is also a participant in that war, because whether it realizes it or not, its policies affect the fortunes of the various belligerents. But Washington is not a primary actor, because it is an outsider in cultural affairs and has only a limited ability to define for believers the role of Islam in public life.

The war between extremist Salafis and the broader populations around them is only the tip of the iceberg. The fight over religion among Muslims is but one of a number of deep and enduring regional struggles that originally had nothing to do with the United States and even today involve it only indirectly. Nonetheless, U.S. policies can influence the balance of power among the protagonists in these struggles, sometimes to a considerable degree.

Until the Arab and Muslim worlds create political orders that do not disenfranchise huge segments of their own populations, the civil war will continue and will continue to touch the United States. Washington can play an important role in fostering authentic and inclusive polities, but ultimately Arabs and Muslims more generally must learn to live in peace with one another so as to live comfortably with outsiders. Whether they will do so is anybody's guess.

It is a stark political fact that in the Arab and Muslim worlds today economic globalization and the international balance of power both come with an American face, and neither gives much reason for optimism. Osama bin Laden's rhetoric, dividing the world into two camps—the *umma* versus the United States and puppet regimes—has a deep resonance because on some levels it conforms, if not to reality, then at least to its appearances. This is why, for the first time in modern history, the extremist Salafis have managed to mobilize mass popular opinion.

This development is troubling, but the United States still has some cards to play. Its policies, for instance, on both West Bank settlements and Iraq, are sorely in need of review— but only after bin Laden has been vanquished. These policy changes might help, but the root problem lies deeper. Once al Qaeda has been annihilated without sparking anti-American revolutions in the Islamic world, the United States should adopt a set of policies that ensure that significant numbers of Muslims—not Muslim regimes but Muslims—identify their own interests with those of the United States, so that demagogues like bin Laden cannot aspire to speak in the name of the entire *umma*. In 1991, millions of Iraqis constituted just such a reservoir of potential supporters, yet America turned its back on them. Washington had its reasons, but they were not the kind that can be justified in terms of the American values that we trumpet to the world. Today we are paying a price for that hypocrisy. This is not to say that we caused or deserved the attacks of September 11 in any way. It is to say, however, that we are to some extent responsible for the fact that so few in the Arab and Muslim worlds express vocal and unequivocal support for our cause, even when that cause is often their cause as well.

Since the events of September 11, innumerable articles have appeared in the press discussing America's loss of innocence. To foreigners, this view of Americans as naive bumpkins, a band of Forrest Gumps who just arrived in town, is difficult to fathom. Whether the MTV generation knows it or not, the United States has been deeply involved in other peoples' civil wars for a long time. A generation ago, for example, we supposedly lost our innocence in Vietnam. Back then, Adonis, the poet laureate of the Arab world, meditated on the ambivalence Arabs feel toward America. In the aftermath of the September 11 attacks, his poem seems prophetic:

> New York, you will find in my land
> . . . the stone of Mecca and the waters of the Tigris.
> In spite of all this,
> you pant in Palestine and Hanoi.
> East and west you contend with people
> whose only history is fire.

These tormented people knew us before we were virgins.

3

HOMEGROWN TERRORISM
IN THE UNITED STATES

Resistance to tyrants is obedience to God.

—Thomas Jefferson

John Brown has been called the father of American terrorism. His army was made up of 18 men, including several of his sons. They took prominent citizens hostage and captured the federal arsenal in Harpers Ferry, Virginia, in 1859. Brown's intention was to liberate slaves from the surrounding territory, form them into an army, and free all the slaves in the South. His group was surrounded and overcome by local militia and later captured by federal troops. The raid itself was a fiasco. Many in the group were killed during the battle; the rest were hanged later (Oates, 1979). Brown was seen as a fanatic and murderer by slaveholders against whom his uprising was aimed, but abolitionists who agreed with his philosophy saw Brown as the embodiment of all that was noble and courageous (Chowder, 2000). The attack on Harpers Ferry polarized the nation and helped propel it into the Civil War.

The United States has a long history of political violence, but until recently, few scholars characterized the experience as terrorism (White, 1998). This limited perspective has resulted in a lack of systematic knowledge and research about terrorism throughout the history of this country. The Uniform Crime Report, since its inception in the 1930s, has continually improved the reporting of other types of criminal behavior, but there is no similar source for domestic terrorism, and official data remain sketchy (Hamm, 1998). The full extent of death and injury that has resulted from homegrown terror will never be known because hate crimes in the United States are likely to be recorded as arsons, homicides, and assaults rather than as terrorism (American Psychological Association, 1998).

For analytical purposes, we have divided homegrown terrorist campaigns waged in the United States into five different categories, based on their ideologies. The discussion of homegrown terror begins with state-sponsored terror conducted by authorities.

AUTHORS' NOTE: Richard Boltz provided research background for this chapter.

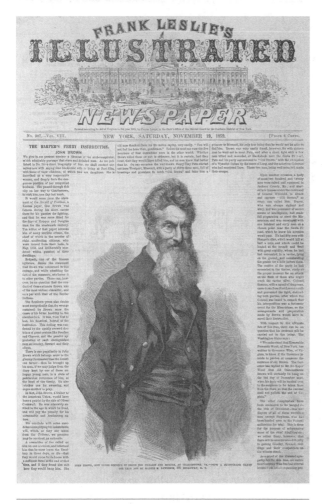

Portrait of John Brown, whose assault on the U.S. arsenal at Harpers Ferry further fueled regional animosity and drove the nation closer to civil war.

Photo from CORBIS. Reprinted with permission.

Next, left-wing class struggles including those of communists and socialists are covered. The third category includes anarchists, whose ecoterrorism may be in aid of animals or the Earth itself. The last two categories may both be considered right-wing, but separation has been made based on their aims. The resulting right-wing categories are white supremacists and religious extremists. These two categories often overlap, but they have also developed separately—white supremacists without religion, and religious extremists without racism (Harmon, 2000; White, 1998; Zulaika & Douglas, 2000).

Some striking similarities exist among all terrorist ideologies, regardless of the terrorists' political affiliation, from self-styled defenders of liberty in the United States to Islamic extremists in Iran (McGuckin, 1997). Religious fanatics are emphasized here because they do not appear to recognize any of the political, moral, or practical considerations that constrain other terrorist groups from causing mass death and destruction (Hoffman, 1998). As the following analysis makes clear, these are not discrete categories. Of more concern than analytical categories are the actual connections between groups from across the spectrum in the United States, connections based on hatred and an antiglobalization ideology.

STATE-SPONSORED TERRORISM

Terror from above relies on the manufacture and *wholesale* spread of fear by authorities, Congress, and the president (Herman, 1982). U.S. citizens are likely to think that wholesale terror is sponsored by tyrannical governments in the Middle East or Latin America, but there have also been violent martial actions taken by U.S. authorities against U.S. citizens. Indigenous Americans were attacked and their culture all but eradicated by official government policy throughout the 19th century. For example, the Removal Act of 1830 caused the forced march of the five great Indian tribes (Cherokee, Choctaw, Chickasaw, Creek, and Seminole) from their farms and businesses along the eastern seaboard to the badlands of Oklahoma. Many died from the harsh conditions along the way, known as the Trail of Tears. Those who survived found the way of life under government control on the reservations to be treacherous and bleak. Domination and genocide characterized many of the policies carried out by U.S. government agencies against Native Americans (Golden Ink, n.d.; "A Brief History of the Trail of Tears," n.d.).

Labor organizers were also systematically besieged by government forces during their struggle to form unions throughout the early decades of the 20th century. The Ludlow massacre in Colorado in 1914 is one example of the use of government agents as terrorists. National Guardsmen attacked a tent colony during a strike against the Colorado Fuel and Iron Co. Wives and children of workers were set aflame, adding another chapter to the bloody history of the labor movement in the United States (Millies, 1995).

In both of these examples, and many others, formal policies were developed to carry out a campaign of terror. Official U.S. forces were used by authorities to threaten or deliver violence, as a means of furthering political agendas. It is essential to understand the impact of state-wholesale (state-sponsored) terrorism to understand *retail* terrorism (Herman, 1982). Retail terrorists are isolated individuals and small groups. A substantial proportion of them arise from official failures and wholesale injustices. Terrorism prevention thus begins with dealing intelligently and humanely with local and regional grievances, abandoning wholesale (state-sponsored) violence. A government perceived as menacing or predatory provokes extremists who feel threatened and forced to withdraw into heavily armed, seething compounds or to engage in preemptive acts of violence (Hoffman, 1998).

LEFTIST CLASS STRUGGLES

Most of the insurgent movements in the United States, such as the Weather Underground, the Black Panthers, and the Puerto Rican Nationalists (FALN), which were well known during the 1960s and 1970s, have been inactive since the 1980s. The Puerto Rican FALN was the last leftist group to continue a terrorist campaign within the United States. Beginning in the 1950s, it conducted bombings, armored car robberies, and assassinations; it even launched a rocket attack against FBI headquarters in San Juan (White, 1998).

Leftist terrorists of the 1970s identified with class struggles and Marxist or Maoist communist ideologies. Many of them were involved with universities and were brought together because of antiwar and civil rights issues that were highly politicized during the decade. They turned to underground guerrilla combat when their street demonstrations were insufficient to end the Vietnam War. During their campaigns, leftist insurgent groups planted countless bombs in banks and public areas, in military and police stations, and twice on successive days in the U.S. Capitol. They were responsible for highly publicized kidnappings, prison breaks, and other events designed to get the attention of the mainstream of U.S. society. Typical of the rhetoric of the time was the *Weather Report*, published by the Weather Underground. In a *Weather Report* issue sent to the Associated Press, a communiqué signed only "weatherman" claimed responsibility for bombing the New York City Police headquarters. It read, in part: "The time is now. Political power grows out of a gun, a Molotov, a riot, a commune and from the soul of the people" (as cited in Jacobs, 1997, p. 111).

In the late 1960s, radicals in the United States calling themselves "The New Left" focused on conflicts over racial disparities and economic inequality. They agreed that their enemies resided in the corporate imperialist system. Their cause was to wage revolutionary war against the United States from within. Attempts were made to forge links between leftist groups including the Black Panthers, Students for a Democratic Society, and the Weather Underground; however, the radical left was fragmented and worked at cross purposes. The united front that would have been necessary to pursue common radical political aims in the United States never materialized. A large number of arrests added to the disorder of the organizations. With the conservative turn of culture in the United States immediately following the 1970s, leftist guerrilla groups like the Weather Underground died out (Jacobs, 1997).

However, the Black Panthers re-emerged at the end of the 20th century. The new groups have the same name and appearance as the earlier groups, but their ideology evolved into a rhetoric of hate and black separatism. The modern Black Panthers are heavily armed. Their mission is to provide protection to African Americans who are being victimized in hate crimes by white supremacists. They have become a group of vigilantes, not followers of the leftist ideology that was the original organizing principle for the Black Panthers (Southern Poverty Law Center, 2000a).

The Symbionese Liberation Army (SLA) are leftist terrorists from the 1970s who returned to the news in the 21st century. The SLA was formed in the fall of 1973 by a group of Berkeley student radicals led by an escaped convict, Donald De Freeze. They grabbed headlines in 1974 by kidnapping newspaper heiress Patricia Hearst. She was found by the police in 1975, but rather than being seen as a victim, Hearst was arrested for her involvement with the terrorists. She was convicted and sentenced to a 7-year prison term for her participation in a bank robbery. In 1979, President Jimmy Carter commuted her sentence, and in 2001 she was pardoned by President Bill Clinton (Staples, 2002).

The rest of the SLA had either died or were fugitives in 1999, when the television show *America's Most Wanted* aired a picture of Kathleen Soliah on the 25th anniversary of the SLA's most notorious crimes. The former terrorist was sought for planting bombs and robbing banks. Police in St. Paul, Minnesota, were able to identify Sara Jane Olson, a suburban housewife, from the photo. In 2002, two other members of the SLA were brought to justice for shooting a bank customer with a sawed-off shotgun during a robbery that netted the SLA $15,000. Kathleen Soliah was included in this robbery, although Emily Harris was accused of the shooting. Also indicted were William Harris and Michael Bortin. The arrests were based on corroborating forensic evidence using 21st-century technology to prove a case that had been languishing before Kathleen Soliah's arrest. The prosecution granted immunity to another former gang member and to Kathleen Soliah's brother for their testimony against the four defendants (Sterngold, 2002; Wasserman, 2002). The most notorious evidence in the case came from a book written by Patricia Hearst and published by Doubleday in 1982. In *Every Secret Thing*, Hearst described the bank robbery in detail, admitting that she drove a getaway car, but she was granted immunity for her testimony against the SLA. Her case is still considered newsworthy despite the changing environment of terrorism in the 21st century.

Anarchists/Ecoterrorists

The "Ecoterror" movement in the United States began with a biocentric ideology that put humans in a position of equality with all forms of life. Those in the movement abhorred the notion of human dominance implied by constant development and encroachment on nature. Their concerns involved preserving wilderness and thwarting expansion. Their actions followed the "monkey-wrenching" dogma, which concentrated on sabotage of equipment and machinery and destruction of property. Ecoterror exploded in the anti-industrialism of the Unabomber, Ted Kaczynski, who made it clear: "The people we are out to get are the scientists and engineers, especially in critical fields like computers and genetics" (as quoted in Sadler & Winters, 1996, p. 76).

The Luddites in Nottingham, England, were an Ecoterror group that originated two centuries ago. They were thought of as the "antimachine" people because they wanted to stop the Industrial Revolution that began in the late eighteenth century. The Luddites didn't want a life where they were forced into factories, to work with machines they couldn't control, and forced from village self-sufficiency into urban dependence and servitude (Sale, 1995). Ecoterror groups today are concerned with the technological revolution that began late in the 20th century. "Technophobes" and "technoresisters" believe that an inevitable eco-catastrophe will strike the world around the year 2020. The coming catastrophe will be based on a combination of rising sea levels, a decrease in the ozone layer, and the social decay that goes along with disastrous corporate global practices (Kupfer, 2001).

The Earth Liberation Front (ELF) targeted urban sprawl in Long Island, New York, at the end of 2000 and the early months of 2001 with nine acts of economic sabotage against luxury homes under construction. The slogan "If you build it, we will burn it" was left on one of the homes. Windows were smashed, sites were vandalized, and bulldozers were decommissioned (Earth First!, 2001). According to ABC News (2001), ELF carried out more than 100 acts of destruction beginning in 1997, causing $37 million in damage. The group claimed responsibility for $2.2 million worth of damage in the year 2000 alone. Its campaign focuses not only on land use and development but also on the destruction of biogenetic research centers.

At the end of the 20th century, ecological terrorists focused their movement in two directions: land-use issues, attacking developers and loggers; and protests against the abuse of animals (White, 1998). The growing membership of the Animal Liberation Front (ALF) targets farmers for their supposed mistreatment of animals. Scientists and researchers are targets for their use of animals in research. Different businesses are targeted for different reasons, among them lumber companies, meat markets, and restaurants (Miller & Miller, 2000).

According to ALF guidelines, "The ALF carries out non-violent direct action against animal abuse by rescuing animals and causing financial loss, usually through the damage and destruction of property, to animal abusers. ALF actions are illegal and therefore activists work anonymously, either individually or in groups, and do not have any centralized organization or address" ("Guidelines," 2000, p. 25).

Ecoterrorists use the "secret cell" structure that has been noted in other terrorist organizations. A member of the ALF reported, "You get a call from someone you trust, about an activity which needs to be undertaken. If you trust them, you go out and do it and don't ask many questions. It's much more effective run on a cell-based structure like that" (Arnold, 1997, p. 242).

RACIAL SUPREMACY

The ideology for white supremacists arose from the ashes of the Civil War. For example, the Ku Klux Klan (KKK), which continued carrying out deliberate racist terrorism for more than a century, was spawned by the era of Reconstruction. Some of the KKK groups of the 21st century still reenact pre–Civil War ceremonies and revere the Confederate flag. For many white supremacists, though, the swastika now symbolizes their agenda for a pure Aryan race. During the 1960s, when cultural changes in race relations were a source of conflict and controversy, white ethnic nationalists from many different groups carried out a systematic campaign of terror against black community leaders and gathering places, especially churches.

A Ku Klux Klan ceremony, with Klansman holding a cross, Stone Mountain, Georgia, near Atlanta.

Photo from Bettmann/CORBIS. Reprinted with permission.

There are also black separatist groups in the United States. Calling themselves the "Nation of Islam," they consider themselves to be the followers of the Messenger Elijah Muhammad. His objective was clear: "I am doing all I can to make the so-called Negroes see that the white race and their religion (Christianity) are their open enemies, and to prove to them that they will never be anything but the devils' slaves and finally go to hell with them for believing and following them and their kind" (Muhammad, 1999, My Objective section). Notable organized efforts took place during the late 1950s and early 1960s in the form of arson and assassination. The movement went underground after many of the leaders were kept under surveillance and jailed. There were notable rifts in the black militant organizations, and public support waned after the 1960s. In the 1990s, a black separatist movement came to public notice again, under the guidance of Minister Louis Farrakhan. Thousands of African Americans were involved in marches and demonstrations. Despite the black racist oratory of the latest movement in the United States, there have been no reported connections to terrorist activities (Anti-Defamation League, 1999).

White supremacists often focus on the illegitimacy of the U.S. Constitution, and therefore of the entire U.S. government. An obsessive suspicion of the government is common, along with beliefs in various conspiracy theories (Snow, 1999). Issues such as gun control, United Nations involvement in international affairs, and clashes between dissidents and law enforcement provided the momentum for rightist groups at the beginning of the 21st century (Simonsen & Spindlove, 2000). Many right-wing groups purport to rely on a "common law" system rather than the U.S. system of justice. Even though the system does not exist, common law adherents involve themselves and government agencies in bogus legal manipulations that are both costly and time-consuming. Their idea is to sabotage U.S. government courts and offices with an inundation of writs, suits, and court orders until officialdom collapses under mountains of paper. In recent years, the rightists in the United States have diversified. A list of types of rightist rebels includes militant right-wing gun advocates, antitax protesters, survivalists, far right libertarians, traditional racists, anti-Semitic Nazi or neo-Nazi movements, and separatist advocates of sovereign citizenship, along with various other groups having negative, hateful attitudes toward the federal government (Abanes, 1996).

Since 1996, the number of known armed militias in the United States has declined, but the militia movement managed to survive despite disorganization, infighting, and a number of highly publicized arrests (Snow, 1999). Core leaders have developed a communications system using the Intenet, radio, and clandestine meetings that has allowed the surviving militia groups to develop consensus around key issues having to do with firearms (Pitcavage, 2001). Other indications suggest that the American right-wing, white supremacist movement is still alive. An alarming connection has been made between the forces of hate in the United States. In 2000, William Pierce, arguably the most influential white supremacist in the world, bought an underground "black metal" hate music company called Resistance. Black metal is a kind of white racist rock music that has been popularized in Europe as well as in the United States by young neo-Nazis. William Pierce, founder of the National Alliance, wrote *The Turner Diaries* (1996), a novel that provided the blueprint for many right-wing terrorist attacks (Blythe, 2000).

A connection between the well-established white supremacists, whose active arm was the militias in the 1990s, and the racist skinheads, who are the agents of terror most like them to emerge in the new century, is a chilling possibility. The connection between white supremacists and racist skinheads is significant for both strategic and analytical reasons. Racist skinheads can best be characterized as a terrorist youth subculture (Hamm, 1998). They provide an avenue for propagating the ideology of hate into the future and upgrading it in more modern cultural terms.

Racist skinhead groups generally accept Nazi, white supremacist, homophobic, and anti-Semitic themes, but these younger neo-Nazis may not espouse the Christian religious messages included with most radical right music and literature in the United States. Their viewpoints may be purely secular, or there may be an affiliation between racist skinheads and pagan religions older than Christianity and even more shrouded in legend and mythology (Southern Poverty Law Center, 2000b).

RELIGIOUS EXTREMISTS

The growth of religious terrorism worldwide appears to account for the increased severity of terrorist attacks since 1991 (Enders & Sandler, 2000). For zealots, violence was established as the only means to overthrow a reviled secular government and attain religious redemption (Hoffman, 1998). Messianic concepts of deliverance, legitimized by theological imperative and achieved through personal action that entails mass indiscriminate murder, are of increasing concern.

Religious extremists prepared for a major crisis at the millennium because they believed that the year 2000 signaled the beginning of the world's end. They foresaw political and personal repression enforced by the United Nations and carried out with the support of the U.S. government. This belief is commonly known as the New World Order Conspiracy. It has survived into the 21st century. Both white supremacists and Christian Identity followers in the United States dread the "One World Government" that they expect will arise in the face of chaos. They look forward to an upcoming catastrophe as a step toward God's government (Hoffman, 1998).

Rubenstein (1987) asserts that there is no unified domestic terrorist threat but rather a context for social protest arising from a moral and social crisis in the United States. Though lacking unity in nature and scope, religious terrorism is anything but disorganized or random. It is driven by an inner logic common among diverse groups and faiths that use political violence to further their sacred causes (Ranstorp, 2000).

THE NEW CENTURY

Michel Wieviorka (1993) explains that acts of terrorist violence are inversions of the ideals under which the movements began. The organized practice of indiscriminate and irredeemable violence is not a faltering movement's last best hope or final act of desperation but rather a substitute for a movement that has either become imaginary or has fallen out of sync, along with the hopes pinned on it. Wieviorka (1993, p. 29) clarifies the course taken by terrorist groups, showing that extreme violence is an ideological and pragmatic attempt to recover a meaning that has been lost.

Democratically run governments such as that of the United States promise empowerment, but the vote does not give the individual much power. Democracies often produce groups that feel marginalized and are willing to attack those deemed responsible for their condition. Majority rule works well only when minorities consider themselves part of the political body (Rapoport, 2000). The United States has a history of disgruntled minorities that turn to violent political action, so it is not likely that we have seen the end of terrorism from within. What is most disturbing is the tendency for the various types of terrorists to work collectively as their ideologies increasingly come together. The separate types of terrorists described above are seldom seen in isolation. Increasingly, radical groups on all sides have come to agree on an antigovernment, antimilitary, anticorporate worldview. Common action by groups coming from different ideological positions has been demonstrated in resistance to global economics and the opening of international markets. Violent extremists from the left and the right have adopted the secret cell form of organization for leaderless resistance (Arnold, 1997).

The outcome of the battle against the forces of economic globalism, or McWorld, waged by the forces of jihad, or religious extremism by whatever name, remains unresolved. This essential conflict between universalism and separatism continues to fuel domestic and international terrorism into the 21st century (Barber, 1992).

HIGHLIGHTS OF REPRINTED ARTICLES

The two readings selected for this chapter are particularly relevant to the right-wing radical terrorism that was of concern in the United States at the end of the 20th century, but their significance carries forward into the future. The concerns expressed by the authors are relevant whether terrorism is transnational or homegrown in the United States.

Jonathan R. White. (2001). "Political Eschatology: A Theology of Antigovernment Extremism." *American Behavioral Scientist*, 44(6), 937-956.

Jonathan White considers the connections between racist and religious violence in the United States. The term *eschatology* derives from Greek and is usually interpreted as "the final judgment." White finds that an eschatological philosophy is tailor-made for terrorists who have rejected the material world and believe that the norms of social behavior no longer matter. He describes the extremist right and its objective of restating religious mythology as a call to violence. As the extremist movements intertwined racism with religion, common elements appeared. According to White, one of the most prominent features is rejection of modernity. Another factor is the belief in a conspiracy of evil forces. Still another common theme running through the extremist right is anti-Semitism. What is of most concern is the utter endorsement of firearm ownership and belief in guns as the mainstays of U.S. society.

Philip Jenkins. (1999). "Fighting Terrorism as if Women Mattered: Anti-Abortion Violence as Unconstructed Terrorism." In Jeff Ferrell & Neil Websdale (Eds.), *Making Trouble: Cultural Constructions of Crime, Deviance, and Control.* New York: Aldine de Gruyter.

Philip Jenkins covers the impact of definition on how terrorism is treated. Using the example of anti-abortion violence, which was identified by law enforcement agencies and justice system policies as protest rather than terrorism, Jenkins points out the significance of labels for policy and the particular bias of the FBI definition of terrorism. The article also discusses the dependence of news organizations and academics on official voices about terrorists. The author's premise is that although actions of the Christian ultraright members involved in anti-abortion violence do not reflect orders from some organizational center, they parallel the actions of other violent groups classified as terrorists.

EXPLORING HOMEGROWN TERRORISM FURTHER

- Two organizations provide in-depth and up-to-date information about hate crimes and hate groups: Southern Poverty Law Center (www.splcenter.org) and the Anti-Defamation League (www.adl.org).
- The Court TV Web site (www.courttv.com) provides extensive information about the Symbionese Liberation Army (SLA), including a chronology of its terrorist actions.
- To follow the operations and ideology of terrorists active in the United States today, it is useful to spotlight two groups: the Animal Liberation Front (ALF) and Earth Firsters or Earth Liberation Front (ELF). A good source for information is the Terrorist Research Center (www.terrorism.com), but stories about these organizations pop up in many sites.
- For more analysis and suggestions for strategies to reduce the violence of neo-Nazi skinheads see Blazak (2001).

VIDEO NOTES

Homegrown, right-wing, white supremacist, anti–U.S. government inspired terrorism has seldom been scrutinized in films. *Betrayed* (Metro-Goldwyn-Mayer, 1988, 112 min.) is one chilling, though dated, exception.

REFERENCES

Abanes, Richard. (1996). *American militias: Rebellion, racism and religion*. Downers Grove, IL: InterVarsity Press.

ABC News. (2001, January 30). ELF making good on threat. Retrieved June 6, 2002, from http://abcnews.go.com/sections/us/DailyNews/elf010130.html

American Psychological Association. (1998). Hate crimes today: An age-old foe in modern dress. Retrieved June 6, 2002, from www.apa.org/pubinfo/hate

Anti-Defamation League. (1999). *The Farrakhan library.* Retrieved June 6, 2002, from www.adl.org

Arnold, Ron. (1997). *Ecoterror*. Bellevue, WA: The Free Enterprise Press.

Barber, Benjamin R. (1992). Jihad vs. McWorld. *Atlantic Monthly, 169*(3), 53-65.

Blazak, Randy. (2001). White boys to terrorist men. *American Behavioral Scientist, 44*(6), 982-1000.

Blythe, Will. (2000, June 8). The guru of white hate. *Rolling Stone*, p. 99.

A brief history of the Trail of Tears. (n.d.). Retrieved June 25, 2002, from www.cherokee.org/culture/historypage.asp?ID=2

Chowder, Ken. (2000). The father of American terrorism. *American Heritage, 51*(1), p. 68.

Earth First! (2001, February-March). *21*(3).

Enders, Walter, & Sandler, Todd. (2000). Is transnational terrorism becoming more threatening? *Journal of Conflict Resolution, 44*(3), 307-322.

Golden Ink. (n.d.). *About North Georgia: The Trail of Tears*. Retrieved June 25, 2002, from http://ngeorgia.com/history/nghisttt.html

Guidelines. (2000, Spring). *Underground*, p. 25.

Hamm, Mark. (1998). Terrorism, hate crime, and antigovernment violence. In Harvey Kushner (Ed.), *The future of terrorism*. Thousand Oaks, CA: Sage.

Harmon, Christopher. (2000). *Terrorism today*. London: Frank Cass.

Hearst, Patricia. (1982). *Every secret thing*. Garden City, NY: Doubleday.

Herman, Edward S. (1982). *The real terror network*. Boston: South End Press.

Hoffman, Bruce. (1998). *Inside terrorism*. New York: Columbia University Press.

Indian Removal Act of 1830, 4 Stat. 411 (1830).

Jacobs, Ron. (1997). *The way the wind blew.* London: Verso.

Jenkins, Philip. (1999). Fighting terrorism as if women mattered: Anti-abortion violence as unconstructed terrorism. In Jeff Ferrell & Neil Websdale (Eds.), *Making trouble: Cultural constructions of crime, deviance, and control*. New York: Aldine de Gruyter.

Kupfer, David. (2001, February/March). Luddism in the new millennium: An interview with Kirkpatrick Sale. *Earth First!, 21*(3). Retrieved June 25, 2002, from http://yeoldeconsciousnessshoppe.com/art42.html

McGuckin, Frank. (Ed.). (1997). *Terrorism in the United States.* New York: H. W. Wilson.

Miller, Joseph, & Miller, R. M. (2000). *Ecoterrorism and ecoextremism against agriculture*. Chicago: Miller Publications.

Millies, Stephen. (1995, January 26). The Ludlow Massacre and the birth of company unions. *Workers World*. Retrieved June 26, 2002, from www.Hartford-hwp.com/archives/45b/030

Muhammad, Elijah. (1999). My mission and objective. *The Supreme Wisdom, 2*. Retrieved June 25, 2002, from www.muhammadspeaks.com/Objective.html

Oates, Stephen B. (1979). *Our fiery trial: Abraham Lincoln, John Brown, and the Civil War era*. Amherst: University of Massachusetts Press.

Pierce, William (writing as Andrew MacDonald). (1996). *The Turner diaries* (2nd ed.). Hillsboro, WV: National Vanguard Books.

Pitcavage, Mark. (2001). The militia movement from Ruby Ridge to Y2K. *American Behavioral Scientist, 44*(6), 957-981.

Ranstorp, Magnus. (2000). Religious terror. In Laura Egendorf (Ed.), *Terrorism: Opposing viewpoints*. San Diego: Greenhaven Press.

Rapoport, David C. (2000). Democracy encourages terror. In Laura Egendorf (Ed.), *Terrorism: Opposing viewpoints*. San Diego: Greenhaven Press.

Rubenstein, R. E. (1987). *Alchemists of revolution*. New York: Basic Books.

Sadler, A. E., & Winters, Paul A. (1996). *Urban terrorism*. San Diego: Greenhaven.

Sale, Kirkpatrick. (1995). *Rebels against the future*. New York: Addison-Wesley.

Simonsen, Clifford E., & Spindlove, Jeremy R. (2000). *Terrorism today: The past, the players, the future*. New York: Prentice Hall.

Snow, Robert. (1999). *The militia threat: Terrorists among us.* New York: Plenum.

Southern Poverty Law Center. (2000a, Fall). Snarling at the white man. *Intelligence Report.* Retrieved June 25, 2002, from www.splcenter.org/cgi-bin/printassist.pl?page=intelligence-project/ip-4p2.html

Southern Poverty Law Center. (2000b, Fall). The new romantics. *Intelligence Report.* Retrieved June 25, 2002, from www.splcenter.org/cgi-bin/printassist.pl?page=intelligenceproject/ip-4q9.html

Staples, Brent. (2002, February 1). Enter Patty Hearst, and other ghosts from the 60's. *The New York Times.* Retrieved June 6, 2002, from www.crimelynx.com/patty60.html

Sterngold, James. (2002, January 18). New evidence paved way for arrests in a '75 killing. *The New York Times.* Retrieved June 6, 2002, from www.rickross.com/reference/symbionese/symbionese16.html

Wasserman, Jim. (2002, February 1). Ex-SLA members get $1M bail. *Associated Press.* Retrieved February 4, 2002, from http://story.news.yahoo.com/news?tmpl=story&u=/ap/20020201/ap_on_re_us/sla_bail_1&printer=1

White, Jonathan R. (1998). *Terrorism.* Belmont, CA: Wadsworth.

White, Jonathan R. (2001). Political eschatology: A theology of antigovernment extremism. *American Behavioral Scientist, 44*(6), 937-956.

Wieviorka, Michel. (1993). *The making of terrorism.* (David G. White, Trans.). Chicago: University of Chicago Press.

Zulaika, Joseba, & Douglas, William. (2000). Variations on terrorism. In Laura Egendorf (Ed.), *Terrorism: Opposing viewpoints.* San Diego: Greenhaven Press.

POLITICAL ESCHATOLOGY

A Theology of Antigovernment Extremism

JONATHAN R. WHITE

This article explores apocalyptic theology in four American extremist religions: Christian Identity; Nordic Christianity and Odinism; violent, "freewheeling" fundamentalism; and Creatorism. It is argued that violent eschatology interacts with criminology in the sense that politicized religions produce criminal behavior and, at times, terrorism. A brief history of the relationship between religion and racist violence is presented as well as an analysis of the social factors that produce political eschatology. The article concludes with an examination of religious terrorism and technological weapons. Mass destruction is the greatest threat of religiously motivated terrorism.

Religious violence in the name of a holy cause is nothing new in the history of conflict, and terrorism in the new millennium will be influenced by resurgent fundamentalism and religious doctrines of violent intolerance. This will be especially true when religious dogmas embrace eschatological or "end-of-time" theology. The purpose of this article is to explore criminological aspects of eschatology as it is expressed in domestic, right-wing, racist violence and extremism. Two methodologies are employed: historical-descriptive analysis and theological explication. After defining some basic parameters, the article begins by placing right-wing extremism in the context of American history. This is followed by a description of recent events that have spurred the growth of the radical right. A theological discussion follows the historical segment. It is composed of an analysis of commonalties among right-wing religions, an examination of factors that must be present to form a theology of hate, and a critique of the mythology of hate.

It is legitimate to ask if a theological analysis of terrorism is criminologically valid. After all, criminology deals with the science of human behavior, whereas theology deals with an investigation of a divine realm outside objective experience. On the surface, it would appear that theology and criminology cannot be satisfactorily combined. Yet, beneath the surface lies a conjunction that invites a combination of methods. Religious behavior is a factor that shapes social constructs, and it may be positive or negative, social or antisocial. Theological constructs interact with criminology when they are the bases for negative human behavior and when they influence moral, conforming actions. The theological analysis in this article focuses on racist religion as a motivation for violent behavior. In essence, it is an attempt to explain the ideology of hate in religious terms. As such, it presents a valid topic for criminological analysis.

DEFINITIONS

Before beginning the historical and theological analyses of right-wing extremism, it is necessary to define basic terms and parameters. The term *eschatology* derives from the Greek word εσχατοζ, a concept dealing with the end of all material and purpose in time and space. In the hellenized version of the Hebrew Bible, eschatology is usually interpreted as the "day of Yahweh"; that is, a final judgment and the realization of God's purpose for creation. This Jewish idea influenced early Christian writers, but the meaning of God's final presence fluctuated in early Christian dogma (Kittel, 1964, p. 697). Christians have expected God's final judgment for 2,000 years, yet they have not agreed on the form it will take. Crossan (1999, pp. 257-287) describes four commonly held eschatological frameworks: ascetic, apocalyptic, ethical, and political. Ascetic eschatology refers to the process of self-denial, whereas the apocalyptic version envisions God's destruction of the existing order. Ethical eschatology, according to Crossan, is quite different. It calls for followers to embrace radically moral behavior in recognition of God's imminent reign. Crossan says that political eschatology is frequently ignored today because it combines expectations of religious judgment with political action. People fear political eschatology. Lewy (1974, p. 40) agrees, arguing that linking political beliefs with an end-of-time theology is a prescription for violence. Given the variety of meanings attached to eschatological expectations, it is not surprising to find that American right-wing extremists have developed their own philosophy of the "end of the age" in various apocalyptic theologies. As Lewy implies, some of these theologies are indeed quite dangerous.

As the new millennium conjures prophecies of doom in some circles, it also brings the threat of increased terrorist violence. There are people who would like to violently usher in the new *eschaton*, and religious terrorism has increased over the past decade (Hoffman, 1995). An eschatological philosophy is tailor made for individual terrorists who have rejected both the material world and the norms of social behavior. It provides a cosmic battlefield where forces for good are called to fight some unspeakable evil.

The consequences are dramatic; indeed, they are cosmic in proportion. All deterrents to violence have been rendered meaningless by the promise of the new *eschaton*. When violent eschatology is politicized on a cosmic battlefield, Armageddon's warriors need no further justification to bear arms. They fight for a holy cause, and all actions are justified.

The term *right-wing religion*, as used in this article, refers to belief systems that incorporate some form of hatred or racism in their basic doctrines. There are four prominent forms of these theologies in America today: Christian Identity, Nordic Christianity or Odinism, freewheeling fundamentalism, and Creatorism. These theologies are extremist religions based on the demonization of other racial, religious, or national groups. This article neither refers to mainstream conservative American religious movements nor attempts to critique Christian fundamentalism. Fundamentalists and conservative Christians differ from their racialist counterparts in that the conservatives base their value system on universal love, they believe that God's actions in history have yet to take place, and they feel they will be raptured into heaven prior to a general tribulation (Barkun, 1997, pp. 105-119; White, 1986). The militant extremists examined in this article believe they must fight to create conditions conducive for the *eschaton*.

Christian Identity is a theology that grew from a 19th-century concept known as Anglo-Israelism. Its basic tenet is that the ancient tribes of Israel were Caucasians who migrated to Europe shortly after the death of Jesus. Whites are actually the descendants of the chosen tribes of Israel, and Whites are asked to identify with the Israelites of old. Christian Identity is strongly anti-Semitic, claiming that humans originated from "two seed lines." Whites are directly descended from God, whereas Jews originated from an illicit sexual union between the devil and the first White woman. Non-White races evolved from animals and are categorized as subhumans. Identity Christians believe that biblical covenants apply only to the White race and that Jesus of Nazareth was not a Jew but the White Israelite son of God. Christian Identity views are championed by Aryan Nations, a variety of prominent Identity pastors, Posse Comitatus, and the American Institute of Theology.

Nordic Christianity or Odinism is a hybrid form of Christianity and old Norse religion. It exists in two forms. On one hand, Nordic Christianity combines a pantheon of Nordic gods under the triune deity of Christianity. Odin, Thor, and other Nordic gods serve Christ by militantly protecting the White Norse race. Pure Odinism, on the other hand, ignores Christian concepts. It simply involves the resurrection of old Nordic mythology and the acceptance of the Nordic pantheon. After enjoying a rebirth in 19th-century Germany, Odinism migrated to the United States through the neo-Nazi movement. Both forms of Nordic religion call for the militant defense of race, bloodlines, and homeland.

Another form of militant, right-wing Christianity can simply be called free-wheeling fundamentalism. This form of religion rejects both the blatant racism of Christian Identity and the hybrid nature of Nordic religions. The free-wheelers are fiercely patriotic and use religion to reinforce social beliefs, values, and behavior. They tend to believe that the federal government is not mystically evil but that it is opposed to the reign of God. They also believe that agents of the government are in conspiracy to destroy America's monetary system and national sovereignty. Many of these groups oppose racism, and some claim that they are not anti-Semitic. Freewheeling fundamentalism is the religion of the patriot movement and the gun-show circuit.

The last form of religion discussed in this article is called Creatorism, a religion originating with the World Church of the Creator (WCOTC). Founded by Ben Klassen, the WCOTC is secular, deistic, and racist. Klassen's purpose was to divorce White people from weak, theistic religions, claiming that such religions were ridiculous expressions of utopian ideals. The Creator, Klassen said, placed things in motion and left people on their own. Klassen's slogan was "Our race is our religion." Creating his own mythology in tracts on naturalistic health and in *The White Man's Bible* (Klassen, 1986), he called on White people to fight Jews, non-White races, and Whites who disagreed with racist philosophy. His successor, Matt Hale, who has taken the secular title Pontifex Maximus from Julius Caesar, endorses conflict to protect the White race. The cry of Creatorists is "RAHOWA," an acronym for "racial holy war."

A HISTORY OF RIGHT-WING RELIGIOUS HATE

In 1995, when reports of the bombing of the federal building in Oklahoma City began to flow from the media, many Americans were surprised to hear of a twisted religion called Christian Identity. Some of them asked about its origins and questioned the belief system of its strange ideology. Was it a new racist religion? Did it have a theological base? Were Christian Identity churches included in mainstream Protestantism? The answer to these and many other questions can be found in the history of ethnocentrically based right-wing religions.

When the first Congregationalists landed at Plymouth in 1620, they brought a feeling of Protestant determinism to the shores of the new world. Hudson (1981, pp. 36-41) states that the Congregationalists hoped to create a new city set on a hill to shine a religious light for the entire world. Albeit unintentionally, the light soon refracted into a multiplicity of scattered divisions. Such continual divisions characterized early American religion.

Marty (1984) states that America has been a land of many religions despite the dominant influence of Protestantism on the popular culture. Native Americans had their own forms of religion, and each group of immigrants came to America with its unique mores, culture, and religious values. Every religious congregation became, in Marty's words, a Pilgrim in its own land, but this did not sit well with the established original Protestant settlers. Beginning in the 19th century, groups of "native" Americans, primarily Protestant, began to form protective associations to dispel the influence of immigrant groups and "foreign" religions (White, 1986). The emergence of the Know Nothings just before the Civil War serves as an appropriate example. An urban, Protestant movement, the Know Nothings formed a secret anti-Catholic society to discourage emigration from Ireland.

The Know Nothings could not compete with the hate-filled religions that emerged after 1865. The most notorious group in the immediate post-Civil War period was the Ku Klux Klan (KKK). The Klan has undergone three distinct phases in its history, starting with an organizational period after the Civil War (Chalmers, 1987). The 1920s brought a conservative attempt to gain mainstream political power, and the Klan entered its current phase after World War II, emphasizing rhetoric, political violence, and fragmentation. The Klan's initial ideology did not lay the foundation for a unified movement, but one factor has remained constant in KKK history: It is a religious organization, and Klansmen base their hatred on the rhetoric of American Protestantism. As a result, the ideology of the Klan and the theology of Christian Identity go hand in hand (Sargent, 1995, pp. 139-143).

Other extremist, right-wing movements also embraced religious rhetoric. The radical grangers of the far West and other agrarian movements of the 19th century laced their political positions with religious phrases. Xenophobic religious zealots began appearing in the 1930s, calling for an uncompromising ethnocentric adoration of the United States and a blind acceptance of religious doctrine. The Depression witnessed the continued blossoming of militant Protestantism, and elements of the Roman Catholic church joined the fray. Marty (1984, pp. 373-389) argues that the clash between modern and traditional theology provided an environment conducive to linking conservative Protestants and Catholics.

At issue, Marty (1984) states, was the clash between the modern world and the traditional one. Traditional values were challenged by modernity, and all forms of American Christianity had to meet the modern world in one way or another. World War I created a momentary illusion of religious unity in America, but the Jazz Age and the Roaring Twenties brought an end to the superficial unification. A dividing line formed, Marty argues, between traditional values and emerging morality. In separate works, Berger (1980, pp. 56-60) and Berlet (1998) arrive at similar conclusions. The traditional dividing lines between Protestants and Catholics began to fade in the Great Depression as Christians began to argue over the fundamental concepts of religion. Both Catholics and Protestants produced champions who defended traditional fundamentals, while each side also produced

those who embraced modernization. As the Catholic and Protestant conservatives moved closer together, the extremists in each camp were not far behind.

Father Charles E. Coughlin rose to fame in the 1930s through the medium of radio. His message was one of xenophobia, anti-Semitism, and blind patriotism. Although Catholic, his words resonated with fundamental American Protestants. Dr. Theodore Stoddard, for example, joined the fray with a rash of racially motivated, anticommunist rhetoric. He called for selective Nordic breeding to eliminate both racial impurity and communism. Other Protestants turned their concerns to Judaism, blaming the Jews for not only being "Christ killers" but for ushering in the age of modernity (Marty 1984, pp. 390-400). Right-wing extremism was ripe for a champion.

Such a figure emerged in the person of Wesley Swift (Holden, 1986). A California radio preacher, Swift uncovered a 19th-century British doctrine called Anglo-Israelism. In a nutshell, Anglo-Israelism claimed that White people in the British Isles were descended from the tribes of ancient Israel (Barkun, 1997, pp. 1-14). The house of David was, in fact, the ruling house of Scotland. According to this doctrine, the other White nations of northern Europe were the true Israelites and the actual heirs to God's promises to the Hebrew patriarchs. Barkun (1997, p. 60) says that Swift modified the doctrine of Anglo-Israelism to fit the United States so that American Whites could lay claim to being Israelites. He encouraged Whites to identify with the ancient Israelites, giving rise to the notion of Identity or Christian Identity. Two of the people influenced by Swift's message were William Potter Gale and a young engineer named Richard Butler. Gale went on to create a militant antitax group known as Posse Comitatus, while Butler left a corporate job to found the most influential Christian Identity church in America, Aryan Nations.

Conspiracy theories also emerged in the 20th century. The American extremist right held that Christianity was under attack by a secret group of secular scientists known as The Order of the Illuminati. Berlet (1998) argues that Adam Weishaupt, an 18th-century Bavarian professor of canon law, was frustrated by the lack of intellectual activity in the priesthood. As a result, he formed a secret society called the Illuminati in 1775. The purpose of his secret society was to promote knowledge and rational discourse within the church, and branches of the Illuminati spread throughout Western Europe. Skeptical of any society that criticized religion and the social order, the Bavarian government banned the Illuminati in 1786. The Illuminati, however, were too entrenched to be eliminated by the actions of a single German state. Branches appeared in several European cities, and the organization spread.

Holden (1999) points out that the extremist right resurrected fear of the Illuminati after World War II, claiming that it was a secret group of intellectual elitists who systematically attacked Christianity. Today, many members of the patriot movement and other extremist groups believe that the Illuminati operate against White American Christians. They cite the pyramid on the back on the dollar bill as evidence that the Illuminati operate secretly in the American government.

Many sources of conspiracy exist in extremist minds. Berlet (1998) points to the Freemasons as one such source. Masonry had been at odds with the established church in Europe since the 1700s, and some members of the church charged the Masons with devil worship. Such a charge was too tempting for the radical right, and fear of the Masons began to spread in the mid-20th century. Fear of socialism, communism, and economic control also provided Protestant and Catholic extremists with "evidence" that groups of conspirators were plotting to destroy American rights. Berlet also points to the demonization of Judaism as a prime source for conspiracy theories.

Animosity between Judaism and Christianity originated in early Christian apologetics, and the history of Christianity is darkened with anti-Semitic strains. Yet, the American extremist right gave anti-Semitism a new twist. As Anglo-Israelism gained ground in the religious right, new "proof" of a global conspiracy emerged with the publication of *The Protocols of the Learned Elders of Zion*. Originally published as a French satire, Czarist police used *The Protocols* as an attempt to trump up evidence against Russian Jews. American industrialist Henry Ford's agent, a fierce anti-Semite named William Cameron, published *The Protocols* in English and distributed it to Ford workers (Barkun, 1997, p. 34). It is still cited by radical religious leaders as proof of a Jewish conspiracy against Christianity. Such conspiracy theories provided for the ideological underpinnings of right-wing religion following the World War II (White, 1997).

RECENT HISTORY OF ANTIGOVERNMENT EXTREMISM

American right-wing extremism fell out of vogue when left-wing violence grew in the 1960s and 1970s, but it experienced a rebirth around 1981. The rejuvenation came as shifting economic conditions threatened the social status of working-class Whites. Sapp (1985) describes the resurrection in terms of three distinct trends: White supremacy, religious extremism, and survivalism. The racial aspect of the movement solidified with the ideological unification of White supremacy under the banner of the Aryan Nations. Richard Butler, a disciple of Wesley Swift, formed a compound in Hayden Lake, Idaho, and his Aryan fortress provided the ideological soil to unite various Klan, Nazi, and other White supremacy groups. Butler became the most important actor in the American racist camp.

Sapp (1985) believes that religion played an important role in the right-wing resurgence, and, once again, he points to Butler. The Identity pastor Butler founded the Church of Jesus Christ, Christian in his White supremacy compound. As his power spread among the racists, his church became a beacon to unite Identity ministers throughout the country. Robert Miles of Cohoctah, Michigan, joined Butler with his own Mountain Church of Jesus. James Wickstrom preached an Identity message from the Sheriff's Posse Comitatus. Even William Pierce, the agnostic author of *The Turner Diaries*, joined the trend by sending his fictional protagonist Earl Turner through a religious experience when he encountered *The Book*. Christian Identity was the dominant force in the contemporary period of right-wing extremism.

Sapp (1985) cites survivalism as the third aspect of the rebirth of the extremist right. Spawned by fears of an impending race war and the collapse of government, survivalists retreated to heavily fortified compounds to ready themselves for Armageddon. Sapp also notes that extremists practiced a type of "dualism"; that is, participants in one type of group tended to share membership in another kind of group. For example, members of White supremacy groups could be found in survivalist camps or in Identity churches. Survivalism gave the extremist right its most militant potential.

Despite regeneration in the 1980s, right-wing extremism was in trouble by 1989. Smith (1994), in one of the best examinations of domestic terrorism available to the public, explains why. Right-wingers were simply not effective. The two groups that practiced the most violence, The Order and Posse Comitatus, actually turned other extremists away from the movement because they were appalled by actual murder. Like most potential terrorists, the majority of right-wingers were happier when practicing right-wing rhetoric. Ideology was safe, but violence was another matter. From a religious view, the hate-filled theology of Christian Identity had the same impact (White, 1998, pp. 217-224). Identity preachers called on their congregations to despise non-Whites and Jews. The call for hatred confused many potential followers, even though they believed in their own ethnic superiority. As a result, some Christian extremists evolved into freewheelers, and they broke from Identity congregations to form independent fundamentalist groups. By 1991, it seemed that right-wing extremism would become a thing of the past. Unfortunately, three issues reanimated the extremists (Stern, 1996, pp. 58-60).

After James Brady, President Ronald Reagan's press secretary, suffered a crippling brain injury in the assassination attempt on Reagan, Brady and his family became champions of gun control legislation. A bill named in his honor and subsequent federal gun control legislation sent an alarm throughout the extremist right. Guns, from the extremist perspective the one thing that could save the country, were under attack. As racists, millennialists, Identity theologians, and other extremists closed ranks, they found that they were on the fringe of a mainstream political issue. By 1991, they were taking theology to the gun show circuit to seek converts.

Two other sources of rejuvenation came in the form of armed confrontations with the federal government. In 1992, Randy Weaver failed to appear in court on a federal weapons violation charge. During the attempt to serve Weaver with a bench warrant, Weaver's son and a U.S. marshal were killed. Weaver barricaded his family in a mountain cabin in Ruby Ridge, Idaho, and challenged the government to come and get him. The situation was exacerbated when a Federal Bureau of Investigation (FBI) sniper killed Weaver's wife. Former Green Beret Lieutenant Colonel James "Bo" Gritz came to the scene to negotiate with Weaver, but the attention he drew helped turn Weaver's standoff at Ruby Ridge into a rallying point for the extremist right.

Closely related to the Weaver incident, at least in the minds of the extremist right, was a Bureau of Alcohol, Tobacco, and Firearms (ATF) raid on the Branch Davidian compound at Waco, Texas, in 1993. Armed with probable cause and a search warrant, ATF agents attempted to raid a religious cult compound to seize illegal firearms. They were met with overwhelming firepower and driven back after suffering more than a dozen casualties, including four agents who were killed. Although ATF agents successfully negotiated a cease-fire and managed to retrieve their wounded officers, FBI agents quickly came to the scene and assumed control. Three months later, the FBI assaulted the compound, only to find that the cult leader, Vernon Howell (a.k.a. David Koresh), had soaked the building with gasoline. More than 70 people were killed in the ensuing blaze, including all the children in the compound.

The Branch Davidian compound had little to do with the racist right, but it had all the elements the extremists loved: guns, a compound standing in the face of federal agents, and religion. Shortly after the failed FBI attack, John Trochmann revealed a new creation: the Militia of Montana. It was an organization, he claimed, designed to protect constitutional rights. Within months, militias popped up all over the United States, each with its own commander. The survivalists of the 1980s reemerged in the form of paramilitary groups, and survivalism has become the dominant theme of extremism at the turn of the millennium.

COMMON THEOLOGICAL ELEMENTS OF RIGHT-WING EXTREMISM

As the extremist movement intertwined racism with religion, common elements appeared in the message. One of the most prominent features of the extremist right is its rejection of modernity. It favors biblical literalism over modernism, and it remains centered in Protestantism despite the influence of some Catholic extremists. By the same token, it should not be described as fundamentalism or confused with conservative Christianity. The xenophobic religion of the extremist right does not accept the Christian call for universal love only; it accepts the idea of love for one's own kind. As a result, right-wing extremism is defined by hate. One does not simply love, one loves in conjunction with hate. For example, one loves Christians because one hates everyone who is not a Christian. One loves Whites because one hates everyone who is not White. Religion is defined by exclusivity.

Barkun (1997, pp. 104-108) also notes that racial extremists in the movement have another profound theological difference with American Christian fundamentalists. Both fundamentalists and extremists tend to be premillenialists; that is, they believe that Jesus of Nazareth will return prior to a 1,000-year reign of peace described in Revelation. Most fundamentalists contend that the Second Coming of Christ will unfold according to biblical prophecies, and believers will experience a rapture prior to Christ's return. Extremists, especially in the Christian Identity movement, believe that prophecies have already been fulfilled and that no rapture will take place. As a result, believers will be forced to endure a 7-year tribulation before the Second Coming. Extremists believe that they must be prepared for the tribulation, and survivalism is a common theme in extremist theology. They are called to prepare militantly for Christ's return.

Another factor emerging from the history of the extremist right is the belief in a conspiracy of evil forces. Each group of extremists endorses some concept of conspiracy, and although the source of conspiracy changes, the belief in conspiracy has remained historically constant. In the 1930s, Father Coughlin preached about an antireligious conspiracy of satanic origin, and after World War II, Wesley Swift and others endorsed this view. Reflecting the mainstream culture, preachers pointed to a conspiracy of communism. As conspiracy theories emerged in the second half of the 20th century, right-wing extremists began to develop a list of potential conspirators that included local governments that fluoridated water supplies, U.S. industrial leaders, international economic groups, the U.S. government, and, eventually, the United Nations. Christian Identity ministers could not make peace with either the Roman Catholic church or with conservative Protestants. They added televangelists and the Vatican to groups of conspiracy theories. In such a world, anything that is not in the extremist camp is potentially involved in a conspiracy of evil.

The most common theme running through the extremist right is anti-Semitism. Regardless of who is blamed for the conspiracy against American values, all right-wingers seem to agree on one point: They find Judaism at the base of the problem. Christian Identity sees Judaism as the result of a cosmic battle between God and the Devil. Even extremists who walked away from religion, such as William Pierce, found Jews to be contemptible. Many claimed that Judaism was behind the periodic economic crises of capitalism because they believed that Jewish bankers controlled the money supply. Christian Identity ministers even claimed that Jewish bankers and the Pope worked in collusion.

It is legitimate to ask how such an extreme, almost nonsensical philosophy of hatred could become popular. The answer can be found in the social structure of extremist groups. In many instances, they tend to be lower-working-class Whites with little formal education. They tend to follow the precepts of traditional, literalized religion, and conspiracies of bankers, Jews, communists, and the United Nations seem to make sense. Similar to members of the old Know Nothing movement of the 19th century, they believe that immigrants and racial minorities are at the base of their decreasing economic status. Blood hatred is endemic to right-wing theology.

A final commonality can be found in the utter endorsement of firearms. The only ultimate protection for White, working-class men, in extremist ideology, is the gun. It will stop a variety of social ills and protect true Americans even as the United Nations attempts to trample constitutional rights. Guns are the mainstays of American society. Finch (1983) sums it up well by describing the right-wing movement as "God, guts, and guns." Gibson (1994) describes it as a displaced desire to fulfill the role of the warrior male. Regardless, the extremist right is a full participant in America's love affair with guns.

Theological commonalties in the extremist right separate the realm of God from the realm of evil. Berlet (1998) says that the right wing sees dichotomies between Christ and the Antichrist, between spirituality and materiality, and between fundamentalism and modernism. The nature of such separations gives rise to religious conflict. God is wholly in partnership with Christ, spirituality, and fundamentalism against the Devil and the dark forces of the cosmos. This is a dualistic, Manichaean struggle between right and wrong. In this atmosphere, Christianity must take a stand against Judaism for the sake of creation, and Christians must stand for the constitution in the face of socialism, economic conspiracies, or the New World Order. This process does not simply separate one camp from the other, it calls the chosen into a holy war with drastic consequences. If the holy warrior loses, God's creation is lost.

A THEOLOGY OF TERRORISM

Theology creates neither violence nor terrorist behavior, but it can provide an atmosphere that justifies an attack on social structures. Three circumstances must be present to motivate believers to move from thought to violent action: (a) believers must perceive a terminal threat to their religious values and attitudes; (b) a theology embracing cosmic salvation, universal love, or wordly peace must be transformed into a dogma of nationalistic, racial, or some other ethnocentrically based protectionism; and (c) the true believers among the faithful must embrace violence as a means for preserving the faith. When these three circumstances are present, terrorism becomes part of a theological process.

Perceived Terminal Threat to Religious Values and Attitudes

Walter Laqueur (1996) argues that the structure of terrorism has evolved throughout the 20th century, and the new millennium will witness yet another metamorphosis as religion becomes one of the dominant factors in terrorist violence. Eschatological religious movements are sweeping the globe and affecting violent fringe elements. Referring to this process as "apocalypse soon," Laqueur points to the presence of eschatological references in mainstream politics, and he believes that religion will become the primary influence on terrorist behavior. The danger in the process, Laqueur argues, is that eschatological terrorists want to "give history a push."

Although Laqueur's (1996) primary unit of analysis is international terrorism, his conclusions are applicable to right-wing domestic extremism. Economic changes and global politics have created conditions that threaten the status of White, working-class men. Despite the economic boom of the 1990s, uneducated White men have not prospered in the global economy, and they lack the educational tools to do so (Hamm, 1994, pp. 105-149). Economic displacement is a real threat, and their anxiety has been exacerbated by heated debates in mainstream American Christianity over such issues as the authority of the Bible, the nature of Christ, and the role of culture in religion. The extremists feel that their world is falling apart, and they are looking for a place to stand. Yet, not every threatened group embraces an extremist theology. Why is the right wing so prone to idiosyncratic theologies? Why do some people embrace ethnocentric religion as a means of social salvation? Martin Marty and Peter Berger have separate but complementary answers.

Marty and Appleby (1991, 1993) argue that the movement toward intolerant fundamentalism is part of an international trend. In a lengthy project that resulted in a five-volume series on fundamentalist religions, Marty and Appleby

(1991, pp. vi-xii) find that the retreat to traditional, militant religion is a global phenomenon. They argue that fundamentalism is a defense against forces of change and that people will defend themselves by grabbing the traditions of the past. Militant fundamentalists fight for God, and they fight under God's leadership. Religion becomes the glue that provides group identity and cohesion. It copes with a confusing social situation by rejecting all threats. Only the fundamentals are safe; everything else is relegated to the realm of the unholy.

Berger (1980, pp. 3-29) makes the same argument from a slightly different vantage point. He argues that the modern world is in collision with traditional values. People cope with this situation in one of three differing ways: rejecting change, coping with change, or seeking new ideologies that preserve tradition within change. Those who reject change may turn to militant protectionism. The logical extension of Berger's argument is that violence can become a method for protecting the traditional world. By applying Berger's thesis to the theology of the extremist right, the logic of intolerance becomes apparent. Right-wing extremism is trying to recapture some idealized element of America's past. Extremists long for the days of White American Protestantism, and some of them will fight for it.

The extremist right looks at change through the spectacles of political eschatology. In other words, there are cosmic consequences if they fail to restore White America. Change does not simply represent social evolution, it is a direct confrontation with evil. In right-wing theology, an incarnate evil force is struggling with a creating deity for control of the world, and the Devil has the same power as God. When threatened with modernity, change, multiculturalism, taxes, or any number of other concepts, extremists cannot compromise. Fanatics who cannot compromise are willing, as Laqueur (1996) says, to give history a push.

Carl D. Haggard, commander of the United States Special Field Forces Militia, provides an example of this logic (Bushart, Craig, & Barnes 1998, p. 219). Haggard believes that the U.S. government has declared war on Christian men and women. He claims that he has no concern with racism or multiculturalism but that he fears

the government is out of control. Haggard fears centralized government power, and his faith tells him to expect individual freedom. There are hundreds of Identity Christians, freewheelers, and others who espouse the same beliefs with a few twists. Most of their actions are rhetorical, and most of them retreat from actual violence. Other extremists, such as Timothy McVeigh, feel they must take action. Former Identity pastor Kerry Noble (1998) says the primary motivation for action is religious faith.

Transforming Universality to Ethnocentrism

For religion to play a dominant role in violence, it is necessary to transform a transcendent message of universality into ethnocentric protectionism. In the case of American Protestantism, there is a tension between two poles. On one hand, Christians are told to embrace everyone. The apostle Paul (Gal. 3:28-29, New Revised Standard Version), for example, states that there is neither Gentile nor Jew, slave nor free, nor women nor man; all are one in Christ. He argues (Rom. 8) that the Christ event provided cosmic unification. Some theologians (Fox, 1988, pp. 129-154; Kung, 1995, pp. 782-789; Rowe, 1994, pp. 127-152) argue that this call varies little from many of the world's religions, and it has roots in secular, Western philosophy. Kung even argues that such logic is the basis for unification and understanding among three sister religions: Judaism, Christianity, and Islam. On the other hand, Christian communities have not historically embraced everyone. It is harrowing in some circles—indeed, it is frequently blasphemous—to include those who do not believe, behave, or worship in a particular way. American Protestantism, and most other religions, exist somewhere in the tension between these two poles.

The growth of violent Christian extremism in the United States involves a willingness of some groups to embrace the pole defining orthodox behavior and to subjugate it to ethnocentric rather than transcendent norms. Universalism is out of the question from this perspective. God's love is only applicable to those who believe, look, think, and act like members of the ethnic group. Right-wing love is reserved only for its own kind. This is the logic behind the extremist right's "Christian patriotism." Right-wing theologians have called for the death of lower-case *c* Christians, and White, militant patriots argue that patriotism is reserved only for those with the proper Christian beliefs (White, 1986, 1997).

The WCOTC serves as a perfect example of ethnocentric transformation. The creed of the church is "our religion is our race," and even a cursory review of WCOTC writings reveals the emphasis on love of one's own kind. On the church's Web site, Hale (1999) writes that the Creator makes a distinction between his loved ones and his enemies. In addition, the Creator expects followers to use love and hate in a constructive manner. Whites are to be loved, all other people are to be hated. Hale goes even further in the "Sixteen Commandments":

> Remember that the inferior mud races are our deadly enemies, and the most dangerous of all is the Jewish race. . . . The guiding principle of all your actions shall be: What is best for the White Race? . . . Do not employ niggers or other coloreds. . . . Destroy and banish all Jewish thought and influence from society. . . . Throughout your life you shall faithfully uphold our pivotal creed of Blood, Soil, and Honor. (Hale, 1999)

Ben Klassen (1986) states that Christianity is a suicidal religion indulging in a world of fantasy and make-believe. Nature's religion, on the other hand, calls believers to life by telling them to fight for their survival. A passage from his *The White Man's Bible* is quoted on the WCOTC Web site: "When I say 'our' survival, I am talking about the White Race, since I am not a bird, or an alligator, or a nigger, or an Indian." Such attitudes clearly indicate the nature of right-wing extremism. In a process of ethnocentric transformation, a potential call for universal love is transformed into ethnocentric love. The by-product is hatred for anyone outside the group.

Bruce (1993, pp. 50-67), writing in the Marty-Appleby project, provides a description of the process of ethnocentric transformation. Examining the conflict in Northern Ireland and comparing it to the rise of the mainstream religious right in the United States, Bruce finds two differing trends in fundamentalism. In Ireland, for example, the struggle focuses on ethnic identity and fighting associated with the birth of a political entity. If one is labeled *Catholic*, it does not necessary imply that one's life is subjugated to Catholic theology. Being Catholic can mean that one is fighting for ethnic identity against Protestants. The same principle is applicable to Protestantism in Ireland. Ethnicity takes precedence over religious affinity, and religious identification becomes part of ethnic identity. A religious label in Ireland is synonymous with ethnic identification. Bruce finds the opposite situation in America's Christian right. Mainstream fundamentalism in the United States is not related to ethnic identification because of the American tradition of religious pluralism.

American extremism, however, is not in the same position as mainstream Christian conservatism. Right-wing extremists violently advocate the protection of their ethnic identity, making them more akin to Bruce's (1993) concept of emerging nationalism in Ireland. Ethnicity and political perspectives dominate the right-wing call to religion. Any transcendent experience designed to unite theological expressions is out of the question for right-wing extremists. Their purpose is not to seek compromise or even find their own enclave in a pluralistic environment. The purpose of the extremist right is to destroy the opposition. This becomes the basis for a call to arms.

True Believers and the Doctrine of Necessity

The perception of a threat and ethnocentric protectionism do not necessarily produce religious violence. Extremists need not turn to their weapons. They might, for example, withdraw from society or practice nonviolent forms of confrontation. Indeed, most extremists follow these paths. Violence is an extreme action that is embraced only by a few hard-core believers. The central question is, Why do some extremists cross the line from rhetoric to violence? H.H.A. Cooper (1977) provides the best answer in one of the early works on modern terrorism.

All terrorists must feel justified in their actions, and religious zealots are no different.

Cooper (1977) believes that terrorists are motivated by the same factors that influence everyone else, and they look for similar rewards for their behavior. Like most individuals, terrorists want neither to engage in violence nor to harm innocent victims. Terrorists, however, have a problem. They cannot accept the world as it is. Even though they know they will kill people by engaging in violence, terrorists reluctantly accept this burden because they cannot tolerate the status quo. Terrorists justify violence by convincing themselves that the injustices of society outweigh the amount of harm caused by their actions. Violence becomes necessary to save society from cosmic evil. Cooper refers to this as the "doctrine of necessity."

Cooper's (1977) theory applies to the religious warrior. Most of America's extremists are rhetorical. They call for violence, they go to Identity meetings and KKK rallies, they carry guns with various militias, and they declare "war" on the federal government. Smith (1994) points out that these "militants" quickly retreat from organizations whenever real violence takes place. Yet, there are those who differ from the extremists described by Smith. A violent few have planted bombs, driven through the streets killing minorities, ambushed police officers, attacked homosexuals, and entered day care centers to shoot children. These terrorists act from necessity. To them, maintaining the status quo does more damage than murdering innocent people. In an age when weapons of mass destruction are available to many disenfranchised groups, this becomes a frightening scenario.

RESTATING A MYTH

The theological danger of right-wing political eschatology is profound, perhaps even more profound than its adherents comprehend, and it is laced with potential violence. The reason is simple. In rejecting the dominant mythology of the age, they are restating the basis of human existence in terms of exclusivity and hate. In other words, they are restating mythology.

Eliade (1968) defines mythology as the sacred stories that bind a group together. The truth of the story is not in question, Eliade says;

rather, the myth contains the social truths that a group accepts as normative. Campbell (1990) defines this in terms of common elements. All myths have certain isomorphic properties. The same types of characters, images, and actions manifest themselves in the stories of various religions. A central question for Campbell (1985) focuses on religions based on love and those based on conflict. Mythology and violence can combine in ethnocentric religions.

To be sure, the history of religion is replete with examples of violent mythology used to justify ethnocentrism. Gottwald (1979), for example, traces the social development of ancient Israel in terms of its settlement of Canaan. According to his thesis, two groups of monotheistic Israelites, a group in the north worshipping El and a migrant group from the south loyal to Yahweh, joined forces for the political domination of Canaan. They cast their political struggle in religious terms, while sometimes conquering and sometimes coexisting with the Canaanites. Bright (1981, pp. 144-146) reinforces this view, claiming that the Israelites looked back on their struggle for Canaan and wrote its history through theological eyes. The result was an ethnocentric myth based on conquest.

The structure of modern mythology provides an atmosphere conducive to the birth and growth of new myths. Campbell (1988) states that our age has lost touch with the myths of the past and that we are searching for a grounding of our existence. Spong (1999) says it another way: Christianity (and by implication, Judaism and Islam) is based on mythological concepts that predate the Scientific Revolution, the Enlightenment, Darwin, and Freud. From Spong's perspective, the West is in a state of religious anomie. The myth must be restated, or it will die. This need not be a frightening or destructive process. Borg (1991) believes that it is possible to shape a new myth from the old structure in a very gentle fashion. Unfortunately, this is not the only alternative. Just as monotheistic Israelites pitted a militant God against the baals of the Canaanites, an emerging combative mythology can claim the hearts and minds of its people. In the case of right-wing eschatology, all deities are exceedingly violent.

It is beyond the scope of this article to critique completely the mythology of the extremist right, but it is worthwhile to present examples. Each of the four theologies discussed in this paper attempts to restate the mythological foundations of Christianity in violent terms. Christian Identity attempts to accomplish this by adopting Hebrew arguments of Jewish exclusivity and by embracing militant texts of the Hebrew Bible. For example, the Phinehas Priesthood, a nebulous, "leaderless" organization, justifies its existence by pointing to Numbers 25:1-16. In this text, a Hebrew priest kills an Israelite man and a Midianite woman for intermarrying. Phinehas priests cite this passage as God's call to purify the White race. Identity Christians use this passage to restate the Christian myth with a militant passion. Ironically, it is worth noting that Moses married a Midianite woman (Exod. 2:21). Extremists are not shy about removing biblical passages from their historical and social contexts.

The freewheelers of the patriot movement have also tried to create a mythology of violence by quoting passages out of context. A favorite quotation comes from Luke 22:35-38. In this passage, Jesus tells his followers to sell their cloaks to buy a sword as a symbolic act of spiritual struggle. This passage repeatedly appears at gun shows and was even quoted in The Covenant, the Sword, and the Arm of the Lord's *Defense Manual* (Covenant, the Sword, and the Arm of the Lord, 1982). When the disciples tell Jesus that they already have two swords, Jesus lets them know that they missed the point. Jesus' admonishment, however, is not cited on the gun show circuit. Other partial passages from Joshua, Judges, Daniel, Matthew, and Revelation are used to transform Christianity into a militant religion. John and Matthew are also frequently cited for their anti-Jewish rhetoric. As the Christian myth is restated in terms of hate, many followers believe that this is simply basic Christianity (Bushart et al., 1998, p. 107). They have no idea that by removing concepts from their social, historical, and theological foundations, they are proclaiming a new religion.

Klassen (1986) takes up similar lines in *The White Man's Bible*. In a tract entitled, *Never Again Through the Serpent's Eyes*, Klassen asks readers to imagine a pioneer woman in a cabin with her young children. A rattlesnake has entered the cabin and threatens to strike one of the children. Klassen poses a debate over the issue. From the liberal humanitarian view, he says, the woman should consider the situation from the snake's point of view. He has just as much right to strike the children as the children have to exist. Of course, Klassen concludes, this is foolish. The only sensible answer is to kill the snake. Theologically, the snake and the mother are in natural, eternal conflict. Nature tells her to destroy any species threatening her children. In his final point, Klassen argues that other races and religions are representative of other species.

Of course, Klassen knew that he was replacing mythology in the WCOTC. The same can be said of Nordic Christianity and Odinism. When Thor strikes the sky with his mighty hammer or Odin calls warriors to Valhalla, Odinists are blatantly substituting an ideological call to violence for a religious call to love. Warrior gods replace Christian archetypes, and the race is called to defend itself. A theology of peace will never serve the extremist right, and they seek to restate mythology in a call to violence.

THEOLOGICAL DANGERS

It is difficult to describe the feeling of grace to those who have not had a religious experience of peaceful revelation. Indeed, to many modern skeptics, the nature of religion seems to be bound in social conflict. The results can be seen in Ireland, where Protestants and Catholics still wage war on each other. It is also apparent in the Balkan Peninsula as ethnic hatred and ethnocentric religion result in the modern massacres. Media commentators speak about violent Islamic fundamentalists from the Middle East, and few Americans can forget the devastating scene in Oklahoma City where Identity extremists killed more than 200 people. In the wake of the new millennium, religious zealots seem to be peddling social conflict as they anxiously await the final struggle of Armageddon. To those who have not experienced peaceful transcendence, religion may seem to be a dark force written in a theology of blood.

This essay has examined the dark side of religious behavior. Religious conflict will dominate the early stages of the new millennium, and it will continue to appear in domestic extremism. Religious violence, especially in the form of terrorism, is a result of politicized eschatological expectations. Yet, religious conflict has swirled around the periphery of human experience in struggles ranging from dirty little wars to cataclysmic, long-term massacres. Why should it merit continued review today, especially with respect to right-wing extremism? Chip Berlet (1998) provides one of the best answers.

In an examination of the apocalyptic paradigm, Berlet (1998) argues that the extremist right's capacity to restate mythology in terms of a cosmic struggle between good and evil is a prescription for violence. Evil is conspiratorial in nature. Extremists believe that secret groups of elites or parasites from lower classes have plotted together to secretly control history. Right-wingers make illogical leaps from evidence to "prove" conspiratorial links, and they simplify social conflicts by blaming problems on a demonized group. They construct theological worlds that are impervious to outside criticism. Such groups have histories of violence.

Walter Laqueur (1999, p. 78) points to the potential for increased violence. The world of terrorism has been limited in the past by the technology available to terrorists and the reluctance of terrorists to use massively destructive force. The world has changed, Laqueur believes, and terrorism is increasingly dominated by religious fanatics. They have access to nuclear devices, chemical and biological weapons, and terminals for computer attacks. Religion gives terrorists the motivation to use such weapons.

Religious doctrines serve as the cement holding right-wing extremism in place. Among its four theological orientations (Christian Identity, Nordic Christianity or Odinism, freewheeling fundamentalism, and Creatorism), beliefs differ, but religion is the basis for claiming ethnic, racial, and national superiority. Other religions are demonized, and the ethnocentric proclamation of theology becomes the basis for violence and terrorism. Extremists have divided the world into the City of God and the City of Satan, and the fundamentalists are God's warriors. With access to weapons of mass destruction, Armageddon beckons warriors who have developed a mythology of hate. Political eschatology is not an abstract theological concept; it is a dangerous reality of the new century.

REFERENCES

Barkun, M. (1997). *Religion and the racist right: The origins of the Christian Identity movement* (2nd ed.). Chapel Hill: University of North Carolina Press.

Berger, P. L. (1980). *The heretical imperative: Contemporary possibilities of religious affirmation.* Garden City, NY: Anchor.

Berlet, C. (1998). *Dances with devils: How apocalyptic and millennialist themes influence right wings scapegoating and conspiracism* [Online]. Available: http://www.publiceye.org/Apocalyptic/Dances_with_Devils_TOC.htm

Borg, M. J. (1991). *Jesus: A new vision: Spirit, culture, and the life of discipleship.* San Francisco: Harper.

Bright, J. (1981). *A history of Israel.* Philadelphia: Westminster.

Bruce, S. (1993). Fundamentalism, ethnicity, and enclave. In M. E. Marty & R. S. Appleby (Eds.), *Fundamentalisms and the state* (pp. 28-49). Chicago: University of Chicago Press.

Bushart, H. L., Craig, J. R., & Barnes, M. (1998). *Soldiers of God: White supremacists and their holy war for America.* New York: Kensington.

Campbell, J. (1985). *The inner reaches of outer space: Metaphor as myth and religion.* New York: A. van der Marck.

Campbell, J. (1988). *The power of myth.* New York: Doubleday.

Campbell, J. (1990). *The hero with a thousand faces.* Princeton, NJ: Princeton University Press.

Chalmers, D. M. (1987). *Hooded Americanism: The history of the Ku Klux Klan.* Durham, NC: Duke University Press.

Cooper, H. H. A. (1977). What is a terrorist? A psychological perspective. *Legal Medical Quarterly, 1,* 8-18.

The Covenant, the Sword, and the Arm of the Lord. (1982). *Defense manual.* Zorapath-Horeb, MO: Author.

Crossan, J. D. (1999). *The birth of Christianity: Discovering what happened in the years immediately after the execution of Jesus.* San Francisco: Harper.

Eliade, M. (1968). *The sacred and the profane: The nature of religion.* New York: Harcourt Brace.

Finch, P. (1983). *God, guts, and guns.* New York: Seaview Putnam.

Fox, M. (1988). *The coming of the cosmic Christ: The healing of mother earth and the birth of a global renaissance.* San Francisco: Harper.

Gibson, J. W. (1994). *Warrior dreams: Paramilitary culture in post-Vietnam America.* New York: Hill and Wang.

Gottwald, N. K. (1979). *The tribes of Yahweh: A sociology of the religion of liberated Israel, 1250-1050 B.C.E.* Maryknoll, NY: Orbis.

Hale, M. (1999). *WCOTC membership manual* [Online]. Available: http://www.rahowa.com/manual.htm.

Hamm, M. S. (1994). A modified social control theory of terrorism: An empirical and ethnographic assessment of American neo-Nazi skinheads. In M. S. Hamm (Ed.), *Hate crime: International perspectives on causes and control* (pp. 105-149). Cincinnati, OH: Anderson.

Hoffman, B. (1995). Holy terror: The implications of terrorism motivated by a religious imperative. *Studies in Conflict and Terrorism, 18*, 271-284.

Holden, R. N. (1986). *Postmillenialism as a justification for right-wing violence.* Gaithersburg, MD: International Association of Chiefs of Police.

Holden, R. N. (1999, March). *Illuminati, Bilderbergers, and the Trilateral Commission: The new world order and global conspiracies.* Paper presented at the Academy of Criminal Justice Sciences Annual Meeting, Orlando, FL.

Hudson, W. S. (1981). *Religion in America: An historical account of the development of American religious life.* New York: Scribner.

Kittel, G. (1964). *Theological dictionary of the New Testament, Vol. II: Delta-eta.* Grand Rapids, MI: Eerdmans.

Klassen, B. (1986). *The White man's Bible.* Costa Mesa, CA: Noontide.

Kung, H. (1995). *Christianity: Essence, history, and future.* New York: Continuum.

Laqueur, W. (1996, September/October). Postmodern terrorism: New rules for an old game. *Foreign Affairs*, 24-36.

Laqueur, W. (1999). *The new terrorism: Fanaticism and the arms of mass destruction.* New York: Oxford University Press.

Lewy, G. (1974). *Religion and revolution.* New York: Oxford University Press.

Marty, M. E. (1984). *Pilgrims in their own land: 500 years of religion in America.* Boston: Little, Brown.

Marty, M. E., & Appleby, R. S. (1991). *Fundamentalisms observed.* Chicago: University of Chicago Press.

Marty, M. E., & Appleby, R. S. (1993). *Fundamentalisms and the state: Remaking policies, economies, and militance.* Chicago: University of Chicago Press.

Noble, K. (1998). *Tabernacle of hate: Why they bombed Oklahoma City.* Ontario, Canada: Voyageur.

Rowe, S. C. (1994). *Rediscovering the West: An inquiry into nothingness and relatedness.* Albany: State University of New York Press.

Sapp, A. D. (1985, March). *Basic ideologies of right-wing extremist groups in America.* Paper presented at the Academy of Criminal Justice Sciences Annual Meeting, Las Vegas, NV.

Sargent, L. T. (1995). *Extremism in America.* New York: New York University Press.

Smith, B. L. (1994). *Terrorism in America: Pipe bombs and pipe dreams.* Albany: State University of New York Press.

Spong, J. S. (1999). *Why Christianity must change or die: A bishop speaks to believers in exile.* San Francisco: Harper.

Stern, K. S. (1996). *A force on the plain: The American militia movement and the politics of hate.* New York: Simon & Schuster.

White, J. R. (1986). *Holy war: Terrorism as a theological construct.* Gaithersburg, MD: International Association of Chiefs of Police.

White, J. R. (1997). Militia madness: Extremist interpretations of Christian doctrine. *Perspectives: A Journal of Reformed Thought, 12*, 8-12.

White, J. R. (1998). *Terrorism: An introduction.* Belmont, CA: Wadsworth.

FIGHTING TERRORISM AS IF WOMEN MATTERED

Anti-Abortion Violence as Unconstructed Terrorism

PHILIP JENKINS

Interviewer: What do you recommend that concerned citizens do at this time?

Army of God member: Every Pro-Life person should commit to destroying at least one death camp, or disarming at least one baby killer. The former is a relatively easy task—the latter could be quite difficult to accomplish. The preferred method for the novice would be gasoline and matches. Straight and easy. No tracks. You've kind of got to pour and light and leave real fast because of the flammability factor. Kerosene is great, but a little more traceable, so you would not want to buy it and use it in the same day.

Interviewer: What about explosives?

Army of God member: With time delays, a most wondrous method, and my personal favorite. ("The Army of God" 1996.)

Violent acts against abortion clinics and providers have often been in the headlines over the last decade. One notorious recent incident involved the attack on a Birmingham, Alabama, women's clinic in early 1998, which resulted in the death of a security guard and the maiming of a clinic nurse. Shortly afterwards, the police named a suspect in this attack, who was also wanted for questioning in connection with another clinic bombing the previous year, in Atlanta: the man wanted in these attacks soon found himself on the FBI's celebrated list of the ten most-wanted offenders. Media reports of the Birmingham incident left no doubt that the act was seen as a heinous terrorist crime, and one newspaper showed the scarred and blinded face of the wounded nurse under the powerful caption, "The Face of Terror" (Smith 1998; compare Greenberg 1998). The act was contextualized alongside other threatening political trends on the extreme right, especially the growth of well-armed paramilitary organizations (Archibald, Robinson, and Sanford 1998; Bragg 1998a, 1998b; Reeves 1998). This interpretation seems natural enough given the heinous character of the crime, but it is remarkable how only recently it has become possible to express such a view, i.e., to describe a clinic attack as terrorism.

Though numerous acts of violence have been associated with prolife militancy over the past two decades, including dozens of bomb and arson attacks, it is only since about 1993 that such incidents have generally been described with the damning label of "terrorism." This important omission long protected violent antiabortion groups and individuals from the full weight of official investigation and state sanction.[1] While media and government sources condemned the individual acts, the terminology used fell well short of that normally employed to categorize the most serious forms of organized political violence. Literally thousands of separate acts of politically motivated criminal violence were not constructed as a distinctive social problem urgently demanding an official response, but were seen rather as congeries of isolated and almost random phenomena. For almost twenty years, this particular subset of domestic terrorist violence remained an unconstructed social problem, acknowledged neither by government nor media, and ignored by almost all writers on terrorism and political crime. Not until 1993 was the language of "terrorism" applied, a change that permitted a rapid process of construction and contextualization, both in public discourse and in official policymaking.

The long refusal to employ "terrorist" was striking because in definitional terms, prolife extremism lacked none of the criteria that would characterize this behavior as terrorist. However, the semantic question so crucial to constructing the wider problem has been shaped throughout by political factors, and especially interest-group politics. Throughout the 1980s, the federal agencies that dominated the official interpretation of political violence and criminality were controlled by partisans of the political Right, many of whom sympathized with the goals if not the methods of prolife extremism. The shift toward seeing the violence as terrorism reflects changes in federal perceptions. At its simplest level, the movement toward denouncing anti-abortion violence as terroristic was a direct outcome of the 1992 election. This is a clear case study of the subjective and ideological nature of the concept of terrorism, as well as of any responses ostensibly designed to combat the perceived menace.

If indeed prolife extremism merits the name of terrorism, this affects our understanding of political violence in the United States, not least in vastly expanding the amount of recorded political violence in the last two decades, and making even more fatuous the periodically asked question, Can terrorism come to the United States? Moreover, the acts in question appear to form a systematic pattern. While they do not reflect orders from some organizational center, the tactics and chronology of the militant antiabortion campaign closely parallel the actions of other violent groups on the extreme Right, which unquestionably do constitute armed terrorism, and which have been so classified by all relevant law enforcement agencies. These parallels extend to individual actions undertaken by "lone assassins" ostensibly operating free from any organizational context.

If this is correct, then antiabortion violence should properly be viewed not merely as terrorism, but as an integral part of the broader pattern of ultraright terrorism that has been so prevalent in the United States since the early 1980s, and that attracted so much public attention after the Oklahoma City bombing of 1995. Even so, sections of the media continue to contextualize antiabortion "protest" quite separately from the "terrorism" of the far Right.

This story illustrates familiar themes in the academic study of how the media approach and interpret crime and deviance, and how they consistently present a narrative that exaggerates the role of relatively powerless offenders, while ignoring or distorting the misdeeds of the powerful and well-connected. The case of prolife violence shows how social constructions of criminality and violence depend on the decisions of agencies of social control, and specifically upon their powers to apply labels and subsequently collect statistics. It also provides a case study of how effectively government agencies can deny or ignore quite blatant endemic public violence and mayhem, with little danger of challenge or contradiction from any outside group or institution. Reactions to prolife violence provide a stark reminder of the dependence of both news organizations and academics on official voices (Sanders and Lyon 1995.) If the aim of journalism is to speak truth to power, then this is one area where the American media have been inexplicably and shamefully silent. And, if anything, the record of academics has been even worse, in that terrorism "experts" have systematically relied on statistics carefully predefined and selected for them by agencies of law enforcement, above all in the federal government.

THE VIOLENCE

There is no serious debate about the reality of the acts under consideration here, nor their frequency (Blanchard 1994; Blanchard and Prewitt 1993; "Abortion," 1995.) Since 1977, antiabortion violence has been traced and catalogued by the National Abortion Federation and other prochoice and feminist groups, whose statistics indicate the extent of extralegal activity. Even so, it should be noted that the figures are

Table 15.1 Abortion Violence in the United States 1977-1995

	Murder	Attempted Murder	Bombing	Arson	Attempted Bombing/Arson
1977-1983	0	0	8	13	5
1984	0	0	18	6	6
1985	0	0	4	8	10
1986	0	0	2	7	5
1987	0	0	0	4	8
1988	0	0	0	4	3
1989	0	0	2	6	2
1990	0	0	0	4	4
1991	0	2	1	10	1
1992	0	0	1	16	13
1993	1	1	1	9	7
1994	4	8	3	5	4
1995	0	0	0	8	0
Total	5	11	40	100	68

SOURCE: "The Abortion Rights Activist," National Abortion Federation, website maintained by Adam Guasch-Melendez.

minima, and that incidents were less likely to be recorded in the earlier years (see Table 15.1).

Opposition to abortion emerged very shortly after the Supreme Court's *Roe v. Wade* decision of 1973, and a direct action campaign emerged about 1976 (see Risen and Thomas 1998; Solinger, Ginsburg and Anderson 1998; Gorney 1998). The direct action movement reached a new degree of organizational maturity in the mid-1980s, and though the groups then formed were not necessarily linked to the ensuing violence, at least some of the militants emerged from their ranks. In 1985, Joseph Scheidler published the influential book *Closed: 99 Ways to Stop Abortion* and his Pro-Life Action League became the most visible activist group until the formation of Operation Rescue in 1986-1987, under Scheidler's influence. These movements used tactics of direct physical confrontation, seeking to close abortion facilities by demonstrations, sit-ins, and invasions.

A violent phase of the antiabortion campaign began in 1977 with an arson attack at a clinic in St. Paul, Minnesota, and a bombing the following year in Cincinnati, Ohio. There were twenty-six incidents and attempts between 1977 and 1983. A firebombing and kidnapping incident in 1982 marked the first appearance of the "Army of God," a name that has since appeared in the context of the most extreme actions, including the recent Birmingham attack

(Bragg 1998b; "The Army of God" 1996; U.S. House of Representatives 1987; Stoddard and Norwick 1978). Violence escalated sharply in 1984-1985, when there were at least fifty-two actual and attempted bombings and arsons. On Christmas Day, 1984, two clinics and a doctor's office in Pensacola, Florida, were bombed as "a gift to Jesus on his birthday." The rate of attacks then fell steeply, to revive in 1991. Between 1991 and 1994, seventy-one actual and attempted arsons and bombings were recorded. It was also in these years that the campaign shifted to direct assaults and murders of physicians and clinic staff. The most serious acts recorded in the period 1977-1995 include over two hundred actual and attempted bombings and arsons, in addition to five murders and eleven attempted murders. This list does not include acts of violence and intimidation such as clinic invasions (347), vandalism (596), assault and battery (96), death threats (238), kidnapping (2), burglary (37), and stalking (214). Nor does it include many thousands of disruptive acts using hate mail, phone calls, and bomb threats. Picketing and clinic blockades have led to tens of thousands of arrests.

Several recent incidents illustrate the nature of the violence. In February 1995, for example, at least five clinics in California were struck by deliberately set arson fires in a three-week period: at Ventura, Santa Barbara, San Luis

Table 15.2   Major Violent Actions Directed Against Abortion Clinics and Providers

Date	Action
March 10, 1993	Dr. David Gunn murdered by Michael Griffin outside clinic at Pensacola, FL
August 19, 1993	Attempted murder of Dr. George Tiller in Wichita, KS, by Rachelle "Shelley" Shannon
July 29, 1994	Dr. John Britton and volunteer escort James H. Barrett murdered by Paul Hill near The Ladies' Center in Pensacola, FL
November 8, 1994	Abortion provider Dr. Garson Romalis shot and wounded in Vancouver, Canada
December 30, 1994	Two women killed by John Salvi at clinics in Brookline, MA
January 16, 1997	Two bombs destroy an Atlanta building containing an abortion clinic
January 29, 1998	Bomb at abortion clinic in Birmingham, AL, kills an off-duty police officer and severely wounds a clinic nurse

Obispo, Santa Cruz, and San Francisco (Burghardt 1995a). While the acts were not unusual in themselves, they offered unusually clear evidence of a deliberate conspiracy. Moreover, the geographical context appeared to link the actions to an earlier protest campaign by an antiabortion group. In a single month in early 1997, "a doctor at a Baton Rouge, LA., abortion clinic was stabbed; a Planned Parenthood office in Dallas was robbed at gunpoint; a Phoenix clinic was the site of three unsuccessful arson attempts; and a Tulsa, OK., clinic was bombed" (Bragg 1997). This particular sequence culminated in the wrecking of an Atlantic clinic by two powerful bombs. Shortly afterwards, a man attempted unsuccessfully to blow up a clinic in Bakersfield, California, using a truck filled with propane and gasoline ("Man Sentenced" 1998).

In 1993 and 1994, antiabortion protesters carried out their most notorious crimes to date, with the murders of doctors who performed the operations (Risen and Thomas 1998; see Table 15.2).

After years of near-fatal attacks, the watershed came on March 10, 1993, when Dr. David Gunn was shot at a Pensacola, Florida, clinic that had earlier been the scene of repeated protests and violence. The same city provided the venue for another attack on July 29, 1994, when Dr. Paul Britton and a clinic escort were murdered. The assassin in this case was Paul Hill, who had earlier persuaded thirty prolife activists to sign a petition justifying killing abortionists as a form of "defensive action" (Hill 1994). In December 1994, two clinic workers were killed at facilities in Brookline, Massachusetts, by protester John Salvi. Assassinations and murder attempts also occurred in Canada. There were numerous other offenses where a political and antiabortion motive was commonly suspected, though not proven, most strikingly the August 1994 murder of Dr. Wayne Patterson in Alabama.

The violent actions have resulted in numerous arrests, including those of some committed and quite professional militants. In the 1980s, Dennis Malvasi undertook several potentially devastating bomb attacks in the greater New York City area (Freedman 1987). Army of God "soldier" Michael Bray was convicted of conspiracy in the bombing of ten clinics and facilities in 1984 and 1985, and in 1994 published a tract entitled *A Time to Kill*, justifying antiabortion violence (Naylor 1989). He was also a signatory to Hill's "Defensive Action" petition. From the same organization, Rachelle "Shelley" Shannon earned celebrity for a 1994 murder attempt on a clinic doctor in Wichita, and was also convicted of firebomb and butyric acid attacks on clinics in 1992 and 1993. She had been active in several western states, and had been arrested some thirty-five times for various protests. She had also corresponded with Michael Griffin, assassin of Dr. Gunn. The federal judge at her 1995 trial described her concisely as a terrorist ("Woman Gets Twenty Year Sentence" 1995; Egan 1995b; Hall 1994; compare Johnson 1993).

Though bombings and shootings were disavowed by other antiabortion activists, many stressed that violence was understandable, and perhaps justifiable in view of what was perceived as the annual legal holocaust of babies: in fact, the Army of God is also known to its supporters as the underground wing of the American Holocaust Resistance Movement ("The Army of God" 1996). Within militant profile circles, the legitimacy of armed violence was discussed widely, to an extent that would have caused serious official concern had it occurred in other political contexts.[2] Extreme prolife views received a wide airing in the best-selling evangelical novel *Gideon's Torch*, cowritten by Chuck Colson (aide to former president Richard Nixon), which describes revolutionary violence against abortion facilities by the so-called Holocaust Resistance: though attacks are not explicitly justified, the prolife pastor imprisoned for inspiring them by his writings is the hero of the novel, and he is even compared to St. Paul (Colson and Vaughn 1995).

Organized Terrorism?

At first sight, there is no doubt that we are dealing with quite numerous and active terrorists, and prochoice leaders have suggested that even the apparent "lone nuts" might have been subject to some degree of organization. This is a controversial issue: the broad national right-to-life organizations strictly disavow street activism or violence; the hard-core activists do not possess a "high command," and a federal investigation of a possible national conspiracy in 1995 was inconclusive. In fact, the groups engaged in militant protest are divided among a great many splinter factions including Operation Rescue, the Lambs of Christ, Missionaries to the Preborn, and Rescue America, while the actual assassins and bombers who have been identified never admit participation in organized plots or conspiracies. However, drawing analogies from other organizations engaged in illegality raises the question whether this apparent lack of centralization conceals real structure and direction. At its simplest level, this is suggested by the clear patterns or trajectories of violence nationwide, which developed and faded at very much the same time in widely different parts of the country.[3]

It has long been common for violent activists to carry out their operations under the cover of bogus front groups, partly in order to confuse

law enforcement, partly to divert blame for actions that attract significant negative public reaction. This pattern of subterfuge has been common in both Middle Eastern and European terrorism, where false flag activities have been a prominent feature of terrorist campaigns in the last three decades. This type of cover is all the more essential in the legal environment of the United States, where federal laws provide devastating civil and criminal penalties for groups that can be shown to have organized or supported a pattern of illegal acts: among the most fearsome is RICO, the Racketeer Influenced and Criminal Organization law (Greenhouse 1994). The antiabortion movement has often been threatened with such sanctions, and has responded by creating a plethora of small and transient entities to carry out protests.

Investigators from prochoice groups like the Bay Area Coalition for Reproductive Rights (BACORR) argue that the dozens of militant organizations are usually thinly disguised offshoots of a larger network (Burghardt 1995b). While rejecting concepts of an overarching national conspiracy, BACORR argues that within this network can be found a "category of activists who, though related to the public 'rescue' groups, constitute a unique sub-set of cadres whose organizational principles are markedly different: the free-floating agents of terror; the miscellaneous clinic bombers, arsonists, saboteurs, drive-by shooters and assassins." Though not subject to direct control from any central group, these activists are organized in cells in the form of the shepherding groups that have developed in Evangelical and Pentecostal churches in the last two decades (Burghardt 1995d; Diamond 1989). Under the shepherding system, small groups of up to a dozen fundamentalist believers are subject to the guidance of a charismatic group leader, in an authoritarian relationship that ventures far into personal and secular matters.

Evidence of organized prolife terrorism is reinforced by parallels with white supremacist and extreme right movements also active in these years. Prolife violence, like that used by ultraright and racist terror movements, peaked in the years 1984-1985 and 1992-1994. Moreover, both for anti-abortion and racist terror movements, the two eras were marked by a similar change of tactics and strategy. Inspired by texts like William Pierce's novel *The Turner Diaries*, white supremacists began a campaign of terrorist violence in 1983 and 1984, at precisely the point that the campaign against abortion facilities turned to systematic violence and sabotage. Not surprisingly, there was an interchange of ideas between prolifers on the one hand, and the radical Patriot right on the other. Already in the mid-1980s, bomb attacks on abortion clinics were a major emphasis in the guerrilla war planning of the extremist Arizona Patriots (Hall 1986). The post-Oklahoma City exposés of the militia movement have detailed the links to prolife movements, and demonstrated the centrality of abortion in much militia rhetoric (Berlet 1995; Junas 1995; Burghardt 1995c, 1995e).

For the far Right, the evils of abortion are transparent, and the issues involved are very close to those raised by other secular concerns. Shortly after the Oklahoma bombing, one Patriot activist at a convention in Missouri defended the bombing by setting it in the broader context of the "abortion holocaust": "And we will ask *them*, how many babies were killed by abortion today?" ("Militia Enemy List Uncovered" 1995; Jasper 1995). The prolife extremists also share much of the conspiracy theory approach found among the paramilitary Right. Apart from the obligatory attack on the New World Order, both also share tendencies to identify Masonic or illuminati conspiracies as the roots of present evils. A tract alleging Masonic persecution of Catholics was found on the person of John Salvi following his rampage at two clinics in Brookline, Massachusetts. Both Patriot and prolife movements are in addition influenced by Christian Reconstructionism, which holds that Christians have a right and duty to exercise theocratic authority in the contemporary world, with the detailed application of the moral and criminal laws laid down in the Old Testament. The theory has been especially significant for groups like Operation Rescue (Berlet 1995). Media reports have linked Eric Rudolph, the suspect in the Birmingham clinic bombing, with Christian Identity views (Manuel 1998).

LONE RANGERS

Since the late 1980s, these connections and parallels have become even more evident, as both prolife and white supremacist activists have developed the concept of "leaderless resistance." This shrewd if desperate strategy was a necessary reaction to the numerous arrests and prosecutions of far Right leaders during the mid- and late 1980s. If even the allegedly tightest of cell systems could be penetrated by federal agents, why have a hierarchical structure at all? Why not simply move to a *non*structure, in which individual groups circulate propaganda, manuals, and broad suggestions for activities, which can be taken up or adapted according to need by particular groups or even individuals? To quote rightist Louis Beam, "Utilizing the leaderless resistance concept, all individuals and groups operate independently of each other, and never report to a central headquarters or single leader for direction or instruction. . . . No-one need issue an order to anyone" (Quoted in Burghardt 1995c). The strategy is ideal in that attacks can neither be predicted nor prevented, and that there are no ringleaders who can be prosecuted. The Oklahoma City bombing was presumably the work of one such "autonomous cell" (Hamm 1998).

The issue of individual action is significant here. Each of the militants arrested in antiabortion violence has appeared to be acting at least on the surface as a "lone fanatic," but it might be asked whether coordination is so wholly lacking as it appears. The years in which prolife extremists were beginning to carry out lone murders of abortion providers were precisely the period in which the far Right was exploring notions of leaderless resistance, undertaken by the "Phantom Cell or individual action." This type of individual warfare is amply portrayed in the 1989 novel *Hunter*, by Andrew MacDonald (i.e., William Pierce), the author of the *Turner Diaries*: this second book depicts a lone assassin seeking to provoke a racial war by means of individual acts of terrorist violence. Berlet reports a 1994 meeting in Massachusetts in which a prominent organizer of antiabortion protests appeared together with members of the John Birch Society and other far-right pressure groups (Berlet 1995). Among the books on sale on this occasion were militia texts and arms manuals, and copies of *Hunter*. One Army of God militant expresses the concept perfectly: "We desperately need single lone-rangers out there, who will commit to destroy one abortuary before they die" ("The Army of God" 1996).

For both the far Right and the antiabortion movement, the years between 1992 and 1994 were critical (Dees and Corcoran 1996; Stern 1996; Gibson 1994; Merkl and Weinberg 1993). Rightist outrage at the twin incidents at Ruby Ridge and Waco initiated a new wave of organization and arming, which found its most visible public manifestation in the militia movement. At the same time, the leaderless resistance concept was intensely discussed both in print and on the Internet. The formation of new groups and militias reached a climax in 1994-1995, though this was stemmed somewhat by public horror at the Oklahoma City attack. On the abortion front, 1993 witnessed the critical shift in the nature of violence, with direct assassinations and murder attempts on the doctors themselves. Though ostensibly the work of lone fanatics, these attacks might well be fitted into the broader concept of leaderless resistance, which presupposes a constellation of highly motivated activists or berserkers who receive propaganda but not direct orders from partisan media. When sufficiently galvanized by these sources, or when the movement appears to demand such extreme action, the individuals arise to perform the violence required.

WHY NOT TERRORISM?

Following the clinic bombings of 1984, the Justice Department and the FBI came under intense pressure from liberal political leaders to investigate the antiabortion violence as an aspect of domestic terrorism (U.S. House of Representatives 1986). However, the bureau refused on the explicit grounds that the acts, however reprehensible, constituted criminal rather than terrorist violence, and therefore fell under the jurisdiction of the Bureau of Alcohol, Tobacco and Firearms. In practice, the refusal to recognize the prolife campaign as terrorism

meant that for a decade, there was no systematic federal response to the violence, which continued largely unchecked. As the problem was unconstructed, individual crimes were counted and collated not by a federal agency, but by private groups, usually prochoice activists.

In retrospect, the FBI's decision seems astonishing. Leaving aside the apparent links with ultraright groups, the sheer volume and severity of anti-abortion violence would seem prima facie to constitute political terrorism. As early as 1988, political scientist David Nice published an important scholarly analysis of the antiabortion bombings, which he contextualized together with other forms of political violence, and that was before the worst upsurges of terrorism and criminality (Nice 1988). However, the application of the terrorist label has proved controversial. That the term is pejorative rather than "objective" is indicated by the fact that no so-called "terrorist" group either foreign or domestic acknowledges that title, and prefers some other terminology: they are instead soldiers, partisans, guerrillas, the resistance. One prolife militant has published what is described as *A Guerrilla Strategy for a Pro-Life America* (Crutcher 1992). The cliché justly holds that "one person's terrorist is another person's freedom fighter," or indeed, "defender of life."

In contrast to other countries, the United States has no legal definition of terrorism; thus no prisoner has ever been accused or tried on the simple offense of terrorism. Laws ostensibly designed to combat the behavior have generally focused on certain specific actions, such as bomb-making, arms offenses, and hostage taking. Individual agencies have therefore enjoyed considerable latitude in applying this evocative term. The standard FBI definition presents terrorism as "the unlawful use of force or violence against persons or property to intimidate or coerce a government, the civilian population, or any segment thereof, in furtherance of political or social goals" (Smith 1994:18). The problems here are manifold, for example, in setting all governments on a moral par, so that an act of resistance against the most savage dictatorship is treated as indistinguishable from that against a liberal democracy, while "unlawful" could mean an act contrary to any statutes, however repressive. The definition makes no allowance for justified resistance, and in fact uses terrorism as a blanket term for any act of political violence that the U.S. government happens to stigmatize.

During the 1980s, the imposition of sanctions against "terrorists" of various kinds led to years of intense controversy among academics and policy specialists about whether this label could properly be applied to those engaged in a paramilitary struggle against an oppressive regime. The two cases most frequently mentioned were the IRA and the South African ANC, both of which commanded broad sympathy in North America. The focus of the definition has subsequently shifted from the armed nature of the violence to its indiscriminate character, and the U.S. government now tends to accept the State Department view of terrorism as premeditated, politically motivated violence directed against noncombatant targets. Even this delineation is flexible, and on other occasions, the definition is expanded to include factors like the following: the acts must be clandestine or surreptitious in nature; they are random in their choice of victims; they are intended to create an overwhelming sense of fear; and they should be undertaken by a nonstate or subnational group. Other violent actions that do not fall within these categories might be variously classified as acts of war or resistance, of partisan or guerrilla conflict, of subversion or sabotage.

Antiabortion terrorism would seem to fit either the State Department or the FBI definitions perfectly. In the California arson fires, for example, or the murders of Drs. Gunn and Britton, the actions were premeditated, politically motivated violence directed against targets that by common consensus would be noncombatant. Moreover, the arson fires at least were clandestine or surreptitious in nature, and a primary goal was to create an overwhelming sense of fear among providers and supporters of abortion, virtually to provide general deterrence by the threat of privately administered capital punishment. While prolife extremists would argue that the doctors and clinics targeted are "combatants" in the sense of being engaged in killing, and must be prevented by whatever means are necessary, no government or court would currently accept such a perspective.

In the face of so much evidence to the contrary, the FBI's refusal to acknowledge prolife terrorism depended on two factors, both of which seem, to say the least, tenuous. One was the apparent lack of structure, direction, or organization in the attacks, so that incidents appeared to be the work of numerous lone individuals, rather than any concerted conspiracy. As we have seen, this perception depended on a limited and highly traditional notion of how terrorist campaigns were and should be directed, assuming the necessity for some kind of highly organized general staff or command center. Related to this was the question of the *political* character of the antiabortion crimes. The political motivation might seem self-evident, in that the violence resulted from protests against the operation of a law that the activists profoundly wished to change. However, the FBI was influenced by the argument that these acts represented protests by angry individuals rather than deliberate political action, and moreover did not seek to change national policy in a manner that would denote behavior as "political." It was social protest, rather than political—though interestingly, the FBI's own criteria for terrorism specified violence "in furtherance of political *or social* goals" (emphasis added). The unwillingness to see clinic bombers as terrorists was all the more surprising in view of the obvious parallels and linkages to the ongoing neo-Nazi campaign, which during 1984-1985 represented the agency's prime domestic priority.

The FBI reached its position by the most specious and improbable arguments, which egregiously contradicted their own definitions and policies, to say nothing of common sense. In reality, it is difficult to avoid the conclusion that the bureau's aversion to focusing on the topic was chiefly partisan and political, and above all reflected a fear of alienating the broad right-wing political constituency that supported the goals of the antiabortion movement. The Reagan administration elected in 1980 was strongly prolife: the president himself declared a National Sanctity of Life Day, and used audio links to address huge prolife rallies in Washington D.C. It was wildly improbable that only a few months after Reagan's stunning electoral victory in November 1984, his administration might have extended the terrorist label to a section of the prolife movement, especially when the embarrassing consequences of such an action might have resulted in the investigation of large sections of the mainstream movement. There is thus no need to postulate any kind of official conspiracy or connivance to explain the official underplaying of terrorism, which arose predictably out of the political alignments of the day.

POLICY IMPLICATIONS

For whatever constellation of reasons, antiabortion violence did not receive the FBI's imprimatur as authentic terrorism, and this decision had far-reaching social and legal consequences. The decision was particularly critical in the legal arena, where such a definition would have opened the potential for a whole new panoply of official sanctions, which would have in turn affected the whole prolife movement rather than only the extremists.

Prior to the 1970s, the FBI enjoyed enormous latitude, formal and otherwise, to decide which political groups might legitimately be investigated, bugged, and penetrated by agents, a pattern that led to widespread abuses. Following a series of Watergate-era scandals, Congress introduced severe limitations on the powers of this and other federal agencies, with the goal of preventing the intimidation of organizations that merely opposed or criticized official policies, or even the actions of a particular party or administration. There were, however, due exceptions where imminent violence might be prevented, and the Reagan administration refined these rules so that a clear warning of a terrorist act or campaign would bring a suspect group within the proper domain of federal investigation. Wiretapping and surveillance would become far easier in such cases, and it would be possible to investigate the group by means of infiltrators and defectors. Proof of organized terrorist activity would also expose the network involved to action under civil and criminal RICO laws, under which property could be seized prior to trial, and heavy fines and lengthy prison terms imposed. In summary, the "terrorist" label would summon forth the same range of powers that caused the decimation

of traditional organized crime groups since the early 1980s, and that led to the uprooting of the right-wing terrorist band known as the Order during 1984 and 1985.

In practical terms, federal definition of conduct as "terrorist" means a far more proactive (rather than reactive) stance in the face of a given campaign, a stance that virtually all observers view as the only potentially successful strategy. Decades of experience have suggested that terrorist groups tend to operate in certain ways, and need certain facilities that if properly observed and investigated can provide rich opportunities for security forces. Often, groups exist simultaneously both above and below ground: a mass party or pressure group provides a cover for illegal underground operations, as well as channeling money for clandestine operations, and providing potential recruits. It is thus essential to observe the legal arm of a movement as a way of identifying the armed illegals.

Let us for example imagine a number of attacks on the embassies and facilities of a particular nation in the United States, and messages to the media that have linked these attacks to the grievances of a dissident party or ethnic group. A reactive stance might consist of improving security at these installations, and perhaps for any diplomats or business people connected with them, followed by intense criminal investigation to determine the individuals or groups directly responsible for given acts. This would, however, be immensely labor-intensive and time-consuming, and would make no progress whatever in rooting out the terrorist factions responsible. A proactive position would rather involve identifying the public or above-ground organizations associated with the suspected dissidents. These would be subject to surveillance with a view to compiling a network analysis to see if links to violent groups might be identified, or even chains of command and communication between the legal and the clandestine arms of the movement. A similar endeavor might also take the form of tracing individuals within the broader movement who have given signs of sympathy for violent action, for example, by writing articles or signing petitions to this effect, or by campaigning on behalf of imprisoned militants. Crucially, infiltrators would have to be placed inside the terrorist organization, initially by making contact through the above ground party. Effective counterterrorism must be proactive, interventionist, and firmly based on the widespread collection and collation of intelligence, and these are all strategies that can only be achieved legally once the crucial designation of "terrorism" has been affixed to the movement in question. Ideally, authorities could gain such a stranglehold on the group's potential operations that it would be induced to cease its campaign.

The investigative scheme outlined here would currently be absolutely illegal in the context of the antiabortion movement, but once the terrorist label had been applied, restraints would be removed accordingly. If it was agreed that the shooting of doctors constituted organized terrorism, then detailed investigation and surveillance could begin in earnest, beginning with the signatories to petitions advocating violence or murder, and the memberships of all groups involved with such documents. Networking would be pursued wherever leads suggested, which in the case of the prolife movement would assuredly mean through the fundamentalist churches and underground religious networks, and perhaps sections of the organized religious Right that was so critical to the Republican electoral effort in these years. In reality, however, the lack of a terrorist definition prevents a proactive response of the sort that would alone be effective against such a threat. The FBI's failure to respond did not only mean that investigators were deprived of the assistance of one agency; rather it implied the absence of all those tactics that are the core of any policy of prevention and eradication.

To understand the potential scope and implications of a proactive antiterrorist investigation, we need only consider other events in progress at precisely the time that the FBI was refusing to regard a series of bombings as evidence of an organized terrorist campaign (Gelbspan 1991). In the early 1980s, the FBI desperately wished to investigate the quite legal and pacific movement against U.S. intervention in Central America, an investigation that could not be pursued unless a "terrorist connection" could be established, however implausibly. With minimal difficulty, informers were found to assert that Central American solidarity groups were, in fact, covers for terrorist plots and assassination schemes, and these claims provided the rationale for a vast campaign of bugging, infiltration, and dirty tricks, much of which was directed against churches, religious communities, and individual church workers. Though such actions were controversial in terms of violating constitutional guarantees of freedom of religion, the argument was that the actions were essential to prevent the outbreak of violence, even though no criminal or terrorist act had been committed. In this instance, the mere suggestion that such events could potentially occur was sufficient to invoke law enforcement agencies engaging in quite intrusive behavior. There is a stark contrast to the antiabortion situation, in which armed attacks were commonplace by mid-1980s. The inescapable conclusion is that the terrorist label was applied too generously when dealing with opponents of government policy, but with astonishing parsimony in the case of political friends and sympathizers.

Unconstructed Terrorism

The consequences of the FBI's attitude have reached far beyond the realm of law and policing, and have ensured that antiabortion violence has been essentially invisible in the mass media and in scholarly sources. This is striking, as the extreme wing of the prolife movement would deserve to be listed among the most active of domestic American terrorist groups, whether this is assessed in terms of the frequency of incidents, the number of fatalities, or the extent of property damage inflicted. In terms of endurance, moreover, the extremist prolife campaign has been one of the hardiest of such movements, quite comparable to other more celebrated insurgencies like that of militant Puerto Rican nationalists, or domestic neo-Nazis.

In terms of scholarship, most published works on terrorist activity in the United States do not even discuss antiabortion violence, still less contextualize it together with other forms of acknowledged terrorism. For example, the pages of the prestigious journal Terrorism have included articles on virtually every violent and secessionist movement around the world, but very little on the abortion theme; and the issue does not even rate an index entry in standard works like Brent L. Smith's otherwise compendious *Terrorism in America* (1994). The abortion issue receives sparse if any coverage in most of the major works on terrorism from these years (Smith 1994; compare O'Sullivan 1986; Wilkinson 1986; Livingstone and Arnold 1986; Merkl 1986; Laqueur 1987; Poland 1988; Stohl 1988; Wardlaw 1989; Livingstone 1990; Vetter and Perlstein 1991; Crenshaw 1995). In one commonly used college textbook on terrorism, the issue receives a page and a half out of nearly three hundred pages—relatively generous compared with most of the literature! (White 1991:179-80). The reasons for this systematic omission are straightforward, in that most academic sources tend to rely on official categories and designations to define the scope of their study, so that when the FBI made its *ex cathedra* pronouncement that abortion violence was not terrorism, the topic was thereby excluded. With the FBI deciding not to cover the topic, the agency could provide no convenient speakers, experts, or statistics to use on news shows to discuss and contextualize new acts of violence. Without such resources, profile violence attracted little academic interest, and offered no attraction for the army of "true crime" authors who normally flock to sensationalistic subjects. We have no such true crime studies of the murders of abortion providers, no case studies of the most notorious bombers and arsonists. The omission of this sort of crime from the scholarly and professional literature is a stark demonstration of the thorough reliance such works normally place on federal sources and information.

Though it is difficult to illustrate a negative, prolife violence was also largely absent from the mass media throughout the years of its sharpest intensity. In general, the topic of terrorism has often been addressed in movies, TV movies, and dramatic series, with Middle Eastern militants a common feature of popular fiction. Groups closer to home have nearly always been treated with somewhat greater sensitivity for fear of offending domestic constituencies, and character portrayals have usually been more subtle than in the depictions of evil Muslim fundamentalists or Palestinians. Nevertheless, domestic terrorist groups have featured in films and television dramas, often in works involving major stars and directors. The fascist Right was the subject of films like *Talk Radio* and *Betrayed*, the violent Left of the film *Running on Empty*, while the Puerto Rican situation has also featured sporadically. On television, neo-Nazi, white supremacist, and militia groups have appeared increasingly as themes since the sudden spotlight cast on such groups by the Oklahoma City bombing. In contrast, abortion in general has always proved a very delicate theme, and the media have been reluctant to approach antiabortion protest in general, and still less the violent extremes. Only in 1993-1994 did the issue emerge, and then chiefly in stand-up comedy shows mocking the hypocrisy of "profile" advocates who supported the assassins of abortion workers. When antiabortion violence eventually appeared in television movies, as late as 1996, such a portrayal was still too daring for the networks: the films *If These Walls Could Talk* and *Critical Choices* were both broadcast on pay cable channels, respectively, HBO and Showtime (James 1996).

Why did the antiabortion theme not attract the same media fascination as other forms of terrorism? Certainly it was not for lack of intrinsic interest, and one can easily construct the sort of fictional themes that might have been employed. Imagine for example the obvious film that could have been made about a determined female investigator rooting out a network of fanatical clinic bombers and assassins, and in so doing uncovering highly placed sympathizers for the terrorists within her own organization, perhaps among her superiors at the FBI or the Justice Department. One would have thought the subject overwhelmingly attractive, offering as it does the adaptation of familiar genres such as the antiterrorist film, the lone investigator, and the conspiracy story. The hypothetical film would also present a superb opportunity for a strong female lead, and could have been expected to have enormous demographic appeal to younger women. Of course, there never was such a feminist *Mississippi Burning*, and the issue has been as absent from cinema screens as from TV movies. If only for the basest financial motives, one would have thought that filmmakers would have been attracted to such conflicts.

The lack of attention is far more than a historical curiosity, because the media serve such a critical role in constructing an issue for public consumption, and thereby in establishing both public and official priorities for responding to it. Some degree of interpretation is inevitable: if the media are to report on any question, they must attempt to give it some meaning, to place it in a frame of reference that will be familiar to the assumed audience. To quote Stuart Hall et al., "If the world is not to be represented as a jumble of random and chaotic events, then they must be identified (i.e. named, defined, related to other events known to the audience), and assigned to a social context (i.e. placed within a frame of meanings familiar to the audience). This process—identification and contextualization—is one of the most important through which events are 'made to mean' by the media" (Hall, Critcher, Jefferson, Clarke, and Roberts 1978:54). If, however, the abortion violence issue is simply absent, while other forms of terrorism receive intense attention, the message is clearly that this form of violence either does not exist or has no real significance. In turn, this lack ensures that there is no public pressure on elected and appointed officials, no cry for a "war on terror" in this particular form; and no rewards for the bureaucratic agencies that achieve success in such a struggle. Throughout the 1980s, the phenomenon remained unconstructed, and thus did not exist as a social problem.

Conversely, the absence of federal sanction leaves the issue as the preserve of prochoice, feminist, and liberal groups, who are alone left to make the point that the behavior in question is authentic terrorism. In this context, the fact of expressing concern about anticlinic violence, or even using the word "terrorism," is perceived as making a partisan political statement. A filmmaker who addressed the issue from this standpoint would thus be denounced by the prolife movement for "extremism" and "hysteria" in the prochoice cause, and the studio or network in question would certainly attract commercial boycotts, and possibly political sanctions. The FBI's stance of magisterial "objectivity" effectively delegitimated any potential movement to expose and counter prolife violence.

CONSTRUCTING TERRORISM 1993-1995

Official attitudes to clinic violence began to change during 1991, following Operation Rescue's mass blockades, which sought to close abortion facilities in Wichita, Kansas, and other areas ("Wichita's Long Hot Summer" 1991). These actions entered the national political arena following the refusal of federal authorities to defend the clinics, apparently aligning the Republican administration not only with the prolife cause, but with its militant direct-action wing. The 1992 elections brought to office the first Democratic president in twelve years, and one moreover supported by liberal and feminist groups. In the aftermath of Wichita, the Clinton administration took seriously the demands of prochoice advocates for federal measures to defend clinics, while prolife militants were discouraged and outraged. In his first month in office in 1993, Clinton lifted several federal restrictions on abortion policy imposed during the Reagan and Bush administrations. The change of regime may well have encouraged the desperation that erupted in the new tactical direction of the extremist movement, and specifically the decision to employ personal violence against abortion providers. Furthermore, the blockade movement had peaked after the 1991 Wichita operation, and subsequent campaigns in 1992 were embarrassing failures.

The crescendo of violence in 1993 and 1994 brought demands for these acts to be counted as terrorism and to be treated with appropriate seriousness. Such calls had been frequently heard in the prochoice and feminist press for years, but now each major attack called forth a chorus of support in the mainstream media, and the murders of doctors and clinic workers were especially influential ("Anti-Abortion Acts" 1992). The volume of coverage, as measured by electronic databases such as *Newspaper Abstracts* and *Periodical Abstracts*, now increased dramatically. *Newspaper Abstracts* offered 208 entries under "abortion violence" for the years 1989-1995, only sixteen of which appeared in the three years 1989-1991. The murder of Dr. David Gunn in March 1993 caused a dramatic upsurge of coverage, as did the Britton shooting in July 1994. Over half the total, 120 items, appeared between the Britton murder and the end of 1995. The changed climate appears to be a direct response to the new attitude of the federal government, and the consequent change in tone of statements from federal law enforcement. However, the relationship between governmental definitions of terrorism and media products regarding antiabortion violence cannot be simply reduced to a linear causal model. For example, the definitional imperatives apparently emanating from the Clinton administration were continuous with the claims-making activities of diverse groups that fed the formal polity at a number of levels. These claims-making activities were not distinct from media sources but were at times an articulation of those forces. If any model is appropriate in terms of understanding the relationship between governmental definitional initiatives and the media portrayal of anti-abortion violence as terrorism, that model would have to acknowledge the synergistic reciprocal relationship between government and media or the shifting ideological homologies between those two seemingly distinct entities. This does not mean that at certain pivotal moments the motive force behind definitional drives does not tend to emanate primarily from either the government or the media.

The terminology applied by the media also changed. In the databases, before 1992 the word "terrorism" was very rarely found in conjunction with the words "abortion," "antiabortion," or "prolife," although specific arson and bomb attacks were very widely reported.[4] From 1992 onwards, however, the conjunction "prolife terrorism" becomes quite frequent, with about twenty-five entries between 1992 and 1995, most occurring immediately after one of the best-known attacks. The shooting of Dr. Gunn caused a particular media outcry, and the *Atlanta Constitution* typically asserted that "Christian terrorists" were incited by the extravagant vocabulary of the prolife leadership (Teepen 1993; Karten 1993; Barringer 1993). The timing of events was particularly important here, in that the first Pensacola shooting occurred only two weeks after the World Trade Center bombing, as a result of which the media had regularly been denouncing terrorism and

religious fanaticism on American soil. Late February had also marked the beginning of the Branch Davidian siege in Waco, Texas, an event that culminated in April with the massacre of seventy-five people. This affair further drew attention to the apocalyptic views and fanatical behavior of the Christian ultra-Right, and its penchant for armed violence.

This far graver perspective influenced the deliberations of a House Judiciary subcommittee, which was then considering measures to protect clinics, and which was told by the son of the murdered doctor that "these antichoice groups, I can't refer to them as pro-life anymore, are using terrorist tactics" (Orman 1993; U.S. House of Representatives 1993; Corbin 1993). In addition, the American Medical Association used the attacks to draw attention to violence against doctors both from prolife extremists and animal rights activists (Gravois 1993). Though religious Right leaders like Chuck Colson and Ralph Reed naturally rejected the "terrorist" label and complained that Christians were being unjustly pilloried as fanatics, the image of prolife terrorism appeared widely in the media, and endured over the following months. An editorial in the *Denver Post* asserted, "Shooting of abortion doctor was terrorism, not just assault," while *the Atlanta Constitution* warned of "Domestic Terrorists at Work." ("'Pro-life' Terrorism" 1993; "Shooting of Abortion Doctor Was Terrorism, Not Just Assault" 1993; Abcarian 1993; "Domestic Terrorists at Work" 1993). The Britton attack in July 1994 was equally influential in promoting the concept of the violent prolife activist as not merely a terrorist but also a "fanatic," a word commonly used previously in the context of Middle Eastern violence and Muslim fundamentalism ("When Extremism Becomes Terrorism" 1994; Risen 1994; O'Connell 1994; Hedges 1994). The radically changed tone of press coverage was suggested by a spate of headlines associating antiabortion violence with terms like "terrorist" and "fanatic," and with the state of war in which clinics now found themselves.

An increasingly hostile media atmosphere culminated following the Brookline attacks that December. These attacks were explicitly described as "domestic terrorism" by President Clinton (Puga 1994a, 1994b; "Pro-Life Terrorism: A How-to" 1995). The days following the Brookline shootings were marked by the starkest media condemnations yet of antiabortion violence (Goodman 1994; "Vigilance and Violence at Abortion Clinics" 1995; Abcarian 1995). Headlines variously proclaimed: "Clinic Killings Another Form of Terrorism" (*Boston Globe*), "Abortion Clinic Killers: Terrorists, Not Saviors" (*USA Today*), and "Pro-Choice Forces Urge War on 'Organized Terrorism'" (*Houston Post*) (Shea 1995; "Abortion Clinic Killers" 1995; Freelander 1995; Swarr 1995). An article in the *Houston Chronicle* was typically entitled "Call Them As They Are: Anti-Abortion Terrorists" (Pike 1995:C11; Wicklund 1995; Parshall 1995). This grim vision was further reflected in cartoons depicting those who attacked abortion facilities and providers as savage fanatics. In the *Washington Post*, Herb Block depicted an antiabortion fanatic declaring, "They should lock up those foreign nuts that are told what to do by some other god," and the cartoonist returned to these themes on several occasions during 1994 and 1995 (Block 1994, 1995a, 1995b). This perception was reflected in some of the media reaction to the Oklahoma City bombing, and specifically the new attention that it attracted to the violent actions of the political extreme Right ("Taking the Measure of Terrorism" 1995). The fact that this incident seemed designed to avenge the Waco massacre further suggested linkages between the violence of secular and religious extremists. Meanwhile, arguments about the political and gender-based nature of clinic violence were reinforced by the growing influence of feminist views in the shaping of federal crime policy. Nineteen ninety-four was the year of the sweeping Violence Against Women Act, which radically reformulated official responses to crimes like stalking and domestic violence.

In the face of such rapidly changing attitudes, the federal government came under heavy pressure to use its power to deter further prolife attacks, both to offer immediate protection to the clinics, and to provide longer-term security. In the immediate aftermath of the Pensacola killings, federal marshals were dispatched to protect clinics across the country in August 1994, while the Justice Department made the critical decision in July 1994 to create a task force to investigate any organized national campaign or conspiracy in the violence ("Federal Marshals Have Been Sent" 1994; Sharp 1994). Though the task force established by Attorney General Reno found no such evidence, the mere reporting of its activities served to focus media attention on prolife violence as a systematic threat, and potentially a form of organized terrorism (Egan 1995a; Johnson 1994). Also critical was the new Federal Access to Clinics legislation, which was credited with suppressing the worst of the street disruptions that had hitherto been permitted in anti-abortion protests (Navarro 1996; Pear 1996; U.S. Senate 1995).

The reduction of street violence may have contributed to the decline in outright terrorism, in that unstable individuals now found less in the way of blatant stimuli encouraging direct violence against clinics and providers. The changed environment was epitomized by prolife militant Andrew Burnett, a friend of militant Shelley Shannon. Interviewed in 1995, he complained, "The pro-life movement has changed radically. Funds are down. People are discouraged. They call us terrorists. But those who have chosen violence have made a big bang." We note that the simple fact of being named as terrorists is listed as one of the major elements in the discrediting of the militant campaign (cited in Egan 1995b).

Between early 1993 and early 1995, anti-abortion violence came to be constructed as a significant social problem. In explaining the remarkably rapid transition in attitudes, one obvious factor was that the nature of the behavior in question had changed quite radically in degree, in that while scattered arsons could be played down in the press or treated as isolated incidents, a campaign of assassination obviously demanded a major official response. It now became difficult for the FBI and other agencies to ignore the violence, especially when the new administration clearly shared feminist and liberal perceptions of the nature and scale of the threat. With administration sanction, the media could now turn its full attention to the violence, and portray it as at least parallel to other forms of terrorism that attracted public concern in these years. In fact, these linkages were so powerful that the question is less why the problem came to be constructed in this way in the mid-1990s, than why it had not been so regarded a decade earlier.

REAL POLITICS AND REAL TERRORISM

During the 1992 election campaign, abortion providers made the grim joke that the only way that they could obtain government protection from assault would be to paint American flags on the walls of their buildings, so that attackers could at least be prosecuted for desecrating the national symbol. The humorous observation raises a serious point, about why politicians and official agencies so long failed to accord due seriousness to an authentic terrorist threat, rather than to such symbolic issues as flag protection. If a group of Middle Eastern or Muslim orientation had carried out assaults against life and property on American soil on a scale far smaller than prolife extremists, official agencies would have made its suppression an absolute priority, and Congress would have passed whatever draconian legislation might have been perceived necessary for this purpose.

In the case of prolife extremism, two critical factors permitted the official refusal to accept the diagnosis of terrorism. One was the identity of the perpetrators, whose affiliations were with groups and ideologies that retained official favor, and the other was the nature of the real and potential victims, who were seen as representing women's causes. It is tempting, but simplistic to suggest a mere imbalance of power here, in that the perpetrators represented groups with far more power and access to authority than did the victims. According to classic conflict theory, the more powerful group exercised the ability to grant or withhold a label of severe deviance according to its own interests (Sanders and Lyon 1995).

However, the real problem was more fundamental, in that the conflict not only concerned the appropriate targets for the imposition of state power, but the appropriate limits of that power. Gender played a vital role in this ideological division. For women's groups, it was natural to insist that the state should intervene forcefully to protect the exercise of a constitutional right,

but the conservative administrations of the 1980s largely denied that such enforcement fell within the legitimate scope of state operations. However much this flouted common sense and consistency, antiabortion violence of whatever scale was not until 1993 recognized as a political problem, as it was directed against one segment of the population, namely women. As such, it was only "social" in nature and therefore beneath the dignity of federal intervention. We are reminded of the old argument that violence and rape in the domestic context did not constitute "real" crime, as these acts were a private domestic transaction in which legal authorities should not interfere.

The modern American experience with terrorism provides rich ammunition to support the feminist argument that matters of grave concern to women are not currently regarded as appropriate for serious political discourse, and in fact do not merit a political label at all. This was the attitude that for many years led to women being appointed to government office in departments responsible for matters such as health and welfare, family and children, where they could fulfill what was virtually an extended domestic role. Confined to the realm of the "merely social," women's issues were not to intrude on the pressing concerns of the state and its proper functions, such as war and peace, law and order, and national security. In this view, the merely personal is emphatically not political. The official depiction of abortion violence as a women's issue, or still more damning, a feminist issue, meant that the problem was framed as a conflict between two groups of zealots, in which the state could and should play no role. The administrations in power between 1981 and 1993 largely shared the view of the antiabortion movement that the staff and patients in an abortion clinic were participating in a morally tainted activity, and could not be regarded as fully innocent victims even if attacks occurred. From such a perspective, conservative administrations felt that treating a "women's issue" like clinic violence under the grave label of terrorism would be frivolous, and a diversion of resources badly needed in the struggle against "real" terrorism. Changing attitudes to prolife terrorism thus symbolize and encapsulate crucial changes in popular views of the appropriate scope and function of politics, and the place of women in the polity. For a grim decade, violence was allowed to flourish precisely because women's concerns were not believed to matter. A proper response could only be formulated once this form of ideological exclusion had been confronted and removed.

NOTES

1. The term "prolife" is the one generally employed by members of the movement itself, though it is highly value-laden in implying that opponents or nonmembers oppose life, or are even "prodeath." For convenience, the term "prolife" will here be employed without quotation marks, though this should not be taken to suggest the author's acceptance of these implications. I am aware of the consequent absurdity involved in using terms such as "prolife killings."

2. From a large literature, see, for example, Risen and Thomas (1998), Solinger et al. (1998), Gorney (1998), Manegold (1995:26), Vrazo (1995), Kerrison (1994), Lewin (1994), Hunter (1994), Rimer (1993), Hertz (1991), Condit (1990), Faux (1990), Terry (1988).

3. Examples include the bombing wave of 1984, the upsurge of arson between 1991 and 1993, and most sensationally, the emergence of assassination as a tactic in 1993-1994.

4. For the tone of earlier coverage, see for example Cleninden (1985).

REFERENCES

Abcarian, Robin. 1993. "A War of Attrition against Abortion." *Los Angeles Times*, October 20.

Abcarian, Robin. 1995. "Where Does Free Speech End, Terrorism Begin?" *Los Angeles Times*, January 4.

"Abortion." 1995. *MS Magazine*, special feature, May-June, pp. 42-66.

"Abortion Clinic Killers Terrorists, Not Saviors." 1995. *USA Today*, editorial, January 3.

"Anti-Abortion Acts a Form of Terrorism, Court Is Told." 1992. *Chicago Tribune*, February 20, p. 2C.

Archibald, John, Carol Robinson, and Peggy Sanford. 1998. "Officer Dies, Nurse Hurt in Abortion Clinic Blast." *Birmingham News*, January 30.

"The Army of God Overview." 1996. *The Abortion Rights Activist*, National Abortion Federation, WWW site maintained by Adam Guasch-Melendez. http://www.cais.com/agm/main/aoginter.htm

Barringer, Felicity. 1993. "Slaying Is a Call to Arms for Abortion Clinics." *New York Times*, March 12.

Berlet, Chip. 1995. "Armed Militias, Right Wing Populism, and Scapegoating." *Political Research Associates*, April 24. http://burn.ucsd.edu/archives/ats-1/1995.May/0027.html.

Blanchard, Dallas A. 1994. *The Anti-Abortion Movement and the Rise of the Religious Right*. New York: Twayne.

Blanchard, Dallas A. and Terry J. Prewitt. 1993. *Religious Violence and Abortion*. Gainesville: University Press of Florida.

Block, Herb. 1994. "Shooting Doctors? Bombing Clinics? How Could People Think of Doing Such Things?" Cartoon, *Washington Post*, August 3, p. A16.

Block, Herb. 1995a. "They Should Lock Up Those Foreign Nuts That Are Told What to Do by Some Other God." Cartoon, *Washington Post*, January 19.

Block, Herb. 1995b. "Greetings, Brother." Cartoon, *Washington Post*, July 19.

Bragg, Rick. 1997. "Abortion Clinic Hit By Two Bombs." *New York Times*, January 17.

Bragg, Rick. 1998a. "Bomb Kills Policeman at Alabama Abortion Clinic." *New York Times*, January 30.

Bragg, Rick. 1998b. "Group Tied to Two Bombings Says It Set Off Clinic Blast." *New York Times*, February 3.

Burghardt, Tom. 1995a. "Anti-Abortion Terror Escalates in California: Four Women's Clinics Attacked in February." Bay Area Coalition for Our Reproductive Rights. http://www.webcom.com/pinknoiz/right/bacorr6.html.

Burghardt, Tom. 1995b. "Dialectics of Terror: Anti-Abortion Direct Action." Bay Area Coalition for Our Reproductive Rights. http://www.webcom.com/pinknoiz/right/terror1.html.

Burghardt, Tom. 1995c. "Leaderless Resistance and the Oklahoma City Bombing." Bay Area Coalition for Our Reproductive Rights. http://nwcitizen.com/public-good/reports/leadless.htm.

Burghardt, Tom. 1995d. "Church Cells." Bay Area Coalition for Our Reproductive Rights. http://www.webcom.com/pinknoiz/right/churchcells.html.

Burghardt, Tom. 1995e. "Neo-Nazis Salute the Anti-Abortion Zealots." *Covert Action Quarterly* (Spring):52.

Cleninden, Dudley. 1985. "Abortion Clinic Bombings Have Caused Disruption for Many." *New York Times*, January 23.

Colson, Chuck and Ellen Vaughn. 1995. *Gideon's Torch*. Dallas: Word.

Condit, Celeste Mishelle. 1990. *Decoding Abortion Rhetoric*. Urbana: University of Illinois Press.

Corbin, Beth. 1993. "Florida Physician Murdered by Clinic Terrorist." *National NOW Times* (April):1.

Crenshaw, Martha, ed. 1995. *Terrorism in Context*. University Park: Pennsylvania State University Press.

Crutcher, Mark. 1992. *Firestorm: A Guerrilla Strategy for a Pro-Life America*. Lewisville, TX: Life Dynamics.

Dees, Morris, and James Corcoran. 1996. *Gathering Storm*. New York: Harper-Collins.

Diamond, Sara. 1989. *Spiritual Warfare*. Boston: South End.

"Domestic Terrorists at Work." 1993. *Atlanta Constitution*, editorial, October 4.

Egan, Timothy. 1995a. "Seeking a National Conspiracy. Abortion Task Force Is Set Back." *New York Times*, June 18.

Egan, Timothy. 1995b. "Shooter Falls Silent about Anti-Abortion Terrorism." *Tacoma News Tribune*, June 18.

Faux, Marian. 1990. *Crusaders*. New York: Carol.

"Federal Marshals Have Been Sent." 1994. *Wall Street Journal*, August 2.

Freedman, Samuel G. 1987. "Abortion Bombings Suspect: A Portrait of Piety and Rage." *New York Times*, May 7.

Freelander, Douglas. 1995. "Pro-Choice Forces Urge War on 'Organized Terrorism.'" *Houston Post*, January 4.

Gelbspan, Ross. 1991. *Break-Ins, Death Threats, and the FBI*. Boston: South End.

Gibson, James William. 1994. *Warrior Dreams*. New York: Hill and Wang.

Goodman, Ellen. 1994. "Danger Closes In on Us." *Boston Globe*, December 31.

Gorney, Cynthia. 1998. *Articles of Faith*. New York: Simon & Schuster.

Gravois, John. 1993. "AMA-Led Coalition Seeking Protection from 'Terrorism.'" *Houston Post*, March 17.

Greenberg, Mary Lou. 1998. "The Fire This Time: When Pro-Life Means Death." *On The Issues* (Summer):24ff.

Greenhouse, Linda. 1994. "Court Rules Abortion Clinics Can Use Rackets Law to Sue." *New York Times*, January 25.

Hall, Andy. 1986. "Secret War Patriots Have Loose Ties to Rightists Nationwide." *Arizona Republic*, December 21.

Hall, Mimi. 1994. "Indictments Tie Oregon Woman to Clinic Attacks." *USA Today*, October 25.

Hall, Stuart, Chas Critcher, Tony Jefferson, John Clarke, and Brian Roberts. 1978. *Policing the Crisis: Mugging, the State, and Law and Order*. London: Macmillan.

Hamm, Mark. 1998. *Apocalypse in Oklahoma*. Boston: Northeastern University Press.

Hedges, Stephen J. 1994. "Abortion: Who's behind the violence?" *U.S. News & World Report*, November 14, pp. 50-67.

Hertz, Sue. 1991. *Caught in the Crossfire*. New York: Prentice Hall.

Hill, Paul. 1994. "Should We Defend Born and Unborn Children With Force?" http://www.webcom.com/pinknoiz/right/knowenemy.html.

Hunter, James Davison. 1994. *Before the Shooting Begins*. New York: Free Press.

James, Caryn. 1996. "Choices and No Choices in the Abortion Wars." *New York Times*, December 18.

Jasper, William F. 1995. "The Rise of Citizen Militias." *New American*, February 6, p. 1

Johnson, David. 1994. "No Link Found to Connect Abortion Clinic Violence." *New York Times*, December 31, p. A9.

Johnson, Dirk. 1993. "Abortions, Bibles and Bullets." *New York Times*, August 28.

Junas, Daniel. 1995 "The Rise of Citizen Militias: Angry White Guys with Guns." *Covert Action Quarterly* (Spring).

Karten, Howard A. 1993. "A Disdain for Political Theology." *Wall Street Journal*, April 15.

Kerrison, Ray. 1994. "The Real Abortion Violence Is inside Clinics." *Human Life Review* 20(Winter):108-9.

Laqueur, Walter. 1987. *The Age of Terrorism*. Boston: Little Brown.

Lewin, Tamar. 1994. "A Cause Worth Killing For?" *New York Times*, July 30.

Livingstone, Neil C. 1990. *The Cult of Counter-Terrorism*. Lexington, MA: Lexington.

Livingstone, Neil C. and T. E. Arnold, eds. 1986. *Fighting Back*. Lexington, MA: D.C. Heath.

Manegold, Catherine S. 1995. "Anti-Abortion Groups Disavow New Killings." *New York Times*, January 1.

"Man Sentenced for Attempt to Bomb Abortion Clinic." 1998. *Los Angeles Times*, February 10.

Manuel, Marlon. 1998. "Clinic Blast Witness May Have Shared Group's Views." *Atlanta Constitution*, February 5.

Merkl, Peter, ed. 1986. *Political Violence and Terror*. Berkeley: University of California Press.

Merkl, Peter H. and Leonard Weinberg 1993. *Encounters with the Contemporary Radical Right*. Boulder, CO: Westview.

"Militia Enemy List Uncovered." 1995. Institute for First Amendment Studies. http://www.body-politic.org/mag/back/art/O5Oipg25.htm.

Navarro, Mireya. 1996. "Abortion Clinics Report Drop in Harassment." *New York Times*, April 4.

Naylor, Janet. 1989. "Bomber of Clinics Won't Halt Opposition." *Washington Times*, July 4.

Nice, David C. 1988. "Abortion Clinic Bombings as Political Violence." *American Journal of Political Science* 32:178-95.

O'Connell, Lorraine. 1994. "Fanatics Differ from the Rest of Us in Absoluteness of Their Thinking." *Atlanta Journal Constitution*, August 7.

Orman, Neil. 1993. "Slain Doctor's Son Accuses Abortion Foes." *Houston Chronicle*, April 2.

O'Sullivan, Noel, ed. 1986. *Terrorism, Ideology and Revolution*. Boulder, CO: Westview.

Parshall, Gerald. 1995. "Abortion: Violence Begets Violence," *U.S.News & World Report*, January 9, p. 10.

Pear, Robert. 1996. "Protests at Abortion Clinics Have Fallen, and New Law Is Credited." *New York Times*, September 24, p. A18.

Pierce, William. 1980. *The Turner Diaries*, 2nd edition. Arlington, VA: National Vanguard.

Pierce, William. 1989. *Hunter*. Hillsboro, VA: National Vanguard.

Pike, Otis. 1995. "Call Them as They Are: Anti-Abortion Terrorists." *Houston Chronicle*, January 4.

Poland, James M. 1988. *Understanding Terrorism*. Englewood Cliffs, NJ: Prentice Hall.

"'Pro-Life' Terrorism." 1993. *Progressive*, December 10.

"Pro-Life Terrorism: A How-to." 1995. *Harper's*, January, pp. 19-22.

Puga, Ana. 1994a. "'Newcomers' Preach Violence." *Boston Globe*, October 30.

Puga, Ana. 1994b. "Pressed, More Providers Halting Their Practices." *Boston Globe*, November 1.

Reeves, Jay. 1998. "1 Killed in Abortion Clinic Bombing." *Birmingham News*, January 29.

Rimer, Sara. 1993. "Abortion Foes Boot Camp Ponders Doctor's Death." *New York Times*, March 18.

Risen, James. 1994. "Shooting Suspect Has Advocated Clinic Violence." *Los Angeles Times*, July 30.

Risen, James and Judy Thomas. 1998. *Wrath of Angels*. New York: Basic Books.

Sanders, Clinton R. and Eleanor Lyon. 1995. "Repetitive Retribution." Pp. 25-44 in *Cultural Criminology*, edited by Jeff Ferrell and Clinton R. Sanders. Boston: Northeastern University Press.

Scheidler, Joseph M. 1985. *Closed: 99 Ways to Stop Abortion*. San Francisco: Ignatius.

Sharp, Deborah. 1994. "Abortion Foes Speak Up to Reject Attacks." *USA Today*, August 1.

Shea, Lois. 1995. "Clinic Killings Another Form of Terrorism." *Boston Globe*, January 8.

"Shooting of Abortion Doctor Was Terrorism, Not Just Assault." 1993. *Denver Post*, editorial, August 25.

Smith, Brent L. 1994. *Terrorism in America*. Albany: SUNY Press

Smith, Gita M. 1998. "The Face of Terror." *Atlanta Constitution*, March 3.

Solinger, Rickie, Faye Ginsburg and Patricia Anderson, eds. 1998. *Abortion Wars*. Berkeley: University of California Press.

Stern, Kenneth S. 1996. *A Force upon The Plain*. New York: Simon & Schuster.

Stoddard, Thomas B. and Kenneth P. Norwick. 1978. *Denying the Right to Choose*. New York: American Civil Liberties Union's Campaign for Choice.

Stohl, Michael, ed. 1988. *The Politics of Terrorism*, 3rd edition. New York: Dekker.

Swarr, Amanda. 1995. "Terrorism and Murder." *Off Our Backs*, May.

"Taking the Measure of Terrorism." 1995. *St. Louis Post-Dispatch*, editorial, May 14.

Teepen, Tom. 1993. "First Amendment Doesn't Protect Abortion Terrorism." *Atlanta Constitution*, March 16.

Terry, Randall. 1988. *Operation Rescue*. Springdale, PA: Whitaker House.

U.S. House of Representatives. 1987. Abortion Clinic Violence: Oversight Hearings before the Subcommittee on Civil and Constitutional Rights of the Committee on the Judiciary, House of Representatives, 99th Congress, first and second sessions, March 6, 12, April 3, 1985; and December 17, 1986. Washington, DC: GPO.

U.S. House of Representatives. 1993. Abortion Clinic Violence. Hearings before the Subcommittee on Crime and Criminal Justice of the Committee on the Judiciary, House of Representatives, 103rd Congress, first session, April 1, June 10, 1993. Washington, DC: GPO.

U.S. Senate. 1995. Violence at Women's Health Clinics. Hearing before a subcommittee of the Committee on Appropriations, U.S. Senate, 104th Congress, first session, special hearing. Washington, DC: GPO.

Vetter, Harold and Gary R. Perlstein. 1991. *Perspectives on Terrorism*. Monterey, CA: Brooks-Cole/Wadsworth.

"Vigilance and Violence at Abortion Clinics." 1995. *St. Louis Post-Dispatch*, editorial, January 4.

Vrazo, Fawn. 1995. "Abortion Fight's Lethal Side." *Philadelphia Inquirer*, January 8.

Wardlaw, Grant. 1989. *Political Terrorism*, 2nd rev. edition. Cambridge: Cambridge University Press.

"When Extremism Becomes Terrorism." 1994. *Los Angeles Times*, editorial, July 30.

White, Jonathan R. 1991. *Terrorism*. Monterey, CA: Brooks-Cole/Wadsworth.

"Wichita's Long Hot Summer." 1991. *Christianity Today*, September 16, pp. 44-46.

Wicklund, Susan. 1995. "An Abortion Doctor's Diary of Terror." *Glamour* 93(4):282ff.

Wilkinson, Paul. 1986. *Terrorism and the Liberal State*. New York: New York University Press

"Woman Gets Twenty Year Sentence in Attacks on Abortion Clinics." 1995. *New York Times*, September 9.

4

REPORTING TERRORISM

If only there were evil people somewhere insidiously committing evil deeds and it were necessary only to separate them from the rest of us and destroy them. But the line dividing good and evil cuts through the heart of every human being, and who is willing to destroy a piece of his own heart?

—Alexander I. Solzhenitsyn

The relationship between journalists and terrorists is both basic and complex. To paraphrase Carlos Marighella, who wrote the manual for urban guerrillas: "the media are important instruments of propaganda for the simple reason that they find terrorist actions newsworthy" (Weimann & Winn, 1994, p. 112).

Interaction between the media and terrorism intensified throughout the 20th century because of the increase of available information and around-the-clock news coverage. With news being presented in multimedia packages and delivered in innovative ways, revolutionaries with political agendas have many more avenues for promoting their ideologies. At the same time, state-sponsored terrorism has a broader audience for mass propaganda campaigns and manipulation of news.

Although government influence on the media is still evident, Internet technology makes it possible for disenfranchised individuals to have access to information. The Net has brought about a democratization of the media. Some would argue that anyone with a Web site is capable of being a journalist online (Kees, 1998).

MEDIA, LAW, AND TERRORISM

Freedom of speech is guaranteed by the First Amendment to the U.S. Constitution. Its central meaning, according to President James Madison, was that the people had the power of censorship over the government, and not the government over the people. He considered this fundamental to the U.S. form of authority (FindLaw, 1998). Even with this protection in place, there have been many attempts to regulate malicious writings. One of the first was the Sedition Act of 1798, which prohibited utterances that excited the hatred of the people against the government.

Media law historically has been divided into two areas: telecommunications and print. The growth of the Internet and digital media has begun to blur the boundaries between the segments, and the bases for the distinctions in law between the two areas are no longer clear (Legal Information Institute, 2001). The Antiterrorism and Effective Death Penalty Act of 1996 included one legislative effort to regulate media cooperation with insurgents (Cole, 1996). Journalists were concerned that, broadly interpreted, the law of 1996 prohibited them from developing valid stories about terrorist groups (Hudson, 2000). The more recent antiterrorism legislation of 2001, the USA PATRIOT Act (2001), is viewed similarly.

Opposition to government through speech alone has been subject to punishment throughout much of U.S. history, but laws criminalizing speech have been struck down regularly by higher courts as inconsistent with the First Amendment (FindLaw, 1998). Some defenders of First Amendment liberties insist that terrorism exists because, in a larger sense, justice does not exist. According to those in opposition, the present corrupt legal system protects the guilty and persecutes the innocent. The ideology of a terrorist group identifies the "enemies" of the group, giving rise to the idea that certain people or things are somehow legitimate targets (Drake, 1998). U.S. citizens may believe they have the constitutional right to join a militia group, become a recluse anarchist, or join violent demonstrations to get political power if they perceive the government as illegal (Hinckley, 1996).

Other countries with democratic forms of government have different histories. Former prime minister of Israel Benjamin Netanyahu (1995) asserted "there is apparently a moment of truth in the life of many modern democracies when it is clear the unlimited defense of civil liberties has gone too far and impedes the protection of life and liberty, and governments decide to adopt active measures against the forces that menace their societies" (p. 32).

The "moment of truth," as Netanyahu terms it, involves the decision to limit the democratic process. Some of the limits to civil liberties imposed in response to the attacks of September 11, 2001, include maintaining close control over media access to information about the investigation into the hijacking and counterterrorist operations. The outcome of tight media controls in the United States remains to be seen, but the experience of other nations that have responded to terrorists by limiting civil liberties is revealing for the rest of the world.

In Peru, for example, the threat of the Shining Path terrorist group generated drastic limits to the democratic process in the late 1980s. Peru's congress, which had become ineffectual, was shut down by President Alberto Fujimori. The courts, which had been accused of complicity with terrorists, were turned into faceless, hooded tribunals with extended judicial powers. All citizens were forced to restrict their activities and were required to provide documents at multiple checkpoints for all movement. Along with increased police powers came increased corruption, and a great deal of brutality was authorized by the state (Palmer, 1994).

In response to terrorism, direct, state-imposed censorship has been common throughout the world. In France, "Bastille Syndrome" is the term used to describe various presidents' intensive interference in broadcasting (Weimann & Winn, 1994). Creating a generalized fearfulness and irrationality gives state leaders greater freedom of action. Terrorism has been used repeatedly to advance tyrannical agendas, justify exceptional legislation, encroach on individual rights, increase internal surveillance, enlarge the role of military forces, and put pressure on journalists to cooperate with agents of the state (Herman & O'Sullivan, 1989). A fear of terrorism has contributed to the vulnerability of democracies to repressive tendencies (Weimann & Winn, 1994). A real threat of subversion is posed not only by guerrillas but also by the reaction of the forces of authority. A common reaction involves censorship and control of public information.

In covering terrorism, the media are damned if they do and damned if they do not exercise self-restraint (Nacos, 1994). The public's need to be informed has to be balanced by journalists' responsibility to prevent unnecessary harm. Three issues are at stake when media sources provide information about terrorism: interference, cooperation, and commercialism.

Interfering in State Operations Against Terrorism

Journalists have become targets of terrorist activity and are repeatedly threatened for expressing opinions contrary to terrorist goals. Throughout Spain, for example, ETA (Euskadi ta Askatasuna or Basque Fatherland and Liberty) terrorists describe journalists and the media who do not share their radical nationalist ideology as Basque traitors or Spanish invaders. According to ETA pronouncements, the media are the mouthpiece for a strategy of news manipulation and instigation of war in Basque Country, an area that lies along the border between Spain and France. Some 100 journalists have been placed under police protection in response to mail bombs and attacks against two of the largest newspapers in the Basque region. Still other journalists were exiled (Mater, 2000). In the United States, NBC newscaster Tom Brokaw and other media-related targets were the intended victims of anthrax sent by mail by terrorists in 2001. Many U.S. journalists have been held hostage, assassinated, or threatened by homegrown and transnational terrorists at home and abroad. Journalists may be targeted because of their views or what they have reported. It is just as likely that their notoriety makes reporters valuable as hostages regardless of their opinions.

How reporters and photographers should act in tense terrorist situations is only one part of the equation for measuring journalistic responsibility. Another is how news managers decide under enormous pressure what should be aired live, what should be aired later, and what should never appear before the public. According to many in law enforcement, the public does not need to see tactical police activity live (Shepard, 2000). Although this may make sense from the standpoint of law enforcement, from a First Amendment standpoint it provides opportunities for police tactics to be obfuscated. Terrorist attacks can be re-created to fit particular political agendas unless they are recorded for the public by journalists and others who represent outside interests on the scene. The U.S. attacks on Afghanistan in 2001 provide a good example. It is essential that journalists observed the bombings as they occurred rather than reporting what authorities directed them to announce after the fact.

Many questions have been raised about the impact of the media on terrorism. The sheer volume of information provided makes a difference with regard to the outcome of terrorist events. When the group Black September took hostages at the Munich Olympics in 1972, the media became involved in the minute details. Because media coverage of the Olympics was already in place, the attack became the center of attention for the entire world. The kidnapping of Israeli Olympic athletes increased worldwide support and sympathy for Israel. The media coverage created the image of hooded, enigmatic, and angry Arab terrorists armed with machine guns who cold-bloodedly killed 11 hostages. The complexities of the conflict were not explored, and the incompetence and misdirection of the authorities in Munich were never explained (Morrison, 2000).

Other aspects of the form and presentation of news may affect terrorism in unknown ways (Barnhurst, 1991). Journalists amplify, arbitrate, and create their own rhetoric about terrorist acts. According to Picard (1991), reporters can choose from four different traditions of reporting to relate terrorist events. In the *information* tradition, reports are expected to be factual and reliably documented. News about terrorism is notably poorly corroborated, although it may appear to be in the information tradition. In the more *sensationalist* tradition, coverage includes emotions, alarm, threat, anger, and fear. Tabloids have an extremely large audience for sensationalized coverage not only in the United States but also globally, and the tabloid style is sometimes found in mainstream daily newspaper reporting about terrorism. When the tradition is toward *feature stories*, the focus is on individuals as heroes, villains, victims, and perpetrators. Feature stories provoke readers with an actual person with whom to relate in emotional ways, using methods similar to the tabloid style, but they are taken more seriously. Features are expected to be reliable reporting. In the *didactic* tradition, the report is intended as an explanation, and the goal is purported to be educating the public. Documentaries about terrorists and terrorism reveal a particular perspective and also support news industry agendas and pander to sponsors' interests. Explanations carry a slant and a viewpoint that reflect the people and organizations making them, though these individuals and groups may present themselves as neutral. Each of these four traditions is useful in different ways and times to both journalists and terrorists.

The impact of media accounts also varies based on the audience receiving the reports, the types of events being reported, and other events that may preempt public attention. Complex factors must be considered in assessing the media's responsibilities in reporting terrorist events.

News organizations have sets of standards and policies on how to react to a variety of conditions in reporting the news. Few of these organizations, however, were prepared to deal with the questions and issues raised by a case such as that of the Unabomber in 1995. Theodore Kaczynski was a disenchanted mathematics professor turned anarchist who espoused an "earth first" ideology. By sending mail bombs to researchers and others in academia, he attacked the representatives of modernity and biotechnology in particular. Now serving an unconditional life sentence, the Unabomber built explosives in a remote, ramshackle cabin where he lived in isolation in Montana. His terrorist pursuits spanned 17 years, killed 3 people, and maimed 29 others. The FBI called the case UNABOM after the first targets, *UN*iversity researchers and *A*irline executives (Walton, 1997). Kaczynski was the author of lengthy diatribes against the course of development and the federal government. The decision by *The Washington Post* and *The New York Times* to publish the Unabomber's 35,000-word manifesto against technology is one instance of media cooperation that has long-term troubling implications for media managers everywhere. The decision was debated heatedly and widely (Harper, 1995). Critics insist that publication of the manifesto set a precedent that encourages terrorists to use the mass media to promote their political views. Since then, the Unabomber has become an icon on the Internet, and his manifesto is available in its totality on several Web sites (Walton, 1997).

Cooperating With Terrorists or With Government Control

News stories are symbolic expressions that create but also are created by culture. The ideal of media objectivity and the reality of subjective bias is a good example of a basic conflict in U.S. culture. According to Solomon (1999), there is an Orwellian logic behind calling bombings by Third World countries "terrorism," while bombings by the United States are righteous "strikes against terror." Herman and O'Sullivan (1989) pointed out that media accounts in the United States seldom cover the precipitating events from which subsequent terrorist events have sprung. Instead, terrorism is commonly reported as an isolated event, out of context, making the perpetrators seem unprovoked and inexplicably evil. Nevertheless, most of the concern about media cooperation has to do with journalists' support for terrorist interests, whereas the cooperation of the media with government interests frequently goes unnoticed.

A study of 258 reports about 127 incidents of political violence showed that the media quoted primary sources less than 6% of the time. That proportion is far below what would normally be considered good practice (Picard & Adams, 1991). Indications are that journalists rely on government sources, particularly the FBI, for most of the information that is reported about terrorists in the United States. What the public knows about terrorists is largely filtered through a process of government control of information. Although the First Amendment prohibits censorship, it makes no reference to restricting information by ensuring that journalists voluntarily rely on only one official source of information.

Wilkinson (1997) asserts that it is intrinsic to the very activity of terrorization that some form of media, however crude, is utilized as an instrument to disseminate the messages of threat and intimidation. The theory that the media are, in part, a cause of terrorism is based on the assumption that by attacking a Western democracy, terrorists will receive benefits from the media through coverage of the incident. The three primary benefits that terrorists may expect are publicity to spread their message, opportunities to provide background and interpretation for their actions, and a level of legitimacy that would otherwise be unobtainable (Becker, 1996).

Targets of terror do not lose their usefulness to terrorists even when violent incidents result in negative media coverage, public outcries against brutality, and widespread sympathy for victims. A nation enraged over terrorism either encourages or inhibits governmental responses in ways that may serve terrorist aims (Nacos, 1994), yet it is often difficult to see the gain obtained through media spotlights on terrorist events. As one example, U.S. public opinion data show conclusively that the bombing of the Murrah Federal Building in Oklahoma City did not provoke personal apprehension and therefore failed as an act of terrorism. It changed neither the public's assessment of danger nor their reported behavior (Lewis, 2000).

It would be simplistic and naïve, however, to presume that media impact may be measured by the response to one event. Media images may influence subjects at a deeper level. In Tel Aviv, Slone (2000) found that media portrayals of terrorism, political violence, and threats to national security provoked anxiety in individual viewers. In an environment where bombings are frequent occurrences, she questioned the veracity of studies claiming that the influence of the mass media is negligible and benign. There is no simple index of negative or positive impact that can determine how the media and terrorism are related.

In the search for a simple explanation, the idea that media are the contagion of terrorism has been widely heralded. According to the theory of contagion, terrorism is cultivated and spread by media coverage. The fear of an epidemic of violence has been used repeatedly to justify efforts to alter media coverage even though there is no significant evidence that media act as a contagion (Picard, 1991). Because terrorism is a "creature" of the media, according to widespread public belief, the media are expected to be aware of their operative role in the terror syndrome and to cooperate with law enforcement (Onder, 1999). Media cooperation with law enforcement in support of government is more likely than media cooperation with terrorist aims. Journalists have more to gain from upholding the status quo than from attacking it.

In the United States, the media are responsible for vast and intractable errors involving a highly skewed perspective about the Middle East and the Southern Hemisphere. A preeminence of belief in Israelis as victims and a pattern of preference for news about Muslim terrorists accompanies a general disposition of the press to downplay terrorist events on the predominantly Spanish-speaking continent of South America. The media perspective in the United States obscures the complete picture readers deserve (CAMERA Media Report, 1995; "Media Coverage Related to Terrorism," 1999; Weimann & Winn, 1994). This is a good example of the way government biases are reflected in information management.

Selling Terrorism: Commercial and Political Interests in Media Reports

The mass media are large, profit-seeking corporations, owned and controlled by wealthy people, heavily dependent on advertising for revenue, and interlocked with other members of the corporate system. The media focus on non-state terrorism, with themes often based on a threat to democracy. State terrorism, when it is reported, is rarely that committed by the United States or its allies. The specific dramatic terrorist events emphasized divert public attention away from "wholesale" terror that is compatible with corporate, state, political, and propaganda interests. The basic rule has been that if foreign violence clashes with capitalism, it may be designated "terrorist"; if not, the word is not applied (Herman & O'Sullivan, 1989).

A survey of journalists in association with the *Columbia Journalism Review* in 1999 found that newsworthy stories have been purposely avoided, and good stories all too frequently are not pursued because of commercial and competitive pressures (Pew Research Center, 1999). At the same time, the global media have been accused of "overkill." For instance, it is widely agreed that in 1996, TV news and the weekend news analysis programs overplayed the Olympic park bombing in Atlanta and the crash of TWA Flight 800. They were accused of pandering to the public's supposed need for instant villains by overhyping the unproved terrorism angle (Douglas, 1996).

News about terrorism may be manufactured in several different ways. One is inflating the menace on the basis of modest, not very threatening, but real actions. Another is the false transfer of responsibility for a terrorist act to a convenient scapegoat. Terrorism is also manufactured in the private sector, sometimes in collusion with agents of the state, to incriminate organizers, resisters, activists, and political enemies (Herman & O'Sullivan, 1989). Although news of terrorist events is seldom outright fabrication, the stories may be manufactured from selected elements and assumptions, with the support of both commercial and government interests. Journalists are being asked to achieve an equilibrium between market orientation and a mission to bolster public confidence (Rosenfeld, 1996). This balance has nothing to do with either validity or impartial reporting of events.

Two elements are necessary for the temperate, considered reporting of terrorism: audiences who prefer reasoned discourse on the news over "infotainment" and "terrorvision" and a professional culture of journalists who have sensitivity to the impact of reporting (Weimann & Winn, 1994). Regulation of the media, by either internal or external authority, will not provide these elements, nor will limiting the democratic process. The relationship between the media and terrorism is much too complex; it is controlled by the culture, not regulations from any single source.

MAKING MARTYRS: TERRORISTS AND THE DEATH PENALTY

The execution of Oklahoma City bomber Timothy McVeigh in 2001 brought up many profound conflicts about terrorists that reflect the impact of culture on the media. Jessica Stern, a lecturer at Harvard University's Kennedy School of Government who served on the National Security Council, has argued that when it comes to terrorism, national security concerns about the effectiveness of the death penalty should be paramount. According to Stern (2001), executions play right into the hands of the country's adversaries, turning criminals into martyrs, inviting retaliatory strikes, and enhancing public relations and fund-raising for national enemies. Moreover, dead terrorists don't talk, whereas live terrorists can become an intelligence asset because they are sources of much-needed information.

McVeigh was 29 years old when he was captured in 1995, very shortly after the bombing of the federal building in Oklahoma City in which 168 people were killed. He was convicted in 1997 of what was then considered the single worst terrorist act in U.S. history. Even though his biography describes an unremarkable, lonely life marked by frustration and an obsession with guns, the former Army corporal became one of the best known and least understood media figures of the 1990s (CNN, 1998; Pastore, 1997). His execution raised concern that he may become an inspiration to a new generation of terrorists. His death may serve the cause of antigovernment, right-wing militias and lead to more deaths rather than ending the threat.

Timothy McVeigh being escorted to his arraignment for bombing the Alfred P. Murrah Federal Building in Oklahoma City. McVeigh was put to death by lethal injection.

Photo copyright © by Reuters NewMedia Inc./CORBIS, April 22, 1995. Reprinted with permission.

A comparison of the reaction to the execution of McVeigh by the American public with the reaction in Peru when the leader of the Shining Path, Abimael Guzman, was captured in 1992 is a remarkable illustration of cultural influences on the media. Guzman's career in terror spanned more than 10 years in Peru. The terrorist era destabilized Peru, causing both social and economic crises (Barnhurst, 1991). The Shining Path is not typical of modern terrorist organizations because it eschewed media

A night photo of the Alfred P. Murrah Federal Building shows the scope of the destruction caused by the blast, which killed 168 people and injured hundreds more.

Federal Emergency Management Agency (FEMA).

attention. The group used violent tactics as the most potent tool with which to communicate with the public.

On the other hand, Peruvian antiterrorist sources were ambivalent about media attention. From the standpoint of propaganda and manipulating public opinion, journalists appeared useful, but from the perspective of reporting police brutality and the corruption of counterterrorist forces, journalists were a threat. Opinion polls in several Latin American countries indicate that the news media are held in high public regard, outstripping all other national institutions, including the Roman Catholic Church (Bilello, 1998). The status of journalists made them a formidable interest group with which Peruvian authorities needed to cooperate and over which they wanted control.

When he took office in 1990, President Fujimori demonstrated single-minded manipulation of the media. He used the press to promote his political agenda and excluded it from areas of potential scandal in the name of national security against the threat of terror. Because the threat was real, public opinion generally was influenced in favor of strict measures to control the threat. The counterterrorist squad was given a new name to attract the public's attention. The celebrated officer in charge had a strong presence in both the press and television news. Media reports were dependent on government sources, or hearsay, for the most part because the terrorists distrusted journalists and the misuse of information. During his years in hiding, personal reports from Guzman were limited to two videos and some writings that surfaced during his life underground. Most of the details about the leaders of the Shining Path still have not come to light because of the strong code of secrecy that protected the group (Mahan, 1997).

The details that were made public were disseminated by government news authorities. From the picture that emerged in the press, Guzman was an unlikely terrorist. A former university professor, he was said to be both weak and unyielding. His capture was a special event, planned and staged for the media. In the video of his first statement, Guzman, who was seriously myopic, did not have his glasses and appeared befuddled and goofy. Later, in custody, Guzman was dressed in a special uniform designed expressly for press appearances by notorious terrorists. The huge black and white stripes of his outfit, a technique of theatrical costuming, were designed to make him appear guilty and powerless.

In his first appearance in custody, Guzman was shown in a large, cagelike structure. The cameras were set up a good distance from him, as they might be when filming a dangerous animal. The microphone was installed inside the cage. In the video, which was shown on all major news outlets throughout the world, Guzman appeared to be ranting and raging because he was yelling at the cameras, not realizing the microphone was nearby. The image is dramatic and at the

Abimael Guzman, the leader of Peru's Sendero Luminso (Shining Path), shortly after his capture in September 1992. His "speech from the cage" was manipulated by the Peruvian government and witnessed by over 200 international journalists.

Photo copyright © AFP/CORBIS. Reprinted with permission.

same time laughable. Through staging, the man who had been considered powerful and even immortal throughout Peru became instantly foolish and impotent.

In the media rush following his capture, the skills and cunning of the agents of antiterrorism were glorified. At the same time, the weaknesses of the enemy were exposed. The public found out that Guzman, 55 years of age, had been tracked by his use of medications for his psoriasis and tendency toward upper respiratory illnesses. The agents found bottles in the trash that led them to his last hideout. He was captured after more than 15 years of clandestine life because of his known ailments. In short order, Guzman went from being a threat to being a joke in journalists' reports about him (BBC, 1999; *Dr. Abimael Guzman's [Chairman Gonzalo] "Speech from a Cage,"* 2000).

Some of the final images the Peruvian public has of Guzman are the impression they were given by the media of the stronghold set up to hold him and the barren island where he will spend the remainder of his days. Guzman is completely closed off from the rest of the world but exists just out in the harbor from the capital in Lima, never to be forgotten. He will die in ignominy as far as most Peruvians are concerned. They see little reason to fear that he will be viewed as a martyr or incite more violence.

HIGHLIGHTS OF REPRINTED ARTICLES

The two articles that follow provide contrast and variation to the theme of media and terror. They were selected because they offer contrasting views on the subject. The first is a broad, informative study of perspectives, trends, and options; the second presents a personal point of view from dramatic experiences with the power of the media in the global system.

Raphael F. Perl. (1997, October 22). *Terrorism, the Media, and the Government: Perspectives, Trends, and Options for Policymakers* (Congressional Research Service Issue Brief). Retrieved June 7, 2002, from http://usinfo.state.gov/topical/pol/terror/crs.htm

Raphael F. Perl provides an overview while examining the competing perspectives in the arena of world terrorism. A specialist in international affairs, foreign affairs, and national defense, Perl provides a clear examination of the opposing interests involved in reporting terrorism. Because his analysis was prepared for government officials, though, Perl does not consider the dilemmas that arise from state control of information during terrorist events. Instead, his coverage is divided into discussion of what terrorists want, what the media wants, and what government wants. A useful section of the article includes options for improving government/media interaction that take the three different interest groups into account.

Perl noted an underlying dilemma faced by legitimate authorities seeking to create public policy concerning terrorism. The conflict is based on common interests in freedom of the press in contrast with the threat that the media may promote the cause of terrorism or its methods. This dilemma is not likely to be resolved soon. On one hand, concern is raised over restricting members of the media from having access to sources of facts to report terrorism; on the other, the fear is raised of irresponsible reporting by misguided and manipulated journalists. Perl notes the danger of eroding constitutional freedoms, especially the freedom of the press—one of the pillars of democracy.

Terry Anderson. (1993). "Terrorism and Censorship: The Media in Chains." *Journal of International Affairs*, *47*(1), 127-136.

Terry Anderson is a well-known journalist who was taken hostage in Lebanon in 1985. He provides a valuable perspective on conflicts of interest between terrorists, the authorities, and the media. From his experience, Anderson raises many disturbing questions about national security and journalistic responsibility to victims. He concludes that there can be no standard for the media to which all situations of terrorism could be applied. Instead, he has concluded that the questions about responsibility for the lives of hostages and about the risks involved with reporting terror that journalists encounter in their work can be answered only individually, and as each occurs. Anderson's article shows how one reporter has struggled with the questions of balancing the public's right to know with the culpability and obligation for those involved that journalists must carry.

EXPLORING MEDIA AND TERRORISM FURTHER

- To see the source of much of the information that is used by the media, go to the FBI Web page (www.fbi.gov/homepage.htm), which provides numerous links to the official U.S. government versions of terrorist events.
- The Web sites of all the global news services—CNN, Reuters, ABC, NBC, CBS, BBC, and others—maintain archives of information about terrorism, which makes it possible to compare viewpoints and check facts about specific groups and events. These sites can be found through various search engines.
- The Pew Research Center for the People and the Press (www.people-press.org) is a good source of research and policy suggestions for the media with regard to terrorism.
- For the complete record of the trial of Unabomber Theodore Kaczynski, see the Time/CNN site www.time.com/time/reports/unabomber/manifesto_toc.html

VIDEO NOTES

How terrorism was actually reported in one extreme example is documented by the film *One Day in September* (Columbia TriStar, 1999, 91 min.), which details the kidnapping of Israeli athletes at the Munich Olympics in 1972.

REFERENCES

Anderson, Terry. (1993). Terrorism and censorship: The media in chains. *Journal of International Affairs, 47*(1), 127-136.

Antiterrorism and Effective Death Penalty Act of 1996, Pub. L. No. 104-132, 110 Stat. 1214 (1996).

Barnhurst, Kevin G. (1991). Contemporary terrorism in Peru: Sendero Luminoso and the media. *Journal of Communication, 41*(4), 75-89.

BBC. (1999, July 15). Peru's Shining Path—Who are they? Retrieved June 7, 2002, from http://news.bbc.co.uk/hi/english/world/americas/newsid_395000/395370.stm

Becker, Jon B. (1996). The news media, terrorism, and democracy: The symbiotic relationship between freedom of the press and acts of terror. Retrieved June 7, 2002, from http://205.158.5.90/lasd-eob/eob-tr2

Bilello, Suzanne. (1998, October 7). Popularity of Latin American press outstrips other institutions. *Freedom Forum.* Retrieved June 17, 2002, from www.freedomforum.org/templates/document.asp?documentID=4880

CAMERA Media Report (The Committee for Accuracy in Middle East Reporting in America). (1995). *Media bury Israeli dead, 6*(1). Retrieved June 7, 2002, from http://world.std.com/~camera/docs/cmr61/bury61.html

CNN. (1998). Timothy McVeigh: Convicted Oklahoma City bomber. *CNN Newsmaker Profiles.* Retrieved June 7, 2002, from www.cnn.com/resources/newsmakers/us/newsmakers/mcveigh.html

Cole, David. (1996) Terrorizing the Constitution. *The Nation.* Retrieved June 17, 2002, from http://past.thenation.com/issue/960325cole.htm

Douglas, Susan. (1996). Terror and bathos. *The Progressive, 60*(9), 40.

Dr. Abimael Guzman's (Chairman Gonzalo) "Speech from a cage," September 24, 1992. (2000). International Emergency Committee to Defend the Life of Dr. Abimael Guzman-U.S. Retrieved June 17, 2002, from www.csrp.org/speech.htm

Drake, C. J. M. (1998). The role of ideology in terrorists' target selection. *Terrorism and Political Violence, 10*(2), 53-85.

FindLaw. (1998). U. S. Constitution: First Amendment: Annotations. Retrieved June 7, 2002, from http://caselaw.lp.findlaw.com/data/constitution/amendment01/18.html

Harper, Christopher. (1995). Did the Unabomber decision set a precedent? *American Journalism Review, 17*(9), 13-15.

Herman, Edward S., & O'Sullivan, Gerry. (1989). *The terrorism industry: The experts and institutions that shape our view of terror.* New York: Pantheon.

Hinckley, Thomas. (1996). TWA 800 Terrorist Cover up? "The media makes terrorism possible and profitable. Retrieved June 7, 2002, from www.chuckbaldwinlive.com/twa2.html

Hudson, David. (2000, March 8). Federal appeals panel finds anti-terrorism law unconstitutionally vague. *Freedom Forum.* Retrieved June 17, 2002, from www.freedomforum.org/templates/document.asp?documentID=11831

Kees, Beverly. (1998, August 12). Net can renew democracy for disenfranchised. *Freedom Forum.* Retrieved June 17, 2002, from www.freedomforum.org/templates/document.asp?documentID=11300

Legal Information Institute. (2001). Media law: An overview. Retrieved June 7, 2002, from www.law.cornell.edu/topics/media.html

Lewis, Carol W. (2000). The terror that failed: Public opinion in the aftermath of the bombing in Oklahoma City. *Public Administration Review, 60*(3), 201-210.

Mahan, Sue. (1997, March). *Women of the Shining Path: A new model for terrorism in Peru.* Paper presented at the Academy of Criminal Justice Sciences, Louisville, KY.

Mater, Gene. (2000, July 7). Basque separatists threaten safety of journalists, says reporters group. *Freedom Forum.* Retrieved June 17, 2002, from www.freedomforum.org/templates/document.asp?documenteID=2967

Media coverage related to terrorism. (1999, December 27). Retrieved June 7, 2002, from www.musalman.com/islamnews/ing-mediacoverageterrorism.html

Morrison, Mike. (2000). Munich massacre: The worst tragedy in modern Olympic history. Retrieved June 7, 2002, from www.infoplease.com/spot/mm-munich.html

Nacos, Brigitte. (1994). *Terrorism and the media.* New York: Columbia University Press.

Netanyahu, Benjamin. (1995). *Fighting terrorism: How democracies can defeat domestic and international terrorists.* New York: Farrar Straus Giroux.

Onder, James J. (1999). Media & law enforcement relations during hostage-taking terrorist incidences: A cooperative decision. *Responder Magazine, 6*(1), 26-33.

Palmer, David S. (Ed.). (1994). *Shining Path of Peru* (2nd ed.). New York: St. Martin's Press.

Pastore, Nick. (1997, June 11). Execution would make Timothy McVeigh a martyr. *USA Today.* Retrieved June 17, 2002, from www.cjpf.org/pubs/mcveigh.html

Perl, Raphael F. (1997, October 22). *Terrorism, the media, and the government: Perspectives, trends, and options for policymakers* (Congressional Research Service Issue Brief). Retrieved June 7, 2002, from http://usinfo.state.gov/topical/pol/terror/crs.htm

The Pew Research Center for the People & the Press. (1999). Self censorship: How often and why. Retrieved June 7, 2002, from http://208.240.91.18/jour00rpt.htm

Picard, Robert G. (1991). Journalists as targets and victims of terrorism. In Yonah Alexander & Robert G. Picard (Eds.), *In the camera's eye.* Washington, DC: Macmillan-Brassey's.

Picard, Robert, & Adams, Paul. (1991). Characterisations of acts and perpetrators of political violence in three elite U.S. daily newspapers. In A. O. Alali & K. K. Eke (Eds.), *Media Coverage of Terrorism.* Newbury Park, CA: Sage.

Rosenfeld, Shalom. (1996). *Blood-red headlines feed terrorist propaganda* (IPI Report). Vienna: International Press Institute.

Sedition Act of 1798. (1798). An act in addition to the Act, entitled An Act for the Punishment of Certain Crimes against the United States, 1 Stat. 112 1790.

Shepard, Alicia C. (2000). Safety first. *American Journalism Review, 22*(1), 22-28. Retrieved June 7, 2002, from www.ajr.org/Article.asp?id=518

Slone, Michelle. (2000). Responses to media coverage of terrorism. *Journal of Conflict Resolution, 44*(4), 508-522.

Solomon, Norman. (1999). *The habits of highly deceptive media*. New York: Common Courage Press.

Stern, Jessica. (2001, February 28). Execute terrorists at our own risk. *New York Times*. Retrieved June 7, 2002, from www.ksg.harvard.edu/news/opeds/stern_terrorism_nyt.htm

USA PATRIOT Act of 2001. Uniting and Strengthening America by Providing Appropriate Tools Required to Intercept and Obstruct Terrorism Act, Pub. L. No. 107-56 (2001).

Walton, Andrew. (1997). Unabomber became an icon on the 'Net. Retrieved June 7, 2002, from www.cnn.com/SPECIALS/1997/unabomb/investigation/icon

Weimann, Gabriel, & Winn, Conrad. (1994). *The theater of terror: Mass media and international terrorism*. New York: Longman.

Wilkinson, Paul. (1997). The media and terrorism: A reassessment. *Terrorism and Political Violence*, *9*(2), 51-64.

TERRORISM, THE MEDIA, AND THE GOVERNMENT

Perspectives, Trends, and Options for Policymakers

Raphael F. Perl

Summary

Terrorists, governments, and the media see the function, roles and responsibilities of the media when covering terrorist events from differing and often competing perspectives. Such perspectives drive behavior during terrorist incidents—often resulting in both tactical and strategic gains to the terrorist operation and the overall terrorist cause. The challenge to both the governmental and press communities is to understand the dynamics of terrorist enterprise and to develop policy options designed to serve the interests of government, the media, and the society.

Terrorists must have publicity in some form if they are to gain attention, inspire fear and respect, and secure favorable understanding of their cause, if not their act. Governments need public understanding, cooperation, restraint, and loyalty in efforts to limit terrorist harm to society and in efforts to punish or apprehend those responsible for terrorist acts. Journalists and the media in general pursue the freedom to cover events and issues without restraint, especially governmental restraint.

Three new trends appear to be emerging which impact on the relationship between the media, the terrorist, and government. These include: (1) anonymous terrorism; (2) more violent terrorist incidents; and (3) terrorist attacks on media personnel and institutions.

A number of options, none without costs and risks, exist for enhancing the effectiveness of government media-oriented responses to terrorism and for preventing the media from furthering terrorist goals as a byproduct of vigorous and free reporting. These include: (1) financing joint media/government training exercises; (2) establishing a government terrorism information response center; (3) promoting use of media pools; (4) promoting voluntary press coverage guidelines; and (5) monitoring terrorism against the media.

The media and the government have common interests in seeing that the media are not manipulated into promoting the cause of terrorism or its methods. But policymakers do not want to see terrorism, or anti-terrorism, eroding freedom of the press—one of the pillars of democratic societies. This appears to be a dilemma that cannot be completely reconciled—one with which societies will continually have to struggle. The challenge for policymakers is to explore mechanisms enhancing media/government cooperation to accommodate the citizen and media need for honest coverage while limiting the gains uninhibited coverage may provide terrorists or their cause. Communication between the government and the media here is an important element in any strategy to prevent terrorist causes and strategies from prevailing and to preserve democracy.

From "Terrorism, the Media, and the Government: Perspectives, Trends, and Options for Policymakers," Perl. Retrieved from U.S. Department of State (1997), International Information Programs, http://usinfo.state.gov/topical/pol/terror/crs.htm

This document is dated October 22, 1997.

INTRODUCTION

This paper responds to a range of inquiries received by CRS on the nature of the relationship of terrorist initiatives, publicity, and governments. The media are known to be powerful forces in confrontations between terrorists and governments. Media influence on public opinion may impact not only the actions of governments but also on those of groups engaged in terrorist acts. From the terrorist perspective, media coverage is an important measure of the success of a terrorist act or campaign. And in hostage-type incidents, where the media may provide the only independent means a terrorist has of knowing the chain of events set in motion, coverage can complicate rescue efforts. Governments can use the media in an effort to arouse world opinion against the country or group using terrorist tactics. Public diplomacy and the media can also be used to mobilize public opinion in other countries to pressure governments to take, or reject, action against terrorism.[1]

Margaret Thatcher's metaphor that publicity is the oxygen of terrorism underlines the point that public perception is a major terrorist target and the media are central in shaping and moving it. For terrorism, the role of the media is critical.

This report examines competing perspectives on the desired role for the media when covering terrorist incidents: what the terrorist wants, what the government wants, and what the media wants when covering a terrorist event. These are classic perspectives drawn from the experiences of this century. It then addresses three recent trends that impact on the relationship between terrorism and the media and concludes with options for congressional consideration.

COMPETING PERSPECTIVES ON THE ROLE OF THE MEDIA WHEN COVERING TERRORIST EVENTS

Terrorists, governments, and the media see the function, roles and responsibilities of the media, when covering terrorist events, from differing and often opposing perspectives. Such perceptions drive respective behaviors during terrorist incidents—often resulting in tactical and strategic gains, or losses, to the terrorist operation and the overall terrorist cause. The challenge to the governmental and press community is to understand the dynamics of terrorist enterprise and to develop policy options to serve government, media and societal interests.

What Terrorists Want From Media

- Terrorists need publicity, usually free publicity that a group could normally not afford or buy. Any publicity surrounding a terrorist act alerts the world that a problem exists that cannot be ignored and must be addressed. From a terrorist perspective, an unedited interview with a major figure is a treasured prize, such as the May 1997 CNN interview with Saudi dissident, terrorist recruiter and financier Usama Bin Ladin. For news networks, access to a terrorist is a hot story and is usually treated as such.

- They seek a **favorable understanding of their cause**, if not their act. One may not agree with their act but this does not preclude being sympathetic to their plight and their cause. Terrorists believe the public "needs help" in understanding that their cause is just and terrorist violence is the only course of action available to them against the superior evil forces of state and establishment. Good relationships with the press are important here and they are often cultivated and nurtured over a period of years.

- Terrorist organizations may also seek to court, or place, sympathetic **personnel in press positions**—particularly in wire services—and in some instances may even seek to control smaller news organizations through funding.

- Legitimacy. Terrorist causes want the press to give **legitimacy to what is often portrayed as ideological or personality feuds or divisions between armed groups and political wings**. For the military tactician, war is the continuation of politics by other means; for the sophisticated terrorist, politics is the continuation of terror by other means. IRA and Hamas are examples of groups having "political" and "military" components. Musa Abu Marzuq, for example, who was in charge of the political wing of Hamas is believed to have approved specific bombings and assassinations.[2] Likewise, the "dual hat" relationship of Gerry

Adams of Sinn Fein—the purported political wing of the IRA—to other IRA activities is subject to speculation. Distinctions are often designed to help people join the ranks, or financially contribute to the terrorist organization.

- They also want the press to notice and give **legitimacy to the findings and viewpoints of specially created non-governmental organizations (NGOs) and study centers** that may serve as covers for terrorist fund raising, recruitment, and travel by terrorists into the target country. The Palestinian Islamic Jihad-funded and controlled World and Islam Studies Enterprise is but one known example. The Hamas-funded Islamic Association for Palestine (IAP) in Richardson, Texas, is another of many.[3]

- In **hostage situations—terrorists need to have details on identity**, number and value of hostages, as well as details about pending **rescue attempts**, and details on the public exposure of their operation. Particularly where state sponsors are involved, they want details about any plans for military retaliation.

- Terrorist organizations seek media coverage that **causes damage to their enemy**. This is particularly noticeable when the perpetrators of the act and the rationale for their act remain unclear. They want the media to amplify panic, to spread fear, to facilitate economic loss (like scaring away investment and tourism), to make populations lose faith in their governments' ability to protect them, and to trigger government and popular overreaction to specific incidents and the overall threat of terrorism.

What Government Leaders Want From the Media

Governments seek understanding, cooperation, restraint, and loyalty from the media in efforts to limit terrorist harm to society and in efforts to punish or apprehend those responsible for terrorist acts, specifically:[4]

- They want coverage **to advance their agenda and not that of the terrorist**. From their perspective, the media should support government courses of action when operations are under way and disseminate government provided information when requested. This includes understanding of policy objectives, or at least a balanced presentation, e.g., why governments may seek to mediate, yet not give in to terrorist demands.

- An important goal is to **separate the terrorist from the media**—to deny the terrorist a platform unless to do so is likely to contribute to his imminent defeat.[5]

- Another goal is to **have the media present terrorists as criminals** and avoid glamorizing them; to foster the viewpoint that kidnapping a prominent person, blowing up a building, or hijacking an airplane is a criminal act regardless of the terrorists' cause.

- In hostage situations, governments often prefer to exclude the media and others from the immediate area, but they want the news organizations to **provide information to authorities** when reporters have access to the hostage site.

- They seek publicity to help **diffuse the tension of a situation**, not contribute to it. Keeping the public reasonably calm is an important policy objective.

- It is generally advantageous if the media, especially television, **avoids "weeping mother" emotional stories on relatives of victims**, as such coverage builds public pressure on governments to make concessions.

- During incidents, they wish **to control terrorist access to outside data**—to restrict information on hostages that may result in their selection for harm; government strongly desires the media **not to reveal planned or current anti-terrorist actions** or provide the terrorists with data that helps them.

- After incidents, they want the media not to reveal government secrets or detail techniques on how successful operations were performed—and not to publicize successful or thwarted terrorist technological achievements and operational methods so that copycat terrorists do not emulate or adapt them.[6]

- They want the media **to be careful about disinformation** from terrorist allies, sympathizers, or others who gain from its broadcast and publication. Many groups have many motives for disseminating inaccurate or false data, including, for example, speculation as to how a plane may have been blown up, or who may be responsible.

- They want the media **to boost the image of government agencies**. Agencies may carefully control leaks to the press giving scoops to newsmen who depict the agency favorably and avoid criticism of its actions.
- They would like **journalists to inform them** when presented with well grounded reasons to believe a terrorist act may be in the making or that particular individuals may be involved in terrorist activity.
- In extreme cases, where circumstances permit, vital national security interests may be at stake, and chances of success high, they may seek **cooperation of the media in disseminating a ruse** that would contribute to neutralizing the immediate threat posed by terrorists. In common criminal investigations involving heinous crimes, such media cooperation is not uncommon—when media members may hold back on publication of evidence found at a crime scene or assist law enforcement officials by publishing misleading information or a non-promising lead to assist authorities in apprehending a suspect by, for example, lulling him or her into a false sense of security.

What the Media Want When Covering Terrorist Incidents or Issues

Journalists generally want the freedom to cover an issue without external restraint—whether it comes media owners, advertisers, editors, or from the government.

- Media want **to be the first with the story**. The scoop is golden, "old news is no news." Pressure to transmit real time news instantly in today's competitive hi-tech communication environment is at an all-time high.
- The media want **to make the story as timely and dramatic as possible**, often with interviews, if possible. During the June 1985 TWA Flight 847 hijack crisis, ABC aired extensive interviews with both hijackers and hostages. (A photo was even staged of a pistol aimed at the pilot's head.[7])
- Most media members want **to be professional and accurate** and not to give credence to disinformation, however newsworthy it may seem. This may not be easily done at times, especially when systematic efforts to mislead them are undertaken by interested parties.

- They want **to protect their ability to operate as securely and freely as possible** in the society. In many instances, this concern goes beyond protecting their legal right to publish relatively unrestrained; it includes personal physical security. They want protection from threat, harassment, or violent assault during operations, and protection from subsequent murder by terrorists in retaliation providing unfavorable coverage (the latter occurring more often abroad than in the United States).
- They want **to protect society's right to know**, and construe this liberally to include popular and dramatic coverage, e.g., airing emotional reactions of victims, family members, witnesses, and "people on the street," as well as information withheld by law enforcement, security, and other organs of government.
- Media members often have no objection to **playing a constructive role in solving specific terrorist situations** if this can be done without excessive cost in terms of story loss or compromise of values.

New Trends Impacting on Terrorism and the Media

A series of recent terrorist acts indicates the emergence of trends that impact on the relationship between the media, the terrorist, and government. These include: (1) a trend towards anonymity in terrorism; (2) a trend towards more violent terrorist incidents; and (3) a trend towards attacks on media personnel and institutions.

Anonymous Terrorism

Today we see instances of anonymous terrorism where no one claims responsibility and no demands are made. The World Trade Center bombing is but one example. This allows the media a larger role in speculation, and generally removes most basis for charges that they are amplifying a terrorist's demands or agenda. Reportage is inevitable; especially if it includes unbridled speculation, false threats or hoaxes, coverage can advance terrorists' agendas, such as spreading panic, hurting tourism, and provoking strong government reactions leading to unpopular measures, including restrictions on individual liberties.

More Violent Terrorism

In the context of advanced information and technology, a trend suggesting more violent terrorism cannot be ignored. The Department of State's *Patterns of Global Terrorism: 1996* notes that while worldwide instances of terrorist acts have dropped sharply in the last decade, the death toll from acts is rising and the trend continues "toward more ruthless attacks on mass civilian targets and the use of more powerful bombs. The threat of terrorist use of materials of mass destruction is an issue of growing concern. . . ."[8] If, and as, terrorism becomes more violent, perceptions that the press is to some degree responsible for facilitating terrorism or amplifying its effects could well grow. Increasingly threatened societies may be prone to take fewer risks in light of mass casualty consequences and may trust the media less and less to police itself.

Attacks on Media Personnel and Institutions

Attacks on journalists who are outspoken on issues of concern to the terrorists seem to be on the rise. Recent attacks occurred in Algeria, Mexico, Russia, Chechnya, and London, but there have been cases as well in Washington, D.C. at the National Press Building and at the United Nations in New York. One private watchdog group estimates that forty-five journalists were killed in 1995 as a consequence of their work.[9]

OPTIONS FOR CONSIDERATION

A number of options might be considered to improve government/media interaction when responding to or covering terrorist incidents. These include: (1) financing joint media/government training exercises; (2) establishing a government terrorism information response center; (3) promoting use of media pools for hostage-centered terrorist events; (4) establishing and promoting voluntary press coverage guidelines; and (5) monitoring terrorism against the media.[10]

Financing Joint Government/Media Training Exercises

Effective public relations usually precedes a story—rather than reacts to it. Nations can beneficially employ broad public affairs strategies to combat terrorist-driven initiatives, and the media can play an important role within the framework of such a strategy. Training exercises are vital: exercises such as those conducted by George Washington University and the Technology Institute in Holon, Israel, which bring together government officials and media representatives to simulate government response and media coverage of mock terrorist incidents. Promoting and funding of similar programs on a broad scale internationally is an option for consideration.

Establishing a Government Terrorist Information Response Center

One option Congress might consider would be establishment of a standing government terrorist information response center (TIRC). Such a center, by agreement with the media, could have on call (through communication links) a rapid reaction terrorism reporting pool composed of senior network, wire-service, and print media representatives. Network coverage of incidents would then be coordinated by the network representative in the center. Such a center could be headed by a government spokesperson (the Terrorism Information Coordinator, TIC) who could seek to promptly seize the information and contexting initiative from the particular terrorist group.

Too often, when incidents happen in the United States there is a vacuum of news other than the incident itself, and by the time the government agencies agree on and fine tune what can be said and what positions are to be taken, the government information initiative is lost.

Promoting Use of Media Pools

Another option that has been mentioned specifically for coverage of hostage type events, would be use of a media pool where all agree on the news for release at the same time. A model would need to be established. However, media agreement would not be easily secured.

Promoting Voluntary Press Coverage Guidelines

Another option would be establishment by the media of a loose code of voluntary behavior or guidelines that editors and reporters could access for guidance.[11] Congress could urge the President to call a special media summit, national or perhaps international in scope under the anti-terrorism committed G-8 industrialized nations summit rubric, for senior network and print media executives to develop voluntary guidelines on terrorism reporting. Another option might be to conduct such a national meeting under the auspices of a new government agency.

Areas for discussion might be drawn from the practices of some important media members and include guidelines on:

- Limiting information on hostages which could harm them: e.g., number, nationality, official positions, how wealthy they may be, or important relatives they have;
- Limiting information on military, or police, movements during rescue operations;
- Limiting or agreeing not to air live unedited interviews with terrorists;
- Checking sources of information carefully when the pressure is high to report information that may not be accurate—as well as limiting unfounded speculation;
- Toning down information that may cause widespread panic or amplify events which aid the terrorist by stirring emotions sufficiently to exert irrational pressure on decisionmakers.

Even if specific guidelines were not adopted, such a summit would increase understanding in the public policy and press policy communities of the needs of their respective institutions.

Tracking Terrorism Against the Media

Finally, a trend toward terrorist attacks against media personnel and institutions may be emerging. This issue was addressed by President Clinton in a meeting with members of the press in Argentina during a state visit there October 17, 1997, when the President expressed concern over the issue of violence and harassment of the press in Argentina and suggested that the Organization of American States (OAS) create a special unit to ensure press freedom similar to the press ombudsman created by the Organization on Security and Cooperation in Europe (OSCE).[12] Notwithstanding, comprehensive and readily available government statistics are lacking. One

way to approach this problem would be for government reports on terrorism, such as the U.S. Department of State's *Patterns of Global Terrorism*, to include annual statistics showing the number of journalists killed or injured yearly in terrorist attacks and the annual number of terrorist incidents against media personnel or media institutions.

CONCLUSION

The media and the government have common interests in seeing that the media are not manipulated into promoting the cause of terrorism or its methods. On the other hand, neither the media nor policymakers want to see terrorism, or counter terrorism, eroding constitutional freedoms including that of the press—one of the pillars of democratic societies. This appears to be a dilemma that cannot be completely reconciled—one with which U.S. society will continually have to struggle. Communication between the government and the media is an important element in any strategy designed to prevent the cause of terrorism from prevailing and in preserving democracy. By their nature, democracies with substantial individual freedoms and limitations on police powers offer terrorists operational advantages. But terrorists and such democracies are not stable elements in combination. If terrorism sustains itself or flourishes, freedoms shrink, and in societies run by ideological authoritarians, thugs, or radical religious extremists, a free press is one of the first institutions to go.

NOTES

1. An example would be to mobilize the tourist industry to pressure governments into participating in sanctions against a terrorist state.

2. See: *Islamic Terrorism from Midwest to Mideast* by Steven Emerson, Christian Science Monitor, August 28, 1996.

3. See: *Terrorism and the Middle East Peace Process: The Origins and Activities of Hamas in the United States*, testimony by international terrorism consultant, Steven Emerson, before the Senate Subcommittee on the Near East and South Asia, March 19, 1996, p. 11. The IAP also publishes al-Zaitonah, one of the largest indigenous Arabic-language publications in the United States.

4. Note that in April 1994, the House Foreign Affairs Committee held hearings on the impact of

television on U.S. foreign policy. Scholarly and media viewpoints were presented on what, if anything, the media might do to avoid inadvertently "skewing" U.S. foreign policy one way or another and setting media foreign policy agendas. Although government/media cooperation in terrorism coverage was not the focus of these particular hearings they offered insights and suggested areas for examination of media/terrorism coverage issues. See: *Impact of Television on U.S. Foreign Policy*, April 26, 1994, U.S. Congress, House Committee on Foreign Affairs, 103rd Congress, 2nd Session, GPO, Washington, 1994, 53 p.

5. In the case of the anonymous "Unabomber", it was publication of a manifesto in the *New York Times* and *Washington Post* that triggered the leads and actions by the suspect's family, which resulted in an arrest.

6. Publication of details on the arrest in Pakistan and return to the United States of CIA shooting suspect, Mir Amal Kansi, has raised concern in the foreign policy, law enforcement, and intelligence communities that nations may be reluctant to cooperate with the United States under similar circumstances in the future. This sequence of events is one recent illustration underscoring the issue of media coverage of events relating to terrorism, the potential negative consequences of some reporting, and the need to explore mechanisms to enhance media/government cooperation in efforts to accommodate the media's need for coverage while limiting the gains such coverage may provide terrorists or their cause.

Kansi was arrested on June 17, 1997 with the help of Pakistani authorities and rendered to the United States. State Department Spokesman Nicholas Burns, in his June 18 daily briefing, remarked to journalists that "the secret of our success is that we are disciplined, and that we are not going to spill our guts in public and say exactly how all this came about; because perhaps we'll want to do the same thing to some other terrorist in the future. . . . Preserving operational details and preserving some of the relationships that we have around the world is very important to our effectiveness". This policy of silence was reportedly ordered by President Clinton so as not to break faith with foreign governments that assisted.

Several days later, after extensive reporting detailing and praising CIA cooperation, FBI planning and how the FBI finally got its man, several of Pakistan's leading newspapers published editorials demanding that their government explain why Pakistani law was waived to allow the suspect to be whisked away from his homeland. See: "Spiriting Off of Fugitive by U.S. Irks Pakistanis" by John F. Burns, *New York Times*, June 23, 1997, p. A9.

7. On June 13, 1985, two Hizballah affiliated Shi'a gunmen hijacked TWA flight 847 en route from Athens to Rome and murdered U.S. Navy diver Robert Stethem after the plane left Algiers and touched down in Beirut for the second time. The hijackers terminated negotiations with the Red Cross and forced the pilot to fly to Beirut after a wire

service report that the Delta Force had flown to the region and other erroneous media reports that the Delta Force was headed to Algeria. All but the three crew members were taken from the plane and held by Amal and Hizballah until released. ABC's coverage of the event drew strong criticism from the U.S. Department of State. Pentagon spokesman Michael Burch on June 19, 1985, accused the American news media of providing information on U.S. military and diplomatic moves that might prove useful to the hijackers: "For the price of a 25-cent newspaper or a 19 inch television, a group of hijackers who only represent the back of a pew of some mosque have a very elaborate intelligence network." Media representatives countered with the response that coverage served to protect rather than endanger the lives of the hostages—that the hijackers would have no benefit from killing the goose (hostages) that lays the golden egg (ongoing publicity).

8. U.S. Department of State, *Patterns of Global Terrorism: 1996*, April 1997, p. iii.

9. According to the New York based Committee to Protect Journalists (CPJ) more than 300 journalists have been murdered since 1986 as a consequence of their work and in 1995 alone 45 were killed. See website address http://www.CPJ.ORG/. See also the *World Press Freedom Review* published by the International Press Institute (IPI) in Vienna, Austria. Concern over a surge in killings of, and assaults against, journalists was also expressed at the opening of the Inter-American Press Association's annual meeting in Mexico City on October 20, 1997. See: West's Leading Press Group Decries Attacks on Journalists by Eloy O. Aguilar, *A.P.* dispatch of October 20, 1997.

10. Another issue for consideration beyond the scope of government and media policymaking is the degree to which a public interest group might be useful in advocating hostage rights and protection with the media, and in raising awareness of the issue of balancing the public's right to know against the rights of hostages and the public to have their safety respected by the media.

11. Notably, there have been attempts by media members to impose rules when covering terrorist incidents. Standards established by the *Chicago Sun-Times* and *Daily News* include paraphrasing terrorist demands to avoid unbridled propaganda; banning participation of reporters in negotiations with terrorists; coordinating coverage through supervising editors who are in contact with police authorities; providing thoughtful, restrained, and credible coverage of stories; and allowing only senior supervisory editors to determine what, if any, information should be withheld or deferred. Such standards are far from uniformly accepted. See: *Terrorism, the Future, and U.S. Foreign Policy*, by Raphael F. Perl, CRS Issue Brief 95112, updated regularly.

12. See: Clinton Suggests OAS Tackle Press Freedom Issue, by Lawrence McQuillan, Reuters dispatch of October 17, 1997.

TERRORISM AND CENSORSHIP

The Media in Chains

*W*hen Israel invaded south Lebanon on 6 June 1982, 1 had been covering southern Africa out of Johannesburg *for nearly a year and was eager to get out. Southern Africa was quiet and I was restless. Lebanon was a war—the world's biggest story—and I was a journalist. The Middle East was the natural place to go.*

Lebanon was exciting. The country fascinated me with its religious diversity, its endless complications, its small feuds and larger wars. The Maronites, the Sunnis, the Shi'a, the Druze, the Palestinians—each had splintered factions and shifting goals. There was incredible violence at a scale and intensity I had never seen before in my six years as a foreign correspondent. But there were also the stubborn, brave, independent people who somehow survived the brutality.

By 1982, Western reporters had become accustomed to wandering freely around Lebanon—subject to the occasional verbal abuse or roughing up—but accepted by even the most radical of factions as journalists, independent of and apart from the U.S. and British governments. A year later, however, the atmosphere had begun to change.

Beginning with the victory of Ayatollah Khomeini in Iran, Iranian money poured into Lebanon to influence the Shi'a, a Muslim sect disaffected with their native leadership. Religious conflicts intensified, and Washington's shifted position on Lebanon inspired a more personal hatred for the United States in particular, and the West in general. In Beirut, more and more bearded men—young Shi'a—appeared on the streets, carrying signs echoing Iran's revolutionary fervor and anti-Western propaganda. Journalists' encounters with such bitter gunmen became a little harder to escape without injury.

In December 1983, a group of Iranian-inspired Shi'a launched an attempt to destabilize Kuwait with attacks on the U.S. and French embassies, power stations and other installations. Despite the destruction, the attempt failed miserably. Hundreds of Shi'a were rounded up, and 17 were charged. Some were given long prison terms and others were handed death sentences. As it took place far off in the Gulf, the event was soon forgotten—at least by the West. There was no immediate connection with events in Lebanon, no hint that the repercussions would involve half a dozen countries and leave Westerners, including me, in chains for months or years.

By the time I was kidnapped in March 1985, the U.S. embassy and the Marine barracks had been bombed; Malcolm Kerr, the president of the American University, Beirut had been murdered; and a handful of Westerners had been

From "Terrorism and Censorship: The Media in Chains," Anderson, *Journal of International Affairs*, *47*(1), 127-136. Copyright © 1993. Reprinted by permission of the *Journal of International Affairs* and the Trustees of Columbia University.

taken hostage. Beirut had turned into a kind of perpetual chaos.

The U.S. embassy had been quietly warning Americans to leave Beirut—a warning that most news people just ignored, although a few took the advice or moved to East Beirut, which was considered a much safer place. I stayed, determined to cover the story. On 16 March 1985, I was kidnapped.

The Islamic Jihad claimed responsibility and demanded the release of the Da'wa 17, the 17 jailed in Kuwait. Thus began my almost seven years in captivity—seven years during which I witnessed firsthand the tenuous and powerful relationship between terrorism and the press.

The Media-Terrorism Relationship

There can be no denying it: The media are part of the deadly game of terrorism. Indeed, the game can scarcely be played without them. In my experience, publicity has been at once a primary goal and a weapon of those who use terror against innocent people to advance political causes or to simply cause chaos. And they are quite good at the public relations game—which is why their attacks, kidnappings and murder are usually so spectacularly vicious.

In my opinion, the very reporting of a political kidnapping, an assassination or a deadly bombing is a first victory for the terrorist. Without the world's attention, these acts of viciousness are pointless. Furthermore, unless the terrorist can attach his political message to the headlines he has caused, he has failed. When newspapers run long analyses about the Islamic Jihad, its hatred of Israel and the West and its reliance on fundamentalist interpretations of Islam, "Islamic Jihad" becomes a legitimate force—something politicians and civilians alike must take seriously.

No matter that the analyses may be uniformly condemnatory, and that the reader has automatically and completely rejected the organization's premises. The acts that have won terrorists this public notice—whether kidnapping or bombing or murder—are seen by terrorists as successful. They have forced the world to take notice of them, indicating their sense of self-importance.

The Role of the Media

Everyone uses the media, journalists are accustomed to being used by presidents, kings, parliaments, entertainers, political activists or ordinary citizens trying to attract the world's attention—that's a major part of the media's role. The media carry messages to anyone from anyone with the knowledge, skill or importance to make use of them. It may be propaganda or it may be truth, but either way, the media carry powerful influence.

I was raised in journalism by old-fashioned editors who ingrained in me a fundamental belief in objectivity. According to my teachers, journalists were meant to present the facts and the facts only, and the audience—armed with seemingly unbiased material—was appointed to analyze and draw conclusions. The journalistic ideal means by allowing the public access to the widest possible range of information, they will be able to judge that which rings true and seems useful, and then utilize it to develop informed opinions and make wise decisions. The ideal is tested constantly in this age of mass marketing, public relations and so-called spin doctors who attempt to distribute information with a specific goal in mind.

But there are facts and there is truth. During my years in captivity, I had plenty of time to reassess the journalist's role in covering news. Objectivity and neutrality are vital, but they do not necessarily entail putting aside a personal desire to see the violence that we cover come to an end.

Terrorist Manipulation of the Media

I am not the first to question the precarious relationship between media and terrorism. A wide-ranging debate about the subject was initiated after the 1979 seizure of the U.S. embassy and the taking of American hostages in Iran in 1979. The Teheran hostage crisis dominated network television coverage of Iran—indeed, the percentage of stories about that country escalated from about one percent in the early 1970s to over 30 percent by 1980.[1]

A half decade later, one event in particular made clear the symbiotic relationship between the media and terrorism, setting off a second flurry of analysis: the hijacking of TWA Flight 847 to Beirut. Here, the media—television in particular—became the primary conduit between the terrorists and the governments.[2]

During the hijacking, the captors set up televised interviews with the hostages and held the first televised hostage news conference. Early on, the event turned into a shameful circus with one television network buying the rights to the story from the Shi'a Amal militia, and thereafter taking over the Summerland Hotel where the hostages were trotted out to meet the press. The amount of money involved is unknown except to those who paid and received it, but rumors suggested it was in the tens to hundreds of thousands of dollars, cash. Regrettably, the fact that one American, Navy diver Robert Stethem, had already been murdered by the hijackers and dozens of lives were in the balance became only a reason for more hype—not for caution and prudence. This was a big story; it was especially a television story and the media were not about to turn off their cameras.[3]

In my situation, the Islamic Jihad did not wage a similar all-out public relations campaign. For months on end, they offered the media so little information that we hostages were deemed forgotten, and friends, relatives and colleagues felt compelled to wage their own campaign for publicity. But when the Islamic Jihad did use tactics to manipulate the media, they were generally successful.

The players on both sides of this long game displayed their understanding of the media in many ways. The Reagan administration first tried to cut the press out of the game. They insisted that there would be no "deals with terrorists," while pursuing the favorite tactic of diplomats—secret negotiations.[4] When the so called arms-for-hostages deal blew up in their faces, they tried to use the press, through purported unofficial leaks in a campaign to "devalue" the terrorists.

When that failed as well, they sent signals to Iran, which sponsors and funds Hizballah, that they were willing, even eager to discuss the matter.[5] Iran returned the signals frequently. Yet it was in comments to independent newspapers, or by government-controlled newspapers in Iran, that the idea of a swap of hostages for Lebanese prisoners held by Israel was first publicly suggested.[6] The kidnappers blatantly used the press to push their agenda, finally signalling their willingness to talk, and even to publicize their disagreements with Iranian sponsors.

Similar manipulation of the media was shown by captors of American officials at the U.S. embassy in Iran five years earlier. Hostage-takers aired their demands through staged demonstrations scheduled to coincide with nightly newscasts and ABC's "America Held Hostage" program, now known as "Nightline."[7] Many terrorist organizations have press offices, complete with spokesmen, press releases and audiovisual material.

In our case, photographs and videos were released along with demands as if our faces—mine in particular—were some sort of instantaneous press pass. No media outlet could deny their audience, and especially not a hostage's relatives, a glimpse of the Americans held in Lebanon. It was a natural way to grab the world's attention.

Still, the videos—a clear manipulation of the media by our captors—were also our only connection to our families, and for that reason alone, allowed us a bit of hope. At least the world would know we were alive. It was by no means an easy thing to do. When one day one of my keepers told me to make a videotape, I thought long and hard about whether I should refuse. I reflected on my Marine Corps training about how to behave as a prisoner, and struggled with the notion of aiding and comforting the enemy.

But in the end, I decided nobody would believe any of it; nobody would really think these were my opinions, and it was likely to be the only way I could reassure my family that I was alive and well. So I read their propaganda—rationalizations of their actions, attacks on President Reagan, vague but ominous threats couched in harsh language—and by so doing, I played a part in the media game.

There were times, however, when the media game—especially the release of videos—backfired on our captors. Terrorists pay enormous attention to the news reports about the things they do. In 1986, when Father Martin Jenco was released, he carried with him a videotape made by fellow hostage David Jacobsen. In the tape, Jacobsen sent his condolences to the "wife and children" of William Buckley, who had died some time before in prison.[8] Jacobsen did not know that Buckley was not married.

An over-enthusiastic journalist used that discrepancy to construct a theory that there was a so-called secret message on that tape. Worse, his television network prominently speculated on the theory. We were allowed by our captors to watch the first few television news reports of our companion's release. I remember seeing a yellow banner across the television screen in one report, emblazoned "Secret Message?" The question mark, I guess, was meant to justify use of the story.

Our captors also saw the story. They were very paranoid people, and believed it. They were extremely angry. We suffered, losing the few privileges we had—books, pen, paper—and were dumped in a vile and filthy underground prison for the next six months. We were lucky one or more of us was not killed.

THE QUESTION OF CENSORSHIP

How do we balance the public's right to know—so vital to our society—and the duty of the press to reveal, with the knowledge that publicity seems so often to serve the purposes of terrorists? Because terrorists want and need publicity, should we therefore not give it to them? Should there be censorship, imposed or voluntary, about such news reports?

Persistent analyses of how the media should and should not respond to terrorism will continue as long as such activities take place, and we may never come up with satisfactory answers. I believe—like all journalists I know—that the press must fulfill its duty to expose and present information objectively, thereby serving the public good. Censorship by government officials would be a grievous mistake, and so-called general guidelines are too often vague or unsuited to particular events to be useful in these kinds of situations.

However, when lives are at stake, journalistic self-restraint may be necessary. In some cases, it will be imperative that information be reported even if the result is loss of life. In others, a journalist will have to choose whether to release, delay or withhold information. In each case, the individual journalist must ask him or herself: Should I report this if it jeopardizes a human life?

When the arms-for-hostages deal was revealed in the press, I was due to be the next hostage released. New clothes to wear home had been bought for me. But the news reports blew the whole deal out of the water. It was five years before I would finally be free. Nonetheless, I agree with the decision my colleagues in the press made to make the negotiations public. The very highest officials in the land, even the president, were engaged in talks that directly contradicted their public statements, indeed broke both U.S. law and violated the Constitution. That was more important than my fate, or that of the others still held.

Such is not often the case. There are times, I have learned, when information should be withheld. In early 1983, when I was reporting on the Middle East out of Beirut, I became aware through impeccable sources that the Palestine Liberation Organization was negotiating with the kidnappers of David Dodge, another president of the American University, Beirut who had been snatched in 1982. The PLO believed it had some hope of winning Dodge's freedom, and at the very least had confirmed he was alive and well—something no one had been able to do in the six months since his abduction.

Though I had second thoughts about the wisdom of reporting the negotiations, I allowed my boss to talk me into filing the story. It got "good play"—headlines in many papers in the United States. My sources, who had not realized how much they were telling me, were furious, and fearful that reports would kill the negotiations. As it happens, they did not: Dodge was eventually released. Still, I knew I had made a mistake. The story served no purpose and advanced no ideal, except maybe my career. If I had wanted Dodge's family to know I had learned he was alive and well, I could have told them privately. As it was, my report could very well have blown the secret talks away, as publicity later did to the arms-for-hostages deal. It could be have cost the elderly Dodge more years in filthy prisons.

That realization had a strong effect on me. When I later had occasion to learn information about people who had been kidnapped, I was very, very careful how I used it, and often did not.

There is no simple formula. My experience as both journalist and hostage has provided me with a personal look at terrorists' manipulation of the media and the impact of the media's coverage of such events. The reply seems obvious: Don't give the terrorists what they want. Don't give them publicity. Don't report on their demands, or even—for the most adamant of media critics—on their actions. If they cannot expect publicity, they will go away.

As with the most obvious answers, this one is both philosophically mistaken and practically impossible. We are, after all, a democracy. That means at least theoretically—and I believe in practice to a greater extent than cynics would have us believe—that the public decides important issues by electing its representatives and changing them when they do poorly. They cannot do so intelligently without a free press, for any controls on the press become rapidly political ones, and in my opinion, will be used by those in power to keep themselves there.

But even if the theory behind full reporting of terrorist acts is sound, what about the practice? Surely the media behave irresponsibly often in the single-minded pursuit of headlines or air time.

We are a nation that has learned to be very suspicious of our leaders, and in particular any attempt by them to overtly control the information to which we have access. A bomb in a public place, or even the kidnapping of a prominent person, are not events that can be easily hidden or ignored. Trying to do so simply gives rise to rumors and false reports—always exaggerating the extent of the incident, and therefore giving the terrorist something he likes even more than publicity—the spreading of fear. I have found that the best antidote to fear is information, even if the information is bad.

Furthermore, the media are not a single entity that can be cautioned, leaned on or controlled. It is difficult to get a group of journalists to agree on something as simple as a basic code of ethics. It is unrealistic to expect any widespread voluntary restraint in matters that involve such attention-grabbing events as terrorist attacks.

Another factor that mitigates against control is that the public does not want it. Despite disparagement of the media for its so-called sensationalism, people seem to want blood-and-guts reports in their daily newsfare. A news organization that does not supply this kind of variety will not last long.

CONCLUSION

The philosophical justification for full reporting on terrorist acts does not give journalists a free hand. In each case they must weigh the theoretical or philosophical value of what they do with the fact that individual human lives are at stake. What they report can have a direct impact on the victims, as terrorists pay enormous attention to the news reports about the things they do.

I tell my colleagues: In each and every report you do where a human life is at risk, you must see in your mind that person's face. You must understand that what you report might well kill the person, and accept the responsibility for that. That doesn't mean you will abandon or even tone down your report. In some cases, one person's life, or even the lives of several people, cannot outweigh the necessity to publish the story.

When a government pleads with journalists to withhold stories about terrorists or terrorist incidents because of national security, or danger to negotiations involving hostages, should the journalist bow to those entreaties? Should the well-being of the hostages override all other considerations, as far as journalists are concerned? Or are there other things that are more important? I believe that each of these questions that so many journalists encounter in their work can only be answered individually, and as each case occurs. They should be, and I believe for the most part are, answered with intelligence and responsibility, and a full and careful regard for the lives that may be at stake. But general "guidelines" too often do not fit all cases. Certainly, we should not allow, or implicitly approve censorship by government officials, who will try to impose censorship in any case. Public approval of their acts simply encourages an even heavier hand.

NOTES

1. James F. Larson, "Television and U.S. Foreign Policy: The Case of the Iran Hostage Crisis," Journal of Communication 36 (1986) p. 116.

2. Patrick O'Heffernan, "TWA Flight 847: Terrorism that Worked (Almost) . . .," in Patrick O'Heffernan, Mass Media and American Foreign Policy: Insider Perspectives on Global Journalism and the Foreign Policy Process (Norwood, NJ: Ablex, 1991).

3. For more specific analyses of TWA incident, see Robert G. Picard, Media Portrayals of Terrorism: Functions and Meaning of News Coverage (Ames, IA: Iowa State University Press, 1993).

4. Los Angeles Times, 28 July 1986.

5. "Bush Seems to Appeal to Iran on Hostage Issue," Washington Post, 21 January 1989.

6. The Washington Post, 30 April 1990.

7. Picard, p. 53.

8. William Buckley was a CIA bureau chief stationed in Beirut. He was kidnapped, tortured and killed by the Islamic Jihad.

5

WOMEN AS TERRORISTS

To be a revolutionary you have to be a human being. You have to care about people who have no power.

—Jane Fonda

A meaningful area for study is the consistent finding that there are far fewer women than men involved in terrorist actions. Some female terrorists have created immense climates of fear, however. Females carried on long-term, low-level conflict at a deadly rate in disparate countries at different times. Their highest leadership has included female cadres, and their ideology has dealt explicitly with gender-related issues. Study of these exceptional women can reveal a lot about the society and culture against which they revolt.

Female terrorists described by news reports today take roles similar to those held by women in revolutionary organizations from earliest times. Knight (1979) pointed out that in the 1905 Revolution in Russia, women showed dogmatic devotion to violence and a strong tendency toward extremism. "Several became fanatics, seeing terror and their own heroic self-sacrifice as an end in itself. The ultimate test of their commitment and devotion to the revolution was their willingness to die" (p. 149).

At the beginning of the 21st century, women continue to be willing to die for their revolutionary ideals. Two current examples illustrate the significance of women for terrorism: The GAM (Free Aceh Movement) separatist movement in Indonesia and the LTTE (Tamil Tigers) separatists in Sri Lanka. Human rights abuses by state-supported military authorities, including disappearances, murders, rapes, and torture, have been well documented in both Indonesia and Sri Lanka. Women have become involved in violence in response to crimes of domination and repression on the part of their national governments. In both countries, the terrorists are Muslim, and both countries' histories and cultures include important roles for women.

The female cadres of the GAM in Indonesia are often widows who enlist for an intensive induction in military operations and intelligence gathering along with ideology, law, and Islamic culture. After training, they return to their places ready to defend their people (Koch, 2000). The GAM has trained thousands of women in military tactics. The leaders of the Aceh movement claim with pride that their female fighters are extremely effective. One indication of how bitter the conflict has become is the widely feared and elusive "widows' battalion" of the GAM (Gaouette, 1999).

For the LTTE in Sri Lanka, female warriors are among the deadliest weapons in the group's arsenal. As suicide bombers, they took thousands of lives, left countless others injured, and cost millions of dollars in damage to property. It has been estimated that women make up fully half of the rebels and that they are also highly represented among the deadly Black Tigers who are trained as suicide bombers. A female LTTE Black Tiger killed herself and Indian prime minister Rajiv Gandhi in 1991 ("Emergency Rule in Sri Lanka," 2002; Schweitzer, 2000).

In the rebel army training camps in Pakistan-occupied Kashmir, girls are being inducted into hostilities as couriers in moving firearms and planting explosives. Some were reportedly getting training in handling of sophisticated weapons (Pargal, 2001). Police around the world have been alerted to the possibility of attacks by suicide squads sent by Kashmiri separatist organizations, a significant number of which are women (Overseas Advisory Security Council, 2001).

For several decades, Palestinians also have included women in suicide attacks as part of their arsenal of terror (Scripps Howard, 2002). This situation was exacerbated when the High Islamic Council in Saudi Arabia issued a *fatwa*, or edict, that decreed that women should join men as suicide martyrs for Islam (Hoffman, 2002). Inviting women to take a larger part in what previously had been a virtually all-male endeavor in the Middle East has grave security implications.

Women also have been well-publicized members of several Western terrorist organizations (Radu & Tismaneanu, 1990). The Zapatistas (EZLN) in the Southern Mexican state of Chiapas provide an example of a revolutionary group in which more than one third of the members are women. The EZLN decided from its inception that to be truly revolutionary, it would have to include women in formulating policies. Women's Revolutionary Laws were hotly debated but eventually became a decree within the movement. Analysts now agree that their influence has reshaped Mexican politics and challenged the nation's prevailing gender stereotypes (Clayton, 1997, Rojas, 1994).

ROLES AND ACTIVITIES FOR FEMALE TERRORISTS

Women have performed many, significantly different kinds of activities for revolutions down through the ages, but their leadership roles were limited (Vetter & Perlstein, 1991). Guerrilla groups include four different levels of action with a focus on women: sympathizers, spies, warriors, and dominant forces.

Sympathizers

At one end of the spectrum are rebel groups for which women are camp followers. Women perform cooking, sewing, and other household chores for the revolution and also may be available for sex. They are involved in the struggle through their relationships with male terrorists. For example, during the early 1800s, as Simón Bolívar pressed the revolution for independence from Spain through what is now Venezuela, Colombia, Peru, and Bolivia, his troops were followed by dozens of *Juanas Cholas*. These women managed to survive by serving the needs of the insurgents (Cherpak, 1978).

At the same level of involvement are female sympathizers who provide access to resources and the ability to carry on a clandestine life in the midst of warfare. Supportive women provide food and hiding places. These women might be called on only once or at irregular intervals to give shelter, donations, weapons, or time and effort to the rebel cause. Their participation in the terrorists' campaign is less direct, and of necessity they are not usually identified publicly with the group. The roles of these female sympathizers nevertheless are crucial to successful terrorist attempts to disrupt the social order.

Spies

In other groups, women are more active in the struggle. Their more prominent roles include those of decoys, messengers, intelligence gatherers, and spies. Women's work and women's status may be exploited for the cause; baby carriages and women who are actually or pretending to be pregnant prove useful for hiding weapons of war. Women working in banks may be helpful to insurgents, as are other women with respectable positions who can provide essential financial and strategic support for the rebels. These women may be above suspicion by virtue of their traditional roles in their societies. Without the assistance of mothers and sisters, wives, aunts, daughters, and female friends, the success of an uprising is not likely. In most groups, female rebels maintain their traditional sex roles while working for the army. They do not expect to have a political impact in the upcoming society they are helping to forge. Like the camp followers, these female revolutionaries have no political agenda for themselves as women after the revolution is over. They expect to return to their previous sex roles as mothers and wives.

Warriors

At the next level are women who are actively recruited into terrorist groups. In these groups, women act as warriors, using weapons and incendiary devices. They fight in the battles on an equal status with men, but they are not leaders. They seldom have any say in the policies or plans they are carrying out. When the revolution is over, there is no explicit scheme to change their status in society. For example, Tatiana Leontiev, a lady-in-waiting to the Russian tsar in the late 1800s, planned to shoot him with a revolver concealed in a bouquet of flowers. She was arrested in the attempt. Her wealthy family passed her off as insane and she was banished to a hotel in Switzerland, but she eventually served a long prison sentence for shooting a businessman journeying through Switzerland because she believed he was the Russian minister of the interior traveling incognito. She was no more than 20 years old at the time (Vetter & Perlstein, 1991, p. 106).

In Bolivia, Tamara Burke became well known because of her connections to Che Guevara and the revolution in which he lost his life. Known as Camarada Tania, she established and controlled urban guerrilla warfare in her country during the 1960s. Because of her brave and forceful reputation, the Symbionese Liberation Army in California used the *nomme de guerre* of Tania for heiress Patricia Hearst after they kidnapped her and she joined their cause in 1974. As a prototype of a female warrior, Camarada Tania was the perfect propaganda image (Radu & Tismaneanu, 1990, p. 112).

Dominant Forces

At the other end of the spectrum are women who are dominant forces within terrorist groups. They are not only actively recruited but also actively involved. Women provide ideology, leadership, motivation, and strategy for their groups. When women are included in the commando group at the center of a terrorist organization, they may

A photograph of kidnapping victim Patty Hearst sent by her captors, the Symbionese Liberation Army, to a Berkeley radio station. On an accompanying audio message, Hearst claimed support for the SLA cause.

Photo © Bettmann/CORBIS, April 1974. Reprinted with permission.

inspire greater fear than do men because their actions are so far outside the traditional behavior expected from women.

When the revolution is over, these commanders envision a society in which the role of women will be changed drastically. Instead of returning to their lives at home, when the war is over, they plan to be running the country and carrying on the international struggle. In the United States, Bernardine Dohrn was an example of a dominant force in the Weather Underground of the 1970s. Hers was a prominent voice in the ideology of the New Left movement that hoped to redefine the nature of society to eliminate the dominance of white males. She is known to have asserted that "The best thing that we can be doing for ourselves, as well as for the . . . revolutionary black liberation struggle is to build a f---ing white revolutionary movement" (Jacobs, 1997, from the book cover).

TWO EXCEPTIONAL TERRORIST GROUPS

Women dominated in the RAF (Rote Armee Fraktion or Red Army Faction) in Germany in the 1970s and 1980s (Huffman, 1999) and in the SL (Sendero Luminoso or Shining Path) in Peru in the 1980s and early 1990s (Poole & Rénique, 1992). Their roles were noteworthy within the RAF and SL, beyond the level of a few select women. In these groups, women were as important as men from many standpoints.

Terrorist organizations in which women establish control are exceptional because of the ways the early leaders develop ideology for the group. Two exemplary female terrorists, Ulrike Meinhof of the RAF and Augusta La Torre Guzman of the SL, were instrumental in developing similar revolutionary ideologies in two very disparate countries in different historical settings during which women became the most nefarious terrorists of all (Demaris, 1977; McClintock, 1986).

The RAF in Germany

The RAF began developing the ideas for its campaign of terror in Germany in the late 1950s. By the late 1960s, its systematic bombings of department stores had made the RAF famous. RAF members were leftists allied with Palestinians, trained in tactics of guerrilla warfare, which was directed primarily toward "imperialists" at U.S. installations in Germany and German sites connected with the military-industrial complex. They were known for the daring nature of their attacks, the sophistication of their planning, and the extent of strategy and organization involved in carrying out their campaigns of terror. Much of the support for the group developed while the early leaders were in custody, and it was fueled by the suspicious deaths of four noted members of the group while they were being held in prison. The RAF was responsible for drastic changes in German life, including a new level of security force to combat insurgencies and a huge new prison complex for holding terrorists and conducting trials. The RAF's campaign of terror also increased levels of suspicion and repression, affecting all of German society (Becker, 1977; Horchem, 1986; Rojahn, 1998).

The Sendero Luminoso in Peru

In Peru, the SL began developing its ideas for a campaign of terror in the 1960s and carried on strikes and marches during the 1970s. As the government's reaction grew more repressive, many of the leaders were forced into a clandestine life at the end of the 1970s. The group's first known guerrilla action took place in 1980. The SL managed to hold the country in fear with unpredictable violent attacks until its leaders finally came to light as a result of a score of high-profile arrests in the early 1990s.

Like the RAF, the members of the SL were leftists. They studied guerrilla tactics in China. Support in the press began after national forces were believed to have massacred hundreds of members of the SL who were being held in prison. The deaths occurred during an uprising over inhuman conditions. In the end, the SL was responsible for the economic and social devastation of one state in Peru and guilty of wreaking havoc with the way of life of the entire nation (DeGregori, 1994; Palmer, 1994; Tarazona-Sevillano, 1990).

Two Female Terrorists

Ulrike Meinhof

Ulrike Meinhof's parents died young, leaving her and her sister in the care of a devoted socialist who had been their mother's friend. After marrying the publisher of a left-wing student newspaper, Meinhof joined more radical student movements and ultimately became the celebrity of the RAF. Beginning in the late 1950s, she was called a media gadfly, well known and outspoken. She maintained a high profile and asserted her opinions on questions of women's rights and the double-bind existence of working mothers. She publicized the situation of youth of the lower social classes, particularly young women in reformatories. After giving birth to twins and having her marriage fail in the 1970s, Meinhof became armed and militant. A suspected brain tumor left her unable to care for her children at times and eventually led to surgery. This was said to be a turning point for her. She became an outlaw when she united with Gudrun Ensslin and Andreas Baader, robbing banks and bombing buildings. The three joined Horst Mahler in Berlin and made plans for continued violence against the government they saw as fascist. They were known to the press as the Baader-Meinhof gang and later as the first generation of the RAF.

Meinhof was seized by authorities in 1972 and held in isolation for 4 years. She and other RAF leaders took part in high-profile hunger strikes backed by leftist lawyers who openly supported their ideals. It took 3 years to bring her and other prominent RAF leaders to trial. She was sentenced to 8 years in custody for assisting in a prison escape for Andreas Baader. When they were moved to a special facility built to house terrorists, discord reigned among the prisoners. Those accused of terrorism were allowed only written communication, and that was manipulated by the authorities and the press. Meinhof faced the possibility of an even longer prison sentence when all the charges were decided. She hacked off her hair carelessly so that it stood in tufts on her head. She wrote at her typewriter daily up until her death. She was alleged to have committed suicide, but she left no farewell note.

The lingering doubts about the state's version of her suicide led many to conclude that Meinhof's death had only been portrayed as a suicide and that the authorities had covered up the actual cause. Following her death, rumors circulated that she had been raped. Tests were inconclusive, so the possibility of rape was never ruled out. Three more deaths of RAF leaders in prison were suspected of being murders by officials.

Meinhof was mourned by thousands of followers, though no members of her family appeared at her funeral. She was eulogized as one of the most significant women in German politics at her grave site on May 15, 1976 (Becker, 1977; Demaris, 1977; Huffman, 1999; Vague, 1994).

Augusta La Torre Guzman

Augusta La Torre was born in the remote foothills of the Andes mountains in a small town located in a state known as the hotbed of resistance to the central government in Lima, Peru. Her father was a politician. In his house, she met her future husband, Abimael Guzman, when he came to plot liberal political strategy with her father and his cronies. La Torre was 18 years old and her husband 27 when they married. Many have credited La Torre for the dramatic origins of the SL. Her husband was considered an intellectual, with deep and complex theories, not much of a speaker and hard to understand. She was the spark who set the ideas on fire.

The couple never had a child. Instead of being a mother or a wife, La Torre was a comrade, a follower, a faithful disciple. She was intensely concerned for the downtrodden in

Peruvian society, especially the indigenous peoples living in the Andes altiplano region. She was recognized throughout the area in her typical costume of trousers and an old baggy sweater, and she was well known as an organizer and a strategist for Guzman. She was seen as Guzman's eyes and ears. When he went to China, she went along. They both studied revolutionary tactics.

La Torre was described as a woman with passionate convictions and final decisions. Hers were the ideas and the policies behind the formation of the original central committee of the SL. She attracted the ideas of female scholars and professionals into the movement in defiance of the established order. After her prominence in the founding of the SL, however, little was heard of La Torre. She went into hiding with Guzman in 1978; after that, the stories about her were few and mostly rumors.

It is believed that La Torre died in 1988. In 1991, the police made public a video describing her funeral. No one in appeared in the video except Guzman, who directed the camera to film a woman's body wrapped in a red flag bearing the communist symbol of a hammer and sickle. In a distant and confused voice, he delivered the formal SL version of La Torre's death. He showed no feeling on the video except when telling the audience that she "annihilated herself." The police doubted the story, and journalists raised serious questions whether her death was suicide or murder. The press speculated that La Torre's death resulted from a split in the SL and that she died as punishment for disloyalty. Her corpse was never found (Kirk, 1993; McClintock, 1986; Palmer, 1994).

IDEOLOGY AND FEMALE TERRORISTS

The terrorist groups with women as dominant forces are set apart by their ideologies from other groups, in which women remain in the roles of supporters and sympathizers. Female terrorists' worldviews about the causes for their acts of violence are often utopian. It is likely that the goal for prominent female terrorists involves creating a new society, not restoring a traditional way of life. Demoralization and a sense of hopelessness with the existing system was the psychological root of both the German RAF and the Peruvian SL movements (Andreas, 1985; Becker, 1977). They saw themselves as being consciously advanced and intellectually superior. They were spawned by academics and philosophers. The university was their fostering mother, although many of the members were not students. They based their ideologies on critical sociological theories that originated among scholars. They saw violence as the only tool for political change. For the members of the RAF and the SL, there was only one course of action to be followed, and that was armed struggle (Becker, 1977; DeGregori, 1994).

Intellectuals in both Germany and Peru fueled the flames of resentment into guerrilla war. Their ideologies advocated action over intellectualizing. They took popular liberal rhetoric and pushed it to extremes. They thought of themselves as the beacons of world revolution and the vanguards of global communism. They sneered at other intellectuals whose weapons were no more than pens. For the members of the RAF and the SL, everyday life was war. The propaganda of the deed attracted militant women who were frustrated by conventional society. They planned to revise the entire global order (Aust, 1987; Grant, 1994; Herzog, 1993).

Terrorist groups in which a significant number of the members of the high command are women are likely to be guided by an ideology developed with consideration for females. Including women in multiple roles in the earliest stages of development sets these groups apart from others in which women's roles are subordinate. The ideology of female-dominated terrorists groups varies considerably from group to group and time to time; however, one consistent belief in the groups' ideologies is the empowerment of women, along with a redefinition of the functions of women in the division of labor.

Hate groups in the United States today are not likely to consider women's issues in their ideology, but they may have plenty of female members. Women may be actively recruited because they are less likely to have arrest records and are more likely to be able to avoid police attention (Blee, 2002). They may provide assistance and support, may seek out information and resources, and may be trained in warfare and participate in attacks. There is little evidence, however, of changes in women's traditional roles within these right-wing extremist groups. There were no reports of female commanders or strategists among racist or Christian Identity terrorist groups in the United States at the end of the 20th century (Potok, 1999).

Researchers have pointed out that rather than revising the traditional female gender roles of caregiving and nurturing, terrorist women have played these same roles with greater fervor in a different direction (Andreas, 1990; O'Connell, 1993). Rather than being liberated from traditional sex roles, female terrorists replaced the restrictions of marriage with fanatic attachment to a leader or cause. Instead of the responsibilities of motherhood, they were burdened with passionate concern for society at large. Female terrorists may be even more fanatic than males. In negating conventional roles, they turn their traditional roles against themselves (Neuburger & Valentini, 1996).

HIGHLIGHTS OF REPRINTED ARTICLES

The two readings about women in terrorism that follow show that despite their rhetoric, female militants have not been liberated from traditional roles by becoming terrorists.

Robin Morgan. (1989). "Token Terrorist: The Demon Lover's Woman. In *The Demon Lover: The Roots of Terrorism*. New York: W. W. Norton & Company.

The selection from Morgan (1989) includes many examples of women who were active as terrorists in all parts of the world. According to Morgan, however, they were not involved in struggles for liberation because of their own political aspirations. Rather, Morgan believes they were involved because of their attachments to lovers. She sees female warriors as devoted to their lovers' ideologies and lifestyle rather than to personal efforts to achieve political benefits for women. They were not feminists, and many went on record to deny their regard for feminist philosophies. Instead, they were committed to a cause that transcended women's concerns.

At the same time, from a historical perspective, Morgan provides a clear analysis of the essential nature of women's participation in revolution: "From Marx through Nechaev to Ortega, they have used her and acknowledged it. They have proclaimed aloud their exploitation of her, written it out in print, denied it and then reaffirmed it, practised it, and practise it still. *They have made it plain: they need women. They cannot do it without women*" (p. 216).

Alison Jamieson. (2000). "Mafiosi and Terrorists: Italian Women in Violent Organizations." *SAIS Review*, *20*(2), 51-64.

Jamieson analyzes the role women played in two very different violent organizations in Italy. Though feminism was a powerful ideological stimulus to the terrorist women of the Red Brigades, their social estrangement and dedication to violent methods alienated them from the genuine concerns of the women's movement. The roles of women involved with the Cosa Nostra are in distinct contrast. Deference to male authority keeps mafiosi women trapped inside traditional behavioral patterns. Women assume more responsibility than before in the Mafia, but their gender roles have remained rigidly circumscribed.

EXPLORING WOMEN AS TERRORISTS FURTHER

- Background on the "Women Behind the Masks" among the Zapatistas (EZLN) in Mexico can be obtained in Spanish at the EZLN Web site (www.ezln.org), and www.eco.utexas. edu links "Zapatistas in Cyberspace" and gives access to numerous different viewpoints about their movement.
- For more information about the German Red Army Faction (RAF), see www.baader-meinhof. com; for more on the Shining Path (SL), see www.csrp.org, a site for the Committee to Support the Revolution in Peru.
- The novel *The Dancer Upstairs* by Nicholas Shakespeare (1997) is a fictionalized account of the Shining Path that sticks remarkably true to the history and social situation in Peru and is still clear and fascinating.
- Today three groups deserve investigation because of the position of women within them: the Tamil Tigers (LTTE) of Sri Lanka, the Free Aceh of Indonesia (GAM), and the Nepalese Maoists. The region of Southeast Asia is the focus because of large numbers of women terrorists there and because there is a need for timely information about their ideology and leadership. Numerous Internet sites and sources exist for them and can be found through most search engines. What are most interesting for further study are the ongoing developments in these contemporary movements.

VIDEO NOTES

Women's role in terrorism may be a conflicted one. *The Demon Lover* described by Morgan is cleverly interpreted in *The Little Drummer Girl* (Warner Bros., 1984, 130 min.).

REFERENCES

Andreas, Carol. (1985). *When women rebel: The rise of popular feminism in Peru.* Westport, CT: Lawrence Hill.

Andreas, Carol. (1990). Women at war. *NACLA Report on the Americas, 24*(4), 20-27.

Aust, Stefan. (1987). *The Baader-Meinhof group: The inside story of a phenomenon* (Anthea Bell, Trans.). London: Bodley Head.

Becker, Jillian. (1977). *Hitler's children: The story of the Baader-Meinhof terrorist gang.* Philadelphia: Lippincott.

Blee, Kathleen. (2002). *Inside organized racism: Women in the hate movement.* Berkeley: University of California Press.

Cherpak, E. (1978). The participation of women in the independence movement in Gran Colombia. In A. Lavrin (Ed.), *Latin American women: Historical perspectives.* Westport, CT: Greenwood.

Clayton, Lea. (1997, March). Revolutionary Zapatista women in cultural perspective. *The Prism* (University of North Carolina), pp. 1-5.

DeGregori, C. (1994). The origins and logic of the Shining Path. In D. Palmer (Ed.), *Shining Path of Peru.* New York: St. Martin's.

Demaris, Ovid. (1977). *Brothers in blood: The international terrorist network.* New York: Scribner.

Emergency rule in Sri Lanka. (2002, January 6). Retrieved June 17, 2002, from http://abcnews.go.com/sections/world/DailyNews/srilanka000106_blast.htm

Gaouette, Nicole. (1999, June 23). Muslim women in freedom fight. *The Christian Science Monitor*. Retrieved June 9, 2002, from www.csmonitor.com/atcsmonitor/specials/women/world/world062399.html

Grant, M. (1994). *Critical intellectuals and the new media.* Unpublished doctoral dissertation, Cornell University.

Herzog, Kristin. (1993). *Finding their voice: Peruvian women's testimonies of war.* Valley Forge, PA: Trinity Press International.

Hoffman, Lisa. (2002, February 6). *Women change the terrorist profile.* Washington, DC: Scripps Howard News Service.

Horchem, H. (1986). Terrorism in West Germany. *Conflict Studies, 186*, 1-21.

Huffman, R. (1999). *This is Baader-Meinhof.* Retrieved June 9, 2002, from www.baader-meinhof.com

Jacobs, Ron. (1997) *The way the wind blew: A history of the Weather Underground.* London: Verso.

Jamieson, Alison. (2000). Mafiosi and terrorists: Italian women in violent organizations. *SAIS Review, 20*(2), 51-64.

Kirk, R. (1993). *Las mujeres de Sendero Luminoso.* Lima, Peru: Instituto Estudios Peruanos.

Knight, Amy. (1979). Female terrorists in the Russian Socialist Revolutionary Party. *Russian Review, 38*, 139-159.

Koch, Jacqueline. (2000, December 9). "Widows" of Aceh fight for freedom in a bitter land. Retrieved June 9, 2002, from www.theage.com.au/news/2000/12/09/FFXXZ1S5HGC.html

McClintock, C. (1986). *Sendero Luminoso guerrillas maoistas del Peru.* Lima, Peru: University of Lima, Faculty of Law and Political Sciences Research Publications.

Morgan, Robin. (1989). Token terrorist: The demon lover's woman. In *The demon lover: The Roots of terrorism.* New York: W. W. Norton & Company.

Neuburger, Luisella de Cataldo, & Valentini, Tiziana. (1996). *Women and terrorism* (Leo Michael Hughes , Trans.). New York: St. Martin's.

O'Connell, H. (Ed.). (1993). *Women and conflict.* Oxford, UK: Oxfam.

Overseas Security Advisory Council. (2001, January 24). Daily global news. Retrieved June 17, 2001, from www.ds-osac.org/globalnews/story.cfm?KEY=10858

Palmer, David Scott. (Ed.). (1994). *The Shining Path of Peru* (2nd ed.). New York: St. Martin's.

Pargal, Sanjeev. (2001, July 30). Pakistan army trains 100 young girls in two Pakistan occupied Kashmir camps. *The Daily Excelsior* (New Delhi), p. 1. Retrieved June 9, 2002, from www.dailyexcelsior.com/01july30/news.htm#8

Poole, Deborah, & Rénique, Gerardo. (1992). *Peru: Time of fear.* London: Latin America Bureau.

Potok, Mark. (1999, Summer). All in the family: Women in the movement. *Intelligence Report* (Southern Poverty Law Center), pp. 12-22.

Radu, Michael, & Tismaneanu, Vladimir. (1990). *Latin American revolutionaries: Groups, goals, methods.* Washington, DC: Pergamon-Brassey's International Defense Publishers.

Rojahn, Christoph. (1998). Left-wing terrorism in Germany: The aftermath of ideological violence. *Conflict Studies. 313*, 1-21.

Rojas, Rosa. (1994). *Chiapas, and the women?* Mexico, DF: Editiones La Correa Feminista, Centro de Investigation y Capacitacion de las Mujer. Mexico, DF.

Schweitzer, Yoram. (2000, April 21). *Suicide terrorism: Development & characteristics.* Institute for Counter Terrorism. Retrieved June 17, 2001, from www.ict.org.il/articles/articledet.cfm?articleid=112

Scripps Howard. (2002, February 6). *Women suicide bombers since 1985.* Washington, DC: International Database.

Shakespeare, Nicholas. (1997). *The dancer upstairs.* Thorndike, ME: G. K Hall & Co.

Tarazona-Sevillano, Gabriela. (1990). *Sendero Luminoso and the threat of narcoterrorism.* New York: Praeger.

Vague, Tom. (1994). *Televisionaries: The Red Army Faction story 1963-1993.* San Francisco: AK Press.

Vetter, Harold J., & Perlstein, Gary R. (1991). *Perspectives on terrorism.* Pacific Grove, CA: Brooks/Cole.

TOKEN TERRORIST

The Demon Lover's Woman

ROBIN MORGAN

Anyone who knows anything of history knows that great social changes are impossible without the feminine ferment. Social progress can be measured exactly by the social position of the fair sex—the ugly ones included.

—KARL MARX

Women should be divided into three main types: first, those frivolous, thoughtless, and vapid women whom we may exploit as confused liberals; second, women who are ardent, gifted, and devoted, but who do not belong to us because they have not yet achieved a real revolutionary understanding; and finally there are the women who are with us completely, who have been fully initiated and who accept our program in its entirety. We should regard these women as the most valuable of our treasures, without whose assistance we cannot manage.

—SERGEI NECHAEV

> *Kiss me with your blood*
> *before the next war.*
> *Kneeling before you*
> *I see the sabre medals mirroring*
> *tortures to come, prisoners to hunt.*
> *I am then the*
> *silence that shall be.*
> *Kiss me, nail me against you*
> *and allow a new cataclysm of death,*
> *of civilizations,*
> *to whirl.*

—ISEL RIVERO

CHERCHEZ L'HOMME

It always happens when women become at last the subject and not the object: in order to define what women, or a group of women, or an individual woman are/is, first one must define what this subject is *not*. So thorough is the stereotyping, the perception of female as Other, the deliberate misinterpretation of motive, that the lies must be peeled away before a female reality can even be approached.

Perhaps the most common misapprehension is the one that blurs together women who participate in general uprisings and "terrorist" women. For the record, then. Women taking to the streets banging pots and pans during food-shortage riots are not engaged in terrorist activity. Women marching in a public demonstration against a colonial government are not engaged in terrorist activity. Peasant women agitating for land rights, squatting on their small share-cropped farms, are not engaged in terrorist activity. Honduran campesino organizer Elvia Alvarado speaks indignantly about such calculated miscategorization:

> The military has started accusing us of . . . being Sandinista terrorists, . . . of working with the Salvadoran guerrillas. . . . I don't know anything about Nicaragua, . . . I don't know what's going on in El Salvador. Hondurans have to worry about what's going on *here*. . . . They always try to say we're part of some big conspiracy, when we're just a handful of poor campesinos. . . . Before, when we used to try to recover the land, we were charged with damaging private property. Now we're still charged with that, but also with being terrorists, . . . you can't even get out on bail. . . . Where do they get off calling us terrorists just because we try to recover the land? We don't want to hurt anyone. We don't even have weapons. So why do they call us terrorists?[3]

A second kind of predictable analysis bases itself on that old stand-by, Blame the Victim. Who is responsible for intensified violence in terrorist groups? Women. J.K. Zawodny writes:

> This problem has never been publicly aired for fear of . . . being charged with antifeminist bias. . . . [Women] do produce tensions within extralegal organizations. . . . it is inevitable (although never admitted formally) that there is conscious or unconscious competition for them . . . affecting relationships among the men. Women's ability to manipulate the membership of the organization on an informal level is another problem. . . . Men who compete for women try to "outdo" each other, often initiating violence first;

looking for a formalized excuse afterward. The fact that the women observe the actions as direct participants is quite an incentive. In this type of cultural setting, the presence of women within a terrorist organization is a psychological inducement to violence that is constantly present on all organizational levels.[4]

As an afterthought, Professor (of International Relations) Zawodny adds, "On the other hand, in some cultures, [women's] presence may serve as a brake on violent actions."[5] But he says no more about *that*—for fear of being accused of a profeminist bias?

Moving right along from blaming all women in general to blaming some women in particular (and don't forget that male terrorism is the fault of the terrorists' mothers), authorities not infrequently cite feminism as the culprit in female terrorism. A rare voice does disagree—but for the wrong reasons. Vera Broido, in her book *Apostles into Terrorists: Women and the Revolutionary Movement in the Russia of Alexander II*, sneers, "To assign to revolutionary women the narrow partisan role of feminists is to distort their position in the revolutionary movement and to diminish their contribution to Russian history."[6] (That silly, narrow, partisan role again, selfishly addressing itself to the majority of the human species.) Most of the terrorism "experts," however, when they decide to examine women's participation at all, claim a direct connection between feminist foment and female violence. Daniel E. Georges-Abeyie is a special favorite of mine. In an article entitled "Women as Terrorists," he reviews the literature on women and criminality, from Cesare Lombroso (criminal women exhibit primitive traits, considerable body hair, lower intelligence), to Freud (they're anatomically inferior, attempting to be men), through Otto Pollak (the rising female crime rate is the result of sexual emancipation), M. Rappaport (female criminals are psychological misfits), J. Cowie, V. Cowie, and E. Slater (there is a chromosomal explanation: such women are more masculine than the normal female), H. C. Vedder and D. Sommerville (they show maladjustment to the normal feminine role), F. Adler (they're a side product of the women's liberation movement), and R. Simon (women's violence is created by a shift in patterns of sexual inequality and the rise in female labor-force participation).[7]

Georges-Abeyie himself does not agree with all of the literature. In fact, he finds some of the conclusions "laughable." He is a modern scholar, rational, one of the "honorable men." But he does feel that "there is some merit to a less extreme interpretation of some of the correlates to these and other theories of this specific form of female criminality [terrorism]." He even adds some correlates of his own, focusing on such Northern American groups as the Weatherpeople and the SLA, with "sizable numbers of female cadres [who] proselytized female homosexuality and bisexuality as well as pansexualism and feminist ideology."[8] His empirical research apparently did not include the later public statements and writings of women previously involved in such groups, to wit, that pressure for rejection of monogamy and for lesbian acts (but never for *male* homosexuality) as forms of "sexual liberation" emanated *from the male leadership of those groups as direct orders*. Rejection of monogamy was to make the women available to all the men, and lesbianism (under male direction and control) was thought by the men to be titillating.[9] Georges-Abeyie notes that "various social-control agencies" today share the assumption that women terrorists have masculine psychologies and even body types, and (contradictorily) that most of the acts committed by such women are "emotive rather than instrumental, i.e., emotional rather than well-thought-out acts with a rational program of action not tied to a love interest, such as an attempt to free a captured husband or lover." (Masculine psychologies but feminine emotions: this is called eating your analysis and having it, too.) These "social-control authorities," according to Georges-Abeyie, are certain that female terrorists are much more likely than men to commit acts of "senseless or nongoal-oriented violence"—as opposed to sensible and goal-oriented violence, I presume. For himself, he theorizes that we can expect a further increase in women's participation in terrorism, because of "changing role-sets" for women in general; the influence of feminism in raising women's expectations of society; and the likelihood that "women who lack the characteristics . . . that society

considers appropriate [gentleness, seductiveness, physical attractiveness, etc.] . . . may seek success in some non-feminine realm, by displaying aggression, unadorned faces and bodies, toughness, or other masculine qualities."[10] (Run for the Revlon, quick, before the shoot-out.) He anticipates that the women in this rise will be seen integrated into national-liberation and socialist struggles, "and not as autonomous legions of Amazon-oriented warriors"—yet he does not ask *why*. Being a good liberal, he feels it imperative to factor into his hypothesis the influence of feminist demands "both logical *and* irrational"; he will decide which is which.

Well. It's difficult to know where to start, with such a barrage of imbecilities. So why not start with feminism? Need it be said that Georges-Abeyie (and Vera Broido, too) would not recognize feminism were it to appear and introduce itself in person? An even more tragic truth is that women who become involved in terrorist acts wouldn't recognize it either, despite claims on their part that they are acting as "liberated" women. How and why feminism eludes them—or, rather, how and why they elude it— is a story unique to them yet familiarly parallel to the story of every woman.

As we've seen, all women share the cross-cultural burden of being viewed as the repositories of (male-defined) morality. Therefore, women must never be wrong doers. To encroach beyond present boundaries—to trespass, disobey, transgress—is a far more censurable act for a woman than for a man. It's the old double standard, as in sex, drinking (a male drunk is a jolly good fellow; a female drunk is disgusting), drug abuse, and prostitution (in the statutes of most countries, the male buyer goes free, while the female seller is jailed). If, then, transgression for a woman is made into an unthinkable act, or at least one for which she knows she will pull down much more opprobrium than a male, *she must transgress via a man.* She believes she has no access to transgression by and for herself. She must try to androgynize herself, combine herself with him. "Wow, what a trip!" reminisced Charles Manson "family" member Susan Atkins while in prison. "I thought 'To taste death, and yet give life.'"[11] As with everything else in her vicarious existence, her rebellion can be conceived by society *and by her* only through him, his modes, his means.

It wasn't a historical coincidence that the nineteenth- and twentieth-century waves of feminism in the United States were born out of the abolition and civil-rights movements respectively. Women, black and white, were in the forefront of those movements, their rebellion always in the context of altruistic struggle for the good of the whole, for the suffrage rights of their men, and later for the rights of *manhood*. All of which was a historical prerequisite to their articulating the smallest revolt on behalf of their own female predicament.

Just as the structure of the male corporate world is the means for a woman to rise in our economy (playing the game by following his rules), so is the structure of a male revolution the means for a woman to rebel (overthrowing the rules by playing his game). The knowledge that she is exchanging one form of male leadership and style for another is not always tolerable, certainly not at first—and then, suddenly, it can be too late.

The "revolutionary" woman has bought into the male "radical" line, as articulated from Nechaev through Castro. She has learned that in order to be a *real* revolutionary, she must disassociate herself from her womanhood, her aspirations, her reality—and most of all, from other women. She must integrate into herself the alarm and disgust with which such men regard "women's issues." Two cases in point: Nadeshda Krupskaya, Lenin's wife, was in her time and fashion a feminist and an advocate of women's sexual freedom—as was his mistress, Inessa Armand. Both have been virtually erased from the official canons, though these two, together with Clara Zetkin, created the idea of International Women's Day (March 8). Lenin was appalled when Armand wanted to write a pamphlet on female sexual liberation; he worried that she was promulgating "adultery" and "freedom from child-bearing."[12]

So the woman who wishes to rebel learns yet another of man's realities. As wife, sister, and mother, she has mouthed his patriotism during national wars, carried his flags, waved at his parades, driven his ambulances. She has tried for millennia to demonstrate her loyalty, to win his acceptance; Jean Bethke Elshtain has

thoroughly documented that fealty in her book *Woman and War*. All the while, though, she has been petitioning, pleading, organizing—for peace. (Is this one reason why his approval has never been forthcoming?) And when her rage at his ignoring her reaches a certain point of necessary expression, she finds again that the only model for it is a male one: *his* revolution.

"By God, I shall exceed my sex," are words attributed to Jeanne d'Arc. They are the words required of the woman who would "succeed" in the man's world (his State or his State-that-would be). *She may not rise with her people.* She must abandon them, abandon her own experience, and, more important, her own intuited, envisioned possible transformation. If she wants power, she must learn that power is synonymous with *his power*— and *his means* of seizing it. If she wants freedom she must learn that this too is synonymous with *his* definition of it and his struggle for it. Neither will save her. Both will destroy her. *But she has found a way to transgress which is acceptable*. She has entered the harem of the Demon Lover.

Her own psychology, ethics, desires, and truths, go underground in her soul. She must deny and deny and deny them. Listen to the court testimony of Vera Zasulich, who in 1878 shot and wounded General Dmitri Trepov, the governor of St. Petersburg, in reaction to hearing about the torture of political prisoners: "Such degradation of human personality should not be allowed to be inflicted. . . . *I could find no other way* of drawing attention to what had happened. . . . *But it is a terrible thing to lift one's hand against another human being*. . . . I fired without aiming [she instantly threw the gun away] . . . I was afraid it might go off again . . . *I did not want this*."[13](Italics mine.) (Zasulich, by the way, was described in the press of the day as being a "spinster" of noble birth, twenty-eight years old—and plain-looking.) In her later life a critic of Lenin, Zasulich wrote in 1892 that "terrorist acts cannot make a movement more powerful, no matter how popular they may be. Terrorism is too morbid a form of struggle. However great the delight it sometimes arouses, in order to carry out terrorist acts all of one's energies must be expended, and a particular frame of mind almost always results: either one of great vanity or one in which life has lost all its attractiveness."[14]

Vanity and despair could comprise an excellent description of patriarchy.

The woman trapped in this position must not only pledge her fealty but defend her commitment—and defend her denial of herself—with a vehemence sufficient to convince her own troubled soul as well as her vigilant male colleagues. So the great Rosa Luxemburg suffered indignities from her long-term lover Leo Jogiches, and insults for being "the last man in the German Social Democratic Party." Luxemburg was torn all her life between a relentless political activism and her yearning for a contemplative life of writing, thinking, and caring for plants and animals; torn between her own insistent pacifism and the cynical prowar position of her own party; torn between what she herself saw as her dependent need for men and her knowledge that the need was self-destructive; torn between her friend Clara Zetkin's feminist influence and her own decision to oppose women's suffrage as diversionary to the workers' cause. Though her courage never failed her (she denounced Lenin as practicing a "Tatar-Mongolian savagery"), the resolve to use that courage on her own behalf and that of other women did.[15] Similarly, Emma Goldman denounced women's suffrage as a joke and a diversion, and sublimated her radical transgressions under the banners of male politics. When Goldman gave us the audacious phrase "If I can't dance to it, it's not my revolution," did she think she would exceed her sex and be dancing only with her brothers?[16]

What we glimpse in the life-loving personal temperaments of Luxemburg and Goldman—the longing for peace and for joy—shines like silver streaked through caverns of a so-called revolutionary male politics grimy with hatred and revenge, with manipulation, petty ambition, and violence. But their lives of torment have been bequeathed to the women who still dance in the Demon Lover's revolutionary State-that-would-be.

"We are becoming the men we wanted to marry" is a consciousness-raising phrase some of us coined in the early 1970s, as women began to look at their own potential instead of gazing vicariously at life through a male-imposed scrim, began to pour into law and medical schools, began to found small businesses, start

magazines, break into nontraditional jobs. It was a useful phrase for its time. In retrospect, it has a built-in danger: the *terms* of our "becoming" remain defined by the men we may (or may not) want to marry. For the rebel woman, who is "becoming" the man she wanted to follow through the revolution, there's no time to question that the role she dons was cut like a uniform for him, not for her. In the act of donning it, she not only delays her own revolution, but in fact *obstructs* it: she reinforces both his priorities and his means.

It's certainly understandable why Nechaev considered such women "treasures." They will dare more, fight harder, work longer, and try to prove themselves to their comrades more than any man will (and more than any man needs to). And the men will exploit them ruthlessly—in the name of the cause the *men* have defined.

During the Chinese Revolution, the single most controversial issue was women's right to divorce; the most persecuted cadres were women trying to organize against foot-binding, wife-beating, and rape. In the 1927-30 purge of Communists by Chiang Kai-shek's Kuomintang, thousands of young women were identified as "radicals" because of bobbed hair, and were accused of "sexual license and free love" politics. Many were wrapped in cotton wadding, doused in oil, and burnt alive.[17]

> Not all were communists, some were bourgeois, and there were many students . . . I think the brutality of the killing has no parallel in all the world . . . When girls [*sic*] were arrested in Hunan they were stripped naked, nailed on crosses, and their noses and breasts were cut off before they were killed . . . [After beheading] their heads were put into men's coffins and the gendarmes said "you have your free love now." . . .[18]

And in the wake of the sacrifice by women cadres? In 1942, Ding Ling, China's greatest novelist and herself a revolutionary, loosed a scathing criticism of the Communist party's betrayal of women in her famous "Thoughts on March 8, International Women's Day." Women, she claimed, were still being subjected to the old oppressive treatments, new ones had been added, and to boot women were being told they were now emancipated. For this cry of truth, she was publicly attacked by Mao, accused of being a reactionary, and sentenced to two years of "thought reform." In and out of official favor for the rest of her life, Ding Ling continued to speak her mind *and* her feminism. In 1956, she was again charged, this time with the crime of refusing to accept party supervision; she had been fighting literary censorship and speaking publicly about women's oppression. The following year, she was denounced by the official writers' union, denied citizenship, expelled from the party, and sentenced to a term of hard labor in Manchuria—where she remained for almost twenty years. "Rehabilitated" and brought back into public favor after Mao's death (when she was seventy-seven) she lived out her last years without bitterness—still writing, and still calling on younger women to free themselves—until her death in 1986.[19]

The "revolution in the revolution"—to borrow and give new meaning to Régis Debray's phrase—does not always take such a long-term or principled form. Sometimes it's simply a cry for immediate help. On May 8, 1972, a Sabena Airlines plane over Yugoslavia was hijacked by a four-person Palestinian team, in what would be a failed attempt to free some prisoners being held in the Israeli prison at Ramallah in the Occupied West Bank. Brought to trial in Israel, the defendants were charged with terrorist acts as well as with the crime of being members of the outlawed Al Fatah. Two of the team were young women, and both pleaded the "defence of constraint," under an inherited British statute then still on the Israeli lawbooks. Their attorney argued that they had been constrained to carry arms under threat of death, and had been involved in the hijacking against their will. One of the women was an addict whose drug dependency had been used to force her participation; the other pleaded that she had been kidnapped by the guerrillas and had been unable to escape. At the trial and later at the appeal, these defenses were rejected and both women were found guilty.[20] In the Sharia (the legal code of Islam) as well as in the Halacha (the legal code of Judaism) women are legally "irresponsible"; in the former, a woman's testimony is rated at half the value of a man's, and in the latter women are considered unreliable or illegal signatories to legal documents. Yet when the State-that-would-be and the State-that-is wish it otherwise, suddenly women are legally responsible for their views and their acts.

The coercion is not always so direct. Equally pernicious and far more common is the use of sex and "love" to enmesh women—and, in turn, the use of women's sexuality to further the cause. This form of coercion—recruitment by romance—is, after all, what the Demon Lover's message is about.

Colin Smith's biography of Ilich Ramirez Sanchez, *Carlos: Portrait of a Terrorist*, is one long saga of Carlos's proud seductions of women into the stable of his revolution:

> One of Carlos's greatest joys was that he was able to claim an energetic sex life as a legitimate working expense, part of the important business of establishing cover and hide-outs . . . he was quite capable of ruthlessly exploiting his sexual conquests, . . . [at one point] he had four regular girl friends, two either side of the [English] Channel, whose homes he sometimes used as safe-houses to hide arms, explosives and false documents. They were also places of sanctuary, somewhere he could be assured, without warning, of getting a bed for the night—preferably a warm one.[21]

Most of these women wound up serving jail sentences, while their Lothario has not yet been caught. That Carlos was notorious among these women for his acutely masculinist attitude toward cooking and housework (he never helped) will strike some readers as amusing, considering the circumstances. That he lived the life of a *bon vivant*—enjoying gourmet food, Napoleon brandy, imported cigars, and designer clothes—often supported by these women, may seem more distasteful. That in country after country—in the Middle East, Turkey, Greece, Germany, Italy, France, England, Scandinavia—he literally recruited women from his bed onto his battlefront, at last seems serious. (Yet all three stages are common, and are related.) Many of the women came in time not only to hide the documents but to smuggle them, not only to secrete the weapons but to shoot them, not only to store the bombs but to plant them. Some of these women are dead. Some are in prison for life. Some are still in hiding. Some are still dancing to his tune.

Each one was certain she was his true love.

Sometimes the Demon Lover pimps for the cause. The use of women as "Mata Hari" sexual bait is by now a cliché. (A subtle form of this was the slogan "Girls say Yes to Boys Who Say No" during the 1960s New Left campaign to encourage draft resistance. Change the letter *A* to *R* and color it scarlet for Revolution.)

Possibly the most famous contemporary case of a woman as sexual lure is that of the late Nora Astorga, the young, beautiful Nicaraguan attorney who was in sympathy with the Sandinista insurgents against the tyrannical Somoza dictatorship. General Reynaldo Perez Vega—called "El Perro" ("The Dog")—a ranking officer in Somoza's notorious human-rights-violating National Guard, had been pursuing her. Finally, in March 1978, she invited Perez to her home, dismissed his bodyguard, brought him to her bedroom, and undressed and disarmed him. Guerrilla men, hiding in her closet, then jumped out and slit his throat. They left his body, draped with the Sandinista flag, behind them when they fled. Astorga disappeared into the revolutionary ranks, leaving behind the message "I want it known that I participated in the operation of bringing to justice this bloody henchman." Later, she would revise her version of the event, claiming that the plan—merely to kidnap and hold Perez Vega for ransom—had gone awry when he attacked the guerrillas.[22] Whatever the real story, the State-that-would-be in this case won. The Sandinistas formed a revolutionary government. Possibly because there had been rumblings of discontent from too many women in Third World revolutionary ranks, it was decided that Astorga need not meet the fate of such forerunners as Haydee Santamaría of Cuba, a liberation heroine who was relegated to a minor "cultural" post and who later committed suicide; or Nguyen Thi Binh of reunited Vietnam, assigned the traditional female portfolio of minister of education and the young. The women were getting restless. So Astorga was rewarded with a rare token position of power: Nicaraguan ambassador to the United Nations, a post she handled with intelligence and dignity, while carefully presenting herself, nonetheless, as a beautiful and chic woman. When I met her in 1987, I couldn't help noticing how her self-discipline overrode what was clearly great fatigue. I didn't know at that time that she was seriously ill with cancer, but was remaining at her post like a "good soldier"; she kept her illness a secret until a few months before her death, in the spring of 1988. So, in person, I merely expressed my solidarity with Nicaraguan women. That elicited a sharp response: "Not solidarity with the Nicaraguan *people*?" "Women," I responded politely, though perhaps a bit wearily, "are my priority." There was no way to ask why solidarity with the majority of the Nicaraguan people—women—was insufficient, why specific solidarity must be expressed for the minority—men—in order to prove one's revolutionary mettle. And there was no way to ask about the rumors of the special man, for there had been one, whom she had loved and whose rebellion she had made her own.

Cherchez l'homme. He is there, one way or the other. In a study of Italian woman terrorists done by Leonard Weinberg and William Lee Eubank, more than two-thirds of the case histories showed women who had become involved because they were married to terrorist men, and in most of the other cases the woman had become involved via a male sibling. A significantly higher number of the women than of the men had had prior blood- or love-relationship ties with terrorists; for those few men who were involved because of family ties, the connections were fraternal or paternal rather than marital or romantic. Furthermore, the men had a history of political involvement predating their terrorist activities; most of the women did not.[23] In effect, the men became involved because of politics and the women became involved because of the men. That too is "political."

The women became involved because men constituted the sole route of transgression available against a system the women knew enough to oppose (though not to oppose *enough*). That rebellion shows itself in the numbers. The study examined terrorist groups of the neo-Fascist Right as well as of the Left: the former had "little allure for women," who were to a significant degree more drawn to the revolutionary Left. In another survey of Italian terrorism, Vittorfranco Pisano found that women's "organizational abilities" were in high demand among Leftist terrorist groups, in particular the Brigate Rosse (Red Brigades).[24] Margherita ("Mara") Cagol was reputedly a paragon of such abilities. Her husband, Renato Curcio, is considered to be the founder of the Red Brigades: *cherchez l'homme*.

Mara Cagol and Renato Curcio are one pair among many in what I would term "couple terrorism." Another is Jean-Marc Rouillan and Nathalie Menignon of Action Directe, a couple known as the Bonnie and Clyde of French terrorism. There are Alexander Yenikomechian and Suzy Mahseredjian of ASALA (the Armenian Secret Army for the Liberation of Armenia) and, also with ASALA, Hratch Kozihioukian and his wife Siranouche Kozihioukian. In the United States, there were Sam Melville and Jane Alpert, and at the pinnacle of the Weather Underground Organization Central Committee, Bernardine Dohrn and Bill Ayers. The Weather Underground Organization could also boast of Kathy Boudin and David Gilbert, among other pairs, but in that case the woman apparently coupled with the wrong man. Gilbert never rose to a position of power with the Weatherpeople and, as one WUO faction later charged, "In an organization dominated by male supremacy, how a woman got to be a leader was to line up with the Central Committee men, on the backs of women." Consequently, Boudin's "relationship with Gilbert kept her down."[25] She may therefore have felt the need to prove herself all the more keenly: she is currently serving a twenty-years-to-life sentence for second-degree murder and first-degree robbery in a 1981 attack on a Brink's van.

These women would have died—as some did—rather than admit that they acted as they did for male approval and love. It takes time, perspective, and courage to hazard such an admission. In 1987, after thirteen years of forced exile from her native Chile, Carmen Castillo was permitted home for a visit to her ailing father. When she had been sent into exile, she was recuperating from bullet wounds and was seven months pregnant with a child fathered by her lover, Miguel Enriquez; he had died at her side in a shoot-out with General Pinochet's military-intelligence forces. It has taken Castillo over a decade of suffering, and of learning to live again, to be able to say as she does now that although she still opposes Pinochet's bloody regime, she would not stoop

to bloody means of contesting. "All that I did back then was for love," she says simply. "It had a logic, and the logic was love."[26]

Carmen Castillo is one of the lucky ones. In a different way, so is Anna-Karin Lindgren. A college graduate, she met Norbert Kroecher at a 1972 New Year's Eve party in Sweden. He was already married, as well as involved with two other women back in his home city of Berlin, but she didn't know that. She fell in love with him. He moved in with her. He had no job, so she supported them both by working as a teacher. Sometimes he came and went without explanation. As Lindgren's friend Pia Lasker testified at her later trial, "Kroecher was a genuine male chauvinist who did not do anything in the home but only exercised Anna-Karin.... Often he lay sleeping until late in the afternoon. He had a room of his own at his disposal in Anna-Karin's apartment." Kroecher "easily grew angry and he often snapped at [Anna-Karin]. Probably he found her irritating. One reason for this was certainly that he was very dependent on her.... Anna-Karin herself was not politically attached to any particular movement and her relationship with Kroecher was not marked by any political will or idea, but was exclusively of an emotional character."[27]

Kroecher was a fugitive from West Germany and a former fringe member of the circle of people around the Baader-Meinhof Group, the Movement 2 June, and the SPK (the German Socialist Patients' Collective).[27a] Now, in Sweden, Kroecher was building a new terrorist group. Over the following five years, his gang robbed banks for funds, planned several bombings, and plotted Operation Leo, an abortive attempt to kidnap a Swedish woman cabinet minister. A number of Swedish men became involved—all of them pulling in their girlfriends. Gradually, some of Kroecher's German friends appeared and became active (along with *their* girlfriends), as did Armando Carillo, from Mexico (and *his* wife, Maria). But in the midst of their activity—after five years of paying for it and committing crimes she never understood—Lindgren was purged, ostensibly for political reasons. In reality, Kroecher had found himself a new woman. "Kroecher was not satisfied with Anna-Karin, who had shown passive resistance against his plans.... Their relationship had progressively worsened. . . . [At the meeting] it was said that Anna-Karin was unreliable and unpolitical. . . . there was some kind of voting. Nobody was against the decision. Anna-Karin wondered what they were doing but she did not ask since she felt there was no point in asking."[28]

The women who recognize their own power-lessness in such a context are "simple-mindedly" more intelligent than those who cling to the illusion that they exceed their sex. "Unpolitical," passively resistant Anna-Karin Lindgren is at least still alive.

Ulrike Meinhof is not.

The Baader-Meinhof Group/Red Army Faction is sometimes cited as unusual both for the number of women involved and for their presence in leadership positions. Less attention is paid to subtler facts. The group was actually begun by two men—Horst Mahler and Andreas Baader. Baader and his woman, Gudrun Ensslin, were members of German SDS. After an attempt was made on the life of their colleague, radical organizer Rudi Dutschke, Baader began calling for violent action against the State, and he and Ensslin adopted the name Wetterleute (Weatherpeople) for themselves in imitation of the U.S. group. Ensslin previously had been calling herself an evangelical paci-fist.[29] Ulrike Meinhof, also a declared pacifist, had been Dutschke's lover. They had worked together at *Konkret*, a "revolutionary pornogra-phy" magazine owned by Meinhof's husband. After the shooting, Dutschke dropped out of politics entirely and left the country—and Meinhof. She then joined Ensslin and Baader, to forge a "guerrilla" group that would, according to their propaganda, expose the contradictions of the Federal Republic of Germany and force the State to show its fascism openly. The Red Army Faction called for terrorism to accomplish this purpose. Ensslin became the operational commander of the group (because of her "orga-nizational abilities"), but Meinhof had led a successful and highly publicized attempt to free Baader after his arrest in 1970, and the Red Army Faction informally came to be named after the two of them. From its founding in 1968-69 until 1972, by which time the original members had been mostly killed or captured, the group carried out bombings, arson, kidnappings, hijackings, and assassinations. It sometimes

worked with Carlos (at Entebbe and in the assault on the OPEC ministers), and is also thought to have had links with the Japanese Red Army, the Italian Red Brigades, the Dutch Red Help cells, the Palestinian Black September faction, and Wadi Haddad's breakaway PFLP. At Entebbe, Red Army Faction member Brigitte Kohlmann, together with her man and teammate Wilfried Bose, was killed by Israeli comman-dos. Ulrike Meinhof committed suicide in her prison cell, as did Ensslin (some factions of the Left in Germany claimed the suicides were mur-ders by prison authorities). Today, the group has fragmented, but some "second-generation" members are thought to be still working throughout Europe, in isolation or in periodic contact with other self-proclaimed terrorist groups.[30] One former member, Beate Sturm, claims in retrospect that the Red Army Faction members were "naive and incurably romantic" with regard to the role their terrorist acts played in furthering world revolution.[31] Anna Mendleson, formerly of the Angry Brigade in the United Kingdom, takes a similar view: "It hasn't changed anything. It hasn't changed anything at all."[32] Dismissing such statements as standard recantations of aging radicals would be easy, except that they have the ring of dis-illusion uniquely voiced by women betrayed in love.

Whether as troops or as "leaders," these women were followers. Their "rebellion" for love's sake is classic feminine—not feminist—behavior. Ulrike Meinhof was no more of a rebel than Sheela P. Silverman, who took the name of Ma Anand Sheela in the community headed by Indian guru Bhagwan Shree Rajneesh. The guru, infamous for his 64,000-acre thirty-million-dollar Oregon ranch and his fleet of eighty-five Rolls Royces, was charged in 1984 with election fraud: he had imported thousands of followers to the area in an attempt to take over control of the county. He is now comfortably back at his ashram in Poona, India, having paid a fine. Sheela Silverman, however, is serving a federal prison sentence for wiretap-ping, attempted murder, and "causing a salmo-nella epidemic by tainting salad bars, poisoning more than 750 people in Waco County." Silverman has said that she acted "as the fall-guy" for the guru's machinations—but she still reveres him.[33] Sandra Good, a Manson "family" member, still apparently revered *her* guru (who had seen his name as a pun on "Man's Son") even after ten years in prison. In March 1986, she refused her first parole because it was conditional on her not visiting Manson, who is still serving a life sentence.

Of the so-called independents—women who appear unattached to men—the two most famous are probably Fusako Shigenobu and Leila Khaled.

Shigenobu allegedly heads the "Arab Committee" of the JRA (Japanese Red Army, Sekigun faction); she has worked closely with Carlos and with Wadi Haddad of the PFLP, and has been shuttling back and forth to Beirut since 1971. Born in Tokyo only a few weeks before the atomic bombing of Nagasaki and Hiroshima, she is the daughter of a shopkeeper who, in his own youth, was a member of the Blood Oath League, an extremist Right-wing group pledged to "cleanse" Japan of corrupt politicians by selectively assassinating them. Shigenobu wanted to write poetry and fiction but was forced to end her education after high school because the family couldn't afford college tuition. She married a Left-wing radical and cofounder of the JRA, Tsoyoshi Okudaira, and at one point supported him by working as a topless dancer in the Ginza red-light district. Of this period, she wrote, "I hated the men who pawed me and used my body to satisfy their lust. . . . I had murder in my heart. But I smiled, for I saw every kiss turn into a rice ball for the Red Army."[34] When Okudaira, one of the JRA terrorists involved in the 1972 PFLP attack on Lod airport, killed himself with his last bullet rather than surrender to the Israelis, his widow moved up into the leadership echelons of the JRA. Since then, it is rumored that the "marriage" between the PFLP and the JRA was "quite literally consummated when [PFLP leader] Habash, who is a good-looking man in a Thirties matinee idol sort of way, and Shigenobu became lovers."[35]

Leila Khaled burst into world headlines on August 29, 1969, when she led the Palestinian hijacking team that commandeered a TWA jet and force it to land in Damascus. She was young, she looked like Audrey Hepburn, and she was the first "female terrorist" to hit the news in mid-action; the press had a field day. Khaled came from a middle-class background; her family had fled Haifa in 1948 and settled eventually in Tyre, in Lebanon. She attended the American University in Beirut and later taught at an elementary school in Kuwait. She joined the PFLP as it was about to splinter from Arafat's more mainstream Al Fatah, in 1967. Her 1975 autobiography, *My People Shall Live*,[36] was ghost-written by George Hajjar, a member of the PFLP's political think tank,[37] which may explain why the book avoids details of her own life and hews more to a line of political rhetoric. In early interviews, too, she would say only, "I am engaged to the Revolution." This was not totally true: she was also engaged to a man, an Iraqi Palestinian militant, whom she subsequently married and later divorced. At the 1980 Mid-Decade United Nations World Conference on Women in Copenhagen, Khaled was lionized by the press, to the dismay of the entire Palestinian delegation. The men, who headed the delegation even though this was a women's conference, were furious that so much attention was being paid to a woman. The women expressed irritation (off-stage and unofficially in private conversations) because Khaled never spoke about *women*. But her reasons came out a year later in an interview with a German feminist newspaper. She displayed the elite disdain for which PFLP commandos are notorious—a contempt for the *fedayeen* who make lowly border raids on Israeli kibbutzim—compounded with a double message about being female:

> When I speak at an international conference, as in Copenhagen, *I represent Palestinians, not women.* . . . Although in Arab society to be married and have children is very important, in my case, nobody wonders about it. A woman who fights politically is respected. . . . *The organizers and organizations would not take us seriously if we were to begin speaking about it* [women's rights]. They would say we wish to be like European women . . . *and they would reject us.* So we try instead to say that honor means more than virginity, that there is honor in recovering our homeland.[38] (Italics mine.)

Khaled has survived assassination attempts by the Israeli secret service, survived prison and release (in a hostage exchange), survived being married and divorced. Of late, she seems to have disappeared into the PFLP bureaucracy, her much-photographed face now making her a liability on terrorist missions. One wonders what that means to her. For she has not survived being female. It's clear in the interview: even for the unattached women, the gestures of obeisance, the protestations of denial, must be made. The woman who rebels via the male mode can do so only to the point where her own rebellion might begin.

Feminist writer Andrea Dworkin is one woman who embarked on that rebellion in the midst of what she had thought was going to be "the revolution":

> I married an anarchist, an ex-Provo,[38a] a proven urban guerrilla. I woke up three years later and the total substance of my concern was housework. I was virtually catatonic; I didn't know who I was anymore. "Love" turned to violence and abuse. Some revolutionaries, after all, have to fight all the time—if not on the streets, then in the home. When one loses all hope of ever changing anything (which he did), one must live out the despair somehow. Some commit suicide, some commit assault. I finally recognized myself as a woman: . . . I had been a victim, of a particular man, of a whole sexist system, of my own illusions. . . . my marriage taught me, much as prison had, the nature and dimension of oppression—in my own body, where I learn best.[39]

That insight came at the beginning of what would be a long journey toward self-discovery, self-invention, self-affirmation. Back in 1972, though, her voice was still tentative; she was still reaching out to understand him, still comprehending his motivation, his despair, more than her own.

For how long must our voices hover in the tentativity of that insight?

We pose the insight, as did the collective voice of the Portuguese writers "the Three Marias," in rumination:

> I wonder whether the *guerrillera* who battles side by side with her brothers . . . is fighting side by side with her real brothers, or whether these brothers may not still bear within themselves the

roots of treason, both in the dialogue of the present struggle and in the future City.[40]

We pose the insight, as does the insurgent Association of Salvadoran Women, in a question:

> The parties and movements of . . . the Left have, in general, not dealt with the problems of women with the same consistency with which they confront other social problems, . . . [but] conceived of women's liberation . . . as technical and private, . . . becoming collective and social only *after* the exploited sectors have won their liberation, that is to say, in some distant and unpredictable future. . . . Will the people's organizations be capable of focusing on the specifics of daily life, or will they leave this to the mercy of the dominant ideology?[41]

More and more, we dare to pose the insight as fact. Inevitably, that daring has come from Third World women who are themselves veterans of liberation struggles. Marie Angélique Savané of Senegal has termed all contemporary "governments—of the Right and the Left—"phallocracies."[42] Fatima Mernissi of Morocco has written about nationalism having repeatedly betrayed women.[43] Lidia Falcón has exposed how the Spanish Communist party first capitalized on and then jettisoned the feminist movement.[44] Ama Ata Aidoo of Ghana writes, "If, as a woman, you try to flex your muscles as a revolutionary cadre where your comrades are predominantly male, you can hit the concrete wall with such force that you might never recover your original self. . . . And don't be shocked if—when victory is won—they return you to the veil as part of the process of consolidating the revolution."[45]

To pose the insight as *action* is most difficult of all.

Elsewhere and at length[46] I've constructed a detailed analogy between women and colonized peoples, observing that colonization requires at least three elements: first, control over the land, so that it can be mined for its natural resources—in the case of women, the "natural resources" of our bodies, in sex and in reproduction; second, the enforced alienation of the colonized from their own territory by a system based on exclusion and mystification—in the case of women, alienation from one's own flesh (lack of reproductive freedom and freedom of sexual preference) and alienation from one's own self-defined existence; and third, a readiness on the part of the colonizer to meet all demands for self-determination with a repertoire of repression, from ridicule through tokenism to brutality—in the case of women, a repertoire spanning derision, individual cooptation, and the more blatant forms of response: rape, battery, *sati*, purdah, erasure, prostitution, and other such means of enslavement.

I would now add a fourth element. The colonized are an invaluable resource (veritable "treasures") in the colonizers' wars *against one another*: in fact, this is one of the reasons for and conveniences of an empire. The examples are many: the all-black division (in a segregated army) fighting for the United States in World War I; men of France's Pacific Island colonies battling for France in the Indo-China War; thousands of "Gunga Dins" supporting the British Empire; the fierce, much-acclaimed Nepalese Gurkha troops in the Indian Army—commanded by British officers—fighting in Britain's wars; the New Zealand and Australian troops massacred at Gallipoli, for the sake of the British Empire; the colonial and Commonwealth nationals used by that empire in the Boer War . . . one could go on and on.

Some of the colonized served in their masters' armies reluctantly. Some were drafted and had no choice. Some enlisted voluntarily. Some served in order to learn how the master wages war, the better to someday wage it against him. Some fought willingly out of an ironic but undeniably powerful *identification* with him, since to be him was to be human. (And they stood a chance of becoming him, after all, since they were men.) The frantic desire to prove oneself loyal to the colonizer has shown itself like a pathetic refrain. Men of color have fought and killed and died for the white man in the hope of winning his approval and respect—and their freedom.

Is it any wonder, then, that women identify men's interests as their own? All women, at some time or other, in one way or another, are forced to do so. The rebel woman in a male-defined State-that-would-be is merely acting out another version of the party woman running for office in the State-that-is. And the terrorist woman is doing the same thing, writ large in letters of fire.

I can hear her now, in furious rebuttal: "To say that my revolutionary struggle is a male-defined one is to trivialize me the way you feminists claim men trivialize women. You refuse to take me, my politics, my militance, seriously as my own. You treat me as a pawn in a game between men. Is this your support? Is this what you call sisterhood?"

And I would reply: "*Yes*. Trying to name the truth, however painful, to one another is the highest respect sisterhood can offer. To dance with the Demon Lover is only to dance oneself toward the false liberation of death. To rebel on his terms is only to rebel against the challenge of living on your own terms."

He tells her (he tells us all) how women's issues are narrow and marginal. Sometimes he tells us that these issues are already solved and we are greedy and spoiled to complain. Sometimes he tells us that these issues can never be solved and we are countering "nature." Sometimes he tells us both lies at once. Always he tells us that our freedom depends on his. So long as she (and we) believe that feminism concerns solely what he defines as women's issues—reproduction, pay equity, child care (however vital each of these is in itself)—she (and we) will remain in conflict. Not until she, and you, and I, fully comprehend the enormity—that all issues are women's issues *to be defined in women's ways and confronted in women's ways*—can any of us break free and refuse to settle for rebellion within his deadly context.

The woman who lies in terror's arms is clasped in an intricate emotional bondage. One cord, coiled around her brain, is her own justifiable human indignation at the suffering of her people, her country, or her planet. This anger has never been taken seriously, since being female, she is expected to be altruistic, and besides, she is less than human anyway. So another bond slips into place—her rage at being a woman in what appears to be a male universe of perception, thought, and action. There is, too, the silken rope of what Nechaev termed "initiation," the bond of her own lust for approval, respect, an acceptance which might mean (as it did for Khaled) relative freedom and power; it loops around her spine. In his world, the elite are those who claim to fight and sacrifice on behalf of those *beneath* them; to confront on your *own* behalf means the humiliation of acknowledging your own oppression, as well as the risk of being accused of selfishness. So she who lies in terror's arms clutches for another bond of reassurance, and it is waiting to curl and knot around her loins: charisma. The men will initiate her and she will be (almost) one of them; other women will look upon her with awe. The charisma attaches because of her intensifying proximity to death: she becomes even more of a treasure to him, since she will be lost to him and since he loves only what he can lose or kill. How well this skein meets now around her throat with another—her well-fostered nurturant "mothering instinct," which longs to interpose her between death and others. At best, then, she believes he can free her by annihilating the sub-human female persona she has worn. At worst, she will still be released from that old non-self. If she is to be consumed in his fires they will grant her her version of his definition of ecstasy—a "standing outside of" the self he never permitted her to have. In all this she is allowed to feel that she is heroic, altruistic, noble—and an exception to her sex. And the final bond, pure satin steel the color of blood ruby, is knotted tight around her heart: it is, in almost every case, her own personal passion for an individual man.

And will she struggle now? Not likely. The combination of promised rewards—from rebellion through respect, charisma, relative freedom and power, requited love, and becoming in his terms nearly human—is one she finds irresistible.

From Marx through Nechaev to Ortega, they have used her and acknowledged it. They have proclaimed aloud their exploitation of her, written it out in print, denied it and then reaffirmed it, practised it, and practise it still. *They have made it plain: they need women. They cannot do it without women.* The State-that-would-be will never become the State-that-is without our aid. The State-that-is cannot sustain itself without our support.

If they cannot do it without us, then what will happen if we turn from them, turn to our own definitions, means, and energies?

Such a message of selfhood and sisterhood is more than terrifying. It takes time for that message to filter through the thick hangings that curtain terror's bed, time we have less of each day. The women there are literally *in terror* of hearing it. The women there lie, not fully living yet undead as Dracula's legion of brides, in the Demon Lover's embrace, trusting him, trusting his love, trusting his promise of immortality, trusting their own lies that they have chosen this. And somewhere, in the deepest recesses of her soul, each one suspects otherwise.

I know these women.

I was one of them.

NOTES

Only those notes from the original material that correspond to text excerpted here are reproduced. The original note numbering has been preserved for those notes. Notes 27a and 38a appear in the original text as asterisked notes at the bottoms of pages 206 and 211, respectively.

3. Elvia Alvarado, *Don't Be Afraid, Gringo: A Honduran Woman Speaks from the Heart*, trans. Medea Benjamin (San Francisco: The Institute for Food and Development Policy, 1987), p. 133.

4. J. K. Zawodny, "Internal Organizational Problems and the Sources of Tensions of Terrorist Movements as Catalysts of Violence," *Terrorism: An International Journal*, Vol. 1, Nos. 3/4 (1978), pp. 280-81.

5. Ibid., p. 281.

6. Vera Broido, *Apostles into Terrorists: Women and the Revolutionary Movement in the Russia of Alexander II* (New York: Viking Press, 1977), p. vi.

7. Daniel E. Georges-Abeyie, "Women as Terrorists," *Terrorism: An International Journal*, Vol. 1, No. 1 (1977), pp. 77-81.

8. Ibid., p. 77.

9. See Susan Stern, *With the Weathermen: The Personal Journal of a Revolutionary Woman* (Garden City, N.Y.: Doubleday, 1975); and Jane Alpert, *Growing Up Underground* (New York: William Morrow, 1981).

10. Georges-Abeyie, "Woman as Terrorists," pp. 82-84.

11. Quoted in Vincent Bugliosi, with Curt Gentry, *Helter Skelter* (New York: Norton, 1974), p. 85.

12. William H. Blanchard, "V. I. Lenin: The Stoic," in Blanchard, *Revolutionary Morality* (Oxford, England, and Santa Barbara, Calif.: ABC-Clio Information Services, 1984), p. 223.

13. Quoted in Adam B. Ulam, *In the Name of the People* (New York: Viking Press, 1977), pp. 146-47. See also Broido, *Apostles into Terrorists*; and Jay Bergman, "Vera Zasulich, the Shooting of Tropov and the Growth of Political Terrorism in Russia, 1878-1881," *Terrorism: An International Journal*, Vol. 4 (1980), p. 37.

14. V. I. Zasulich, *Sbornik statei* (St. Petersburg, 1907), quoted in Bergman, "Vera Zasulich," p. 45.

15. See Elzbieta Ettinger, *Rosa Luxemburg: A Life* (Boston: Beacon Press, 1987); and Peter Nettl, *Rosa Luxemburg* (London: Oxford University Press, 1969).

16. Emma Goldman, *Living My Life*, 2 vols. (New York: Alfred A. Knopf, 1931).

17. Statistical Preface to "China," in *Sisterhood Is Global: The International Women's Movement Anthology*, ed. Robin Morgan (Garden City, N.Y.: Anchor Press/Doubleday, 1984), p. 149.

18. Ts'ai Ch'ang, eyewitness recollection, quoted in Joan M. Maloney, "Women in the Chinese Communist Revolution," in *Women, War, and Revolution*, ed. Carol R. Berkin and Clara M. Lovett (New York: Holmes and Meier, 1980), p. 169.

19. Statistical Preface to "China," in *Sisterhood Is Global*, ed. Morgan, pp. 148, 150. See also "Ding Ling: To Write What Others Would Not Dare," *Connexions*, Spring 1982; and *Ting Ling—Purged Feminist* (Tokyo: Femintern Press, n.d.).

20. Jacob W. F. Sundberg, "Lawful and Unlawful Seizure of Aircraft," *Terrorism: An International Journal*, Vol. 1, Nos. 3/4 (1978), pp. 428-29.

21. Colin Smith, *Carlos: Portrait of a Terrorist* (London: Deutsch, 1976) p. 149.

22. Craig Canine et al., "What Becomes a Legend Most," *Newsweek*, April 2, 1978, p. 49; and Elaine Sciolino, "Nicaragua's U.N. Voice," *New York Times Magazine* cover story, September 28, 1986.

23. Leonard Weinberg and William Lee Eubank, "Italian Women Terrorists," *Terrorism: An International Journal*, Vol. 9, No. 3 (1987), pp. 255, 259.

24. Vittorfranco S. Pisano, "A Survey of Terrorism of the Left in Italy, 1970-78," *Terrorism: An International Journal*, Vol. 2, Nos. 3/4 (1979), p. 180.

25. John Castellucci, *The Big Dance: The Untold Story of Kathy Boudin and the Terrorist Family That Committed the Brink's Robbery* (New York: Dodd, Mead, 1986), p. 126. See also Ellen Frankfort, *Kathy Boudin and the Dance of Death* (New York: Stein and Day, 1983).

26. Shirley Christian, "Santiago Journal: The Exile Returns, Embodying the Agony of '73," *New York Times*, July 2, 1987.

27. Testimony of Pia Lasker, *Judgment Proceedings*, pp. 188, 93, 46, 94, quoted in Jacob W. F. Sundberg, "Operation Leo: Description and Analysis of a European Terrorist Operation,"

Terrorism: An International Journal, Vol. 5, No. 3 (1981), pp. 210-11.

27a. The German Socialist Patients' Collective was the bizarre brainchild of Dr. Wolfgang Huber, who in 1969 alchemized the theories of R. D. Laing and David Cooper into his own political dreams. He began organizing his patients at the Psychiatric Neurological Clinic of Heidelberg University into "working circles"—one on radio transmission, one on judo/karate, and one on explosives. His wife, Ursula Huber, headed the explosives group. The point of the SPK was that "The System has made us sick. . . . there must be no therapeutic act which has not been previously clearly and uniquely shown to be a revolutionary act. . . . Let us strike a deathblow at the sick system." ("Patient Info No. I," pamphlet by the SPK, quoted in Jacob W. F. Sundberg, "Operation Leo: Description and Analysis of a European Terrorist Operation," *Terrorism: An International Journal*, Vol. 5, No. 3 [1981], p. 203.) In 1971, the SPK was raided by the police, shortly after announcing its merger with Baader-Meinhof.

28. *Judgment Proceedings*, p. 122, quoted in Sundberg, "Operation Leo," p. 221.

29. Sundberg, "Operation Leo," pp. 200-202.

30. Ibid. See also Jillian Becker, *Hitler's Children* (London: Grenada Publishing, 1977); Becker, "Another Final Battle on the Stage of History," *Terrorism: An International Journal*, Vol. 5, Nos. 1/2 (1981); and Christopher Dobson and Ronald Payne, *The Weapons of Terror: International Terrorism at Work* (London: Macmillan, 1979).

31. *Der Baader-Meinhof Report*, Aus Akten des Bundeskriminalamtes, der "Sonderkommission Bonn" und des Bundesamts für Verfassungsschutz (v. Hase und Koehler Verlag Mainz, 1972), p. 97, quoted in translation in Raymond R. Corrado, "Ethnic and Student Terrorism in Western Europe," in *The Politics of Terrorism*, ed. Michael Stohl (New York and Basel: Marcel Dekker, 1979), p. 241.

32. Quoted in Anthony M. Burton, *Urban Terrorism: Theory, Practice and Response* (London: Leo Cooper, 1975), p. 33.

33. "Guru's City in Desert Sits Nearly Empty," *New York Times*, August 9, 1987.

34. Quoted in Smith, *Carlos*, p. 111.

35. Smith, *Carlos*, pp. 113-14.

36. Leila Khaled, *My People Shall Live: The Autobiography of a Revolutionary* (New York: Bantam Books, 1975).

37. Smith, *Carlos*, p. 83.

38. Quoted in Elvira Ganter, "Conversation with Leila Khaled," *Courage Aktuelle Frauenzeitung*, West Berlin, No. 8 (August 1981).

38a. The Provos were a loose movement in the Netherlands in the late 1960s, a mix of counterculture lifestyle and "revolutionary" militant tactics. The first issue of a magazine they published was confiscated because it carried a recipe for making bombs. As Dworkin wrote, "The idea was to make the information available; the idea was to provoke the police."

("Whatever Happened to Provo or The Saddest Story Ever Told," unpublished essay written in 1968, quoted by the author's permission.)

39. Andrea Dworkin, "Amsterdam," unpublished essay written in 1972, quoted by the author's permission.

40. The Three Marias, *New Portuguese Letters* (New York: Bantam Books, 1975), p. 87.

41. Association of Salvadoran Women, "We Cannot Wait . . .," in *Sisterhood Is Global*, ed. Morgan, p. 213.

42. Marie Angélique Savané, "Elegance amid the Phallocracy," in *Sisterhood Is Global*, ed. Morgan, p. 598.

43. Fatima Mernissi, "The Merchant's Daughter and the Son of the Sultan," in *Sisterhood Is Global*, ed. Morgan, pp. 447-53.

44. Lidia Falcón, "Women Are the Conscience of Our Country," in *Sisterhood Is Global*, ed. Morgan, pp. 636-31.

45. Ama Ata Aidoo, "To Be a Woman," in *Sisterhood Is Global*, ed. Morgan, p. 264.

46. Robin Morgan, "On Women as a Colonized People" (originally published in *Circle One* [Colorado Springs: Colorado Women's Health Network, 1974], collected in Morgan, *Going Too Far: The Personal Chronicle of a Feminist* [New York: Random House/Vintage Books, 1977]).

MAFIOSI AND TERRORISTS

Italian Women in Violent Organizations

Alison Jamieson

This short paper analyzes and compares the role that women have played in two very different violent organizations in Italy, the leftist terrorist Red Brigades (BR) and the Sicilian Mafia. While sexual equality and autonomy from traditional forms of authority were a dominant factor in Italian far-left groups, the Mafia's hierarchical structure has retained its patriarchal authoritarianism and male exclusivity despite the expanding role of women in its administrative and commercial functions.

In order to understand how this polarization could exist in two contemporary Italian organizations it is necessary to look first at the historical and cultural context in which each developed. The Red Brigades were children of their time, baby boomers in a rapidly industrializing society caught up in a tide of popular protest—a heterogeneous mix of partisan heroics, anti-Vietnam War militancy, and revolutionary zeal—of which they believed themselves to be the vanguard. Feminism was a minority motivation within the minority that opted for armed struggle, but the protest that nurtured it was a mainstream movement grounded in the relatively emancipated society of Italy's industrial north. The founding principles of Cosa Nostra, the Sicilian Mafia, were constructed in mid-nineteenth century Sicily around archaic rituals and vows of honor and silence, whose defining ethos of *omertà* literally signifies "the ability to be a man." Female exclusion from the patriarchal order is not simply the consequence of the chauvinistic nature of the organization *Cosa Nostra* but a projection, albeit distorted, of a set of traditions and a value system, which still survive in southern Italy today.

VIOLENCE

The Italian Red Brigades and the Cosa Nostra have a number of features in common: a hermetic and hierarchical structure, a clear division of roles and responsibility, and the premeditated use of violence for specific goals. But here the similarities end. The most striking difference lies in the purpose and nature of violence in the two organizations. Left-wing violence derives from Marxist-Leninist revolutionary theory, is altruistic, symbolic, and has long-term aims; its targets are the representatives of a power system to be overthrown in favor of a dictatorship of the proletariat. Mafia violence, by contrast, is immediate and pragmatic, aimed solely at the pursuit of profit and the conservation of power and influence for the clan. Rather than overthrow institutional authority, the Mafia prefers to erode and suborn it; hence its essentially conservative nature. However, the purpose of this article is not to compare the Red Brigades with the Mafia, but to focus on gender roles in two types of organizational structure in which the practice of violence is a defining characteristic.

FEMINISM IN ITALY

In the postwar period until the mid-1960s, Italian society was characterized by a political and cultural paternalism that was promulgated by the Catholic Church and both principal political parties, the Christian Democratic Party (DC) and the Communist Party (PCI). Although women had fought alongside men as partisans in the Second World War and assumed an increasingly important role in the workplace, trade unions, and political formations, the law discriminated heavily against them and in favor of men. Women were essentially defined by their roles as daughters, wives, and mothers. Divorce was only legalized in 1970; before that, marital unfaithfulness was a crime applicable to women and punishable with three months of imprisonment. A man could beat his wife with impunity; his adultery was not a criminal offence, and a wife could only be granted grounds for legal separation if the husband's infidelity had caused a public scandal. Moreover, abortion was a crime until 1978.

Against this background, the women's movement grew rapidly from the late 1960s onward. The momentum was strongest in northern Italy, where the female workforce in the factories of the industrial triangle of Milan, Genoa, and Turin became the focal point for political mobilization on behalf of women's causes. In the more rural southern regions, high unemployment rates and the preponderance of the male as family breadwinner meant that women had fewer opportunities to work outside the home or make autonomous choices concerning social and political aggregation.

Feminism became a driving force within the numerous political protest groups that mushroomed in the late 1960s. It sharpened the politicized woman's perspective on social injustice and intensified her rejection of existing power structures. Feminist groups marched together in demonstrations, occupied courtrooms during abortion trials, and lobbied parliament for the introduction of a housewives' wage that would allow them to have an independent political voice without the need to take up conventional employment. For the majority of women adherents, the feminist cause was an end in itself, but within the growing militancy of the extra-parliamentary Left it was a political exercise ground for a more radical battle and more extreme methods.

ARMED STRUGGLE

Susanna Ronconi entered the Red Brigades at the beginning of 1974 at the age of twenty-three, having been active in the feminist movement since the late 1960s. In her case, militancy was determined "first and foremost by feminism, the need for liberation and to live out the contradiction of the 'feminine difference' which had always been latent in me."[1] This contradiction that set her simultaneously *with* and *against* men in the political struggle was sometimes hard to reconcile.

> Feminism never became a "separate militancy" but it served to reinforce in a visceral way my conviction of being totally extraneous to the current social and cultural model. Feminism would make my extraneousness to existing society more radical, would make the word "liberation" a concrete object which became a "force" against marginalization, broke with any theory that saw emancipation of the woman as a trailing appendix of the working class movement and focussed on the originality of the female condition in itself, without the need to submit to alliances and hegemony.[2]

By insisting on a separate identity and a set of demands that explicitly excluded men, and by rebelling against the woman's habitual relegation to clerical or logistical tasks within political organizations, the feminist movement drove a wedge through the entire extra-parliamentary Left. According to former militant Mario Massardi,

> The Left in general (and the New Left was no exception) had paid scant attention to the ideology of women's liberation, entrusting the task of resolving all the contradictions and evils generated by the society of profit to the cathartic flames of revolutionary fire. But women, and especially those who were the most politicized, rejected the tradition that united them with the proletariat in the struggle for common emancipation in a common cause against a common enemy, and claimed

the right to their own individuality. You could compile entire volumes of letters written to "our newspapers" in which former militants-turned-feminists accused their partners of "domestic fascism" or protested about the tedium of the work they were obliged to do in back offices amid ink and paper—"angels of the photocopier," just as their mothers had been "angels of the fireside."[3]

For Ronconi and her companions, the split with mainstream feminism involved embracing a broader set of goals whose realization explicitly required the use of violence. Many joined the armed struggle not only to bring down capitalist society but, after a spate of indiscriminate bomb attacks and presumptions of institutional protection for right-wing terrorism, also out of the perceived need to fight a return of fascism. The experience of violence given and received was not new for those who had taken part in workers' and student demonstrations of the 1960s or the protest movements of the early 1970s. Police had intervened forcibly to break up sit-ins, occupations, demonstrations, and street battles between militants of extreme Right and Left. Whereas truncheons were used against male demonstrators, police officers removed their belts and lashed out at female protestors.

Ronconi recalls that the choice to abandon the feminist groups in which she had militated overtly in favor of clandestine armed struggle had been particularly difficult because it implied breaking off all contact with her mother, who had shared some of her non-conformist and feminist views. It was more radical still for Adriana Faranda, who left her young daughter to join the BR as a "regular," that is, a fully clandestine member ("irregulars" maintained ordinary jobs and lives):

> More than a point of no return it was a choice: choosing to enter the Red Brigades, to become clandestine and therefore to break off relations with your family, with the world you'd lived in until the day before is a choice so total that it involves your entire life, your daily existence. It means choosing to occupy yourself from morning till night with problems of politics, organization and fighting, and no longer with normal life—culture, cinema, your children and their education, with all the things that fill other people's lives.[4]

The Red Brigades justified the use of violence in terms of an inevitable and necessary starting point in a process of societal change.

> You convince yourself that to reach this utopia it is necessary to pass through the destruction of the society which prevents your ideas from being realized—violence is a necessary component of this destruction. The concept of the purifying bloodbath is axiomatic to the model of the socialist revolution. There was a whole series of cultural models which indicated that any major change in history had always passed through conflicts of the most violent type between those defending the old social order and those wanting to impose the new. If you accept the premise of the inevitability of violence you accept that it is a necessary price to pay, even though it has absolutely nothing to do with what will come afterwards.[5]

In clandestinity, feminism took a variety of forms, such as the acquisition of particular expertise in the use of firearms or the refusal to perform tasks considered women's work. Mara Cagol, co-founder with Renato Curcio and Alberto Franceschini of the Red Brigades, never cooked meals for her companions, "saying, with the same tone of voice used by the other female companions of the movement, that she was incapable."[6]

In February 1975, Cagol led a commando unit to free her husband, Curcio, from Casale prison in a perfectly executed and bloodless action, but was killed a few months later in a shoot-out with the police. Some years later, a four-member, all-women unit was formed within another leftist group, Front Line, to carry out and claim responsibility for actions of particular relevance to the feminist cause and to "advance the protagonism of women within the armed struggle."[7] Among the actions carried out by the unit was the shooting of a female prison guard accused of maltreating women political prisoners.

Female participation in politically motivated violence has been consistently high not only in Italy but also elsewhere in Western Europe; indeed, it has been higher than in common criminal activity. Criminologists estimate that just 6 percent of all violent crime is committed by women, most of which is directed against their

Table 5.1   Incidence of Reported Cases of Criminal Conspiracy and Mafia Association in Italy 1990-1995

	Criminal Conspiracy			Mafia Association		
	Men	*Women*	*Total*	*Men*	*Women*	*Total*
1990	975	142	1,117	80	1	81
1991	1,778	203	1,981	132	1	133
1992	1,938	243	2,181	215	10	225
1993	2,670	361	3,031	232	9	241
1994	4,597	1,024	5,621	1,214	16	1,230
1995	7,114	1,193	8,037	1,888	89	1,977

SOURCE: Ditezione in Investigativa AntiMafia, from data supplied by the Justice Ministry.

own children. Between 1969 and 1989, 945 women were investigated for left-wing terrorist crimes in Italy, out of a total of 4,087 individuals—that is 23.1 percent of all those investigated. The share of females among left-wing political prisoners in 1986 was somewhat lower, at around 10 percent, a gender ratio that was also reflected in BR membership. Female membership of the Red Army Faction in Germany was estimated at around 50 percent, while the Irish Republican Army (IRA), the Spanish separatist group *ETA*, and *Action Directe* in France have all had female members involved in the direct exercise of violence.

In general, former female members of the Red Brigades report that gender equality was maintained in the organization. But Faranda, a member of the Rome column that carried out the 1978 kidnapping and murder of former Prime Minister Aldo Moro, recalls that at the time of her arrest in 1979, no woman had ever sat on the BR's strategy-making body, the Executive Committee.

> I can't say there was any real discrimination, but I felt that the men were listened to more. Also, if any uncertainty or doubt were shown by a woman it would seem more serious.[8]

A significant exception to the principle of gender equality was an unwritten rule that, because of the limited sexual opportunities in clandestinity and the male/female ratio in the organization, gave regular male BR members the right to have sexual relations with the female irregular member in whose name the base where they lived would be officially rented or owned. This was notionally introduced to oppose the "bourgeois morality" of the PCI, but it caused considerable rebellion on the part of the women. Faranda and her partner, Valerio Morucci, succeeded in living together during the entire period of their clandestinity, but their case was an exception, only permitted because of a lack of bases. The concept of "the couple" was held to be soft and incompatible with the dedication required for a revolution.

Gender per se does not seem to have determined differences in attitudes to the exercise of violence, which were the product of individual character and experience. Ronconi recalls being told by several men that they could not have shot someone in cold blood, whereas she and other companions achieved this by a conscious process of abstraction and depersonalization, both of themselves and their victims. Nonetheless, from interviews about the armed struggle conducted with female terrorist group members, some differences of attitude and perception emerge which can be defined in terms of gender. The first is the way the "just cause" and feelings of injustice are experienced. According to Faranda:

> In general I think for the men it was a more rational problem; for the women it was an involvement more at the level of tangible emotion, more maternal, if you like, as if they felt things more directly—disasters and injustices which happened on the other side of the world. The involvement of women was in one way more rational, but in another more visceral, more immediate.[9]

When questioned, few Italian women terrorists have been able to describe concretely what form their idealized society would take, other than by citing the absence of negative characteristics. Faranda explains this as an abhorrence of authority, rooted in feminist principles:

> Women remain enemies of any type of power whatsoever; they have a feeling of real hostility towards it. Even when talking about the seizure of power, there is always a trace of recalcitrance, almost an identification of the evils of humanity with the very existence of a power exercised over others. It's something they always feel, continually. It's rebellion but it's more than rebellion, rather a conviction that the power of one individual over another is a source of disaster and injustice.[10]

A further gender distinction emerges in the relationship to weapons, and in particular to the automatic pistol or revolver which every clandestine group member was obliged to carry. Ronconi, who spent eight years underground, first in the BR and then in Front Line, and who was held responsible for five murders in the years 1979-80, claims she saw her weapon primarily for her own defense, and only occasionally as an offensive instrument. She and other female companions had occasion to laugh at the posturing of their gun-toting male companions: "Some of the younger men had a mania for guns and treated them a bit like a fetish, in a kind of infantile, typically masculine way."[11] Not uncommonly, male revolutionaries mythologized the power of the gun, handled and cleaned their weapons obsessively, and fantasized about heroic acts of daring do. Their idols did not come solely from Marx and Lenin, but also from the writings of Jack Kerouac, George Jackson, and Franz Fanon, from the books of R.L. Stevenson, John Buchan, and T.E Lawrence, and even from cult movies.

> With Vietnam over and disillusioned by post-Maoist China, we were obliged to create new poles of reference: the cult of what I would call "our America" was born: America as a country where you could solve any social conflict merely by picking up your Winchester. I remember people who on the eve of an action would go to see Sam Peckinpah's *The Wild Bunch* if it were on in some part of the city. One lad confessed to me in prison that he had seen it twenty-two times. I never asked him how many charges he was standing trial for—it seemed totally irrelevant.[12]

If some tentative conclusions can be drawn about gender distinction in Italian left-wing terrorism on the basis of the subjective accounts of participants, one could suggest, firstly, that the feminist cause was a powerful lens through which feelings of injustice—initially perceived in terms of male oppression—were focussed and then diffused. Secondly, the "call to arms"—the woman's ideological impetus to act to change society through violence—was rawer and more passionately felt than that of the male, and was conspicuously devoid of the elements of fantasy, heroism, and noble death with which her male counterpart clothed his idealism.

WOMEN OF THE COSA NOSTRA

The militant feminism of the Italian extreme Left stands in sharp contrast to the deference to male authority that characterizes the majority of Mafia women. Whereas the Italian woman terrorist adopted a consciously exaggerated stand against institutional and societal paternalism, the women of Cosa Nostra have remained trapped inside traditional behavioral patterns. Gender roles remain rigidly circumscribed, even if, functionally speaking, women have assumed a greater variety of responsibilities than was once the case. In Sicily, membership of Cosa Nostra, the "honorable society," has always been and remains exclusively male. Women do not participate directly in acts of violence, nor do they occupy positions within the decision-making hierarchy. Despite this, for women whose husbands or fathers are mafiosi, Cosa Nostra rules govern the minutiae of their daily lives; they are Mafia property and party to most of its secrets. According to Piera Aiello, who turned state's witness after the murder of her mafioso husband,

> [t]he wives, whether they are Mafia women themselves, Sicilian or not, hear everything, take everything on themselves. I was just a sponge. If

you ask Mafia husbands questions, they refuse to answer, but if you're good and keep quiet, then, because they're just as stupid as all other men, they confide in you, because it makes them feel important.[13]

Those who enter Cosa Nostra are bound to exercise "self control, a negation of sentiment in oneself and in others and the rejection of any 'feminine' qualities in other men."[14] Women are perceived as untrustworthy because prone to irrationality and uncontrollable emotion. At the same time there is an ambiguity toward the woman: in all-male conversations they are discussed with contempt or as sexual objects; yet they are also idealized through the stereotypes of "mother" and "mother of my children."[15]

The apparent passivity of Mafia women should not necessarily be taken for weakness. In many respects the need to stay silent and to accept the rules made by others calls for considerable reserves of self control, loyalty, and sacrifice, particularly as regards affective relationships, which are constantly overshadowed by the possibility of violent death. In this sense the Mafia woman's resilience may surpass that of the female revolutionary, who renounces family relationships and the trappings of social intercourse, but does so as a conscious choice.

The wife of mafioso Natale L'Ala, who also turned state's witness after her husband's death, states:

I loved Natale, but I know now that I spent 25 years in hell. The life fascinated me . . . then it became an inferno. I just couldn't stand it any more seeing all those people die. All that cruelty. Wives without husbands, mothers waiting for their sons to grow up in order to be avenged. I was terrorized, I was afraid for him and for me. I would have liked to break the circle of violence but if I had done it when he was still alive Natale wouldn't have understood. He would have squeezed the life out of me, or else I would have had to leave. And I loved him. . . .[16]

THE FUNCTION OF WOMEN

Women occupy several crucial roles within the Mafia world, which includes the biological family of a mafioso, the Mafia "family" or clan, and the clan's illicit activities. The Mafia wife/ mother is an important figure in that her life is conducted largely within the conventional social structures of her neighborhood and within the *mandamento* or zone controlled by her husband's Mafia clan. Wives of important Mafia bosses enjoy considerable privileges, even if they live in partial or total clandestinity. Their status guarantees obsequious respect, physical protection, and the right to indulge in conspicuous consumption. The wife of Cosa Nostra's *capo dei capi* Totò Riina allegedly kept an entire cellar filled with fur coats, even though she had been in hiding with her husband for thirty years and had never left Sicily's generally warm shores.

The Church represents a crucial area of intersection between the Mafia as a criminal organization and the society within which it moves. A profession of faith in the values of honor, chastity, sacrifice, and obedience, as well as respect for family unity are common to both, while the rites of baptism, communion, marriage, and funeral are rigorously followed by Mafia families, even when participants in these ceremonies are fugitives from justice. The Sicilian mafioso is permitted to have a mistress but divorce is frowned upon, as is blatant womanizing. The principal role of a Mafia wife/ mother is to raise her children according to Mafia principles, ensuring that the two worlds of Mafia and family become indistinguishable. Continuity is crucial because children are the future of the organization.[17]

Women also have an important strategic function in that the linking of two Mafia clans through marriage can consolidate or mend relations between them, sometimes to the detriment of an opposing faction. The arranged marriage has not disappeared in southern Italy, while the traditional pattern of reinforcing clan strength by intermarriage has been observed even among second generation Calabrian Mafia families in Canada.

When their menfolk are incarcerated, Mafia women become vital conveyors of messages and orders between prison and the outside world at a time when other visitors are not permitted. On one occasion, the videotape of a prison encounter between a husband and wife was used to indict the wife on the charge of Mafia association. Replay of the tape had shown that an apparently innocuous conversation, conducted through a glass screen and accompanied by graphic facial expressions and gestures, had been a cover for issuing instructions to murder.

The significance of women within Mafia operations expanded considerably in the late 1970s and early 1980s with the growth of heroin production and trafficking, when five refineries operating in Sicily satisfied an estimated 30 percent of the entire North American demand. Women, often ignorant of the risks they ran, were used as transatlantic drug couriers; others were involved in cutting and adulterating drug consignments for retail sale, in dealing, and in the safekeeping of heroin stocks.

In the wake of successful anti-Mafia efforts since 1992—resulting in some eight thousand individuals reported in Sicily for Mafia crimes— the participation of women in illicit activities has undoubtedly increased, even if in many cases they are merely acting on the orders of their menfolk. Their more active involvement is reflected by the rise in the incidence of cases involving women being reported for Mafia association, from one in 1990 to eighty-nine in 1995.[18] Other growth areas for female participation include money laundering and illicit commercial operations such as false accounting practices.

REBELLION

The Sicilian Mafia wife generally knows what to expect after marriage and is unlikely to rebel against convention unless, following the murder of a husband or son, she is provoked to seek justice by collaborating with the authorities. Those who do so are shunned by their neighbors, threatened, or killed. A seventeen year old girl from a Mafia family who had seen both her father and her brother murdered decided to turn state's witness in 1991, and was removed to a safe house. Her mother's response was to report the magistrate in charge of the case for kidnapping. When the magistrate himself was murdered six months later the girl committed suicide but her mother, unrepentant, desecrated her grave.

Some Mafia women have encouraged their men to repent and turn state's witness, but others have ostentatiously criticized the choice— out of shame or from fear, perhaps of a loss of status, or for physical safety. The mother, sister, and aunt of one Mafia turncoat were murdered one month after he had begun to collaborate; they had refused state protection in apparent dissent with his choice but had maintained secret contact with him. The sister of another collaborator publicly disowned her brothers, calling them "vile traitors," and tried to commit suicide.

Although some Mafia groups, such as the *Camorra* of the Naples region, have occasionally accepted women as equal participants in the organization's activities, they remain a minority. Meanwhile Cosa Nostra continues to derive strength from its mandatory ban on female affiliates. Rarely if ever do Sicilian women contribute to the effective force of the Mafia association, defined under Italian law as "the power of intimidation afforded by the associative bond and the state of subjugation or criminal silence which derives from it." In other words, to borrow a division of roles coined by Alan Block,[19] women have entered the "enterprise syndicate" but not the "power syndicate" of organized crime.

If feminism has made barely perceptible inroads into the culture of Cosa Nostra, the militant form in which it was transposed to the Red Brigades cannot with hindsight be said to have brought any tangible benefits, either to the organization or to the feminist cause. Although feminism was a powerful ideological stimulus to the women of the Red Brigades, their social estrangement and dedication to violent methods alienated them from the genuine concerns of the women's movement. Several former women terrorists have admitted that the infliction of violence was also a form of self-mutilation, and that to equate the woman's role as giver of life with the right to take it, as Susanna Ronconi did, was a tragic illusion. Were an articulate repudiation of violence to extend to the women of Cosa Nostra the organization would be in serious difficulty, for their silence guarantees its survival. Breaking it would indeed signify a resounding victory for feminism.

NOTES

1. Interview with Susanna Ronconi in D. Novelli and N. Tranfaglia, *Vite Sospese: Le Generazioni del Terrismo*, (Milan: Garzanti, 1988) pp. 199-120.

2. *Ibid.*

3. Mario Massardi, former member of *Comitati Comunisti Rivoluzionari*, in Alison Jamieson, *The Heart Attacked: Terrorism and Conflict in the Italian State* (London: Marion Boyars, 1989) pp. 236-7.

4. The author conducted three interviews with Adriana Faranda and her partner, Valerio Morucci, in the top security prison of Paliano during 1987 and 1988, in which they described their experiences in the armed struggle, including the kidnap and murder of former Prime Minister Aldo Moro. The first interview, with Faranda alone, is reproduced in full in Alison Jamieson, *The Heart Attacked: Terrorism and Conflict in the Italian State*.

5. Interview with Adriana Faranda.

6. A. Franceschini, *Mara, Renato e lo, Storia dei fondatori delle BR* (Milan: Arnaldo Mondadori Editore, 1988) p. 18.

7. Silveria Russo, member of Front Line, in D. Novelli and N. Tranfaglia, *Vite Sospese: Le Generazioni del Terrorismo*, p. 316.

8. Interview with Adriana Faranda.

9. *Ibid.*

10. *Ibid.*

11. Interview with Susanna Ronconi in E. MacDonald, *Shoot the Women First* (London: Fourth Estate, 1991) p. 190.

12. Mario Massardi in Jamieson, *The Heart Attacked*, p. 243.

13. R. Siebert, *Mafia e Quotidianità* (Milano: II Saggiatore, 1996) p. 74.

14. R. Siebert, "La Mafia e le Donne," in L. Violante, ed., *Mafia e Società Italiana, Rapporto '97* (Bari: Laterza, 1997) p. 110.

15. Siebert, *Mafia e Quotidianità*, p. 76.

16. Ministero dell'Interno, *Rapporto Annuale sul Fenemono della Criminalità Organizzata per il 1995* (Rome: 1996) p. 274.

17. C. Longrigg, *Mafia Women* (London: Chatto & Windus, 1997) p. 101.

18. Alison Jamieson, *The Antimafia: Italy's Fight against Organized Crime* (New York: St. Martins Press, 2000) p. 231.

19. A. Block, *East Side-West Side: Organizing Crime in New York 1930-1950* (New Brunswick, NJ: Transaction Press, 1982).

6

CONVENTIONAL TERRORIST TACTICS

Fighting terrorism is like being a goalkeeper. You can make a hundred brilliant saves but the only shot that people remember is the one that gets past you.

—Paul Wilkinson

Albrecht (2001) described conventional terrorism as "a collusive, symmetrical dance of reciprocal suicide" (p. 1 of 3 on Web site). This chapter details the deadly tactics of terrorists at the beginning of the 21st century, but many of the strategies are ages old. Despite the basic repetitive patterns in the terrorist dance macabre, a consensus exists among analysts that the face of terrorism is changing, as are its methods. A new breed of terrorists is said to be seeking out and using weapons of extreme deadliness that create ever greater numbers of victims spread over larger areas (Cilluffo & Tomarchio, 1998).

According to Bruce Hoffman (1999), terrorism is where politics and violence intersect in hopes of producing power. Violence (or the threat of violence) is thus the essential tactic of terrorism. Terrorists strongly maintain that only through violence can their cause triumph and their long-term political aims be attained. Rather than being indiscriminate or senseless, terrorism is actually a very deliberate and planned application of violence. It may be designed to achieve attention, acknowledgment, or even sympathy and support for the terrorists' cause. A goal of terrorist violence might also be to achieve recognition of their rights and of their organization. Their intention may be to take complete control of the national government, their separate homeland, and/or their people by force. Although some terrorist movements have been successful in achieving the first objectives, rarely in modern times has any group attained the latter (Bruce Hoffman, 1997).

All terrorists have one trait in common: They live in the future (Bruce Hoffman, 1998a). Every terrorist is driven by burning impatience coupled with an unswerving belief in the potency of violence. Terrorist attacks generally are as carefully planned as they are premeditated. A terrorist campaign must keep moving forward, no matter how slowly, or it will die (Bruce Hoffman, 1998a).

Some categories of terrorist groups have better chances of survival than others. Historically, religious movements persisted for centuries, but in modern times

A member of the International Olympic Committee (bottom right) speaks with a masked member of Black September (top photo and bottom left), the PLO faction that invaded the Olympic Village in 1972, killing 11 members of the Israeli Olympic Team.

Photo © Bettmann/CORBIS, September 5, 1972. Reprinted with permission.

ethnonationalist/separatist terrorist groups typically have lasted longest and been the most successful (Bruce Hoffman, 1998a). For one example, armed Muslim separatist rebellions have persisted in Southeast Asia since the 1940s. Although the amount of violence has varied over time, the Muslim separatists have raised credible challenges to the authority of their central governments for more than half a century. For example, the Abu Sayyaf, which split from the Moro National Liberation Front in 1991, has its roots in colonial history in the southern Philippines. The Aceh rebellion in Indonesia is also based on long-standing demands for a distinct Islamic state (Tan, 2000).

CHILDREN AT WAR

Often forgotten in analyses of terrorist tactics is the most horrific element of terrorism. At the beginning of the 21st century, more than 300,000 children, some as young as 7 years old, were being used as combatants, sometimes after being kidnapped. They are exploited by both established governments and rebel movements in at least 30 armed conflicts around the world. Whether or not the conflicts are defined as terroristic, children are trained in violent tactics by their involvement (Hansen, 2001; Human Rights Watch, 1999).

Table 6.1 Child Soldiers Fighting in Recent and Ongoing Conflicts

Colombia	(P, O)	Algeria	(P, O)	Afghanistan	(all groups)
Mexico	(P, O)	Angola	(G, O)	India	(P, O)
Peru	(O)	Burundi	(G, O)	Indonesia	(P, O)
		Chad	(G)	Myanmar	(G, O)
Russian Federation	(O)	Republic of Congo	(G, O)	Nepal	(O)
Turkey	(O)	Democratic Republic of Congo	(G, O)	Pakistan	(O)
Yugoslavia	(P, O)	Eritrea	(G)	Philippines	(O)
		Ethiopia	(G)	Solomon Islands	(O)
Iran	(G, O)	Rwanda	(G, O)	Sri Lanka	(O)
Iraq	(G, O)	Sierra Leone	(all groups)	East Timor	(P, O)
Israel and Occupied Territories	(G, O)	Somalia	(all groups)	Tajikistan	(O)
Lebanon	(O)	Sudan	(all groups)	Papua New Guinea	(O)
		Uganda	(G, O)	Uzbekistan	(O)

SOURCE: Data were retrieved June 18, 2000, from www.child-soldiers-org/report2001/map.html
NOTE: G = government armed forces; P = paramilitaries; O = armed opposition groups.

Young combatants participate in all aspects of contemporary political strife. They wield AK-47s and M-16s on the front lines of combat, serve as human mine detectors, participate in suicide missions, carry supplies, and act as spies, messengers, or lookouts. Physically vulnerable and easily intimidated, children typically make obedient soldiers. In Sierra Leone, at present, children forced to take part in atrocities are often given drugs to overcome their fear or reluctance to fight. In addition to combat duties, girls are subject to sexual abuse and may be taken as "wives" by rebel leaders. Because of their immaturity and lack of experience, child soldiers suffer higher casualties than adults. Schooled only in war, even after a conflict is over, former child soldiers are often drawn into crime or become easy prey for future recruitment (Human Rights Watch, 2001).

In India, the Inter-Parliamentary Union issued a statement following a conference on cross-border terrorism. The chairperson noted: "In their most impressionable age these terrorist groups are inculcating racial and sectarian hatred among children. Religious and cultural bigots are misleading future citizens of the world into cults of hatred and intolerance" ("Najma's Call," 2001, p. 1). According to Israelis, for example, in Palestine a sermon by Sheik Mohammed Ibrahim as-Madhi, broadcast on state-controlled TV, admonished: "We must educate our children on the love of holy war for the sake of God and the love of fighting for the sake of God" ("Palestinian Women and Children," 2001).

Many young children had parents who were terrorists. Some grew up in terrorist camps and among a cult of extremists. Many of them are nobody's children now. They may have seen their fathers or mothers brutally killed. Some may even have been born shortly after their mothers had died, many more were delivered underground, and a few had their umbilical cords cut inside jail. Most of the children remember the gruesome scenes they experienced, but few know what their parents fought for or why they were gunned down. Militants' widows and widowers may be forced to abandon their children out of sheer desperation. Isolation and hopelessness are common in these children. Efforts to restore the families of terrorists to the mainstream are rare (Pushkarna, 1998).

CONVENTIONAL TACTICS BECOMING MORE DEADLY

Terrorist tactics have not grown increasingly complex, nor are terrorists' weapons likely to be technologically more demanding today. Instead, conventional terrorist weapons have been used in successive incidents with increasing sophistication. Three events in the transnational terrorist campaign against the United States of the 1990s and the early 21st century provide examples of the ways in which rising levels of lethality have been achieved without more complex munitions. The most deadly terrorism has resulted from using conventional weapons with intense planning and some innovation.

The chain of events linking the United States directly with transnational terror began with the first World Trade Center bombing in 1993, moved to the continent of Africa, and returned to the World Trade Center in 2001, with a vengeance. In 1993, the weapon was an explosive device of 1,200 pounds of combustible material left in a rented van in a basement parking garage. In that bombing, 6 people died and 1,042 were injured. Before that first World Trade Center bombing, international terrorism was considered somebody else's problem by most U.S. citizens, who were reluctant to believe that New York had just joined the roster of international cities where terrorism is expected (Greenberg, 1994; Kelly, 1998; Reeve, 1999).

The perpetrators of the 1993 bombing were captured and the damage to New York from the incident was limited. Though the plot may have been flawed technically, it was shrewd socially in making the point that the very heart of the U.S. economy, located in a major population center, was vulnerable to the crippling blows of a dedicated group of believers (Kelly, 1998). Islamic extremists were charged with the 1993 bombing. Connections to Afghanistan and training in terrorist tactics were uncovered. The terrorists were said to be furious over U.S. support of Israel and the treatment of Palestinians. They were outraged by the presence of Western control in sacred Muslim sites in Saudi Arabia (Reeve, 1999).

After the attack, Ramsi Yousef, who was eventually charged as the leader of the operation, returned to his wife and children living in Pakistan just across the border from the Afghan town of Kandahar. The links between Yousef and Osama bin Laden have been shrouded in secrecy and confusion. Initially, the connection appeared tenuous, only one of thousands of leads, but investigators believe Yousef received support and funding from bin Laden via his relatives and associates (Reeve, 1999). After his capture in Pakistan, Yousef was returned to the United States, where he was sentenced to 240 years in prison for the bombing ("World Trade Center Bombing," 2001).

Five years later, terrorists demonstrated how this same tactic of truck bombing could be used with increasing deadliness. On the morning of August 7, 1998, in Dar es Salaam, Tanzania, an attack on the U.S. embassy killed 12 people and injured another 85. Most of the victims were Africans. The bomb vehicle was blocked by an embassy water truck at the closed embassy gates and did not succeed in penetrating the embassy's outer perimeter. Five local guards in the vicinity of the bomb vehicle were killed. Just 30 minutes prior to the bombing, the embassy had conducted its weekly "alarm recognition" drill, and mission personnel were familiarized with emergency procedures, though there was no specific drill for vehicle bombs (Accountability Board Report, Dar es Salaam, 1998).

At approximately the same time, on the same morning of August 7, 1998, terrorists driving another truck detonated a large bomb in the rear parking area of the U.S. embassy in Nairobi. A total of 213 people were killed. An estimated 4,000 in the vicinity of the embassy were injured by the blast (Accountability Board Report, Nairobi, 1998).

The incidents in Dar es Salaam and Nairobi gave notice that although transnational terrorism would be an unparalleled threat to U.S. security in the 21st century, tactics would remain conventional. The embassy bombings also show the increased deadliness of the tactics, because suicide bombers proclaimed their message with their lives. The East African bombings occurred in a region of the world that had been considered outside the maelstrom of international terrorism. The embassies presented excellent targets both because security was lax and because they were centrally located. They were symbols of the vulnerability of U.S. power, even though most of the victims were not Americans (Simonsen & Spindlove, 2000). The operations did not appear to have been undertaken by a local terrorist organization. Instead, the massive attacks involved ad hoc amalgamations of like-minded individuals who seem to have been brought together for a specific mission (Bruce Hoffman, 1998b). Terrorist cells had been carefully and patiently built in Africa, and the simultaneous bombs demonstrated a high level of operational skill (Harmon, 2000). Although no one took credit for or explained the violence, evidence shows that the embassy strikes were financed by Osama bin Laden as part of his worldwide declaration of war against the United States. The bombings were demonstrations of an ideology that encouraged violence as retribution for the desecration of Muslim holy places in Mecca and Medina. They promised to pursue U.S. forces and strike at U.S. interests everywhere. The motivation to do violence to U.S. symbols persisted.

Immediately after the embassy bombings, security measures were strengthened at embassies and military facilities throughout the region and around the world. A reward of $2 million was offered for information about the East African bombings. Increased security after these and further attacks did not prevent the attacks with airliners against the World Trade Center on September 11, 2001, or numerous other terrorist incidents since 1998. Security technologies can provide more "hardened targets," but terrorists will seek out overlooked weaknesses. Even without specialized skills and technical resources, the level of lethality of terrorists may continue to escalate because conventional tactics remain a significant threat.

LEADERLESS RESISTANCE

Fundamentalist Islamic terrorists are not the only extremists who have threatened the United States. Serious threats have been made by self-styled defenders of righteousness from within as well. Transnational and homegrown terrorists have striking similarities. Both promote urban guerrilla warfare conducted by subversives who use the cellular model of organization. Both Islamic and homegrown ad hoc groups may be well funded and have support networks that provide them with freedom of movement and opportunities to attack U.S. interests on a global basis. These groups are more dangerous than traditional hierarchical organizations because they decentralize and compartmentalize their actions (DoCeuPinto, 1999). They advocate the use of the same violent methods and the same goal of destruction of the U.S. government. According to the public voice of neo-Nazis in the United States, William Pierce, "When people are pushed as far as they are willing to go and when they have nothing to lose, then they resort to terrorism. There will be more and more such people in the future" (Grigg, 1996, p. 5 of 8 on the Web site).

The tactic of leaderless resistance is commonly linked with Louis Beam in the late 20th century (Harmon, 2000), but this type of organization is identical to the methods used by the Committees of Correspondence during the U.S. Revolutionary War. Using this tactic, all individuals and groups operate independently of each other and do not report to a central headquarters or single leader for direction or instruction. According to Beam, this is not as impractical as it appears, because in any movement, all persons involved have the same general outlook, are acquainted with the same philosophy, and usually react to given situations in similar ways. Beam proposed: "America is quickly moving into a long dark night of police state tyranny . . . let the coming night be filled with a thousand points of resistance. Like the fog which forms when conditions are right and disappears when they are not, so must the resistance to tyranny be" (Beam, 1992, p. 6).

The bombing of the Murrah Federal Building in Oklahoma City is almost a textbook case of what Beam termed leaderless resistance. To a lesser degree and on a smaller scale, factions within the direct action anti-abortion movement have systematically applied the doctrine for a number of years (Burghardt, 1995). The Aryan Republican Army, charged with 22 bank robberies in eight U.S. states, openly promoted leaderless resistance in a video. Members use the Bible to justify their actions. "Study your Scriptures," they say. "Then you'll understand why you have to go out and kill" (Pattillo, 1998).

Leaderless resistance is a tactic, not an ideology, and as such it can be applied by anyone opposing an overwhelming force. Leaderless resistance allowed the Unabomber to elude the FBI for 18 years. It is the tool of the disenfranchised, the poor, and the weak, who have neither the status, the power, nor the resources to confront those they wish to fight on even terms. Its greatest strength is that although it is easy for the state to infiltrate a large, anonymous organization, it's much harder to slip undercover agents into small cells where everybody knows everybody else (Kaplan, 1997).

GUIDEBOOKS OF TERROR TACTICS

Some people believe that Mao Zedong's *Little Red Book* is the world's most widely read manual on the strategy and tactics of terror. Carlos Marighella's *Manual of the Urban Guerrilla* (1985) and William Pierce's *The Turner Diaries* (1995) are also well-known guidebooks for terrorists. Those interested in directions for staging a terrorist incident can find them in many places. Not only can readers find philosophical and strategic directions, but detailed plans and instructions also are published. Some guerrillas develop tactics from studying counterterrorist strategy manuals developed by police or military forces to direct their own proactive strikes.

Technical details and up-to-date intelligence about strategic targets are also available in public policy manuals and on Internet sites (The Sans Institute, 2001). The intelligence community is hard at work with other researchers creating sophisticated detection programs capable of identifying incidents of online steganography. Derived from the Greek words meaning "covered writing," steganography refers to hiding information or communications inside something so unremarkable that no one would suspect it is there. Steganography is a good way for terrorist cells to communicate. The sender can transmit a message without ever communicating directly with the receiver. It's an old concept described by Herodotus. According to Greek history, a secret message was tattooed on the scalp of a slave. When his hair grew back, he was dispatched to the Greeks, who shaved the slave's head and recovered the message (Lisa Hoffman, 2001).

Among Islamic extremists, the members of "God's Brigade" are reported to have an 11-volume Arabic-language encyclopedia of *jihad* that serves as a guidebook. It has 6,000 pages detailing practices of terror and urban-guerrilla warfare (Jacquard, 2001). Many other documents recovered in Afghanistan after the fall of the Taliban documented the tactics planned and carried out by warriors for *jihad*. Guidebooks for terrorists were available in written, electronic, and video formats.

Following the September 11 bombings of the World Trade Center, three identical letters, handwritten in Arabic, surfaced. They linked three of the nineteen hijackers who crashed into the World Trade Center and the Pentagon and who were forced into a crash landing in western Pennsylvania. According to Attorney General John Ashcroft, "It is a disturbing and shocking view into the mind set of these terrorists. The letter provides instructions to the terrorists to be carried out both prior to and during their terrorist attacks" (as quoted in Ross, 2001). It is illustrative that the instructions for this deadly incident were handwritten as letters, the most conventional of all forms of communication.

THE BASICS

As fanatical or irrational as the terrorists of today may seem, they have remained remarkably conventional operationally. Terrorists continue to rely on the same basic weapons that they have used successfully for more than a century (Bruce Hoffman, 2001). Terrorists of the 21st century adhere to the familiar and narrow tactical patterns because they have mastered them. Equally important, they are likely to believe that conventional tactics optimize their likelihood of success (Bruce Hoffman, 2001). The four basic tactics that singly or jointly make up most terrorist incidents continue to include (a) assassinations of public figures, murder of civilians, and genocide; (b) hijackings; (c) kidnapping, hostage taking, and barricade incidents; and (d) bombings and armed assaults.

Terrorists in the 21st century have demonstrated the ease with which modifications and combinations of basic tactics can be made across the technological spectrum. Terrorists have shown their willingness to adapt technology as opportunities present themselves (Bruce Hoffman, 1997). Death and destruction from multifarious attacks with conventional high explosives have been far higher than in cases involving unconventional weapons (Bruce Hoffman, 2001).

Assassinations

Assassinations have always been basic to terrorists. One of the most noted examples was the death of Israeli Prime Minister Yitzhak Rabin on November 4, 1995. Rabin had become noteworthy because of his involvement in peace negotiations with the Palestinians. His progress toward a settlement was celebrated by many, but it aroused the ire of extremists. Rabin was a target because he was perceived as a significant leader whose removal would change the course of global relations. Shortly before his murder, there were documented threats against Rabin's life, and he was advised not to make public appearances. He refused to avoid crowds and was not willing to wear a bullet-proof vest to the peace rally in Malchei Yisrael Square in Tel Aviv where he was shot.

His assassin, Yigal Amir, had been arrested twice before at demonstrations in opposition to Rabin's policies of negotiation. Amir was a 25-year-old Israeli student who belonged to a loosely organized group of dissidents opposed to any concessions toward Palestine. He disguised himself as a driver and waited with other chauffeurs near Rabin's limo. His Beretta pistol was loaded with hollow-point bullets. Amir hit Rabin in the thorax and abdomen with two bullets, and Rabin was dead within hours. Amir was apprehended at the scene of the crime, arrested by security officers (Praesidia-Defence, 1996), and charged with conspiracy to kill the prime minister. A huge arms cache was found in his home (Israeli Ministry of Foreign Affairs, 1995).

Analysts debate the impact of Rabin's death on the Israeli-Palestinian peace process. For a time, some believed that his death blazed a path toward unity. Critics asserted that his assassination was part of a larger plot and pointed out attempts to cover up complicity in the murder by the Israeli secret service (Shuman, 2001).

The amount of social change and upheaval that has resulted from assassinations is immeasurable. As a tactic of war, a single strategic fatality can have an impact that makes an assassination a compelling choice for a strike against an enemy.

The United States has witnessed many attempts and several successful assassinations of public figures by individuals considered to be mentally unstable rather than terrorists. The prevailing explanations of their actions included personal conflicts and religious delusions. Despite a number of conspiracy theories that question whether the assassins of political and public figures, including John F. Kennedy and Dr. Martin Luther King, Jr., really acted alone, links between assassins in the United States and recognized group interests remain in question. Members of one celebrated terrorist group, however, were convicted for carrying out a well-planned, although inept, assassination attempt of an American president.

Various factions of the Puerto Rican terrorist group known as the FALN (Fuerzas Armadas Liberación Nacional) were active in the United States for more than four decades (Tooley, 1999). In addition to pulling a high-profile armored car robbery, the group conducted bombings, assassinations, and even a rocket attack against FBI headquarters in San Juan (McLaughlin, 1999). Two Puerto Rican extremists attempted to assassinate President Harry Truman on November 1, 1950. One of the terrorists died in the attempt, along with a police officer, while Truman watched from an upstairs window. Two other security guards and the surviving assassin were wounded. He was later convicted of first-degree murder and sentenced to die; however, his sentence was commuted by President Truman, without explanation, to life in prison. On December 10, 1979, President Jimmy Carter, also without explanation, commuted his sentence, and he was released at age 64. An estimated crowd of 5,000 supporters greeted him when he returned to San Juan, Puerto Rico, 29 years after the attempt, refusing to denounce the use of violence and vowing to continue his struggle for Puerto Rican independence (Poland, 1988, p. 183).

An alternative form of assassination may be focused on unknown victims whose deaths are meant to harm a notorious or corporate target. Product tampering and poisoning are variations on the ancient tactic of assassination that may appeal to those whose adversary can be affected through their products (Dietz, 1988). Product tampering is included here as a conventional tactic because it is likely to be based on low-end technology and usually targets a limited number of victims.

Another variant on assassination is genocide. Extremists intent on removing all of their enemy, rather than a symbolic few, have resorted to mass murder. In the worst massacres, entire kinship groups and subcultures have been destroyed. In many of the cases of genocide and attempted genocide, the members of a targeted group were assassinated by state-sponsored terrorist organizations (Simonsen & Spindlove, 2000).

Hijacking

Hijacking gained increased attention in 2001, but it was a conventional terrorist weapon long before that. The basis for hijacking is taking over a vehicle on the public thoroughfare and turning it into a terrorist weapon. Terrorists may target autos, buses, trains, ships, military vehicles, aircraft, or even spacecraft depending on their technical resources and development. Car theft at knife point or gunpoint has become one of the

Israeli Prime Minister Yitzhak Rabin shakes hands with PLO chief Yasser Arafat at the Erez Checkpoint in Gaza, Israel. Rabin was assassinated for his efforts at peace making.

Photo copyright © by David Rubinger/CORBIS, 1994. Reprinted with permission.

most serious threats to motoring overseas. Statistics are lacking, but there are many reports that seizing vehicles is a common terrorist tactic (The Bush Telegraph, 1997). There is no way to determine how many international hijackings of autos are politically motivated acts of terrorists or to separate them from those of criminally motivated perpetrators.

One of the most dramatic hijackings in history occurred on October 7, 1985, when the *Achille Lauro*, a luxury cruise ship flying the Italian flag, was seized while sailing from Alexandria to Port Said. The hijackers were members of the Palestine Liberation Front (PLF), a faction of the Palestine Liberation Organization (PLO), who had boarded the ship in Genoa, posing as tourists. They held the ship's crew and passengers hostage, and they threatened to kill the passengers unless Israel released 50 Palestinian prisoners. They also threatened to blow up the ship if a rescue mission was attempted. When their demands had not been met by the following afternoon, the hijackers shot Leon Klinghoffer, an American Jew who was partly paralyzed and in a wheelchair. They threw his body and wheelchair overboard (Halberstam, 1988). The perpetrators surrendered in exchange for a pledge of safe passage, but the Egyptian jet that was to fly the hijackers to freedom was intercepted by U.S. Navy F-14 fighters. The terrorists were forced to land in Sicily and were taken into the custody of Italian authorities. At least two of the most notorious of the convicted terrorists escaped from Italian jurisdiction. Twelve years later, the mastermind of the *Achille Lauro* hijacking, Mohammed Abu Abbas, was a public figure in Palestine, a notorious supporter of the peace process and a close associate of PLO chairman Yasser Arafat (Goldenberg, 2000; Simonsen & Spindlove, 2000). He was sentenced in absentia to five life terms in Italy and is wanted in the United States, but Abbas remains a free man (Horan, 1998; Najib, 1999; Reynolds, 1996).

Kidnapping and Hostage Taking

Kidnapping and hostage taking are included among the basic terrorist tactics. The act involves seizing, detaining, or threatening to kill, injure, or continue to detain someone. The victim is held to compel a third party to act or abstain from acting as a condition for the release of the seized person (Simonsen & Spindlove, 2000, p. 24). The tactic of seizing captives has been used to terrorists' advantage and disadvantage throughout the ages. Despite their common elements, it is possible to distinguish between kidnapping and hostage taking. Kidnappers confine their victims in secret locations and make ransom demands, threatening to kill the victim if these demands are not met. Hostage takers openly confront the police or military, in known locations, with the objective often being to make demands with full media coverage (Poland, 1988).

Hostage taking has a long relationship with rebellion and warfare. A well-publicized incident that involved barricading and hostage taking began on December 17, 1996, and ended when Peruvian armed forces stormed the residence of the Japanese ambassador in Lima on April 22, 1997. An armed group of approximately 20 members of the Tupac Amaru Revolutionary Movement (MRTA) held 400 people hostage, including a government minister, several ambassadors, and members of the Peruvian congress. The guerrillas, disguised as waiters and carrying champagne and canapes, sneaked into a celebration on the birthday of Japan's emperor. The terrorists demanded the release of their leaders and some 300 other members of their group who were in state custody. Their long-term goal entailed reconstructing Peru's economic model to benefit the masses. To ensure their escape, they also asked for transport of the rebel commandos to a jungle location, with a number of dignitaries as hostages. The siege of the Japanese embassy lasted for 126 days. Some of the hostages were released in the early hours of the takeover, and some reportedly were sent out of the embassy because of health problems. Others were traded for concessions during the negotiations. Seventy-two hostages were held through the entire 18-week siege. When Peruvian counterterrorist forces stormed the embassy, at least 14 of the terrorists were alive. Reports followed of extrajudicial executions of the MRTA rebels after they had been captured. All the terrorists were reportedly shot in the head by the Peruvian military (Derechos Human Rights, 1997). A hostage and two Peruvian soldiers also lost their lives. This attack led to the defeat of the MRTA as an organization.

The Peruvian president's mother and sister were among the more than 150 hostages released by the MRTA in the early hours of the first morning of the attack. President Alberto Fujimori was of Japanese descent, and the attack on Japanese interests was in opposition to his policies of cooperation with Japan (CNN, December 18, 1996; December 19, 1996; April 22, 1997). His prominent role in ending the five-month siege left him highly regarded in Japan despite scandal that later forced his exile from Peru in disgrace (Millett, 2000). He was able to retain Japanese citizenship even though dual citizenship was not allowed in Japan or for a head of state in Peru. His unusual status means that the former president is safe from Peruvian prosecution for corruption.

In general, hostage taking is costly, with little positive return for terrorists. On the other hand, kidnapping victims for ransom has provided significant financial resources to perpetrators. Many groups, such as the ELN in Colombia and the Abu Sayyaf Group in the southern Philippines, periodically kidnap foreign employees of large corporations and hold them for huge ransom payments (Federation of American Scientists, 1998). Kidnapping may be more of an economic expediency than a strategy for political advance, but targets are often among those considered enemies to the terrorists. The kidnapping of important businesspeople, corporate executives, and members of their families has provided terrorist groups with a lucrative, low-risk source of revenue for a very long time (Poland, 1988).

U.S. citizens may be favorite targets of kidnappers because it is not U.S. government policy to intercede. Terrorists as well as professional kidnappers also may believe that many U.S. firms carry vast sums in kidnapping and ransom insurance protection (Clancy, 2001). In the late 1990s, Latin America was the region where kidnapping was most prevalent and where ransom demands were highest. More incidents took place in Colombia than in any other country (Shepherd, 1997), but kidnapping is also a threat outside Latin America. The BBC reported in 1999 that kidnapping was "almost a national sport among terrorists in Yemen" (Fryer, 1999).

Bombing

Bombing is another essential tactic for terrorists. With advancing technology, the types of bombs available continue to proliferate. The history of terrorist bombing begins with dynamite, black powder, and Molotov cocktails, and carries on with Semtec and daisy cutters. The real hazard of conventional explosives persists despite concerns about the threat of nuclear bombs. The objective of bombing remains essentially the same regardless of the technology employed. The purposes of bombing are to blow up a notable target and gain attention for a cause, slow down the opposition, get rid of political adversaries, and destroy property. Some bombings intend to achieve all these goals, whereas others are meant simply to gain attention.

The suicide bombings at the embassies in Tanzania and Kenya brought U.S. attention to this terrorist tactic. The suicide bombing of the USS *Cole* in October of 2000 was another in the series of incidents directed against the United States (Daly, 2001). On September 11, 2001, the use of suicide bombs became an even more salient threat to U.S. interests. Analysts determined that suicide terrorists were the last link of a long organizational chain that involved numerous actors (Sprinzak, 2000, p. 66).

A perspective on the lives and worlds of those who become suicide bombers is provided by Charu Lata Joshi's article about Sri Lankan suicide bombers titled "Ultimate Sacrifice" (2000). She describes the 17-year war for independence fought by the Liberation Tigers of Tamil Eelam (LTTE). That war created a pantheon of martyrs. Each one's picture is framed, garlanded, and hung on the wall of his or her training camp to be revered by hundreds of other teenagers willing to sign their lives away for the cause. They will receive the title *mahaveera* (brave one), and their mothers will be called *veeravati*, or brave mother.

In rural areas of Sri Lanka, farming is no longer reliable as a source of employment and income. For young Tamils who do make it to secondary school, jobs are scarce and movement within the country is restricted. The lack of opportunity and work in an area that has exhibited no visible signs of development for a decade is often cited to explain wide support for the LTTE. "The war that has consumed more than 70,000 lives and drained the economy [of Sri Lanka] continues to find human ammunition" (Joshi, 2000, p. 6).

An 18-year-old volunteer explained: "This is the most supreme sacrifice I can make. The only way we can get our homeland is through arms. That is the only way anybody will listen to us. Even if we die." Another volunteer, age 19, asked "I lost two brothers in the war. Why should I stay behind?" (Joshi, 2000, p. 3).

HIGHLIGHTS OF REPRINTED ARTICLES

The two articles that follow examine the basic tactic of bombing and how it has continued to influence both the face of terrorism and the structure of history.

James Dingley. (2001). "The Bombing of Omagh, 15 August 1998: The Bombers, Their Tactics, Strategy, and Purpose Behind the Incident." *Studies in Conflict and Terrorism, 24,* 451-465.

James Dingley describes a specific bombing while tracing the background of the Irish Republican Army's conflict. The author gauges the impact of this "ideal type" terrorist campaign that has rocked Northern Ireland since before 1920.

This selection was chosen because it describes an extended terrorist conflict that has depended on bombing as its primary method for confronting the enemy. It shows the essential nature of bombing as a form of terrorism as well as describing strategies and planning that go along with bombing. The bombing in a small market town in Northern Ireland is reviewed. Twenty nine people were killed in the blast and 200 wounded, most of whom were bystanders and civilians. The factions of the IRA are explored, including the motives and ideas of those who carried out the bombing. The aftereffects of the bombing are described in the context of what has been happening for the last 30 years. Although the IRA announced a complete disarmament late in 2001, the peace process in Northern Ireland has been sidetracked many times in the past. The United States has increased pressure on the IRA to disarm in conformity to a global campaign against terrorism. World revulsion against terrorism may propel Northern Ireland to negotiate sharing power (Cowley, 2001).

Rohan Gunaratna. (2000, October 20). "Suicide Terrorism: A Global Threat." *Jane's Intelligence Review.* Retrieved June 9, 2002, from www.janes.com/security/regional_security/news/usscole/jir001020_1_n.shtml

Rohan Gunaratna shows the tactical role suicide bombing has taken in transnational terror. The article was informed by the First International Conference on Countering Suicide Terrorism, held in Israel from February 21 to February 23, 2000. The author provides background on the tactic of suicide bombing and a summary of suicide terrorism incidents since the 1980s, although suicide attacks by terrorists were documented during the 1st century (Schweitzer, 2000).

When he wrote this article, the author had not considered suicide bombers in large commercial airliners, but he includes discussion of aerial explosive devices as one of the basic types known to have been used in suicide bombings. He also explains the types of terrorist groups that have employed suicide bombing. This article was selected because it provides a detailed explanation of the modus operandi for carrying out suicide bombings and a look at the responses available for confronting this tactic.

EXPLORING CONVENTIONAL TERRORIST TACTICS FURTHER

- The journal *Terrorism and Political Violence* (see www.frankcass.com/jnls/tpv.htm) provides research articles about assassination, hijacking, kidnapping, and bombing.
- The PBS series for Frontline, *The IRA & Sinn Fein*, is available on the Web at www.pbs.org/wgbh/pages/frontline/shows/ira/. It includes interviews and historical and cultural information as well as maps and other links.
- The global intelligence organization Interpol presents information about terrorist tactics at www.interpol.int
- For details and findings about the bombing of the Murrah building in Oklahoma City in 1993, enter the terms "Murrah" and "Oklahoma City" into any good search engine.

VIDEO NOTES

A fascinating drama about conventional terrorism enfolds in *Four Days in September* (Miramax, 1998, 110 min.). The film relates both the political and the personal demands inflicted when an ambassador is kidnapped by terrorists.

REFERENCES

Accountability Board Report, Dar Es Salaam. (1998). Bombings of the US embassy in Dar es Salaam, Tanzania—Discussion and findings. *The Terrorism Research Center.* Retrieved June 17, 2002, from www.terrorism.com/state/board_daressalaam.html

Accountability Board Report, Nairobi. (1998). Bombings of the US embassy in Nairobi, Kenya—Discussion and findings. *The Terrorism Research Center.* Retrieved June 17, 2002, from www.terrorism.com/state/board_nairobi.html

Albrecht, Karl. (2001). World-wide women. *The Futurist.* Retrieved June 10, 2002, from www.wfs.org/esalbrecht.htm

Beam, Louis. (1992, February). Leaderless resistance. *The Seditionist.* Retrieved June 10, 2002, from www.louisbeam.com/leaderless.htm

Burghardt, Tom. (1995). *Leaderless resistance and the Oklahoma City bombing.* Bay Area Coalition for Our Reproductive Rights. Retrieved June 10, 2002, from http://www2.mo-net.com/~mlindste/beam.html

The Bush Telegraph. (1997, December 17). *Mission and project support.* Retrieved June 17, 2002, from www.mapsupport.com/thedatabase/bushtel/Default.htm

Cilluffo, Frank, & Tomarchio, Jack T. (1998). Responding to new terrorist threats. *Orbis, 42-43,* 439-452.

Clancy, Cordelia. (2001, September 21). Kidnapping businesspeople has become big business. *Business Journal.* Retrieved June 10, 2002, from http://sanjose.bizjournals.com/sanjose/stories/2001/09/24/smallb2.html

CNN. (1996, December 18). Tupac Amaru—Peru's smaller guerrilla group. *World News.* Retrieved June 10, 2002, from www.cnn.com/WORLD/9612/18/peru.sidebar/

CNN. (1996, December 19). Red Cross official named hostage negotiator in Peru. *World News.* Retrieved June 10, 2002, from www.cnn.com/WORLD/9612/19/peru/

CNN. (1997, April 22). 1 hostage killed in daring Peru rescue. *World News.* Retrieved June 10, 2002, from www.cnn.com/WORLD/9704/22/peru.update.late/

Cowley, Martin. (2001, October 23). *IRA says it takes historic step to disarm.* Reuters/Breaking News from Around the Globe. Retrieved June 17, 2002, from www.reuters.com/printer-friendly.jhtml?type=topnews&StoryID=313439

Daly, John. (2001, September 17). Suicide bombing: No warning, and no total solution. *Jane's Terrorism & Security Monitor,* pp. 1-5. Retrieved June 17, 2002, from www.janes.com/security/international_security/news/jtsm/jtsm010917_1_n.shtml

Derechos Human Rights. (1997, April 25). Peru: Possible extra-judicial executions of MRTA rebels. Retrieved June 10, 2002, from www.derechos.org/human-rights/actions/peru.html

Dietz, Park Elliott. (1988). Dangerous information: Product tampering and poisoning. *Journal of Forensic Sciences, 33*(5), 1206-1217.

Dingley, James. (2001). The bombing of Omagh, 15 August 1998: The bombers, their tactics, strategy, and purpose behind the incident. *Studies in Conflict and Terrorism, 24,* 451-465.

DoCeuPinto, Maria. (1999). Some U.S. concerns regarding Islamist and Middle Eastern terrorism. *Terrorism and Political Violence, 11*(3), 72-96.

Federation of American Scientists. (1998, August 8). National Liberation Army (ELN)—Colombia. *Intelligence Resource Program.* Retrieved June 10, 2002, from www.fas.org/irp/world/para/eln.htm

Fryer, Jonathan. (1999, January 14). Yemen: Arabia's Wild West. *BBC Online Network.* Retrieved June 10, 2002, from http://news.bbc.co.uk/hi/english/world/from_our_own_correspondent/newsid_253000/253004.stm

Goldenberg, Suzanne. (2000, April 29). Israel lets in Achille Lauro hijacker turned peacemaker. *The Guardian* (Manchester, UK). Retrieved June 10, 2002, from www.guardian.co.uk/international/story/0,3604,215428,00.html

Greenberg, Keith. (1994). *Terrorism, the new menace.* New York: The Millbrook Press.

Grigg, William Norman. (1996). Hard left's 'right-wing' kin. *New American, 12*(13). Retrieved June 10, 2002, from www.thenewamerican.com/tna/1996/vol2no13/vol2no13_right.htm

Gunaratna, Rohan. (2000, October 20). Suicide terrorism: A global threat. *Jane's Intelligence Review.* Retrieved June 9, 2002, from www.janes.com/security/regional_security/news/usscole/jir001020_1_n.shtml

Halberstam, Malvina. (1988). Terrorism on the high seas: The Achille Lauro, piracy and the IMO Convention on Maritime Safety. *American Journal of International Law, 82*(2), 269-310.

Hansen, Brian. (2001, August 31). Children in crisis. *Congressional Quarterly Researcher, 11*(2), 657-680.

Harmon, Christopher. (2000). *Terrorism today.* London: Frank Cass.

Hoffman, Bruce. (1997). The confluence of international and domestic trends in terrorism. *Terrorism and Political Violence, 9*(2), 1-15.

Hoffman, Bruce. (1998a). The modern terrorist mindset: Tactics, targets and technologies. In *Inside terrorism.* New York: Columbia University Press.

Hoffman, Bruce. (1998b, August 16). The new terrorist: Mute, unnamed, bloodthirsty. *Los Angeles Times.* Retrieved June 10, 2002, from www.rand.org/hot/op-eds/081698LAT.html

Hoffman, Bruce. (1999). Terrorism trends and prospects. In Ian Lesser et al. (Eds.), *Countering the new terrorism.* Santa Monica, CA: RAND—Project Air Force.

Hoffman, Bruce. (2001). Change and continuity in terrorism. *Studies in Conflict and Terrorism, 24*, 417-428.

Hoffman, Lisa. (2001, October 4). How terrorists hide messages online. Scripps Howard News Service. Retrieved June 10, 2002, from www.s-t.com/daily/10-01/10-05-01/a02wn021.htm

Horan, Deborah. (1998, June 7). Mohammad Abu Abbas stops running. World News Inter Press Service. Retrieved June 17, 2002, from www.oneworld.org/ips2/june98/04_04_010.html

Human Rights Watch. (1999). Children's rights—Human rights developments. *HRW World Report.* Retrieved June 17, 2002, from www.hrw.org/worldreport99/children/index.html

Human Rights Watch. (2001). Children's rights—Stop the use of child soldiers. *HRW World Report.* Retrieved June 10, 2002, from www.hrw.org/campaigns/crp/index.htm

Israeli Ministry of Foreign Affairs. (1995, December 6).Yigal and Haffai-Amir, and Dror Adani indictments. Communication by Ministry of Justice Spokesperson. Jerusalem. Retrieved June 17, 2002, from www.israel-mfa.gov.il/mfa/go.asp?MFAH01gn0

Jacquard, Roland. (2001, October 29). The guidebook of jihad. *Time.* Retrieved June 17, 2002, from www.time.com/time/magazine/article/0.9171.1101011029-180519.00.html

Joshi, Charu Lata. (2000, June 1). Ultimate sacrifice—Sri Lanka suicide bombers. *Far Eastern Economic Review,* p. 64. Retrieved June 17, 2002, from www.feer.com/2000/0006_01/p64currents.html

Joyce-Hasham, Mariyam. (2000, July). *Emerging threats on the Internet.* The Royal Institute of International Affairs, Briefing Paper. New Series No. 15. Retrieved June 10, 2002, from www.riia.org/pdf/briefing_papers/emerging_threats_on_the_internet.pdf

Kaplan, Jeffrey. (1997). The American radical right's leaderless resistance. *Terrorism and Political Violence, 9*(3), 218.

Kelly, Robert J. (1998). Armed prophets and extremists: Islamic Fundamentalism. In H. Kushner (Ed.), *The future of terrorism.* Thousand Oaks, CA: Sage.

Marighella, Carlos. (1985). *Manual of the urban guerrilla.* Chapel Hill, NC: Documentary Publications.

McLaughlin, Martin. (1999, September 27). U.S. liberals join right-wing attack on clemency for Puerto Rican nationalists. Retrieved June 10, 2002, from www.wsws.org/articles/1999/sep1999/clem-s27.shtml

Millett, Michael. (2000, December 13). Citizenship ruling to save Fujimori from Lima's Wrath. *Sydney Morning Herald* (Sydney, Australia). Retrieved June 10, 2002, from http://old.smh.com.au/news/0012/13/text/world7.html

Najib, Mohammed. (1999, May 17). Abu Abbas, now an Arafat intimate, feels no remorse for Klinghoffer killing. Retrieved June 10, 2002, from www.worldtribune.com/x74.html

Najma's call to save children from terrorists. (2001, September 11. *The Hindu.* Retrieved June 10, 2002, from www.hinduonnet.com/thehindu/2001/09/11/stories/02110006.htm

Palestinian women and children encouraged to become suicide bombers. (2001, August 5). Israel News Agency. Retrieved June 10, 2002, from www.israelnewsagency.com/suicide.html

Pattillo, Linda. (1998, April 24). Shadowy threat of extremist hate groups quietly growing. Retrieved June 10, 2002, from www.cnn.com/SPECIALS/views/y/9804/pattillo.unholywar/

Pierce, William (writing as Andrew MacDonald). (1996). *The Turner diaries* (2nd ed.). Hillsboro, WV: National Vanguard Books.

Poland, James M. (1988). *Understanding terrorism.* Englewood Cliffs, NJ: Prentice Hall.

Praesidia Defence. (1996, September 6). How Operation Sunrise failed—Lessons learned of the assassination of Rabin. Retrieved June 10, 2002, from www.praesidia.de/Welcome/ Press_and_publications_on_terr/Assassination_of_Rabin_-_how_O/hauptteil_assassination_ of_rabin_-_how_o.html

Pushkarna, Vijaya. (1998, April 19). Terrorists' children. Retrieved June 10, 2002, from www.the-week.com/98apr19/life1.htm

Reeve, Simon. (1999). *The new jackals.* Boston: Northeastern University Press.

Reynolds, Rob. (1996, May 10). Abu Abbas: From terrorist to peace activist. Retrieved June 10, 2002, from www.cnn.com/WORLD/9605/10/abu.abbas/

Ross, Wendy. (2001, September 28). *Identical letters link terrorists on three hijacked flights September 11.* Washington, DC: U.S. Department of State, International Information Programs. Retrieved June 17, 2002, from http://usinfo.state.gov/topical/pol/terror/01092810

The Sans Institute. (2001, October 4). *Daily news report.* Dartmouth's Institute for Security Technology Studies. Retrieved June 10, 2002, from www.incidents.org/ists/100501.php

Schweitzer, Yoram. (2000, April 21). *Suicide terrorism: Development & characteristics.* Institute for Counter Terrorism. Retrieved June 17, 2001, from www.ict.org.il/articles/articledet. cfm?articleid=112

Shepherd, Nigel. (1997). *Kidnapping and extortion liability.* New York: Converium North America. Retrieved June 10, 2002, from www.zreclaim.com/closerLook/kidnap.asp

Shuman, Ellis. (2001, November 1). Trial of agent provocateur Raviv postponed, again. *Israel Insider.* Retrieved June 17, 2002, from www.israelinsider.com/channels/politics/articles/ pol_0068.htm

Simonsen, Clifford, & Spindlove, Jeremy. (2000). *Terrorism today.* Upper Saddle River, NJ: Prentice Hall.

Sprinzak, Ehud. (2000, September/October). Rational fanatics. *Foreign* Policy, pp. 66-73. Retrieved June 17, 2002, from www.foreignpolicy.com

Tan, Andrew. (2000). Armed Muslim separatist rebellion in Southeast Asia: Persistence, prospects and implications. *Studies in Conflict and Terrorism, 23,* 267-288.

Tooley, Mark. (1999, August 18). *Clinton offers to free Puerto Rican terrorists.* Institute on Religion and Democracy, UM Action News. Retrieved June 17, 2002, from www. umaction.org/mtooley46.htm

World Trade Center bombing in New York 2/26/93. (2001, May 15). *The Washington Post.* Retrieved June 17, 2002, from www.washingtonpost.com/c.../terror&appestat=detail& resulttype=attack&entityId=14

THE BOMBING OF OMAGH, 15 AUGUST 1998

The Bombers, Their Tactics, Strategy, and Purpose Behind the Incident

JAMES DINGLEY

The purpose of this article is to review the above incident: what happened, how it happened and who did it and why. Also, to place it in the context of the current "peace process," Irish history and the history of Irish Republican violence. In looking at who carried out the bombing there is also an attempt to explain the split between the Provisional and Real IRA, their motives and ideas, the complex relationship between the two and what they hope to achieve. This is then followed by an analysis of the actual bombing, the tactics involved in carrying it out and what went wrong. And finally to look at the after effects of the bombing. In many ways the bombing was not as unusual as portrayed by the media, just a continuation of what had been happening for the last 30 years; thus, it is instructive in itself as an "ideal" terrorist operation.

Saturday, 15 August 1998, saw one of the worst terrorist incidents in the history of the current Northern Ireland troubles. A car bomb exploded in the center of the small County Tyrone market town of Omagh killing 29 people and injuring over 200 others, many seriously and permanently disabled as a result. All of those killed and nearly all of those injured had no connection with the security forces; some were even Spanish tourists. Not only were most of the victims civilians, but a majority of them were Catholics, and some were even active Republicans. This adds a certain degree of irony since the "Real" IRA, who planted the bomb, are an ostensibly Catholic Republican group who espouse a distinctly Catholic form of nationalism.[1]

The attack caused deep outrage and shock in Northern Ireland, the Republic of Ireland, and Britain, which was later mixed with a sense of perplexity at what the purpose of such an atrocity could be. After all, the attack came after the Province had decidedly voted in favor of the 1998 Good Friday "peace agreement" in the previous elections of 22 May 1998. This peace agreement was effectively a negotiated settlement between the British government (the sovereign authority over Northern Ireland), the Republic of Ireland (who had a latent territorial claim over Northern Ireland), and the majority of the constitutional political parties within Northern Ireland. The Agreement was to form a power-sharing, devolved government within Northern Ireland, recognizing its constitutional

Address correspondence to James Dingley, Faculty of Business and Management, University of Ulster, Newtownabbey, County Antrim BT37 OGB Northern Ireland, UK. E-mail: j.c.dingley@ulst.ac.uk

From "The Bombing of Omagh, 15 August 1998: The Bombers, Their Tactics, Strategy, and Purpose Behind the Incident," Dingley, *Studies in Conflict and Terrorism, 24,* 451-465. Copyright © 2001. Reproduced by permission of Taylor & Francis, Inc., http://www.routledge-ny.com

position within (and majority support for) the United Kingdom. Crucially, it required that such power-sharing did not imply that any of the participating parties give up their objectives of either seeking to remain part of the United Kingdom (the Unionist Parties) or of aspiring to join the Republic of Ireland (Nationalist and Republican Parties). On this basis the main Republican Party, Sinn Fein, the political wing of the Provisional IRA (the major paramilitary group that had waged a 30-year terrorist campaign against the British State) agreed to call off their "military" campaign, the aim of which was to force Northern Ireland into the Republic.

Views and opinions over whether the Agreement was a triumph or a solution, and for whom and what varied greatly. However, the majority of the Northern Ireland electorate supported the Agreement, as did most of Sinn Fein's electoral supporters. And, quite remarkably, it also saw the situation where the representatives of a major terrorist organization (Provisional IRA) found themselves sitting in constitutional government, holding ministerial offices alongside previously bitterly opposed Unionist opponents. However, Republicans were expected to concede the democratic will of the majority in Northern Ireland to remain part of the United Kingdom (something their terrorist campaign had fought against) and the Republic of Ireland gave up its territorial claim over Northern Ireland.

Meanwhile, many ambiguities remained both in the formal wording of the Agreement and in what precisely it meant in overall terms, but such "constructive ambiguity" was hailed by some as part of the Agreement's success, allowing all sides to see in the Agreement what they wanted. Most important was the precise role of terrorist weapons and the vexed question of their decommissioning. A major purpose of the Agreement was to remove the terrorist violence from Northern Ireland's politics, yet that violence had been at the heart of Sinn Fein and the IRA for 30 years. And although that violence had played a major role in propelling a minority party like Sinn Fein into the center of government it had not, as yet, brought about their ideal of making Northern Ireland part of the Republic of Ireland. Thus, although a significant proportion of Unionists had grave doubts about

entering government with former, and still armed, terrorists a section of Republican support had equally grave doubts about entering any government but that of a united Irish Republic; for those Republicans the Agreement was a "sell out."[2]

However, in terms of popular perception, an Agreement had been made that effectively appeared to end 30 years of "troubles" and had led the major terrorist organization involved, Provisional IRA, to at least call a halt to its operations. Sinn Fein had actively canvassed for the Agreement during the elections. And Omagh was something of a Republican bastion as it had not only strong local support but also a Sinn Fein mayor. Consequently, the condemnation of the bombing was almost universal, including not only the Provisional IRA, but the Irish National Liberation Army (INLA, a smaller republican terrorist group), and Continuity IRA (another splinter group from the Provisional IRA).

The purpose of this article is thus to explore the dynamics behind the bombing of Omagh. This will involve a review of the terrorist group involved, namely the so-called Real IRA; who they are and what their purpose is and their relationship to other republican groups. Next, by looking at their choice of Omagh as a target, the intention is to understand their tactics and strategy, what they thought they were trying to do and why. This article will then analyze the bombing operation itself; how the operation was carried out, what actually happened, and what the intention was. Finally, this study will discuss the repercussions of the bombing and how it fit in with the wider political picture within the Province and between Republican groups.

THE REAL IRA AND
THE REPUBLICAN TRADITION

The Real IRA is a splinter group from the Provisional IRA. The Provisionals, who have waged the main terrorist campaign against the British State for the last 30 years, were in turn the product of a split in 1970 within the old IRA between themselves and what became known as the "Official" IRA. The Officials had majority support within the Republican movement at the time of the split but the Provisionals claimed to be the true spiritual heirs of the Republican movement and the Irish Republic proclaimed by Patrick Pearse during the Dublin Easter Rising of 1916.

Republicanism is usually a reference to the more militant strand of Irish nationalism, a nationalism that appeals almost solely to the Catholic population of Ireland, Catholics being the overwhelming majority in the Republic of Ireland but a minority in Northern Ireland. This religious difference, along with the economic difference of a largely rural economy in the Republic and a predominantly industrial economy in the North, became the basis for the partition of Ireland into what became the Republic and Northern Ireland (or, according to nationalists, "the North"). It has been this partition that the almost wholly Catholic Republican movement, which is mostly constituted by Sinn Fein and the IRA, wish to end.

The Official IRA had long ago called off its terrorist campaign to concentrate on purely political work and metamorphosed itself into the Workers Party. The Officials subscribed to an openly Marxist analysis (unlike the Provisionals's vaguely socialist ideology). Interestingly, the Officials's Marxist analysis had led them to question the material benefits (for the working class) of a united Ireland and led them to see the Republican terrorist campaign in Northern Ireland as inherently sectarian. They have now become closely associated with the modern school of revisionist history that questions many of the old assumptions of Irish nationalism and the iniquities of British rule.[3]

To many traditional Republicans the metamorphosis of the Officials and their new revisionist attitudes stand as an example of how politics leads to a compromise, corruption, and loss of ideals. Nonviolent politics, which is explicitly stated in the Agreement as the sole means by which to attain political objectives, as such, equates with a "sell out" in the pure Republican mind. Only violence is pure and uncorrupted and uncompromising. This is a core theme of many nationalist movements.[4]

The Reals, in turn, split away from the Provisionals in protest at the involvement of Sinn Fein, the political wing of the Provisional IRA, in the "peace process." The appellation of the word "Real" is an invention of the press and

is based on the tactics that these dissident Provisional members use when recruiting. It was first used in South Armagh, long a center of hardline Republicanism in the North[5] by dissident Provisionals who claimed that they were the "real" IRA when out talking to local Republicans who asked them who they were. They attempted to convey the message that the Provisionals were no longer acting in the real spirit of the IRA but that they, the Reals, were the real spirit and embodiment of the IRA; that they were the IRA, in practice, now that the Provisionals had called off the "armed struggle" (how republicans refer to their terrorist campaign).[6]

Essentially, the Reals appealed to those members of the Provisionals who distrusted talk of compromise over the principle of an all-Ireland Republic as the only solution to the "troubles" (the troubles being the local euphemism for the 30-year terrorist campaign that followed the riots and civil disturbances of the late 1960s in the North). This was in response to the Provisionals's apparently growing acceptance of the idea that an interim-type arrangement would be acceptable as the basis for a cease-fire, followed by a period of power-sharing. In other words, the Reals had a vision or belief in pursuing a "military" campaign until they achieved a united Ireland, whereas the Provisionals appeared to be edging toward an interim compromise of some kind, prompting traditional Republican fears of a sell out.

It should be said that any compromise envisaged by the Provisionals is only regarded as a short- or medium-term one that would presage some kind of transition to an all-Ireland state.[7] But compromise is always a difficult concept for those having a purist vision to accept or come to terms with and nearly all nationalist and religious beliefs tend to be built on fairly uncompromising premises. Hence Whyte's observation that ". . . conflicts about religion and nationality are non-bargainable and therefore much harder to resolve."[8] Nations and Gods, to believers, either exist and simply are, or they are not. Halfway houses and compromises tend to deny the reality of a nation's or God's existence, and such a failure to permit the full being of the reality is often the essence of related claims of discrimination and oppression. That is to say, believers are unable to realize their pure vision in their daily lives and this denies them their true expression and being. It also explains why many sympathizers often become detached from the purist/visionary, as they have to deal with the reality of their everyday lives, which frequently makes compromise a necessity. After 30 years of sustained terrorist activity republicans had failed to shift their opponents or come anywhere nearer success than the Good Friday Agreement offered. By recognizing this reality the Provisionals had made substantial political gains and the bulk of their supporters backed them in compromising with what they saw as reality.

However, it is precisely the visionarys' and purists' rejection of what is presented as conventional reality and their search for an alternative higher reality that drives them on. It is an alternative to conventional wisdom and an appeal to higher, "other," values and goals that they seek; this is part of the very nature of the religious appeal. What is done, religious and nationalist activists reason, is not to be explained in terms of the ordinary and conventional, namely within the confines of the existing state, but by an appeal to a higher authority, the pure ideal, the idealized state. Thus do many writers on nationalism note its conflation with religion and the origins of national identity in religious groups and the religious nature of nationalist violence as sanctifying, purifying, and inspiring; its costs are not to be measured in ordinary mortal and material terms but in idealized terms.[9] Perhaps the Easter Rising of 1916 in Dublin was one of the best examples of this, as even those participating knew it to be doomed to failure before they even started. During the rising and in its immediate aftermath, the rebels were ridiculed by most of the population, even most of Catholic Ireland. But what the nationalist rebels themselves saw as their "blood sacrifice," with all its overtly Catholic religious overtones, came later to be seen as the catalyst for the triumph of Republicanism. The rebels inspired the insurrection of 1919-21, which later paved the way for an independent Republic of Ireland.[10]

The question of compromise over pure ideals is something that has split Irish Republicans for much of the twentieth century. This was the principal cause of the Irish Civil War (1921-23),

which was even more brutal than the preceding secessionist campaign of the "Anglo-Irish war" between 1919 and 1921. The Anglo-Irish Treaty of 1921 that ended the campaign provided a settlement between secessionist Irish Republican forces and the British government. However, the Treaty fell short of republican ideals on two points. First, although offering all the substance of independence it retained the symbolic trappings of the British State as the nominal sovereign authority in Ireland, and second, the Treaty provided for the partition of Ireland into what became the Irish Free State (now the Republic of Ireland) and Northern Ireland, whose majority Protestant population insisted on remaining an integral part of the United Kingdom, although with their own provincial government in Belfast.

Republicans had demanded both an independent republic and a united Ireland and thus its purists became anti-Treaty, although pro-Treaty factions accepted the Treaty as providing the substance of independence (if not all of its overt forms) and the best deal available given the reality of the situation. The pro and anti factions then became locked in the Irish Civil War that ended up killing more people than the insurrection against Britain.[11]

Once again purist Republicans look over their shoulders at the history of the Treaty and partition. They view it as indicating how once politics and compromise enters into their schema of things the ideal gets lost or forsaken.

Although the anti-Treaty faction lost the civil war they never disbanded and maintained their organization and insistence that they were still the true heirs of the Easter Rising and the true republican authority. As such, although not organizing any campaign against the Free State (restyled the Republic of Ireland in 1949), they did organize insurrectionary campaigns against both Northern Ireland and mainland Great Britain in the 1920s, 1930s, and from 1956-62, "to remove the British presence." Eventually, all of these campaigns folded for lack of any popular support.

The IRA then reemerged in 1969-70 as a result of the widespread sectarian riots and civil disorder in Northern Ireland in the late 1960s. At first they defined their role as mainly defenders of the minority Catholic population, but after a while sought to go on the offensive against Northern Ireland and indeed the British State itself in order to force Northern Ireland into a united Ireland. This caused a further split in 1970, between the Official IRA, who placed material and objective benefits before pure ideals (for example, not only Protestants but Catholics also were much better off materially in a Northern Ireland that was part of the United Kingdom) and the Provisionals who placed pure ideals, a united Ireland, before all else. This ended in bloody feuds and a permanent split, with the Officials stigmatized as compromisers and betrayers of the cause of an independent united Ireland.[12]

Thus, undoubtedly, the Reals look over their shoulders at a history whereby compromises and material deals and calculations lead to splits and to betrayal of the pure ideal (that the pure ideal has invariably been rejected by the popular majority does not inhibit them). This rejection of compromise is also behind the existence of another faction emerging from the Provisionals—"Continuity" IRA. Continuity, whose name, again, is symbolic of fears of splits and sell outs and the need to maintain the pure vision.

Fears of splits within the movement haunt much of Republican thinking and are thus an important factor in all their calculations. However, so are fears of sell outs and compromise, and what motivates most of the splinter groups from the IRA is a fear that any compromise, even if realistic, is a betrayal of all that they stand for and have fought for over the years. Continuity feared betrayal of the cause to such an extent that they were prepared to risk splitting the Republican movement, but also hoped to take enough people with them to become the catalyst of a rejuvenated IRA.

The Reals similarly fear that the talks already represent a surrender, to be confirmed if any weapons are ever decommissioned. Weapons decommissioning has become a major issue surrounding the Agreement. Most people in the North, and outside, assumed that all terrorist weapons would be either handed over to the authorities or destroyed and that this was part of the Agreement that they voted for; Republicans claim that it was not. The Agreement itself is very ambiguously worded[13] and the last two years have seen much debate over the issue. But, for many Republicans, the idea of decommissioning any weapons at all has come to be seen as an act of surrender that they will not tolerate, because this would equal the ultimate betrayal.

Security sources claim that the Reals are publicly represented by their political wing, the "32 County Sovereignty Committee." They are based in the Southern border town of Dundalk, and associated with figures such as Bernadette Sands-McKevitt, whose brother, Bobby Sands, a convicted Provisional IRA terrorist, died on a hunger strike in a British prison in 1981. Bobby Sands became something of an icon for republicans and thus the presence of his sister in any republican organization has great symbolic and emotional power. Both the Reals and the 32 County Committee are believed to operate mostly from the Republic, where they are based, only crossing into the North for specific operations. They are also believed to have recruited very strongly from the old border county areas, picking up strong support from areas such as Fermanagh, South Tyrone, and South Armagh.

Most Reals were—and security sources believe many still are—existing members of the Provisionals, dissidents from within and not a totally new group. As such most Reals would be known to members of the Provisional IRA, just as the security forces know who many of them are. The Reals are not regarded as a shady new group, but a continuance of a hard-line and purist tradition within old-style republicanism.[14]

The Reals come mostly from the border counties, which have always been areas of strong republican support and regarded as more militant and less politically sophisticated. Many rural areas in Northern Ireland, particularly in border areas, with long memories of past wrongs and grievances, are predominantly Catholic, smaller, closer knit, and exclusive communities with closer ties to the Republic. This makes terrorist operations easier to plan and execute from just across the border, a short run in and then an easy escape route out, all based on local knowledge.[15] Areas such as South Armagh are colloquially referred to as "Indian" or "bandit" country and are notoriously difficult to police. They have also seen some of the worst terrorist incidents of the troubles, such as the 1976 Kingsmill massacre of ten Protestants coming home from work in a mini-bus or the 1983 Darkley killing of three Protestants at a church service.[16]

The border areas contrast with Gerry Adams's West Belfast heartland. Adams is the President of Sinn Fein, a former Belfast IRA commander, an elected Member of Parliament in the UK Parliament (although he declines to take his seat), and the prime mover in the peace process. His Belfast constituency is more isolated in the middle of a predominantly Protestant city, where even many Catholics are very anti-IRA, and a long way from the border.

Martin McGuiness is the other notable figure in the republican camp and often thought of as Adams's second in command in Sinn Fein. His base is in the city of Londonderry, where he was known to security forces as the local IRA commander. Although the border is nearby, it has been easier to police and the effectiveness of the IRA has been much reduced. Also, Londonderry has a sizeable Protestant population and contains a substantial proportion of Catholics who do not sympathize with the IRA.

Given the urban and rural nature of the wider republican constituency, the Provisionals have a more complicated reality with which to come to terms. Security sources have long emphasized the difference between the rural- and border-based republicans as compared with their city-based compatriots. These differences are represented in different priorities and tactics required in rural border areas compared with those relevant in an urban and more religiously and ethnically mixed area. Also, a small town and local farming economy compared with a city-based industrial economy with extensive relations beyond the Province creates different perceptions of interest and reality.[17]

Consequently, urban-based republicans found themselves coming to terms with a more complex operating environment with a greater ideological mix than the rurally based Reals. It is easier for the Reals to think like purists in their environment, thus helping to orientate them toward a less compromising outlook.[18]

Real IRA also had two additional major factors working in their favor in terms of mounting and sustaining their own terrorist campaign. First, their leading organizer and founder, whose name is well known to the security forces, is reputed to be a former quartermaster-general of the Provisionals who left in disgust at the talks process.[19] As such, he has full knowledge of all the weapons available to the IRA, where they are, and how to use them.[20] Second, the Reals have the support of major American groups and individuals who have the ability not only to raise public support for them abroad but also to raise funds. One such individual is the former director of Noraid, Martin Calvin:

> . . . who through most of the 1980s and 1990s successfully raised millions of dollars for the Irish Republican cause. He has long been a man of considerable stature among Irish Americans, blessed with a smooth tongue and persuasive charm. And he is openly opposed to the peace agreement.[21]

This contrasts with the Continuity IRA, who have had to rely heavily on bank raids to raise funds for operations and arms purchases, which leaves them more vulnerable to public opprobrium and police investigation. Continuity also lack the leadership of such "big players" as the former quartermaster-general of Provisional IRA or the sister of an IRA hunger-striker. Additionally they are believed to be more of an internal faction of dissidents within the Provisionals who have not formally broken away.[22]

At this point the start of the run up to the Omagh bombing can be seen. The Reals had also tried bank raids and robberies as well. It was one of their attempts in May 1998, in County Wicklow in the Republic, that went seriously wrong. Here, an attempted raid on a security van was intercepted and one of their members shot dead. This indicated a serious internal security problem as it followed the interception of an attempted bombing raid on mainland Britain, where a complete bombing squad was intercepted and its members picked up at the south Dublin port of Dun Laoghaire in April 1998. Here a car containing a large viable bomb, primer, and detonator were intercepted.[23]

Both of these interceptions were the result of a tip-off and coincided with several other operations in the Newry area of Northern Ireland being interdicted as well. This led to a temporary suspension of operations until the source of the leaks was identified and dealt with. But once this was done, believed to be by July, the Reals were ready to restart their campaign and build heavily on the disaffection of many hard-line Republicans over the May referendum and the political line being pursued by the Provisionals.[24]

The Reals had also had problems in some of their early bombings. Often they gave what they considered too long a warning time to security forces to evacuate an area. This gave the Army's ATO (Ammunition Technical Officer) the time to move in and disarm the bomb. But by late July they had solved most of these problems and launched a series of devastating bomb attacks in rural market towns in Northern Ireland. The best example was probably Banbridge, County Down, on 1 August 1998, which was devastated when a bomb was successfully placed and detonated in the center of town. The 30-minute warning time proved just adequate to evacuate the relevant area but much too short to permit the ATO to move in. In brief, this became the model for Omagh two weeks later.[25]

The Reals were now in a strong position to develop the bombing campaign they had started. It should be stated here that after the Omagh bombing itself they were firmly warned off further activities by the Provisionals[26] and appear to have heeded this warning, at least until 2000. Presumably they did not feel strong enough to take on the Provisionals in a full confrontation. Current security briefings describe the bulk of those remaining in the Provisionals as cohesive and although there is a critical internal analysis of their progress going on the majority are well enough disciplined not to get involved in any more splits or feuds with other republican groupings.[27]

However, had the Omagh bomb gone according to plan (that it did not is discussed later) it may well have been a catalyst of some sort. The Reals were beginning to establish genuine momentum, and they were starting to pick up recruits from old and current Provisionals as well as from newcomers. According to security sources they were possibly on the verge of a substantial increase in numbers and could have started to make large inroads into traditional Provisional support. The Provisionals were

already hurt by the quartermaster-general's defection, as he not only took weapons with him but support, goodwill, and much infrastructure.[28]

After Omagh the Reals kept a relatively low profile, as have the Provisional IRA, up to 2000. Since then both the Continuity and Reals have set off small bombs, and both had been foiled in other attempted bombings in the first eight months of 2000.[29] What now waits to be seen is whether their intended campaigns will grow into anything more substantial. Arms decommissioning is still an important issue on which major calculations concerning the future success of the peace process and implementation of the Agreement hinges. If nothing else the Reals have sent a clear message of fear and potential trouble if there is any dilution of purist goals, namely, the acceptance of partition, or appearance of surrender such as the decommissioning of terrorist weapons. The calculation that would then arise is whether the Real IRA and Continuity IRA would form the basis for a mass defection from the Provisionals or merely become a catalyst for a purging of the Provisionals leadership.

WHY OMAGH? THE CHOICE OF A TARGET

Omagh stood out as a good symbolic target for the Real IRA. It is an economic, administrative, legal, and military center and thus can be identified with an attack on the British presence and rule as a whole. Like many terrorist bombings it was aimed to send a message of an ability to strike at the heart of its opponents and register ubiquity, as well as simply causing economic, material, and disruptive damage.

Omagh is a mixed Catholic and Protestant town with a small Catholic majority. It is in the county town of Tyrone and thus a local center of administration. It also contains a crown courthouse, thus making it the center of the local judicial system. In addition, for many years it has been a garrison town of the regular army in the Province (as distinct from the locally recruited part-time Ulster Defence Regiment/ Royal Irish Regiment who also have a base there). In this way Omagh may be seen as something of a local center for the normal civil and military apparatus of the state. In addition it is also a major market town and consequently a local economic center.

As a center for most of County Tyrone any event occurring there would naturally have greater follow on effects both in terms of practical disruptions of services and in generating gossip and word of mouth propaganda.[30] Media reporting would also be relatively easy as it not only has its own local newspaper with all its reporting facilities and links to the national media but also houses local studios of the regional branches of both national broadcasting organizations (the British Broadcasting Corporation and Independent Television). Propaganda by deed as well as by media was thus ensured.

As a center Omagh would expect to have lots of people coming and going, especially on a Saturday, including a higher number of strangers. The bustle of activity, particularly just prior to the start of a new school year with parents buying items for their children's return to school, would also create better cover for the bombers. More people and more activity than normal would help to mask the movements of the bombers and divert police attention from any slightly abnormal events. This helped to provide good cover for a good target.

Omagh also had the advantage, from a bomber's point of view, of providing an ideal location for surveillance and logistics. It is in an area of above-average Republican support where operatives cannot only move easily and without comment but also can find easy and relatively willing popular refuge. The bombers could also rely on a steady stream of locally provided information in addition to conducting their own surveillance without generating adverse attention. Even known terrorists could pass by the security forces without attracting comment as they would be local people. The Provisionals in the mid-Tyrone area have long had an active presence and the depth of their support is indicated in the Sinn Fein mayor of Omagh.[31]

Omagh consequently provided an ideal target in terms of set up and operation, and for similar reasons provided an easy location in which to make good an escape. The risks involved in driving a car bomb in, parking the car, and then walking away were greatly reduced, particularly given the more relaxed attitude to security that

existed with the Provisionals cease-fire. And although Omagh is not a border town it is relatively close to the border, so there is neither too great a distance in to it nor out of it (less than half an hour). Omagh thus constituted both a safe target as well as an easy and symbolic one.

On a more speculative level there is also the possibility of some kind of internal logic in the symbolic status of Omagh. That is, because the town does have a Sinn Fein mayor and is a traditional Provisional area of support this made it a target of particular significance for the Reals. In bombing Omagh they were also sending a message to the Provisionals, both "cocking a snook" at them and reminding them of their treachery in dealing with the Brits. A target that permitted an attack on both the British and the Provisionals at the same time could be both good publicity for their cause and a good campaigning call for recruits, a large part of the purpose of their campaign.[32]

This line of reasoning would further blend with the fact that Omagh is a mixed town and that, after the cease-fire, Protestants and Catholics appeared to be mixing freely and normally. The fear and distrust that both sides had of each other was being overcome and normality returning. This is not what is needed to mount a sectarian terrorist campaign; what is required is fear and division. The terrorist wants to be able to evoke a sense of threat emanating from the "other" side. This is a major objective of many terrorist tactics. By creating a fear that members of the other community may not only be collecting information on you but actively plotting to harm members of your own community, perhaps even yourself, individuals are discouraged from mixing with others. In this way, distorted images and fears are raised about the other community and they become demonized and feared. From this perspective it becomes much easier to identify the other community as a hated enemy and an oppressor to be fought against while at the same time enhancing one's own community's internal cohesion in the face of a stereotyped threat from the other. As a consequence, different groups are kept apart, as has long been the case in Northern Ireland between Protestants and Catholics. By helping to break down this fear of the "other," as a result of the cease-fire, the Provisionals could be perceived as undermining the cause of the Republican movement by weakening the communal fears and attachments that help sustain the Republican cause.

By maintaining a separation it is much easier to build up communal images and fears and thus continue the enmity that helps legitimate the cause. An integrated and harmonious Omagh would be the last thing a Republican purist would want, except under their terms and jurisdiction. This helps maintain the momentum of the campaign—you can't trust the other side, you never know when they will bomb you. The free and easy mixing of a prosperous and bustling market town, in which old quarrels and divisions were being forgotten, was just the kind of target to appeal to either Continuity or the Reals.

WHAT HAPPENED AND WHAT WENT WRONG

The bombing followed a fairly conventional pattern for a car bombing in Northern Ireland. The explosive was homemade, based on commercial fertilizer and detonated with the aid of a small charge of semtex. It was loaded into a red Vauxhall Cavalier saloon that had been stolen in Carrickmacross, across the border in County Louth in the Republic, and fitted with false number plates (in this case it was fitted with "ringer" plates, that is, ones that tally with a real car of a similar description). It was then kept in a secluded lock-up garage until the time for the operation, when it was driven over the border by two men to be parked in Omagh. Once across the border the two drivers picked up a local guide to take them to their predetermined destination and place the bomb.[33]

The plan was to park the car outside the courthouse, something not possible in the pre-cease-fire days, and then to phone a warning through giving half an hour notice to clear the area. The original plan was not to cause death but mass destruction of property. In particular, the aim was to destroy the courthouse—the symbol of British law and order. However, the car was parked on Market Street, leading down from the courthouse. Sources in the security forces now firmly believe that this was a mistake and that

for some reason the bombers panicked or feared detection and deliberately parked the car away from the courthouse.

At this point details become a little murky. Why the bombers panicked is unclear, but what is known is that two calls were made giving coded warnings from telephone boxes in South Armagh. These, it must be presumed, were the result of the bombers phoning some kind of signal back to their base in North Louth or South Armagh. It is unlikely that they would have said "We planted the bomb" or anything similar. Instead, they probably had an agreed signal of letting the phone ring a certain number of times to be repeated another number of times. This would have made it difficult to communicate any change in location.[34]

However, a warning, using a known codeword, was phoned through to Ulster Television and to the Samaritans, but it was based on the false premise of the original plan to bomb the courthouse. On receiving the warning the police proceeded to clear the area around the courthouse and quite logically directed many of the evacuees down Market Street as an easy escape route and presumed safe area.[35]

The bomb then went off at the prescribed time, only on Market Street, where a large number of evacuees were surrounding the car containing the bomb, hence the large number of casualties. Many of those killed and most seriously injured were actually leaning against the car or huddled closely around it. This was not the intention, and the police believe it was genuinely a mistake on the part of the Real IRA.[36]

Up to the placing of the bomb everything had gone well for the bombers and their tactics are worth noting as being exemplary for this kind of operation. The choice of car was important, a common enough family car unlikely to attract attention on a crowded family shopping day. The car had been recently stolen from across the border and kept concealed until needed, thus limiting knowledge of the stolen vehicle becoming available in the country in which the crime was to be committed. Moreover, being fitted with ringer plates meant that if checked by the police the vehicle would appear to correspond with a legitimate car registration. It was driven in and parked only at the time of priming the bomb and during the early afternoon when the town was likely to be very busy, again limiting the amount of attention a single car would draw. Everything was designed to maximize an image of normality and blending in with the surrounding environment and at a time when most people would be too busy to notice any slight abnormality anyway.

A major cause of the final disaster is believed by the security forces to have been inexperience on the part of the operatives. Although the planning and logistics appear to have had the hallmarks of experienced terrorists the final execution appears to have been the work of novices. Why novices should have been used is an open question but is assumed to imply a lack of experienced operatives in this particular aspect of terrorist operations. This is deduced from the wrong warning being given and the sudden change of plan and failure to communicate it adequately. However, by the time the bomb exploded those who had planted it had been picked up by their getaway and were probably safe across the border in the Irish Republic.[37] This more than anything illustrates the effective use of international borders to frustrate the security forces' ability [to] follow up and investigate terrorist acts.

AFTERWARDS

If the intention of the bombers was to make themselves internationally known they certainly succeeded. However, they failed in one of the most important aspects of political-military terrorist strategy; that is, to use just enough violence to be known and feared, but not enough to invoke excessive counter-reaction. The bombers also illustrated the failure of staying within defined limits of violence as set by your own constituency of supporters. As Eamon Collins, a former Provisional IRA operative has stated, the Provisionals:

> . . . tried to act in a way that would avoid severe censure from within the nationalist community; they knew they were operating within a sophisticated set of informal restrictions on their behaviour.[38]

In this sense the Reals "blew it" very badly. They were utterly condemned by every political party in Northern Ireland, the Republic, and Britain, and almost as importantly, the United States. American reaction was especially swift and strong, emotions and sentiment being heightened by America's own recent experiences of being bombed in Nairobi and Dar es Salaam, only weeks before Omagh, with massive loss of life. This represented an unfortunate juncture of the international and domestic for the Reals with their dependence on American support and finance.

At home the Reals also managed, inadvertently, to reconfirm the Provisionals as the Republican authority in Northern Ireland. Abhorrence of the bombing, and outrage at the casualties (particularly Catholic and republican) caused many republican doubters to fall back in line with the Provisionals. Indeed, they almost benefited from it as Gerry Adams and Martin McGuiness were able to be seen on news reports visiting the scene and comforting bereaved relatives. (Such scenes have been strangely lacking after other bombing incidents.) This helped to foster a statesmanlike image of Sinn Fein, encouraging the view that its peace process policy was based on courage, wisdom, and discipline.[39] The bombing also conveyed another unspoken message with which the Provisionals could not have been at all unhappy to see transmitted—"If you don't deliver to us just look and see what mad men you will have to deal with then."

Although no one is suggesting that the entire Omagh bombing was deliberately set up by the Provisionals, the after effects did play neatly into their hands. The horrors of a return to violence were vividly illustrated without them having to initiate that violence themselves and be the recipients of all the related opprobrium. They could even be seen to condemn violence and project a sympathetic image of themselves as the peacemakers.

What is also interesting in the aftermath of the bombing is that no one has yet been convicted. This is strange since most of the Reals are known to be former Provisionals. Moreover, the names of the suspected bombers are known not only to the security forces but also to the Provisionals, including Sinn Fein.[40] Indeed, shortly after the bombing representatives of the Provisionals visited prominent members of the

Reals and reminded them that " . . . they were in violation of IRA rules. Some were reportedly told that they would be shot if they continued their activities."[41] Whatever the new Provisional stance on constitutional politics it certainly does not seem to extend to providing information about serious crimes to either the British or the Irish police.[42] And although the Provisionals gave an excellent impression of condemning that particular act of violence they carefully avoided condemning the use of terrorist violence per se. Indeed, the message they seemed to send was that they reserved to themselves the exclusive right to use political violence on behalf of the Republican constituency. In this way the Provisionals used the situation to reconfirm their own discipline and control while at the same time maintaining an air of moral indignation on behalf of an outraged citizenry. But at the same time they did not alienate their wider constituency of support by "shopping" fellow republicans to either the British or Irish authorities.

The Provisionals played the situation with consummate skill and turned a tragedy into a useful platform to both play the international press and politicians and also to reestablish their hegemony over the Republican movement. Sinn Fein could now portray themselves as serious men of peace by condemning and restraining the Reals for what the Provisionals had been doing for 30 years, and without giving up a thing.

There is even a school of thought among some security analysts that Omagh may have helped to solve a rather awkward problem for the Provisionals. This school regards the Reals as having been a useful adjunct for the Provisionals. The Real IRA's bombs helped to exert a violent threat to the State, during the peace process, that the Provisionals could not themselves exercise directly since they were on cease-fire, which was part of the condition for their inclusion in the peace process. The Real IRA's bombs had all the required effect of the Provisionals's own bombs but could be disowned and allow the Provisionals to continue in the talks as peaceful participants. There are conspiracy theorists who think that the British and Irish governments may have colluded in this by not acting on intelligence reports that suggested that the Reals may have had tacit support from the Provisionals. The Reals could be publicly disowned while working within a Provisional plan to maintain the violent pressure on government while at the same time negotiating under the guise of a cease-fire.

The reasons for thinking this are not just political calculation but also consideration of the Reals's sphere of operations in North Louth in the Irish Republic and South Armagh in Northern Ireland. This area is the home territory of the Provisionals's chief of staff, recently named in a Dublin court case and book as Thomas "Slab" Murphy.[43] That the Provisionals would not know what was going on their own patch and allow it to happen without their tacit approval beggars belief.

Further, when the quartermaster-general left the Provisionals to form the Reals and took all his knowledge, skills, and materials with him he was in contravention of the IRA's "Green Book," and its general order 14.[44] This order states that to use knowledge, skills, and stock gained while in the IRA for the benefit of any other organization will lead to a court-martial and if found guilty the penalty is execution. Nearly all of the Reals's acts have used IRA weapons stocks and techniques. Yet no Real has as yet been tried or executed, not even following Omagh.

For the Provisionals the Reals were becoming an increasing problem, for, although serving a useful indirect purpose, their very success was leading them to get out of control. However, to formally pursue any Real meant disciplining and probably executing men, often former colleagues, for doing what the Provisionals had been doing for nearly 30 years. There were also quite a few Reals with a much larger well of sympathy among republican supporters. Any disciplining acts could have led to major splits and recriminations, even an internal war. Yet at the same time the Reals were starting to pose a serious challenge to the Provisionals's hegemony over militant Republicanism. Omagh solved the problem nicely, if by accident. It enabled the Provisionals to resume control while only having to issue threats against the Reals.

To summarize, there is a strong suspicion that the Provisionals knew all about the Reals and their campaign, although they might not have known that Omagh was a specific target. Before the bombing there was probably a fine calculation for the Provisionals as to whether they were prepared to let the Reals continue with their campaign, weighing up the advantages of the campaign and the costs of stopping it. When the bombing went so disastrously wrong it provided the Provisionals with the pretext and opportunity to decisively step in and reassert their authority. However, whether the recent upsurge in the Reals's campaign in 2000 falls within the same category of Provisional "proxy bombing" is less certain, but so far there have been few signs of the Provisionals actively discouraging the Reals.

Following the Omagh bombing, constitutional politicians on both sides of the border expressed outrage and used the opportunity to push through new antiterrorist legislation, although to little immediate effect. But, given that the bombing could have been used to great advantage in pressurizing terrorist groups to decommission their weapons, one may be a little surprised at the speed with which the whole issue appears to have been forgotten. If it has not been forgotten it is certainly not being publicized. Indeed, beyond the victims of the bombing there is an awful sense of Who remembers Omagh? now starting to emerge. The outrage felt at the time has quickly been superseded by other events, with the Omagh bomb becoming just another atrocity in the long catalogue of the "troubles."

Meanwhile, security briefings have continually suggested that both the Real IRA and Continuity IRA were just biding their time until enough of the dust had settled on Omagh to start up again. After that, the Provisionals might not be far behind. Given that most serious and authoritative security analysts doubt the sincerity of their commitment to the peace process, the current phase of the Provisionals's strategy can be seen merely as an integral, and continuing, part of their long-established strategy of "the armalite and the ballot box."[45]

NOTES

1. *Sunday Times* (London), 16 August 1998; *Independent on Sunday* (London), 16 August 1998; and *The Independent* (London), 17 August 1998, all provide detailed reports of the bombing.

2. For a discussion of the "peace process," sometimes also referred to as the "talks" and the negotiations leading up to the 1998 Good Friday Agreement; see Paul Bew, Henry Patterson, and Paul Teague, *Between War and Peace* (London: Lawrence & Wishart, 1997), part III; Arthur Aughey and Duncan Morrow, *Northern Ireland Politics* (London: Longman, 1996), postscript; and Jonathan Tonge, *Northern Ireland: Conflict and Change* (Hemel Hempstead: Prentice Hall), chapters 9-11. For the Good Friday Agreement see *The Agreement* (Belfast: HMSO, 1998).

3. For an introduction to the revisionist debate see Virginia Crossman in *Ireland in Proximity* (London: Routledge, 1999). For the full range of the debates see D. George Boyce and Alan O'Day, eds., *Modern Irish History* (London: Routledge, 1996) or Ciaran Brady, ed., *Interpreting Irish History* (Dublin: Irish Academic Press, 1994).

4. See Oliver MacDonagh, *States of Mind* (London: Allen & Unwin, 1983) for the application of this in Ireland or Elie Kedourie, *Nationalism* (Oxford: Blackwell, 1993) for its application in nationalism generally.

5. For a history of the IRA in South Armagh and the origins of the Reals see Toby Harnden, *Bandit Country* (London: Hodder & Stoughton, 1999).

6. Security briefing. This term, both here and in later notes, refers specifically to interviews with either members of the local police (Royal Ulster Constabulary, the RUC) or members of the armed forces serving in Northern Ireland. Invariably such briefings are confidential and "off the record" and given by personal contacts who agreed to speak on the basis of private contacts and relationships built up over a period of years. Although this is obviously unsatisfactory from a purely academic point of view, in terms of referencing and validation, it is often the only way in which contemporary events can be effectively recorded and reported. Because of the legal, operational, and security problems involved in responding to a contemporary terrorist campaign (in whose midst both the author and informants have to live) and the political calculations of governments, much of the relevant information and intelligence exists only in the nonpublic domain. Access to relevant information is thus often restricted to what can be gleaned from personal contacts who will only agree to discuss matters on the basis of complete confidentiality. However, every attempt to verify such briefings is made, via reference to previous incidents, known strategy and tactics, using more than one contact, and finally via discussions with other academic and journalists working in the same area.

7. During the whole of the peace process, Provisional IRA have constantly reiterated their commitment to an united Ireland—2016 being the target date, to coincide with the centenary of the Easter Rising.

8.   John Whyte, *Interpreting Northern Ireland* (Oxford: Clarendon Press, 1991), p. 192.

9.   See Elie Kedourie, *Nationalism* (Oxford: Blackwell, 1993) or Liah Greenfeld, *Nationalism: Five Roads to Modernity* (Harvard: Harvard University Press, 1993); Adrian Hastings, *The Construction of Nationhood* (Cambridge: Cambridge University Press, 1997); and Anthony Smith, *National Identity* (London: Penguin, 1991).

10.   See MacDonagh, op. cit., chapter 5 and M. L. R. Smith, *Fighting For Ireland? The Military Strategy of the Irish Republican Movement* (London: Routledge, 1995), chapter 2.

11.   Smith, op. cit., chapter 2; and J. Bowyer Bell, *The Secret Army* (Dublin: Poolbeg, 1989), part 1.

12.   See Smith, op. cit., pp. 87-90; Thomas Hennessey, *A History of Northern Ireland, 1920-1990* (Dublin: Gill & Macmillan), chapter 4; and Tim Pat Coogan, *The IRA* (Glasgow: Fontana, 1989), chapters 18 & 20.

13.   *The Agreement*, op. cit., p. 20.

14.   Security briefing.

15.   Harnden, op. cit.

16.   Harnden, op. cit., pp. 185-190 on Kingsmills and Tim Pat Coogan, *The Troubles* (London: Random House, 1995), pp. 278-279 on Darkley.

17.   See James Dingley and Michael, Kirk-Smith, "How Could They Do It? The Bombing of Omagh, 1998," *Journal of Conflict Studies* (Spring 2000), pp. 105-126.

18.   Security briefing.

19.   Security briefing.

20.   See John Horgan and Max Taylor, "The Provisional Irish Republican Army: Command and Functional Structure," *Terrorism and Political Violence* 9(3) (1997); for an explanation of who does what in the IRA.

21.   *The Independent* (London), 5 September 1998, p. 4.

22.   Security briefing.

23.   *The Independent* (London), 3 April 1998, p. 1.

24.   Security briefing.

25.   Security briefing.

26.   *The Independent* (London), 9 September 1998.

27.   Security briefing.

28.   Security briefing.

29.   The most recent bombing operation undertaken by the Reals at the time of writing (25 August 2000) was an attempt to plant a 500 lb bomb in Londonderry, probably aimed at an Orange parade in the city. It was intercepted before it could be planted. See *The Independent* (London), 12 August 2000, p. 1. For other bombings or attempts see *The Independent* (London), 7 February 2000, p. 1; 26 February 2000, p. 2; 17 March 2000, p. 2; and 17 April 2000, p. 2.

30.   David Rapoport, "Fear and Trembling in Three Religious Traditions," *American Political Science Review* 78 (1984). This article particularly stresses the assassinations carried out in Biblical and medieval times, whose very openness appears to be a deliberate attempt to publicize the acts. Media relations appear to be a very old aspect of terrorism.

31.   *The Economist* (London), 22 August 1998, pp. 21-22.

32.   See Dingley and Kirk-Smith, "How Could They Do It?" for a discussion of the bombers' emotional and symbolic motivations.

33.   Security briefing.

34.   Security briefing.

35.   For reports on the bombing in detail and how the police responded to the warning given see the *Sunday Times* (London), 16 August 1998, p. 1 and *The Independent* (London), 17 August 1998, p. 1.

36.   Security briefing.

37.   Security briefing.

38.   Bruce Hoffman, *Inside Terrorism* (London: Victor Gollanaz, 1998), p. 164.

39.   *The Independent* (London), 18 August 1998, p. 4.

40.   Security briefing.

41.   *The Independent* (London), 9 September 1998, p. 1.

42.   This point was recently reconfirmed by Martin McGuiness on a BBC TV interview (14 May 2000) in which he stated that he could not ask any of his community to cooperate with the police given the way they are currently constituted.

43.   Harnden, op. cit., writes extensively on the role of "Slab" Murphy in both South Armagh and in the IRA.

44.   The Green Book is the IRA's formal statement of aims and objectives, plus its standing orders and commands; codes of practices; and punishments.

45.   Smith, *Fighting for Ireland*, pp. 172-178.

SUICIDE TERRORISM

A Global Threat

ROHAN GUNARATNA

Traditionally viewed as a problem affecting the Middle East and South Asia, the threat posed by suicide terrorism is spreading around the globe. Rohan Gunaratna assesses the nature of the threat, preventive and reactive security measures, and examines future trends.

The enhanced international and domestic threat of suicide terrorism from terrorist groups in the Middle East and South Asia was the focus of the First International Conference on Countering Suicide Terrorism, held in Israel between 21-23 February 2000. The conference brought together some 80 police, military, intelligence and security specialists to share their national experiences, and was prompted by the growing need for governments to identify the threat and co-operate at strategic and tactical levels to disrupt suicide terrorism.

THE THREAT

Suicide terrorism is the readiness to sacrifice one's life in the process of destroying or attempting to destroy a target to advance a political goal. The aim of the psychologically and physically war-trained terrorist is to die while destroying the enemy target.

In the 1980s suicide terrorism was witnessed in Lebanon, Kuwait and Sri Lanka. In the 1990s it had spread to Israel, India, Panama, Algeria, Pakistan, Argentina, Croatia, Turkey, Tanzania and Kenya. With enhanced migration of terrorist groups from conflict-ridden countries, the formation of extensive international terrorist infrastructures and the increased reach of terrorist groups in the post Cold War period, suicide terrorism is likely to affect Western Europe and North America in the foreseeable future.

There are now 10 religious and secular terrorist groups that are capable of using suicide terrorism as a tactic against their governments and/or foreign governments. They are: the Islam Resistance Movement (Hamas) and the Palestinian Islamic Jihad of the Israeli occupied territories; Hizbullah of Lebanon; the Egyptian Islamic Jihad (EIJ) and Gamaya Islamiya (Islamic Group—IG) of Egypt; the Armed Islamic Group (GIA) of Algeria; Barbar Khalsa International (BKI) of India; the Liberation Tigers of Tamil Eelam (LTTE) of Sri Lanka; the Kurdistan Worker's Party (PKK) of Turkey; and the Osama bin Laden network (Al Quaida) of Afghanistan.

There were also four pro-Syrian, Lebanese and Syrian political parties engaged in suicide terrorism in the 1980s, but they are currently inactive in the terrorist front. These groups staged around 25 suicide attacks in Lebanon. As

From "Suicide Terrorism: A Global Threat," October 20, 2000. Gunaratna. Reproduced with permission from Jane's Information Group—Jane's Intelligence Review.

Number of Suicide Attacks Between 1980-2000

The Liberation Tigers of Tamil Eelam (LTTE) in Sri Lanka and in India	168
Hizbullah and pro-Syrian groups in Lebanon, Kuwait and Argentina	52
Hamas in Israel	22
The Kurdistan Worker's Party (PKK) in Turkey	15
The Palestinian Islamic Jihad (PIJ) in Israel	8
Al Quaida in East Africa	2
The Egyptian Islamic Jihad (EIJ) in Croatia	1
The Islamic Group (IG) in Pakistan	1
Barbar Khalsa International (BKI) in India	1
The Armed Islamic Group (GIA) in Algeria	1

more than one group claimed some of the attacks, perhaps to diffuse the threat to the group, it is difficult to identify the group responsible. The groups engaged in suicide operations in Lebanon alongside Hizbullah were the Natzersit Socialist Party of Syria; the Syrian Nationalist Party; the Lebanese Communist Party; and the Baath Party of Lebanon.

There are two types of suicide operations: battlefield and off the battlefield. In battlefield operations, suicide bombers are integrated into the attacking groups. Most off-the-battlefield operations have involved single suicide bombers. In the case of the LTTE and Hamas, there have been multiple suicide bombers. The targets have been static and mobile, against infrastructure and humans. Suicide bombers have destroyed military, political, economic and cultural infrastructure. They have committed terrorist attacks by killing civilians in buses, crowded places and in buildings. Suicide bombers have also assassinated political and military VIPs.

KEY CHARACTERISTICS

Examination of suicide terrorism across a range of groups has revealed that terrorist groups use suicide bombers when they are both strong and weak. In terms of military and economic power, Hizbullah and the LTTE lead the list of suicide operations. In terms of numbers, the LTTE has conducted the largest volume of suicide operations, followed by Hizbullah, Hamas and the PKK. In terms of range, only some of the groups have operated beyond their territories.

As well as abortive attempts to conduct suicide operations in Israel, Hizbullah has successfully conducted suicide operations in Argentina. The LTTE has conducted one suicide operation in India. It is the only group to have killed two world leaders—the former prime minister of India, Rajiv Gandhi, and the president of Sri Lanka, Ranasinghe Premadasa—using male and female suicide bombers.

The Egyptian groups have conducted suicide operations in Croatia against a police station and in Pakistan against the Egyptian embassy. Al-Quaida used at least one Egyptian suicide bomber in the 1998 East African embassy bombings. All the other active groups have conducted suicide operations within their own territory. The PKK has threatened to conduct suicide operations in Germany where there is a large Kurdish diaspora.

All the suicide terrorist groups have support infrastructures in Europe and in North America. Leaders and members of these groups are known to travel to the West, and key activists live either in Europe or in North America distributing propaganda, raising funds, and in some instances procuring weapons and shipping them to the various theatres of conflict.

Suicide-capable groups differ in form, size, orientation, goal and support. A review of the key characteristics of the 10 suicide-capable groups reveals that any group can acquire suicide bomb technology and engage in suicide terrorism:

• Al Quaida is a mix of several associate groups that are internationally dispersed. From Afghanistan, Bin Laden provides the overall direction to the organisation. Al Quaida efforts are primarily directed against the USA ('Great Satan') and Israel ('Little Satan'), and their allies. More recently, Al Quaida has directed its efforts against India on the issue of Kashmir, a territory disputed between India and Pakistan. The USA has directed its resources to disrupting Al Quaida support operations in the USA, especially after the 1998 embassy bombings in Kenya and Tanzania.

- The Indian counter insurgency specialist, K P S Gill, broke the backbone of the Sikh insurgents in Punjab, northern India. BKI is fighting for an independent 'Khalistan' in the predominantly Sikh state of Punjab. It has a small presence in the target country—India— but enjoys a significant presence in the diaspora—UK and Canada. In January 2000, when BKI was planning to conduct its second suicide operation, the Indian security forces apprehended the bomber.

- The GIA has staged only one suicide operation as part of its fight to establish an Islamic state in Algeria.

- Hizbullah, responsible for suicide bombing the US Marine Corps barracks and the headquarters of the French paratroopers in Lebanon in 1983, is fighting to oust the Israelis from southern Lebanon. Hizbullah is supported by Iran, a steadfast state sponsor. Today, Hizbullah is also a political party.

- Hamas and PIJ, operating in Gaza and West Bank, have vowed to destroy the 'Zionist state of Israel'. Currently, Hamas and PIJ are controlled by the Palestinian Authority under its President, Yasser Arafat. Shin Bet (the Israeli security agency) and the Mossad (the Israeli external intelligence agency) have regulated the efficacy of these two groups by removing their key operatives and military leaders.

In a deep-penetration operation, Shin Bet agents placed a micro explosive device in the mobile phone of the Hamas suicide bomb maker, Yahiya Aiyyash, killing him. Due to the efficiency of the countermeasures adopted by Israeli police, military, intelligence and security organisations, the number of fatalities and casualties caused by Hamas, the PIJ and Hizbullah bombing has steadfastly declined. Towards the last few bombings, the explosions only killed the bomber. Although Hamas is likely to retain a military capability, the group will probably join the political mainstream in the foreseeable future. The PIJ became weak after the Mossad assassinated Shikaki, its military and political commander in Malta.

- The two Egyptian groups—IG and EIJ— are fighting to establish an Islamic state in Egypt. The leader of the EIJ, Dr Ayman Al-Thawaheri, lives in Afghanistan and works closely with Bin Laden.
- Until the capture of PKK leader Abdullah Ocalan, the PKK fought for an independent Kurdistan in southeastern Turkey. Today, the PKK is demanding autonomy and equal cultural rights.
- The LTTE is fighting for an independent Tamil state in northeastern Sri Lanka. As the quality of targets chosen by the LTTE is high, it has a sophisticated training programme that lasts for about a year. As well as training the bomber, the LTTE research unit tests the effects of explosives on dogs and goats to ensure that the attack is successful. The list of Sri Lankan VIPs killed in suicide attacks includes one president, one presidential candidate, the State Minister of Defence, the Navy Chief and various area commanders. No country has lost so many leaders in such a short period of time as Sri Lanka has to the LTTE suicide bombers.

MOTIVATION

Some suicide groups are motivated by religion, religious/ethnic nationalism, or ethnic nationalism. Al Quaida's religious philosophy transcends territorial borders. Hamas, the PIJ and Hizbullah are primarily religious groups, but they are also driven by ethno-nationalism. BKI is the only non-Islamic religious group. While the LTTE and the PKK are driven by ethno-nationalism, the PKK is also infused with Marxist-Leninist ideology. As such, the motivation of Hamas, the PIJ and Hizbullah suicide bombers is primarily Islam. The motivation of the LTTE and the PKK suicide bombers is mainly Tamil and Kurdish nationalism respectively.

Dependent on the political environment and potential and actual donors, a new ideological orientation can be built into a group. With the end of the Cold War, most groups are abandoning Marxist, Leninist and Maoist ideologies and embracing ethno-nationalist and/or religious ideologies.

There are some constraints that affect the deployment of female suicide bombers. An examination of the groups driven by religious ideology reveals that Islam has constrained the use of women suicide bombers. Nevertheless, about five of the suicide operations in Lebanon were women. Although the PIJ once planned to use a woman to suicide bomb the Israeli prime minister's residence in Jerusalem, the operation was thwarted. About 30% of the suicide operations in Sri Lanka have been conducted by women.

A higher percentage of women have featured in off-the-battlefield suicide operations, which requires infiltration, invisibility and deception. A woman staged the suicide operation that killed Rajiv Gandhi in India. Most suicide operations in Turkey are by women. For many reasons, women are the preferred choice of secular groups when it comes to infiltration and strike missions. First, women are less suspicious. Second, in the conservative societies of the Middle East and South Asia, there is a hesitation to body search a woman. Third, women can wear a suicide device beneath her clothes and appear pregnant.

Modus Operandi

The organisation of suicide operations is extremely secretive. The success of the mission depends on a number of elements: level of secrecy; thorough reconnaissance; and thorough rehearsals. Secrecy enables the preservation of the element of surprise, critical for the success of most operations.

Thorough reconnaissance enables the group to plan, often by building a scale model of the target. Thorough rehearsals allow the bomber to gain stealth and speed. There are other elements, such as getting the bomber to the target zone and then to the target itself. The bomber is usually supported by an operational cell, responsible for providing accommodation, transport, food, clothing and security to the bomber until he/she reaches the target. Resident agents help generate intelligence for the operation, from target reconnaissance to surveillance. The cell members confirm the intelligence. Often, immediately before the attack, the bomber conducts the final reconnaissance.

As a comprehensive knowledge of the target is essential for the success of a suicide operation, terrorist groups depend on building solid agent-handling networks. Some security and intelligence agencies have succeeded in penetrating the agent-handling network of various terrorist groups. In some cases, the only form of defence is to penetrate the terrorist group itself. This is because bombers penetrate governments or societies as sleepers and gradually gain acceptance as a trusted member. Thus the bomber can reach and destroy a valuable target—human or infrastructure.

In such cases, even the presence of a few hundred bodyguards or guards assigned to protect sensitive installations cannot serve as a counter measure. As such, penetration of the terrorist group is the first line of defence. The last line of defence is hardening the vulnerable and likely targets.

There are six types of suicide improvised explosive devices (IEDs). These are: the human-borne suicide IED, also known as the suicide bodysuit; the vehicle-borne suicide IED; the motorcycle-borne suicide IED; naval craft-borne suicide IED; scuba diver-borne suicide IED; and aerial- (microlight, glider, mini-helicopter) borne suicide IED. All these categories have been used in South Asia and the Middle East.

The largest number of suicide IEDs used has been the suicide bodysuit. As terrorists are cost conscious, there have been only a few cases of bombers using aerial-borne suicide IEDs. Yet these are the most difficult to thwart. Their small size makes them hard to detect on radar, but the range of a light aircraft is limited, weather sensitive and lacks accuracy.

The traditional concept of security is based on deterrence, where the terrorist is either killed or captured. The success of a suicide terrorist operation is dependent on the death of the terrorist. The suicide terrorist is not worried about capture, interrogation (including torture), trial, imprisonment and the accompanying humiliation.

Furthermore, in suicide attacks, there is no need to provide an escape route, or for the extraction of the attacker/attacking force. The group does not have to concern itself with developing an escape plan, often the most difficult phase of an operation. Therefore, a suicide terrorist could enter a high security zone and accomplish his/her mission without worrying about escape or evasion. The certain death of the attacker enables the group to undertake high quality operations while protecting the organisation and its cadres. As every prisoner has a point of breaking under psychological or physical pressure, the certain death of the attacker or attackers prevent the captor extracting information.

LIKELY DEVELOPMENTS

The development of counter measures has led to a decline in the number of suicide attacks. In Israel, several rings of security prevent the suicide bomber from reaching the intended target. In response, groups try out novel methods of infiltration. In this game of 'cat and mouse', one side can learn from the other in an attempt to 'checkmate' the opponent. While most groups can improvise, only a few are innovative.

To detect persons carrying explosives, security authorities have used sniffer dogs, with a maximum attention span of 30 minutes. One terrorist group has hired the services of a dog handler from France to monitor the ability of sniffer dogs. It is likely that this group will develop a suicide body suit with a repellent to evade the attention of sniffer dogs. With these developments, it is likely that the role of the sniffer dog will diminish with time and more innovative mechanisms will be necessary to detect the bomber.

The suicide body suit has evolved to improve concealment and is becoming increasingly small. Initially, the device was a square block of explosives worn in the chest and the belly area. Gradually, the device evolved into a heart shaped block of explosives placed just above the navel. As body searches for suicide devices are usually conducted around the abdomen, a group is also developing breast bombs.

Most suicide body suits have no/little electronics, making it difficult for security agencies to develop counter-technologies to detect these devices. A suicide body suit can be made from commercial items. With the exception of the malleable plastic explosives and detonator, all the other components can be purchased from a tailor shop (stretch denim) and an auto shop (steel ball bearings, wires, batteries and switches). Furthermore, when a device is sophisticated it becomes difficult to operate, as well as fixing it when it fails to function. Suicide devices will thus remain simple.

However, there are likely to be variations of suicide devices. Terrorists tend to select from a repertoire of tactics. This is to retain an element of surprise and to evade the attention of security authorities directed at countering a standard set of tactics.

STATE RESPONSES

Terrorist groups learn from one another. Unlike in the 1970s and the 1980s, post-Cold War groups share resources intelligence, technology, expertise and personnel.

However, due to the need to preserve counter-technologies or political rivalry, there is either a lack of co-operation or no co-operation at all between affected countries. For instance, the British do not share counter remote-control bomb technologies against the Provisional IRA (PIRA) with their US counterparts. This is primarily due to suspicion of access or infiltration of the US military and security industries by PIRA activists and supporters. Similarly, there is no co-operation between Israel and Sri Lanka, the most affected countries. During the Cold War, Indian pressure, and subsequently, the Sri Lankan Muslim lobby led to a rupture of Israeli-Sri Lankan ties that included Israeli technical co-operation in training Sri Lankan bomb technicians.

An example of how a lack of co-operation between the VIP security divisions of India and Sri Lanka affected security was the failure of the Sri Lankan Presidential Security Division to estimate the kill radius of the suicide device. In India, over 18m is maintained between the political VIP and the public. The distance between the LTTE female suicide bomber and President Chandrika Bandaranaike Kumaratunge, who was partially blinded by an explosion in December 1999, was less than 12m.

Other than co-operation at strategic and tactical levels between VIP security divisions, the lack of research into the technical capability of terrorist groups has gravely weakened the ability of security divisions to protect their VIPs.

Strategic and tactical countermeasures can be used against suicide operations. They could be preventive and reactive. Preventive measures range from propaganda directed against potential suicide bombers, to infiltrating the suicide organisations of terrorist groups. Reactive measures range from the hardening of targets, to using dummy cars to protect VIPs. Yet security agencies agree that suicide terrorism is hard to fight. The US secret service argues that if an assassin is willing to die, it is impossible to protect the president. Nonetheless, affected governments have tried to protect their VIPs and critical infrastructure.

A GROWING THREAT

The threat of suicide terrorism is likely to spread with time. As many second-generation operations have been conducted away from the theatre of war, it is likely that suicide terrorism will affect Western Europe and North America in the future.

Terrorist groups are increasingly providing intensive training to their bombers, with the intention of increasing their endurance. For instance, the suicide bomber who destroyed the US embassy in Nairobi in 1998 had been resident in Kenya for four years. He had married in Kenya and lived in the capital before carrying out the suicide operation. Similarly, the suicide bomber who assassinated President Premadasa of Sri Lanka had lived in the capital, Colombo, for three years before carrying out the attack.

Terrorist groups are setting a dangerous trend of using suicide bombers to destroy targets far away from their theatres of war. Many groups are likely to use suicide bombers to infiltrate target countries and conduct suicide attacks against Western VIPs and critical infrastructure in the foreseeable future.

7

UNCONVENTIONAL
TERRORIST TACTICS

Violence does, in truth, recoil upon the violent, and the schemer falls into the pit which he digs for another.

—Sir Arthur Conan Doyle

Conventional terrorist activities, including assassinations, hijackings, kidnappings, and bombings, are still the first choice of most terrorists. The September 11, 2001, attack on the World Trade Center and the Pentagon demonstrated that these traditional methods can be used to inflict horrifying devastation. The threat posed by contemporary terrorism is increased even further by the availability of weapons of mass destruction (WMD) and the growth of cyberterrorism. Today's terrorists can choose from a potent arsenal of weapons capable of destroying large portions of our planet. WMD (made from nuclear, biological, and chemical materials) and cyberterrorism (the use of computers to spread information and paralyze vital infrastructures) could cause hundreds of thousands, even millions, of deaths and injuries. Unconventional weapons could incite global panic and paralyze governments' attempts to respond to the ensuing crisis.

For more than a century, terrorists have fantasized about weapons that could obliterate large portions of the earth. Karl Heinzen, the mid-19th century German radical philosopher who thought prizes should be given for inventing new poisons and explosives (Laqueur, 1977, p. 27), fantasized about weapons like "rockets, poison gases, and land mines, that one day would destroy whole cities with 100,000 inhabitants" (Laqueur, 1999, p. 13). The difference between now and then is that today the raw materials for producing and dispersing WMD are readily available, especially since the breakup of the Soviet Union, which left immense amounts of high-quality nuclear and other materials susceptible to theft.

The decline in the 1990s of left-wing terrorist groups, which flourished in the 1970s and 1980s, was accompanied by a rise in right-wing groups. Where left-wing terrorists focused primarily on economic and political causes, many of today's right-wing terrorists, like those accused of the September 11, 2001, attacks, are driven by religious zealotry (Laqueur, 1999). Thus, the growing availability of unconventional weapons comes at a time when right-wing, fanatical terrorism is also growing.

The increase in the fanaticism of religious or apocalyptic terrorists means that more terrorists are willing to use unconventional weapons. The consequences of just one doing so are extraordinarily high. Some terrorists are deterred by the horrific consequences of attacks with WMD, but extremists who are willing to die for their cause may also want to maximize fatalities with unconventional weapons. Rogue governments may be afraid to use such weapons against more powerful enemies for fear of retaliation, but they may nevertheless be willing, either for profit or to further their political agenda, to supply terrorists with the raw materials to produce them.

The FBI released these images of the envelope (above) and the threatening letter (right) containing anthrax that was sent to U.S. Senator Thomas Daschle (D-South Dakota).

Photo courtesy of the Federal Bureau of Investigation.

The danger of bioterrorism became apparent for the first time to many people in the United States a few weeks after the September 11 attacks. Letters containing anthrax were sent through the U.S. mail: 5 people died from anthrax exposure and another 18 were known to be infected. More than a thousand people were tested for contact with anthrax, and about 30,000 people were given antibiotics to prevent infection.

Hundreds of other people reported substances that they feared were anthrax; most were false alarms. Health care professionals raised concern that the supply of antibiotics to counter anthrax was inadequate, and the Bush administration announced that it would buy antibiotics that could be made available quickly to treat up to 12 million people.

The ensuing investigation of the anthrax attacks found no clear links to the September 11 attacks, and many officials speculated that homegrown bioterrorists were responsible. Subsequently, President Bush sent to Congress a proposed budget for fiscal 2003 that sought an additional $11 billion over 2 years to protect the nation against biological terrorism, quadrupling what was spent before the September 11 attacks to counter bioterrorism. Money also was earmarked in the president's budget for improving the nation's public health system and for pumping up budgets of federal agencies involved in biodefense. Money also would be provided to expand the national stockpile of vaccines and antibiotics, build anticontamination laboratories, research new drugs, and improve coordination among local, state, and federal emergency preparedness teams.

THE 21ST CENTURY ARSENAL

Chemical Weapons

Chemical agents can be gases or liquids. They include poisons, such as arsenic and strychnine, and nerve gases, such as sarin and tabun. Mustard gases, which are blistering

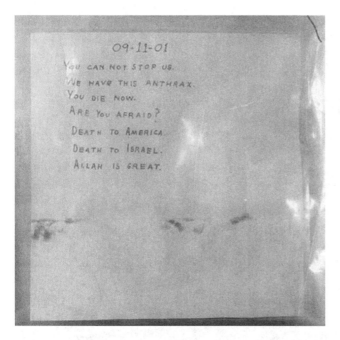

agents that affect the eyes, respiration, and skin, were widely used in World War I. Chemical weapons were also used in the Russian Civil War of 1919-1921, by Spain against Morocco in 1925, and by Italy against Ethiopia in the 1930s. They were used more recently in the Iran-Iraq War of 1983-1988, by Libya against Chad in 1987, and by Iraq against the Kurds in 1988 (Falkenrath, Newman, & Thayer, 2000, p. 91). Many chemical agents are used for legitimate medical, insecticide, and cleaning purposes and are thus readily available and often relatively cheap to purchase.

Biological Weapons

Biological weapons were used by ancient Romans, who contaminated their enemies' water supply with dead animals. In the 14th century, the Tartars are believed to have catapulted plague-infected corpses over the walls of their enemies' castles, initiating the Great Plague, also called the "Black Death," that eventually devastated much of Europe. Scientists confirmed that Japan used biological weapons against China and the Soviet Union during the early years of World War II (Falkenrath et al., 2000, p. 91).

In addition to spreading plagues, biological weapons can be used to spread smallpox, typhus, tuberculosis, Legionnaires' Disease, Ebola virus, and other infectious diseases. Anthrax spores could kill hundreds of thousands of people, even if only tiny amounts were disseminated effectively into the atmosphere. Biological weapons are relatively easy to produce and hide. A small amount can wreak havoc through the contamination of food and water.

Nuclear Weapons

The world has witnessed two nuclear attacks: In 1945, the United States detonated nuclear bombs on the Japanese cities of Hiroshima and Nagasaki. The bombings brought a quick end to World War II. The ability to manufacture nuclear weapons depends on the availability of high-quality uranium and plutonium. These materials are frequently in transit from one nuclear reactor site to another, making them vulnerable to theft. Domestic pressures and international political differences make it difficult for the key nuclear states of Russia, China, France, India, and the United States to agree on methods for stopping the growth of nuclear weaponry (Barletta, 2001, p. 4). Pakistan recently tested a nuclear device, and North Korea, Iran, and Iraq have developed or tried to develop nuclear capacity.

Hazardous materials decontamination specialists from the FBI and the Environmental Protection Agency work to identify anthrax-contaminated mail sent to Capitol Hill, following the discovery of letters containing anthrax.

Photo courtesy of the Federal Bureau of Investigation.

Cyberterrorism

Like WMD, cyberterrorism can cause widespread damage. Cyberterrorists use the Internet to contact colleagues, disseminate their views to a wider audience, and tap new sources of financial support. The Internet also provides an abundance of detailed instruction for anyone interested in making bombs, rockets, flamethrowers, and dozens of other lethal weapons and poisons.

The Internet has another sinister potential. Theoretically, it would take but one talented terrorist to devastate a country's infrastructure and generate panic and death. Military bases, hospitals, airports, banks, power plants, and other critical components of daily life depend on computers. Boilers could be programmed to explode, national security data could be altered, air traffic control systems could be sabotaged, food and water sources could be poisoned through changes in computer-driven controls—the possibilities are limited only by the cyberterrorists' skill and imagination.

How Real Is the Threat?

There have been many more hoaxes, pranks, and unconfirmed allegations reported than there have been actual uses of unconventional weapons. The Center for

Nonproliferation Studies at the Monterey Institute of International Studies maintains a database of all known criminal and terrorist incidents worldwide involving WMD agents by non-state actors. From 1900 to April 2001, the database lists more than 940 incidents; more than 700 of these occurred after 1990 (Monterey Institute for International Studies, 2001). The database includes information on use and threatened use, possession and attempted possession, and hoaxes and pranks. The vast majority of incidents were failed attempts to acquire WMD materials, hoaxes, and pranks. Relatively few incidents resulted in death or serious injury.

The Monterey data suggest that the actual use of nonconventional weapons may be growing. The number of incidents in the database stayed relatively stable between 1999 and 2000, but hoaxes declined by almost half and deaths increased tenfold.

Most of the weapons were simple "household" agents, which are unlikely to cause massive casualties. Roughly half of the incidents were criminally motivated, and the other half were categorized as politically motivated (Pate, Ackerman, & McCloud, 2001).

There are also many unconfirmed allegations of WMD attacks. For example, the United States has accused the Soviet Union of using toxic weapons against the Hmong tribesmen in Laos and against civilians and Khmer Rouge forces in Cambodia in the 1970s. South Africa was accused of using anthrax in the Rhodesian civil war of 1978-1980 and of releasing a deadly strain of malaria in Angola in the 1980s. Fidel Castro repeatedly has accused the United States of conducting biological attacks against Cuban crops (Falkenrath et al., 2000, p. 79). In January 2000, a Russian general accused Chechen rebels of giving toxic wine and fruit to Russian soldiers in Chechnya (Pate et al., 2000).

A Misguided Response to the Threat?

In a report issued prior to September 11, the Henry L. Stimson Center, a nonprofit public policy research organization, maintained that the United States was poorly prepared to react in the event of a significant attack using unconventional weapons (Smithson & Levy, 2000). The Stimson Center's study criticized the federal government for underfinancing the disease surveillance and hospital systems that would be overwhelmed in a large-scale WMD attack. In 2000, only $222 million, or about 14%, of the federal unconventional terrorism budget was earmarked for hospital preparations, public health infrastructure, and biomedical research. Only 6% of the budget was devoted to strengthening public hospitals, clinics, and emergency health facilities.

According to the study, the government has funded emergency response teams of dubious value (Smithson & Levy, 2000). For example, more than $134.7 million was spent to prepare and train National Guard teams to help in the event of a germ or chemical terrorist attack, but the study found that the teams probably would not arrive in time to provide significant help to local populations because the germs and chemicals spread so quickly.

The Stimson Center study recommended that the United States stop funding emergency preparedness training programs and abolish the National Guard units responsible for WMD attacks. Instead, it urged that money should be used to outfit hospitals and fire stations with decontamination capabilities and to increase research and training. Further, the study criticized the lack of coordination of federal efforts, which resulted in the creation of about 90 terrorism training preparedness courses with different missions, resources, and requirements, resulting in "a confusing mess." Whether the $11 billion budget requested by President Bush for bioterrorism will remove the deficiencies noted by the Stimson Center remains to be seen.

AUM SHINRIKYO: A TERRORIST CULT

Only one large-scale attack with WMD by non-state terrorists has been confirmed. The March 20, 1995, chemical weapons attack on Tokyo's subways by the Aum Shinrikyo apocalyptic and millenarian cult was said to herald a new age of "catastrophic" terrorism (Smithson & Levy, 2000, p. xi).

Aum Shinrikyo was controlled by the messianic and highly eccentric Shoko Asahara. A large and wealthy cult, the members of which included several scientists, Aum Shinrikyo experimented with both chemical and biological weapons. It was able to obtain many of its raw materials from Russia and the United States.

Although Aum Shinrikyo may be the first nongovernmental terrorist organization to engage in widespread use of WMD, it does not stand as a worthy model for replication. Aum Shinrikyo was "a terrorist nightmare—a cult flush with money and technical skills led by a con-man guru with an apocalyptic vision, an obsession with chemical and biological weaponry, and no qualms about killings" (Smithson & Levy, 2000, p. xii). The group nevertheless could not overcome the technical and scientific difficulties in WMD production and dissemination, and the death toll from the attack fell far short of Aum Shinrikyo's intent. Put in another perspective, the attacks "were less deadly than some single-person shooting sprees, and required considerably more effort to prepare and carry out" (Falkenrath et al., 2000, p. 23).

Shoko Asahara: A Chaotic Leader

Shoko Asahara's background seems bizarre for a terrorist leader (see, e.g., Cameron, 1999; Falkenrath et al., 2000; Laqueur, 1999; Mullins 1997; Walsh, 1995). Born Chizuo Matsumoto in 1955 on Kyushu, one of Japan's major islands, he was blind in one eye and partly blind in the other. At the age of 5, he was sent to a special school for the blind, where his partial sight gave him a big advantage over the other students. He quickly turned the advantage into a position of power. With partial vision, Matsumoto helped his classmates, but in return he bullied and intimidated them into doing his bidding. After graduating from the school in 1977, Matsumoto moved to Tokyo. When he was refused entry into Tokyo University, he started studying acupuncture and herbal medicine. He married, and he and his wife opened a small shop selling traditional Chinese herbs and health tonics. The business went bankrupt after Matsumoto was arrested and fined for selling fake cures.

In 1984, Matsumoto opened a yoga school, began to gather disciples, and founded Aum Shinrikyo. Two years later, as his following grew, Matsumoto traveled to India, where he claimed to have become enlightened while alone in the Himalayan mountains. Upon returning to Japan, he changed his name to the "holy" Shoko Asahara. *Aum* in Sanskrit symbolizes the "powers of destruction and creation in the universe," and *shinrikyo* means the "teaching of the supreme truth" (Reader, 2000, p. 15). As the name suggests, its leader's mission was to teach his followers the truth about the universe.

As a religion, Aum was "a hodgepodge of ascetic disciplines and New Age occultism, focused on supposed threats from the U.S., which [Asahara] portrayed as a [conspiracy] of Freemasons and Jews bent on destroying Japan. The conspiracy's weapons: sex and junk food" (Walsh, 1995). Asahara was demanding of his followers in Aum; for example, they were supposed to kiss his feet before addressing him.

From Bizarre to Dangerous

Aum was approved as a religion under Japan's Religious Corporations Law, which meant that the group had tax benefits, the right to own property, and protection from government interference. It soon grew into a large organization with thousands of members. It also became rich with the money demanded from members: the group's assets were estimated to be between $300 million and $1 billion. (Senate Permanent Subcommittee, 1996). Aum owned many companies worldwide, including "a computer firm, a chain of restaurants and a fitness club in Japan; a Taiwanese import/export company; and a tea plantation in Sri Lanka" (Cameron, 1999, p. 284). It also had extensive land holdings in Japan and elsewhere. Many of Asahara's followers were well educated, and several were doctors, engineers, and computer experts.

Shoko Asahara, whose doomsday cult, Aum Shinrikyo, spread sarin gas in the Tokyo subway system in 1995.

Photo copyright © by AFP/CORBIS. Reprinted with permission.

Why was Aum able to attract so many followers? One observer offers this explanation: "The time was ripe for gurus. Japan's galloping economic miracle in the 1970s and '80s also spawned a boom in new religions offering spiritual refuge to Japanese alienated by materialism. Asahara's messianic self-image expanded to help fill this void" (Walsh, 1995). Aum targeted people who were alienated from society, including lonely and emotionally needy people (Cameron, 1999, p. 284).

Asahara discouraged dissent and promoted his own unchallenged authority. To ensure obedience, he used brainwashing techniques including sleep deprivation, poor diet, electric shock treatments, and physical isolation. The cult also manufactured its own LSD and may have sold it to others (Sayle, 1996). Leaving the cult was not easy. Members were frightened, and some apparently were murdered for trying to escape. Outsiders who criticized the cult were also murdered, including a lawyer, his wife, and their baby. The lawyer had been planning to sue Aum on behalf of some of the cult members' parents (Kaplan & Marshall, 1996, pp. 37-43).

Aum continued to grow and expanded to Russia. Asahara once preached to a crowd of 15,000 in a Moscow sports stadium (Walsh, 1995). At its height, the cult was estimated to have 50,000 followers, of whom 10,000 were in Japan and up to 30,000 were in Russia (Cameron, 1999, p. 284).

In 1989, Asahara formed the Shinrito ("Supreme Truth") political party in an effort to expand Aum's base of support. In 1990, the party ran 25 candidates in the election of Japan's Lower House Diet. All of them lost. Legal problems mounted when hundreds of the group's followers were accused of falsifying their legal residence so they could vote in Asahara's district (Reader, 2000, p. 44).

Stunned and humiliated by the defeat at the polls, Asahara became further alienated from the rest of Japanese society. His ambition switched from simply controlling Japan to destroying it (Cameron, 1999, p. 280). It is roughly around this time that Asahara became obsessed with the idea of the coming of Armageddon (Senate Permanent Subcommittee, 1996). He decided to fulfill this prophecy himself.

Aum apparently tried and failed several times to develop and disseminate biological weapons. The cult experimented with anthrax, Q fever, and botulinum, as well as trying to collect samples of the Ebola virus. In 1990, cult members drove around the area outside the Japanese parliament spraying a botulinum toxic aerosol. The Japanese Crown Prince's wedding in 1993 was targeted for biological attack, but the group's toxin was not ready in time. Cult members again drove around the city spraying the toxin. In 1993, they tried to spray anthrax spores from the rooftop of their Tokyo headquarters (Cameron, 1999, p. 295). None of these events caused any deaths (Kaplan & Marshall, 1996).

Aum had more success with developing chemical agents. The cult tested sarin gas on sheep at its farm in Australia (Cameron, 1999, p. 293). The group again encountered numerous technical difficulties. For example, attempts to manufacture sarin gas were accompanied by problems building electrolysis tanks and reactor vessels, as well as by the crash of their Russian-made helicopters, which were to have been used to spray and disperse the gas (Cameron, 1999, p. 294). In 1994, they nevertheless produced enough sarin gas to attack three judges who were presiding over a land fraud suit against the cult. The attack killed 4 and injured 150 people (Falkenrath et al., 2000, p. 20).

Not until 1995, however, did the Tokyo Metropolitan Police begin to seriously investigate Aum's role in these assaults. Under Japan's laws, religious organizations generally are exempt from official investigation. Its status as a recognized religion enabled Aum to keep its plans secret. Now, with the police investigating, Asahara felt pressured to quickly launch Armageddon, and he hatched a flimsy plan to release sarin gas in the Toyko subway. The group did not wait to secure sufficiently pure sarin or to devise an effective dissemination strategy, dooming its plan for Armageddon.

The Attack

On the morning of March 20, 1995, five members of Aum Shinrikyo boarded subway trains at five different stations around Tokyo. Each member carried two sealed plastic pouches of sarin nerve gas and a sharpened umbrella. As the trains neared the center of the city, the terrorists put the plastic pouches on the floor and punctured them with the umbrellas. They then fled the subways as the liquids leaked quickly out of the bags. The effects were almost instantaneous: Passengers began to sweat, their noses ran, they coughed and wheezed, some vomited, and others had seizure-like symptoms.

Twelve people died and more than 5,000 were injured (Senate Permanent Subcommittee, 1996). It could have been much worse. Had a more scientifically sophisticated approach been used, thousands could have been killed.

The Aftermath

After the attack, the police focused immediately on Aum Shinrikyo and raided the cult's facilities. Large stockpiles of chemicals were seized, including ingredients for nerve gases such as sarin, VX, tabun, soman, and hydrogen cyanide (Cameron, 1999, p. 293). On May 16, 1995, Asahara was arrested and charged with masterminding the subway attacks, as well as with 16 other crimes, including murders, attempted murders, manufacture of illegal drugs, and production of WMD. Japan's so-called "trial of the century" began.

Japan's court system is complex, and Asahara's trial was expected to last as long as 10 years. The 200th hearing in the trial was conducted on June 22, 2001. Asahara began his trial by firing his lawyer, and he refused to cooperate with any of his court-appointed attorneys. Often pictured wearing pajamas and reported to be sleeping or mumbling to himself during the court proceedings, the bushy-bearded Asahara has used his prosecution to reinforce his eccentric reputation.

After the attack, many members of Aum Shinrikyo tried to distance themselves from Asahara. The cult was reorganized, and its name was changed to Aleph, a name that symbolizes renewal. The cult apparently has renounced the belief that it is acceptable to commit murder to achieve its goals, but many Japanese still believe that Asahara controls the group.

HIGHLIGHTS OF REPRINTED ARTICLES

The articles selected to accompany this chapter address the two different forms of unconventional terrorism: WMD and cyberterrorism. The first article examines the past, present, and future of biological, chemical, and nuclear weapons. The second article applies historical and legal analysis to cyberterrorism in the United States.

Walter Laqueur. (1999). "Weapons of Mass Destruction." In *The New Terrorism: Fanaticism and the Arms of Mass Destruction.* New York: Oxford University Press.

Walter Laqueur places contemporary WMD in the context of science fiction. The article highlights some of literature's more famous "mad scientists" and their efforts at mass destruction. The line between fiction and reality is often blurry, and real-life terrorists have devised plots that fiction writers envy.

The article presents a brief history of chemical, biological, and nuclear weapons, then summarizes international efforts to stop their proliferation. The many examples discussed in the article include chemical gas attacks by the Germans in World War I that killed thousands of Allied soldiers, to which the Allies retaliated, killing thousands of Germans. Chemical weapons subsequently were banned by international agreements, but that did not stop Adolf Hitler from using nerve gases against Jews in concentration camps. More recently, Iraq used nerve gas against Iran, killing thousands. Biological weapons also were used by the Germans during World War I, when they tried to use cholera bacilli, the plague, and anthrax against their enemies. In addition to discussing the past and present uses of WMD, the article assesses the future of these weapons.

Brian Levin. (2002). "Cyberhate: A Legal and Historical Analysis of Extremists' Use of Computer Networks in America." *American Behavioral Scientist, 45*(6), 958-988.

Levin considers how homegrown extremists use the Internet to promote their agendas. Right-wing hate groups, like the Imperial Klansmen of America and the White Aryan Resistance, and left-wing environmentalists and animal-liberation extremists use Web sites for spreading propaganda and promoting violent leaderless resistance. The article analyzes the history of several homegrown terrorist groups' use of the Internet as well as the Supreme Court's decisions on offensive speech in cyberspace. The article also discusses issues surrounding criminal prosecutions and the impact of the USA PATRIOT Act of 2001 on cyberterrorism.

EXPLORING UNCONVENTIONAL TERRORIST TACTICS FURTHER

- The Center for Nonproliferation Studies at the Monterey Institute (http://cns.miis.edu/index.htm) maintains WMD databases and issues reports, such as "Anthrax and Mass Casualty Terrorism: What Is the Bioterrorist Threat After September 11?"
- The Carnegie Endowment for International Peace's Non-Proliferation Project (www.ceip.org/files/nonprolif/default.asp) posts news and analysis on a variety of problems associated with WMD. These include critiques of the Bush Administration's WMD policies as well as threats and capabilities of nations around the globe.
- The United Nations has a branch devoted to WMD. Topics include treaties and conventions on nuclear, chemical, and biological weapons, as well as transcripts from the latest symposiums on terrorism and disarmament. The Web address is www.un.org/Depts/dda/WMD/WMD.htm
- The Henry L. Stimson Center (www.stimson.org), a nonprofit, nonpartisan organization, posts online publications such as "Beyond Deterrence: A Global Approach to Reducing Nuclear Dangers" and "'House of Cards': The Pivotal Importance of a Technically Sound BWC Monitoring Protocol."

VIDEO NOTES

Although weapons of mass destruction may seem like something from a movie plot, modern films contain few good studies of the threat of biological and chemical weapons. A celebrated drama about a global nuclear crisis spawned by terrorists is *Crimson Tide* (Hollywood Pictures, 1995, 115 min.).

REFERENCES

Barletta, Michael. (2001). *WMD threats 2001: Critical choices for the Bush administration* (Monterey Proliferation Strategy Group Occasional Paper #6). Monterey, CA: Monterey Institute of International Studies, Center for Nonproliferation Strategies.

Cameron, Gavin. (1999). Multi-track microproliferation: Lessons from Aum Shinrikyo and Al Qaida. *Studies in Conflict and Terrorism, 22*, 277-309.

Falkenrath, Richard A., Newman, Robert D., & Thayer, Bradley A. (2000). *America's Achilles' Heel: Nuclear, biological, and chemical terrorism and covert attack*. Cambridge, MA: MIT Press.

Kaplan, David E., & Marshall, Andrew. (1996). *The cult at the end of the world: The incredible story of Aum*. London: Arrow Books.

Laqueur, Walter. (1977). *Terrorism*. Boston: Little, Brown, and Company.

Laqueur, Walter. (1999). *The new terrorism: Fanaticism and the arms of mass destruction*. New York: Oxford University Press.

Levin, Brian. (2002). Cyberhate: A legal and historical analysis of extremists' use of computer networks in America. *American Behavioral Scientist, 45*(6), 958-988.

Monterey Institute for International Studies. (2001). *WMD database*. Monterey, CA: Monterey Institute of International Studies, Center for Nonproliferation Strategies. [Electronic version available by subscription.]

Mullins, Mark R. (1997). Aum Shinrikyo as an apocalyptic movement. In Thomas Robbins & Susan J. Palmer (Eds.), *Millennium, messiahs, and mayhem: Contemporary apocalyptic movements*. New York: Routledge.

Pate, Jason, Ackerman, Gary, & McCloud, Kimberly. (2001). *2000 WMD terrorism chronology: Incidents involving sub-national actors, and chemical, biological, radiological, or nuclear materials*. Monterey, CA: Monterey Institute of International Studies, Center for Nonproliferation Strategies.

Reader, Ian. (2000). *Religious violence in contemporary Japan: The case of Aum Shinrikyo*. Honolulu: University of Hawaii Press.

Sayle, Murray. (1996, April 1). Nerve gas and the four noble truths. *The New Yorker*, pp. 56-71.

Senate Permanent Subcommittee on Investigations of the Committee on Governmental Affairs. (1996). Staff statement, global proliferation of weapons of mass destruction: A case study of the Aum Shinrikyo. *Global proliferation of weapons of mass destruction, part I, hearings before the Permanent Subcommittee on Investigations of the Committee on Governmental Affairs, U.S. Senate, 104th Cong., 1st Sess*. Washington, DC: Government Printing Office.

Smithson, Amy E., & Levy, Leslie-Anne. (2000). *Ataxia: The chemical and biological terrorism threat and the U.S. response* (Report #35). Washington, DC: Henry L. Stimson Center.

USA PATRIOT Act of 2001. Uniting and Strengthening America by Providing Appropriate Tools Required to Intercept and Obstruct Terrorism Act, Pub. L. No. 107-56 (2001).

Walsh, James. (1995, April 3). Shoko Asahara: The making of a messiah. *Time Magazine*.

WEAPONS OF MASS DESTRUCTION

Walter Laqueur

Weapons of mass destruction have long been a subject of the human imagination, in both the literary and literal sense. The use of biological and chemical weapons in war can be traced back for centuries; nuclear weapons, of course, appeared more recently, and have been used only twice, by one country. And there is even a new weapon, the potential of which is only now being understood: the computer. But as the twentieth century comes to a close, all these weapons, particularly biological/chemical, or so-called B/C weapons, are increasingly available to more states and, what is more frightening, to small groups, even individuals.

Imagining Doomsday

The idea that life on earth will come to a violent end is ancient and has often been envisioned as the result of some giant conflagration, a flood, a collision with a comet, or some mysterious plague. The god or gods have been held responsible, either out of caprice or annoyance with what humankind had wrought. But the idea of human beings playing god is more recent, and for a long time was the preserve of science fiction writers, who, in the last century or so, have raised the specter of the mad scientist (or mere technician) capable of destroying whole cities, continents, perhaps even the planet.

Jules Verne and H. G. Wells are the best-known early practitioners of this type of fiction. Robur, the mad genius in Wells's *Invisible Man*, saw himself as the master of the world, and while many have read the book or watched one of the several film versions, very few remember that Robur's main purpose was to spread terror, as he himself put it. At about the same time—that is to say, the last decade of the nineteenth century and the first of the twentieth—stories with titles such as "The Last Days of Earth," "The Purple Cloud," "Crack of Doom," and "Lord of the World" were widely read. Critics interpreted their popularity as a symptom of the decline of religious faith, of the displacement of religion by science, or of general moral degeneracy.

This fiction, in which some scientifically inclined madman would deliberately bring about the end of life on earth, became a whole subgenre of literature, not well received critically but widely read and quite influential. No scientist in that age of great scientific achievement came forward to criticize these stories, and some of them, such as the French astronomer Flammarion, even made notable contributions to this literature.

Instead of summarizing a whole field, we will focus on two fairly typical examples. One is "The Enemy of All the World," a short story by Jack London. The hero, Emil Gluck, born in Syracuse, New York, in 1895, had a most unhappy childhood. He studied chemistry at the University of California but was thrown out for using the word *revolution* in a public speech. Even though he was persecuted, maligned, and misunderstood, this forlorn and lonely human being at first made no attempt at retaliation. But after being unlucky in love, failing in business, and being wrongfully arrested for murder, the patience of this almost saintly man snapped and he became a violent nihilist. Utilizing his scientific training, he came up with an invention that made it possible for him to dispose of all his enemies. Another of his inventions provided the money for carrying out his schemes. And so he became a mysterious terror, destroying property, taking countless lives, and causing frightful havoc. He caused a German-American war in which 800,000 people were killed, and from a little launch blew up seven warships. Then he destroyed the Atlantic seaboard from Maine to Florida, which was followed by the destruction of the northern shore of the Mediterranean from Gibraltar to Greece. "There was no defense against this unknown and all-powerful foe," London wrote, until Silas Bannerman, a U.S. secret service agent, arrested him. Gluck was executed on December 4, 1941. Earlier the French government had offered him a billion francs for his invention, which had something to do with powerful electrical discharges. But Gluck, a man of principle, indignantly rejected the offer: "Why sell you what would enable you to enslave and maltreat suffering humanity?"

The story of Emil Gluck, "one of the world's most unfortunate geniuses whose mighty powers were so twisted and warped that he became the most amazing of criminals," was first published in 1907 in a collection titled *Eccentricities of Crime*.

Fifteen years after London's story, a novel in installments appeared in Germany's leading illustrated weekly, *Berliner Illustrirte Zeitung*. Titled *Dr. Mabuse: The Gambler*, the novel proved to be the most popular ever published by this venerable periodical. It sold half a million copies in Germany alone (and there were many translations) and gave rise to a whole Mabuse industry. Millions who never read the book saw the silent film based on the book, produced by Fritz Lang. Seventy-five years later, the name Mabuse still crops up in Germany and to a lesser extent elsewhere in Europe, in rock music, as the title of an alternative-medicine journal, in advertisements for cars, and in books for young readers.

The author, Norbert Jacques, was born in Luxembourg and made a modest name for himself as the author of travelogues to exotic countries. Then he created the Mabuse character, a demonic criminal, a Nietzschean nihilist turned supergangster who believed that "there is no love, only desire, no happiness, only will to power." Mabuse wanted to show the world that he was a giant, a titan, and not bound by morality or religion. The Mabuse books would be of only limited interest to us except for the fact that, as Jacques went on producing sequels to the original work, he came to describe the Mabuse phenomenon more and more in terms of a terrorist group led by a fanatical madman out to dominate the world. Terrorists like Mabuse think of themselves as the vanguard of a regenerated mankind, but only if everyone else alive is destroyed. The salvation of mankind, by their logic, demands millions of corpses. In Jacques's books a chemist named Null, who is a scientific genius and an escapee from a lunatic asylum, discovers the power to realize their aim. The last Mabuse novel, titled *Chemiker Null*, deals with the terrorists out to decimate mankind. It was published in installments in a Swiss daily newspaper (*Neue Zuercher Zeitung*), but there was not sufficient interest at the time for publishing it as a book.

Jacques was never to repeat the success of the first Mabuse book. His character vanished from later novels, largely because the Mabuse phenomenon had been declared undesirable in Nazi Germany. Then Dr. Mabuse reappeared after the Second World War on the movie screen. No fewer than eight films with him as the chief villain were produced in the 1950s and 1960s; however, they were grade-B horror movies and did not deal with the theme of Nietzschean-scale terrorism.

Throughout history world destruction has usually been imagined as taking the form of, say, an all-consuming fire or global inundation. After the invention of dynamite by Alfred Nobel, these concerns were replaced by the concept of powerful explosives. With the progress in natural science around the last turn of the century, the search for such weapons proceeded in various directions and served as inspiration for doomsday writers. H. G. Wells was among the first to envisage nuclear war and biological warfare, in *War of the Worlds* (1898), a subject later taken up by Harold Nicolson (*Public Faces*, 1932) and others. Jules Verne's ultimate weapon was an unspecified combination of flying machines and powerful explosives. In one of his novels, *The Begum's Fortune*, a malevolent German scientist builds a shell filled with enough gas to kill the inhabitants of Franceville, a fictional French city with a population of 250,000. In the early works of Wells and some French novels of the period (notably Robida's *La Guerre aux Vingtième Siecle*), bacteriological and chemical warfare make an appearance; in Well's case, interplanetary warfare is seen. Death rays (called Z rays, K rays, or other catchy names) also appeared before the First World War. They are imagined as bringing down the German zeppelins, at the time one of the most fearsome forms of modern warcraft. In the novels of Aleksei Tolstoi, such rays are used to destroy the moon, among other targets, not because the moon is thought to be of great strategic importance but because its destruction would occasion a great panic from which capitalist speculators would benefit.

Poison gas as a means of mass destruction had been described before 1914, but in World War I it was actually used. Then the effects of a coming gas war became a major topic in countless books and stories in many languages. At that time more rays—heat rays, disintegrator rays, cosmic rays, infrasound rays, and other deadly rays—emanated from the fertile imaginations of science fiction writers. Just before World War I, the character of Dr. Fu Manchu was created. The prototype of the evil scientist bent on world domination, he successfully experimented with deadly and exotic poisons rather than with the commonplace microbes, such as bubonic plague, introduced by earlier writers.

Planetary horror featuring alien invasion and interplanetary warfare were grist for the science fiction writer's mill even before the Second World War. Edmond Hamilton's "Crashing Suns" appeared in 1928, and Jack Williamson's *Space Patrol* novels about a doomsday device called "AKKA" a few years later. In these books, whole galaxies disappear at the press of a button. (Hamilton was given the affectionate nickname "World Wrecker" and "World Destroyer" for his imagined catastrophes.) In

H. G. Wells's *War of the Worlds*, Martians use a destructive ray of sorts. Alfred Noyes's 1940 novel *The Last Man* features the invention of a heart-stopping ray. Not surprisingly, when the laser beam was invented in 1960, it inspired many new fictional death rays.

Biological terrorism has become quite commonplace in today's horror-science fiction. A few examples are Richard Preston's *Hot Zone* (1994) and *The Cobra Event* (1998). In the first novel, the villain is a mad scientist named Archimedes who uses the Ebola virus in attempts to destroy New York, London, Calcutta, and eventually the whole world. In *The Cobra Event*, the madman works for a small New Jersey biotech company and his methods are both more complicated and more nefarious.

Science fiction writers have been more creative with regard to technology than with the psychology of their heroes and villains. Quite frequently, weapons are used to aid a good cause, such as defending earth against the invasion of evil aliens from other planets. But the mad scientist is typically represented as a villain, simply because of his wish to dominate the world or because of his intrinsic evil. Interestingly, religious belief, the fanaticism of sects that believe in impending doom, seldom, if ever, plays a role. Sometimes, a quasiplausible justification for the desire to dominate the world is proposed, such as a plan to end further destructive world wars. Other times, horrific destruction is seen as a just punishment to a generation who has sinned, deteriorated morally, or succumbed to a blind belief in uncontrolled scientific progress. The question of whether or not life will continue after a general holocaust is occasionally raised. Some writers conjecture that even if life on the face of the earth ceased to exist, it might still continue in the oceans or elsewhere in the cosmos as the result of the migration of survivors to another galaxy.

In view of the great cost of producing weapons of mass destruction, one would think that science fiction writers would imagine these endeavors as being undertaken only by governments with unlimited resources at their disposal. But this has not been the case. In the fictions, the deadly inventions are always made by individuals or small groups of people rather than states. This probably has had more to do with the needs of the literary genre and the market for the stories. Whatever the reason, criminals and small terrorist groups figure far more often than geopolitics in this branch of prophetic literature.

On March 20, 1995, life imitated art. That morning a Japanese cult called Aum Shinri Kyo (Supreme Truth) placed containers of sarin poison gas on five trains of the Tokyo underground network that converged in the Kasumigaseki station, where many government offices are situated. The attack resulted in 12 dead, 5,500 injured, and, of course, a great deal of chaos.

[. . .]

Although hardly a doomsday event, Aum's attack gave the world a sense of the magnitude of destruction a few lunatics or terrorists can inflict on the public and the ease with which it can be caused.

A BRIEF HISTORY OF CHEMICAL WARFARE

Weapons technology during the twentieth century has caught up with the imaginations of earlier science fiction writers and in some respects exceeded them. The idea of using poison gas against one's enemies occurred first to the Fenians in the 1870s, who intended to spray it in the House of Commons in London. There seem to have been similar plans during the Boer War and the Japanese war with the Russians in 1905, but these did not go beyond an amateurish experimental stage.

Gas was first used on a massive scale in 1915 by the German High Command in the battle of Ypres. The substance used, chlorine gas, came as a total surprise to the Allies. The result was five thousand Allied dead, more injured, and a German breakthrough of four miles. There were two more German gas attacks within the next few days, but they led to no decisive victory. Although the concentration of gas was high and the clouds carried the poisonous substances miles away, only a small sector of the front line was affected, reducing the effectiveness of the gas. The German command, furthermore, failed to follow up the initial panic with a determined advance. Whether it would have been possible to advance into the territory that had been infected with poison gas is not known.

Seen in retrospect, this gas warfare was a failure at the time; the intention had been to put an end to the indecisiveness of trench warfare, and this was not achieved. The first poison-gas attack by the Allies came in Loos, Belgium, five months later. The immediate effects were horrible, as the Germans were as unprepared there as the Allies had been at Ypres. But again there was no decisive breakthrough. Gas subsequently played a considerable role in the battle of Fey-en-Haye, and gas artillery shells were fired in the battle for Verdun in 1916 and in the Battles of the Somme.

In the meantime, the use of phosgene and mixtures of phosgene and chlorine had been introduced into the war; mustard gas, which worked more slowly but produced equally deadly effects, was also used. The clouds of gas could penetrate up to twelve miles behind the front line. But while the psychological impact was enormous, poison gas had no decisive effect in any major battle, even though it is believed to have killed or injured hundreds of thousands of soldiers and civilians. The exact number of gas casualties is not known and will never be; estimates vary between 500,000 and 1.2 million, the lower figure being the more likely. The effects of poison gas were perhaps most devastating when it was used by the Germans against the Russians, east of Warsaw, in 1915. The Russians were unprepared and reportedly lost some 25,000 soldiers in the first attack. But the total number of Russian civilians killed and incapacitated is not known. Some deaths certainly occurred in the factories where gas was produced or where shells were filled with poison gas. Furthermore, civilians were killed and injured in villages and towns near the front line. The great shock of gas warfare is seen in many World War I memoirs. The painful, slow death of a poison-gas victim was never more starkly described than in Roger Martin du Gard's novel *Antoine Thibault*.

In the end, some twenty-five poison gases were used in the First World War. Some, like the chlorine and phosgene gases, were of use only against unprotected troops. The blistering gases, like mustard gas, were somewhat more effective, and had the war continued longer, the British would have used yet another family of gases consisting of arsenic compounds.

The idea that gases might be used in a coming war had occurred to politicians at the Hague peace conference of 1907, and the signatories of the protocols had agreed not to use projectiles diffusing asphyxiating and harmful gases, including tear gas. Poison gas was again banned in the Geneva protocols of 1925, which were signed mainly by the European powers; it was not specified in these documents what sanctions could be taken against the transgressors. The possibility that gas might be released from cylinders on the ground apparently had not occurred to them and was not banned. These protocols notwithstanding, the general public and many military writers took it for granted that poison gas would be used after all, and there was a huge literature describing its horrors. Such literature was not unwarranted. Poison gas was applied by the Italians in Ethiopia in the thirties; according to some estimates, almost one-third of the casualties of the Ethiopians following the Italian invasion were due to poison gas.

All powers prepared themselves for this eventuality to at least some degree. The Germans built gas-producing laboratories in the Soviet Union in accordance with a secret treaty with Moscow. Eventually, the Soviet Union made a great effort to have vaster quantities of poison gas at its disposal than any other power.

Why, then, were poison gases not used in the Second World War? It was certainly not a matter of humanitarian scruples. On a number of occasions the two sides seem to have been close to deploying these weapons. For the Germans, the use of gas would have been more a hindrance than an advantage in the early phase of the war, when their units were advancing rapidly. After 1942 the Allies had air superiority, and if the Germans had used gas they would have been more exposed to retaliation than their enemies. Another important consideration was the German army's use of horses, which could not be effectively protected in a gas attack. There were an insufficient number of horse gas masks, and a gas attack would have effectively immobilized the German artillery. What is more, the German civilian population was quite unprepared for gas attacks. A victim of a gas attack in World War I, Hitler himself had an aversion to the use of gas on the field of battle, though he did consider using gas when the tide

of war turned against him. The temptation for the Germans was all the greater because they had gained an important advantage over the Allies in their manufacture of nerve gases, especially tabun and sarin, in the late 1930s. By 1944 the Germans had a huge arsenal of nerve-gas bombs. Several times after Stalingrad, when the Allied troops landed in Normandy, the use of the new gases was considered; Hitler's decision against it was based on the assumption that the Allies were bound to have these gases too, as his experts had told him. These substances had been known about for decades; only the extent of their lethal properties was not known. But the Allies did not have tabun and sarin. When they made their landings on the beaches of France they did not even carry gas masks.

The full extent of German superiority in chemical weaponry became known only after the war. The secret had been kept from the Allies for almost eight years; the Allies were aware of German experiments in nuclear science but were in the dark with regard to tabun and sarin. However, the use of the nerve gases would not have resulted in a German victory; it would probably have led to the use of nuclear bombs against Germany rather than Japan. But the war might have lasted a bit longer. In the end poison gases were used by the German leadership only against civilians, in the extermination camps of Eastern Europe—mainly against Jewish civilians—and also, to a lesser degree, against Soviet prisoners of war and others.

Since World War II, poison gas has been used mainly in the Middle East, specifically by Iraq against Iran. Mustard gas was employed in August 1983 at Haj Umran, and a year later, at Al Basra, when the Iraqis were on the defensive in a war they had provoked, they again used nerve gases. In 1985 and 1986, at Um Rashrash, Hawiza marsh, and elsewhere, thousands of Iranian soldiers were reportedly killed as the result of gas attacks. Saddam Hussein used poison gas against the Kurds at Panjwin and in March 1987 at Halabjah. In the 1980s, tabun was Saddam Hussein's weapon of choice. Gas was also reported to have been used by Nasser's Egypt during its military expedition in Yemen and possibly on a few other occasions.

The poisons originally used were chlorine and mustard gases, which affect the eyes, the upper and lower respiratory tract, and the skin. Although these gases are highly toxic, extremely painful, and often deadly, their effect was not immediate, whereas the substances discovered after World War I, such as sarin, GB, and VX, can cause instantaneous death. (The G family of gases enters the human organism by way of the respiratory tract; the V family penetrates through the skin.) The toxicity of the nerve gases manufactured during and after World War II was infinitely greater than that of their predecessors.

CHEMICAL WEAPONRY TODAY

In contrast to biological warfare, chemical warfare has already been waged on a massive scale. If there are in theory many thousands of biological agents that terrorists could use, there are probably even more poisonous chemical substances. Most chemical agents are not gases but liquids dispensed in droplets. They can be divided according to their chemical composition. Among the old, "classic" poisons, which appeared in the earliest detective novels, are Prussic acid, arsenic, and strychnine. Choking agents were used in World War I, including chlorine and phosgene, which cause pulmonary edema. The blistering agents used in that war were mustard gas, lewisite, and others that cause chemical burns and destroy lung tissue. Hydrogen cyanide and cyanogen chloride attack the respiratory system and result rapidly in coma and death. The nerve gases tabun, sarin, soman, and VX affect the neuromuscular system. They block the enzyme cholinesterase, causing paralysis of the neuromuscular system and thus death. Tabun and sarin are organophosphates, discovered in Germany as a by-product of the search for new insecticides. Even more poisonous are the gases of the V (VX) series that penetrate the skin as well as the respiratory tract and bring about respiratory failure and death within a very short time. Also worth mentioning are LSD and other hallucinogenic agents, although they are not among the most likely agents to be used by terrorists at present.

Most of these chemical substances have a legitimate use. Arsenic and strychnine in small doses were once used for medical purposes.

Eserin, one of the first of the nerve gases, was originally used as a drug against glaucoma. Some of the substances are insecticides, others are used in the pharmaceutical industry, and still others are compounds employed as cleaning agents, herbicides, or rodenticides. Therefore, many are available commercially. They can be stolen not only from military installations but from civilian laboratories; one writer has noted that truckloads of the insecticide parathion are on the roads every day. The quantities stored by both the armed forces and industry are so large that sizable amounts could easily go unaccounted for.

If terrorists want, they can manufacture potent chemical poisons from such substances as isopropyl alcohol, which is readily available, or from various pesticides and herbicides. Experts agree that the technical knowledge and experience needed to produce a chemical weapon is less than that required for manufacturing a biological weapon, probably on the level of a moderately conscientious graduate student. Some substances and compounds are, of course, more difficult to produce than others, but there is no reason to assume that a terrorist will choose the most complicated rather than the least sophisticated weapon. Experts also agree that virtually all the materials and equipment can be bought commercially, but there is no unanimity as to whether one chemist would be sufficient for an operation of this kind.

It is generally assumed that the real difficulty in waging chemical warfare is not the manufacture or acquisition of the poison but its dissemination. This refers to both volatile and nonvolatile agents. Vapors are affected by the direction of the wind as well as the temperature of the air. Nerve gases quickly hydrolize in water and are therefore not suitable for poisoning water reservoirs. Dispersal by means of an aerosol always involves a high loss of toxicity. While in laboratory conditions a few milligrams might be sufficient to kill several thousand human beings, experts believe that tons of poison would be needed in the open air or in water because there are always biological activities that diminish the toxicity of the agent. Thus, it was not an accident that the Japanese terrorists chose an enclosed space and preferred sarin, which is less volatile, to more toxic agents.

There are other ways of disseminating chemicals, such as by firing a mortar or artillery shell (an unlikely means to be chosen by a terrorist group) or crashing a van or a truck loaded with chemical substances against a building. But all of these involve many uncertainties, and though they might succeed in the case of a single building or enclosed space, it would become progressively more difficult to repeat the act in the future because of far greater police and public awareness.

Past threats or actual attempts to use chemical weapons have been made in several countries: by terrorists of the extreme right, by animal-liberation militants, by Tamil separatists on several occasions, by Palestinian terrorists, by the Alphabet bomber, by Minutemen, by Russian (or rather, ex-Soviet) extortionists, and by an ex-Stasi agent. Other incidents have been reported in Italy, the Philippines, Chile, Iraq, Tadzhikistan, Turkey, the United Kingdom, and at least a dozen other countries. A closer examination of these attempts reveals no evidence that the markers of the threats had, in fact, amounts of chemical agents sufficient to carry them out, and that most of the attempts themselves were amateurish. However, the fear of poison is great and the panic caused by an attack of this kind is bound to be enormous. It might cause more psychological than physical havoc. Even the authors of books on gas warfare in the 1930s warned that an enemy would launch such an attack mainly because of its devastating psychological impact.

A Brief History of
Biological Warfare

The history of biological warfare goes back much further than the use of poison gases, but the biological agents that threaten us today are of recent invention. The great plague of the fourteenth century, which is said to have killed about one-third of the population of Europe, was allegedly spread by the Tartars besieging the fortress of Caffa in the Crimea. The Tartars catapulted plague-infected corpses into the fortress; according to reports, ships from Genoa carried the disease to northern Italy and the rest of Europe.

Another oft-cited example of early biological warfare occurred during the Indian wars in North America in the 1760s. It seems certain that local British commanders planned to give the Indians, as a peace offering, blankets from military hospitals that had been infected by smallpox. A smallpox epidemic did break out among the Indians of Pennsylvania, but it is not certain whether the blankets played any role in its spread.

During the First World War, Germans were charged with trying to spread cholera bacilli in Italy, the plague in St. Petersburg, and anthrax in Mesopotamia and Rumania, intending to kill cattle and horses. There were unconfirmed reports about all kinds of exotic biological agents being transmitted to other countries by such unlikely means as the ink containers of fountain pens. In Silver Spring, a Washington, D.C., suburb, a small German laboratory headed by one Dr. Anton Dilger produced a liter of anthrax and glanders (*Pseudomonas gladei*) intended to infect horses and mules that were to be shipped from Baltimore to the western front in Europe. The original seed culture had allegedly been supplied from Berlin. While these early attempts to engage in biological warfare were unsuccessful, research and stockpiling continued after the end of the First World War.

All major nations engaged in these preparations, but only the Japanese actually carried out biological warfare, dropping plague-infested fleas and grain over Chinese cities after the invasion of 1937. In the mid-1930s, a special biological-warfare unit called 731 was established under a General Ishi in Manchuria. Many biological agents were produced in the laboratories of this unit, including plague, smallpox, typhus, and gas gangrene. In tests on Chinese prisoners of war and civilians, about ten thousand people were killed. Toward the end of the war the production of these agents was stepped up; hundreds of millions of plague-infested fleas were bred and scheduled to be dropped over American airfields. In the end the order to use biological weapons against the Americans was not given, in part because an American submarine sunk the ship carrying key members of unit 731 in the Pacific. While the biological agents used by the Japanese were among the most toxic known, the means of spreading them were primitive; aerosols did not yet exist.

Whether and where biological agents were used after World War II is a matter of some dispute, but there is no doubt that all major powers and some smaller countries engaged in research and built up their stockpiles. Iraq under Saddam Hussein has been particularly active in this respect. The installations established in Iraq were far bigger and more advanced than outsiders had assumed. They had been built up within a short period, about five years, with the help of various European firms, and it proved easy to hide them. Even UNSCOM, the United Nations investigation committee that tried to locate them after Iraq's defeat in 1991, discovered only a small part. Had it not been for the defection in August 1995 of Husain Kamal, Saddam Hussein's son-in-law, who brought with him many documents, the number of laboratories found would have been only a tiny percentage of the total. If the Iraqi dictator eventually decided not to use these weapons, the reason seems to have been that retaliation would be swift and devastating.

Iraq, however, was not the only country in the Middle East to build up such weapons. Iran, Syria, and, above all, Libya were reported to have followed Baghdad's example. Altogether up to fifteen countries in the Middle East and Asia developed these weapons, and the number of countries that had missiles with which to deliver them was even larger. Libya attracted the most attention, owing to the erratic behavior of Colonel Khadafi. With the help of German, Swiss, and other biological firms, large underground laboratories were built at Tarhuna and Rabta. These could be transformed within less than twenty-four hours from weapons factories into innocuous-looking pharmaceutical laboratories. Some foreign delegations were invited to inspect them, and a few even believed the official version put out by Tripoli. But parliamentary delegations do not normally include experts carrying detection equipment.

The Middle East countries are hardly alone in their production of these weapons. According to the U.S. State Department, "yellow rain," an agent difficult to classify but belonging to the general family of the mycotoxins, was applied in Laos, Kampuchea, and Afghanistan by Communist forces. Some five hundred instances of its use were documented and the number of

fatalities was alleged to be in the thousands, but there have been doubts expressed at the time by some American scientists with regard to the use of this specific agent.

There was no doubt, however, about assassination attempts carried out by the KGB using biological agents. In the 1970s, sophisticated agents called ricin were employed against two Bulgarian émigrés, Georgi Markov in London and Vladimir Kostov in Paris. Markov was stabbed with the tip of an umbrella and killed. In Kostov's case, the pellet did not penetrate the skin and he lived to tell the story. During the *glasnost* period there was access to some KGB sources, and more details became known about its laboratories; the poisons that had been developed there had been employed not only against foreign enemies but also against Soviet citizens.

Accidents occurred in the germ-warfare installations, the most famous of which was the anthrax epidemic at Sverdlovsk, in the Urals, in April 1979. The details were kept secret by the Soviets, which was not difficult because Sverdlovsk was a city closed to foreigners. According to the assessment by American intelligence, a huge airborne (aerosol) release of anthrax spores used for bacteriological warfare resulted in many fatalities. But according to the initial Soviet version, some careless workers had thrown anthrax-infected meat on garbage heaps, causing the outbreak. The Soviet version seemed plausible, but because of the secrecy surrounding it—for five years the Russians had denied the accident altogether—the official version was not widely believed, even inside the Soviet Union. Under *glasnost* it became known that the initial Western suspicions were correct and that, furthermore, there had been several other minor such accidents that had not become known at all.

THE FUTURE OF GERM WARFARE

For decades interest in biological warfare has grown because it is thought to be the most cost-effective method to kill or incapacitate people. In war many shells and bullets are expended, often without killing or disabling a single human being. Even during World War I gas was far more efficient than bullets, and today the botulinum toxin is a thousand times more toxic than sarin, one of the most deadly of the early nerve gases. It is cheaper to produce, and little sophisticated knowledge is needed to manufacture it. Colin Powell, former U.S. Chief of Staff, said in 1993, "The one that frightens me to death, perhaps even more so than tactical nuclear weapons, and the one we have the least capability against, is biological weapons." Other political and military leaders have expressed similar fears in recent years.

Americans, British, Russians, and Japanese have been working since the late 1930s on biological arms, yet they remain one of the least predictable of all weapons. They could continue to be unpredictable or they could become one of the most deadly weapons of all. Epidemics throughout history in Europe, Asia, and the Americas have killed many more people than wars, and diseases of a new kind might become the weapon of choice of a new genus of terrorists.

Scientists and science fiction writers have presented a great many scenarios of biological warfare, all of them frightening. Consider these: According to a study published in 1972, an anthrax spore aerosol attack on New York could result in 600,000 deaths. According to a 1980 study, spreading one ounce of anthrax spores, which are far more deadly than the botulinum toxin, in a domed stadium could infect 60,000 to 80,000 people within an hour. Another scenario concerns threats to major water reservoirs. Research shows that only a pound or two of *Salmonella typhi* or botulinum toxin would be required to effect the same horrid result as ten tons of potassium cyanide. Anthrax is also frequently mentioned as a contaminant. Both anthrax and botulinum cause respiratory failure as well as external and internal bleeding within one to three days, and are usually fatal.

Other agents reportedly explored for military purposes are *Yersinia pestis*, which causes the bubonic plague, and tropical diseases such as Ebola, a highly contagious virus that leads within two or three days to bleeding, convulsions, and death. In principle, many agents of human and animal disease could be possible weapons. The list of potential agents is long, ranging from smallpox and psittacosis (parrot fever) to old diseases such as tuberculosis and pneumococci, which were once believed conquered but new

strains of which have developed that are resistant to antibiotics and immunization. New diseases with possible appeal to terrorists have recently appeared, such as Lassa fever, which is spread by wild rodents in West Africa, Legionellosis (Legionnaire's disease), and fatal toxic septicemia (flesh-eating bacteria).

Nor can diseases affecting animals be excluded: Ebola fever appeared first as a disease affecting apes, and Creutzfeldt-Jakob disease, or mad cow disease, first appeared in cattle. The fact that a disease is seldom, if ever, fatal does not necessarily mean that terrorists in search of biological-warfare agents won't use it. Severe forms of conjunctivitis, to choose but one example, may effectively disable its victims. Whereas the military would hardly be interested in the application of a disease such as leprosy or AIDS because the incubation period is measured in years rather than months, this consideration may not be relevant to a small group of fanatics. Even diseases for which there are treatments might be used by those interested primarily in causing a panic rather than a pandemic.

Biological arms have a few well-known advantages over other weapons. They are easy to produce, and difficult to detect, once created. They are cheap and likely to cause not only human fatalities but economic damage by ruining crops. And they are as likely to cause as much panic as a gas attack. How easy is it to acquire a biological-weapons capability? On this issue expert opinions diverge. Some experts have maintained that biological agents can be produced in a garage, a toolroom, or a kitchen. The ease of making a biological weapon can be compared to that of brewing beer. According to one author, preparing the growth medium for bacteria is not more complicated than preparing Jell-O. Experts believe an amateur or a second- or third-year biology student could easily obtain the knowledge needed to create lethal weapons. Others, however, believe that those who want to engage in even the most primitive level of biological warfare must have the equivalent of a graduate science degree, and others believe even greater education is necessary. An individual would need knowledge and experience not only in microbiology and aerosol physics but three or four other fields as well, so it is more likely that a small group of experts would be needed. One expert believes that at least five specialists, including a pathologist and a pharmacologist, are needed. These experts also tend to dismiss the "kitchen table" argument and believe that access to a bacteriological laboratory is crucial. There are similar differences in estimates concerning the cost of such a venture, ranging from a few thousand to a few million dollars.

While a small crew working with primitive tools might produce bacteria of one form or another, dissemination of the weapon could present insurmountable obstacles. Unlike a scientist, the terrorist need not engage in experimental animal tests to check the toxicity of his agents. On the other hand, it is difficult to imagine from a practical point of view how best to utilize a weapon that has not been tested.

Which are the most likely biological agents to be used in the future? Various lists have been published over the years, including ones identifying agents combining the greatest toxicity with ease of production (or acquisition), cultivation, hardiness, immunity to detection and counter-measures, and rapidity of effect. According to estimates published in 1997 in the *Journal of the American Medical Association*, Rift Valley fever and tick-borne encephalitis, assuming a downwind reach of one kilometer, could cause between 400 and 9,500 fatalities and incapacitate approximately 35,000 people. Typhus and brucellosis, with a downwind reach of 5-10 kilometers, could kill up to 19,000 people and affect 85,000 to 125,000 more. Most deadly are tularemia and anthrax, which, with a downwind reach of about 20 kilometers, might kill 30,000 to 95,000 and incapacitate 125,000.

Experts believe that bacterial rather than viral agents are more likely to be chosen because viruses are difficult to cultivate and more perishable. In a list by Berkowitz published in 1972, eight bacterial agents are most likely to appeal: anthrax, brucellosis, coccidioidomycosis, cryptococcosis, pneumonic plague, psittacosis, Rocky Mountain spotted fever, and tularemia. According to Berkowitz, plague and psittacosis can cause epidemics, and anthrax, plague, and Rocky Mountain spotted fever are highly lethal. Some of the bacilli are common, others less so, but all are highly infectious.

In a list compiled by Wayman Mullins published in 1992, *escherichia coli*, hemophilus influenzae, malaria, cholera, *Yersina pesti*, typhoid, bubonic plague, cobra venom, and shellfish toxin are also potential candidates for use in biological warfare. Coccidioidomycosis, Rocky Mountain spotted fever, and pneumonic plague were dropped from this list, possibly because these diseases are now treatable. Rocky Mountain spotted fever is seldom fatal and can be controlled by tetracycline. For the pneumonic plague, streptomycin or gentamycin are both quite effective if used early. Tetracycline and chloramphenicol are also effective against typhoid fever. There are cures for illness caused by most of the other epidemic agents if treatment is given early.

The U.S. Congress Office of Technology Assessment lists eight biological agents most likely to be used as weapons: anthrax, tularemia, *Yersina pestis, Shigella flexneri* (which causes a bacillary dysentery), another shigella, various salmonella species, botulinum, and staphylococcus enterotoxin B. This list seems to be based on the assumption that terrorists would decide to contaminate drinking water and food supplies. Other authors have mentioned ricin as a likely terrorist agent of choice. Ricin, which can be extracted from the castor bean, is highly toxic, but far less so than botulinal toxin, and probably more difficult to spread. It has, however, been successfully used in the assassination of individuals.

Even smallpox, a highly infectious and lethal disease that has been extinct for more than twenty years, might be used for offensive military or terrorist purposes, since considerable stockpiles of smallpox vaccine exist.

The most recent and authoritative list of possible biological agents is that published in the *Journal of the American Medical Association* in 1997. This list was based on biological agents that have already been made into weapons, not merely on theoretical considerations. Anthrax and botulinum figure prominently in this list; both were weaponized by Iraq and presumably by other countries. Brucellosis, plague, Q fever, tularemia, smallpox, viral encephalitis, viral hemorrhagic fever (which includes a whole group of tropical diseases, such as Lassa fever), and staphylococcal enterotoxin B are also on this list. Anthrax is the only agent that appears on every list; there are differences of opinion about the others.[1]

To prepare a biological weapon, one needs a seed culture that can be obtained from the natural environment. This is the most secure way, but also the one that demands the most skill. The agent, be it anthrax, botulism, or one of the others, has to be identified, isolated, and cultivated, processes that require considerable knowledge and experience. There are, however, other ways to obtain seed cultures. They can be stolen from laboratories, bought on the black market, gained under false pretenses, or even commissioned by mail order. Civilian laboratories are not well guarded, nor are military installations impregnable. Commercial firms offer specimen cultures for a few dollars, and they rarely check whether those placing an order are acquiring it for a legitimate use.[2] Lastly, those eager to engage in biological terrorism could obtain seed cultures from states supporting terrorist groups.

There has not yet been a single successful biological-weapons attack by terrorists. Most have been undertaken by blackmailers or people with a grudge rather than political terrorists or religious fanatics. However, there is evidence that terrorist groups of all stripes have shown interest in this new form of warfare. A Russian microbiologist, Viktor Pasechnik, who defected to the West at a scientific congress in London in 1989, reported that Russia, in contravention of the 1972 Biological Convention, had continued to engage in such research, including work on a biologically engineered dry form of super-plague. The Russians had also discussed providing terrorist groups with biological-warfare agents. According to official Soviet spokesmen, biological-warfare work continued up to 1992, but after the defection of Pasechnik and Ken Alibek, the latter a highly placed Russian official in the biological-weapons program, there were strong Western protests, which apparently led to a sizable reduction in the production of biological weapons, though probably not its cessation.

In the 1990s the Russians have developed new and very dangerous strains of biological agents (including a new form of anthrax and one of the Marburg virus). It has also become apparent that the United States, having stuck to the treaty banning these weapons, does not know how to cope with the agents. It is fairly certain that some of the scientists who participated in this Russian program and still eager to make use of their know-how have found their way to countries in the Middle East and Asia.

Threats to use biological-warfare agents have been reported from the Arab world, the Baader Meinhof gang in Germany, British Columbia, Queensland (Australia), Great Britain, and the United States, but in no case has it been proven that those threatening attacks had such agents in their possession. Media reports that terrorists were trying to obtain biological agents and were training specialists in this field have also come from the United States, Canada, Germany, the Arab world, and other countries. Several of these reports concerned a Rockville, Maryland, laboratory where telephone orders for botulinal toxin were received. Some of the reports were denied by the authorities; others were not.

In the 1980s, in a safe house of the Red Army faction in Paris, quantities of botulinal toxin were found, and in another safe house in Germany were found considerable quantities of organophosphorous compounds from which nerve gases are made. Mustard gas was stolen from a U.S. installation in Stuttgart, Germany, apparently by Baader Meinhof followers, and earlier there was an attempt by the Weather Underground to steal biological agents from a U.S. Army laboratory in Fort Derrick, Maryland.

In more than a few cases, lone individuals have posed a threat. In 1995, a man was arrested in Little Rock, Arkansas, charged with trying to bring 130 grams of ricin into Canada. He also carried $89,000 in cash, four guns, and 20,000 rounds of ammunition. According to his lawyer, the individual in question needed the ricin to kill coyotes threatening his chickens. The prosecutor commented that this was tantamount to claiming that a thermonuclear device was needed to protect one's home against burglary. There have been dozens of similar cases in which toxins were acquired and arrests made, and it stands to reason that there have been others which never came to light. The same is probably true of the purchase or theft of seed cultures. Among those who have been apprehended and arrested are extreme rightists who possessed ricin.

There was a successful small-scale attack in Oregon, where members of a religious cult (former members of Bhagwan Shree Rajneesh's group) contaminated salad bars with *Salmonella typhi*, poisoning some 750 people. Ma Anand Sheela, one of the principal aides of Rajneesh, was arrested on charges of attempted murder and assault.

The attractions of biological weapons are obvious: easy access, low cost, toxicity, and the panic they can cause. But there are drawbacks of various kinds that explain why almost no successful attacks have occurred. While explosive or nuclear devices or even chemical agents, however horrific, affect a definite space, biological agents are unpredictable: they can easily get out of control, backfire, or have no effect at all. They constitute a high risk to the attackers, although the same, or course, is true of chemical weapons. This consideration may not dissuade people willing to sacrifice their own lives, but the possibility that the attacker may kill himself before being able to launch an attack may make him hesitate to carry it out.

Biological agents, with some notable exceptions, are affected by changes in heat or cold, and, like chemical agents, by changes in the direction of the wind. They have a limited life span, and their means of delivery are usually complicated. The process of contaminating water reservoirs or foodstuffs involves serious technical problems. Even if an agent survives the various purification systems in water reservoirs, boiling the water would destroy most germs. Dispersing the agent as a vapor or via an aerosol system within a closed space—for instance, through the air-conditioning system of a big building or in a subway—would appear to offer better chances of success, but it is by no means foolproof.

There are well-known defenses against biological weapons, ranging from immunization, to gas masks and other protective clothing, to decontamination processes. Antibiotics are effective against many bacteria if applied soon after infection; and there are also various antifungal medicines. Although not much progress has been made so far in the field of early detection, research in this area is under way. At the same time, researchers may be creating new strains of genetically engineered germs that are able to resist drug therapy. According to Dr. Joshua Lederberg, a Nobel prize-winning scientist, at the present time, there is no technical defense against biological weapons, only an ethical solution. But as Lederberg asked, Would an ethical solution deter a sociopath?

There are also political considerations that argue against the use of biological weapons. Weapons of mass destruction will not appeal to terrorists pursuing clear political aims, especially if friends might be among the victims. A biological weapon launched by terrorists in Northern Ireland would affect Catholics as well as Protestants; in India, it would affect Hindus as well as Muslims; in Israel, Arabs as well as Jews; in Spain, Basques as well as Spaniards. Ecoterrorists cannot be sure that a certain agent will wipe out only human beings, leaving animals and plants unaffected. But the most obvious political reason biological terrorism is risky is that it could produce an enormous backlash against those who perpetrated the attack. Another consideration is psychological in character: Most terrorists need the demonstration effect—that is, showy attacks producing a great deal of noise. A biological campaign would be silent.

Only the most extreme and least rational terrorist groups, or those motivated not by distinct political aims but by apocalyptic visions or by some pan-destructionist belief, are likely to employ weapons of this kind. This may reduce the risk that biological weapons will be used, but it does not rule it out.

THE NUCLEAR THREAT

The great fear of the post-Second World War years was of nuclear weapons. After the detonation of nuclear bombs over Hiroshima and Nagasaki, people were understandably anxious about what would happen if weapons somehow found their way into the hands of terrorists.

But the fear was not limited to the use of weapons like those employed at the end of World War II. A 1996 study called "Proliferation: Threat and Response," prepared by the Office of the American Secretary of Defense, said: "Mixed isotope plutonium (reactor-grade material) can be used in nuclear weapons; such a device would be less efficient and might have a less predictable yield. A weapon using non-weapon grade plutonium was successfully detonated in the 1960 test. Another alternative would be a radiological weapon that employed conventional explosives, or other means to scatter radioactive material. Such a weapon would not produce a nuclear yield; however, it could spread contamination. While such weapons would have less military significance than devices that result in nuclear detonations, radiological weapons have enormous potential for intimidation. Targeting a nuclear reactor in an antagonist's territory to produce an accident releasing nuclear material would be another option."

Fears were further fueled by accidents or near accidents at nuclear reactors, culminating with the meltdown at Chernobyl, and by the emergence of a black market in nuclear materials. There is good cause to fear because proliferation continues, and successful work is being done on nuclear devices in many states, some of which either openly or surreptitiously support terrorist groups.

After World War II, the fear of atomic war dominated the public consciousness in America and Western Europe, although it seemed less of a threat to Eastern Europeans and hardly bothered the Third World. As early as 1951, Hollywood produced a film titled *Fire* about life after an atomic holocaust. This was followed by works of fiction such as Nevil Shute's *On the Beach* (1957), Walter Miller's *Canticle for Leibowitz* (1959), Mordecai Roshwald's *Fail Safe* and *Level 7*, and, best remembered, Stanley Kubrick's 1964 film *Dr. Strangelove*.

After 1975, the number of movies and novels on this subject declined, partly because the public's interest had been satiated. But the idea that nuclear weapons could fall into the wrong hands, whether of rogue states or terrorists, continued to preoccupy the experts. The number of specialized papers on the subject and consideration of various nuclear scenarios grew from year to year in Washington and the military academies. Nuclear proliferation, the experts argued, was apparently unstoppable, particularly as popular magazines, and more recently the Internet, began to provide reliable information on how to produce nuclear devices cheaply in a nonlaboratory setting.

This information leads the reader step by step through the process of becoming an atom bomb designer. First, weapons-grade uranium must be acquired. Then one has to decide on the type of bomb to be made, preferably a small plutonium device, for which at least 2.5 kilos of plutonium is needed. Next the bomb's core has to be assembled, which entails putting a sphere of compacted plutonium oxide crystals in the center of a large cube of Semtex (one of the newer, more powerful explosives). The finished product will weigh about a ton and, in the absence of an aircraft or a missile powerful enough to deliver the bomb, will need a van or a truck to get to the target. All these steps, though intricate, do not in theory present insurmountable difficulties for determined amateurs with a little knowledge of nuclear physics and access to the literature available in many public libraries. The greatest challenge to making a bomb has always been the means to obtain uranium or plutonium.

At the same time that knowledge about how to make nuclear weapons has spread, however, the nuclear industry has grown. The number of reactors worldwide has increased, as have strategic and tactical nuclear weapons themselves, which are stored in a variety of places, with uranium and plutonium constantly in transit. Gradually a nuclear black market has come into being. What initially been an American-Soviet issue has over the years became a global problem.

The issue of nuclear proliferation has been discussed ever since the first nuclear bomb was exploded. So far only governments have had the resources to produce nuclear devices and the planes and rockets to deliver them. However, nuclear terrorism has never been ruled out, and, indeed, acts of nuclear sabotage, by radical ecologists albeit on a minor scale, took place during the 1970s and '80s. One of the first occurred in 1973 when a commando from a left-wing Argentinian group, the ERP, entered the construction site of the Atucha atomic power station north of Buenos Aires. In 1976, bombs were thrown at an atomic power plant in Britany, France, but the nuclear reactor was not damaged. During the following years, several attacks against the Lemoniz nuclear power station near Bilbao, Spain, were undertaken by the ETA, the Basque separatist organization. These attacks, and threats of further attacks, were also supported by Spanish radical ecologists who wanted the stations removed. Other attacks were directed against plants near San Sebastian, Pamplona, Tafalla, Beriz, and other sites in northern Spain. They included the murder of the head of the Lemoniz plant and the abduction of its chief engineer. In 1979, a nuclear instruments factory near Santander in northern Spain was attacked. Though there is no evidence that the attack was intended to bring about an explosion or massive contamination (the main victims of such an event would have been the Basques themselves), it is still possible that a major accident might have occurred as a result of mishap or the ignorance of the attackers.

In 1982, the terrorist wing of the African National Congress (ANC) sabotaged two South African nuclear plants, causing substantial damage. Both nuclear reactors were damaged, but since they were not operational at the time there was no emission of radiation. Most other such incidents have involved either individuals of uncertain motivation or have been directed against factories supplying machinery for nuclear installations, as has happened in Canada, Belgium, Holland, and Italy. In 1985, Philippine terrorists blew up the transmission cables of the country's first nuclear plant. It is impossible to speculate on the potential damage had any of these actions generated a major accident, but the accident at Chernobyl offers us clues.

What if a home-produced or stolen nuclear device did explode? A ten-to fifteen-kiloton device strategically placed in a major city would devastate several square miles and could cause 30,000 to 100,000 casualties. A thermonuclear device of greater size could devastate an area twenty times as large and the number of victims would be correspondingly larger. The bombing or sabotage of a civilian reactor might cause relatively little direct damage, provided it is located far from major cities; the ecological damage, on the other hand, would be great and lasting. But in view of the fact that so many reactors now exist around the globe, that many of them are located in or near major cities, and that radiological materials are also stored in laboratories and hospitals, even a small amount of radiological contamination could have major consequences.

For a long time public and specialist concern was focused on the danger of a nuclear device being used by a rogue state or terrorist group. Only more recently has attention been given to possibilities that do not involve fissionable radioactive materials, such as uranium and plutonium, but nonfissionable radioactive materials, such as cesium 137, strontium, and cobalt-60. Weapons using these materials could be exploded by conventional means, and though they would not cause as many fatalities as a nuclear device, they could lead to disruptions in the physical infrastructure of a locality—by contaminating water supplies and other essential facilities.

In a statement in March 1996, John M. Deutch, director of the CIA, mentioned that during the war in Chechnya, Chechen leaders threatened to turn Moscow into a desert by using radioactive waste. To make the threat more credible, the police were directed by anonymous callers to a container in a Moscow park in which cesium 137 was hidden. The quantities discovered were small and could not have done much harm, but it stands to reason that if the Chechen rebels had access to radioactive materials widely used for medical and industrial purposes, other terrorists could obtain greater quantities and use them if they so desired.

Though the danger of a nuclear attack by a hostile country or a terrorist group has figured prominently in the public consciousness and expert commentary, after more than fifty years of books, movies, and war games, the horrible event has not yet come to pass. It is not surprising, then, that there is now a belief among some experts that nuclear terrorism has been an overrated nightmare.

Belittlers of the threat argue as follows: In the past, threats of nuclear terrorism have almost always come from mentally disturbed people and the occasional criminal blackmailer who, it turned out, was bluffing. Real terrorists—that is to say, those pursuing political aims—are more interested in publicity than in a great number of victims. Furthermore, the use of the weapons of superviolence could likely lead to estrangement between the nuclear terrorists and their sympathizers, who might abhor mass murder.

Furthermore, it has been widely assumed that since the design of atomic bombs was more or less in the public domain, it was only a matter of time until the terrorists would build their own. But they have not. Critics point to the fact that even sovereign states with substantial resources at their disposal have failed to construct nuclear devices. After twenty years of trying and the outlay of more than a billion dollars, Iraq had not produced a single nuclear device by the time the Gulf War broke out. This may have been the result of the destruction by the Israelis of their main reactor, which set their program back years. Also, critics doubt that even governments that sponsor terrorism would give nuclear devices to their surrogates, because these sorcerer's apprentices might get out of control and even turn against their patrons. Critics believe it is unlikely that terrorists could steal a nuclear weapon—from the former Soviet Union—for instance, and even if they succeeded, they might not be able to detonate it. These and other reasons have led skeptics to doubt that nuclear terrorism is a real threat at the present time.

During the Cold War, the threat of nuclear war was perhaps exaggerated in Europe, even more so than in America. Now that the Cold War has ended, the tendency to doubt a continuing threat is perfectly understandable. The fact that so many years have passed since Hiroshima and Nagasaki without any nuclear attacks also has influenced thinking on the matter. It seems likely that if there is a nuclear incident in the years to come, it will occur in the context of a regional war or as the result of a Chernobyl-like accident a rather than in the form of a terrorist attack. It is also true, as the critics argue, that sovereign states, however aggressive, will not easily give up control over their nuclear material or nuclear weapons.

But it is by no means certain that this reasoning is foolproof. There could always be an exception or two—for example, governments desperate and reckless enough to accept the risks. Furthermore, global nuclear proliferation has continued, and with the breakdown of the Soviet Union, the large of amounts of nuclear

material that exist there could attract smugglers if the price is right. A large-scale sophisticated nuclear program is expensive, but countries who really wanted the nuclear bomb have acquired it, and others are sure to follow. Iraq in its war against Iran is a good example of a state that, had it possessed nuclear weapons, might well have used them. The situation in the Indian subcontinent is similar. Almost any country, forced to choose between defeat and the use of nuclear weapons, might just opt for the latter.

[. . .]

Chemical agents, biological agents, nuclear devices, and cyberterrorism all have precedents in this century, if not before, and the technology needed to obtain and use each form of weapon has become increasingly available to the fanatic, the disgruntled, and the mentally unbalanced.

NOTES

1. The literature on biological and chemical weapons of mass destruction is huge and highly technical. It is impossible to cover it all in this book. The most important studies are mentioned in the bibliography. I am particularly grateful to Jessica Stern for having shared with me the substance of her book *Risk and Dread: Preempting the New Terrorists* (Cambridge, Massachusetts, 1999) before publication. Her study deals with the technical aspects of the issues involved in far greater detail. An agency of the U.S. Department of Defense published in February 1998 the most authoritative collection of facts and figures so far available about Iraqi weapons of mass destruction, titled "Iraqi Weapons of Mass Destruction Programs." An exhaustive historical survey of the illicit use of biological agents in the twentieth century is provided by Seth Carus in "Bioterrorism and Biocrimes," National Defense University, August 1998.

2. The first such recorded use occurred before World War I. The details emerged in the trial in 1914 of Hans Hopf, who poisoned several family members in Frankfurt, Germany. He had ordered the cultures he needed from a laboratory in Vienna. W. Seth Carus, *Bioterrorism and Biocrimes: The Illicit Use of Biological Agents in the 20th Century* (National Defense University, 1998).

CYBERHATE

A Legal and Historical Analysis of Extremists'
Use of Computer Networks in America

BRIAN LEVIN

American extremists have traditionally cultivated technology to enhance efficiency and promote goals. This article concentrates on how domestic right-wing and other extremists have used computer networks to these ends. Although the concept of a guerrilla insurgency through "leaderless resistance" became a factor in right-wing extremist movements before the Internet's advent, cyberspace hastened its popularity. The Internet has been useful to hatemongers and extremists because it is economical and far reaching, and online expression is significantly protected by the First Amendment. Various court decisions have established that not all communication is protected, in cyberspace or elsewhere. Although the government cannot regulate Internet expression because it offends sensibilities, it can regulate expression that constitutes crimes that fall under various unprotected areas of speech. Courts have convicted hatemongers who use the Internet to communicate threats rather than merely ideas. Private service providers and foreign governments have greater latitude to prohibit offensive and hateful expression that does not constitute a threat.

From his modest home in Washington State, Buford Furrow was one of tens of thousands who went online in the summer of 1999 to access Stormfront.org, the flagship American hate Web site founded in April 1995 by neo-Nazi and ex-Klansman Don Black (Backover, 1999). The site features numerous links as well as essays and graphics promoting the concepts of White supremacy, Jewish conspiracies, government atrocities, Black inferiority, Nazism, and guerrilla warfare tactics. In addition to Stormfront.org and various other racist Web sites, Furrow accessed a macabre site called Gore Gallery, on which explicit photos of brutal murders are posted. He also used the services of a mapping site to chart cross-country route instructions from his home in the Pacific Northwest to the offices of the civil rights group Southern Poverty Law Center in Montgomery, Alabama, where he planned to undertake a murderous terror spree. When Furrow determined that the journey to Alabama was too long a drive, he set his sights on Southern California, where he again located

AUTHOR'S NOTE: Special thanks to my good friends Ken Stern of the American Jewish Committee; Gail Gans, Dr. Mark Pitcavage, Brian Mareus, and Jordan Kessler of the Anti-Defamation League; Joe Roy and Mark Potok of the Southern Poverty Law Center; David Goldman of HateWatch; and Chip Berlet of Political Research Associates and Michael Gennaco for their time, brilliant research, and analysis. They have been invaluable toward this piece, and the world is a better place for each of their efforts to combat hatred and violence.

potential targets on a printout he got from the same mapping Web site.

Furrow's planned Los Angeles terrorist target sites were all Jewish-based cultural and educational entities: the Simon Wiesenthal Center's Museum of Tolerance, the University of Judaism, and the Skirball Cultural Center. With his Internet-produced map in his vehicle, Furrow drove to Los Angeles with a cache of weapons, cash, and extremist literature. After staking out the Wiesenthal Center, Furrow decided that the premises were too well guarded for him to generate enough casualties, and he abandoned his plan for an attack there.

About 2 weeks later, Furrow had driven off a freeway in the San Fernando Valley to refuel when he happened on the North Valley Jewish Community Center. The facility, which was hosting a nondenominational day school for children, became the place for Furrow to undertake his "wake-up call" to Americans to kill Jews. When Furrow entered the building with an assault rifle blazing, he first shot an elderly receptionist and a teenage girl who cared for the young students attending the summer day school. He continued shooting, hitting three children, one as young as 5 years old, before leaving the facility.

Shortly thereafter, Furrow fatally shot a Filipino American postal delivery worker named Joseph Illeto because he worked for the federal government and was not White. Furrow also carjacked a woman's automobile in the course of his immediate flight but did not injure her (C. Witkoff, personal communication, August 14, 2001).

Furrow's case is illustrative of the perplexing legal and social issues presented by the emerging use of the Internet by extremists. Furrow did not commit his atrocities merely because of the Internet. Indeed, Furrow had been entrenched in the hate movement for some time, including a stint in the now defunct Aryan Nations hate group in the mid-1990s. He had a history of mental illness and was under correctional supervision, which was supposed to have prohibited him from possessing weapons at the time of his rampage. Furthermore, masses of Web surfers accessed the same sites without resorting to violence. Still, whether inspirational or instructional, the Internet supplied information that clearly helped fuel the explosion of a ticking human time bomb. For today's violent extremists, the Internet has emerged as a possible solution to the legal, organizational, and logistical issues facing the increasingly embattled world of extremism (C. Witkoff, personal communication, August 14, 2001).

EXTREMISM HISTORY: TYING THE MESSAGE TO NEW MEDIA

The Internet is just the latest technological innovation utilized by domestic extremists over the past century to spread their philosophy and to increase their ranks. In 1915, 12 years before the creation of the Academy Awards, self-proclaimed Grand Wizard Colonel William J. Simmons had meticulously planned to launch the second revival of the Ku Klux Klan to coincide with the introduction of the world's first modern, full-length, feature film. One week before the much anticipated Atlanta premiere of the racist and pro-Confederate motion picture *Birth of a Nation*, Simmons bussed 15 men from Atlanta to Stone Mountain for the formal Klan revival ceremony, complete with a ritual cross lighting. The day of the Atlanta premiere, Simmons carefully placed his revival announcement in the local newspaper right next to the advertisement for the film. The film, based on Thomas Dixon's (1905) best-selling novel *The Clansman: An Historical Romance of the Ku Klux Klan*, was a national cause célèbre because never before had a film combined a story line with modern production techniques. Although the film proved a useful promotional tool, new technology was not the only force at play in the Klan's renaissance. The group's major expansion during the period did not come until 5 years later, when the Klan's promotional methods became much more sophisticated, and its leadership expanded to include two experienced marketers. At its political and membership peak in 1925, the Klan controlled state and national politicians and had 4.5 million members (Chalmers, 1981).

By the 1930s, the Ku Klux Klan had succumbed to tales of violence, fraud, and sex scandals, leaving the right-wing extremist world to others, such as the pro-Nazi Silver Shirts and the German-American Bund. Around the time that the Third Reich was using radio broadcasts and propaganda films to promote anti-Semitism in Germany, America had its own new medium extremist pioneer. A right-wing, fiery, populist Catholic preacher named Father William Coughlin gained a national following through a xenophobic and increasingly anti-Semitic radio program that was broadcast from coast to coast. The power of Coughlin's message and the radio medium, however, was no match for the changing sentiments of the American public, which had shifted with America's entry into World War II in 1941 (Southern Poverty Law Center, 1996; Walker, 1994).

The Early Computer Age of Right-Wing Extremism

The next significant communication advance for right-wing extremists came about in 1983, when West Virginia neo-Nazi publisher George Dietz established the first computer bulletin board system (BBS), called alternatively Liberty Bell Net or Info. International Network, to post racist, anti-Semitic, and Holocaust denial material. With an Apple II computer, Dietz was "apparently the first White supremacist to launch his material in cyberspace," according to researcher Chip Berlet (2001, p. 1). Dietz's Liberty Bell publication was at one time described by the Anti-Defamation League (ADL) as "perhaps the largest pro-Nazi and anti-Jewish propaganda mill in the United States" (Schwartz, 1996, p. 31). Dietz's bulletin boards, accessible to those with computers and dial-up telephone modems, were text postings arranged by title, including "The Jew in Review," "The Holohoax," "WVA Real Estate Bargains," and "Prof. R.P. Oliver's Postscripts." Professor Revilo P. Oliver was a virulent bigot whose epithet-laden writings were frequently featured in Dietz's publications. Dietz's text-only bulletin boards relied heavily on his existing racist publication, *Liberty Bell*, for content. Dietz also allowed space for additional comment and for the downloading of files by interested users (Berlet, 2001; Lowe, 1985).

Shortly thereafter, the Aryan Nations and White Aryan Resistance (WAR) set up BBSs of their own to spread their supremacist ideology. The men behind these BBSs, the Aryan Nations' Louis Beam and WAR's Tom Metzger, are still influential White supremacists. Both vigorously promote ideologies that encourage followers to undertake random racist and antigovernment violence, a message well suited for the anonymous and far-reaching medium of computer networks (Berlet, 2001).

Even though he stands only 5'7'' and weighs only 130 pounds, Louis Beam is one of the most imposing figures in the White supremacist world. A former helicopter tail gunner during the Vietnam War who sports a "Born to Lose" tattoo on his arm, Beam first entered the Ku Klux Klan in 1968. Beam eventually rose through the ranks of David Duke's Klan faction, in which he became the group's Grand Dragon for the state of Texas. Beam was notorious not only for his fiery rhetoric but for his ability to get acquittals on the various criminal charges he faced during his White supremacist career (Dees, 1996; Schwartz, 1996).

In Texas, Beam created and trained a private Klan army called the Texas Emergency Reserve (TER). In 1981, the TER's primary activity was terrorizing Vietnamese refugee fishermen. One year later, the TER was forced to disband after the Southern Poverty Law Center and the Texas attorney general prevailed in a lawsuit (Dees, 1996).

Beam's next position was "ambassador at large" for one of America's most influential neo-Nazi groups: Aryan Nations, based in Hayden Lake, Idaho. At Aryan Nations, Beam split his time between cross-country recruiting and publishing. His work often revolved around bigotry and military themes, particularly guerrilla warfare tactics. In *Essays of a Klansman*, Beam (1983) developed an assassination point system by which extremists could attain "Aryan Warrior" status: a murderous tactic allegedly used by The Order, an Aryan Nations terrorist spin-off organization (Dees, 1996; Schwartz, 1996).

In June 1984, Beam created Aryan Nations' BBS to aid recruiting and increase communication efficiency between existing bigoted extremists throughout the nation. The BBS's first message was as follows:

MSG LEFT BY: SYSTEM OPERATOR—FINALLY, WE ARE ALL GOING TO BE LINKED TOGETHER AT ONE POINT IN TIME. IMAGINE IF YOU WILL, ALL OF THE GREAT MINDS OF THE PATRIOTIC CHRISTIAN MOVEMENT LINKED TOGETHER AND JOINED INTO ONE COMPUTER. ALL THE YEARS OF COMBINED EXPERIENCE AVAILABLE TO THE MOVEMENT. NOW IMAGINE ANY PATRIOT IN THE COUNTRY BEING ABLE TO CALL UP AND ACCESS THOSE MINDS, TO DEAL WITH THE PROBLEMS AND ISSUES THAT AFFECT HIM.

YOU ARE ON LINE WITH THE ARYAN NATIONS BRAIN TRUST. IT IS HERE TO SERVE THE FOLK. (Berlet, 2001, p. 2)

Various sections included the following:

1. NOTICE TO ALL ARYANS

2. AT LAST UNITY!!!

3. ESSAYS OF A KLANSMAN

4. FROM THE MOUNTAIN

5. WHO IS THE U.S. RUN FOR?

6. 1984 IS HERE FOR CANADA

7. NATION IS RACE!

8. MORRIS DEES QUEER

9. JOKE OF THE 20TH CENTURY

10. FROM INSIDE CANADA (Berlet, 2001, p. 2)

The network, called Aryan Nations Liberty Net, consisted of a variety of dial-up bulletin boards connected to telephone numbers in the states of Texas, Idaho, and North Carolina. According to extremism expert Chip Berlet (2001), the systems ran on Radio Shack and Apple computers using standard BBS software. Access to the BBS's content was controlled through passwords that were distributed to preapproved authorized users, who also paid a $5 fee. Beam noted that the BBS was a "patriotic brain trust" where computers brought "their power and capabilities to the American Nationalist Movement" (Lowe, 1985, p. 1). Beam explained to members that the BBS was designed "for Aryan Patriots only" and was a "pro-American, pro-White, anti-Communist network of true believers who serve the one and only God—Jesus, the Christ" (Berlet, 2001; Lowe, 1985, p. 1).

A contemporary ADL analysis divided Liberty Net's content into three main areas. The first and predominant area was "hate propaganda," which consisted of new and reprinted material as well as member contributions. The second section was a fee-based listing of racist and antigovernment organizations. Another section identified groups and individuals designated as enemies and traitors of the Aryan cause. Members could locate ADL offices or "ZOG" informers. *ZOG* is an acronym for *Zionist Occupational Government*, a term used by extremists to identify the purported Israeli-controlled American government. The listings were often coupled with invectives from hate-mongers. For instance, a Beam Klan protégé in North Carolina promoted the BBS in print offline to other extremists by stating, "We have an up-to-date list [on the BBS] of many of the Jew headquarters around the country so that you can pay them a friendly visit" (Lowe, 1985, p. 2). A BBS-posted message was even more ominous: "According to the word of our God, Morris Dees earned two death sentences. . . . Thy will be done on earth as it is in heaven" (Berlet, 2001; Dees, 1996, p. 40; Lowe, 1985, pp. 2, 5-6).

Former California Ku Klux Klan Grand Dragon Tom Metzger soon followed with a racist BBS of his own offering content from his organization, WAR. Like Beam, Metzger had a military background, having achieved the rank of colonel in the U.S. Army. He migrated to California in 1961 from the Midwest to obtain employment in the field of electronics. He eventually settled in the north San Diego community of Fallbrook, where he worked as a television repairman. Beginning in 1975, Metzger joined, led, and later seceded from Duke's California Klan faction. While directing the California Ku Klux Klan, Metzger operated a "border patrol" to harass undocumented Mexican nationals and a paramilitary-style "security force" that was involved in violent confrontations with police and demonstrators. After he lost a bid for a seat in Congress, Metzger founded the White American Political Association, which became WAR in 1983 (Lowe, 1985, p. 5).

As the head of WAR, Metzger expanded the reach of his organization through a variety of bigoted media exercises that included at various times a monthly WAR newspaper, videos, books, pamphlets, jewelry, audiotapes, a nation-wide network of telephone message banks, rallies, and cable-access television shows distributed to providers throughout the United States. In the mid-1980s, however, Metzger's latest propaganda foray involved WAR's bigoted BBS. Metzger's goal of inciting random acts of racial violence, particularly by young neo-Nazi skinheads, however, eventually proved costly. In October 1990, Metzger, his son, and his WAR organization were found tortuously liable in the amount of $12.5 million by an Oregon civil court jury in the killing of a young Ethiopian immigrant by Portland skinheads who were linked to the California bigot (Schwartz, 1996, p. 79-81).

By early 1985, the activities of extremists became publicized by monitoring groups and the press. Chip Berlet, then of Midwest Research Associates, issued a brief memorandum on January 5, 1985, at a conference of researchers. On January 24, 1985, the ADL released a longer fact-finding report, *Computerized Networks of Hate* (Lowe, 1985), which described in detail the characteristics of racist BBSs. The report's analysis of racists' BBSs during the 1980s appears to be equally applicable to today's Internet. Although taking a generally cautious tone, the report stated, "Many users of computerized data banks are impressionable young people vulnerable to propaganda." The report further stated, "The use of computer technology marks a new departure for hate groups and represents an effort to give right-wing extremism a modern look." The report continued, "More troubling, the use of new technology to link together hate group activists coincides with an escalation of serious talk among some of them about the necessity of committing acts of terror" (Berlet, 2001; Lowe, 1985, p. 1; Schwartz, 1996, p. 79-81).

By 1986, Aryan Nations Liberty Net had grown to include phone numbers in Houston, Dallas, and Chicago in addition to Idaho and North Carolina, while WAR continued to operate its California-based BBS. By the early 1990s, BBSs were supplanted by a new form of computer-oriented textual exchange, called discussion boards, such as those on Usenet. These new message exchanges are arranged by topic and generally open to the public for response or rebuttal. Although many discussion boards revolve around mainstream areas of discussion, some are bigoted or extremist in nature. By the mid-1990s, antigovernment, "patriot" groups added this technology to an array of communication media that included fax networks and shortwave radio broadcasts (Berlet, 2001; Southern Poverty Law Center, 1996).

The Emergence of "Leaderless Resistance"

By the 1990s, a key trend in the world of American right-wing extremism was that of leaderless resistance. The concept was first popularized among modern right-wing ideologues as a tool to combat communism by Colonel Ulius Amoss. The White supremacist version of the strategy advocates that individuals or small autonomous guerrilla cells target government officials, civil rights advocates, minorities, and infrastructure sites for violent strikes. There were several factors that influenced the emergence of this trend (*Nature and Threat*, 1995).

First, the folklore and icons of right-wing extremists increasingly revolved around Aryan-style warriors who battled a conspiratorial array of evil enemies responsible for wresting control of America from White racialists. This theme is present in books by prominent White supremacists such as Richard Kelley Hoskins's (1990) *Vigilantes of Christendom: The History of the Phineas Priesthood*, William Pierce's fictional novel *The Turner Diaries: A Novel* (Macdonald, 1978), and its follow-up, *Hunter: A Novel* (Macdonald, 1989). The World Church of the Creator promoted "RAHOWA" (racial holy war), while Pierce's National Alliance promoted *The Turner Diaries*, and WAR (1988) distributed a flyer to skinheads stating, "TRASH EM! SMASH EM! [swastika symbol] MAKE EM DIE!" A vast array of hate rock bands with names such as Skrewdriver, Aggravated Assault, Aryan, and RAHOWA also glorified bigotry and random violence (Resistance Records, 2001). Real-life racial terrorists such as murderers David Tate, Gordon Kahl, and Richard Wayne Snell, as well as The Order's ringleader, Robert Mathews, achieved cult status among right-wing extremists after violent confrontations with law enforcement (*Klanwatch Intelligence Report*, 1989).

Second, organized hate groups dissolved or splintered because of criminal prosecutions and civil lawsuits arising out of their connections to violent bigotry. These losses resulted in the imprisonment of many racist leaders and the crippling of several prominent violent hate groups, including Alabama's United Klans of America, California's WAR, the Invisible Knights of the Ku Klux Klan, the World Church of the Creator, the Arizona Patriots, and Arkansas's Covenant, Sword and Arm of the Lord militia. Starting in the late 1970s, the Southern Poverty Law Center pioneered a strategy of suing hate groups civilly under traditional tort law claims relating to agency and negligence theories for their part in promoting hate violence by their members or agents. Staggering monetary judgments, usually far in excess of the groups' assets, bankrupted various Klan and neo-Nazi groups and their leaders. As a solution to these difficulties, some hatemongers successfully promoted leaderless resistance as an alternative. In this way, hatemongers can legally encourage utilitarian violence by those with whom they have no direct connection. Still, some remaining hatemongers who did switch from violent acts to mere rhetoric lost credibility with their desired audience (Levin, 1998). In addition, guerrilla violence served a different purpose for certain right-wing extremists as time progressed. As certain right-wing movements saw their goals diverge from those of mainstream society, guerrilla violence gained currency among those who felt wholly disenfranchised. In the hate movement, as well as the extreme offshoots of the antiabortion, gun rights, and taxpayer movements, fanatics viewed themselves as at war with various societal institutions. The tactical value of leaderless resistance was promoted by Louis Beam (1983, 1992) in *Essays of a Klansman* and his journal *The Seditionist*, by the Militia of Montana in its newsletter *Taking Aim* (1994), and in an underground antiabortion terrorist instruction manual entitled *Army of God* (*Nature and Threat*, 1995).

Finally, by the mid-1990s, technology evolved to a point at which leaderless resistance could be promoted with far greater efficiency through the Internet. As Southern Poverty Law Center analyst Mark Potok observed,

> The Internet is an important piece of the leaderless resistance strategy. It allows lone wolves to keep abreast of events, changes in ideology and discussions of tactics—all of which may influence his own choice of target. Far more than hard copy publications, the Internet allows the lonewolf to remain a part of a larger movement even though he attends no meetings, puts his name on no lists, and generally tries to remain invisible. A good example of this is Matthew Williams, the self-confessed murderer of a gay couple in California, who used the Internet to privately explore a variety of extremist ideologies before picking up the gun. (personal communication, September 6, 2001)

Scholar Roger Eatwell cites the following reasons for the Internet's popularity among extremists: (a) the low-cost and potentially high-quality presentation and distribution of information, (b) the ability to tailor messages to specific audiences who self-select the type of information they seek, (c) the ability to create an effective image of ideological community, and (d) the ease of global distribution across jurisdictional boundaries (Griffin, 1997).

In addition, Mark Potok also observed that the Internet complements existing media and reaches a wider audience:

> [The Internet] allows those interested to privately peruse the group's materials without making any overt commitment, meaning that people who in the past who would have not gotten near these groups—middle and upper-middle class teenagers, in particular—are now being exposed to the white supremacist message. That said, however, the real extremist action on the Internet is in interactive venues like discussion groups, closed E-lists and person-to-person E-mail. Other media [are still being] used by extremists—radio, cable television, underground publications, even "earned" mainstream media. (personal communication, September 6, 2001)

THE WORLD WIDE WEB

In April 1995, Don Black unveiled what is generally regarded as the first major "hate site" on the World Wide Web: Stormfront.org. The ADL's Mark Pitcavage (personal communication, September 6, 2001) pointed out that there were small, individual Web sites that promoted hatred and antigovernment conspiracies before Stormfront.org, but Black's site, by virtue of the depth of its content and its style of presentation, represents a new period for right-wing extremism online. Its home page proclaims, "White Pride World Wide: White Nationalist Resource Page," and continues, "Stormfront is a resource for those courageous men and women fighting to preserve their White Western culture, ideals and freedom of speech and association—a forum for planning strategies and forming political and social groups to ensure victory" (Stormfront.org, 2001).

Don Black grew up in Alabama and attended the University of Alabama. Shortly thereafter, he became involved with David Duke's Klan faction, in which he became the Alabama Grand Dragon and eventually its national leader after Duke's departure in 1980. Black and other extremists were tried and convicted in federal district court for their role in a plot to overthrow the Caribbean nation of Dominica. Black learned computer technology and worked as a computer consultant after moving to Palm Beach, Florida. He continues to run Stormfront.org from his Florida home (Schwartz, 1996).

After Black launched Stormfront.org, other extremists soon followed with sites of their own. The nation's largest neo-Nazi organization soon staked its own position in cyberspace. Retired physicist William Pierce's National Alliance registered domain names for its site starting in July 1995 (J. Roy, personal communication, September 5, 2001).

Originally from Atlanta, Pierce received his Ph.D. in physics in 1962 from the University of Colorado. Dr. Pierce taught physics at Oregon State University for 3 years. Following a short-lived scientific job, he joined the American Nazi Party under the stewardship of firebrand extremist George Lincoln Rockwell. Following the killing of Rockwell in 1967 at the hands of another Nazi, Dr. Pierce became a leader in the American Nazi Party.

In 1970, Pierce left his position at the American Nazi Party to assist in the development of the National Youth Alliance. Pierce soon wrested control of the group from another prominent bigot named Willis Carto. In 1971, hostilities between Pierce and Carto became public following a dispute over mailing lists. In 1974, 4 years after taking control of the organization, Pierce changed the name of the fledgling organization to the National Alliance. In 1978, the Internal Revenue Service rejected Pierce's attempt to gain tax-exempt status for the National Alliance as an educational organization.

That same year, Pierce published *The Turner Diaries* under the pseudonym Andrew Macdonald (1978). The book is a glorified, fictional account of an anti-government race war by a band of White supremacists who perpetrate atrocities against government officials, Jews, intellectuals, and Blacks. After Pierce proclaimed the novel a "handbook for White victory," American neo-Nazis embraced it as a call to action.

A group of neo-Nazis including National Alliance and Aryan Nations members from the American Northwest organized the terrorist group The Order, named for the fictional criminal group featured in Pierce's *The Turner Diaries* (Macdonald, 1978). The real group, led by the National Alliance's Pacific Northwest leader Robert Mathews, issued a "declaration of war" against American society that culminated in the largest armored car heist in American history and the assassination of a prominent antiracist radio personality, Alan Berg, in 1984. In December 1984, Robert Mathews died in a fire ignited after a pitched battle with federal authorities in Washington State. The other living members of The Order were captured and convicted on federal charges, although millions of dollars from the armored car heist were never recovered. It is alleged by authorities, but not proved, that the money was circulated among prominent American White supremacists. After the heist, Pierce paid $95,000 in cash for 346 acres of land in rural West Virginia as the new site for the National Alliance's headquarters (Southern Poverty Law Center, 1999, p. 15).

Over the next several years, Pierce continued regular publication of newsletters, periodicals, and books. The March/April 1989 issue of the

Table 1   Early Hate Sites on the World Wide Web

Organization	Type	Web Publisher	Location	Time
Stormfront.org	Web-based hate entity	D. Black	Palm Beach, Florida	1995 to present
National Alliance	National neo-Nazi group	W. Pierce	West Virginia	1995 to present
Cyberhate	Web-based hate group	"R. Lodgson"	Texas	1995 to present
White Aryan Resistance	White supremacist group	T. Metzger	San Diego County, California	1996 to present
World Church of the Creator	White supremacist religious group	M. Hale	East Peoria, Illinois	1996 to present
Alpha HQ	Web-based neo-Nazi group	R. Wilson	Philadelphia	1996 to 1998
Zundelsite	U.S. Web portal for material of Canadian neo-Nazi and Holocaust denier E. Zundel	I. Rimland	United States	1996
Imperial Klansmen of America	Ku Klux Klan faction		Powderly, Kentucky	1997

National Vanguard featured a full-page cover photo of Adolph Hitler, and the interior proclaimed him "the greatest man of our era." Pierce's follow-up racist novel, *Hunter* (Macdonald, 1989), was dedicated to Joseph Paul Franklin, a violent racist felon who assassinated two innocent Black joggers in Salt Lake City, Utah.

In 1995, Pierce received more publicity when it was revealed that convicted Oklahoma City bomber Timothy McVeigh was fixated with *The Turner Diaries* (Macdonald, 1978) and had made calls to the National Alliance in the period before the bombing. Part of the book glorifies an antigovernment terrorist who blows up a federal building in an early-morning truck bomb blast. In 1996, a National Alliance member, Todd Vanbiber, was implicated in three bank robberies after police responded to an accidental bomb blast at his home. It was alleged in court testimony that Dr. Pierce was to have received at least $2,000 in proceeds from Mr. Vanbiber's criminal gang (Schwartz, 1996, pp. 106-112; Southern Poverty Law Center, 1999).

Pierce's (1994) promotion of a plan for a White revolution against Jews, minorities, and other enemies is illustrated by his statements in the *National Alliance Bulletin*:

> The Christians who now talk about the impiety of opposing Jews because they are God's chosen people can be made to talk instead about the impiety

of collaborating with Jews because they are the spawn of Satan. . . . All the homosexuals, racemixers, and hard-case collaborators in the country who are too far gone to be re-educated can be rounded up, packed into 10,000 or so railroad cattle cars, and eventually double-timed into an abandoned coal mine in a few days time. All of these people simply don't count, except as a mass of voters. . . . Those who speak against us now should be looked at as dead men—as men marching in lockstep toward their own graves—rather than as people to be feared or respected or given any consideration. (p. 5)

By 2001, Pierce was promoting his ideology through multiple forms of media, including magazines, newsletters, leafleting, radio broadcasts, a comic book, an exclusive catalogue of hate rock compact discs, and an Internet Web site (National Alliance, 2000).

By the end of 2000, Hate Watch counted about 400 bigoted Web sites, and the Southern Poverty Law Center counted 366 "hate Web sites" on the Internet: 97 for the Ku Klux Klan, 80 for neo-Nazi organizations, 19 for racist skinhead organizations, 30 for the Christian Identity movement, 7 for Black separatist organizations, 18 for neo-Confederacy organizations, and 115 containing other material (D. Goldman, personal communication, September 5, 2001; J. Roy, personal communication, September 5, 2001). Some of the more well known websites are found in Table 1.

OTHER INTERNET EXTREMISTS IN THE NEW CENTURY

Although domestic hatemongers were among the first extremists to exploit the efficiencies of the Internet, they are now far from the only ones to make active use of the Internet to target America for propaganda or attack. In addition, Web sites are not the only way contemporary extremists use the Internet. Extremists today use the Internet to access private message boards, e-mail, research, hacking, hidden instructions, listservs (closed e-mail networks), and chat rooms where conversations take place in real time.

Leftist environmental- and animal-liberation extremists have dozens of Web sites that provide information on legal activism, news, and disfavored institutions, as well as downloadable sabotage manuals—accompanied by carefully worded disclaimers. While their philosophies are different from those of online bigots, their use of the Web as a tool for propaganda and violent leaderless resistance is strikingly similar. A prominent animal liberation site offers a downloadable "do it yourself booklet" for "every animal rights activist" on "basic incendiary mixes from easily acquired materials, popular with ALF activists wordl [sic] wide." (Animal Liberation Front, 2001a). Another similar animal liberation site has similar material but also has a password protected section that is not available to casual users. (Animal Liberation Front, 2001b).

A related offshoot movement, the Earth Liberation Front (ELF), has a support Web site that promotes similar tactics and philosophies:

As the ELF structure is non-hierarchical, individuals involved control their own activities. There is no a centralized organization or leadership tying the anonymous cells together. Likewise, there is no official "membership." Individuals who choose to do actions under the banner of the E.L.F. are driven only by their personal conscience or decisions taken by their cell while adhering to the stated guidelines.

Lone wolfs or cells called "elves" by the ELF have committed over 100 acts of property destruction since 1997 that have resulted in 37 million dollars in damage, but no human deaths. (Earth Liberation Front, 2001)

A radical anti-Abortion Web site that has been on and off the Internet over the past several years called for future Nuremburg-style trials for abortion providers and listed extensive personal information about them that included driver's license information, social security numbers, home addresses, vehicles, and their travel information. The site also provided streaming video from abortion clinics and a list of doctors who perform abortions, with slash marks through the names of those who have been murdered (*Planned Parenthood v. American Coalition of Life Activists*, 2001; Christian Gallery, 2001).

In November 2001 an Internet savvy armed fugitive on the FBI's 10 Most Wanted list allegedly visited the home of the publisher of the Nuremberg Files site, Neal Horsley, and held him at gun point. The fugitive and convict, Clayton Waagner, was allegedly staking out abortion clinics when he was previously arrested. When first captured Waagner mentioned the Nuremberg Files website and also told authorities that he used various email accounts of his own to hide information. Waagner demanded that Horsley use his website to post proof that 42 abortion clinic employees who Waagner had targeted for attack had quit their jobs in order to get off his hit list (Roddy, 2001a). Upon his arrest in December 2001 it was confirmed that he posted threats to abortion clinic workers via the Internet and monitored the web through a laptop and on computers at Kinkos copy stores (D. Roddy, 2001b).

While Middle Eastern terrorist groups such as Hamas and Hizbollah have support Web sites in both English and Arabic that promote anti-Israeli and anti-American propaganda and their "martyrs," Al Qaeda had no such permanent presence on the World Wide Web (Hizbollah, 2001; Hamas, 2001). However, in the period after the devastating September 11, 2001 terror attacks, authorities have pieced together a disturbing composite that indicates Al Qaeda was a computer-savvy terrorist conglomerate. The September 11th hijackers made reservations via AmericanAirlines.com, exchanged e-mail via Yahoo!, and conducted online research about the effectiveness of crop-dusting aircraft as a means to disperse chemical agents (Cohen, 2001).

A former French official stated that authorities there also believe that suspected Al Qaeda terrorists were awaiting instructions to destroy the American embassy in Paris in September 2001, through the Internet via a method known as *steganography*. Steganography, Greek for hidden writing, is a method of encrypting hidden messages in photo or audio files implanted in e-mails or on Web sites. Steganographic software, readily available on the Internet, enables the sender and recipient to exchange communications with messages that are invisible to the unaided eye but identifiable to those clued into where it is implanted. Investigators too, can detect the presence of steganographic devices via algorithms, which hunt for deviations in patterns found in online photographic or audio files (Cohen, 2001a).

The nerve center of the secretive Al Qaeda organization also apparently used the Internet for other purposes as well. At hastily abandoned operations centers in Kabul, Afghanistan journalists uncovered remaining evidence suggesting that Al Qaeda "used the Internet to research rudimentary bomb-making and chemical weapons development and to track news coverage of Mr. bin Laden" (Rhode, 2001, p. 1).

THE FIRST AMENDMENT

The use of the Internet by various groups and individuals to disseminate controversial and hateful content reignited debate on the status of the First Amendment. Over the past century, the Supreme Court has established new standards relating to the protection of expressive rights from governmental interference, and these rulings have a direct impact on Internet expression. Specifically, the Court has identified various circumstances in which the government has greater latitude to interfere with or punish expression. The relevant factors include

1. the time, place, or manner (as opposed to the content) of the expression in the context of a particular setting;

2. whether the expression's character falls into an area of speech the Court has deemed "unprotected";

3. whether the expression constitutes behavior traditionally regarded as criminal; and

4. whether there is a compelling governmental interest in restricting the speech.

THE INTERNET AS A MODERN PUBLIC SQUARE

A central issue regarding the government's ability to regulate expression on the Internet revolves around how the medium is legally categorized. The Supreme Court has held that the government has greater flexibility in regulating expression when it occurs in certain outlets. In *Hague v. Committee for Industrial Organization* (1939), the Supreme Court held that public areas serve an important role in the furtherance of discourse in a democratic society. In *Hague*, union members fought the enforcement of a Jersey City municipal code that prohibited the distribution of printed material and assemblies in public places without a permit issued at the discretion of a city official. The Court's decision threw out the ordinance, maintaining,

> Whenever the title of streets and parks may rest, they have immemorially been held in trust for the use of the public and, time out of mind, have been used for purposes of assembly, communicating thoughts between citizens, and discussing of public questions. Such use of the streets and public places has, from ancient times, been a part of the privileges, immunities, rights, and liberties of citizens. The privilege of a citizen of the United States to use the streets and parks for communication of views on national questions may be regulated in the interest of all; it is not absolute, but relative and must be exercised in subordination to the general comfort and convenience, and in consonance with peace and good order; but it must not, in the guise of regulation be abridged or denied. (pp. 515-516)

The *Hague* (1939) decision represents a fairly good articulation of the principle at issue in public forum cases. As legal scholar Harry Klaven pointed out, "In an open democratic society the streets, the parks, and other public places are an important facility for public discussion and the political process" (Cohen & Danelski, 1997, p. 375). Klaven maintained that a citizen's access to public forums for communication is an "index of freedom." If the

Supreme Court were to find that the Internet is the equivalent of a public forum, then expression on it would have the greatest protection from governmental regulation.

The *Hague* (1939) decision is still good law, although the contours of its doctrine have been better established by subsequent cases. Later decisions better defined what entities constitute public forums and what types of regulations of them are permissible. Streets, parks, and sidewalks are areas where speech is most protected. Other places, such as libraries, schools, and their surrounding areas, are in an intermediate category (*Grayned v. City of Rockford*, 1972). It appears that the courts will allow regulation of expression when the manner is incompatible with the routine activity of a particular place at a particular time.

Lastly, the Supreme Court found that nonpublic forums offer the government the most leeway to interfere with speech. In these places, the Court approved of nondiscriminatory restrictions that are reasonable to the efficient functioning of a facility. For instance, the Court held that airport terminals, while open to the public, are not places related to expression. Maintaining that airport terminals are not "public fora," the Court upheld a ban on solicitations and dispersal of literature (*International Soc. for Krishna Consciousness v. Lee*, 1992).

The Supreme Court addressed the legal status of the Internet and the regulation of controversial content on it in *Reno et al. v. American Civil Liberties Union et al.* (1997). The decision in *Reno et al. v. American Civil Liberties Union et al.* invalidated two parts of the Communications Decency Act of 1996 that restricted the display of sexually oriented content. However, the decision had a significant impact on Internet regulation in general. In relevant parts, the act punished the "knowing" communication to minors of "obscene or indecent" messages. It also banned the knowing communication of messages to minors or the display of messages that could be viewed by minors. The prohibited messages related to material that was "patently offensive as measured by contemporary community standards, sexual or excretory activities or organs" (§ 223[d]).

The decision was a landmark for two reasons. First, the justices gave broad First Amendment protection to Internet-based communications, dismissing government claims that they should be restricted in the same manner as radio and television frequencies. The justices also dismissed the notion that the government can ban communications between adults on the grounds that minors might receive messages for which they are unfit.

The Court instead contended that the Internet was more like a public square than a television broadcast:

> Through the use of chat rooms, any person with a phone line can become a town crier with a voice that resonates farther than it could from any soapbox. Through the use of Web pages, mail explorers and newsgroups, the same individual can become a pamphleteer. As the District Court found, the content of the Internet is as "diverse as human thought." We agree . . . that our cases provide no basis for qualifying the level of First Amendment scrutiny that should be applied to this medium. (*Reno et al. v. American Civil Liberties Union et al.*, 1997, pp. 896-897)

The justices found that the Internet differs from television and radio broadcasts because there are unlimited available outlets, there is no precedent of governmental restrictions, and the recipient of a message actively searches for it with some foreknowledge of its content. On the basis of this, the Court offered a heightened level of scrutiny to analyze governmental restriction on expression. The government may restrict expression on the Internet only when it is necessary to further an important governmental interest and is narrowly tailored to achieve that interest. The Court also attacked the statute's vagueness, particularly in its invocation of the terms *indecent* and *patently offensive*.

The Supreme Court's ruling in *Reno* (1997) established the Internet as a public forum: a place where speech is most protected from governmental regulation. However, the decision did not completely insulate the Internet from regulation. Even when expression takes place in public forums, it can still be regulated when the communication is of a certain character.

After the Supreme Court's ruling in *Reno v. ACLU*, Congress undertook a more focused attempt to regulate expression on the Internet. In the Child Online Protection Act (COPA) (47 U.S.C. § 23), restrictions are more narrow than those found in the CDA in that COPA's restrictions apply only to commercial websites. COPA makes it a criminal offense to provide material that is "harmful to minors" and defines such as "patently offensive" material involving lewd nudity or sexuality. The law was immediately challenged in federal court by the ACLU. The organization, however, did not challenge the law's possible application to obscene speech, an area of expression involving extreme pornographic depictions that has traditionally been regarded as unprotected by the First Amendment. The trial court held that the law impermissibly punished expressive content protected by the First Amendment without the requisite presence of a compelling governmental interest. In an appeal, the United States Court of Appeals for the Third Circuit invalidated the law, but for a different reason. The Court of Appeals held that a provision of the statute basing punishment on the "contemporary community standards" of individual municipalities was too burdensome to webpublishers. The Supreme Court heard oral argument on the constitutionality of COPA on November 28, 2001, and a decision is expected by June 2002. The case is significant because the decision could affect the way that extremist or controversial speech designated as "harmful to minors" is regulated on the Internet. (*ACLU v. Reno*, 2000; on appeal as *Ashcroft v. ACLU*, 2002).

GOVERNMENT'S POWER TO REGULATE EXPRESSION VARIES BY CATEGORY

The Internet is home to a broad spectrum of content. Generally, governmental regulations based simply on the content of the idea expressed will be overturned. For instance, in *Boss v. Barry* (1988), the Supreme Court invalidated a law that prohibited the display of insulting signs near foreign embassies that hold other countries out to "public odium" or "public dispute." In these instances, courts impose a standard on governmental conduct called strict scrutiny. Under this standard, the government must establish two things about official restrictions on expression for them to be held constitutional: (a) They are

necessary to achieve a compelling state interest, and (b) they are narrowly tailored to achieve that compelling interest (*Boos v. Barry*, 1988; *Widmar v. Vincent*, 1981).

If, however, the expression falls under an "unprotected" area of speech, the government has far greater ability to regulate or proscribe it. When speech falls into a category that is unprotected, it can be prohibited outright as long as the government can demonstrate a rational nexus between the regulation and a legitimate governmental purpose. Unprotected areas of speech include defamation, fraudulent commercial speech, obscenity, and incitement to criminality. Technically, another unprotected category called "fighting words" exists but is considered by many to be dormant because the Court has refused to invoke the category in upholding a speech restriction in five decades.

Fighting Words and Offensive Speech

Controversial content that causes anger, disgust, or offense in many viewers has a home on the Internet. A line of Supreme Court decisions has set forth standards relating to the government's ability to regulate controversial content. In 1942, the Supreme Court created the unprotected category of fighting words and defined them as those words that by their very utterance would arouse a violent response in a listener (*Chaplinsky v. State of New Hampshire*, 1942). Presumably, then, very offensive speech could often be banned as fighting words. Although the Supreme Court has never officially abandoned this category, its recent opinions cast significant doubt on the category's continued vitality. First, the Supreme Court has failed to identify any fighting words fit for governmental proscription for five decades. Second, the Court has consistently held that the mere offensiveness of speech is not a basis for restricting it, a doctrine that appears to undercut the purpose of the fighting words exception in the first place.

When the first fighting words decision in *Chaplinsky v. State of New Hampshire* (1942) was handed down, the Court appeared to accept the notion that merely offensive speech might be punishable without contravening the First Amendment. Similarly, in *Beauharnais v. Illinois* (1952), the Supreme Court affirmed

Illinois's "group-libel" statute. In 1917, in the aftermath of violent race rioting, Illinois (and later other states) passed a group-libel statute that punished those who made bigoted, "defamatory" statements against racial, religious, or ethnic groups. Although never technically overturned, subsequent Supreme Court decisions have clearly rejected all the foundational arguments on which the *Beauharnais* decision relied, and the case is no longer regarded as sound law. Illinois's group-libel law was repealed in 1961 (Walker, 1994).

In the decades that followed, the Court shifted toward far greater protection of offensive racist or political speech. In a Vietnam War-era case, *Cohen v. California* (1971), Paul Cohen challenged his conviction under a breach of the peace statute that criminalized "offensive conduct." Cohen was arrested for wearing a jacket reading "Fuck the Draft" as he walked the corridors of the Los Angeles Municipal Court. The *Cohen* case is considered a landmark not only because it squarely addressed the issue of offensive speech but also for its cogent analysis of a number of other significant free expression issues.

Justice John Harlan, writing for the majority, rejected a variety of assertions before addressing the issue of criminalizing offensiveness. He rejected the assertion that the wording fell under the unprotected category of "obscenity" because it was not of a sexual nature. Obscenity is one of several areas of unprotected speech that the government has almost unbridled authority to punish. Next, Justice Harlan rejected the contention that Cohen was punished for violating the decorum of a court building. The statute was a broadly applicable one whose text did not take into account the location of the "crime."

Harlan also rejected the notion that government had the authority to protect "unwilling or unsuspecting" people from receiving distasteful messages while in public places. This notion of course reflects the longstanding view that speech is most protected from restrictions based on content when it is made in public forums. Those in public places, Harlan maintained, do not have the same privacy expectation to be free from the intrusion of unwanted views and ideas that exists for those in their homes. "We are often captives outside the sanctuary of the home and subject to objectionable speech," the Court

held in a case from the previous year (*Rowan v. U.S. Post Office Depart.*, 1970, p. 738). Seizing on that notion, Justice Harlan maintained that those in public places "could effectively avoid further bombardment of their sensibilities simply by averting their eyes" (p. 22).

Justice Harlan was particularly forceful in dismissing California's most broad grab at power: the ability to punish speech on the basis of offensiveness, a notion Harlan labeled "inherently boundless":

> How is one to distinguish this from any other offensive word? Surely the State has no right to cleanse public debate to the point where it is grammatically palatable to the most squeamish among us. For, while the particular four-letter word being litigated here is perhaps more distasteful than most others of its genre, it is nevertheless often true that one man's vulgarity is another's lyric. Indeed, we think it is largely because governmental officials cannot make principled distinctions in this area that the Constitution leaves matters of taste and style so largely to the individual. (*Cohen v. California*, 1971, p. 25).

In *Texas v. Johnson* (1989), the Supreme Court held that the Constitution protects even the most unpopular and offensive type of speech in a case involving flag burning. While protesting outside city hall near the site of the 1984 Republican National Convention in Dallas, Gregory Johnson set fire to an American flag.

After the incident, Johnson was charged and convicted under a Texas law that criminalizes the desecration of "venerated objects" such as monuments, houses of worship, and cemeteries. Also included as a protected object is "a state or national flag." Johnson was the only person at the event who was charged, and he faced only the single "desecration" charge. The statute states that the desecration of a covered object means to "deface, damage, or otherwise physically mistreat [it] in a way that the actor knows will seriously offend one or more persons likely to observe or discover his action." At trial, various observers of the flag immolation stated that they had indeed been "seriously offended" by it (*Texas v. Johnson*, 1989, p. 399). Johnson was sentenced to 1 year in prison and assessed a $2,000 fine (*Texas v. Johnson*, 1989, p. 400).

On appeal from the Texas state courts, the Supreme Court held that the law was unconstitutionally used against the flag burner. Technically, the appeal to the Supreme Court addressed only the narrow issue of the statute's application to Johnson. However, the reasoning of the opinion made it a virtual certainty that the Court would have thrown out the law if it had been asked to do so.

The Court noted that offensiveness was protected speech, unlike the unprotected categories of incitement to criminality or fighting words. The Court stated that government may not "ban the expression of certain disagreeable ideas on the unsupported presumption that their very disagreeableness will provoke violence" (*Texas v. Johnson*, 1989, p. 409). After rejecting Texas's contention that offensive flag burnings were equivalent to breaches of the peace, the Court addressed the state's second contention. Texas authorities also maintained that the state had an interest "in preserving the flag as a symbol of nationhood and national unity" (*Texas v. Johnson*, 1989, p. 410). The majority held that Texas's interest in that regard directly and impermissibly implicated the idea being expressed. The punishment unconstitutionally was linked to the unpatriotic idea associated with the flag's offensive destruction. Patriotic burnings of worn flags that conveyed respect for the national symbol would not be punished. Thus, the same act was being treated differently on the basis of the particular idea promoted.

Because the state's action was based on the content of the idea expressed, the Court applied strict scrutiny analysis. Under strict scrutiny, a state must establish that its actions furthered a compelling state interest in the least restrictive way possible. The Court found, as it usually does when applying strict scrutiny analysis, that Texas failed to meet its burden.

Justice William Brennan, speaking for the five-person majority, stated, "If there is a bedrock principle underlying the First Amendment, it is that the government may not prohibit the expression of an idea simply because society finds the idea itself offensive or disagreeable" (*Texas v. Johnson*, 1989, p. 414). He continued, "To conclude that government may permit designated symbols to be used to communicate a limited set of messages would be to enter territory having no discernible or defensible boundaries" (*Texas v. Johnson*, 1989, p. 414).

In a separate concurrence, Justice Anthony Kennedy described the majority decision as "painful to announce." Perhaps recognizing the firestorm of popular criticism to come, Justice Kennedy attempted to explain the decision more in philosophical terms than technical legal ones:

> Though symbols often are what we ourselves make of them, the flag is constant in expressing beliefs Americans share, beliefs in law and peace and that freedom which sustains the human spirit. The case here today forces recognition of the costs to which those beliefs commit us. It is poignant, but fundamental that the flag protects those who hold it in contempt. (p. 421)

In light of *Cohen v. California* (1971), *Texas v. Johnson* (1989), and other cases, some observers have concluded that the unprotected speech category of fighting words no longer exists. Technically, it does exist, because the category has never been officially and explicitly overruled by any Supreme Court decision. Realistically, however, case law subsequent to *Chaplinsky v. New Hampshire* (1942) indicates that the conceptual support for the fighting words category has been undermined to the point at which current controlling case law is in direct conflict. That is probably why the Supreme Court has failed to identify and punish a fighting words utterance in half a century.

The *Texas v. Johnson* (1989) case was a landmark for many reasons, especially so for those analyzing speech on the Internet. It stands for the proposition that governmental laws cannot single out the nonviolent expression of even the most offensive and disquieting ideas. Furthermore, the United States will not extradite individuals whose offensive expression violates the laws of another nation when that expression is legal in America.

Internet Companies and the Display of Objectionable Content

Many major Internet service providers (ISPs), such as America Online, as private companies can and often do set contractual requirements relating to the conduct and expression of their customers. These restrictions are found in the "terms of service" (TOS) agreements to which customers consent as a condition of access to providers' systems. ISPs are free to include provisions that restrict content for a variety of reasons, including the fact that the material is bigoted, offends sensibilities, or is fraudulent. As long as they abide by their TOS agreements, ISPs are free to delete content or cancel service if someone improperly uses the service or posts objectionable content (Kessler & Rosenberg, 2000).

In the United States section 230 of the CDA protects ISPs from being subjected to civil or criminal culpability for the improper online communications of its clients. However, the American Internet company, Yahoo!, recently won a cross border dispute involving French litigants. The litigants were French civil rights [groups] who won a case in France to prevent the company's French and American sites from hosting online auctions of Nazi memorabilia. France's Nazi Symbols Act, La Nouveau Penal Code Art. R.645-2 prohibits the display of Nazi "uniforms, insignia or emblems." In November 2001, a United States District Court in San Jose, California, refused to honor France's restrictive orders relating to the conduct of Yahoo!'s American auction site. Because the United States' First Amendment protects controversial speech that is banned elsewhere, America will continue to be a legal refuge for Internet speech that is illegal elsewhere in the world. (*Yahoo! v. La Ligue Contre Racism*, 2001).

Criminal Incitement

Another unprotected area of speech that directly applies to Internet extremists, particularly those who promote violence, is that of criminal incitement. In the case of *Brandenburg v. Ohio* (1969), the Supreme Court articulated what is now the current test to determine the contours between lawful, protected advocacy and unprotected, illegal incitement to criminality. Currently, for dangerous advocacy to be classified as illegal incitement, two conditions must be met. First, the speech must be directed toward inciting or producing imminent lawless action. Second, the speech must be likely to incite or produce such action.

The case came about from an incident in the early 1960s. Klansman Clarence Brandenburg invited a television news crew to film a Ku Klux Klan rally on a private farm in Hamilton County, Ohio. The prosecution of Brandenburg was based primarily on news footage taken at the private event, where only Klansmen and the news crew were present. The news footage showed a dozen people with hoods assembled around a large wooden cross, which was set ablaze. Some of the Klansmen appeared to be armed, and the microphone picked up only "scattered phrases" that derided African Americans and Jews. Elsewhere in the news clip, Brandenburg addressed the assemblage unarmed but dressed in full Klan regalia. In a bigoted speech at the rally, Brandenburg said in part,

> The Klan has more members in the State of Ohio than does any other organization, but if our President, our Congress, our Supreme Court, continues to suppress the White, Caucasian race, it's possible that there might have to be some revengeance [*sic*] taken.
> We are marching on Congress July the Fourth, four hundred thousand strong. From there we are dividing into two groups, one group to march on St. Augustine, Florida, the other group to march into Mississippi. Thank you. (*Brandenburg v. Ohio*, 1969, p. 446)

Later, Brandenburg added the following opinion to a substantially similar statement at the same event: "Personally, I believe the nigger should be returned to Africa, the Jew returned to Israel" (*Brandenburg v. Ohio*, 1969, p. 446).

Brandenburg was convicted under Ohio's Criminal Syndicalism Act, which punished

> advocat[ing] . . . the duty, necessity, or propriety of a crime, sabotage, violence, or unlawful methods of terrorism as a means of accomplishing industrial or political reform [and for] voluntarily assembl[ing] with any society, group, or assemblage of persons formed to teach or advocate the doctrines of criminal syndicalism. (§ 2923.13)

Brandenburg was sentenced to 10 years in state prison and assessed a $1,000 fine for his conduct at the rally. The Supreme Court, in a unanimous opinion, overturned the flawed statute on its own wording without ever actually applying it to Brandenburg's speech. The *Brandenburg* (1969) decision provides significant protection to online extremists as long as their violent advocacy is abstract in nature.

Traditional Crimes

As new communication technologies such as the Internet arise, they give malefactors new ways to manifest traditional forms of criminal behavior. Some communications have been by tradition considered so dangerous that the law views them solely as criminal conduct rather than expressive speech related to the First Amendment, and this applies equally to the Internet. The most prominent examples of this are threats, conspiracies, criminal solicitation, and certain types of fraud. In law, a threat is defined as a statement communicating an intent to injure another or damage the property of another. The Supreme Court addressed the issue of criminalizing threats in *Watts v. United States* (1969). The *Watts* case involved an 18-year-old African American Vietnam War protester who was convicted under a law making it a crime to threaten the life of the president. At an antiwar rally in August 1966, Watts stated,

> And now I have already received my draft classi-fication as 1-A and I have got to report for my physical this Monday coming. I am not going. If they ever make me carry a rifle the first man I want to get in my rifle sights is L.B.J. [President Lyndon Johnson]. They are not going to make me kill my black brothers. (*Watts v. United States*, 1969, p. 706)

Unbeknownst to Watts, an investigator with the Army Counter Intelligence Corps secretly noted what he was saying.

The law under which Watts was convicted made it a federal crime to "knowingly and will-fully [make] any threat to take the life of or inflict bodily harm upon the President of the United States" (*Watts v. United States*, 1969, p. 708).

The Supreme Court threw out Watt's convic-tion but upheld the law. Watts's statement was deemed by the Court to be a "crude offensive" political statement of constitutionally protected

speech rather than a genuine threat. The Court stated that although the law itself was consti-tutional, its application to Watts's political expression was not. The government has an overwhelming interest in both protecting the president's life and allowing him to perform his duties without the obstruction that results from violent threats, the Court found. In contrast, the Court also found, "[There is] a profound national commitment to the principle that debate on public issue should be uninhibited, robust, and wide open, and that it may well include vehement, caustic, and sometimes unpleasantly sharp attacks on government and public officials" (*Watts v. United States*, 1969, p. 708).

Threats are not the only kinds of statements that are criminal by their very nature. Con-spiracies and criminal solicitation have traditionally been regarded as crimes. A con-spiracy is an agreement by two or more people to commit a crime or to solicit or aid others in the commission of a crime (American Law Institute, 1985). Some conspiracy statutes also require an overt step in furtherance of the planned offense by one of the parties, although that step could be a very small one, such as obtaining a tool or drawing a sketch. Conspiracy prosecutions do not require that the target crime ever be carried out. In contrast to incitement prosecutions, then, there is no requirement of imminence at all for a conviction to take place. Conspiracy is a separate offense from the crime actually planned by the instigators. Criminal solicitation punishes those who ask, direct, or encourage another to commit a crime (American Law Institute, 1985).

Fraud (i.e., depriving someone of money or property by misrepresentation or deception) and other economic crimes can result in both civil and criminal liability (Black, 1979, p. 337). It is a federal crime to commit fraud by telephone lines or mail. White supremacist and Middle Eastern extremists movements have traditionally encouraged economic crimes ranging from bank robberies to financial frauds. Over the past quar-ter century, right-wing extremists such as The Order and the Montana Freemen have counter-feited financial instruments as a method of fund-ing their activities. The ADL's Mark Pitcavage (personal communication, September 6, 2001) has found that various recent frauds involving right-wing extremists have had a direct connection to the Internet. Dr. Pitcavage observed that some of the most common types of these frauds involve "sham trusts, tax protest schemes, and pyramid investment schemes." He further observed that other schemes are directed against the government, such as those dealing with money laundering and tax evasion. All these various criminal provisions are considered crimes no matter in what mode of communication they manifest, whether online, in person, by telephone, or by letter.

In December 2001 President George W. Bush announced that one of the largest charitable organizations in the United States that provide aid to Palestinians was under investigation for funding the terrorist group Hamas. The Texas headquarters of the Holy Land Foundation was raided by federal agents and its assets were frozen. The organization, a tax-exempt charity, markets itself online (www.hlf.org, 2001; President Announces Progress, 2001). Infocom, a computer and web support company that provides services to various Arab businesses and charities, had its offices in Texas raided and its assets frozen by federal agents in September 2001 after authorities alleged that a Hamas militant was an investor. Infocom is the web service company for the Holy Land foundation (Cohen, 2001a).

Although traditional laws can sometimes be used to prosecute computer crime, the federal government and all 50 states now have additional criminal legislation specifically addressing computer crime (Pennsylvania Crimes Code; 18 U.S.C. § 1029; 18 U.S.C. § 1030). Current cybercrime laws punish those who commit fraud by computer as well as those who use or damage data or hardware without authorization (Schmalleger, 1999). The FBI reports that computer network intrusions doubled from 1997 through 1999. The agency also reports a rise in the dissemination of computer viruses and the use of "hacktivism"—politically motivated attacks on publicly accessible computer systems operated by government and businesses (FBI, 1999). These new computer laws address such things as unauthorized computer tampering, fraud, trespass, and theft of services, but they do not create a distinct charge for cyberthreats.

Cyberthreats

Much of the media attention on the Internet and extremism has focused on offensive Web sites. However, the medium has recently emerged as a vehicle for bigots to transmit threats. The ease with which large numbers of victims can be threatened by mass e-mailings and the potential reach of Web site-posted threats warrant an examination of existing law. The character of certain Web site threats can be more complex than a solitary threat delivered in person or by letter. These threats can be and often are designed to deliver not only a threat to an intended target but also a de facto solicitation to action to numerous other violence-prone extremists. It is this de facto solicitation component and the use of a wide-ranging instrument that weigh in favor of new legislation specifically addressing Web site threats.

Enhancing punishment for a crime because the offender uses a particular instrument or new technology is nothing new in criminal law. Existing law enhances punishment when a crime involves an aircraft, automatic weapons, or the use of a telecommunications system. Arguably, threats and other online crimes undertaken by White supremacists and others are substantively different because of the ubiquitous nature of the Web. A threat divulging private information broadcast over the Internet, for example, not only can intimidate its target but can also be a criminal solicitation to others unknown, complete with valuable information that aids in the proposed crime's commission.

Currently, though, federal prosecutors have tried online bigoted criminals under existing law. On September 26, 1996, Richard Machado, using a university computer, sent a racist, epithet-filled threat to about 60 mostly Asian students at the University of California, Irvine (UCI). Machado, who had flunked out of UCI, warned, "I personally will make it my life career to find and kill everyone of you personally. OK?????? That's how determined I am. Get the fuck out, Mother Fucker (Asian Hater)" (*United States v. Machado*, 1998, Government's Exhibit, p. 1).

In February 1998, Machado became the first individual to be convicted in the United States of a so-called hate crime over the Internet. After a jury deadlock in his first trial, a subsequent jury convicted Machado of violating 18 U.S.C. §245 (1968) for interfering with the students' right to attend a public college. Machado was sentenced to 1 year in prison (*United States v. Machado*, 1998).

Less than a month later, in March 1998, 67 Latino students and employees of California State University, Los Angeles; the Massachusetts Institute of Technology; and other institutions received a threatening e-mail that read in part, "I hate your race. I want you all to die. will [*sic*] do kill all your people for me, wetback. . . . I'm going to come down and kill your wetback, affirmative action ass. . . . I hate wetbacks!!! Kill all wetbacks!!!" (*United States v. Machado*, 1998, Government's Exhibit).

In June 1999, Kingman Quon, an Asian American college student in California, received a 2-year sentence under 18 U.S.C. § 245 (1968) for sending those threatening e-mails. His probation bars him from using a computer or going online for a year once he is released from prison (*United States v. Quon*, 1999).

Online haters face prosecution for violating not only traditional civil rights statutes but also other statutes dealing with telecommunications. Under the Communications Decency Act (1996), those who seek to threaten, annoy, or harass others through the use of a telecommunications device by making lewd, indecent, or anonymous contact face up to 2 years in prison. In addition 18 U.S.C. § 875 (1934) provides for up to 2 years of incarceration for threats communicated through interstate commerce, which can include phone or computer lines.

In October 1998, a neo-Nazi hate site, Alpha HQ, run by longtime Philadelphia racist Ryan Wilson, became the first hate site to be removed from the World Wide Web by court order after the Pennsylvania deputy attorney general, Trent Hargrove, obtained a civil injunction. The attorney general's office contended that the site was in violation of state laws that generally prohibit harassment, terrorist threats, and ethnic intimidation. Wilson failed to appear in his own defense.

The site published threats against two Pennsylvania civil rights workers. One was Bonnie Jouhari, a fair housing and hate crime official from Berks County. The site showed one photograph of Jouhari and another of her office exploding into flames. The site labeled her a "race traitor," a term commonly used by White supremacists to label an individual as a target of violence. The site, in referring to Jouhari, also stated, "[She] has received warnings in the mail that she is a race traitor. . . . Traitors like this should beware, for in our day, they will be hung from the neck from the nearest tree or lamp post" (*Commonwealth v. Wilson et al.*, 1998, Attorney General's Exhibit II). It also stated that Jouhari's fair housing work was injurious to society. After he was interviewed by the Federal Bureau of Investigation, Wilson put up a disclaimer relating to violent acts, which a judge later held to be ineffective (*Commonwealth v. Wilson et al.*, 1998).

In July 2000, Department of Housing and Urban Development officials successfully sued Wilson for using his Web site and other media to violate the Fair Housing Act. The charge stated that he violated the act by threatening Jouhari and her daughter to prevent Jouhari from enforcing the act and living in her home. Jouhari's job obligated her to assist victims of housing discrimination in filing discrimination complaints pursuant to the act. Wilson, who did not contest the suit, was held liable for over $1 million by an administrative law judge (Lichtblau, 2000).

In *Planned Parenthood v. American Coalition of Life Activists* (2001), a jury found a consortium of radical antiabortion organizations liable for $107 million in a case arising out of "wanted poster"-type literature that was distributed both online and offline. The online literature included detailed personal information about abortion doctors along with a list of doctors that specifically referenced those who had been assaulted or murdered, indicating them with lines through their names or by changing the color of the type. Although the site did not explicitly direct readers to kill the doctors listed, it labeled them murderers who needed to be brought to justice. After an injunction was issued, the Web site was taken offline, but it was sporadically available. On March 28, 2001, the U.S. Court of Appeals for the Ninth Circuit reversed the jury verdict and dissolved the lower court's injunction. The decision reaffirmed protection to leaderless resistance-type Web activity. Judge Alex Kozinski declared, "Political speech may not be punished just because it makes it more likely that someone will be harmed at some unknown time in the future by an unrelated third party" (*Planned Parenthood v. American Coalition of Life Activists*, 2001, p. 1015). On October 3, 2001, the full Ninth Circuit Court of Appeals vacated the March decision of its own three judge panel and scheduled the case for a brand new hearing. This action had the effect of nullifying the legal status of the Court's March 2001 ruling (*Planned Parenthood* v. *American Coalition of Life Activists*, 2001).

AIDING AND ABETTING

Generally the publication of potentially dangerous information to a broad audience, like that found on the Internet, is protected by the First Amendment, even if it is foreseeable that someone down the line might use that knowledge for illegal ends. However, if the distribution of information is targeted to specific wrongdoers or is designed to facilitate or assist a terrorist act or crime, the sender can face criminal and civil liability under a theory of aiding and abetting. Usually, this involves a sender who either knows the recipient or who desires to aid in the commission of a particular crime. In certain circumstances, however, courts have held that aiding and abetting liability can extend to situations where criminal instructions are broadly disseminated to people such as large groups of would-be tax evaders and drug customers (*United States v. Barnett*, 1982; *United States v. Buttorff*, 1978). In a civil case involving Palladin Press's "Hitman" murder-instruction manual, a federal appeals court held that a civil jury could find aiding and abetting liability in a case where a publisher specifically markets mail-order homicide instructions to a narrow audience consisting substantially of would be assassins. The court maintained this position despite the fact that the publisher did not have personal knowledge of purchasers or of their possible criminal plans. (*Rice v. Paladin Enterprises, Inc.*, 1997). These rulings could be applicable to instances where the Internet is used as an instrument to aid and abet terrorist acts.

NEW TERRORISM LEGISLATION AND THE INTERNET

In the aftermath of the September 2001 terror attacks, President Bush signed the Patriot Act of 2001. The lengthy legislative package has various provisions that specifically address computers and the Internet. The act allows the issuance of nationwide wire and search warrants by one federal judge. In addition, the statute enhances the ability of authorities to monitor the flow of Internet and e-mail traffic by terrorist suspects. The law also requires ISPs to deliver information to authorities relating to Internet communications when there is a reasonable belief that there is an imminent risk of violence. The statute further allows interception of communications in which authorities have a reasonable belief that they are relevant to an investigation and being used by a computer trespasser. The Act permits the deportation of foreigners who commit criminal incitement, who materially support designated terrorists groups, or who further terrorist acts. Last, the Patriot Act overlays enhancements on to an earlier statute, the Computer Fraud and Abuse Act (CFAA 18 USC § 1030). The CFAA establishes penalties for those who use the Internet to deface Web sites, or those who damage or interfere with computer networks without authorization. In addition to the Patriot Act the federal government may intercept criminal wire and electronic transmissions, including Internet communications, under Title III of the Omnibus Crime Control and Safe Streets Act of 1968 and its amendments, and sections of the Electronic Communications Privacy Act of 1986 and its amendments.

The Patriot Act also allows the use of an FBI Internet surveillance filter known as "Carnivore" in situations where the sought after electronic evidence is relevant to the pursuit of an existing criminal investigation. According to FBI Assistant Director Donald Kerr: "It works by 'sniffing' the proper portions of network packets and copying and storing only those packets which match a finely defined filter set programmed in conformity with the court order. This filter set can be extremely complex, and this provides the FBI with an ability to collect transmissions which comply with pen register court orders, trap & trace court orders, Title III interception orders, etc." (Kerr, 2000).

Federal authorities have other electronic surveillance tools at their disposal as well. In November 2001 it was revealed that the FBI has developed an eavesdropping software called Magic Lantern which is delivered to a suspect's computer via email. The software records every keystroke made by a suspect for use by authorities. It is particularly useful for finding passwords and keys to encrypted messages send by suspects. There is debate as to whether a standard search warrant would legally suffice for its application, or whether more restrictive wiretap rules apply instead (Bridis, 2001).

Lastly, the National Security Agency in conjunction with the governments of Australia, New Zealand, the United Kingdom and Canada allegedly operates a transnational electronic surveillance operation called Echelon which is capable of intercepting land and cellular phone communications, e-mails, fax transmissions, web browsing, browsing history, and satellite signals (BBC, 2001).

CONCLUSION

The Internet has become the latest technology to be exploited by extremists and hatemongers. After a series of disastrous criminal and civil judgments over the past two decades, modern American hatemongers have refined both their message and their tactics. For a variety of reasons, including legal developments and technological advances in communications, many contemporary hate leaders are more willing to merely inspire violence than their predecessors were. In the past, groups like the Klan believed they shared the goals, if not the tactics, of their overall community. Today, an array of ideological and religious extremists see their role changed from enforcers of a majoritarian status quo to warriors in a guerrilla insurgency called "leaderless resistance."

Technological innovations such as the Internet have allowed extremists to inexpensively spread their rhetoric and strategies to a wider audience of potential would be terrorists without the necessity—and legal risks—of maintaining a more direct relationship with them. Violence or property destruction directed by hate groups and other terrorists is no longer insulated from punishment by a laissez faire legal system. The Supreme Court and lower tribunals have sculpted an important niche to protect the rights of bigots and other extremists who vigorously promote hateful and distasteful views, in cyberspace and other public fora. Contractual terms set forth by service providers can, however, restrict expression by customers. Because American law is more protective of speech than laws elsewhere, there will be continued litigation to determine which nation has jurisdiction over cyberspeech that breaks the laws.

Although American law protects offensive content on the Internet, cyberspace by itself may be no more effective to extremism's long-term existence than the film *Birth of a Nation* was to the Klan. More secretive foreign groups like Al Qaeda, hampered by a lack of Internet access to much of their impoverished potential audience, relied on the Internet as a tactical tool, bypassing its marketing efficiencies. The most successful domestic purveyors of hate, however, are people like William Pierce, who uses the Internet as a gateway marketing tool to expose his audience to a variety of messages from other media including books, periodicals, radio shows, and hate-rock compact discs.

As analyst Mark Potok observed,

> Although the Internet is important in bringing extremist messages to the general population, it is only a start in the recruitment process. No one becomes a Nazi simply by going up on a Web page. Ultimately, it is through white power music concerts, speeches by charismatic leaders and face-to-face interactions that the movement really brings in new participants. (personal communication, September 6, 2001)

Nonetheless, the FBI has observed that a new 21st Century terrorist threat has emerged from the use of computers and the Internet: "Terrorists are known to use information technology and the Internet to formulate plans, raise funds, spread propaganda, recruit new members, and communicate securely. However, there have also been cases of terrorists using cyber-based attacks. . . . The threat of cyberterrorism will grow in the new Millennium, as the leadership positions in extremist organizations are increasingly filled with younger, 'Internet-savvy' individuals." (FBI, 1999).

References

ACLU v. Reno, 217 F.3d 162 (3rd Cir. 2000); cert. granted (U.S. May 21, 2001), Ashcroft. v. ACLU (No. 00-1293).

American Law Institute. (1985). *Model penal code and commentaries*. Philadelphia: Author.

Animal Liberation Front. (2001a, November). Available from www.animal-liberation.com

Animal Liberation Front. (2001b, November). Available from http://members.tripod.com/alfsg/join.html

Backover, A. (1999, November 8). Hate sets up shop on Internet. *The Denver Post*, p. E-01.

Beam, L. (Ed.). (1983). *Essays of a Klansman: Being a compendium of Ku Klux Klan ideology, organizational methods, history, tactics, and opinions, with interpolations by the author*. Hayden Lake, ID: A.K.I.A.

Beam, L. (1992, February). Leaderless resistance. *The Seditionist, 12*.

Beauharnais v. Illinois, 343 U.S. 250 (1952).

Berlet, C. (2001, April). *When hate went online*. Paper presented at the Northeast Sociological Association Spring Conference, Fairfield, CT.

Black, H. C. (1979). *Black's law dictionary: Definitions of the terms and phrases of American and English jurisprudence, ancient and modern* (5th ed.). St. Paul, MN: West.

Boos v. Barry, 485 U.S. 312 (1988).

Brandenburg v. Ohio, 395 U.S. 444 (1969).

Bridis, T. (2001, November 23). FBI is building a 'Magic Lantern' software: Would allow agency to monitor computer use. *The Washington Post*, p. A15

British Broadcasting Co. (2001, May 29) *Q&A: What you need to know about Echelon, London*. Available from http://news.bbc.co.uk/hi/english/sci/tech/newsid_1357000/1357513.stm

Chalmers, D. M. (1981). *Hooded Americanism: The history of the Ku Klux Klan*. New York: Franklin Watts.

Chaplinsky v. State of New Hampshire, 315 U.S. 568 (1942).

Christian Gallery (2001, November). Available from www.christiangallery.com

Cohen v. California, 403 U.S. 15 (1971).

Cohen, A. (2001a, November 12). When terror hides online: Bin Laden's crew may be using the web to send secret messages. *Time, 158*, 65.

Cohen, A. (2001b, October 8). Who finds terror: Following the money. *Time, 68*, 70.

Cohen, W., & Danelski, D. (1997). *Constitution law: Civil liberties and individual rights*. Westbury, NY: Foundation.

Commonwealth v. Wilson et al., Berks County Court of Common Pleas, (1998, October 21).

Communications Decency Act, 47 U.S.C. § 223 (1996).

Computer Fraud and Abuse Act, 18 U.S.C. § 1030

Dees, M. (with Corcoran, J.). (1996). *Gathering storm: America's militia threat*. New York: HarperCollins.

Dixon, T. (1905). *The clansman: An historical romance of the Ku Klux Klan*. New York: Doubleday.

Earth Liberation Front. (2001, November). Available from www.earthliberationfront.com/about/index.shtml

18 U.S.C. § 245 (1968).

18 U.S.C. § 875 (1934).

18 U.S.C. § 1029 (1991).

18 U.S.C. § 1030 (1991).

Electronic Communications Privacy Act of 1986 (as amended).

Federal Bureau of Investigation, Counterterrorism Division (1999) *Terrorism in the United States*. Washington, DC, p. 40-41.

Grayned v. City of Rockford, 408 U.S. 104 (1972).

Griffin, R. (1997). *Caught in its own net: Postwar fascism outside Europe*. Retrieved August 2001 from http://www.brookes.ac.uk/schools/humanities/Roger/2457/FASOUT.htm

Hague v. Committee for Industrial Organization, 307 U.S. 496 (1939).

Hamas (2001, November). Available from www.palestine-info.com

Hizbollah (2001, November). Available from www.hizbollah.org

Holy Land Foundation (2001, December). Available from www.hlf.org

Hoskins, R. (1990). *Vigilantes of Christendom: The history of the Phineas Priesthood*. Lynchburg, VA: Virginia Publishing.

International Soc. for Krishna Consciousness v. Lee, 505 U.S. 672 (1992).

Kerr, D. (2000, July 24) *Internet and data interception capabilities developed by FBI*. Statement before the United States House of Representatives, The Committee on the Judiciary Sub-committee on the Constitution, Washington, D.C.

Kessler, J., & Rosenberg, D. (2000). *Combating extremism in cyberspace*. New York: Anti-Defamation League.

Klanwatch Intelligence Report. (1989, December). p. 47.

La Nouveau Penal Code, Art. R.645-2.

Levin, B. (1998). The patriot movement: Past, present & future. In H. Kushner (Ed.), *The future of terrorism: Violence in the new millennium* (pp.). Thousand Oaks, CA: Sage.

Lichtblau, E. (2000, July 21). Neo-Nazi must pay $1.1 million to fair housing activist. *Los Angles Times*, p. A19.

Lowe, D. (1985). *Computerized networks of hate.* New York: Anti-Defamation League.

Macdonald, A. (1978). *The Turner diaries: A novel.* Hillsboro, WV: National Vanguard.

Macdonald, A. (1989). *Hunter: A novel.* Hillsboro, WV: National Vanguard.

National Alliance. (2000). *Home page.* Available from http://www.natall.com

The nature and threat of violent anti-government groups in America: Hearings before the Subcommittee on Crime of the House Committee on the Judiciary, 104th Cong. (1995) (testimony of Brian Levin).

Ohio Criminal Syndicalism Act, Ohio Rev. Code Ann. § 2923.13.

Pennsylvania Crimes Code, 18 Penn. Cons. Stat. § 3933.

Pierce, W. (1994, January). Reorienting ourselves for success. *National Alliance Bulletin*, p. 5.

Planned Parenthood v. American Coalition of Life Activists, 224 F. 2d 1007 (9th Cir. March 28, 2001), vacated, en banc rehearing ordered, 268 F.3d 908 (October 3, 2001).

President announces progress on financial fight against terror. (2001, December 4). Press release. Washington, DC: White House.

Provide Appropriate Tools Required to Intercept and Obstruct Terrorism (PATRIOT) Act of 2001; H.R. 2975, Section 201, Title II.

Resistance Records. (2001). *Home page.* Available from http://www.resistance.com

Rhode, D. (2001, November 17) In 2 abandoned Kabul houses, some hints of Al Qaeda Presence. *The New York Times*, p. 1.

Reno et al. v. American Civil Liberties Union et al., 521 U.S. 844 (1997).

Rice v. Paladin Enterprises, Inc., 128 F.3d 233 (4th Cir. 1997), cert. denied, 118 S.Ct. 1515 (1998).

Roddy, D. (2001a, November 25). Fugitive abortion foe: I sent anthrax threats: Waagner makes visit to Web site operator. *Pittsburgh Post-Gazette*, p. A7.

Roddy, D. (2001b, December 6). Abortion clinic stalker arrested in Ohio. *Pittsburgh Post-Gazette*, p. A1.

Rowan v. U.S. Post Office Dept., 397 U.S. 728 (1970).

Schmalleger, F. (1999). *Criminal law today: An introduction with capstone cases.* Upper Saddle River, NJ: Prentice Hall.

Schwartz, A. M. (Ed.). (1996) *Danger: Extremism— The major vehicles and voices on America's far right fringe.* New York: Anti-Defamation League.

Southern Poverty Law Center. (1996). *False patriots: The threat of antigovernment extremists.* Montgomery, AL: Author.

Southern Poverty Law Center. (1999, Winter). The alliance and its allies: Pierce builds bridges at home, abroad. *Intelligence Report, 93.*

Stormfront.org. (2001). *Home page.* Available from http://www.stormfront.org

Taking Aim. (1994, November).

Texas Penal Code Ann. § 42.09 (1989).

Texas v. Johnson, 491 U.S. 397 (1989).

Title III of the Omnibus Crime Control and Safe Streets Act of 1968 (as amended).

United States v. Barnett, 667 F.2d 835 (9th Cir. 1982).

United States v. Buttorff, 572 F.2d 619 (8th Cir. 1978).

United States v. Machado, No. 96-142 (C.D. Ca. 1998).

United States v. Quon, No. 99-76 (C.D. Ca. 1999).

Walker, S. (1994). *Hate speech: The history of an American controversy.* Lincoln, NE: Bison.

Watts v. United States, 394 U.S. 705 (1969).

White Aryan Resistance. (1988). *Flyer.*

Widmar v. Vincent, 454 U.S. 263 (1981).

Yahoo! v. La Ligue Contre Racism, 2001 U.S. Dist. Lexis 18378 (2001).

8

COUNTERTERRORISM

The greatest dangers to liberty lurk in insidious encroachment by men of zeal—well-meaning but without understanding.

—Louis D. Brandeis

The attacks of September 11, 2001, seared the consciousness of the United States, provoking calls for military retaliation abroad and new antiterrorism laws at home. The ensuing military operations to wrest Osama bin Laden away from his hosts, the Taliban government of Afghanistan, have changed the dynamics of world politics in many unanticipated and still unknown ways.

More than ever before, the U.S. government's counterterrorism policy is seen as an integral part of its foreign affairs policy. New alliances and shifting priorities will likely characterize U.S. counterterrorism foreign policy for years to come.

Domestic counterterrorism policies are likewise subject to change in the post–September 11 world. Demonstrating a renewed focus on terrorism, on October 8, 2001, President George W. Bush created an Office of Homeland Security, headed by Tom Ridge, former governor of Pennsylvania. The office's mission was to develop a national strategy for detecting, protecting, and responding to terrorist assaults. Among the priority areas identified by the new office were airport security, emergency response teams, border security, and biodefense.

Likewise, the domestic antiterrorism laws enacted as a response to September 11 present new and difficult challenges to our democracy. To succeed in the long run, domestic counterterrorism strategies must preserve cherished constitutional principles, and officials must resist the temptation to diminish the freedoms upon which the nation is based.

This chapter discusses U.S. counterterrorism policy from two interrelated perspectives: foreign affairs and domestic civil liberties.

COUNTERTERRORISM AND U.S. FOREIGN POLICY

Before September 11, 2001, citizens of the United States and its holdings, both at home and abroad, were increasingly targets of terrorism, but the United States was not the most targeted nation in the world. Colombia suffered the most terrorist incidents in 2000. India was second, and Indians also had been the target of the airline attack that caused the greatest number of deaths before September 11—the 1985 bombing of an Air India jet off the coast of Ireland that killed all 329 people aboard. Sikh and Kashmiri terrorists were blamed by the U.S. Department of State for the attack.

According to the State Department, 423 terrorist attacks occurred worldwide in 2000, an increase of 8% from the 392 attacks recorded during 1999. Much of the increase represented terrorist bombings of a multinational oil pipeline in Colombia; the pipeline, to many people a symbol of the United States, was bombed 152 times. Western Europe had the largest decrease in terrorist attacks between 1999 and 2000: from 85 to 30. The number of casualties caused by terrorists also increased in 2000: 405 were killed and 791 wounded, up from the 1999 totals of 233 dead and 706 wounded (U.S. Department of State, 2001).

In the past two decades, roughly one-third of all terrorist attacks worldwide have been aimed at U.S. citizens or property, and the proportion was higher in the 1990s than in the 1980s (Pillar, 2001, p. 57). The number of anti-U.S. attacks rose from 169 in 1999 to 200 in 2000. Nineteen U.S. citizens were killed in acts of international terrorism in 2000, of whom 17 were sailors who died in the attack against the USS *Cole* in the Yemeni port of Aden.

A Global Perspective on Transnational Terrorism

Varying explanations have been offered as to why the United States and its interests are so attractive to transnational terrorists. Most of the explanations center on the changes wrought in international politics by the collapse of the Soviet Union and the end of the Cold War. The emergence of the United States as the world's only remaining economic and military superpower has fueled resentment in many areas around the globe. In addition, the opportunities for terrorism against the United States are magnified by the open nature of our society; our long, virtually undefended borders; the enormous number of international visitors to our land; and the many visible signs of our presence around the world.

Many observers believe that poverty and injustice contribute to terrorism, and they argue that counterterrorism activities should include attempts to improve living conditions in less prosperous countries (Schweitzer, 1998). Although a long-term strategy to provide disadvantaged people with employment and other opportunities for a better life might deter some potential terrorists, it would be ineffective in discouraging the most fanatic. A "core of incorrigibles," including but not limited to al-Qaeda, seems determined to wreak violence against the United States and its allies.

Chapter 2 of this volume discussed the conceptual clash postulated by Barber (1992, 1995) between "Jihad" and "McWorld." Barber predicted that the cultural differences between religious extremism and global capitalism were on a collision course that inevitably would lead to violent confrontation. Following the September 11 attacks, as many Americans struggled to understand how such horrific events could have happened, Barber's arguments gained renewed attention.

According to Barber, the forces of "McWorld"—which include the international marketing of American pop culture, fast food, and violent video games, among other things—are deeply offensive to the religious value systems of many Muslims and Arabs. In an interview shortly after September 11, Barber said that the aggressive marketing of American products had left many people in other nations with a distorted image of the United States. He observed that "we don't even export the best of our *own* culture, as defined by serious music, by jazz, by poetry, by our extraordinary literature, our playwrights—we export the worst, the most childish, the most base, the most trivial of our culture. And we call that American" (Rosenfeld, 2001, ¶ 20 of print article).

Barber argues that consumerist capitalism and religious fundamentalism are both threats to the development of global democracy. The only way to avoid an unprecedented explosion of violence is to promote democracy around the world: "If we export capitalism without democracy, we breed anarchy and terrorism" (Rosenfeld, 2001, ¶ 16). Few genuine democracies exist in those portions of Africa and Asia believed to be the wellspring of much of the terrorism directed against the United States today; many are ruled by kings, military dictators, or clerics.

Samuel Huntington is another author whose mid-1990s book has been frequently quoted since September 11. In *The Clash of Civilization and the Remaking of the World Order*, Huntington (1996) identified eight civilizations: Sinic (China, Vietnam, Korea), Japanese, Hindu-Indian, Islamic, Orthodox-Russian, Western, Latin American, and African. He predicted that conflicts in the 21st century would not be between nations but between distinct civilizations that have different cultures and religions. This clash of civilizations would dominate global politics and define the battle lines of the future. Huntington predicted that the greatest conflicts would be between the predominantly Christian nations of the West and Muslim nations in Africa and Asia.

In an interview after September 11, Huntington said the current war against terrorism did not meet his definition of clashing civilizations because the governments of many Muslim and Arab nations are cooperating with the United States in fighting terrorism. Huntington expressed concern, however, that the West's counterterrorism strikes, including the war against the Taliban, might enrage citizens of Muslim and Arab nations, spurring attempts to overthrow their governments. Huntington said: "I fear that while September 11 united the West, the response to September 11th will unite the Muslim world" (Healy, 2001). Pakistan may be particularly vulnerable because of its high concentration of ethnic Pashtuns, who are the same ethnicity as the Taliban (Rashid, 2001). Pakistan's nuclear arsenal in the possession of extremists is a frightening scenario.

Huntington's thesis has been criticized for being too simplistic and ignoring the numerous currents and countercurrents that define any religion or culture. Edward W. Said (2001) argues that civilizations are much more complex and varied than Huntington admits:

> the personification of enormous entities called "the West" and "Islam" is recklessly affirmed, as if hugely complicated matters like identity and culture existed in a cartoon-like world where Popeye and Bluto bash each other mercilessly, with one always more virtuous pugilist getting the upper hand over his adversary. (p. 1, ¶ 3)

Said further faults the clash of civilization concept for not recognizing "that the major contest in most modern cultures concerns the definition or interpretation of each culture. . . . [A] great deal of demagogy and downright ignorance is involved in presuming to speak for a whole religion or civilization" (p. 1, ¶ 3). Instead of seeing verification of a clash of cultures in the September 11 attacks, Said argues that we should look at it as a "carefully planned and horrendous, pathologically motivated suicide attack and mass slaughter by a small group of deranged militants" (p. 1, ¶ 5).

International Responses to Terrorism

No international criminal code exists, nor is there an international police force capable of combating terrorism or an international court with jurisdiction over all acts of terrorism. Governments around the globe nevertheless engage in counterterrorism activities, primarily by passing laws against terrorism and entering into cooperative agreements with one another. Many examples of cooperation among nations were seen in the aftermath of the September 11 attacks.

The United Nations (UN), which was founded in 1945 following World War II by 51 "peace loving" nations, has grown to 189 member states that have signed a number of global treaties, regional conventions, and bilateral agreements. The UN's mission is to maintain international peace and security, promote human rights, and help member nations resolve political, cultural, and economic problems.

The UN Charter governs the use of force between states, and several conventions and treaties outline the obligations of the members. At least 11 major multination conventions detail states's responsibilities for combating terrorism (U.S. Office of Counterterrorism, 1998). Among these are several conventions against offenses committed aboard aircraft, against diplomats and senior government officials, against unlawful taking of nuclear materials and plastic explosives, against taking of hostages, and against ships or fixed offshore platforms on the continental shelf. The UN General Assembly and the Security Council also pass resolutions aimed at specific states. For example, in 2000, the Security Council called on Afghanistan's Taliban to close its terrorist training camps, stop providing sanctuary to international terrorists, and cooperate with international efforts to bring indicted terrorists to justice (UN Resolution 1333, December 19, 2000).

The UN has been criticized as being ineffective against terrorism. Member states have been unable to agree on a definition of terrorism, and disputes commonly arise about who are the aggressors and who are the victims. Many nations object when the more powerful members of the UN try to impose their views of what constitutes terrorism. For example, Israel repeatedly has asserted that a state that supports terrorism is guilty of an armed attack on the state that is victimized, but the UN has rejected this argument. Many of the counterterrorism operations conducted by Israel have been condemned by the UN Security Council, or condemnation has been avoided only because of a veto by the United States (Travalio, 2000, p. 156). In addition to the UN conventions, a number of other agreements exist, including extradition treaties between individual nations and smaller multinational alliances such as the North Atlantic Treaty Organization (NATO).

International Cooperation and the Use of Military Forces

Non–state-sponsored terrorism committed against the citizens or holdings of a state generally is not a violation of international law, but rather a violation of the domestic criminal laws of the victim state or the state where the terrorist act occurred. *State-sponsored terrorism* is a violation of international law that invokes the victimized state's right of self-defense (Sharp, 2000, p. 37). Disputes exist about the degree of culpability necessary to label a state a sponsor of terrorism. The UN Charter gives victim states the right to respond with military force in the event of an "armed attack," but that term is not defined. A weak government that cannot prevent terrorists from using its country as a training or recruiting base from which to launch attacks is not considered guilty of an armed attack on another state (Travalio, 2000, p. 152). On the other hand, there is "a raging debate among international lawyers" (Travalio, 2000, p. 152) over whether a state that provides active support for international terrorists is engaged in an armed attack. The Taliban's support of al-Qaeda was clearly considered by the United States and its allies as an armed attack justifying military intervention.

The United States was not alone in its military response to September 11. The day after the attack, the 19-member NATO announced it would invoke the mutual defense clause, which considers an attack on one member an attack on all, as long as the United States supplied evidence of the involvement of bin Laden and al-Qaeda. On October 2, 2001, NATO announced that the United States had provided the necessary "clear and compelling proof." NATO nations granted the United Nations open access to their airfields and seaports and agreed to enhance intelligence cooperation relating to terrorist threats. Putting a stamp of approval on America's decision to attack Afghanistan, NATO also agreed to send its military troops into combat as necessary.

Other nations, including many predominantly Muslim and Arab nations such as Pakistan, Saudi Arabia, and Egypt, also offered to cooperate in the hunt for those behind the September 11 attacks. Governments around the world, including those in Africa, the Middle East, and Asia, are threatened by extremism. A large American military presence, some fear, could provoke a popular uprising capable of toppling the governments that assist the United States. With these concerns in mind, the United States sought other types of support from some countries, including use of airspace and sharing of intelligence information. In Uzbekistan, a primarily Muslim nation that borders Afghanistan, the United States was permitted to station forces to launch search-and-rescue missions. Offers of cooperation even came from Sudan, against which the United States had launched a cruise missile attack in 1998. The United States had believed that the missile target, a suspected chemical weapons factory in the capital, Khartoum, was involved in the bombings of the U.S. embassies in Kenya and Tanzania.

The United States also received considerable international cooperation in seizing terrorists' assets. President Bush issued an expanded list of organizations and suspected associates of terrorists, and he authorized the Treasury Department to halt transactions with any banks that refused to freeze terrorists' assets. Nations were asked to seize the assets of many groups and individuals believed to be associated with global terrorism. Many of these groups, including Hamas, Hizbollah, the Real Irish Republican Army, and the Basque Fatherland and Liberty (Euskadi ta Askatasuna, or ETA), are not clearly linked to al-Qaeda.

Following September 11, the Bush administration warned that its war on terrorism would extend far beyond Afghanistan and bin Laden. Cautioning that the war would be protracted, the president portrayed the war in Afghanistan as only the first stage of a multistage effort. The risks and burdens of America's foreign policy are not fully known, but history suggests that retaliation begets retaliation.

The High Cost of Retaliation

Many terrorist experts and policy makers endorse the concept that a strong offense is the best defense, but some warn that the United States is partially responsible for the heightened threat it faces. The Pentagon's Defense Science Board (1997) noted that "Historical data show a strong correlation between U.S. involvement in international situations and an increase in terrorist attacks against the United States" (p. 15). Eland (1998) further examined the correlations noted by the Defense Science Board and concluded that American military intervention in foreign countries inevitably led terrorists to retaliate against the United States. It is not American pop culture, depravity, or materialism that provokes terrorism, Eland argues; instead, it is America's exercise of its military might overseas.

Eland suggested that the number of attacks against the United States could be reduced if it used military restraint in other countries. Tracing retaliatory terrorist incidents since 1915, Eland (1998) observed that

> the interventionist foreign policy currently pursued by the United States is an aberration in its
> history. Adopting a policy of military restraint would return the United States to the traditional

foreign policy it pursued for the first century and a half of its existence before the Cold War distorted it. (p. 7)

Proposals to return to a less interventionist foreign policy are controversial, and many observers believe that, in the long run, aggressive responses to terrorism will reduce future attacks against the United States. Because there is no agreement on the root causes of terrorism, it is difficult to agree on the proper scope of U.S. foreign counterterrorism policy. Domestic counterterrorism policy is similarly contentious.

DOMESTIC COUNTERTERRORISM POLICY

Counterterrorism activities within the nation's borders must operate within the legal restraints of our democracy. But how vigorously can a democracy fight terrorism and remain a democracy? How can the United States play by the rules of its democracy when terrorists make their own rules? Which of our civil liberties should we be willing to give up, and what kind of proof do we need that sacrificing personal freedom is an effective antidote to terrorism? There are, of course, no easy answers to these questions, and the search for the proper balance between a safe society and a free one is complex and dynamic.

The discussion to follow centers on four aspects of domestic counterterrorism policy: first, the provisions of, and controversies around, recent antiterrorism legislation, including the USA PATRIOT Act (2001) passed in response to September 11; second, the detentions that occurred in the aftermath of the attacks; third, the plan to use military tribunals to try noncitizens accused of terrorism; and fourth, a review of three infamous and overreaching counterterrorism operations from U.S. history.

Legislating Against Terrorism

Most nations treat terrorism as a criminal act, not a political one. Outlawing terrorism implies faith in the legal system, and antiterrorism legislation in democratic countries generally incorporates constitutional rights and judicial review (White, 1998, p. 247). Critics of the government's counterterrorism policy have long argued that lawmakers overrate terrorist threats to achieve their political goals, with the result that civil liberties are sacrificed without an increase in public safety. Similar criticisms have been leveled against the two U.S. antiterrorism laws discussed below: the Antiterrorist Act of 1996 and the USA PATRIOT Act of 2001.

Antiterrorism Act of 1996

The Antiterrorism and Effective Death Penalty Act of 1996 was the culmination and merger of disparate legislative efforts, some of them stretching back more than a decade. The bombings of the World Trade Center in 1993 and the Alfred P. Murrah Federal Building in Oklahoma City in 1995 supplied the impetus for the 1996 law, although other issues such as habeas corpus and immigration aided passage of the bill. Most of the criticism against the legislation focused on the domestic law enforcement provisions, not foreign policy (Pillar, 2001, p. 7).

The 1996 law made some terrorist acts federal crimes punishable by death, thereby avoiding statute of limitation restrictions that apply to non–death penalty crimes. It established a formal list of Foreign Terrorist Organizations (FTOs) designated by the Secretary of State. Blocking FTO financing was an integral part of the bill, and the groups' assets were frozen. Penalties of up to 10 years in prison were established for anyone supplying material support or resources to an FTO. Support for humanitarian purposes, such as operating schools and hospitals affiliated with FTOs, also was prohibited.

The law revived a previous practice of denying visas to foreigners based on membership in terrorist groups. No proof that the individual furthered the illegal activities of the group was necessary. Further, the bill authorized deportation of anyone who was associated with a terrorist group at the time of otherwise legal entry into the United States.

Prior to the law, the FBI had been prohibited from opening or expanding an investigation if the basis for the investigation was an activity protected by the First Amendment, such as speech or assembly. That prohibition was repealed. Private citizens who were victims of terrorism were permitted to file suit for damages against state sponsors in U.S. courts. This provision created an exception to the doctrine of sovereign immunity that normally protects states from being sued. In addition and not directly related to terrorism, the 1996 act placed a 1-year statute of limitations on habeas corpus petitions, which allow federal courts to review cases of inmates who claim that state courts violated their constitutional rights.

Critics argue that the 1996 antiterrorist legislation was "one of the worst assaults on the Constitution in decades" (Dempsey & Cole, 1999, p. 2). The condemnation leveled against the act included the following.

- The bill added to the chaos surrounding a capital punishment system already fraught with error. Further, many foreign nations oppose the death penalty and might be unwilling to cooperate with U.S. efforts to apprehend terrorists on foreign soil if doing so might lead to an execution. Members of the European Union, for example, have not extradited fugitives to the United States without an assurance that the death penalty will not be sought (Pillar, 2001, p. 85).

- Following the money trail is extremely difficult and unlikely to achieve results. Most of the financial transactions of terrorists take place outside the United States, and many of them also take place outside formal banking systems. Terrorists use multiple false names that obscure their ties with one another. Informal money-by-wire arrangements are common, as are the physical movements of currency from the hands of one terrorist to another. Offshore banking businesses make it easier to conceal financial transactions, and the complex organizational links among overlapping groups make it unlikely that terrorists' "lifeblood" can be controlled sufficiently through U.S. legislation.

- Making crimes of activities protected by the First Amendment, including support for peaceful humanitarian and political activities of groups labeled terrorist, resurrects the concept of guilt by association.

- Deportees are denied basic due process rights, especially the right to confront their accusers.

- The law's limits on the "Great Writ" of habeas corpus were unrelated to terrorism and served the political agenda of conservatives without increasing public safety.

Supporters of the bill acknowledged that some of the criticisms might be valid, but they argued that tough measures were needed to protect the public. As will be discussed below, somewhat similar criticisms were leveled against the USA PATRIOT Act, passed in the aftermath of the September 11 attacks.

The USA PATRIOT Act

Shortly after the September 11 attacks, President Bush asked Congress to enact another counterterrorism package. Unlike the 1996 law, which was the product of a full year of legislative debate, the act to "Provide Appropriate Tools Required to Intercept and Obstruct Terrorism" (the USA PATRIOT Act) sailed quickly through Congress, passing the House of Representatives by a vote of 356 to 66 and the Senate by 98 to 1. The sole dissenting senator, Russell D. Feingold (D-Wisc.), said that the bill's search and seizure provisions were unconstitutional, as was punishing people for vague associations with possible terrorist organizations. Nevertheless, the lopsided vote was a clear indication of the mood of Congress about domestic counterterrorism operations.

The USA PATRIOT Act was signed into law by President Bush on October 26, 2001, and included the following provisions:

- *Roving wiretaps.* Law enforcement officials may obtain a warrant from a special intelligence court for a wiretap on any telephone used by a suspected terrorist. Previously, separate judicial authorization had been needed for each phone used by the suspect.
- *National search warrants.* Federal officials can apply for search warrants that can be used nationwide.
- *Detention.* Immigrants suspected of involvement in terrorism can be held for up to 7 days for questioning; the previous limit was 2 days. After a week, they must be charged with a crime or released, although under certain conditions their detentions can be extended by 6-month periods.
- *Wiretaps and purpose of investigation.* Previously, to obtain a wiretap from a special intelligence court, foreign intelligence had to be the only purpose of the investigation. Under the new law, authorities can apply for a wiretap in cases where foreign intelligence is a significant purpose of the investigation but not the sole purpose.
- *Criminal penalties raised.* Sentences for terrorist acts, harboring terrorists, and financing terrorism were increased.
- *Bioterrorism.* The law makes it a crime to possess substances that can be used as biological or chemical weapons for any reason other than a "peaceful" purpose.
- *Monitoring computers.* Computers are likened to telephones, and officials can subpoena e-mail communications of suspected terrorists.
- *Intelligence sharing.* The bill expands the role of local law enforcement officials by authorizing them to share information, including grand jury testimony, with national security officials.
- *Money laundering.* The Treasury Department was given greater authority to force foreign banks to determine the sources of large bank accounts. U.S. financial transactions with foreign banks that refuse to release information on depositors to U.S. investigators can be cut off, even if the foreign bank is following its nation's bank secrecy laws.
- *Shell banks.* The law prohibits dealings with offshore shell banks, which are not regulated by the banking industry.
- *Sunset provisions.* The expanded powers of wiretaps for telephones and computers expire in 4 years.

Like the 1996 legislation, the 2001 legislation has been praised and criticized. In testimony before the U.S. Judiciary Committee on October 3, 2001, several witnesses commented on the strengths and weaknesses of the proposed bill. Douglas W. Kmiec, Dean of the Law School of the Catholic University of America in Washington, D.C., expressed his support for the bill by noting that our founder's conception of freedom was not a freedom to do anything or associate for any purpose, but to do those things which do not harm others and which, it was hoped, would advance the common good. Freedom separated from this truth is not freedom at all, but license. Congress can no longer afford, if it ever could, to confuse freedom and license— because doing so licenses terrorism, not freedom. (Kmiec, 2001, p. 1)

Speaking against the bill, another law professor, David Cole, said that the bill was an overreaction based on fear; that it sacrificed the bedrock principles of political freedom and equal treatment; and that it traded the liberty of vulnerable immigrants for the safety of the rest of society. Cole concluded that the

overbreadth of the bill reflects the overreaction that we have often indulged in when threatened. The expansive authorities that the Administration bill grants, moreover, are not likely to make us safer. To the contrary, by penalizing even wholly lawful, nonviolent, and associational activity, we are likely to drive such activity underground, to encourage extremists, and to make the communities that will inevitably be targeted by such broad-brush measures disinclined to cooperate with law enforcement. As Justice Louis Brandeis wrote nearly 75 years ago, the Framers of our Constitution knew "that fear breeds repression; that repression breeds hate; and that hate menaces stable government.". . . In other words, freedom and security need not necessarily be traded off against one another; maintaining our freedom is itself critical to maintaining our security. (Cole, 2001, p. 8)

Controversial Detentions and Racial Profiling

On the day of the terrorist attacks, federal law enforcement agents began what may end up as the most extensive criminal investigations in U.S. history. Focusing on non-U.S. citizens, particularly immigrants and visitors from Arab and Muslim nations, federal investigators ultimately detained more than 1,000 foreigners. A small number of those imprisoned were held as material witnesses to the September 11 assaults, and the rest were held on immigration violations (e.g., expired visas) and criminal charges, such as traffic violations and misdemeanors unrelated to terrorism. Had it not been for September 11, most of the criminal charges and immigration violations would have been ignored or resolved with paperwork.

Government officials justified the detentions as a necessary response to an extraordinary situation, and they noted that federal agents were merely enforcing existing laws. Mindy Tucker, a spokeswoman for the Justice Department, said that

Sept. 11 has forced the entire government to change the way we do business . . . Our No. 1 priority right now is to prevent any further terrorist attacks. Part of that entails identifying those who may have connections to terrorism who are here in America and making sure they're not in a position to carry out any further terrorism. (as quoted in Wilgoren, 2001, p. 1)

On September 18, the Bush administration announced that it had rewritten the detention rules so as to allow indefinite detention of immigrants suspected of crimes during a national emergency. Human rights groups repeatedly have criticized indefinite detention practices in other countries, and they quickly objected to President Bush's administrative order. Legal scholars noted, however, that indefinite detention of immigrants is consistent with Supreme Court rulings. For example, in 1999, the High Court ruled that immigrants singled out for deportation because they associated with a terrorist organization had no right to challenge their deportation on First Amendment grounds (*Reno v. American-Arab Anti-Discrimination Committee*, 1999). The Court based its holding on the 1996 antiterrorism legislation and the argument that aliens do not enjoy the constitutional rights granted to U.S. citizens. Critics of the Supreme Court's decision noted that "the Court put immigrants on notice that if they engage in political activity of which the government disapproves, they are vulnerable to selective retaliatory enforcement of immigration laws" (Dempsey & Cole, 1999, p. 3).

Despite the Supreme Court's ruling and the Bush administration's policy, human rights advocates argue that noncitizens should be afforded the basic legal protections of the U.S. Constitution. They argue that the nation's Founders intended to protect the natural rights of all human beings, regardless of their citizenship. Among these are the rights to be formally charged, confront accusers, present evidence, and require rigorous standards of proof.

Few, if any, of those arrested are believed to have known some of the suspected hijackers, and as of mid-2002, none of the detainees had been formally accused of assisting in the attack. The U.S. attorney general, however, opined that the roundup had prevented more terrorism, and the Justice Department announced that it would try to interview about 5,000 Arab and Muslim men living in the United States on temporary visas. Immigration attorneys and Arab-American community leaders expressed concern that those who cooperated with government authorities might be detained and deported. Some law enforcement officials spoke out against the interviews as a form of racial profiling. For example, the acting police chief of Portland, Oregon, Andrew Kirkland, refused to assist federal authorities on the grounds that Oregon law prohibits local police from questioning immigrants who are not suspected of a crime (Butterfield, 2001).

Military Tribunals

On November 15, 2001, President Bush signed an executive order allowing foreigners suspected of international terrorism to be tried in special military tribunals. The trials would be presided over by military officers, without a jury, and probably would take place outside the United States. Defendants would have lawyers, but not necessarily those of their choosing. Hearsay evidence, typically barred from civilian trials, would be permitted, and the proceedings could be held in secret if necessary to protect classified information. Sentences, including death, could be imposed with a two-thirds vote of the presiding military officers.

Critics quickly complained that President Bush had seized dictatorial power and betrayed basic American values. The administration responded that the tribunals were necessary in a time of war and that they would make it possible to move quickly and prevent the disclosure of classified national security information.

Subsequent rules drafted by the administration afforded more due process protections for defendants than originally announced. Under the new rules, the death penalty would require a unanimous verdict, although only a two-thirds vote of the panel of military officials would be needed for a guilty verdict. Proof beyond a reasonable doubt would be required, but hearsay evidence would be allowed. Defendants would have military lawyers appointed to their case, although they could also hire their own lawyers.

President Bush's counsel, Alberto R. Gonzales (2001), defended the plan for military tribunals by noting that

> it specifically directs that all trials before military commissions will be "full and fair." . . . The American military justice system is the finest in the world, with longstanding traditions of forbidding command influence on proceedings, of providing zealous advocacy by competent defense counsel, and of procedural fairness. . . . The suggestion that these commissions will

U.S. Army military police escort a detainee to his cell in Camp X-Ray at the U.S. Naval Base at Guantanamo Bay, Cuba. Detainees are suspected members of Afghanistan's Taliban and al-Qaeda.

Photo courtesy of the U.S. Navy.

afford only sham justice like that dispensed in dictatorial nations is an insult to our military justice system." (¶ 6)

Nationally syndicated columnist William Safire (2001) objected to comparing the president's plan with military trials.

Military attorneys are silently seething because they know that to be untrue. The U.C.M.J. [United Code of Military Justice] demands a public trial, proof beyond reasonable doubt, an accused's voice in the selection of juries and right to choose counsel, unanimity in death sentencing and above all appellate review by civilians confirmed by the Senate. Not one of those fundamental rights can be found in Bush's military order setting up kangaroo courts for people he designates before "trial" to be terrorists. Bush's fiat turns back the clock on all advances in military justice, through three wars, in the past half-century." (p. A17)

The idea of military tribunals was also criticized outside the United States. When the United States moved captured Taliban soldiers and al-Qaeda members from Afghanistan to Guantanamo Bay, Cuba, for further investigation and prosecution, many U.S. allies protested U.S. plans for trying them in military tribunals.

Nevertheless, historical precedent exists for using military tribunals during wartime. Major John Andre, a British spy whose capture exposed Benedict Arnold's plan to surrender West Point to the British in exchange for money and a military commission, was tried by a group of 14 military officers in 1780 and hanged after his conviction. During the Civil War, President Abraham Lincoln ordered hearings before military tribunals for Confederate agents suspected of sabotaging railroads. In 1942, 6 months after the attack on Pearl Harbor, the Supreme Court upheld the use of military tribunals for eight spies who had landed submarines on beaches in Florida and Long Island; six of the eight were executed.

Three Infamous Cases from the U.S. History of Counterterrorism

Domestic counterterrorism activities that appear to many people to be justified by the seriousness of the threat may in hindsight be seen as harmful and unnecessary. History has demonstrated that fear and inflamed passions can lead to overzealous enforcement and scapegoating of innocent people. Three examples from the 20th century are presented below: the Palmer Raids, the internment of Japanese Americans, and the House Un-American Activities Committee and McCarthyism.

The Palmer Raids

One infamous example of overreaction occurred shortly after World War I, when America was struggling with rampant inflation, high unemployment, labor strikes, and race riots. A climate of fear and repression centered on the growing Communist Party. The "Red Scare" intensified when A. Mitchell Palmer, President Woodrow Wilson's attorney general, claimed that communism was "eating its way into the homes of the American workman" (Palmer, 1920, ¶ 3 of Web site). Palmer recruited J. Edgar Hoover as his special assistant; together, they used the Espionage Act of 1917 (H. R. 291, 1917) and an amendment to it, the Sedition Act of 1918, to launch a campaign against radicals and left-wing organizations.

A series of bombings began in the late spring of 1919, and on June 2, bombs went off in eight cities, including Washington, D.C., where Palmer's home was partially destroyed. It was never determined who set the bombs, but the communists were quickly blamed. Palmer claimed that the communists were trying to take over the government. In an essay titled "The Case Against the Reds," Palmer (1920) charged that "tongues of revolutionary heat were licking the altars of the churches, leaping into the belfry of the school bell, crawling into the sacred corners of American homes, seeking to replace marriage vows with libertine laws, burning up the foundations of society" (¶ 3 of Web site).

The attorney general retaliated for the bombings by ordering the Justice Department to conduct a number of raids on radical and leftist organizations around the country. On January 2, 1920, 500 FBI agents arrested union leaders, scientists, former antiwar protesters, and others suspected of supporting leftist causes. Federal officials, acting without judicial warrants, broke into offices of labor unions and other targeted groups, rummaging through and destroying political and personal documents. Within a few months, more than 5,000 people were taken into custody; after lengthy detentions, most were released without charges being filed. Among those arrested was Emma Goldman, a well-known feminist and anarchist author. She, along with 249 other aliens, was deported and put on a ship bound for the Soviet Union.

Attitudes against Attorney General Palmer changed when the communist takeover failed to materialize, and he was denounced for violating the arrestees' civil liberties. Some critics claimed that Palmer had devised the "Red Scare" to help him become the Democratic presidential candidate in 1920. Ultimately, Palmer was convicted of misappropriating government funds, and charges against the remaining prisoners were dropped. For more on the Palmer Raids, see Feuerlicht (1971), Hoyt (1969), Labor Research Association (1948), and McCormick (1997).

Japanese American internees line up for the noon meal at the Manzanar War Relocation Authority (WRA) Camp in California in 1943. This photo is part of a series of photographs of the Manzanar internment camp taken by the renowned photographer Ansel Adams.

Photo courtesy of the Library of Congress, Prints & Photographs Division, Ansel Adams, photographer.

Japanese Internment

America's experience with the internment of people of Japanese heritage is another infamous example of overzealous counterterrorism at the expense of cherished American values. World War II was already devastating Europe when Japanese forces attacked the U.S. naval base at Pearl Harbor on December 7, 1941, stunning the nation and pushing it into the war. Anti-Asian prejudice was already strong in the United States, and the attack on Pearl Harbor cast even greater suspicion on people of Japanese ancestry.

Although he had no direct evidence that the Japanese intended to invade the United States, on February 19, 1942, President Franklin D. Roosevelt signed Executive Order No. 9066, authorizing the secretary of war to define military areas from which "any or all persons may be excluded as deemed necessary or desirable." Fearing an attack on the West Coast, the government created military areas in California, Washington, Oregon, and parts of Arizona, from which all persons of Japanese ancestry were banned. The War Relocation Authority was created, and the army forcibly moved more than 110,000 people of Japanese descent, most of whom were American citizens, to one of 10 internment camps set up in California, Idaho, Utah, Arizona, Wyoming, Colorado, and Arkansas. The internment camps were euphemistically called "relocation centers."

The camps were overcrowded and the housing was primitive, with no plumbing or cooking facilities (War Relocation Authority, 1943). Coal for fires was scarce, food was rationed, and many cold nights were faced with just a blanket. Several young Japanese Americans refused to be drafted into the military from the camps, arguing that they were willing to fight for the United States, but not until their families were released; they were prosecuted and imprisoned.

In 1944, President Roosevelt rescinded the order, and the last internment camp was closed at the end of 1945. In addition to being forced to live in squalid conditions, the internees lost their property, businesses, and livelihoods. Four decades later, the government recognized the harm caused by its overzealous counterterrorism efforts, and the Civil Liberties Act of 1988, signed by President Ronald Reagan, "acknowledged the fundamental injustice of the evacuation, relocation, and internment of United States citizens and permanent resident aliens of Japanese ancestry during World War II" (Civil Liberties Act, 1988). Payments of $20,000 were made to each of the approximately 60,000 surviving internees, and the U.S. government issued a formal apology. For more on the Japanese internments, see Harth (2001), Houston and Houston (1983), Myer (1971), and Robinson (2001).

More Red Scares: HUAC and McCarthyism

Guilt by association was the driving force behind the House Un-American Activities Committee (HUAC), which began operations in 1938. Looking to rout out radicals and communists, especially those from Hollywood and members of labor unions, HUAC made vague and sweeping accusations against individuals and asked witnesses to "name names." The hearings seemed designed to get people to renounce their past rather than to establish criminal guilt: HUAC already knew most of the names that it demanded from the witnesses. Many refused, and their careers and reputations were ruined. One group of writers and directors, known as the Hollywood Ten, were sent to prison for not cooperating with HUAC.

With a reputation built on making unsubstantiated accusations that the government had been infiltrated by communists, Senator Joseph McCarthy became chairman of the Senate permanent investigations subcommittee in 1953, a position from which he exercised great power. Through widely publicized television hearings, using unidentified informers, and making outlandish accusations, McCarthy ruined the careers of many people, with little or no evidence. His methods eventually came under attack by the press and his colleagues, and in 1954 the U.S. Senate voted to condemn him for misconduct. McCarthy is remembered today by many as a demagogue and witch-hunter; others treat his legacy more generously, crediting him with bringing the serious threat of communism to the attention of America. For more on the Red Scare, see Fried (1991), Herman (2000), McCarthy (1985), and Schreker (1994).

HIGHLIGHTS OF REPRINTED ARTICLES

The two articles selected to accompany this chapter reflect the two dimensions of U.S. counterterrorism policy discussed in this chapter: foreign affairs and domestic policy.

Paul R. Pillar. (2001). "Lessons and Futures." In *Terrorism and U.S. Foreign Policy*. Washington, DC: Brookings Institution Press.

This chapter was written before September 11, 2001, but its suggestions for U.S. counterterrorism policy remain relevant. Pillar warns against building false expectations that terrorism can be defeated. Counterterrorism, Pillar says, is "a fight and a struggle, but it is not a campaign with a beginning and an end. . . . Terrorism happens. It should never be accepted, but it should always be expected" (p. 218).

Pillar suggests that rather than using a "war" metaphor, policy makers and the public should use a model more akin to that used in public health policies aimed at controlling communicable disease: The government should shift foreign policy emphasis and resources as necessary but never fall prey to the illusion that its efforts can bring total success.

Pillar makes a series of recommendations, including injecting a counterterrorism perspective into all foreign policy decisions. Many of his suggestions mirror policies enacted by the United States after September 11, such as disrupting terrorist infrastructures worldwide and helping other governments to fight terrorism within their borders.

Jeffrey Rosen. (2001, October 7). "A Cautionary Tale for a New Age of Surveillance." *New York Times Magazine.*

Rosen warns against giving up liberties without a corresponding increase in security. After the September 11 attacks, most American stocks plummeted, but the fortunes of many biometrics companies soared. Biometrics is a method of identifying people by scanning and quantifying their unique physical characteristics, such as their retinal patterns or their facial structure. The owners of a program called FaceIt, which creates identification codes based on 80 aspects of facial structure, lobbied lawmakers to install hundreds of cameras at each major airport. A former head of the New York Police Department recommended installing biometric surveillance cameras in Times Square to scan the faces of pedestrians and compare them with a database of suspected terrorists.

Rosen studied biometric surveillance techniques in Great Britain, where fear of the Irish Republican Army led to the installation of an estimated 2.5 million closed circuit television cameras. The British approach has attracted little opposition, but it also has not identified any terrorists. The cameras have succeeded primarily in letting people know that they are being watched at all times, promoting social conformity and conventional behavior. Rosen does not want the United States to go down the same path as the British because the "promise of America" is that we can "escape the Old World [where] people knew their place."

Exploring Counterterrorism Further

- The U.S. Office of Counterterrorism (www.state.gov/s/ct/) is the agency within the Department of State officially responsible for developing, coordinating, and implementing American counterterrorism policy.
- The Web site of the International Policy Institute for Counterterrorism (www.ict.org.il), a private research organization, includes information on UN resolutions, international treaties, and international and national laws against terrorism.
- The Congressional Research Services (CRS) (www.cnie.org/NLE/CRS) publishes a variety of reports on counterterrorism policy. After the September 11 attacks, the CRS updated a report titled "Terrorism and the Law of War: Trying Terrorists as War Criminals Before Military Commissions."
- The international response to U.S. counterterrorism policy in the aftermath of September 11, 2001, is of great concern to human rights organizations. Amnesty International

(www.amnesty-usa.org) issued a report titled "The Backlash: Human Rights at Risk Throughout the World." It also argues that the prisoners held at Guantanamo Bay should be presumed to have prisoner of war status.

VIDEO NOTES

The threat from the military in response to terrorism may be overplayed in *The Siege* (20th Century Fox, 1998, 120 min.), but the film provides some sobering images about fighting violence with violence.

REFERENCES

Antiterrorism and Effective Death Penalty Act, Pub. L. No. 104-132 (2001).

Barber, Benjamin R. (1992). Jihad vs. McWorld. *Atlantic Monthly, 269*(3), 53-65.

Barber, Benjamin R. (1995). *Jihad vs. McWorld.* New York: Times Books.

Butterfield, Fox. (2001, November 22). Police are split on questioning Mideast men." *The New York Times.* Retrieved June 19, 2002, from www.nytimes.com/2001/11/22/national/22POLI.html?ex=1007565080&ei=1&en=07393e2cd9456819

Civil Liberties Act of 1988, 50 App. U.S.C.A § 1989 (1988).

Cole, David. (2001). *On civil liberties and proposed anti-terrorism legislation.* Testimony before the Senate Judiciary Committee. Washington, DC: Senate Judiciary Committee.

Defense Science Board. (1997). *The Defense Science Board 1997 summer study task force on DOD responses to transnational threats* (Final Report, Vol. 1). Washington, DC: U.S. Department of Defense.

Dempsey, James X., & Cole, David. (1999). *Terrorism and the Constitution: Sacrificing civil liberties in the name of national security.* New York: First Amendment Foundation.

Eland, Ivan. (1998). *Does U.S. intervention overseas breed terrorism? The historical record* (Foreign Policy Briefing No. 50). Washington, DC: Cato Institute.

Exec. Order No. 9066, 3 C.F.R. 1092 (1942).

Feuerlicht, Roberta Strauss. (1971). *America's reign of terror: World War I, the Red Scare, and the Palmer raids.* New York: Random House.

Fried, Richard M. (1991). *Nightmare in red: The McCarthy era in perspective.* New York: Oxford University Press.

Gonzales, Alberto R. (2001, November 30). Martial justice, full and fair." *The New York Times.* Retrieved June 19, 2002, from http://usinfo.state.gov/topical/pol/terror/01120302.htm

Harth, Erica. (2001). *Last witness: Reflections on the wartime internment of Japanese Americans.* New York: Palgrave.

Healy, Patrick. (2001, November 6). Harvard scholar's '96 book becomes the word on war. *Boston Globe.*

Herman, Arthur. (2000). *Joseph McCarthy: Reexamining the life and legacy of America's most hated senator.* New York: Free Press.

House Res. 291, 65th Cong., 40 Stat. 553-554 (1917).

Houston, Jeanne Wakatsuki, & Houston, James D. (1983). *Farewell to Manzanar: A true story of Japanese American experience during and after the World War II internment.* New York: Bantam Books.

Hoyt, Edwin P. (1969). *The Palmer Raids, 1919-1920; An attempt to suppress dissent.* New York: Seabury Press.

Huntington, Samuel P. (1996). *The clash of civilizations and the remaking of the world order.* New York: Simon & Schuster.

Kmiec, Douglas W. (2001, October 3). *On the constitutionality of various provisions of the proposed anti-terrorism act of 2001.* Testimony before the Senate Judiciary Committee. Washington, DC: Senate Judiciary Committee.

Labor Research Association. (1948). *The Palmer Raids.* New York: International Publishers.

McCarthy, Joseph. (1985). *The fight for America.* Random Lake, WI: Times Printing Co.

McCormick, Charles H. (1997). *Seeing reds: Federal surveillance of radicals in the Pittsburgh Mill District, 1917-1921.* Pittsburgh, PA: University of Pittsburgh Press.

Myer, Dillon S. (1971). *Uprooted Americans; the Japanese Americans and the War Relocation Authority during World War II.* Tucson: University of Arizona Press.

Palmer, A. Mitchell. (1920). The case against the "Reds." *Forum, 63,* 173-185. Retrieved June 19, 2002, from http://chnm.gmu.edu/courses/hist409/palmer.html

Pillar, Paul R. (2001). *Terrorism and U.S. foreign policy.* Washington, DC: Brookings Institution.

Rashid, Ahmed. (2001). *Taliban.* New Haven, CT: Yale University Press.

Reno v. American-Arab Anti-Discrimination Committee, 117 F. 3d 97-1252 (9th Cir.1999). U.S. Lexis 1514.

Robinson, Greg. (2001). *By order of the president: F.D.R. and the internment of Japanese Americans.* Cambridge, MA: Harvard University Press.

Rosen, Jeffrey. (2001, October 7). A cautionary tale for a new age of surveillance. *The New York Times Magazine.* www.nytimes.com/2001/10/07/magazine/07SURVEILLANCE.html

Rosenfeld, Megan. (2001, November 6). Global thinker. *The Washington Post,* p. C01. [Abbreviated versions of this article appear at www.nikeworkers.org/reebok/global_thinker.html and elsewhere]

Safire, William. (2001, November 26). Kangaroo courts. *The New York Times,* p. A17.

Said, Edward W. (2001, October 22). The clash of ignorance. *The Nation.* Retrieved June 19, 2002, from www.thenation.com/doc.mhtml?i=20011022&s=said

Schreker, Ellen. (1994). *The age of McCarthyism.* New York: St. Martin's.

Schweitzer, Glenn E. (1998). *Super-terrorism, assassins, mobsters, and weapons of mass destruction.* New York: Plenum Trade.

Sedition Act of 1918, 40 Stat. 553-554 (1918).

Sharp, Walter G., Sr. (2000). The use of armed force against terrorism: American hegemony or impotence?" *Chicago Journal of International Law, 1*(1), 37-47.

Travalio, Gregory M. (2000). Terrorism, international law, and the use of military force. *Wisconsin International Law Journal, 18*(1), 145-191.

U.S. Department of State. (2001). *Patterns of global terrorism: 2000.* Washington, DC: Author.

U.S. Office of Counterterrorism. (1998). *International terrorism conventions.* Washington, DC: Department of State.

USA PATRIOT Act of 2001. Uniting and Strengthening America by Providing Appropriate Tools Required to Intercept and Obstruct Terrorism Act, Pub. L. No. 107-56 (2001).

War Relocation Authority. (1943). *Relocation of Japanese Americans.* Washington, DC: Author.

White, Jonathan R. (1998). *Terrorism: An introduction.* Belmont, CA: Wadsworth.

Wilgoren, Jodi. (2001, November 25). Swept up in a dragnet, hundreds sit in custody and ask, "Why?" *The New York Times,* p. 1.

LESSONS AND FUTURES

Paul R. Pillar

Sound counterterrorist policy requires a long and broad perspective. Awareness of past efforts to fight terrorism provides a sense of what is—and just as important, what is not—possible to accomplish in that fight. Sensitivity to other current national interests is needed to understand the immediate limits and complications of counterterrorism. An eye aimed at the future helps to prepare for threats yet to develop and possibilities yet to be exploited.

A PROBLEM MANAGED, NEVER SOLVED

The long history of terrorism is reason enough to expect that it will always be a problem and usually a significant one. It is a product of such basic facts of human existence as the discontent that is sometimes strong enough to impel people toward violence, the asymmetries of the weak confronting the strong, and the vulnerability of almost every facet of civilization to physical harm at the hands of those who find a reason to inflict harm. If there is a "war" against terrorism, it is a war that cannot be won.

Counterterrorism, even though it shares some attributes with warfare, is not accurately represented by the metaphor of *a* war. Unlike most wars, it has neither a fixed set of enemies nor the prospect of coming to closure, be it through a "win" or some other kind of denoue-ment. Like the cold war, it requires long, patient, persistent effort, but unlike it, it will never conclude with the internal collapse of an opponent. There will be victories and defeats, but not big, tide-turning victories. Counter-terrorism is a fight and a struggle, but it is not a campaign with a beginning and an end.

Perhaps a better analogy is the effort by public health authorities to control communica-ble diseases. That effort, like counterterrorism, deals with threats that come in many different forms, some more virulent than others. Some of the threats are waxing; some are waning. Some are old; others are very new. Much of the chal-lenge and the frustration comes from the fact that just as things are going well on one front—and occasionally even so well that a problem is eradicated altogether (smallpox, the Red Army Faction)—a different and perhaps even more threatening problem emerges (AIDS, al-Qaida). Attention and resources get shifted around as threats evolve, but the effort as a whole can never stop.

Analogies aside, a central lesson of counter-terrorism is that *terrorism cannot be "defeated"—only reduced, attenuated, and to some degree controlled*. Individual terrorists or terrorist groups sometimes are defeated; terrorism as a whole never will be. Expectations must be kept realistic. Unrealistically high hopes for counter-terrorism lead to impatience that in turn leads to sweeping (and thus perhaps satisfying) but not necessarily effective measures, such as some of the legislation enacted in 1996. Such hopes also encourage despair when they cannot be achieved. Each terrorist attack becomes that much more of a discouraging setback, and the dashed hopes assist the terrorist in damaging public morale. Moreover, unrealistic striving for zero terrorist attacks (which might mean retrenchment overseas to reduce exposure to terrorism) would be no better for overall U.S. foreign policy interests than striving for zero unemployment (which would exacerbate inflation) would be for U.S. economic interests. Counterterrorist programs will prevent many terrorist attacks but will not prevent them all. Terrorism happens. It should never be accepted, but it should always be expected.

The impossibility of winning a "war" or inflicting an overall defeat raises the question of what standards to use in assessing the success or failure of counterterrorist programs. Terrorist attacks, and people getting killed or wounded in them, are obvious and quantifiable indications of failure. But as noted, zero attacks would be an impossible standard. One could look at trends as a measure—that is, whether terrorism has been up or down lately—but the sporadic and uneven nature of terrorism means that short-term fluctuations have little significance, and the effects of other factors make longer-term trends only an imperfect gauge of the effectiveness of counterterrorist programs. One might also look at counterterrorist achievements such as renditions, prosecutions, or rolled-up plots, but this can never be more than a partial scorecard.

Although there is no simple standard, any assessment of counterterrorist policies should bear in mind that *the purpose of counterterrorism is to save lives (and limbs and property) without unduly compromising other national interests and objectives*. This principle has two elements, one narrow and one broad. The narrow one is that as far as counterterrorism is concerned, anything other than saving lives is but a means to that end. That goes for everything from prosecuting an individual terrorist to placing sanctions on a state sponsor. Some of those means may have come to be seen as ends in themselves for other reasons (such as the satisfaction of seeing justice done that comes from prosecuting a terrorist), but they are not counterterrorist ends. They are good for counterterrorism only if, given the circumstances in which they are used, they are likely to reduce terrorism and save lives.

The broad element is that counterterrorism constantly and inevitably impinges on other important U.S. interests, and so counterterrorist policy must be judged according not only to how many lives it saves but also to how little damage it does to those other interests. This objective is partly a matter of not letting the fear of terrorism, or measures taken to avoid it, so disrupt the other business of the U.S. government or of U.S. citizens that it constitutes a victory of sorts for the terrorists. This means, for example, not making U.S. elements overseas so preoccupied with protecting themselves against terrorism that what is supposed to be their primary mission becomes secondary. The chairman of the Joint Chiefs of Staff saw this happening to some extent to the U.S. military in the wake of the Khubar Towers bombing, given the heavy emphasis on force protection. To correct this imbalance, he issued reminders that the missions of the U.S. armed forces require them to go places and to do things that make some terrorism inevitable, and that the U.S. military "cannot afford to subscribe to a 'zero casualty' mentality."[1]

The broad element is also a matter of staying cognizant of the potentially detrimental side effects of counterterrorist measures and of employing those measures carefully and judiciously, with an eye toward all of the interests they affect. In the United States, awareness of counterterrorism's side effects has focused more intently on domestic concerns such as civil liberties rather than on the many ways in which steps taken in the name of counterterrorism can affect U.S. foreign relations, possibly to the detriment of other U.S. interests or even, in the long run, counterterrorism itself . . . Those potential effects range from resentment over the extraterritorial application of U.S. laws to perpetuation of myths about the anti-Islamic character of U.S. policy, and the rankling of allies—on whom the United States is dependent for so much besides counterterrorism—over what they perceive as obdurate policies toward state sponsors.

The integral link between counterterrorism and other aspects of foreign policy suggests an even broader standard for assessing the success or failure of counterterrorist policy. Besides such measures as plots foiled and fugitives caught, the success of any administration's counterterrorist policy should also be measured according to how more—or less—effective it makes that administration's overall foreign policy. It is a counterterrorist success, for example, if the United States elicits more forth-right cooperation from a foreign government because effective counterterrorist work has made that government less afraid of terrorist reprisals for doing business with Washington. It is a success if U.S. diplomats feel safe enough in a terrorism-prone area to stay focused on their primary mission of advancing U.S. economic and political interests in the country to which they are accredited. And it is a success if the United States enjoys a positive image in a culture (for example, the Islamic world) because the problem of extremists in that culture has been handled in a deft way that does not antagonize the nonextremists, or if alliances are harmonious because policies toward state sponsors of terrorism are handled in a constructive way that influences the state sponsor's behavior without antagonizing the allies.

RECOMMENDATIONS

Some of the most basic and important aspects of good counterterrorist policy—such as a clear national commitment to counter international terrorism and the priority and resources that this effort warrants—are part of the general consensus on the subject and do not need to be restated again. But many pieces of advice have emerged on ways to think about counterterrorism that are not so widely understood and accepted, and ways in which U.S. policies could be beneficially tweaked. The principal recommendations are summarized in the form of the following precepts.

Inject the counterterrorist perspective into foreign policy decisionmaking. Foreign policy should be made with the awareness that many aspects of U.S. foreign relations, although they may not carry the "counterterrorist" label, nonetheless bear on the threat that international terrorism poses to U.S. interests. U.S. initiatives overseas affect the resentments and motivations of those who might resort to terrorism.

A U.S. posture overseas may entail increased vulnerability to terrorism (and in the worst case may involve a Lebanon-type trap in which withdrawals cannot be undertaken without the United States appearing to be defeated by terrorism). And the management of relations with many foreign governments whose cooperation is needed in combating terrorism has major consequences for the effectiveness of the whole U.S. counterterrorist effort. Other important U.S. interests—often more important than counterterrorism in any given case—are also at stake, but the question, "What are the implications of this for terrorism?" should at least be posed and analyzed as part of the decisionmaking process for many foreign policy issues. Those issues include any that involve a physical U.S. presence or a significant U.S. initiative overseas and any that have significant bearing on U.S. relations with a state that poses terrorist problems or is an important U.S. partner in combating terrorism.

Injecting the counterterrorist perspective is partly a matter of who participates in the decisions. The State Department's coordinator for counterterrorism should have a seat at more decisionmaking tables than has been true in the past. At the White House, the national coordinator for security, infrastructure protection, and counterterrorism should similarly have a voice in a wide range of issues (and not just on budgetary guidance). In large measure, however, keeping the implications for counterterrorism in mind is a matter of senior decisionmakers (and those who prepare their decision papers) remembering to do so.

Pay attention to the full range of terrorist threats. International terrorism's impact on U.S. interests covers a very wide range in terms of perpetrators, methods, and the interests affected. The United States cannot afford to focus narrowly on whatever segment of that range currently is in the headlines, given the diversion of attention and resources from other segments (or from terrorism as a whole) that entails. The United States should not become as preoccupied with any one terrorist as it has been with Usama bin Ladin (even given his considerable influence), because in the fractionated world of international terrorism no single individual is responsible for more than a small part of the mayhem. The nation should not be as preoccupied with any one scenario as it has been with mass casualty chemical, biological, radiological, or nuclear (CBRN) terrorism in the United States (even given the calamity that would be, if it occurred), because that is only one of many ways in which international terrorism can seriously affect U.S. interests, and it is not the most likely way. The allocation of counterterrorist attention and resources should be guided not only by the prospect of dead American bodies but also by the harm that international terrorism—by threatening foreigners—does to U.S. interests by wrecking peace processes or by destabilizing or intimidating otherwise friendly regimes. And the United States should look not only for the current bin Ladin but also for the *next* one, and for the circumstances that may cause such a threat to arise.

Disrupt terrorist infrastructures worldwide. Counterterrorism needs to be as far reaching, geographically and functionally, as international terrorism itself. With globe-girdling networks of cells, and peripatetic terrorists whom those networks support, most of the activity that could culminate in terrorist attacks on U.S. interests (including attacks in the United States) takes place far from U.S. shores, and most of it consists of such mundane but essential functions as recruitment, finance, and logistics. The United States should therefore devote a major effort to the piece-by-piece disruption of those terrorist infrastructures. It must rely on cooperative foreign governments to do most of this work, and it should take advantage of the enforcement by those governments of their own laws (including laws having nothing to do with terrorism) to make the terrorists' professional life as difficult as possible in as many places as possible. That this work is less visible and less publicly satisfying than the more dramatic counterterrorist measures the United States sometimes takes should not detract from the priority given to it.

Use all available methods to counter terrorism, while not relying heavily on any one of them. Even the disruption of terrorist infrastructures has shortcomings as well as advantages. The same is true of every other means available to the United States to combat terrorism. The shortcomings are found in basic elements of counterterrorism (such as attacking capabilities or influencing intentions), functional instruments (such as criminal law or military force), and more specific tools or policies (such as formally designating terrorist groups, or applying sanctions to state sponsors). The limitations may involve practical difficulties in implementation (for example, trying to identify terrorist financial accounts), undesirable side effects (for example, public resentment over a military strike), or the inapplicability of a measure to parts of the terrorist problem (true of many measures taken against state sponsors, which do not curb terrorism by independent groups). Some hoped-for effects may be inherently uncertain, such as the deterrent effect that a criminal prosecution may (or may not) have in the minds of other terrorists. Since no single measure can do the job, the United States must extract whatever advantage it can from each measure. This means the *selective* use of counterterrorist tools and instruments, bearing in mind the applicability—or inapplicability—of an instrument to a particular case. Anyone who promotes a single method or approach as the "key" to counterterrorism is selling not keys but snake oil.

The instrument of criminal law—even though it is enshrined in one of the basic tenets of current U.S. policy—should not automatically be given precedence over other instruments. A prosecution in a U.S. court should be viewed as one possible means rather than an end and should be foregone if in any case the use of other means (including, for example, the continued collection of intelligence on the activities of terrorists at large) seems likely to save more lives. The investigative resources of law enforcement agencies should be used to support not only criminal prosecutions but also other counterterrorist measures (such as administrative actions to interdict flows of money). And the United States should be open to seeing justice served in reliable foreign courts even for some terrorists who may have violated U.S. law.

Tailor different policies to meet different terrorist challenges. A foolish consistency is the hobgoblin not only of little minds, as Ralph Waldo

Emerson said, but also of insufficiently flexible counterterrorist policy. In some respects consistency in counterterrorism is indeed desirable, such as in upholding a reputation for firmness against terrorist coercion and in opposing terrorism no matter who is the victim (including adversaries of the United States). But beyond basic commitments, differences are at least as significant as similarities. The terrorist threat is not really "a threat" but rather a method used by an assortment of actors who threaten U.S. interests in varying ways and degrees. There are important differences in the roots of terrorism in various countries, the prospects for resolving conflicts with different terrorist organizations, the degree to which state sponsors are still behind terrorism, the salience of other issues in U.S. relations with states that sponsor or enable terrorism, and other pertinent variables. Such differences should form the basis for tailoring what is, in effect, a different counterterrorist policy for each group or state. Foreign terrorist groups are incredibly diverse—ranging from small bands of fugitives on the run like the Japanese Red Army to politically or militarily potent organizations like the Liberation Tigers of Tamil Eelam. The terrorist methods that each has used should be consistently opposed, and a counterterrorist technique or two (such as catching leading members of a group) might be applied to each, but almost everything else about dealing with them needs to be shaped to meet individual circumstances. Such tailoring may be complicated, difficult, and rhetorically unsatisfying (because it defies generalization), but it is necessary to make counterterrorism more effective and to protect other U.S. interests at stake.

Give peace a chance. Although the objective regarding most terrorist groups should be to eradicate them, with others the most promising (or least unpromising) path toward ending the bloodshed is to enlist the group in a peace process aimed at resolving the underlying conflict. Determining whether this is so requires a careful assessment of the group's political and military strength, the nature of the issues and whether competing demands are bridgeable, and the availability of more moderate interlocutors to represent interests the terrorists claim to

support. If engagement in a peace process seems more feasible than eradication, the United States should encourage the start of such a process or support—even indirectly as an interested outsider—any process that has already begun. The negotiations over Palestine and Northern Ireland (despite the continuing threat of renewed violence in both places) should serve as models of how much such peacemaking can curb terrorism. Colombia may some day become another example.

The legacy of a group's past terrorism, the disruptions caused by its more recent attacks, and even the abhorrence of terrorism that touches U.S. interests directly should not lead the United States to reject peacemaking with a group out of hand. Any road to peace that involves organizations that have used terrorism will be rocky. Infractions should be penalized as appropriate but not allowed to kill a process that otherwise still has a chance to succeed. The label "terrorist" should not be a permanent disqualifier for doing business with the United States or for being part of a U.S.-supported political process. Not only were Yasir Arafat and Gerry Adams leaders of terrorist groups; so were Menachem Begin and Yitzhak Shamir.

Legislate sparingly. The need for well-tailored policies is one reason that legislation—which is inherently better suited to general rules than to specific applications—should play only a limited role in counterterrorist policy. The procrustean nature of much current U.S. counterterrorist law, with uniform penalties or restrictions placed on what are decidedly mixed bags of states or groups, has been its biggest drawback. Other disadvantages include the difficulty in responding quickly to changed circumstances when policies are codified in law, the unfortunate side effects of congressional micromanagement of matters like aviation security, and the defects that stem from the process by which U.S. laws on terrorism get written (that is, in fits and starts corresponding to the fluctuations in public concern about the topic, and with heavy influence by vocal minorities whose first concern is not counterterrorism). Because it needs to be flexible, U.S. counterterrorist policy should largely be a matter of executive discretion—and this includes the application of economic sanctions and most other counter-terrorist measures that currently are constrained or required by law. Congress should refrain from enacting case-specific laws (such as the Iran-Libya Sanctions Act or Helms-Burton) in the name of counterterrorism. It should also resist the tendency to use the passing of still more laws as a gesture to respond to postincident bursts of public concern about terrorism.

Congress's legislative role in combating international terrorism, though limited, still has several important aspects. Besides providing the resources for a sustained counterterrorist effort, it is the job of Congress to declare objectives on matters such as human rights and to set the rules on subjects such as the extraterritorial activities of U.S. law enforcement agencies. Most important, it needs to keep the executive branch supplied with a full set of counterterrorist tools to apply at the latter's discretion, intelligently and flexibly, to individual cases. The International Emergency Economic Powers Act is a good model of such a tool-furnishing law. In the short term, legislation would be needed not just to give the executive branch more such flexibility but to undo some of the less helpful aspects of existing law, particularly on the topic of the next precept.

Keep terrorist lists honest. Official U.S. lists of terrorist states or groups need to be accurate, complete, and up-to-date portrayals of what is really going on in international terrorism, as they currently are not. They need to be in order to keep U.S. counterterrorist policy credible, realize fully whatever value they have as incentives to improve terrorist-related behavior, and provide a fair and useful frame of reference in discussions of terrorism with foreign partners, the American public, and the groups and states that are on the lists (or should be). The lists should be about terrorism, not about other issues, as has too often been the case with the list of state sponsors. And the lists should be promptly changed when terrorist-related behavior changes.

The lists would be more likely to exhibit such truth and responsiveness if they were unshackled from the automatic sanctions, associated criminal penalties, and other measures to which they are currently bound by law. Decisions about whether a state should be designated as a state sponsor or as "not cooperating fully" on counterterrorism under the terms of the Antiterrorism and Effective Death Penalty Act should not have to be surrogates for decisions about sanctions. Decisions about designating Foreign Terrorist Organizations should not depend on the evidentiary problems that lawyers anticipate in defeating future legal challenges. The various sanctions and penalties should be retained as tools for the executive to use selectively, in cases when they—with other counter-terrorist measures and bearing in mind other U.S. interests—seem most likely to be effective.

Encourage reforming state sponsors to reform even more by engaging them, not just punishing them. The United States should seize the opportunity provided by the substantial decline in state sponsorship of terrorism during the past several years to nurture even more improvement on this front, as well as to advance other U.S. interests in the states in question. This means not only keeping lists of state sponsors up to date but also using positive and negative techniques to move bilateral relationships in the desired direction. The economic sanctions and other negative measures on which the United States has primarily relied (and the limitations of which have been amply demonstrated) have a role, but their effectiveness as an inducement to better behavior depends on U.S. willingness to change them when the behavior that was the reason for enacting them in the first place has changed. The United States needs to demonstrate this responsiveness to keep the state directly concerned on the right path and to convince others that supporting—or reducing support for—terrorism makes a difference in what kind of relations they will have with Washington.

The United States should try to make it easier, not harder, for regimes trying to clean up their acts to clean them up further. This requires clear communication of what is expected, which is best done through direct dialogue. It also means not expecting the more difficult reforms to be accomplished quickly. And it means incrementally improving the relationship as terrorist-related behavior incrementally improves. Most important, the United States should avoid postures that lead decisionmakers on the other side (or in other countries) to conclude that relations with Washington will remain poisoned no matter how much support for terrorism is reduced.

Libya and Cuba are clearly candidates for better relations as far as issues (or rather, the paucity of them) of current support for terrorism are concerned. A similar statement could be made on terrorism and North Korea, with which there has already been engagement driven by concerns over weapons proliferation. Even when significant problems of support to terrorism remain (as with Iran), and major improvement in relations with Washington in the near term may not appear feasible, the same principles of structuring incentives to encourage, not discourage, incremental improvement apply.

Of every action (or inaction) regarding relations with state sponsors the question should be asked, "Is this likely to reduce terrorism?" The objective should not be to condemn people for the past but to save lives in the future. Changing a relationship with a foreign leader stained by sins of the past should not require any judgment that he has had a change of heart. What matters is change in this policies, and that might occur (as with Muammar Qadhafi or Fidel Castro) because the circumstances he faces have changed.

Help other governments to help with counterterrorism. The dependence of the United States on a host of foreign governments for much of the counterterrorist work that needs to be done (especially the disruption of terrorist infrastructures) should be recognized in the management of relations with those governments. The needed cooperation often includes measures that are difficult or (from the foreign government's viewpoint) risky, and U.S. assistance and reassurance should be furnished to make the other government willing and able to act. The overall warmth of a bilateral relationship obviously affects willingness, but so do efforts to educate the foreign partner that terrorism is a threat to both countries. Training and other forms of practical assistance to police and security services enhance the ability of many foreign governments (especially in less developed countries) to help, and the United States should be generous in providing such assistance,

through Antiterrorism Training Assistance courses and other departmental training programs. The concerns of cooperating governments about terrorist reprisals should be respected by preserving the secrecy of joint operations, even if this means resisting the urge to trumpet counterterrorist successes.

Work with, not against, allies. With most Europeans and other close allies, what is needed is not technical assistance and reassurance but rather more comity and coordination. The United States should respect (and even learn something from) different perspectives toward countering terrorism and not try to change allied policies that experience and deeply felt national interests dictate will not be changed. It should exploit ways in which policies that are not uniform may nonetheless be coordinated to mutual benefit, especially regarding state sponsors. The United States should also end the use of secondary economic sanctions—which have been ineffective and damaging to intra-alliance relations—in futile efforts to bend allies to its will. When the counterterrorist operations of allies raise human rights concerns (as they have at times with Israel and Turkey), the United States should work within the framework of continued close counterterrorist cooperation—one of the most effective channels the United States has for influencing human rights practices—to discourage such abuses.

Use public diplomacy to elucidate terrorism without glamorizing terrorists. The reaching out for foreign help and cooperation must extend not only to governments but also to their citizens. An active program of public diplomacy should explain why terrorism hurts the interests of those citizens and why U.S. counterterrorist efforts do not. The public diplomacy needs to be adroit, as well as active, to avoid the pitfall of making wanted terrorists appear more like Robin Hoods than like malign criminals.

Level with the American people. The strong domestic public support that is essential for effective counterterrorism—if the support is to be as sustained as it must be, and if public attitudes are not to exacerbate some of the less helpful policy tendencies—should be *informed* support. National leaders must resist the temptation to use emotional or simplistic themes that, although effective at drumming up support in the short term, may reduce the political room for maneuver when it comes to the more complex and delicate issues in counterterrorism. Instead of displaying a bag of sugar on television—as a senior government official once did—and speaking in exaggerated terms about how many people could be killed if it contained anthrax spores, it would be better to give Americans a sense of the different ways that international terrorism can directly affect their interests (which includes, among many other things, low-casualty as well as high-casualty CBRN attacks), and the less apparent but important ways in which it already affects their interests indirectly. Citizens have a right to know what to expect—not just any one way that terrorism could hurt them but the many ways in which it can and the relative likelihood of those different ways materializing.

American citizens, in their capacity not just as potential victims, but as taxpayers and sources of support for their government's policies, must become familiar with several other realities. One is surely the need for sustained, not sporadic, effort and resources to combat terrorism. Political leaders can help by saying more about the subject in the lulls between major terrorist attacks and not confining so much of their oratorical and legislative efforts to the aftermath of such incidents. Another reality is the need for flexibility. Sometimes the most promising way to reduce future terrorism is through the kind of measures, such as engagement of selected terrorist groups or state sponsors, that in a less educated perspective might be seen as going soft on terrorism. And yet another is that terrorism cannot be eliminated, that it will claim more victims, and that any attempt to achieve zero casualties would be in vain.

Remember that more is not necessarily better. U.S. counterterrorist policy needs to exhibit finesse and nuance, not just vigor and oomph. Both sets of characteristics are important, but so far responses to terrorism have emphasized quantity more than quality. Much attention has been paid to making counterterrorist measures stronger, broader, or more numerous (whether the measures are sanctions, lists, criminal penalties, military strikes, or whatever). More needs to be paid to gauging how effective or applicable such measures are to individual cases.

NOTE

1. Statement of General Henry H. Shelton to the House Armed Services Committee, February 9, 2000 (http://www.house.gov/hasc/testimony/ 106thcongress/ 00-02-09shelton.htm [July 24, 2000]).

A CAUTIONARY TALE FOR A NEW AGE OF SURVEILLANCE

Jeffrey Rosen

A week after the attacks of Sept. 11, as the value of most American stocks plummeted, a few companies, with products particularly well suited for a new and anxious age, soared in value. One of the fastest growing stocks was Visionics, whose price more than tripled. The New Jersey company is an industry leader in the fledgling science of biometrics, a method of identifying people by scanning and quantifying their unique physical characteristics—their facial structures, for example, or their retinal patterns. Visionics manufactures a face-recognition technology called FaceIt, which creates identification codes for individuals based on 80 unique aspects of their facial structures, like the width of the nose and the location of the temples. FaceIt can instantly compare an image of any individual's face with a database of the faces of suspected terrorists, or anyone else.

Visionics was quick to understand that the terrorist attacks represented not only a tragedy but also a business opportunity. On the afternoon of Sept. 11, the company sent out an e-mail message to reporters, announcing that its founder and C.E.O., Joseph Atick, "has been speaking worldwide about the need for biometric systems to catch known terrorists and wanted criminals." On Sept. 20, Atick testified before a special government committee appointed by the secretary of transportation, Norman Mineta. Atick's message—that security in airports and embassies could be improved using face-recognition technology as part of a comprehensive national surveillance plan that he called Operation Noble Shield—was greeted enthusiastically by members of the committee, which seemed ready to endorse his recommendations. "In the war against terrorism, especially when it comes to the homeland defense," Atick told me, describing his testimony, "the cornerstone of this is going to be our ability to identify the enemy before he or she enters into areas where public safety could be at risk."

Atick proposes to wire up Reagan National Airport in Washington and other vulnerable airports throughout the country with more than 300 cameras each. Cameras would scan the faces of passengers standing in line, and biometric technology would be used to analyze their faces and make sure they are not on an international terrorist "watch list." More cameras unobtrusively installed throughout the airport could identify passengers as they walk through metal detectors and public areas. And a final scan could ensure that no suspected terrorist boards a plane. "We have created a biometric network platform that turns every camera into a Web browser submitting images to a database in Washington, querying for matches," Atick said. "If a match occurs, it will set off an alarm in Washington, and someone will make a decision to wire the image to marshals at the airport."

Of course, protecting airports is only one aspect of homeland security: a terrorist could be

From "A Cautionary Tale for a New Age of Surveillance," Rosen. This article first appeared in the *New York Times Magazine*, October 7, 2001. Reprinted with permission.

lurking on any corner in America. In the wake of the Sept. 11 attacks, Howard Safir, the former New York police commissioner, recommended the installation of 100 biometric surveillance cameras in Times Square to scan the faces of pedestrians and compare them with a database of suspected terrorists. Atick told me that since the attacks he has been approached by local and federal authorities from across the country about the possibility of installing biometric surveillance cameras in stadiums and subway systems and near national monuments. "The Office of Homeland Security might be the overall umbrella that will coordinate with local police forces" to install cameras linked to a biometric network throughout American cities, Atick told me. "How can we be alerted when someone is entering the subway? How can we be sure when someone is entering Madison Square Garden? How can we protect monuments? We need to create an invisible fence, an invisible shield."

Before Sept. 11, the idea that Americans would voluntarily agree to live their lives under the gaze of a network of biometric surveillance cameras, peering at them in government buildings, shopping malls, subways and stadiums, would have seemed unthinkable, a dystopian fantasy of a society that had surrendered privacy and anonymity. But in fact, over the past decade, this precise state of affairs has materialized, not in the United States but in the United Kingdom. At the beginning of September, as it happened, I was in Britain, observing what now looks like a glimpse of the American future.

I had gone to Britain to answer a question that seems far more pertinent today than it did early last month: why would a free and flourishing Western democracy wire itself up with so many closed-circuit television cameras that it resembles the set of "The Real World" or "The Truman Show"? The answer, I discovered, was fear of terrorism. In 1993 and 1994, two terrorist bombs planted by the I.R.A. exploded in London's financial district, a historic and densely packed square mile known as the City of London. In response to widespread public anxiety about terrorism, the government decided to install a "ring of steel"—a network of closed-circuit television cameras mounted on the eight official entry gates that control access to the City.

Anxiety about terrorism didn't go away, and the cameras in Britain continued to multiply. In 1994, a 2-year-old boy named Jamie Bulger was kidnapped and murdered by two 10-year-old schoolboys, and surveillance cameras captured a grainy shot of the killers leading their victim out of a shopping center. Bulger's assailants couldn't, in fact, be identified on camera—they were caught because they talked to their friends—but the video footage, replayed over and over again on television, shook the country to its core. Riding a wave of enthusiasm for closed-circuit television, or CCTV, created by the attacks, John Major's Conservative government decided to devote more than three-quarters of its crime-prevention budget to encourage local authorities to install CCTV. The promise of cameras as a magic bullet against crime and terrorism inspired one of Major's most successful campaign slogans: "If you've got nothing to hide, you've got nothing to fear."

Instead of being perceived as an Orwellian intrusion, the cameras in Britain proved to be extremely popular. They were hailed as the people's technology, a friendly eye in the sky, not Big Brother at all but a kindly and watchful uncle or aunt. Local governments couldn't get enough of them; each hamlet and fen in the British countryside wanted its own CCTV surveillance system, even when the most serious threat to public safety was coming from mad cows. In 1994, 79 city centers had surveillance networks; by 1998, 440 city centers were wired. By the late 1990's, as part of its Clintonian, center-left campaign to be tough on crime, Tony Blair's New Labor government decided to support the cameras with a vengeance. There are now so many cameras attached to so many different surveillance systems in the U.K. that people have stopped counting. According to one estimate, there are 2.5 million surveillance cameras in Britain, and in fact there may be far more.

As I filed through customs at Heathrow Airport, there were cameras concealed in domes in the ceiling. There were cameras pointing at the ticket counters, at the escalators and at the tracks as I waited for the Heathrow express to Paddington Station. When I got out at Paddington, there were cameras on the platform and cameras on the pillars in the main terminal. Cameras followed me as I walked from the main station to the underground, and there were cameras at each of the stations on the way to King's Cross. Outside King's Cross, there were cameras trained on the bus stand and the taxi stand and the sidewalk, and still more cameras in the station. There were cameras on the backs of buses to record people who crossed into the wrong traffic lane.

Throughout Britain today, there are speed cameras and red-light cameras, cameras in lobbies and elevators, in hotels and restaurants, in nursery schools and high schools. There are even cameras in hospitals. (After a raft of "baby thefts" in the early 1990's, the government gave hospitals money to install cameras in waiting rooms, maternity wards and operating rooms.) And everywhere there are warning signs, announcing the presence of cameras with a jumble of different icons, slogans and exhortations, from the bland "CCTV in operation" to the peppy "CCTV: Watching for You!" By one estimate, the average Briton is now photographed by 300 separate cameras in a single day.

Britain's experience under the watchful eye of the CCTV cameras is a vision of what Americans can expect if we choose to go down the same road in our efforts to achieve "homeland security." Although the cameras in Britain were initially justified as a way of combating terrorism, they soon came to serve a very different function. The cameras are designed not to produce arrests but to make people feel that they are being watched at all times. Instead of keeping terrorists off planes, biometric surveillance is being used to keep punks out of shopping malls. The people behind the live video screens are zooming in on unconventional behavior in public that in fact has nothing to do with terrorism. And rather than thwarting serious crime, the cameras are being used to enforce social conformity in ways that Americans may prefer to avoid.

The dream of a biometric surveillance system that can identify people's faces in public places and separate the innocent from the guilty is not new. Clive Norris, a criminologist at the University of Hull, is Britain's leading authority on the social effects of CCTV. In his definitive study, "The Maximum Surveillance Society: the Rise of CCTV," Norris notes that in the 19th century, police forces in England and France began to focus on how to distinguish the casual offender from the "habitual criminal" who might evade detection by moving from town to town. In the 1870's, Alphonse Bertillon, a records clerk at the prefecture of police in Paris, used his knowledge of statistics and anthropomorphic measurements to create a system for comparing the thousands of photographs of arrested suspects in Parisian police stations. He took a series of measurements—of skull size, for example, and the distance between the ear and chin—and created a unique code for every suspect whom the police had photographed. Photographs were then grouped according to the codes, and a new suspect could be compared only with the photos that had similar measurements, instead of with the entire portfolio. Though Bertillon's system was often difficult for unskilled clerks to administer, a procedure that had taken hours or days was now reduced to a few minutes.

It wasn't until the 1980's, with the development of computerized biometric and other face-recognition systems, that Bertillon's dream became feasible on a broad scale. In the course of studying how biometric scanning could be used to authenticate the identities of people who sought admission to secure buildings, innovators like Joseph Atick realized that the same technology could be used to pick suspects or license plates out of a crowd. It's the license-plate technology that the London police have found most attractive, because it tends to be more reliable. (A test of the best face-recognition systems last year by the U.S. Department of Defense found that they failed to identify matches a third of the time.)

Soon after arriving in London, I visited the CCTV monitoring room in the City of London police station, where the British war against terrorism began. I was met by the press officer, Tim Parsons, and led up to the control station, a modest-size installation that looks like an air-traffic-control room, with uniformed officers manning two rows of monitors. Although installed to catch terrorists, the cameras in the City of London spend most of their time following car thieves and traffic offenders. "The technology here is geared up to terrorism," Parsons told me. "The fact that we're getting ordinary people—burglars stealing cars—as a result of it is sort of a bonus."

Have you caught any terrorists? I asked. "No, not using this technology, no," he replied.

As we watched the monitors, rows of slow-moving cars filed through the gates into the City, and cameras recorded their license-plate numbers and the faces of their drivers. After several minutes, one monitor set off a soft, pinging alarm. We had a match! But no, it was a false alarm. The license plate that set off the system was 8620bmc, but the stolen car recorded in the database was 8670amc. After a few more mismatches, the machine finally found an offender, though not a serious one. A red van had gone through a speed camera, and the local authority that issued the ticket couldn't identify the driver. An alert went out on the central police national computer, and it set off the alarm when the van entered the City. "We're not going to do anything about it because it's not a desperately important call," said the sergeant.

Because the cameras on the ring of steel take clear pictures of each driver's face, I asked whether the City used the biometric facial recognition technology that American airports are now being urged to adopt. "We're experimenting with it to see if we could pick faces out of the crowd, but the technology is not sufficiently good enough," Parsons said. "The system that I saw demonstrated two or three years ago, a lot of the time it couldn't differentiate between a man and a woman." (In a recent documentary about CCTV, Monty Python's John Cleese foiled a Visionics face-recognition system that had been set up in the London borough of Newham by wearing earrings and a beard.) Nevertheless, Parsons insisted that the technology will become more accurate. "It's just a matter of time. Then we can use it to detect the presence of criminals on foot in the city," he said.

In the future, as face-recognition technology becomes more accurate, it will become even more intrusive, because of pressures to expand the biometric database. I mentioned to Joseph Atick of Visionics that the City of London was thinking about using his technology to establish a database that would include not only terrorists but also all British citizens whose faces were registered with the national driver's license bureau. If that occurs, every citizen who walks the streets of the City could be instantly identified by the police and evaluated in light of his past misdeeds, no matter how trivial. With the impatience of a rationalist, Atick dismissed the possibility. "Technically, they won't be able to do it without coming back to me," he said. "They will have to justify it to me." Atick struck me as a refined and thoughtful man (he is the former director of the computational neuroscience laboratory at Rockefeller University), but it seems odd to put the liberties of a democracy in the hands of one unelected scientist.

Atick says that his technology is an enlightened alternative to racial and ethnic profiling, and if the faces in the biometric database were, in fact, restricted to known terrorists, he would be on to something. Instead of stopping all passengers who appear to be Middle Eastern and victimizing thousands of innocent people, the system would focus with laserlike precision on a tiny handful of the guilty. (This assumes that the terrorists aren't cunning enough to disguise themselves.) But when I asked whether any of the existing biometric databases in England or America are limited to suspected terrorists, Atick confessed that they aren't. There is a simple reason for this: few terrorists are suspected in advance of their crimes. For this reason, cities in England and elsewhere have tried to justify their investment in face-recognition systems by filling their databases with those troublemakers whom the authorities can easily identify: local criminals. When FaceIt technology was used to scan the faces of the thousands of fans entering the Super Bowl in Tampa last January, the matches produced by the database weren't terrorists. They were low-level ticket scalpers and pickpockets.

Biometrics is a feel-good technology that is being marketed based on a false promise—that the database will be limited to suspected terrorists. But the FaceIt technology, as it's now being used in England, isn't really intended to catch terrorists at all. It's intended to scare local hoodlums into thinking they might be setting off alarms even when the cameras are turned off. I came to understand this "Wizard of Oz" aspect of the technology when I visited Bob Lack's monitoring station in the London borough of Newham. A former London police officer, Lack attracted national attention—including a visit from Tony Blair—by pioneering the use of face-recognition technology before other people were convinced that it was entirely reliable. What Lack grasped early on was that reliability was in many ways beside the point.

Lack installed his first CCTV system in 1997, and he intentionally exaggerated its powers from the beginning. "We put one camera out and 12 signs" announcing the presence of cameras, Lack told me. "We reduced crime by 60 percent in the area where we posted the signs. Then word on the street went out that we had dummy cameras." So Lack turned his attention to face-recognition technology and tried to create the impression that far more people's faces were in the database than actually are. "We've designed a poster now about making Newham a safe place for a family," he said. "And we're telling the criminal we have this information on him: we know his name, we know his address, we know what crimes he commits." It's not true, Lack admits, "but then, we're entitled to disinform some people, aren't we?"

So you're telling the criminal that you know his name even though you don't, I asked? "Right," Lack replied. "Pretty much that's about advertising, isn't it?"

Lack was elusive when I asked him who, exactly, is in his database. "I don't know," he replied, noting that the local police chief decides who goes into the database. He would only make an "educated guess" that the database contains 100 "violent street robbers" under the age of 18. "You have to have been convicted of a crime—nobody suspected goes on, unless they're a suspected murderer—and there has to be sufficient police intelligence to say you are committing those crimes and have been so in the last 12 weeks." When I asked for the written standards that determined who, precisely, was put in the database, and what crimes they had to have committed, Lack promised to send them, but he never did.

From Lack's point of view, it doesn't matter who is in his database, because his system isn't designed to catch terrorists or violent criminals. In the three years that the system has been up and running, it hasn't resulted in a single arrest. "I'm not in the business of having people arrested," Lack said. "The deterrent value has far exceeded anything you imagine." He told me that the alarms went off an average of three times a day during the month of August, but the

only people he would conclusively identify were local youths who had volunteered to be put in the database as part of an "intensive surveillance supervision program," as an alternative to serving a custodial sentence. "The public statements about the efficacy of the Newham facial-recognition system bear little relationship to its actual operational capabilities, which are rather weak and poor," says Clive Norris of the University of Hull. "They want everyone to believe that they are potentially under scrutiny. Its effectiveness, perhaps, is based on a lie."

This lie has a venerable place in the philosophy of surveillance. In his preface to "Panopticon," Jeremy Bentham imagined the social benefits of a ring-shaped "inspection-house," in which prisoners, students, orphans or paupers could be subject to constant surveillance. In the center of the courtyard would be an inspection tower with windows facing the inner wall of the ring. Supervisors in the central tower could observe every movement of the inhabitants of the cells, who were illuminated by natural lighting, but Venetian blinds would ensure that the supervisors could not be seen by the inhabitants. The uncertainty about whether or not they were being surveilled would deter the inhabitants from antisocial behavior. Michel Foucault described the purpose of the Panopticon—to induce in the inmate a state of conscious and permanent visibility that assures the automatic functioning of power." Foucault predicted that this condition of visible, unverifiable power, in which individuals have internalized the idea that they may always be under surveillance, would be the defining characteristic of the modern age.

Britain, at the moment, is not quite the Panopticon, because its various camera networks aren't linked and there aren't enough operators to watch all the cameras. But over the next few years, that seems likely to change, as Britain moves toward the kind of integrated Web-based surveillance system that Visionics has now proposed for American airports and subway systems. At the moment, for example, the surveillance systems for the London underground and the British police feed into separate control rooms, but Sergio Velastin, a computer-vision scientist, says he believes the two systems will eventually be linked, using digital technology.

Velastin is working on behavioral-recognition technology for the London underground that can look for unusual movements in crowds, setting off an alarm, for example, when people appear to be fighting or trying to jump on the tracks. (Because human CCTV operators are easily bored and distracted, automatic alarms are viewed as the wave of the future.) "Imagine you see a piece of unattended baggage which might contain a bomb," Velastin told me. "You can back-drag on the image and locate the person who left it there. You can say where did that person come from and where is that person now? You can conceive in the future that you might be able to do that for every person in every place in the system." Of course, Velastin admitted, "if you don't have social agreement about how you're going to operate that, it could get out of control."

Once thousands of cameras from hundreds of separate CCTV systems are able to feed their digital images to a central monitoring station, and the images can be analyzed with face- and behavioral-recognition software to identify unusual patterns, then the possibilities of the Panopticon will suddenly become very real. And few people doubt that connectivity is around the corner; it is, in fact, the next step. "CCTV will become the fifth utility: after gas, electricity, sewage and telecommunications," says Jason Ditton, a criminologist at the University of Sheffield who is critical of the technology's expansion. "We will come to accept its ubiquitousness."

At the moment, there is only one fully integrated CCTV in Britain: it transmits digital images over a broadband wireless network, like the one Joseph Atick has proposed for American airports, rather than relying on traditional video cameras that are chained to dedicated cables. And so, for a still clearer vision of the interconnected future of surveillance, I set off for Hull, Britain's leading timber port, about three hours northeast of London. Hull has traditionally been associated not with dystopian fantasies but with fantasies of a more basic sort: for hundreds of years, it has been the prostitution capital of northeastern Britain.

Six years ago, a heroin epidemic created an influx of addicted young women who took to streetwalking to sustain their drug habit. Nearly two years ago, the residents' association of a low-income housing project called Goodwin Center hired a likable and enterprising young civil engineer named John Marshall to address the problem of under-age prostitutes having sex on people's windowsills.

Marshall, who is now 33, met me at the Hull railway station carrying a CCTV warning sign. Armed with more than a million dollars in public financing from the European Union, Marshall decided to build what he calls the world's first Ethernet-based, wireless CCTV system. Initially, Marshall put up 27 cameras around the housing project. The cameras didn't bother the prostitutes, who in fact felt safer working under CCTV. Instead, they scared the johns—especially after the police recorded their license numbers, banged on their doors and threatened to publish their names in the newspapers. Business plummeted, and the prostitutes moved indoors or across town to the traditional red-light district, where the city decided to tolerate their presence in limited numbers.

But Marshall soon realized that he had bigger fish to fry than displacing prostitutes from one part of Hull to another. His innovative network of linked cameras attracted national attention, which led, a few months ago, to $20 million in grant money from various levels of government to expand the surveillance network throughout the city of Hull. "In a year and a half," Marshall says, "there'll be a digital connection to every household in the city. As far as cameras go, I can imagine that, in 10 years' time, the whole city will be covered. That's the speed that CCTV is growing." In the world that Marshall imagines, every household in Hull will be linked to a central network that can access cameras trained inside and outside every building in the city. "Imagine a situation where you've got an elderly relative who lives on the other side of the city," Marshall says. "You ring her up, there's no answer on the telephone, you think she collapsed—so you go to the Internet and you look at the camera in the lounge and you see that she's making a cup of tea and she's taken her hearing aid out or something."

The person who controls access to this network of intimate images will be a very powerful person indeed. And so I was eager to meet the monitors of the Panopticon for myself. On a side street of Hull, near the Star and Garter Pub and the city morgue, the Goodwin Center's monitoring station is housed inside a ramshackle private security firm called Sentry Alarms Ltd. The sign over the door reads THE GUARD HOUSE. The monitoring station is locked behind a thick, black vault-style door, but it looks like a college computer center, with an Alicia Silverstone pinup near the door. Instead of an impressive video wall, there are only two small desktop computers, which receive all the signals from the Goodwin Center network. And the digital, Web-based images— unlike traditional video—are surprisingly fuzzy and jerky, like streaming video transmitted over a slow modem.

During my time in the control room, from 9 p.m. to midnight, I experienced firsthand a phenomenon that critics of CCTV surveillance have often described: when you put a group of bored, unsupervised men in front of live video screens and allow them to zoom in on whatever happens to catch their eyes, they tend to spend a fair amount of time leering at women. "What catches the eye is groups of young men and attractive, young women," I was told by Clive Norris, the Hull criminologist. "It's what we call a sense of the obvious." There are plenty of stories of video voyeurism: a control room in the Midlands, for example, took close-up shots of women with large breasts and taped them up on the walls. In Hull, this temptation is magnified by the fact that part of the operators' job is to keep an eye on prostitutes. As it got late, though, there weren't enough prostitutes to keep us entertained, so we kept ourselves awake by scanning the streets in search of the purely consensual activities of boyfriends and girlfriends making out in cars. "She had her legs wrapped around his waist a minute ago," one of the operators said appreciatively as we watched two teenagers go at it. "You'll be able to do an article on how reserved the British are, won't you?" he joked. Norris also found that operators, in addition to focusing on attractive young women, tend to focus on young men, especially those with dark skin. And those young men know they are being watched: CCTV is far less popular among black men than among British men as a whole. In Hull and elsewhere, rather than eliminating prejudicial surveillance and racial

profiling, CCTV surveillance has tended to amplify it.

After returning from the digital city of Hull, I had a clearer understanding of how, precisely, the spread of CCTV cameras is transforming British society and why I think it's important for America to resist going down the same path. "I actually don't think the cameras have had much effect on crime rates," says Jason Ditton, the criminologist, whose evaluation of the effect of the cameras in Glasgow found no clear reduction in violent crime. "We've had a fall in crime in the last 10 years, and CCTV proponents say it's because of the cameras. I'd say it's because we had a boom economy in the last seven years and a fall in unemployment." Ditton notes that the cameras can sometimes be useful in investigating terrorist attacks—like the Brixton nail-bomber case in 1999—but there is no evidence that they prevent terrorism or other serious crime.

Last year, Britain's violent crime rates actually increased by 4.3 percent, even though the cameras continued to proliferate. But CCTV cameras have a mysterious knack for justifying themselves regardless of what happens to crime. When crime goes up the cameras get the credit for detecting it, and when crime goes down, they get the credit for preventing it.

If the creation of a surveillance society in Britain hasn't prevented terrorist attacks, it has had subtle but far-reaching social costs. The handful of privacy advocates in Britain have tried to enumerate those costs by arguing that the cameras invade privacy. People behave in self-conscious ways under the cameras, ostentatiously trying to demonstrate their innocence or bristling at the implication of guilt. Inside a monitoring room near Runnymede, the birthplace of the Magna Carta, I saw a group of teenagers who noticed that a camera was pivoting around to follow them; they made an obscene gesture toward it and looked back over their shoulders as they tried to escape its gaze.

The cameras are also a powerful inducement toward social conformity for citizens who can't be sure whether they are being watched. "I am gay and I might want to kiss my boyfriend in Victoria Square at 2 in the morning," a supporter of the cameras in Hull told me. "I would not kiss my boyfriend now. I am aware that it has altered the way I might behave. Something like that might be regarded as an offense against public decency. This isn't San Francisco." Nevertheless, the man insisted that the benefits of the cameras outweighed the costs, because "thousands of people feel safer."

There is, in the end, a powerfully American reason to resist the establishment of a national surveillance network: the cameras are not consistent with the values of an open society. They are technologies of classification and exclusion. They are ways of putting people in their place, of deciding who gets in and who stays out, of limiting people's movement and restricting their opportunities. I came to appreciate the exclusionary potential of the surveillance technology in a relatively low-tech way when I visited a shopping center in Uxbridge, a suburb of London. The manager of the center explained that people who are observed to be misbehaving in the mall can be banned from the premises. The banning process isn't very complicated. "Because this isn't public property, we have the right to refuse entry, and if there's a wrongdoer, we give them a note or a letter, or simply tell them you're banned." In America, this would provoke anyone who was banned to call Alan Dershowitz and sue for discrimination. But the British are far less litigious and more willing to defer to authority.

Banning people from shopping malls is only the beginning. A couple of days before I was in London, Borders Books announced the installation of a biometric face-recognition surveillance system in its flagship store on Charing Cross Road. Borders' scheme meant that that anyone who had shoplifted in the past was permanently branded as a shoplifter in the future. In response to howls of protest from America, Borders dismantled the system, but it may well be resurrected in a post-Sept. 11 world.

Perhaps the reason that Britain has embraced the new technologies of surveillance, while America, at least before Sept. 11, had strenuously resisted them, is that British society is far more accepting of social classifications than we are. The British desire to put people in their place is the central focus of British literature, from Dickens to John Osborne and Alan Bennett. The work of George Orwell that casts the most light on Britain's swooning embrace of

CCTV is not "1984." It is Orwell's earlier book "The English People."

"Exaggerated class distinctions have been diminishing," Orwell wrote, but "the great majority of the people can still be 'placed' in an instant by their manners, clothes and general appearance" and above all, their accents. Class distinctions are less hardened today than they were when I was a student at Oxford at the height of the Thatcher-era "Brideshead Revisited" chic. But it's no surprise that a society long accustomed to the idea that people should know their place didn't hesitate to embrace a technology designed to ensure that people stay in their assigned places.

Will America be able to resist the pressure to follow the British example and wire itself up with surveillance cameras? Before Sept. 11, I was confident that we would. Like Germany and France, which are squeamish about CCTV because of their experience with 20th-century totalitarianism, Americans are less willing than the British to trust the government and defer to authority. After Sept. 11, however, everything has changed. A New York Times/CBS news poll at the end of September found that 8 in 10 Americans believe they will have to give up some of their personal freedoms to make the country safe from terrorist attacks.

Of course there are some liberties that should be sacrificed in times of national emergency if they give us greater security. But Britain's experience in the fight against terrorism suggests that people may give up liberties without experiencing a corresponding increase in security. And if we meekly accede in the construction of vast feel-good architectures of surveillance that have far-reaching social costs and few discernible social benefits, we may find, in calmer times, that they are impossible to dismantle.

It's important to be precise about the choice we are facing. No one is threatening at the moment to turn America into Orwell's Big Brother. And Britain hasn't yet been turned into Big Brother, either. Many of the CCTV monitors and camera operators and policemen and entrepreneurs who took the time to meet with me were models of the British sense of fair play and respect for the rules. In many ways, the closed-circuit television cameras have only exaggerated the qualities of the British national character that Orwell identified in his less famous book: the acceptance of social hierarchy combined with the gentleness that leads people to wait in orderly lines at taxi stands; a deference to authority combined with an appealing tolerance of hypocrisy. These English qualities have their charms, but they are not American qualities.

The promise of America is a promise that we can escape from the Old World, a world where people know their place. When we say we are fighting for an open society, we don't mean a transparent society—one where neighbors can peer into each other's windows using the joysticks on their laptops. We mean a society open to the possibility that people can redefine and reinvent themselves every day; a society in which people can travel from place to place without showing their papers and being encumbered by their past; a society that respects privacy and constantly reshuffles social hierarchy.

The ideal of America has from the beginning been an insistence that your opportunities shouldn't be limited by your background or your database; that no doors should be permanently closed to anyone who has the wrong smart card. If the 21st century proves to be a time when this ideal is abandoned—a time of surveillance cameras and creepy biometric face scanning in Times Square—then Osama bin Laden will have inflicted an even more terrible blow than we now imagine.

APPENDIX A: LOCATIONS OF WORLDWIDE TERRORIST ACTIVITY (MAPS 1-8)

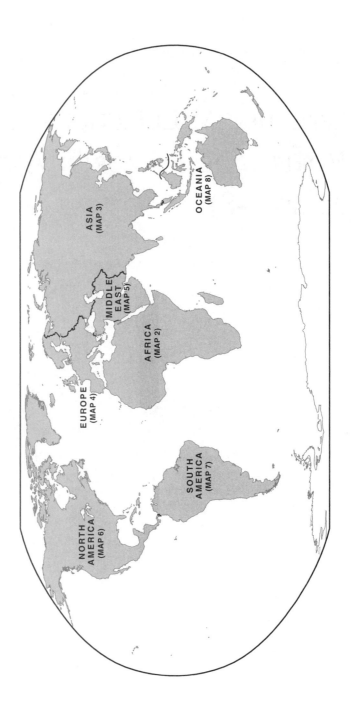

MAP TWO: AFRICA

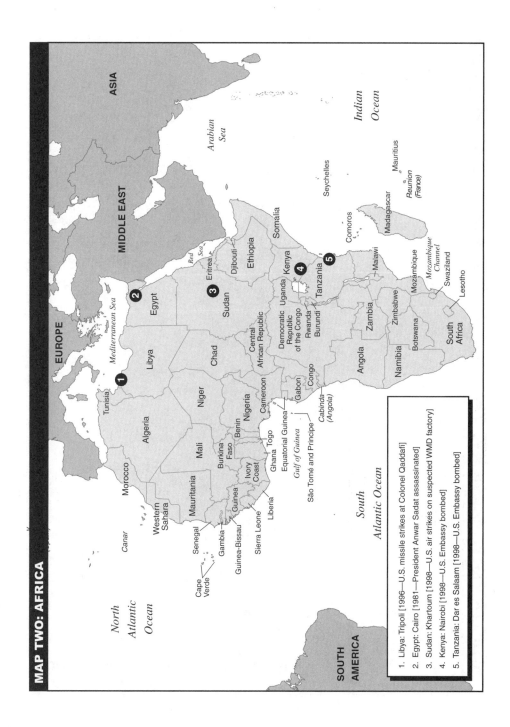

1. Libya: Tripoli [1996—U.S. missile strikes at Colonel Qaddafi]
2. Egypt: Cairo [1981—President Anwar Sadat assassinated]
3. Sudan: Khartoum [1998—U.S. air strikes on suspected WMD factory]
4. Kenya: Nairobi [1998—U.S. Embassy bombed]
5. Tanzania: Dar es Salaam [1998—U.S. Embassy bombed]

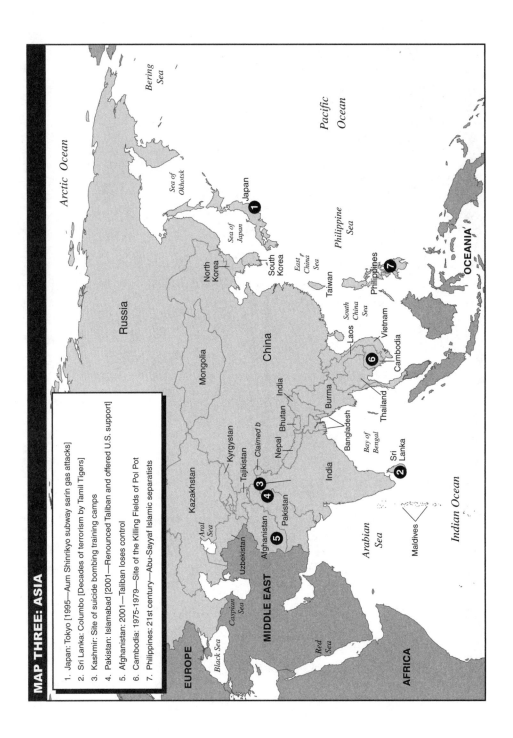

MAP THREE: ASIA

1. Japan: Tokyo [1995—Aum Shinrikyo subway sarin gas attacks]
2. Sri Lanka: Columbo [Decades of terrorism by Tamil Tigers]
3. Kashmir: Site of suicide bombing training camps
4. Pakistan: Islamabad [2001—Renounced Taliban and offered U.S. support]
5. Afghanistan: 2001—Taliban loses control
6. Cambodia: 1975-1979—Site of the Killing Fields of Pol Pot
7. Philippines: 21st century—Abu-Sayyaf Islamic separatists

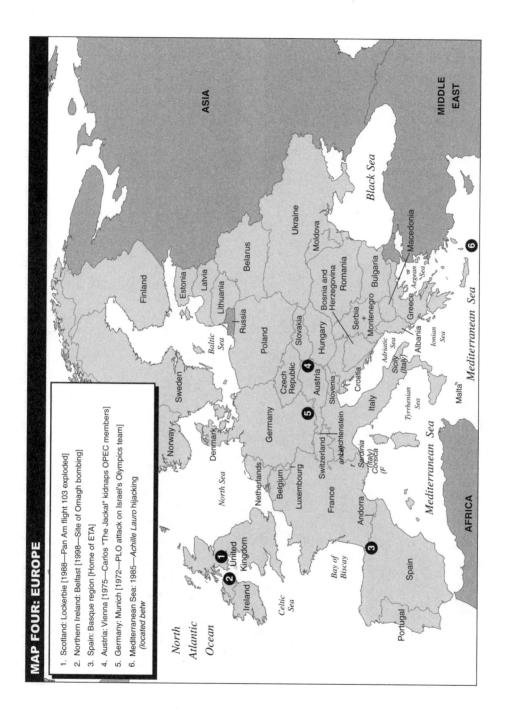

MAP FOUR: EUROPE

1. Scotland: Lockerbie [1988—Pan Am flight 103 exploded]
2. Northern Ireland: Belfast [1998—Site of Omagh bombing]
3. Spain: Basque region [Home of ETA]
4. Austria: Vienna [1975—Carlos "The Jackal" kidnaps OPEC members]
5. Germany: Munich [1972—PLO attack on Israel's Olympics team]
6. Mediterranean Sea: 1985—*Achille Lauro* hijacking
   (located betw

North
Atlantic
Ocean

ASIA

MIDDLE
EAST

Black Sea

AFRICA

Mediterranean Sea

317

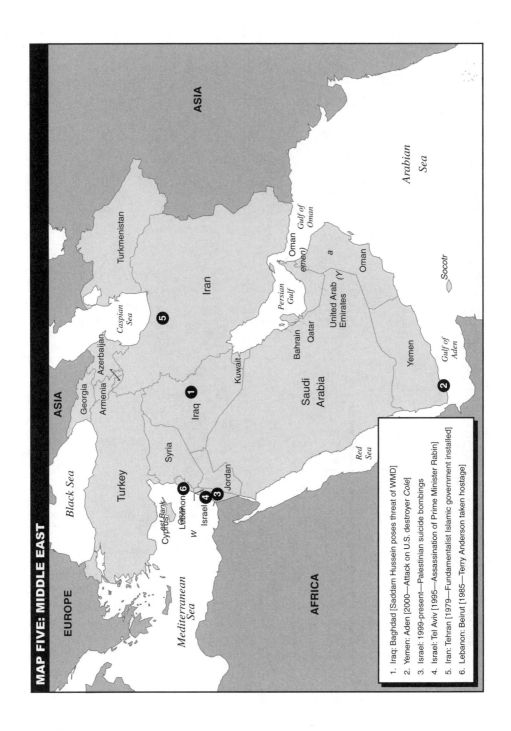

MAP FIVE: MIDDLE EAST

EUROPE

ASIA

ASIA

Black Sea

Turkey

Mediterranean Sea

Cyprus

Georgia

Armenia

Azerbaijan

Caspian Sea

Turkmenistan

⑤

Syria

West Bank

Lebanon ⑥

Israel ④

③

Jordan

Iran

Iraq ①

Kuwait

Red Sea

Saudi Arabia

Persian Gulf

Bahrain

Qatar

United Arab Emirates

Oman (Yemen)

a

Oman

Gulf of Oman

Yemen ②

Gulf of Aden

Socotr

Arabian Sea

AFRICA

1. Iraq: Baghdad [Saddam Hussein poses threat of WMD]
2. Yemen: Aden [2000—Attack on U.S. destroyer *Cole*]
3. Israel: 1999-present—Palestinian suicide bombings
4. Israel: Tel Aviv [1995—Assassination of Prime Minister Rabin]
5. Iran: Tehran [1979—Fundamentalist Islamic government installed]
6. Lebanon: Beirut [1985—Terry Anderson taken hostage]

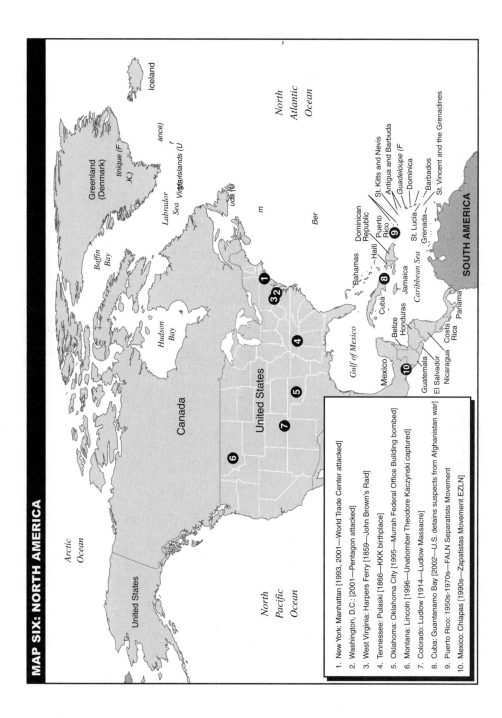

MAP SIX: NORTH AMERICA

Arctic
Ocean

North
Pacific
Ocean

United States

Canada

United States

Baffin
Bay

Hudson
Bay

Greenland
(Denmark)

Iceland

Labrador
Sea

North
Atlantic
Ocean

Gulf of Mexico

Mexico

Belize
Honduras

Guatemala
El Salvador
Nicaragua

Costa
Rica

Panama

Bahamas

Cuba

Jamaica

Haiti

Dominican
Republic

Puerto
Rico

Caribbean Sea

St. Kitts and Nevis
Antigua and Barbuda
Guadeloupe (F
Dominica

St. Lucia
Grenada

Barbados
St. Vincent and the Grenadines

SOUTH AMERICA

1

3 2

4

5

7

6

8

9

10

1. New York: Manhattan [1993, 2001—World Trade Center attacked]
2. Washington, D.C.: [2001—Pentagon attacked]
3. West Virginia: Harpers Ferry [1859—John Brown's Raid]
4. Tennessee: Pulaski [1866—KKK birthplace]
5. Oklahoma: Oklahoma City [1995—Murrah Federal Office Building bombed]
6. Montana: Lincoln [1996—Unabomber Theodore Kaczynski captured]
7. Colorado: Ludlow [1914—Ludlow Massacre]
8. Cuba: Guantanamo Bay [2002—U.S. detains suspects from Afghanistan war]
9. Puerto Rico: 1950s-1970s—FALN Separatists Movement
10. Mexico: Chiapas [1990s—Zapatistas Movement EZLN]

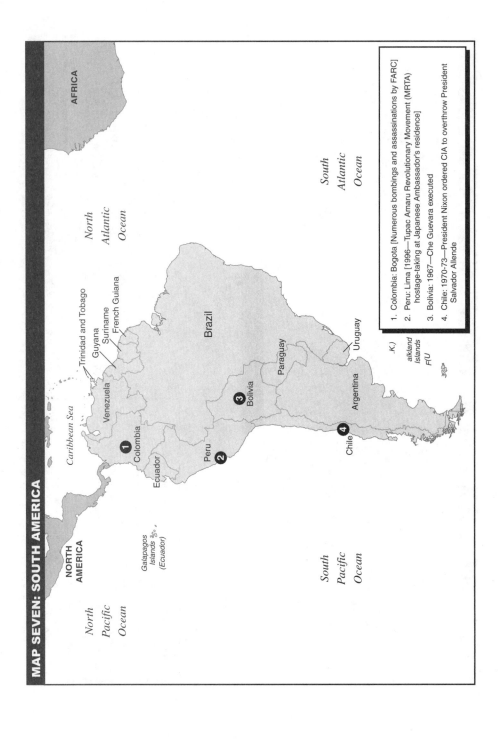

MAP SEVEN: SOUTH AMERICA

1. Colombia: Bogota [Numerous bombings and assassinations by FARC]
2. Peru: Lima [1996—Tupac Amaru Revolutionary Movement (MRTA) hostage-taking at Japanese Ambassador's residence]
3. Bolivia: 1967—Che Guevara executed
4. Chile: 1970-73—President Nixon ordered CIA to overthrow President Salvador Allende

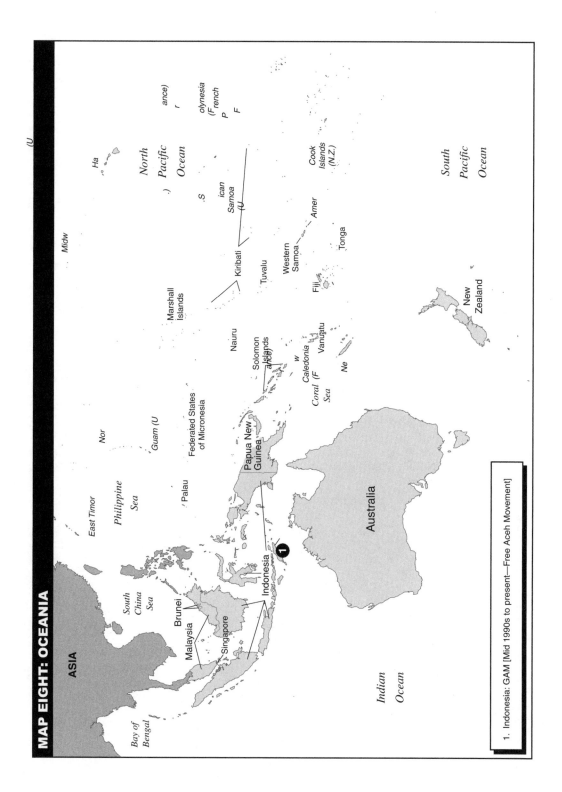

ASIA

Bay of
Bengal

South
China
Sea

Malaysia

Brunei

Singapore

Indonesia

East Timor

Philippine
Sea

Palau

Guam (U

Nor

Federated States
of Micronesia

Papua New
Guinea

Marshall
Islands

Nauru

Solomon
Islands

w
Caledonia (F

Coral
Sea

Ne

Vanuatu

Kiribati

Tuvalu

Western
Samoa

Fiji

Tonga

Amer

Midw

Ha

North
Pacific
Ocean

S

ican
Samoa
(U

.)

ance)

r

olynesia
(French

P

F

Cook
Islands
(N.Z.)

Australia

Indian
Ocean

New
Zealand

South
Pacific
Ocean

(U

1. Indonesia: GAM [Mid 1990s to present—Free Aceh Movement]

APPENDIX B: BACKGROUND INFORMATION ON TERRORIST GROUPS

U.S. DEPARTMENT OF STATE

The information below is taken from *Patterns of Global Terrorism 2001*, released by the Office of the Coordinator for Counterterrorism, U.S. Department of State, May 21, 2002. The annual *Patterns of Global Terrorism* report is submitted by the United States Department of State in compliance with Title 22 of the United States Code, Section 2656f(a), which requires the Department of State to provide Congress a full and complete annual report on terrorism for those countries and groups meeting the criteria of Section (a)(1) and (2) of the Act. The complete report is available on the Web at www.state.gov/s/ct/rls/pgtrpt. This site is managed by the Bureau of Public Affairs, U.S. Department of State. External links to other Internet sites should not be construed as an endorsement of the views contained therein. The first section, on foreign terrorist organizations, can be found at www.state.gov/s/ct/rls/pgtrpt/2001/html/10252.htm. The second section, on other terrorist groups (pp. 346-361), can be found at www.state.gov/s/ct/rls/pgtrpt/ 2001/html/1-254.htm

Background Information on Designated Foreign Terrorist Organizations

Contents

Abu Nidal Organization (ANO)
Abu Sayyaf Group (ASG)
Al-Aqsa Martyrs Brigade
Armed Islamic Group (GIA)
'Asbat al-Ansar
Aum Supreme Truth (Aum) (a.k.a. Aum Shinrikyo, Aleph)
Basque Fatherland and Liberty (ETA) (a.k.a. Euzkadi Ta Askatasuna)
Al-Gama'a al-Islamiyya (Islamic Group, IG)
HAMAS (Islamic Resistance Movement)
Harakat ul-Mujahidin (HUM) (Movement of Holy Warriors)
Hizballah (Party of God)
Islamic Movement of Uzbekistan (IMU)
Jaish-e-Mohammed (JEM) (Army of Mohammed)
Al-Jihad (Egyptian Islamic Jihad)

Kahane Chai (Kach)
Kurdistan Workers' Party (PKK)
Lashkar-e-Tayyiba (LT) (Army of the Righteous)
Liberation Tigers of Tamil Eelam (LTTE)
Mujahedin-e Khalq Organization (MEK or MKO)
National Liberation Army (ELN)—Colombia
Palestine Islamic Jihad (PIJ)
Palestine Liberation Front (PLF)
Popular Front for the Liberation of Palestine (PFLP)
Popular Front for the Liberation of Palestine-General Command (PFLP-GC)
Al-Qaida
Real IRA (RIRA)
Revolutionary Armed Forces of Colombia (FARC)
Revolutionary Nuclei
Revolutionary Organization 17 November (17 November)
Revolutionary People's Liberation Party/Front (DHKP/C)
Salafist Group for Call and Combat (GSPC)
Sendero Luminoso (Shining Path, or SL)
United Self-Defense Forces/Group of Colombia (AUC)

The following descriptive list constitutes the 33 terrorist groups that currently are designated by the Secretary of State as Foreign Terrorist Organizations (FTOs), pursuant to section 219 of the Immigration and Nationality Act, as amended by the Antiterrorism and Effective Death Penalty Act of 1996. The designations carry legal consequences:

- It is unlawful to provide funds or other material support to a designated FTO.
- Representatives and certain members of a designated FTO can be denied visas or excluded from the United States.
- US financial institutions must block funds of designated FTOs and their agents and must report the blockage to the US Department of the Treasury.

* * *

Abu Nidal Organization (ANO) a.k.a. Fatah Revolutionary Council, Arab Revolutionary Brigades, Black September, and Revolutionary Organization of Socialist Muslims

Description
International terrorist organization led by Sabri al-Banna. Split from PLO in 1974. Made up of various functional committees, including political, military, and financial.

Activities
Has carried out terrorist attacks in 20 countries, killing or injuring almost 900 persons. Targets include the United States, the United Kingdom, France, Israel, moderate Palestinians, the PLO, and various Arab countries. Major attacks included the Rome and Vienna airports in December 1985, the Neve Shalom synagogue in Istanbul and the Pan Am Flight 73 hijacking in Karachi in September 1986, and the City of Poros day-excursion ship attack in Greece in July 1988. Suspected of assassinating PLO deputy chief Abu Iyad and PLO security chief Abu Hul in Tunis in January 1991. ANO assassinated a Jordanian diplomat in Lebanon in January 1994 and has been linked to the killing of the PLO representative there. Has not attacked Western targets since the late 1980s.

Strength
Few hundred plus limited overseas support structure.

Location/Area of Operation
Al-Banna relocated to Iraq in December 1998, where the group maintains a presence. Has an operational presence in Lebanon including in several Palestinian refugee camps. Financial problems and internal disorganization have reduced the group's activities and capabilities. Authorities shut down the ANO's operations in Libya and Egypt in 1999. Has demonstrated ability to operate over wide area, including the Middle East, Asia, and Europe.

External Aid
Has received considerable support, including safehaven, training, logistic assistance, and financial aid from Iraq, Libya, and Syria (until 1987), in addition to close support for selected operations.

Abu Sayyaf Group (ASG)

Description
The ASG is the most violent of the Islamic separatist groups operating in the southern Philippines. Some ASG leaders have studied or worked in the Middle East and allegedly fought in Afghanistan during the Soviet war. The group split from the Moro National Liberation Front in the early 1990s under the leadership of Abdurajak Abubakar Janjalani, who was killed in a clash with Philippine police on 18 December 1998. His younger brother, Khadaffy Janjalani, has replaced him as the nominal leader of the group, which is composed of several semi-autonomous factions.

Activities
Engages in kidnappings for ransom, bombings, assassinations, and extortion. Although from time to time it claims that its motivation is to promote an independent Islamic state in western Mindanao and the Sulu Archipelago, areas in the southern Philippines heavily populated by Muslims, the ASG now appears to use terror mainly for financial profit. The group's first large-scale action was a raid on the town of Ipil in Mindanao in April 1995. In April of 2000, an ASG faction kidnapped 21 persons, including 10 foreign tourists, from a resort in Malaysia. Separately in 2000, the group abducted several foreign journalists, 3 Malaysians, and a US citizen. On 27 May 2001, the ASG kidnapped three US citizens and 17 Filipinos from a tourist resort in Palawan, Philippines. Several of the hostages, including one US citizen, were murdered.

Strength
Believed to have a few hundred core fighters, but at least 1000 individuals motivated by the prospect of receiving ransom payments for foreign hostages allegedly joined the group in 2000-2001.

Location/Area of Operation
The ASG was founded in Basilan Province, and mainly operates there and in the neighboring provinces of Sulu and Tawi-Tawi in the Sulu Archipelago. It also operates in the Zamboanga peninsula, and members occasionally travel to Manila and other parts of the country. The group expanded its operations to Malaysia in 2000 when it abducted foreigners from a tourist resort.

External Aid
Largely self-financing through ransom and extortion; may receive support from Islamic extremists in the Middle East and South Asia. Libya publicly paid millions of dollars for the release of the foreign hostages seized from Malaysia in 2000.

Al-Aqsa Martyrs Brigade

Description
The al-Aqsa Martyrs Brigade comprises an unknown number of small cells of Fatah-affiliated activists that emerged at the outset of the current *intifadah* to attack Israeli targets. It aims to drive the Israeli military and settlers from the West Bank, Gaza Strip, and Jerusalem and to establish a Palestinian state.

Activities
Al-Aqsa Martyrs Brigade has carried out shootings and suicide operations against Israeli military personnel and civilians and has killed Palestinians who it believed were collaborating with Israel. At least five US citizens, four of them dual Israeli-US citizens, were killed in these attacks. The group probably did not attack them because of their US citizenship. In January 2002, the group claimed responsibility for the first suicide bombing carried out by a female.

Strength
Unknown.

Location/Area of Operation
Al-Aqsa operates mainly in the West Bank and has claimed attacks inside Israel and the Gaza Strip.

External Aid
Unknown.

Armed Islamic Group (GIA)

Description
An Islamic extremist group, the GIA aims to overthrow the secular Algerian regime and replace it with an Islamic state. The GIA began its violent activity in 1992 after Algiers voided the victory of the Islamic Salvation Front (FIS)—the largest Islamic opposition party—in the first round of legislative elections in December 1991.

Activities
Frequent attacks against civilians and government workers. Between 1992 and 1998 the GIA conducted a terrorist campaign of civilian massacres, sometimes wiping out entire villages in its area of operation. Since announcing its campaign against foreigners living in Algeria in 1993, the GIA has killed more than 100 expatriate men and women—mostly Europeans—in the country. The group uses assassinations and bombings, including car bombs, and it is known to favor kidnapping victims and slitting their throats. The GIA hijacked an Air France flight to Algiers in December 1994. In late 1999 a French court convicted several GIA members for conducting a series of bombings in France in 1995.

Strength
Precise numbers unknown; probably around 200.

Location/Area of Operation
Algeria.

External Aid
Algerian expatriates, some of whom reside in Western Europe, provide some financial and logistic support. In addition, the Algerian Government has accused Iran and Sudan of supporting Algerian extremists.

'Asbat al-Ansar

Description

'Asbat al-Ansar—the Partisans' League—is a Lebanon-based, Sunni extremist group, composed primarily of Palestinians, which is associated with Usama Bin Ladin. The group follows an extremist interpretation of Islam that justifies violence against civilian targets to achieve political ends. Some of those goals include overthrowing the Lebanese Government and thwarting perceived anti-Islamic influences in the country.

Activities

'Asbat al-Ansar has carried out several terrorist attacks in Lebanon since it first emerged in the early 1990s. The group carried out assassinations of Lebanese religious leaders and bombed several nightclubs, theaters, and liquor stores in the mid-1990s. The group raised its operational profile in 2000 with two dramatic attacks against Lebanese and international targets. The group was involved in clashes in northern Lebanon in late December 1999 and carried out a rocket-propelled grenade attack on the Russian Embassy in Beirut in January 2000.

Strength

The group commands about 300 hundred fighters in Lebanon.

Location/Area of Operation

The group's primary base of operations is the 'Ayn al-Hilwah Palestinian refugee camp near Sidon in southern Lebanon.

External Aid

Probably receives money through international Sunni extremist networks and Bin Ladin's al-Qaida network.

Aum Supreme Truth (Aum) a.k.a. Aum Shinrikyo, Aleph

Description

A cult established in 1987 by Shoko Asahara, the Aum aimed to take over Japan and then the world. Approved as a religious entity in 1989 under Japanese law, the group ran candidates in a Japanese parliamentary election in 1990. Over time the cult began to emphasize the imminence of the end of the world and stated that the United States would initiate Armageddon by starting World War III with Japan. The Japanese Government revoked its recognition of the Aum as a religious organization in October 1995, but in 1997 a government panel decided not to invoke the Anti-Subversive Law against the group, which would have outlawed the cult. A 1999 law gave the Japanese Government authorization to continue police surveillance of the group due to concerns that Aum might launch future terrorist attacks. Under the leadership of Fumihiro Joyu the Aum changed its name to Aleph in January 2000 and claimed to have rejected the violent and apocalyptic teachings of its founder. (Joyu took formal control of the organization early in 2002 and remains its leader.)

Activities

On 20 March 1995, Aum members simultaneously released the chemical nerve agent sarin on several Tokyo subway trains, killing 12 persons and injuring up to 6,000. The group was responsible for other mysterious chemical accidents in Japan in 1994. Its efforts to conduct attacks using biological agents have been unsuccessful. Japanese police arrested Asahara in May 1995, and he remained on trial facing charges in 13 crimes, including 7 counts of murder at the end of 2001. Legal analysts say it will take several more years to conclude the trial. Since 1997 the cult continued to recruit new members, engage in commercial enterprise, and acquire property, although it scaled back these activities significantly in 2001 in response to public outcry. The cult maintains an Internet home page. In July 2001, Russian authorities arrested a group of Russian Aum followers who had planned to set off bombs near the Imperial Palace in Tokyo as part of an operation to free Asahara from jail and then smuggle him to Russia.

Strength
The Aum's current membership is estimated at 1,500 to 2,000 persons. At the time of the Tokyo subway attack, the group claimed to have 9,000 members in Japan and up to 40,000 worldwide.

Location/Area of Operation
The Aum's principal membership is located only in Japan, but a residual branch comprising an unknown number of followers has surfaced in Russia.

External Aid
None.

Basque Fatherland and Liberty (ETA) a.k.a. Euzkadi Ta Askatasuna

Description
Founded in 1959 with the aim of establishing an independent homeland based on Marxist principles in the northern Spanish Provinces of Vizcaya, Guipuzcoa, Alava, and Navarra, and the southwestern French Departments of Labourd, Basse-Navarra, and Soule.

Activities
Primarily involved in bombings and assassinations of Spanish Government officials, security and military forces, politicians, and judicial figures. ETA finances its activities through kidnappings, robberies, and extortion. The group has killed more than 800 persons and injured hundreds of others since it began lethal attacks in the early 1960s. In November 1999, ETA broke its "unilateral and indefinite" cease-fire and began an assassination and bombing campaign that has killed 38 individuals and wounded scores more by the end of 2001.

Strength
Unknown; may have hundreds of members, plus supporters.

Location/Area of Operation
Operates primarily in the Basque autonomous regions of northern Spain and southwestern France, but also has bombed Spanish and French interests elsewhere.

External Aid
Has received training at various times in the past in Libya, Lebanon, and Nicaragua. Some ETA members allegedly have received sanctuary in Cuba while others reside in South America.

Al-Gama'a al-Islamiyya (Islamic Group, IG)

Description
Egypt's largest militant group, active since the late 1970s; appears to be loosely organized. Has an external wing with supporters in several countries worldwide. The group issued a cease-fire in March 1999, but its spiritual leader, Shaykh Umar Abd al-Rahman, sentenced to life in prison in January 1996 for his involvement in the 1993

World Trade Center bombing and incarcerated in the United States, rescinded his support for the cease-fire in June 2000. The Gama'a has not conducted an attack inside Egypt since August 1998. Senior member signed Usama Bin Ladin's *fatwa* in February 1998 calling for attacks against US. Unofficially split in two factions; one that supports the cease-fire led by Mustafa Hamza, and one led by Rifa'i Taha Musa, calling for a return to armed operations. Taha Musa in early 2001 published a book in which he attempted to justify terrorist attacks that would cause mass casualties. Musa disappeared several months thereafter, and there are conflicting reports as to his current whereabouts. Primary goal is to overthrow the Egyptian Government and replace it with an Islamic state, but disaffected IG members, such as those potentially inspired by Taha Musa or Abd al-Rahman, may be interested in carrying out attacks against US and Israeli interests.

Activities
Group conducted armed attacks against Egyptian security and other government officials, Coptic Christians, and Egyptian opponents of Islamic extremism before the cease-fire. From 1993 until the cease-fire, al-Gama'a launched attacks on tourists in Egypt, most notably the attack in November 1997 at Luxor that killed 58 foreign tourists. Also claimed responsibility for the attempt in June 1995 to assassinate Egyptian President Hosni Mubarak in Addis Ababa, Ethiopia. The Gama'a has never specifically attacked a US citizen or facility but has threatened US interests.

Strength
Unknown. At its peak the IG probably commanded several thousand hard-core members and a like number of sympathizers. The 1999 cease-fire and security crackdowns following the attack in Luxor in 1997, and more recently security efforts following September 11, probably have resulted in a substantial decrease in the group's numbers.

Location/Area of Operation
Operates mainly in the Al-Minya, Asyu't, Qina, and Sohaj Governorates of southern Egypt. Also appears to have support in Cairo, Alexandria, and other urban locations, particularly among unemployed graduates and students. Has a worldwide presence, including the United Kingdom, Afghanistan, Yemen, and Austria.

External Aid
Unknown. The Egyptian Government believes that Iran, Bin Ladin, and Afghan militant groups support the organization. Also may obtain some funding through various Islamic nongovernmental organizations.

HAMAS (Islamic Resistance Movement)

Description
Formed in late 1987 as an outgrowth of the Palestinian branch of the Muslim Brotherhood. Various HAMAS elements have used both political and violent means, including terrorism, to pursue the goal of establishing an Islamic Palestinian state in place of Israel. Loosely structured, with some elements working clandestinely and others working openly through mosques and social service institutions to recruit members, raise money, organize activities, and distribute propaganda. HAMAS's strength is concentrated in the Gaza Strip and a few areas of the West Bank. Also has engaged in political activity, such as running candidates in West Bank Chamber of Commerce elections.

Activities
HAMAS activists, especially those in the Izz el-Din al-Qassam Brigades, have conducted many attacks—including large-scale suicide bombings—against Israeli

civilian and military targets. In the early 1990s, they also targeted Fatah rivals and began a practice of targeting suspected Palestinian collaborators, which continues. Increased operational activity in 2001 during the *intifadah*, claiming numerous attacks against Israeli interests. Group has not targeted US interests and continues to confine its attacks to Israelis inside Israel and the territories.

Strength
Unknown number of hardcore members; tens of thousands of supporters and sympathizers.

Location/Area of Operation
Primarily the West Bank, Gaza Strip, and Israel. In August 1999, Jordanian authorities closed the group's Political Bureau offices in Amman, arrested its leaders, and prohibited the group from operating on Jordanian territory. HAMAS leaders also present in other parts of the Middle East, including Syria, Lebanon, and Iran.

External Aid
Receives funding from Palestinian expatriates, Iran, and private benefactors in Saudi Arabia and other moderate Arab states. Some fundraising and propaganda activity take place in Western Europe and North America.

Harakat ul-Mujahidin (HUM) (Movement of Holy Warriors)

Description
The HUM is an Islamic militant group based in Pakistan that operates primarily in Kashmir. It is politically aligned with the radical political party, Jamiat-i Ulema-i Islam Fazlur Rehman faction (JUI-F). Long-time leader of the group, Fazlur Rehman Khalil, in mid-February 2000 stepped down as HUM emir, turning the reins over to the popular Kashmiri commander and his second-in-command, Farooq Kashmiri. Khalil, who has been linked to Bin Ladin and signed his *fatwa* in February 1998 calling for attacks on US and Western interests, assumed the position of HUM Secretary General. HUM operated terrorist training camps in eastern Afghanistan until Coalition airstrikes destroyed them during fall, 2001.

Activities
Has conducted a number of operations against Indian troops and civilian targets in Kashmir. Linked to the Kashmiri militant group al-Faran that kidnapped five Western tourists in Kashmir in July 1995; one was killed in August 1995 and the other four reportedly were killed in December of the same year. The HUM is responsible for the hijacking of an Indian airliner on 24 December 1999, which resulted in the release of Masood Azhar—an important leader in the former Harakat ul-Ansar imprisoned by the Indians in 1994—and Ahmad Omar Sheikh, who was arrested for the abduction/murder in January-February 2001 of US journalist Daniel Pearl.

Strength
Has several thousand armed supporters located in Azad Kashmir, Pakistan, and India's southern Kashmir and Doda regions. Supporters are mostly Pakistanis and Kashmiris and also include Afghans and Arab veterans of the Afghan war. Uses light and heavy machineguns, assault rifles, mortars, explosives, and rockets. HUM lost a significant share of its membership in defections to the Jaish-e-Mohammed (JEM) in 2000.

Location/Area of Operation
Based in Muzaffarabad, Rawalpindi, and several other towns in Pakistan, but members conduct insurgent and terrorist activities primarily in Kashmir. The HUM trained its militants in Afghanistan and Pakistan.

External Aid
Collects donations from Saudi Arabia and other Gulf and Islamic states and from Pakistanis and Kashmiris. The HUM's financial collection methods also include soliciting donations from magazine ads and pamphlets. The sources and amount of HUM's military funding are unknown. In anticipation of asset seizures by the Pakistani Government, the HUM withdrew funds from bank accounts and invested in legal businesses, such as commodity trading, real estate, and production of consumer goods. Its fundraising in Pakistan has been constrained since the government clampdown on extremist groups and freezing of terrorist assets.

Hizballah (Party of God) a.k.a. Islamic Jihad, Revolutionary Justice Organization, Organization of the Oppressed on Earth, and Islamic Jihad for the Liberation of Palestine

Description
Formed in 1982 in response to the Israeli invasion of Lebanon, this Lebanon-based radical Shi'a group takes its ideological inspiration from the Iranian revolution and the teachings of the Ayatollah Khomeini. The Majlis al-Shura, or Consultative Council, is the group's highest governing body and is led by Secretary General Hassan Nasrallah. Hizballah formally advocates ultimate establishment of Islamic rule in Lebanon and liberating all occupied Arab lands, including Jerusalem. It has expressed as a goal the elimination of Israel. Has expressed its unwillingness to work within the confines of Lebanon's established political system; however, this stance changed with the party's decision in 1992 to participate in parliamentary elections. Although closely allied with and often directed by Iran, the group may have conducted operations that were not approved by Tehran. While Hizballah does not share the Syrian regime's secular orientation, the group has been a strong tactical ally in helping Syria advance its political objectives in the region.

Activities
Known or suspected to have been involved in numerous anti-US terrorist attacks, including the suicide truck bombings of the US Embassy in Beirut April 1983 and US Marine barracks in Beirut in October 1983 and the US Embassy annex in Beirut in September 1984. Three members of Hizballah, 'Imad Mughniyah, Hasan Izz-al-Din, and Ali Atwa, are on the FBI's list of 22 Most Wanted Terrorists for the hijacking in 1985 of TWA Flight 847 during which a US Navy diver was murdered. Elements of the group were responsible for the kidnapping and detention of US and other Western hostages in Lebanon. The group also attacked the Israeli Embassy in Argentina in 1992 and is a suspect in the 1994 bombing of the Israeli cultural center in Buenos Aires. In fall 2000, it captured three Israeli soldiers in the Shabaa Farms and kidnapped an Israeli noncombatant whom it may have lured to Lebanon under false pretenses.

Strength
Several thousand supporters and a few hundred terrorist operatives.

Location/Area of Operation
Operates in the Bekaa Valley, Hermil, the southern suburbs of Beirut, and southern Lebanon. Has established cells in Europe, Africa, South America, North America, and Asia.

External Aid
Receives substantial amounts of financial, training, weapons, explosives, political, diplomatic, and organizational aid from Iran and received diplomatic, political, and logistical support from Syria.

Islamic Movement of Uzbekistan (IMU)

Description
Coalition of Islamic militants from Uzbekistan and other Central Asian states opposed to Uzbekistani President Islom Karimov's secular regime. Before the counterterrorism coalition began operations in Afghanistan in October, the IMU's primary goal was the establishment of an Islamic state in Uzbekistan. If IMU political and ideological leader Tohir Yoldashev survives the counterterrorism campaign and can regroup the organization, however, he might widen the IMU's targets to include all those he perceives as fighting Islam. The group's propaganda has always included anti-Western and anti-Israeli rhetoric.

Activities
The IMU primarily targeted Uzbekistani interests before October 2001 and is believed to have been responsible for five car bombs in Tashkent in February 1999. Militants also took foreigners hostage in 1999 and 2000, including four US citizens who were mountain climbing in August 2000, and four Japanese geologists and eight Kyrgyzstani soldiers in August 1999. Since October, the Coalition has captured, killed, and dispersed many of the militants who remained in Afghanistan to fight with the Taliban and al-Qaida, severely degrading the IMU's ability to attack Uzbekistani or Coalition interests in the near term. IMU military leader Juma Namangani apparently was killed during an air strike in November. At year's end, Yoldashev remained at large.

Strength
Militants probably number under 2000.

Location/Area of Operation
Militants are scattered throughout South Asia and Tajikistan. Area of operations includes Afghanistan, Iran, Kyrgyzstan, Pakistan, Tajikistan, and Uzbekistan.

External Aid
Support from other Islamic extremist groups and patrons in the Middle East and Central and South Asia. IMU leadership broadcasts statements over Iranian radio.

Jaish-e-Mohammed (JEM) (Army of Mohammed)

Description
The Jaish-e-Mohammed (JEM) is an Islamic extremist group based in Pakistan that was formed by Masood Azhar upon his release from prison in India in early 2000. The group's aim is to unite Kashmir with Pakistan. It is politically aligned with the radical political party, Jamiat-i Ulema-i Islam Fazlur Rehman faction (JUI-F). The United States announced the addition of JEM to the US Treasury Department's Office of Foreign Asset Control's (OFAC) list—which includes organizations that are believed to support terrorist groups and have assets in US jurisdiction that can be frozen or controlled—in October and the Foreign Terrorist Organization list in December. The group was banned and its assets were frozen by the Pakistani Government in January 2002.

Activities
The JEM's leader, Masood Azhar, was released from Indian imprisonment in December 1999 in exchange for 155 hijacked Indian Airlines hostages. The 1994 HUA kidnappings by Omar Sheikh of US and British nationals in New Delhi and the July 1995 HUA/Al Faran kidnappings of Westerners in Kashmir were two of several

previous HUA efforts to free Azhar. The JEM on 1 October 2001 claimed responsibility for a suicide attack on the Jammu and Kashmir legislative assembly building in Srinagar that killed at least 31 persons, but later denied the claim. The Indian Government has publicly implicated the JEM, along with Lashkar-e-Tayyiba . . . for the 13 December attack on the Indian Parliament that killed 9 and injured 18.

Strength
Has several hundred armed supporters located in Azad Kashmir, Pakistan, and in India's southern Kashmir and Doda regions, including a large cadre of former HUM members. Supporters are mostly Pakistanis and Kashmiris and also include Afghans and Arab veterans of the Afghan war. Uses light and heavy machineguns, assault rifles, mortars, improvised explosive devices, and rocket grenades.

Location/Area of Operation
Based in Peshawar and Muzaffarabad, but members conduct terrorist activities primarily in Kashmir. The JEM maintained training camps in Afghanistan until the fall of 2001.

External Aid
Most of the JEM's cadre and material resources have been drawn from the militant groups Harakat ul-Jihad al-Islami (HUJI) and the Harakat ul-Mujahedin (HUM). The JEM had close ties to Afghan Arabs and the Taliban. Usama Bin Ladin is suspected of giving funding to the JEM. The JEM also collects funds through donation requests in magazines and pamphlets. In anticipation of asset seizures by the Pakistani Government, the JEM withdrew funds from bank accounts and invested in legal businesses, such as commodity trading, real estate, and production of consumer goods.

Al-Jihad a.k.a. Egyptian Islamic Jihad, Jihad Group, Islamic Jihad

Description
Egyptian Islamic extremist group active since the late 1970s. Merged with Bin Ladin's al-Qaida organization in June 2001, but may retain some capability to conduct independent operations. Continues to suffer setbacks worldwide, especially after 11 September attacks. Primary goals are to overthrow the Egyptian Government and replace it with an Islamic state and attack US and Israeli interests in Egypt and abroad.

Activities
Specializes in armed attacks against high-level Egyptian Government personnel, including cabinet ministers, and car-bombings against official US and Egyptian facilities. The original Jihad was responsible for the assassination in 1981 of Egyptian President Anwar Sadat. Claimed responsibility for the attempted assassinations of Interior Minister Hassan al-Alfi in August 1993 and Prime Minister Atef Sedky in November 1993. Has not conducted an attack inside Egypt since 1993 and has never targeted foreign tourists there. Responsible for Egyptian Embassy bombing in Islamabad in 1995; in 1998 attack against US Embassy in Albania was thwarted.

Strength
Unknown, but probably has several hundred hardcore members.

Location/Area of Operation
Operates in the Cairo area, but most of its network is outside Egypt, including Yemen, Afghanistan, Pakistan, Lebanon, and the United Kingdom, and its activities have been centered outside Egypt for several years.

External Aid
Unknown. The Egyptian Government claims that Iran supports the Jihad. Its merger with al-Qaida also boosts Bin Ladin's support for the group. Also may obtain some funding through various Islamic nongovernmental organizations, cover businesses, and criminal acts.

Kahane Chai (Kach)

Description
Stated goal is to restore the biblical state of Israel. Kach (founded by radical Israeli-American rabbi Meir Kahane) and its offshoot Kahane Chai, which means "Kahane Lives," (founded by Meir Kahane's son Binyamin following his father's assassination in the United States) were declared to be terrorist organizations in March 1994 by the Israeli Cabinet under the 1948 Terrorism Law. This followed the groups' statements in support of Dr. Baruch Goldstein's attack in February 1994 on the al-Ibrahimi Mosque—Goldstein was affiliated with Kach—and their verbal attacks on the Israeli Government. Palestinian gunmen killed Binyamin Kahane and his wife in a drive-by shooting in December 2000 in the West Bank.

Activities
Organize protests against the Israeli Government. Harass and threaten Palestinians in Hebron and the West Bank. Have threatened to attack Arabs, Palestinians, and Israeli Government officials. Have vowed revenge for the death of Binyamin Kahane and his wife.

Strength
Unknown.

Location/Area of Operation
Israel and West Bank settlements, particularly Qiryat Arba' in Hebron.

External Aid
Receives support from sympathizers in the United States and Europe.

Kurdistan Workers' Party (PKK)

Description
Founded in 1974 as a Marxist-Leninist insurgent group primarily composed of Turkish Kurds. The group's goal has been to establish an independent Kurdish state in south-eastern Turkey, where the population is predominantly Kurdish. In the early 1990s, the PKK moved beyond rural-based insurgent activities to include urban terrorism. Turkish authorities captured Chairman Abdullah Ocalan in Kenya in early 1999; the Turkish State Security Court subsequently sentenced him to death. In August 1999, Ocalan announced a "peace initiative," ordering members to refrain from violence and request-ing dialogue with Ankara on Kurdish issues. At a PKK Congress in January 2000, members supported Ocalan's initiative and claimed the group now would use only political means to achieve its new goal, improved rights for Kurds in Turkey.

Activities
Primary targets have been Turkish Government security forces in Turkey. Conducted attacks on Turkish diplomatic and commercial facilities in dozens of West European cities in 1993 and again in spring 1995. In an attempt to damage Turkey's tourist indus-try, the PKK bombed tourist sites and hotels and kidnapped foreign tourists in the early to mid-1990s.

Strength
Approximately 4,000 to 5,000, most of whom currently are located in northern Iraq. Has thousands of sympathizers in Turkey and Europe.

Location/Area of Operation
Operates in Turkey, Europe, and the Middle East.

External Aid
Has received safehaven and modest aid from Syria, Iraq, and Iran. Damascus generally upheld its September 2000 antiterror agreement with Ankara, pledging not to support the PKK.

Lashkar-e-Tayyiba (LT) (Army of the Righteous)

Description
The LT is the armed wing of the Pakistan-based religious organization, Markaz-ud-Dawa-wal-Irshad (MDI)—a Sunni anti-US missionary organization formed in 1989. The LT is led by Abdul Wahid Kashmiri and is one of the three largest and best-trained groups fighting in Kashmir against India; it is not connected to a political party. The United States in October announced the addition of the LT to the US Treasury Department's Office of Foreign Asset Control's (OFAC) list—which includes organizations that are believed to support terrorist groups and have assets in US jurisdiction that can be frozen or controlled. The group was banned and its assets were frozen by the Pakistani Government in January 2002.

Activities
The LT has conducted a number of operations against Indian troops and civilian targets in Kashmir since 1993. The LT claimed responsibility for numerous attacks in 2001, including a January attack on Srinagar airport that killed five Indians along with six militants; an attack on a police station in Srinagar that killed at least eight officers and wounded several others; and an attack in April against Indian border security forces that left at least four dead. The Indian Government publicly implicated the LT along with JEM for the 13 December attack on the Indian Parliament building.

Strength
Has several hundred members in Azad Kashmir, Pakistan, and in India's southern Kashmir and Doda regions. Almost all LT cadres are non-Kashmiris mostly Pakistanis from madrassas across the country and Afghan veterans of the Afghan wars. Uses assault rifles, light and heavy machineguns, mortars, explosives, and rocket propelled grenades.

Location/Area of Operation
Has been based in Muridke (near Lahore) and Muzaffarabad. The LT trains its militants in mobile training camps across Pakistan-administered Kashmir and had trained in Afghanistan until fall of 2001.

External Aid
Collects donations from the Pakistani community in the Persian Gulf and United Kingdom, Islamic NGOs, and Pakistani and Kashmiri businessmen. The LT also maintains a website (under the name of its parent organization Jamaat ud-Daawa), through which it solicits funds and provides information on the group's activities. The amount of LT funding is unknown. The LT maintains ties to religious/military groups around the world, ranging from the Philippines to the Middle East and Chechnya through the MDI fraternal network. In anticipation of asset seizures by the Pakistani Government,

the LT withdrew funds from bank accounts and invested in legal businesses, such as commodity trading, real estate, and production of consumer goods.

Liberation Tigers of Tamil Eelam (LTTE)

Other known front organizations: World Tamil Association (WTA), World Tamil Movement (WTM), the Federation of Associations of Canadian Tamils (FACT), the Ellalan Force, and the Sangilian Force.

Description
Founded in 1976, the LTTE is the most powerful Tamil group in Sri Lanka and uses overt and illegal methods to raise funds, acquire weapons, and publicize its cause of establishing an independent Tamil state. The LTTE began its armed conflict with the Sri Lankan Government in 1983 and relies on a guerrilla strategy that includes the use of terrorist tactics.

Activities
The Tigers have integrated a battlefield insurgent strategy with a terrorist program that targets not only key personnel in the countryside but also senior Sri Lankan political and military leaders in Colombo and other urban centers. The Tigers are most notorious for their cadre of suicide bombers, the Black Tigers. Political assassinations and bombings are commonplace. The LTTE has refrained from targeting foreign diplomatic and commercial establishments.

Strength
Exact strength is unknown, but the LTTE is estimated to have 8,000 to 10,000 armed combatants in Sri Lanka, with a core of trained fighters of approximately 3,000 to 6,000. The LTTE also has a significant overseas support structure for fundraising, weapons procurement, and propaganda activities.

Location/Area of Operations
The Tigers control most of the northern and eastern coastal areas of Sri Lanka but have conducted operations throughout the island. Headquartered in northern Sri Lanka, LTTE leader Velupillai Prabhakaran has established an extensive network of checkpoints and informants to keep track of any outsiders who enter the group's area of control.

External Aid
The LTTE's overt organizations support Tamil separatism by lobbying foreign governments and the United Nations. The LTTE also uses its international contacts to procure weapons, communications, and any other equipment and supplies it needs. The LTTE exploits large Tamil communities in North America, Europe, and Asia to obtain funds and supplies for its fighters in Sri Lanka often through false claims or even extortion.

Mujahedin-e Khalq Organization (MEK or MKO) a.k.a. The National Liberation Army of Iran (NLA, the militant wing of the MEK), the People's Mujahidin of Iran (PMOI), National Council of Resistance (NCR), Muslim Iranian Student's Society (front organization used to garner financial support)

Description
The MEK philosophy mixes Marxism and Islam. Formed in the 1960s, the organization was expelled from Iran after the Islamic Revolution in 1979, and its primary support

now comes from the Iraqi regime of Saddam Hussein. Its history is studded with anti-Western attacks as well as terrorist attacks on the interests of the clerical regime in Iran and abroad. The MEK now advocates a secular Iranian regime.

Activities

Worldwide campaign against the Iranian Government stresses propaganda and occasionally uses terrorist violence. During the 1970s the MEK killed several US military personnel and US civilians working on defense projects in Tehran. It supported the takeover in 1979 of the US Embassy in Tehran. In 1981 the MEK planted bombs in the head office of the Islamic Republic Party and the Premier's office, killing some 70 high-ranking Iranian officials, including chief Justice Ayatollah Mohammad Beheshti, President Mohammad-Ali Rajaei, and Premier Mohammad-Javad Bahonar. In 1991, it assisted the government of Iraq in suppressing the Shia and Kurdish uprisings in northern and southern Iraq. Since then, the MEK has continued to perform internal security services for the Government of Iraq. In April 1992, it conducted attacks on Iranian Embassies in 13 different countries, demonstrating the group's ability to mount large-scale operations overseas. In recent years the MEK has targeted key military officers and assassinated the deputy chief of the Armed Forces General Staff in April 1999. In April 2000, the MEK attempted to assassinate the commander of the Nasr Headquarters—the interagency board responsible for coordinating policies on Iraq. The normal pace of anti-Iranian operations increased during the "Operation Great Bahman" in February 2000, when the group launched a dozen attacks against Iran. In 2000 and 2001, the MEK was involved regularly in mortar attacks and hit-and-run raids on Iranian military and law enforcement units and government buildings near the Iran-Iraq border. Since the end of the Iran-Iraq War the tactics along the border have garnered few military gains and have become commonplace. MEK insurgent activities in Tehran constitute the biggest security concern for the Iranian leadership. In February 2000, for example, the MEK attacked the leadership complex in Tehran that houses the offices of the Supreme Leader and President.

Strength

Several thousand fighters located on bases scattered throughout Iraq and armed with tanks, infantry fighting vehicles, and artillery. The MEK also has an overseas support structure. Most of the fighters are organized in the MEK's National Liberation Army (NLA).

Location/Area of Operation

In the 1980s the MEK's leaders were forced by Iranian security forces to flee to France. Since resettling in Iraq in 1987, the group has conducted internal security operations in support of the Government of Iraq. In the mid-1980s the group did not mount terrorist operations in Iran at a level similar to its activities in the 1970s, but by the 1990s the MEK had claimed credit for an increasing number of operations in Iran.

External Aid

Beyond support from Iraq, the MEK uses front organizations to solicit contributions from expatriate Iranian communities.

National Liberation Army (ELN)—Colombia

Description

Marxist insurgent group formed in 1965 by urban intellectuals inspired by Fidel Castro and Che Guevara. Began a dialogue with Colombian officials in 1999 following a campaign of mass kidnappings—each involving at least one US citizen—to demonstrate its strength and continuing viability and force the Pastrana administration to negotiate. Peace talks between Bogotá and the ELN, started in 1999, continued sporadically through 2001 until Bogotà broke them off in August, but resumed in Havana, Cuba, by year's end.

Activities
Kidnapping, hijacking, bombing, extortion, and guerrilla war. Modest conventional military capability. Annually conducts hundreds of kidnappings for ransom, often targeting foreign employees of large corporations, especially in the petroleum industry. Frequently assaults energy infrastructure and has inflicted major damage on pipelines and the electric distribution network.

Strength
Approximately 3,000-5,000 armed combatants and an unknown number of active supporters.

Location/Area of Operation
Mostly in rural and mountainous areas of north, northeast, and southwest Colombia, and Venezuela border regions.

External Aid
Cuba provides some medical care and political consultation.

The Palestine Islamic Jihad (PIJ)

Description
Originated among militant Palestinians in the Gaza Strip during the 1970s. PIJ-Shiqaqi faction, currently led by Ramadan Shallah in Damascus, is most active. Committed to the creation of an Islamic Palestinian state and the destruction of Israel through holy war. Also opposes moderate Arab governments that it believes have been tainted by Western secularism.

Activities
PIJ activists have conducted many attacks including large-scale suicide bombings against Israeli civilian and military targets. The group increased its operational activity in 2001 during the *Intifadah*, claiming numerous attacks against Israeli interests. The group has not targeted US interests and continues to confine its attacks to Israelis inside Israel and the territories.

Strength
Unknown.

Location/Area of Operation
Primarily Israel, the West Bank and Gaza Strip, and other parts of the Middle East, including Lebanon and Syria, where the leadership is based.

External Aid
Receives financial assistance from Iran and limited logistic support assistance from Syria.

Palestine Liberation Front (PLF)

Description
Broke away from the PFLP-GC in mid-1970s. Later split again into pro-PLO, pro-Syrian, and pro-Libyan factions. Pro-PLO faction led by Muhammad Abbas

(Abu Abbas), who became member of PLO Executive Committee in 1984 but left it in 1991.

Activities
The Abu Abbas–led faction is known for aerial attacks against Israel. Abbas's group also was responsible for the attack in 1985 on the cruise ship *Achille Lauro* and the murder of US citizen Leon Klinghoffer. A warrant for Abu Abbas's arrest is outstanding in Italy.

Strength
Unknown.

Location/Area of Operation
PLO faction based in Tunisia until *Achille Lauro* attack. Now based in Iraq.

External Aid
Receives support mainly from Iraq. Has received support from Libya in the past.

Popular Front for the Liberation of Palestine (PFLP)

Description
Marxist-Leninist group founded in 1967 by George Habash as a member of the PLO. Joined the Alliance of Palestinian Forces (APF) to oppose the Declaration of Principles signed in 1993 and suspended participation in the PLO. Broke away from the APF, along with the DFLP, in 1996 over ideological differences. Took part in meetings with Arafat's Fatah party and PLO representatives in 1999 to discuss national unity and the reinvigoration of the PLO but continues to oppose current negotiations with Israel.

Activities
Committed numerous international terrorist attacks during the 1970s. Since 1978 has conducted attacks against Israeli or moderate Arab targets, including killing a settler and her son in December 1996. Stepped up operational activity in 2001, highlighted by the shooting death of Israeli Tourism Minister in October to retaliation for Israel's killing of PFLP leader in August.

Strength
Some 800.

Location/Area of Operation
Syria, Lebanon, Israel, West Bank, and Gaza.

External Aid
Receives safehaven and some logistical assistance from Syria.

Popular Front for the Liberation of Palestine–General Command (PFLP-GC)

Description
Split from the PFLP in 1968, claiming it wanted to focus more on fighting and less on politics. Opposed to Arafat's PLO. Led by Ahmad Jabril, a former captain in the Syrian Army. Closely tied to both Syria and Iran.

Activities
Carried out dozens of attacks in Europe and the Middle East during 1970s-80s. Known for cross-border terrorist attacks into Israel using unusual means, such as hot-air

balloons and motorized hang gliders. Primary focus now on guerrilla operations in southern Lebanon, small-scale attacks in Israel, West Bank, and Gaza.

Strength
Several hundred.

Location/Area of Operation
Headquartered in Damascus with bases in Lebanon.

External Aid
Receives support from Syria and financial support from Iran.

Al-Qaida

Description
Established by Usama Bin Ladin in the late 1980s to bring together Arabs who fought in Afghanistan against the Soviet Union. Helped finance, recruit, transport, and train Sunni Islamic extremists for the Afghan resistance. Current goal is to establish a pan-Islamic Caliphate throughout the world by working with allied Islamic extremist groups to overthrow regimes it deems "non-Islamic" and expelling Westerners and non-Muslims from Muslim countries. Issued statement under banner of "The World Islamic Front for Jihad Against the Jews and Crusaders" in February 1998, saying it was the duty of all Muslims to kill US citizens—civilian or military—and their allies everywhere. Merged with Egyptian Islamic Jihad (Al-Jihad) in June 2001.

Activities
On 11 September, 19 al-Qaida suicide attackers hijacked and crashed four US commercial jets, two into the World Trade Center in New York City, one into the Pentagon near Washington, DC, and a fourth into a field in Shanksville, Pennsylvania, leaving about 3,000 individuals dead or missing. Directed the 12 October 2000 attack on the USS *Cole* in the port of Aden, Yemen, killing 17 US Navy members, and injuring another 39. Conducted the bombings in August 1998 of the US Embassies in Nairobi, Kenya, and Dar es Salaam, Tanzania, that killed at least 301 individuals and injured more than 5,000 others. Claims to have shot down US helicopters and killed US servicemen in Somalia in 1993 and to have conducted three bombings that targeted US troops in Aden, Yemen, in December 1992.

Al-Qaida is linked to the following plans that were not carried out: to assassinate Pope John Paul II during his visit to Manila in late 1994, to kill President Clinton during a visit to the Philippines in early 1995, the midair bombing of a dozen US trans-Pacific flights in 1995, and to set off a bomb at Los Angeles International Airport in 1999. Also plotted to carry out terrorist operations against US and Israeli tourists visiting Jordan for millennial celebrations in late 1999. (Jordanian authorities thwarted the planned attacks and put 28 suspects on trial.) In December 2001, suspected al-Qaida associate Richard Colvin Reid attempted to ignite a shoe bomb on a transatlantic flight from Paris to Miami.

Strength
Al-Qaida may have several thousand members and associates. Also serves as a focal point or umbrella organization for a worldwide network that includes many Sunni Islamic extremist groups, some members of al-Gama'a al-Islamiyya, the Islamic Movement of Uzbekistan, and the Harakat ul-Mujahidin.

Location/Area of Operation
Al-Qaida has cells worldwide and is reinforced by its ties to Sunni extremist networks. Coalition attacks on Afghanistan since October 2001 have dismantled the

Taliban—al-Qaida's protectors—and led to the capture, death, or dispersal of al-Qaida operatives. Some al-Qaida members at large probably will attempt to carry out future attacks against US interests.

External Aid
Bin Ladin, member of a billionaire family that owns the Bin Ladin Group construction empire, is said to have inherited tens of millions of dollars that he uses to help finance the group. Al-Qaida also maintains moneymaking front businesses, solicits donations from like-minded supporters, and illicitly siphons funds from donations to Muslim charitable organizations. US efforts to block al-Qaida funding has hampered al-Qaida's ability to obtain money.

Real IRA (RIRA) a.k.a. True IRA

Description
Formed in early 1998 as clandestine armed wing of the 32-County Sovereignty Movement, a "political pressure group" dedicated to removing British forces from Northern Ireland and unifying Ireland. The 32-County Sovereignty Movement opposed Sinn Fein's adoption in September 1997 of the Mitchell principles of democracy and nonviolence and opposed the amendment in December 1999 of Articles 2 and 3 of the Irish Constitution, which laid claim to Northern Ireland. Michael "Mickey" McKevitt, who left the IRA to protest its cease-fire, leads the group; Bernadette Sands-McKevitt, his wife, is a founder-member of the 32-County Sovereignty Movement, the political wing of the RIRA.

Activities
Bombings, assassinations, and robberies. Many Real IRA members are former IRA members who left that organization following the IRA cease-fire and bring to RIRA a wealth of experience in terrorist tactics and bombmaking. Targets include British military and police in Northern Ireland and Northern Ireland Protestant communities. RIRA is linked to and understood to be responsible for the car bomb attack in Omagh, Northern Ireland on 15 August, 1998 that killed 29 and injured 220 persons. The group began to observe a cease-fire following Omagh but in 2000 and 2001 resumed attacks in Northern Ireland and on the UK mainland against targets such as MI6 headquarters and the BBC.

Strength
100-200 activists plus possible limited support from IRA hardliners dissatisfied with the IRA cease-fire and other republican sympathizers. British and Irish authorities arrested at least 40 members in the spring and summer of 2001, including leader McKevitt, who is currently in prison in the Irish Republic awaiting trial for being a member of a terrorist organization and directing terrorist attacks.

Location/Area of Operation
Northern Ireland, Irish Republic, Great Britain.

External Aid
Suspected of receiving funds from sympathizers in the United States and of attempting to buy weapons from US gun dealers. RIRA also is reported to have purchased sophisticated weapons from the Balkans. Three Irish nationals associated with RIRA were extradited from Slovenia to the UK and are awaiting trial on weapons procurement charges.

Revolutionary Armed Forces of Colombia (FARC)

Description
Established in 1964 as the military wing of the Colombian Communist Party, the FARC is Colombia's oldest, largest, most capable, and best-equipped Marxist insurgency. The FARC is governed by a secretariat, led by septuagenarian Manuel Marulanda, a.k.a. "Tirofijo," and six others, including senior military commander Jorge Briceno, a.k.a. "Mono Jojoy." Organized along military lines and includes several urban fronts. In 2001, the group continued a slow-moving peace negotiation process with the Pastrana Administration that has gained the group several concessions, including a demilitarized zone used as a venue for negotiations.

Activities
Bombings, murder, kidnapping, extortion, hijacking, as well as guerrilla and conventional military action against Colombian political, military, and economic targets. In March 1999 the FARC executed three US Indian rights activists on Venezuelan territory after it kidnapped them in Colombia. Foreign citizens often are targets of FARC kidnapping for ransom. Has well-documented ties to narcotics traffickers, principally through the provision of armed protection.

Strength
Approximately 9,000-12,000 armed combatants and an unknown number of supporters, mostly in rural areas.

Location/Area of Operation
Colombia with some activities—extortion, kidnapping, logistics, and R&R—in Venezuela, Panama, and Ecuador.

External Aid
Cuba provides some medical care and political consultation.

Revolutionary Nuclei a.k.a. Revolutionary Cells

Description
Revolutionary Nuclei (RN) emerged from a broad range of antiestablishment and anti-US/NATO/EU leftist groups active in Greece between 1995 and 1998. The group is believed to be the successor to or offshoot of Greece's most prolific terrorist group, Revolutionary People's Struggle (ELA), which has not claimed an attack since January 1995. Indeed, RN appeared to fill the void left by ELA, particularly as lesser groups faded from the scene. RN's few communiqués show strong similarities in rhetoric, tone, and theme to ELA proclamations. RN has not claimed an attack since November 2000.

Activities
Beginning operations in January 1995, the group has claimed responsibility for some two dozen arson attacks and explosive low-level bombings targeting a range of US, Greek, and other European targets in Greece. In its most infamous and lethal attack to date, the group claimed responsibility for a bomb it detonated at the Intercontinental Hotel in April 1999 that resulted in the death of a Greek woman and injured a Greek man. Its modus operandi includes warning calls of impending attacks, attacks targeting property vice individuals; use of rudimentary timing devices; and strikes during the late evening-early morning hours. RN last attacked US interests in Greece in November 2000 with two separate bombings against the Athens offices of Citigroup and the studio of a Greek/American sculptor. The group also detonated an explosive device outside the Athens offices of Texaco in December 1999. Greek targets have included court

and other government office buildings, private vehicles, and the offices of Greek firms involved in NATO-related defense contracts in Greece. Similarly, the group has attacked European interests in Athens, including Barclays Bank in December 1998 and November 2000.

Strength
Group membership is believed to be small, probably drawing from the Greek militant leftist or anarchist milieu.

Location/Area of Operation
Primary area of operation is in the Athens metropolitan area.

External Aid
Unknown, but believed to be self-sustaining.

Revolutionary Organization 17 November (17 November)

Description
Radical leftist group established in 1975 and named for the student uprising in Greece in November 1973 that protested the military regime. Anti-Greek establishment, anti-US, anti-Turkey, anti-NATO, and committed to the ouster of US Bases, removal of Turkish military presence from Cyprus, and severing of Greece's ties to NATO and the European Union (EU).

Activities
Initial attacks were assassinations of senior US officials and Greek public figures. Added bombings in 1980s. Since 1990 has expanded targets to include EU facilities and foreign firms investing in Greece and has added improvised rocket attacks to its methods. Most recent attack claimed was the murder in June 2000 of British Defense Attaché Stephen Saunders.

Strength
Unknown, but presumed to be small.

Location/Area of Operation
Athens, Greece.

Revolutionary People's Liberation Party/Front (DHKP/C) a.k.a. Devrimci Sol, Revolutionary Left, Dev Sol

Description
Originally formed in 1978 as Devrimci Sol, or Dev Sol, a splinter faction of the Turkish People's Liberation Party/Front. Renamed in 1994 after factional infighting, it espouses a Marxist ideology and is virulently anti-US and anti-NATO. Finances its activities chiefly through armed robberies and extortion.

Activities
Since the late 1980s has concentrated attacks against current and retired Turkish security and military officials. Began a new campaign against foreign interests in 1990. Assassinated two US military contractors and wounded a US Air Force officer to protest the Gulf War. Launched rockets at US Consulate in Istanbul in 1992. Assassinated prominent Turkish businessman and two others in early 1996, its first significant terrorist act as DHKP/C. Turkish authorities thwarted DHKP/C attempt in June 1999 to fire light antitank weapon at US Consulate in Istanbul. Conducted its first

suicide bombings, targeting Turkish police, in January and September 2001. Series of safehouse raids and arrests by Turkish police over last three years have weakened group significantly.

Strength
Unknown.

Location/Area of Operation
Conducts attacks in Turkey, primarily in Istanbul. Raises funds in Western Europe.

External Aid
Unknown.

The Salafist Group for Call and Combat (GSPC)

Description
The Salafist Group for Call and Combat (GSPC) splinter faction that began in 1996 has eclipsed the GIA since approximately 1998, and currently is assessed to be the most effective remaining armed group inside Algeria. In contrast to the GIA, the GSPC has gained popular support through its pledge to avoid civilian attacks inside Algeria (although, in fact, civilians have been attacked). Its adherents abroad appear to have largely co-opted the external networks of the GIA, active particularly throughout Europe, Africa, and the Middle East.

Activities
The GSPC continues to conduct operations aimed at government and military targets, primarily in rural areas. Such operations include false roadblocks and attacks against convoys transporting military, police, or other government personnel. According to press reporting, some GSPC members in Europe maintain contacts with other North African extremists sympathetic to al-Qaida, a number of whom were implicated in terrorist plots during 2001.

Strength
Unknown; probably several hundred to several thousand inside Algeria.

Location/Area of Operation
Algeria.

External Aid
Algerian expatriates and GSPC members abroad, many residing in Western Europe, provide financial and logistics support. In addition, the Algerian Government has accused Iran and Sudan of supporting Algerian extremists in years past.

Sendero Luminoso (Shining Path, or SL)

Description
Former university professor Abimael Guzman formed Sendero Luminoso in the late 1960s, and his teachings created the foundation of SL's militant Maoist doctrine. In the 1980s SL became one of the most ruthless terrorist groups in the Western Hemisphere; approximately 30,000 persons have died since Shining Path took up arms in 1980. Its stated goal is to destroy existing Peruvian institutions and replace them with a communist peasant revolutionary regime. It also opposes any influence by foreign governments, as well as by other Latin American guerrilla groups, especially the Tupac Amaru Revolutionary Movement (MRTA).

In 2001, the Peruvian National Police thwarted an SL attack against "an American objective", possibly the US Embassy, when they arrested two Lima SL cell members. Addtionally, Government authorities continued to arrest and prosecute active SL members, including, Ruller Mazombite, a.k.a. "Camarada Cayo", chief of the protection team of SL leader Macario Ala, a.k.a. "Artemio", and Evorcio Ascencios, a.k.a. "Camarada Canale", logistics chief of the Huallaga Regional Committee. Counterterrorist operations targeted pockets of terrorist activity in the Upper Huallaga River Valley and the Apurimac/Ene River Valley, where SL columns continued to conduct periodic attacks.

Activities
Conducted indiscriminate bombing campaigns and selective assassinations. Detonated explosives at diplomatic missions of several countries in Peru in 1990, including an attempt to car bomb the US Embassy in December. Peruvian authorities continued operations against the SL in 2001 in the countryside, where the SL conducted periodic raids on villages.

Strength
Membership is unknown but estimated to be 200 armed militants. SL's strength has been vastly diminished by arrests and desertions.

Location/Area of Operation
Peru, with most activity in rural areas.

External Aid
None.

United Self-Defense Forces/Group of Colombia (AUC—Autodefensas Unidas de Colombia)

Description
The AUC—commonly referred to as the paramilitaries—is an umbrella organization formed in April 1997 to consolidate most local and regional paramilitary groups each with the mission to protect economic interests and combat insurgents locally. The AUC—supported by economic elites, drug traffickers, and local communities lacking effective government security—claims its primary objective is to protect its sponsors from insurgents. The AUC now asserts itself as a regional and national counterinsurgent force. It is adequately equipped and armed and reportedly pays its members a monthly salary. AUC political leader Carlos Castaño has claimed 70 percent of the AUC's operational costs are financed with drug-related earnings, the rest from "donations" from its sponsors.

Activities
AUC operations vary from assassinating suspected insurgent supporters to engaging guerrilla combat units. Colombian National Combat operations generally consist of raids and ambushes directed against suspected insurgents. The AUC generally avoids engagements with government security forces and actions against US personnel or interests.

Strength
Estimated 6000 to 8150, including former military and insurgent personnel.

Location/Areas of Operation
AUC forces are strongest in the northwest in Antioquia, Córdoba, Sucre, and Bolívar Departments. Since 1999, the group demonstrated a growing presence in other northern

and southwestern departments. Clashes between the AUC and the FARC insurgents in Putumayo in 2000 demonstrated the range of the AUC to contest insurgents throughout Colombia.

External Aid
None.

Background Information on Other Terrorist Groups

Contents

Alex Boncayao Brigade (ABB)
Al-Ittihad al-Islami (AIAI)
Allied Democratic Forces (ADF)
Anti-Imperialist Territorial Nuclei (NTA)
Army for the Liberation of Rwanda (ALIR)
Cambodian Freedom Fighters (CFF)
Continuity Irish Republican Army (CIRA)
First of October Antifacist Resistance Group (GRAPO)
Harakat ul-Jihad-I-Islami (HUJI)
Harakat ul-Jihad-I-Islami/Bangladesh (HUJI-B)
Islamic Army of Aden (IAA)
Irish Republican Army (IRA)
Al-Jama'a al-Islamiyyah al-Muqatilah bi-Libya
Japanese Red Army (JRA)
Jemaah Islamiya (JI)
Kumpulan Mujahidin Malaysia (KMM)
Lord's Resistance Army (LRA)
Loyalist Volunteer Force (LVF)
New People's Army (NPA)
Orange Volunteers (OV)
People Against Gangsterism and Drugs (PAGAD)
Red Hand Defenders (RHD)
Revolutionary Proletarian Initiative Nuclei (NIPR)
Revolutionary United Front (RUF)
The Tunisian Combatant Group (TCG)
Tupac Amaru Revolutionary Movement (MRTA)
Turkish Hizballah
Ulster Defense Association/Ulster Freedom Fighters (UDA/UVF)

* * *

Alex Boncayao Brigade (ABB)

Description
The ABB, the breakaway urban hit squad of the Communist Party of the Philippines New People's Army, was formed in the mid-1980s. The ABB was added to the Terrorist Exclusion list in December 2001.

Activities
Responsible for more than 100 murders and believed to have been involved in the murder in 1989 of US Army Col. James Rowe in the Philippines. In March 1997 the

group announced it had formed an alliance with another armed group, the Revolutionary Proletarian Army (RPA). In March 2000, the group claimed credit for a rifle grenade attack against the Department of Energy building in Manila and strafed Shell Oil offices in the central Philippines to protest rising oil prices.

Strength
Approximately 500.

Location/Area of Operation
The largest RPA/ABB groups are on the Philippine islands of Luzon, Negros, and the Visayas.

External Aid
Unknown.

Al-Ittihad al-Islami (AIAI) a.k.a. Islamic Union

Description
Somalia's largest militant Islamic organization rose to power in the early 1990s following the collapse of the Siad Barre regime. Aims to establish an Islamic regime in Somalia and force the secession of the Ogeden region of Ethiopia.

Activities
Primarily insurgent-style attacks against Ethiopian forces and other Somali factions. The group is believed to be responsible for a series of bomb attacks in public places in Addis Ababa in 1996 and 1997 as well as the kidnapping of several relief workers in 1998. AIAI sponsors Islamic social programs, such as orphanages and schools, and provides pockets of security in Somalia.

Strength
Estimated at some 2,000 members, plus additional reserve militias.

Location/Area of Operation
Primarily in Somalia, with limited presence in Ethiopia and Kenya.

External Aid
Receives funds from Middle East financiers and Western diaspora remittances, and suspected training in Afghanistan. Maintains ties to al-Qaida. Past weapons deliveries from Sudan.

Allied Democratic Forces (ADF)

Description
A diverse coalition of former members of the National Army for the Liberation of Uganda (NALU), Islamists from the Salaf Tabliq group, Hutu militiamen, and fighters from ousted regimes in Congo. The conglomeration of fighters formed in 1995 in opposition to the government of Ugandan President Yoweri Museveni.

Activities
The ADF seeks to use the kidnapping and murder of civilians to create fear in the local population and undermine confidence in the Government. The group is suspected to be responsible for dozens of bombings in public areas. A Ugandan military offensive in 2000 destroyed several ADF camps, but ADF attacks continued in Kampala in 2001.

Strength
A few hundred fighters.

Location/Area of Operation
Western Uganda and eastern Congo.

External Aid
Received past funding, supplies, and training from the Government of Sudan. Some funding suspected from sympathetic Hutu groups.

Anti-Imperialist Territorial Nuclei (NTA)

Description
Clandestine leftist extremist group that appeared in the Friuli region in Italy in 1995. Adopted the class struggle ideology of the Red Brigades of the 1970s-80s and a similar logo—an encircled five-point star—for their declarations. Opposes what it perceives as US and NATO imperialism and condemns Italy's foreign and labor polices.

Activities
Criticized US/NATO presence in Italy and attacked property owned by US Air Forces personnel at Aviano Air Base. Claimed responsibility for a bomb attack in September 2000 against the Central European Initiative office in Trieste and a bomb attack in August 2001 against the Venice Tribunal building. Threw gasoline bombs at the Venice and Rome headquarters of the then-ruling party, Democrats of the Left, during the NATO intervention in Kosovo.

Strength
Approximately 20 members.

Location/Area of Operation
Mainly in northeastern Italy, including Friuli, Veneto, and Emilia.

External Aid
None evident.

Army for the Liberation of Rwanda (ALIR)
a.k.a. Interahamwe, Former Armed Forces (ex-FAR)

Description
The FAR was the army of the Rwandan Hutu regime that carried out the genocide of 500,000 or more Tutsis and regime opponents in 1994. The Interahamwe was the civilian militia force that carried out much of the killing. The groups merged and recruited additional fighters after they were forced from Rwanda into the Democratic Republic of Congo (then-Zaire) in 1994. They are now often known as the Army for the Liberation of Rwanda (ALIR), which is the armed branch of the PALIR or Party for the Liberation of Rwanda.

Activities
The group seeks to topple Rwanda's Tutsi-dominated government, reinstitute Hutu-control, and, possibly, complete the genocide. In 1996, a message allegedly from the ALIR threatened to kill the US Ambassador to Rwanda and other US citizens. In 1999, ALIR guerrillas critical of alleged US-UK support for the Rwandan regime kidnapped and killed eight foreign tourists including two US citizens in a game park on the Congo-Uganda border. In the current Congolese war, the ALIR is allied with Kinshasa against the Rwandan invaders.

Strength
Several thousand ALIR regular forces operate alongside the Congolese army on the front lines of the Congo civil war, while a like number of ALIR guerrillas operate behind Rwanda lines in eastern Congo closer to the Rwandan border and sometimes within Rwanda.

Location/Area of Operation
Mostly Democratic Republic of the Congo and Rwanda, but some operations in Burundi.

External Aid
The Democratic Republic of the Congo provides ALIR forces in Congo with training, arms, and supplies.

Cambodian Freedom Fighters (CFF) a.k.a. Cholana Kangtoap Serei Cheat Kampouchea

Description
The Cambodian Freedom Fighters (CFF) emerged in November 1998 in the wake of political violence that saw many influential Cambodian leaders flee and the Cambodian People's Party assume power. With an avowed aim of overthrowing the Government, the group is led by a Cambodian-American, a former member of the opposition Sam Rainsy Party, and its membership includes Cambodian-Americans based in Thailand and the United States and former soldiers from the separatist Khmer Rouge, Royal Cambodian Armed Forces, and various political factions.

Activities
The CFF has on at least one occasion attacked government facilities and planned other bombing attacks. In late November 2000, the CFF staged an attack on several government installations, during which at least eight persons died and more than a dozen were wounded, including civilians.The group's leaders claimed responsibility for the attack. Following a trial of 32 CFF members arrested for the attack, five received life sentences, 25 received lesser jail terms, and two were acquitted. In April 1999, five other members of the CFF were arrested for plotting to blow up a fuel depot outside Phnom Penh with antitank weapons.

Strength
Exact strength is unknown, but totals probably never have exceeded 100 armed fighters.

Location/Area of Operation
Northeastern Cambodia near the Thai border.

External Aid
US-based leadership collects funds from the Cambodian-American community.

Continuity Irish Republican Army (CIRA) a.k.a. Continuity Army Council

Description
Radical terrorist splinter group formed in 1994 as the clandestine armed wing of Republican Sinn Fein (RSF), which split from Sinn Fein in the mid-1980s. "Continuity" refers to the group's belief that it is carrying on the original IRA goal of forcing the British out of Northern Ireland, and CIRA actively seeks to recruit IRA members.

Activities
CIRA has been active in the border areas of Northern Ireland where it has carried out bombings, assassinations, kidnappings, extortion, and robberies. Targets include British military and Northern Ireland security targets and Northern Ireland Loyalist paramilitary groups. Does not have an established presence on the UK mainland. CIRA is not observing a cease-fire and in October said decommissioning weapons would be "an act of treachery."

Strength
Fewer than 50 hard-core activists but is said to have recruited new members in Belfast.

Location/Area of Operation
Northern Ireland, Irish Republic.

External Aid
Suspected of receiving funds and arms from sympathizers in the United States. May have acquired arms and material from the Balkans in cooperation with the Real IRA.

First of October Antifascist Resistance Group (GRAPO)
Grupo de Resistencia Anti-Fascista Primero de Octubre

Description
Formed in 1975 as the armed wing of the illegal Communist Party of Spain during the Franco era. Advocating the overthrow of the Spanish Government and replacement with a Marxist-Leninist regime, GRAPO is vehemently anti-US, calls for the removal of all US military forces from Spanish territory, and has conducted and attempted several attacks against US targets since 1977. The group issued a communiqué following the 11 September attacks in the United States, expressing its satisfaction that "symbols of imperialist power" were decimated and affirming that "the war" has only just begun.

Activities
GRAPO has killed more than 90 persons and injured more than 200. The group's operations traditionally have been designed to cause material damage and gain publicity rather than inflict casualties, but the terrorists have conducted lethal bombings and close-range assassinations. In May 2000, the group killed two security guards during a botched armed robbery attempt of an armored truck carrying an estimated $2 million, and in November 2000, members assassinated a Spanish policeman in a possible reprisal for the arrest that month of several GRAPO leaders in France. The group also has bombed business and official sites, employment agencies, and the Madrid headquarters of the ruling Popular Party, for example, the Barcelona office of the national daily *El Mundo* in October 2000, when two police officers were injured.

Strength
Unknown but likely fewer than a dozen hard-core activists. Spanish and French officials have made periodic large-scale arrests of GRAPO members, crippling the organization and forcing it into lengthy rebuilding periods. The French and Spanish arrested several key leaders in 2001.

Location/Area of Operation
Spain.

External Aid
None.

Harakat ul-Jihad-I-Islami (HUJI)
(Movement of Islamic Holy War)

Description
HUJI, a Sunni extremist group that follows the Deobandi tradition of Islam, was founded in 1980 in Afghanistan to fight in the jihad against the Soviets. It is also affiliated with the Jamiat Ulema-I-Islam Fazlur Rehman faction (JUI-F) and the Deobandi school of Sunni Islam. The group, led by chief commander Amin Rabbani, is made up primarily of Pakistanis and foreign Islamists who are fighting for the liberation of Kashmir and its accession to Pakistan.

Activities
Has conducted a number of operations against Indian military targets in Kashmir. Linked to the Kashmiri militant group al-Faran that kidnapped five Western tourists in Kashmir in July 1995; one was killed in August 1995 and the other four reportedly were killed in December of the same year.

Strength
Exact numbers are unknown, but there may be several hundred members in Kashmir.

Location/Area of Operation
Pakistan and Kashmir. Trained members in Afghanistan until fall of 2001.

External Aid
Specific sources of external aid are unknown.

Harakat ul-Jihad-I-Islami/Bangladesh
(HUJI-B) (Movement of Islamic Holy War)

Description
The mission of HUJI-B, led by Shauqat Osman, is to establish Islamic rule in Bangladesh. HUJI-B has connections to the Pakistani militant groups Harakat ul-Jihad-i-Islami (HUJI) and Harak ul-Mujahidin (HUM), who advocate similar objectives in Pakistan and Kashmir.

Activities
HUJI-B was accused of stabbing a senior Bangladeshi journalist in November 2000 for making a documentary on the plight of Hindus in Bangladesh. HUJI-B was suspected in the July 2000 assassination attempt of Bangladeshi Prime Minister Sheikh Hasina.

Strength
HUJI-B has an estimated cadre strength of over several thousand members.

Location/Area of Operation
Operates and trains members in Bangladesh, where it maintains at least six camps.

External Aid
Funding of the HUJI-B comes primarily from madrassas in Bangladesh. The group also has ties to militants in Pakistan that may provide another funding source.

Islamic Army of Aden (IAA)
a.k.a. Aden-Abyan Islamic Army (AAIA)

Description
The Islamic Army of Aden (IAA) emerged publicly in mid-1998 when the group released a series of communiqués that expressed support for Usama Bin Ladin,

appealed for the overthrow of the Yemeni Government and the commencement of operations against US and other Western interests in Yemen.

Activities
Engages in bombings and kidnappings to promote its goals. Kidnapped 16 British, Australian, and US tourists in late December 1998 near Mudiyah in southern Yemen. Since the capture and trial of the Mudiyah kidnappers and the execution in October 1999 of the group's leader, Zein al-Abidine al-Mihdar (a.k.a. Abu Hassan), individuals associated with the IAA have remained involved in terrorist activities. In 2001 the Yemeni Government convicted an IAA member and three associates for their roles in the October 2000 bombing of the British Embassy in Sanaa.

Strength
Not known.

Location/Area of Operation
Operates in the southern governorates of Yemen—primarily Aden and Abyan.

External Aid
Not known.

Irish Republican Army (IRA) a.k.a. Provisional Irish Republican Army (PIRA), the Provos (Now almost universally referred to as the PIRA to distinguish it from RIRA and CIRA.)

Description
Terrorist group formed in 1969 as clandestine armed wing of Sinn Fein, a legal political movement dedicated to removing British forces from Northern Ireland and unifying Ireland. Has a Marxist orientation. Organized into small, tightly knit cells under the leadership of the Army Council.

Activities
The IRA has been observing a cease-fire since 1997 and in October 2001 took the historic step of putting an unspecified amount of arms and ammunition "completely beyond use." The International Commission on Decommissioning characterized the step as a significant act of decommissioning. The IRA retains the ability to conduct operations. Its traditional activities have included bombings, assassinations, kidnappings, punishment beatings, extortion, smuggling, and robberies. Bombing campaigns were conducted against train and subway stations and shopping areas on mainland Britain. Targets included senior British Government officials, civilians, police, and British military targets in Northern Ireland. The IRA's current cease-fire (since July 1997) was preceded by a cease-fire from 1 September 1994 to February 1996.

Strength
Several hundred members, plus several thousand sympathizers—despite the possible defection of some members to RIRA or CIRA.

Local/Area of Operation
Northern Ireland, Irish Republic, Great Britain, Europe.

External Aid
Has in the past received aid from a variety of groups and countries and considerable training and arms from Libya and the PLO. Is suspected of receiving funds, arms, and

other terrorist related material from sympathizers in the United States. Similarities in operations suggest links to ETA.

Al-Jama'a al-Islamiyyah al-Muqatilah bi-Libya
a.k.a. Libyan Islamic Fighting Group, Fighting Islamic
Group, Libyan Fighting Group, Libyan Islamic Group

Description
Emerged in 1995 among Libyans who had fought against Soviet forces in Afghanistan. Declared the Government of Libyan leader Muammar Qadhafi un-Islamic and pledged to overthrow it. Some members maintain a strictly anti-Qadhafi focus and organize against Libyan government interests, but others are aligned with Usama Bin Ladin's al-Qaida organization or are active in the international *mujahidin* network.

Activities
Claimed responsibility for a failed assassination attempt against Qadhafi in 1996 and engaged Libyan security forces in armed clashes during the mid to late 1990s. Currently engages in few armed attacks against Libyan interests either in Libya or abroad. Some members may be aligned with al-Qaida or involved in al-Qaida activities.

Strength
Not known but probably has several hundred active members.

Location/Area of Operation
Probably maintains a clandestine presence in Libya, but since late 1990s many members have fled to various Middle Eastern and European countries.

External Aid
Not known. May obtain some funding through private donations, various Islamic non-governmental organizations, and criminal acts.

Japanese Red Army (JRA) a.k.a.
Anti-Imperialist International Brigade (AIIB)

Description
An international terrorist group formed around 1970 after breaking away from Japanese Communist League-Red Army Faction. Fusako Shigenobu led the JRA until her arrest in Japan in November 2000. The JRA's historical goal has been to overthrow the Japanese Government and monarchy and to help foment world revolution. After her arrest Shigenobu announced she intended to pursue her goals using a legitimate political party rather than revolutionary violence, and the group announced it would disband in April 2001. May control or at least have ties to Anti-Imperialist International Brigade (AIIB); also may have links to Antiwar Democratic Front—an overt leftist political organization—inside Japan. Details released following Shigenobu's arrest indicate that the JRA was organizing cells in Asian cities, such as Manila and Singapore. The group had a history of close relations with Palestinian terrorist groups—based and operating outside Japan—since its inception, primarily through Shigenobu. The current status of the connections is unknown.

Activities
During the 1970s, JRA carried out a series of attacks around the world, including the massacre in 1972 at Lod Airport in Israel, two Japanese airliner hijackings, and an attempted takeover of the US Embassy in Kuala Lumpur. In April 1988, JRA operative

Yu Kikumura was arrested with explosives on the New Jersey Turnpike, apparently planning an attack to coincide with the bombing of a USO club in Naples, a suspected JRA operation that killed five, including a US servicewoman. He was convicted of the charges and is serving a lengthy prison sentence in the United States. Tsutomu Shirosaki, captured in 1996, is also jailed in the United States. In 2000, Lebanon deported to Japan four members it arrested in 1997 but granted a fifth operative, Kozo Okamoto, political asylum. Longtime leader Shigenobu was arrested in November 2000 and faces charges of terrorism and passport fraud.

Strength
About six hardcore members; undetermined number of sympathizers. At its peak the group claimed to have 30 to 40 members.

Location/Area of Operation
Location unknown, but possibly in Asia and/or Syrian-controlled areas of Lebanon.

External Aid
Unknown.

Jemaah Islamiya (JI)

Description
Jemaah Islamiya is an Islamic extremist group with cells operating throughout Southeast Asia. Recently arrested JI members in Singapore, Malaysia, and the Philippines have revealed links with al-Qaida. The JI's stated goal is to create an Islamic state comprising Malaysia, Singapore, Indonesia, and the southern Philippines. Three Indonesian extremists, one of whom is in custody in Malaysia, are the reported leaders of the organization.

Activities
Began developing plans in 1997 to target US interests in Singapore and, in 1999, conducted videotaped casings of potential US targets in preparation for multiple attacks in Singapore. A cell in Singapore acquired four tons of ammonium nitrate, which has not yet been found.

In December 2001, Singapore authorities arrested 15 Jemaah Islamiyah members, some of whom had trained in al-Qaida camps in Afghanistan, who planned to attack the US and Israeli Embassies and British and Australian diplomatic buildings in Singapore. Additionally, the Singapore police discovered forged immigration stamps, bombmaking materials, and al-Qaida-related material in several suspects' homes.

Strength
Exact numbers are unknown but press reports approximate that the Malaysian cells may comprise 200 members.

Location/Area of Operation
The JI has cells in Singapore and Malaysia; press reports indicate the JI is also present in Indonesia and possibly the Philippines.

External Aid
Largely unknown, probably self-financing; possible al-Qaida support.

Kumpulan Mujahidin Malaysia (KMM)

Description
Kumpulan Mujahidin Malaysia (KMM) favors the overthrow of the Mahathir government and the creation of an Islamic state comprising Malaysia, Indonesia, and the

southern Philippines. Malaysian authorities believe that smaller, more violent, extremist groups have split from KMM. Zainon Ismail, a former mujahid in Afghanistan, established KMM in 1995. Nik Adli Nik Abdul Aziz, currently detained under Malaysia's Internal Security Act (ISA), assumed leadership in 1999. Malaysian police assert that three Indonesian extremists, one of whom is in custody, have disseminated militant ideology to the KMM.

Activities
Malaysia is currently holding 48 alleged members of the KMM and its more extremist wing under the ISA for activities deemed threatening to Malaysia's national security, including planning to wage a jihad, possession of weaponry, bombings and robberies, the murder of a former state assemblyman, and planning attacks on foreigners, including US citizens. Several of the arrested militants have reportedly undergone military training in Afghanistan, and some fought with the Afghan *mujahidin* during the war against the former Soviet Union. Others are alleged to have ties to Islamic extremist organizations in Indonesia and the Philippines.

Strength
Malaysian police assess the KMM to have 70 to 80 members. The Malaysian press reports that police are currently tracking 200 suspected Muslim militants.

Location/Area of Operation
The KMM is reported to have networks in the Malaysian states of Perak, Johor, Kedah, Selangor, Terengganu, and Kelantan. They also operate in Wilayah Persukutuan, the federal territory comprising Kuala Lumpur. According to press reports, the KMM has ties to radical Indonesian Islamic groups and has sent members to Ambon, Indonesia to fight against Christians.

External Aid
Largely unknown, probably self-financing.

Lord's Resistance Army (LRA)

Activities
Founded in 1989 as the successor to the Holy Spirit Movement, the LRA seeks to overthrow the incumbent Ugandan Government and replace it with a regime that will implement the group's brand of Christianity. The LRA frequently kills and kidnaps local Ugandan civilians in order to discourage foreign investment and precipitate a crisis in Uganda.

Strength
Estimated 2,000.

Location/Area of Operation
Northern Uganda and southern Sudan.

External Aid
The LRA has been supported by the Government of Sudan.

Loyalist Volunteer Force (LVF)

Description
An extreme loyalist group formed in 1996 as a faction of the mainstream loyalist Ulster Volunteer Force (UVF) but did not emerge publicly until February 1997. Composed largely of UVF hardliners who have sought to prevent a political settlement with Irish

nationalists in Northern Ireland by attacking Catholic politicians, civilians, and Protestant politicians who endorse the Northern Ireland peace process. In October 2001 the British Government ruled that the LVF had broken the cease-fire it declared in 1998. The LVF decommissioned a small but significant amount of weapons in December 1998, but it has not repeated this gesture.

Activities
Bombings, kidnappings, and close-quarter shooting attacks. LVF bombs often have contained Powergel commercial explosives, typical of many loyalist groups. LVF attacks have been particularly vicious: The group has murdered numerous Catholic civilians with no political or terrorist affiliations, including an 18-year-old Catholic girl in July 1997 because she had a Protestant boyfriend. The terrorists also have conducted successful attacks against Irish targets in Irish border towns. In 2000 and 2001, the LVF also engaged in a violent feud with other loyalists in which several individuals were killed.

Strength
Approximately 150 activists.

Location/Area of Operation
Northern Ireland, Ireland.

External Aid
None.

New People's Army (NPA)

Description
The military wing of the Communist Party of the Philippines (CPP), the NPA is a Maoist group formed in March 1969 with the aim of overthrowing the government through protracted guerrilla warfare. The chairman of the CPP's Central Committee and the NPA's founder, Jose Maria Sison, directs all CPP and NPA activity from the Netherlands, where he lives in self-imposed exile. Fellow Central Committee member and director of the CPP's National Democratic Front (NDF) Luis Jalandoni also lives in the Netherlands and has become a Dutch citizen. Although primarily a rural-based guerrilla group, the NPA has an active urban infrastructure to conduct terrorism and uses city-based assassination squads. Derives most of its funding from contributions of supporters in the Philippines, Europe, and elsewhere, and from so-called "revolutionary taxes" extorted from local businesses.

Activities
The NPA primarily targets Philippine security forces, politicians, judges, government informers, former rebels who wish to leave the NPA, and alleged criminals. Opposes any US military presence in the Philippines and attacked US military interests before the US base closures in 1992. Press reports in 1999 and in late 2001 indicated that the NPA is again targeting US troops participating in joint military exercises as well as US Embassy personnel. The NPA claimed responsibility for the assassination of congressmen from Quezon (in May) and Cagayan (in June) and many other killings.

Strength
Slowly growing; estimated at over 10,000.

Location/Area of Operations
Operates in rural Luzon, Visayas, and parts of Mindanao. Has cells in Manila and other metropolitan centers.

External Aid
Unknown.

Orange Volunteers (OV)

Description
Terrorist group that appeared about 1998-99 and is comprised largely of disgruntled loyalist hardliners who split from groups observing the cease-fire. OV seeks to prevent a political settlement with Irish nationalists by attacking Catholic civilian interests in Northern Ireland.

Activities
The group has been linked to pipe-bomb attacks and sporadic assaults on Catholics. Following a successful security crackdown at the end of 1999, the OV declared a cease-fire in September 2000 and remained quiet in 2001.

Strength
Up to 20 hardcore members, some of whom are experienced in terrorist tactics and bombmaking.

Location/Area of Operations
Northern Ireland.

External Aid
None.

People Against Gangsterism and Drugs (PAGAD)

Description
PAGAD was formed in 1996 as a community anti-crime group fighting drugs and violence in the Cape Flats section of Cape Town but by early 1998 had also become antigovernment and anti-Western. PAGAD and its Islamic ally Qibla view the South African Government as a threat to Islamic values and consequently promote greater political voice for South African Muslims. Abdus Salaam Ebrahim currently leads both groups. PAGAD's G-Force (Gun Force) operates in small cells and is believed responsible for carrying out acts of terrorism. PAGAD uses several front names including Muslims Against Global Oppression (MAGO) and Muslims Against Illegitimate Leaders (MAIL) when launching anti-Western protests and campaigns.

Activities
PAGAD's activities were severely curtailed in 2001 by law enforcement and prosecutorial efforts against leading members of the organization. There were no urban terror incidents from September 2000 through 2001, compared to nine bombings in the Western Cape in 2000 that caused serious injuries and a total of 189 bomb attacks since 1996. PAGAD's previous bombing targets have included South African authorities, moderate Muslims, synagogues, gay nightclubs, tourist attractions, and Western-associated restaurants. PAGAD is believed to have masterminded the bombing on 25 August 1998 of the Cape Town Planet Hollywood.

Strength
Estimated at several hundred members. PAGAD's G-Force probably contains fewer than 50 members.

Location/Area of Operation
Operates mainly in the Cape Town area, South Africa's foremost tourist venue.

External Aid
Probably has ties to Islamic extremists in the Middle East.

Red Hand Defenders (RHD)

Description
Extremist terrorist group formed in 1998 composed largely of Protestant hardliners from loyalist groups observing a cease-fire. RHD seeks to prevent a political settlement with Irish nationalists by attacking Catholic civilian interests in Northern Ireland. In July 2001 the group issued a statement saying it considered all nationalists as "legitimate targets." RHD is a cover name often used by elements of the banned Ulster Defense Association and the Loyalist Volunteer Force.

Activities
In recent years, the group has carried out numerous pipe bombings and arson attacks against "soft" civilian targets such as homes, churches, and private businesses, including a bombing outside a Catholic girls school in North Belfast in September. RHD claimed responsibility for the car-bombing murder in March 1999 of Rosemary Nelson, a prominent Catholic nationalist lawyer and human rights campaigner in Northern Ireland, and for the murder of a Catholic journalist in September 2001.

Strength
Up to 20 members, some of whom have considerable experience in terrorist tactics and bombmaking.

Location/Area of Operation
Northern Ireland.

External Aid
None.

Revolutionary Proletarian Initiative Nuclei (NIPR)

Description
Clandestine leftist extremist group that appeared in Rome in 2000. Adopted the logo of the Red Brigades of the 1970s and 1980s—an encircled five-point star—for their declarations. Opposes Italy's foreign and labor policies.

Activities
Claimed responsibility for bomb attack in April 2001 on building housing a US-Italian relations association and an international affairs institute in Rome's historic center. Claimed to have carried out May 2000 explosion in Rome at oversight committee facility for implementation of the law on strikes in public services. Claimed responsibility for explosion in February 2002 on Via Palermo adjacent to Interior Ministry in Rome.

Strength
Approximately 12 members.

Location/Area of Operation
Mainly in Rome, Milan, Lazio, and Tuscany.

External Aid
None evident.

Revolutionary United Front (RUF)

Description
The RUF is a loosely organized guerrilla force seeking to retain control of the lucrative diamond-producing regions of the country. The group funds itself largely through the extraction and sale of diamonds obtained in areas of Sierra Leone that it controls.

Activities
During 2001, reports of serious abuses by the RUF declined significantly. The resumption of the Government's Disarmament, Demobilization, and Reintegration program in May was largely responsible. From 1991-2000, the group used guerrilla, criminal, and terror tactics, such as murder, torture, and mutilation, to fight the government, intimidate civilians, and keep UN peacekeeping units in check. In 2000 they held hundreds of UN peacekeepers hostage until their release was negotiated, in part, by the RUF's chief sponsor, Liberian President Charles Taylor. The group also has been accused of attacks in Guinea at the behest of President Taylor.

Strength
Estimated at several thousand supporters and sympathizers.

Location/Area of Operation
Sierra Leone, Liberia, Guinea.

External Aid
A UN experts panel report on Sierra Leone said President Charles Taylor of Liberia provides support and leadership to the RUF. The UN has identified Libya, Gambia, and Burkina Faso as conduits for weapons and other materiel for the RUF.

The Tunisian Combatant Group (TCG)

Description
Also referred to as the Tunisian Islamic Fighting Group, the TCG's goals reportedly include establishing an Islamic government in Tunisia and targeting Tunisian and Western interests. Founded probably in 2000 by Tarek Maaroufi and Saifallah Ben Hassine, the group has come to be associated with al-Qaida and other North African Islamic extremists in Europe who have been implicated in anti-US terrorist plots there during 2001. In December, Belgian authorities arrested Maaroufi and charged him with providing stolen passports and fraudulent visas for those involved in the assassination of Ahmed Shah Massood, according to press reports.

Activities
Tunisians associated with the TCG are part of the support network of the international Salafist movement. According to Italian authorities, TCG members there engage in false document trafficking and recruitment for Afghan training camps. Some TCG associates are suspected of planning an attack against the US, Algerian, and Tunisian diplomatic interests in Rome in January. Members reportedly maintain ties to the Algerian Salafist Group for Call and Combat (GSPC).

Strength
Unknown.

Location/Area of Operation
Western Europe, Afghanistan.

External Aid
Unknown.

Tupac Amaru Revolutionary Movement (MRTA)

Description
Traditional Marxist-Leninist revolutionary movement formed in 1983 from remnants of the Movement of the Revolutionary Left, a Peruvian insurgent group active in the 1960s. Aims to establish a Marxist regime and to rid Peru of all imperialist elements (primarily US and Japanese influence). Peru's counterterrorist program has diminished the group's ability to carry out terrorist attacks, and the MRTA has suffered from infighting, the imprisonment or deaths of senior leaders, and loss of leftist support. In 2001, several MRTA members remained imprisoned in Bolivia.

Activities
Previously conducted bombings, kidnappings, ambushes, and assassinations, but recent activity has fallen drastically. In December 1996, 14 MRTA members occupied the Japanese Ambassador's residence in Lima and held 72 hostages for more than four months. Peruvian forces stormed the residence in April 1997 rescuing all but one of the remaining hostages and killing all 14 group members, including the remaining leaders. The group has not conducted a significant terrorist operation since and appears more focused on obtaining the release of imprisoned MRTA members.

Strength
Believed to be no more than 100 members, consisting largely of young fighters who lack leadership skills and experience.

Location/Area of Operation
Peru with supporters throughout Latin America and Western Europe. Controls no territory.

External Aid
None.

Turkish Hizballah

Description
Turkish Hizballah is a Kurdish Islamic (Sunni) extremist organization that arose in the late 1980s in the Diyarbakir area in response to Kurdistan Workers' Party atrocities against Muslims in southeastern Turkey, where (Turkish) Hizballah seeks to establish an independent Islamic state. The group comprises loosely organized factions, the largest of which are Ilim, which advocates the use of violence to achieve the group's goals, and Menzil, which supports an intellectual approach.

Activities
Beginning in the mid-1990s, Turkish Hizballah which is unrelated to Lebanese Hizballah expanded its target base and modus operandi from killing PKK militants to conducting low-level bombings against liquor stores, bordellos, and other establishments that the organization considered "anti-Islamic." In January 2000, Turkish security forces killed Huseyin Velioglu, the leader of (Turkish) Hizballah's Ilim faction, in a shootout at a safehouse in Istanbul. The incident sparked a year-long series of

operations against the group throughout Turkey that resulted in the detention of some 2,000 individuals; authorities arrested several hundred of those on criminal charges. At the same time, police recovered nearly 70 bodies of Turkish and Kurdish businessmen and journalists that (Turkish) Hizballah had tortured and brutally murdered during the mid to late-1990's. The group began targeting official Turkish interests in January 2001, when 10-20 operatives participated in the assassination of the Diyarbakir police chief, the group's most sophisticated operation to date.

Strength
Possibly a few hundred members and several thousand supporters.

Location/Area of Operation
Primary area of operation is in southeastern Turkey, particularly the Diyarbakir region.

External Aid
Turkish officials charge that Turkish Hizballah receives at least some assistance, including training, from Iran.

Ulster Defense Association/Ulster Freedom Fighters (UDA/UVF)

Description
The UDA, the largest loyalist paramilitary group in Northern Ireland, was formed in 1971 as an umbrella organization for loyalist paramilitary groups. It remained a legal organization until 1992, when the British Government proscribed it. Among its members are Johnny Adair, the only person ever convicted of directing terrorism in Northern Ireland, and Michael Stone, who killed three in a gun and grenade attack on an IRA funeral. The UDA joined the UVF in declaring a cease-fire in 1994; it broke down in January 1998 but was later restored. In October 2001, the British Government ruled that the UDA had broken its cease-fire. The organization's political wing, the Ulster Democratic Party, was dissolved in November 2001.

Activities
The group has been linked to pipe bombings and sporadic assaults on Catholics in Northern Ireland; it stepped up attacks in 2001. William Stobie, the group's former quartermaster who admitted to passing information about the UDA to the British Government, was murdered in December; the Red Hand Defenders claimed responsibility for the killing.

Strength
Estimates vary from 2,000 to 5,000 members, with several hundred active in paramilitary operations.

Location/Area of Operation
Northern Ireland.

External Aid
None.

APPENDIX C: VIDEO NOTES

Introduction

State-sponsored terrorism is depicted vividly and validly in *The Killing Fields* (Warner Bros., 1984, 142 min.).

Chapter 1

Many historical films about regional and class conflicts might be useful for envisioning the present global situation. For example, the history of the Irish Republican Army is portrayed in *Michael Collins* (Warner Bros., 1996, 132 min.).

Chapter 2

Background about international terrorism is explained often in documentaries about the Central Intelligence Agency. One noted exploration of the U.S. role in the "blowback" of transnational terrorism is titled *C.I.A.: America's Secret Warriors* (Discovery Channel, 1997, 2 vols., 50 min. each).

Chapter 3

Homegrown, right-wing, white supremacist, anti–U.S. government inspired terrorism has seldom been scrutinized in films. *Betrayed* (Metro-Goldwyn-Mayer, 1988, 112 min.) is one chilling, though dated, exception.

Chapter 4

How terrorism was actually reported in one extreme example is documented by the film *One Day in September* (Columbia TriStar, 1999, 91 min.), which details the kidnapping of Israeli athletes at the Munich Olympics in 1972.

Chapter 5

Women's role in terrorism may be a conflicted one. *The Demon Lover* described by Morgan is cleverly interpreted in *The Little Drummer Girl* (Warner Bros., 1984, 130 min.).

Chapter 6

A fascinating drama about conventional terrorism enfolds in *Four Days in September* (Miramax, 1998, 110 min.). The film relates both the political and the personal demands inflicted when an ambassador is kidnapped by terrorists.

Chapter 7

Although weapons of mass destruction may seem like something from a movie plot, modern films contain few good studies of the threat of biological and chemical weapons. A celebrated drama about a global nuclear crisis spawned by terrorists is *Crimson Tide* (Hollywood Pictures, 1995, 115 min.).

Chapter 8

The threat from the military in response to terrorism may be overplayed in *The Siege* (20th Century Fox, 1998, 120 min.), but the film provides some sobering images about fighting violence with violence.

INDEX

Abbas, Mohammed Abu, 199
Abbas, Muhammad, 76
ABC, 146, 152
Abolitionists, 85
Abortions
    in Italy, 183
    opponents, 115
    supporters of rights, 115, 125
    See also Antiabortion violence
Abu Marzuq, Musa, 144
Abu Nidal Organization (ANO), 47, 322-323
    See also Black September
Abu Sayyaf, 192, 200, 323
Achille Lauro, 199
ACLU. *See* American Civil Liberties Union
Action Directe, 174, 185
Action for National Liberation (ALN), 9, 10
Adams, Gerry, 144-145, 212, 216
Adams, John, 38-39
ADL. *See* Anti-Defamation League
Adonis, 83
Afghanistan
    bin Laden in, 52, 277, 279
    biological weapons used in, 246
    drug trafficking, 65
    Soviet invasion, 52
    terrorist documents, 196-197, 263
    terrorists in, 49, 280
    U.S. attacks following September 11, 73, 131,
        277, 280, 281
    U.S. cruise missile attacks on bin
        Laden camps, 54
    See also Taliban
African American separatists, 88, 90, 261
African National Congress (ANC), 118, 252
Agrarian movements, 100
Aido, Ama Ata, 177
Aiello, Piera, 186-187
Airline crashes
    media coverage, 134
    Pan Am Flight 103, 48, 54-55

    terrorist bombings, 278
    See also September 11, 2001, terrorist attacks
Airline hijackings. *See* Hijackings
Aiyyash, Yahiya, 222
Al Fatah. *See* Fatah, Al
Al Qaeda. *See* Qaeda, Al
Albania, criminal syndicates, 69
Alcohol, Tobacco, and Firearms, Bureau of. *See*
        Bureau of Alcohol, Tobacco, and Firearms
Aleph, 235, 325-326
Alexander II, Tsar, 7
ALF. *See* Animal Liberation Front
Algeria
    Armed Islamic Group (GIA), 220, 222
    FLN, 30-31
    Islamic extremists, 79
Algiers, 38, 40
    See also Pirates, Barbary
Alibek, Ken, 249
Allende, Salvador, 49
ALN. *See* Action for National Liberation
Alpert, Jane, 174
Alvarado, Elvia, 168
America Online, 267
American Civil Liberties Union (ACLU), 264
American Holocaust Resistance Movement, 115
American Institute of Theology, 98
American Medical Association, 123
American Nazi Party, 260
American Revolution, 196, 287-288
American University, Beirut, 150, 153, 176
Amir, Yigal, 197
Amoss, Ulius, 258
Anarchists
    bombings, 43
    in United States, 40
    use of violence, 6-7, 8, 40-41
    See also Ecoterrorists; Unabomber
ANC. *See* African National Congress
Ancient Order of Hibernians, 41
Anderson, Terry, 150, 152, 153

Andre, John, 287-288
Anglo-Israelism, 98, 100, 101
Angry Brigade, 175
Animal Liberation Front (ALF), 89, 262
Animal rights groups, 89, 123, 262
ANO. *See* Abu Nidal Organization
Anonymous terrorism, 146
Anthrax
    accidents, 246
    attacks in United States, 131, 228
    Aum Shinrikyo research in, 234
    German use in World War I, 245
    South African use, 231
    threat of, 229, 247, 248
Antiabortion violence
    as terrorism, 111, 112, 117, 118,
        123-124, 125-126
    assaults and murders, 113, 114, 117, 118,
        122-123, 262
    attacks on clinics, 111, 113-114, 116,
        118, 123-124
    evolution of movement, 113
    extent of, 112-114, 115-116, 120
    federal response, 117, 118-119, 122, 123,
        124, 125-126
    justifications, 114-115
    lack of scholarly attention, 120-121
    laws against, 123, 124
    leaderless resistance, 116-117, 196
    manuals, 259
    media coverage, 112, 120, 121-124
    motives, 118
    organized groups, 113, 115
    similarities to other rightist violence,
        112, 115-116
    Web sites promoting, 262, 271-272
Anti-Defamation League (ADL), 256, 257, 258,
    260, 269
Anti-Semitism
    of rightist religious groups, 98, 100, 101,
        103, 106
    violent attacks, 255
Antiterrorism and Effective Death Penalty
    Act of 1996, 46, 130, 282-283, 286, 300
Arab countries
    divisions within, 82
    See also Islam; Middle East
Arafat, Yasser, 80, 176, 199, 222
Arbenz Guzmán, Jacobo, 50
Argentina
    attacks on journalists, 148
    nuclear reactors, 251
    suicide terrorism, 221
Aristotle, 1-2
Arizona Patriots, 116, 259

Armand, Inessa, 170
Armed Islamic Group (GIA), 220, 222, 324
Armenian Secret Army for the Liberation of
    Armenia (ASALA), 174
Army of God, 113, 114, 115, 117
Arnold, Benedict, 287
Aryan Nations, 98, 100, 101, 255, 256-257, 260
Aryan Nations Liberty Net, 257, 258
Aryan Republican Army, 196
Asahara, Shoko, 47, 232, 233, 234-235
ASALA. *See* Armenian Secret Army for the
    Liberation of Armenia
Ashcroft, John, 197
Asia
    Foreign Terrorist Organizations, 47
    Islamic terrorists in, 49, 192
    See also individual countries
Asian Americans
    Japanese internment in United States, 289-290
    threats received, 270-271
Assassinations
    as terrorist tactic, 197-198
    biological weapons, 246
    impact, 198
    in India, 47, 158, 221, 223
    in Russia, 7-8, 159
    in Sri Lanka, 221, 225
    Mafia, 66
    of presidents, 2, 40, 198
    See also Murders
Assassins (Ismailis-Nizari), 20-24
    comparison to Thugs and Zealots, 11,
        16, 24, 26
    enemies, 22, 23
    goals, 20-21, 24
    methods, 23
    Mohammed as model, 23-24
    murders by, 20, 22-23, 31
    network, 22
    origins, 21
    political organization, 22, 29
    relationships with victims, 22, 24
    supporters, 23
    theology, 21-22
    weapons, 21, 31
Association of Salvadoran Women, 177
Astorga, Nora, 173
Atef, Muhammad, 75
ATF. *See* Bureau of Alcohol, Tobacco,
    and Firearms
Atick, Joseph, 303, 304, 305, 306
Atkins, Susan, 169
Atlanta (Georgia)
    attacks on abortion clinics, 114
    Olympic Park bombing, 134

Aum Shinrikyo, 47, 232-235, 242, 325-326
Australia, electronic surveillance in, 273
Automobiles
    hijackings, 198-199, 255
    used in bombings, 207, 215-216
Ayers, Bill, 174

Baader, Andreas, 162
Baader-Meinhoff group
    goals, 31
    links to other terrorist groups, 174
    members, 51, 162
    threats of biological weapons, 249
    women in, 175
    See also Red Army Faction
Baath Party of Lebanon, 221
BACORR. *See* Bay Area Coalition for
    Reproductive Rights
Bakunin, Michael, 7
Barbar Khalsa International (BKI), 220, 222
Barbary Coast states
    ransom payments to, 38, 39
    wars, 40
Barbary pirates, 38-40
Barlow, Joel, 40
Basayev, Shamil, 69, 70
Basque Fatherland and Liberty (ETA), 326
    asset seizures, 281
    attacks on nuclear reactor, 251-252
    drug trafficking by, 64
    goals, 47
    links to drug cartels, 68
    relations with media, 131
    women in, 185
Bastille Syndrome, 130
Bautista, Fulgencio, 51
Bay Area Coalition for Reproductive Rights
    (BACORR), 115
Beam, Louis, 116, 195, 196, 256, 257, 259
Beauharnais v. State of Illinois, 265-266
Begin, Menachem, 29
Belfast (Northern Ireland), 64, 212
Bentham, Jeremy, 307
Berg, Alan, 260
Berlin, discotheque bombing, 54
Bertillon, Alphonse, 305
Bible, 108
Bin Laden, Mohammed, 52
Bin Laden, Osama, 52-54
    CNN interview, 144
    conceptual world, 74, 82
    "Declaration of War against the Americans,"
      75, 76, 77, 78-79
    family, 52
    funding of terrorist attacks, 194, 195

goals of September 11 attacks, 73, 78, 79
interview, 53
"Jihad Against Jews and Crusaders," 76
October 7, 2001, statement, 73, 74, 82
opposition to U.S. presence in Saudi Arabia,
    52, 74, 76, 78, 80
responsibility for terrorist attacks, xii-xiii
revolutionary goals, 73, 78-79
role in Al Qaeda, 221-222
U.S. attacks on camps, 54
view of United States, 53, 73, 76-78, 81, 82
See also Qaeda, Al
Biological weapons
    accidents, 246
    agents, 247, 248
    assassinations using, 246
    attacks in United States, 131, 228, 249-250
    Aum Shinrikyo research in, 234
    defense against, 228, 231, 248, 250
    dissemination methods, 248, 250
    effectiveness, 246-247, 250
    fictional depictions, 239-242
    future of, 246-250
    history, 229, 245-246
    Japanese army unit, 245
    laws against, 284
    potential terrorist use, 249
    production, 247-248, 249
    threat of, 229, 250
    treatments, 248, 250
    use by states, 229, 231, 245-246
    See also Weapons of mass destruction
Biometrics, 303, 305, 306-307, 310
Birmingham (Alabama), attack on abortion clinic,
    111, 113, 116
Birth of a Nation, 255
BKI. *See* Barbar Khalsa International
Black, Don, 254, 260
Black Panthers, 87, 88
Black September, 131-132, 175, 322-323
    See also Abu Nidal Organization
Blacks. *See* African American separatists
Blair, Tony, 304, 306
Block, Herb, 124
Blood Oath League, 176
Bolivar, Simón, 158
Bolivia
    revolutionaries, 51
    urban terrorism, 159
Bombings
    abortion clinics, 113
    as terrorist tactic, 201
    by IRA, 212, 213, 304
    development of dynamite, 43, 240
    goals, 201

history, 201, 288
in Israel, 133
increase in, 278
leftist groups in 1970s, 87
of airliners, 48, 54-55, 278
See also Omagh bombing; Suicide bombers
Booth, John Wilkes, 2
Borders Books, 310
Bortin, Michael, 88
Bose, Wilfried, 175
Boss v. Barry, 265
Boudin, Kathy, 174
Brady, James, 102
Branch Davidians, 102, 117, 123, 124
Brandenburg, Clarence, 268-269
Brandenburg v. Ohio, 268-269
Bray, Michael, 114
Brennan, William, 267
Brigate Rosse. *See* Red Brigades
Britain
    Angry Brigade, 175
    chemical weapons, 242
    class distinctions, 310, 311
    closed-circuit television cameras, 304-311
    counterterrorism, 224, 304, 310
    electronic surveillance, 273
    Good Friday peace agreement, 207-208, 210
    Gunpowder Plot, 2-4
    IRA bombings, 212, 304
    IRA prisoners, 211
    Luddites, 89
    Pan Am 103 crash, 48, 54-55
    relations with Thugs, 19-20, 29
    rule of India, 8-9
    rule of Ireland, 210
    See also Northern Ireland
Britton, Paul, 114, 118, 122-123
Broido, Vera, 168
Brokaw, Tom, 131
Brookline (Massachusetts), attacks on abortion
    clinics, 114, 116, 123-124
Brousse, Paul, 7
Brown, John, 85
Brutus, 2
Buckley, William, 153
Bulger, Jamie, 304
Bureau of Alcohol, Tobacco, and Firearms (ATF),
    102, 117
Burma, criminal activities of terrorist groups,
    60, 63, 64-65, 67
Burnett, Andrew, 124
Burns, William, 42
Bush, George H. W., 55, 82, 122
Bush, George W.
    counterterrorism budget, 228, 231

response to September 11 attacks, xi, 270,
    272, 277, 281, 284, 286
Butler, Richard, 100, 101

Cagol, Margherita (Mara), 173-174, 184
Cali cartel, 65
California, attacks on abortion clinics,
    113-114, 118
California State University,
    Los Angeles, 270-271
Calvin, Martin, 212
Cambodia, 231, 246
Cameron, William, 101
Camorra, 68-69, 188
Canada
    anti-abortion violence, 114
    electronic surveillance, 273
    Italian Mafia in, 187
Capital punishment. *See* Executions
Carillo, Armando, 174
Carillo, Maria, 174
Carjackings, 198-199
Carlo, Willis, 260
Carlos the Jackal (Ilich Ramirez Sanchez),
    51-52, 54, 172-173, 175, 176
Carnivore, 272-273
Carter, Jimmy, 88, 198
Castano, Carlos, 68
Castillo, Carmen, 174
Castro, Fidel, 9, 47, 50-51, 231
Catholic Church. *See* Roman Catholic Church
CBRN (chemical, biological, radiological,
    nuclear) weapons. *See* Biological weapons;
    Chemical weapons; Nuclear weapons;
    Radiological weapons; Weapons of mass
    destruction
CCTV. *See* Closed-circuit television cameras
CDA. *See* Communications Decency Act
Censorship, 130-131
    See also Freedom of speech
Center for Nonproliferation Studies, 230-231
Central America
    protests against U.S. intervention, 120
    women activists, 168, 173, 177
Central Intelligence Agency (CIA), 49, 51
CFAA. *See* Computer Fraud and Abuse Act
Chaplinsky v. State of New Hampshire, 265, 267
Charan, Bhagwati, 8
Charitable organizations
    as funding source for terrorist groups,
        46, 145, 270
    Web sites, 270
Chechen Mafia, 69, 70
Chechnya
    guerrillas, 69, 70, 231, 252

terrorism in, 49
Chemical weapons
    availability, 244
    dissemination methods, 244-245
    effects, 243-244
    fictional depictions, 239-242
    history, 229, 241, 242-244
    international conventions, 242
    legitimate uses, 244
    manufacture of, 244
    sarin attack in Tokyo subway, 232,
        234-235, 242
    terrorist use of, 245
    types, 228-229, 244
    use in extermination camps of World War II, 242
    See also Weapons of mass destruction
Chernobyl, 251
Chiang Kai-Shek, 171
Chiapas (Mexico). *See* Zapatista National
        Liberation Army
Chicago, Haymarket Square riots, 42
Child Online Protection Act (COPA), 265
Children
    as combatants, 192-194
    of terrorist parents, 193-194
Chile, Pinochet regime, 49, 174
China
    biological weapons used by Japanese, 229, 245
    women's rights, 171-172
Chinese Communist Party, 171-172
Christian Democratic Party (Italy), 183
Christian Identity, 98, 100, 101, 102, 103, 105, 108
    conspiracy theories, 91-92
    links to anti-abortion violence, 116
    Web sites, 261
Christian Reconstructionism, 116
Christianity
    anti-Semitism, 101
    conservatives, 98, 100, 106
    eschatology, 98
    messianic images, 21
    See also Protestants; Religious extremists;
        Roman Catholic Church
Church of England, 3
CIA. *See* Central Intelligence Agency
Cicero, 2
Cincinnati (Ohio), attack on abortion clinic, 113
Citybus (Belfast), 64
Civil liberties, 130, 310
Civil Liberties Act of 1988, 290
Civil War, U.S., 89, 287
Cleese, John, 306
Clement VII, Pope, 3
Clinton, Bill, 88, 122, 123, 124, 148
Closed-circuit television cameras (CCTV)

crime reductions, 307, 309
    criticism of, 309
    in Britain, 304-311
    networks, 308-309
    social effects, 305, 309-310
CNN, 144
Cohen, Paul, 266
Cohen v. California, 266, 267
Cole, David, 285
Cole, USS, 53, 201, 278
Collins, Eamon, 216
Colombia
    criminal activities of terrorist groups,
        60, 64, 65
    drug trafficking, 61, 65-66, 67, 68
    kidnappings, 200, 201
    National Liberation Army (ELN), 47, 66, 68,
        200, 335-336
    terrorism in, 277, 278
    See also Revolutionary Armed Forces of
        Colombia
Colorado Fuel and Iron Co., 87
Colorado, Ludlow massacre, 87
Colson, Chuck, 115, 123
Committees of Correspondence, 196
Communications Decency Act of 1996 (CDA),
        264, 265, 268, 271
Communists
    Chinese, 171-172
    in United States, 87, 288, 290
    Italian, 183, 185
    Latin American, 51
    Lebanese, 221
    Spanish, 177
Computer Fraud and Abuse Act (CFAA), 272
Computers
    bulletin board systems (BBSs), 256-257, 258
    crimes using, 270
    critical systems, 230
    See also Cyberterrorism; Internet
Congregationalists, 99
Congress, U.S.. *See* U.S. Congress
Constitution, U.S., 90, 129
    See also First Amendment
Continuity IRA, 208, 211, 212, 213, 218, 347-348
Conventional terrorist tactics
    effectiveness, 197
    manuals, 9, 196-197, 217
    planning, 195, 223
    sophistication, 194
    use of violence, 191
    See also Assassinations; Bombings; Hijackings;
        Hostage-takings; Murders
COPA. *See* Child Online
        Protection Act

Cosa Nostra
    assassinations of officials, 66
    comparison to Red Brigades, 182
    drug trafficking, 188
    hierarchical organization, 182
    origins, 182
    state's witnesses against, 186-187, 188
    use of violence, 182
    women's roles, 182, 186-188
    See also Mafia
Coughlin, Charles E., 100, 103, 256
Counterfeiting, 269
Counterterrorism
    against suicide terrorism, 223, 224-225
    against weapons of mass destruction, 228, 231
    airport security, 303
    asset seizures and freezing, 281, 282
    biometrics, 303, 305, 306-307, 310
    civil liberties issues, 130, 310
    closed-circuit television cameras, 304, 310
    deportations, 285-286
    distinction from war, 295
    domestic, 119-120, 277, 282, 288-290
    electronic surveillance, 272-273
    evaluations, 296-297
    in Britain, 224, 304, 310
    in Israel, 222, 224, 280
    in Sri Lanka, 224-225
    international cooperation, 279-280, 301
    methods, 298-299, 302
    military tribunals, 286-288
    penetration of terrorist groups, 223
    policy recommendations, 297-302
    public diplomacy, 301
    public support, 301-302
    purpose, 296
    side effects, 296, 298
    U.S. foreign policy and, 277-282, 296-297
    unrealistic hopes, 295-296
    See also Legislation
Covenant, Sword, and Arm of the
    Lord, 108, 259
Creatorism, 98, 99
    See also World Church of the Creator
Criminal organizations. *See* Transnational
    criminal organizations
Criminals, habitual, 305
Croatia, suicide terrorism, 221
Cromwell, Thomas, 3
Crusaders, 80
Cuba
    as sponsor of terrorism, 48, 301
    Guantanamo Bay, 287
    Revolution, 9, 50-51, 173
    suspicions of biological attacks, 231
    women activists, 173

Cultural conflicts, 45-46
Curcio, Renato, 174, 184
Cyberterrorism
    growth, 227
    threat of, 230, 273-274
    threats transmitted on Internet, 270-272
Cyprus, 30
Czolgosz, Leon, 40

Darrow, Clarence, 42-43
Da'wa 17, 151
De Freeze, Donald, 88
Death penalty. *See* Executions
Debray, Régis, 172
Decatur, Stephen, 40
Dees, Morris, 257
Dershowitz, Alan, 310
Deutch, John M., 252
Dietz, George, 256
Dilger, Anton, 245
Ding Ling, 171-172
Ditton, Jason, 308, 309
Dixon, Thomas, 255
Dr. Mabuse: The Gambler (Jacques), 240
Dodge, David, 153
Dohrn, Bernardine, 160-161, 174
Dominica, 260
Drug trafficking
    by terrorist groups, 59, 61, 63, 64-65, 67
    cartels, 61, 62, 65-66, 68
    in Albania, 69
    in Asia, 64-65, 67
    in Colombia, 61, 65-66, 67, 68
    in Italy, 188
    in Mexico, 62
    Mafia involvement, 188
    violence related to, 61
Duke, David, 256, 257, 260
Dutschke, Rudi, 175
Dworkin, Andrea, 177
Dynamite, 43, 240

Earth Liberation Front (ELF), 89, 262
Ecoterrorists, 88-89, 251-252, 262
Egypt
    chemical weapons, 243
    Islamic extremists, 75, 79, 81, 220, 221, 222
    Jewish population, 24
    participation in U.S. war on terrorism, 281
    reactions to September 11 attacks, 76
    Shia state, 21
Egyptian Islamic Jihad (EIJ), 75, 78, 220,
    222, 331-332
El Al airlines, 52
Electronic Communications Privacy
    Act of 1986, 272

Electronic surveillance, 272-273, 284
ELF. *See* Earth Liberation Front
Elizabeth I, Queen of England, 3
ELN. *See* National Liberation Army
Elshtain, Jean Bethke, 170
E-mail, 259, 270, 273
    See also Internet
"The Enemy of All the World" (London), 239-240
England. *See* Britain
Enlightenment, 4
Enriquez, Miguel, 174
Ensslin, Gudrun, 162, 175
Environmental groups. *See* Ecoterrorists
EOKA, 30
ERP, 251
Eschatology, 98, 104, 105, 107, 109
Escobar, Pablo, 68
Espionage Act of 1917, 288
ETA. *See* Basque Fatherland and Liberty
Ethiopia, Italian invasion, 242
Europe
    Foreign Terrorist Organizations, 47
    terrorism in, 49, 278
    See also individual countries
European Union, 283, 308
Euskadi ta Askatasuna. *See* Basque Fatherland
    and Liberty
Executions
    debates on, 135, 283
    guillotine, 4-5
    of McVeigh, 135
EZLN. *See* Zapatista National Liberation Army

FaceIt technology, 306
Face-recognition technology, 303, 305,
    306-307, 310
Al-Fadl, Jama Ahmed, 53
Fair Housing Act, 271
Falcón, Lidia, 177
FALN (Fuerzas Armadas Liberación Nacional).
    See Puerto Rican Nationalists
Faranda, Adriana, 184, 185, 186
FARC. *See* Revolutionary Armed Forces of
    Colombia
Farrakhan, Louis, 90
Fatah, Al, 172, 176
Fawkes, Guy, 2-4
FBI. *See* Federal Bureau of Investigation
Federal Access to Clinics law, 124
Federal Bureau of Investigation (FBI)
    abuse of power, 119
    Branch Davidians and, 102
    cybercrime and, 270, 271
    cyberterrorism threat, 273-274
    definition of terrorism, xiii, 117-118

    electronic surveillance, 272-273
    investigations of antiabortion violence,
        117, 121, 122
    investigations of anti-government protests, 120
    investigatory powers, 283
    Palmer raids, 288
    relations with media, 133
    Ruby Ridge confrontation, 102
    UNABOM investigation, 132
Feingold, Russell D., 284
Female terrorists. *See* Women terrorists
Feminism
    history, 170
    in 1970s, 171
    influence on U.S. crime policy, 124
    Italian, 183-184
    of women terrorists, 168, 169, 183, 184,
        186, 188
Fhimah, Al Amin Khalifa, 54
Fiction
    fear of nuclear war in, 251
    on Ku Klux Klan, 255
    science fiction, 239-240, 241, 247
    stories of biological or chemical weapons
        attacks, 239-242, 247
    See also The Turner Diaries (Pierce)
Fidayeen. See Assassins (Ismailis-Nizari)
Fighting words, 265-266
Figne, Vera, 7
Films, 240, 251, 255
First Amendment, 129, 130, 133, 263, 267
First International Conference on Countering
    Suicide Terrorism, 220
Flag burning, 266-267
FLN (Algeria), 30-31
Ford, Henry, 101
Foreign policy
    counterterrorism and, 277-282, 296-297
    Middle East policies of United States, 76, 81, 82
Foreign Terrorist Organizations (FTOs), 46-48, 49,
    282-283, 300, 321-344
Forsyth, Frederick, 51
Foucault, Michel, 307
France
    Bastille Syndrome, 130
    censorship, 130
    nuclear reactors, 251
    restrictions on sales of Nazi memorabilia, 268
    Revolution, 4-6, 39
    terrorist acts in, 52
    terrorist groups, 174, 185, 262-263
    use of closed-circuit television cameras, 310
Franceschini, Alberto, 184
Franklin, Joseph Paul, 261
Fraud, 269-270

Free Aceh Movement. *See* GAM
Freedom of speech
    application to Internet, 263-265
    categories of speech, 265-267, 268-269
    First Amendment, 129, 130, 133, 263, 267
    in public areas, 263-264
    responsibility of media and, 154
    restrictions, 263, 265-267, 268-269
Freemasonry, 101, 116
Free-wheeling fundamentalism, 98, 99,
    102, 103, 108
French Revolution, 4-6, 39
Freud, Sigmund, 168
Fromkin, David, 73
Front Line, 184, 186
FTOs. *See* Foreign Terrorist Organizations
Fuerzas Armadas Liberación Nacional (FALN).
    See Puerto Rican Nationalists
Fujimori, Alberto, 130, 136, 200
Fundamentalists. *See* Free-wheeling
    fundamentalism; Religious extremists
Furrow, Buford, 254-255

Gale, William Potter, 100
GAM (Free Aceh Movement), 157, 192
Gamaya Islamiya (Islamic Group), 220, 222
Gandhi, Mahatma, 8, 9
Gandhi, Rajiv, 47, 158, 221, 223
Genocide, 198
George Washington University, 147
Georges-Abeyie, Daniel E., 168-169
Germ warfare. *See* Biological weapons
German Socialist Patients' Collective (SPK), 174
Germany
    anti-Semitism, 256
    biological weapons, 245
    chemical weapons, 229, 241, 242
    Kurds in, 221
    Munich Olympics, 51, 131-132
    socialists, 171
    spies in World War II, 287
    terrorist acts in, 54
    use of closed-circuit television cameras, 310
    World War I, 229, 241, 242, 245
    See also Red Army Faction
GIA. *See* Armed Islamic Group
Gilbert, David, 174
Gill, K. P. S., 222
Glasgow (Scotland), 309
Globalization
    cultural conflicts, 45-46, 75, 76, 77, 278-279
    growth, 45
Goldman, Emma, 171, 288
Gonzales, Alberto R., 286-287
Good, Sandra, 176

Gowen, Franklin, 41, 42
Great Britain. *See* Britain
Greece, ancient, 1-2
Greek Orthodox Church, 30
Griffin, Michael, 114
Gritz, James "Bo," 102
Guevara, Ernesto "Che," 9, 47, 50-51, 159
Guillotine, Joseph, 4-5
Gulf War, 52, 82, 83
Gunn, David, 114, 118, 122, 123
Gunpowder Plot, 2-4
Guns
    right to bear arms, 102, 104
    use by women, 186
Guzman, Abimael, 9, 135, 137-138, 162, 163

Habash, George, 51, 176
Haddad, Wadi, 175, 176
Haggard, Carl D., 105
*Hague v. Committee for Industrial
    Organization*, 263-264
Hajjar, George, 176
Hale, Matt, 99, 106
Hamas (Islamic Resistance Movement),
    48, 327-328
    asset seizures, 281
    Covenant, 80
    fund raising, 145, 270
    goals, 48, 79, 222
    political and military components, 144
    relations with secular leaders, 80
    suicide terrorism, 220, 221, 222
    Web site, 262
Hamilton, Edmond, 241
Hargrove, Trent, 271
Harlan, John, 266
Harris, Emily, 88
Harris, William, 88
Hasan Pasha, 40
Hate Watch, 261
Haymarket Square riots, 42
Hearst, Patricia, 88, 159
Heathrow Airport, 304
Heinzen, Karl, 6, 227
Henry L. Stimson Center, 231
Henry VIII, King of England, 3
Herodotus, 18, 196
Hezbollah. *See* Hizbollah
Hijackings
    Achille Lauro, 199
    as terrorist tactic, 198-199
    automobile, 198-199, 255
    by Palestinian groups, 51, 172, 176, 199
    TWA flights, 146, 152, 176
Hill, Paul, 114

Hinduism
    criminal tribes and, 29-30
    extremists, 16-17
    Kali, 17, 18, 19, 29
    view of history, 21
    See also Thugs
Hindustan Socialist Republican Association
    (HSRA), 8-9
Hitler, Adolph, 242, 261
Hizbollah (Party of God), 48, 329
    asset seizures, 281
    funding, 152
    goals, 48, 222
    hostages in Lebanon, 151, 152-153
    Iranian support, 222
    links to drug trafficking, 65
    suicide terrorism, 220, 221, 222
    Web site, 262
Holy Land Foundation, 270
Homegrown terrorism in United States
    animal rights groups, 89, 123
    categories, 85-86
    counterterrorism strategies, 119-120, 277, 282
    ecoterrorists, 88-89, 251-252, 262
    history, 85
    Indian removal, 86-87
    lack of information, 85
    media portrayals, 121
    similarities to international groups, 195
    See also Antiabortion violence; Labor
        movement; Leftist groups; Rightist groups;
        White supremacists
Honduras, women activists, 168
Hoover, J. Edgar, 288
Horsley, Neal, 262
Hoskins, Richard Kelley, 258
Hostage-takings
    as terrorist tactic, 200-201
    by Barbary pirates, 38-40
    distinction from kidnapping, 200
    goals, 200
    in Iran, 151, 152
    in Lebanon, 48, 150-151, 152-153
    Japanese ambassador's residence in Lima, 200
    media coverage, 131-132, 145, 151-153
    Munich Olympics, 51, 131-132
    of journalists, 131, 150
    OPEC ministers, 51, 175
House Un-American Activities Committee
    (HUAC), 290
Howell, Vernon. *See* Koresh, David
HSRA. *See* Hindustan Socialist Republican
    Association
HUAC. *See* House Un-American Activities
    Committee

Hubal, 74, 77, 81
Hulegu, 76
Hull (England), 308-310
Hunter (Pierce), 116-117, 258, 261
Huntington, Samuel, 279
Hussein, Saddam, 51, 82, 243, 246

IAP. *See* Islamic Association for Palestine
Ibn Taymiyya, 77, 78
Identity Christians. *See* Christian Identity
IEDs. *See* Improvised explosive devices
Illeto, Joseph, 255
Illinois, group-libel statute, 265-266
Illuminati, 100-101, 116
Immigrants, detentions of, 284, 285-286
Improvised explosive devices (IEDs), 223, 224
India
    assassinations, 47, 158, 221, 223
    British rule, 8-9
    Inter-Parliamentary Union, 193
    Sikh groups, 222, 278
    terrorism in, 8-9, 220, 277-278
    See also Hinduism; Kashmir; Thugs
Indians. *See* Native Americans
Indonesia
    GAM (Free Aceh Movement), 157, 192
    terrorists in, 49
Industrial Revolution, 89
Info. International Network, 256
Infocom, 270
INLA. *See* Irish National Liberation Army
International Association of Bridge and Structural
    Iron Workers, 42, 43
International Emergency Economic Powers Act, 300
International Monetary Fund, 45
Internet
    abortion provider information on, 262, 271-272
    criminal use of, 269
    democratization of media in, 129
    e-mail, 259, 270, 273
    extremists' use of, 259, 262, 273
    fraud on, 269-270
    free speech on, 263-265
    globalization and, 45
    growth, 130
    hate Web sites, 254, 260, 261, 271
    leaderless resistance promoted through, 259,
        262, 271-272
    mapping sites, 254-255
    monitoring by law enforcement, 272-273
    online auctions, 268
    regulation of sexually oriented content, 264, 268
    steganography, 196, 263
    terrorists' use of, 230, 254-255, 262-263,
        272, 273

Usenet discussion boards, 258
See also Cyberterrorism
Internet service providers (ISPs), 267-268, 272
Inter-Parliamentary Union, 193
Invisible Knights of the Ku Klux Klan, 259
IRA. *See* Irish Republican Army
Iran
American hostages, 151, 152
arms-for-hostages deal, 152, 153
as sponsor of terrorism, 48, 152, 222
biological weapons, 246
Islamic revolution, 150
war with Iraq, 229, 243
Iraq
as sponsor of terrorism, 48, 51
biological weapons research, 246, 248
chemical weapons used, 229, 243
invasion of Kuwait, 52
nuclear weapons research, 253
opposition to Saddam, 83
sanctions on, 76, 81
U.N. weapons inspectors, 246
war with Iran, 229, 243
Ireland
Easter Rising, 47, 209, 210
Good Friday peace agreement, 207-208, 210
history, 210
partition, 209, 210
See also Northern Ireland
Irish Americans, 212
Irish National Liberation Army (INLA), 208
Irish Republican Army (IRA), 350-351
American supporters, 64, 118, 212, 224
Catholics in, 30, 207
criminal activities, 64
Good Friday peace agreement, 207-208, 210
history, 47, 210-211
longevity, 18
political and military components, 144-145, 208
revenue sources, 64
terrorist manual, 9, 217
use of violence, 208, 304
weapons decommissioning, 211, 213
women in, 185
See also Continuity IRA; Provisional IRA; Real
IRA; Sinn Fein
Islam
bin Laden's view of, 53
enmity to West, 80
extremists, 16-17, 29, 75, 76-77, 78, 79, 81
failures of extremists, 79, 81
history, 76, 80
internal ideological conflict, 74, 78, 79, 82
law (*shari'a*), 75, 78, 80, 81, 172
millenarian movements, 21, 23

opposition to secular leaders, 78
rise of, 75-76
Salafiyya reform movement, 74-75, 76-77,
78, 79-81
Sunni, 78
umma (universal community), 73, 74,
77, 80, 82
victims of terrorism, 49
Wahhabism, 75
See also Jihad; Shia Muslims
Islamic Association for Palestine (IAP), 145
Islamic Jihad. *See* Hizbullah
Islamic Resistance Movement. *See* Hamas
Islamic terrorists
FLN (Algeria), 30-31
goals, 49
hijackings, 152
in Asia, 49, 192
in Kuwait, 150, 151
media coverage, 121, 134
relations with secular leaders, 80
religious motives, 75
spread of, 49
suicide terrorism, 220, 221
tactics guidebooks, 196-197
women, 223
World Trade Center bombing (1993), xiii, 53,
77, 78, 123, 146, 194, 282
See also Assassins; Hamas; Hizbullah; Qaeda, Al
Ismailis-Nizari. *See* Assassins
Israel
American support, 81, 82
ancient, 107
Anglo-Israelism, 98, 100, 101
assassination of Rabin, 197-198
athletes killed at Munich Olympics,
51, 131-132
attack on Iraqi nuclear reactor, 253
bombings in, 133, 224
counterterrorism, 222, 224, 280
Entebbe raid, 175
First International Conference on Countering
Suicide Terrorism, 220
intelligence agencies, 222
invasion of Lebanon, 150
Islamic enemies, 79
media coverage of terrorism, 133, 134
peace negotiations, 197
prisoners, 172, 199
relations with Sri Lanka, 224
secret service, 176, 198
Technology Institute (Holon), 147
terrorist acts against, 52, 133, 224
See also Judea; Zionism
Italian Communist Party (PCI), 183, 185

Italy
    feminism, 183-184
    neo-Fascism, 173
    use of poison gas in Ethiopia, 242
    women terrorists, 173-174, 183, 184, 185, 186
    See also Mafia; Red Brigades

Jacobsen, David, 153
Jacques, Norbert, 240
James I, King of England, 2
Japan
    biological weapons used, 229, 245
    hijackings in, 48
    Hiroshima and Nagasaki bombings, 229, 250
    rightist groups, 176
    sarin attack in Tokyo subway, 232, 234-235, 242
Japanese Americans, internment, 289-290
Japanese Red Army (JRA), 47, 175, 176, 351-352
Jefferson, Thomas, 38, 39, 40
Jenco, Martin, 152-153
Jersey City (New Jersey), free speech
    restrictions, 263-264
Jerusalem, 80
Jews. *See* Anti-Semitism; Israel; Judaism
Jihad
    bin Laden on, 53
    cultural struggle against West, 45-46, 75,
        76, 77, 278-279
    extremist view of, 75
    meanings, 45-46
    Shia beliefs, 21
Jogiches, Leo, 171
John Birch Society, 116
Johnson, Gregory, 266-267
Jones, John Paul, 38
Josephus, 26
Jouhari, Bonnie, 271
Journalists. *See* Media
JRA. *See* Japanese Red Army
Judaism
    extremists, 16-17, 29
    law (Halacha), 172
    messianic doctrines, 21, 25, 98
    See also Anti-Semitism; Israel; Zealots
Judea
    rebellion against Roman rule, 2, 24, 25,
        26-28, 29
    See also Zealots
Julius Caesar, 2

Kaczynski, Theodore, 88, 132, 196
Kahl, Gordon, 259
Kali, 17, 18, 19, 29
Kamal, Husain, 246
Kant, Immanuel, 23

Kashmir, terrorists in, 49, 158, 222, 278
Kennedy, Anthony, 267
Kennedy, John F., 198
Kenya, bombing of U.S. embassy, 53-54, 195,
    201, 216, 221, 225, 281
Kerr, Donald, 272-273
Kerr, Malcolm, 150
KGB, 246
Khaled, Leila, 176-177
Kidnappings
    as terrorist tactic, 200-201
    by Red Brigades, 68, 185
    government responses, 201
    ransom demands, 200, 201
    See also Hostage-takings
King, Martin Luther, Jr., 198
Kirkland, Andrew, 286
KKK. *See* Ku Klux Klan
KLA. *See* Kosovo Liberation Army
Klassen, Ben, 99, 106, 108
Klinghoffer, Leon, 199
Kmiec, Douglas W., 284
KNF. *See* Kosovo National Front
Know Nothings, 99
Kohlmann, Brigitte, 175
Kopp, Magdalena, 51
Koresh, David, 102
    See also Branch Davidians
Kosovo, 49, 59, 69
Kosovo Liberation Army (KLA), 59, 69
Kosovo National Front (KNF), 69
Kostov, Vladimir, 246
Kozihioukian, Hratch, 174
Kozihioukian, Siranouche, 174
Kozinski, Alex, 271-272
Kroecher, Norbert, 174-175
Krupskaya, Nadeshda, 170
Ku Klux Klan (KKK)
    Duke faction, 256, 257, 260
    history, 89, 100, 255-256
    membership, 255
    rallies, 268
    religious background, 100
    use of media, 255
    Web sites, 261
Kubrick Stanley, 251
Kumaratunge, Chandrika Bandaranaike, 225
Kuomintang, 171
Kurdistan Worker's Party (PKK), 47, 332-333
    drug trafficking allegations, 65
    goals, 47, 222
    suicide terrorism, 220, 221
Kurds, chemical weapons used on, 229, 243
Kuwait
    Iraqi invasion, 52

Islamic extremists, 150, 151
U.S. support of regime, 82

La Belle Discotheque (Berlin) bombing, 54
La Torre Guzman, Augusta, 161, 162-163
Labor movement, 41, 42-43, 87
Lack, Bob, 306-307
L'Ala, Natale, 187
Lambs of Christ, 115
Lang, Fritz, 240
Laos, 231, 246
Laqueur, Walter, 49
Lasker, Pia, 174
Latin America
    Foreign Terrorist Organizations, 47
    independence movements, 158
    influence of Che Guevara, 50
    media coverage of terrorism, 134
    nationalism, 9
    public esteem for media, 136
    revolutionaries, 51
    urban terrorism, 9-10
    See also Central America; *and*
        individual countries
Law, Islamic (*shari'a*), 75, 78, 80, 81, 172
Laws. *See* Legislation
Leaderless resistance, 116-117, 195-196,
    258-259, 271-272
Lebanese Communist Party, 221
Lebanon
    drug trafficking by terrorist groups, 59
    hostages held in, 48, 150-151, 152-153
    Israeli invasion, 150
    suicide terrorism, 220-221, 222
    terrorist bombings, 48
    U.S. embassy, 151
    Western hostages, 150-151, 152-153
    See also Hizbullah
Lederberg, Joshua, 250
Leftist groups
    in United States, 87-88, 160-161, 174, 288
    Italian, 183-184
    leaderless resistance, 262
    use of Internet, 262
    women in, 160-161, 169, 174
    See also Communists; Red Army Faction
Legislation
    antiterrorism, 46, 130, 272, 277, 282-285,
        286, 299-300
    computer crimes, 270
    Internet regulations, 264-265, 268, 271, 272
    on sedition and espionage, 129, 288
Lenin, Vladimir, 9, 51, 170
Leontiev, Tatiana, 159
Liberation Tigers of Tamil Eelam (LTTE),
    47, 334

drug trafficking allegations, 64
goals, 47, 222
suicide bombers, 158, 201, 220, 221, 222, 225
training, 222
women in, 157, 158, 223, 225
Liberty Bell Net, 256
Libya
    as sponsor of terrorism, 48, 51, 54, 301
    biological weapons, 246
    hijackers, 48, 54
    U.S. bombing, 40, 55
Lincoln, Abraham, 2, 287
Lindgren, Anna-Karin, 174-175
Llewellyn Iron Works, 42
Locations of terrorist activity, 314-320
Lockerbie, Scotland, explosion of Pan Am Flight
    103, 48, 54-55
Lombroso, Cesare, 168
London
    closed-circuit television cameras,
        304-308, 310
    IRA bombings, 304
    police, 305
    Underground, 307, 308
London, Jack, 239-240
Long Island (New York), 89
Los Angeles Times, bombing at, 42
LTTE. *See* Liberation Tigers of Tamil Eelam
Luddites, 89
Ludlow massacre, 87
Lumumba University (Moscow), 51
Luxemburg, Rosa, 171

Ma Anand Sheela, 175-176, 250
MacDonald, Andrew. *See* Pierce, William
Machado, Richard, 270-271
As-Madhi, Mohammed Ibrahim, 193
Madison, James, 129
Mafia
    Albanian, 69
    Camorra, 68-69, 188
    Chechen, 69, 70
    cooperation with Red Brigades, 68-69
    drug trafficking, 69
    lack of cooperation with terrorists, 59-60
    women's roles, 188
    See also Cosa Nostra; Russian Mafia
Magic Lantern, 273
Mahler, Horst, 175
Mahseredjian, Suzy, 174
Major, John, 304
Malvasi, Dennis, 114
Manson, Charles, 169, 176
Manual of the Urban Guerrilla (Marighella),
    9-10, 31, 196
Mao Zedong, 9, 172, 196

Maoism, 87, 223
Marighella, Carlos, 9-10, 31, 129, 196
Markov, Georgi, 246
Marshall, John, 308
Martin du Gard, Roger, 242
Marulanda, Manuel, 67
Marx, Karl, 9
Marxism, 87, 223
Masons, 101, 116
Massachusetts Institute of Technology, 270-271
Massardi, Mario, 183-184
Mathews, Robert, 259, 260
McCarthy, Joseph, 290
McCarthyism, 290
McDonald's, 45
McGuiness, Martin, 212, 216
McKinley, William, 40
McNamara, James B., 42-43
McNamara, John J., 42
McParland, James, 41
McVeigh, Timothy, 105, 135, 261
    See also Oklahoma City, bombing of Murrah
        Federal Building
Medellin cartel, 61, 65-66, 68
Media
    attacks on journalists, 131, 147, 148
    audiences, 134
    biases, 133, 134, 151
    censorship, 130-131, 153
    commercial and competitive pressures, 134
    contagion theory, 133-134
    cooperation with governments, 133, 134
    cooperation with terrorists, 132, 133-134
    coverage of antiabortion violence, 112,
        120, 121-124
    digital, 130
    extremists' use of, 100, 103, 255-256, 258, 261
    in Omagh, 214
    issues in coverage of terrorism, 131-135
    kidnappings of journalists, 131, 150
    manipulation of, 137, 151, 152, 154
    print, 130
    professional culture, 134-135
    regulation attempts, 129, 130-131, 153
    relations with governments, 145-146,
        147-148, 154
    relationships with terrorists, 129,
        131-132, 144-145, 151-153, 154
    reporting traditions, 132
    responsibilities, 131, 153-154
    role in covering terrorism, 144-146
    See also Films; Freedom of speech
Al-Megrahi, Abdelbaset Ali Mohmed, 54
Meinhof, Ulrike, 161, 162, 175
Melville, Sam, 174

Mendleson, Anna, 175
Menignon, Nathalie, 174
Mernissi, Fatima, 177
Metzger, Tom, 256, 257-258
Mexico
    drug trafficking, 62
    See also Zapatista National Liberation Army
Middle East
    anti-American views, 46, 81-82, 83
    Foreign Terrorist Organizations, 47-48, 49
    oil, 82
    See also Islamic terrorists; Palestinian terrorist
        groups; *and individual countries*
Miles, Robert, 101
Military tribunals, 286-288
Militia movement, 91, 102-103, 116, 117, 259
Militia of Montana, 102, 259
Millenarian movements
    Christian, 98
    in United States, 91-92
    Islamic, 21, 23
    Jewish, 25, 98
    use of violence, 98
Miller, Walter, 251
Mineta, Norman, 303
Missionaries to the Preborn, 115
Mohammed, 23-24, 74, 75
Mongols, 76, 77, 80
Montana Freemen, 269
Monterey Institute of International
        Studies, 230-231
Moro, Aldo, 185
Moro National Liberation Front, 192
Morocco, 38
    See also Pirates, Barbary
Morucci, Valerio, 185
Moscow
    apartment bombings, 69
    Lumumba University, 51
Moses, 108
Most, John (Jonathan), 6, 40-41
Movement 2 June, 174
MRTA. *See* Tupac Amaru Revolutionary
        Movement
Mubarak, Hosni, 75, 81
Muhammad. *See* Mohammed
Muhammad, Elijah, 90
Munafiqun (Hypocrites of Medina), 74, 78
Munich Olympics, Israeli athletes killed,
        51, 131-132
Murders
    by product tampering, 198
    genocide, 198
    of tyrants, 1-2
    political, 6

See also Assassinations
Murphy, Thomas "Slab," 217
Murrah Federal Building. *See* Oklahoma City,
    bombing of Murrah Federal Building
Music, hate, 91, 258
Myanmar. *See* Burma
Mythology, 107-108

Naples. *See* Camorra
Narodnaya Volya, 7-8, 31
Nasser, Gamel Abdel, 243
Nation of Islam, 90
National Abortion Federation, 112
National Alliance, 260, 261
National Guard (U.S.), 87, 231
National Liberation Army (ELN; Colombia), 47,
    66, 68, 200, 335-336
National Security Agency, 273
National Security Archives, 49
National Youth Alliance, 260
Nationalism
    in India, 8-9
    Irish, 207, 209, 210
    Latin American, 9
    Palestinian, 79, 80
    Puerto Rican, 87, 198
    seen as idolatry by Muslims, 79-80
    terrorism motivated by, 8-9
Native Americans
    religions, 99
    removal from territories, 86-87
    smallpox infections, 245
NATO (North Atlantic Treaty Organization),
    46, 280-281
Natzersit Socialist Party, 221
Naval Postgraduate School, Dudley Knox
    Library, 46
Nechaev, Sergey, 7, 31, 171, 178
Neo-Nazis, 91, 118, 195, 258, 260, 261, 271
Netanyahu, Benjamin, 130
New Left, 87, 160-161, 173
New World Order, 91-92, 116
New York City
    bombings, 87
    surveillance cameras, 304
    See also September 11, 2001, terrorist attacks
New York City Police Department, 87
New York Times, 132
New Zealand, electronic surveillance, 273
News media. *See* Media
Nguyen Thi Binh, 173
Nicaragua, 173
Nice, David, 117
Nicolson, Harold, 241
Nixon, Richard M., 49

Nobel, Alfred, 43, 240
Noble, Kerry, 105
Nordic Christianity, 98, 99, 108
Norris, Clive, 305, 307, 309
North Atlantic Treaty Organization (NATO),
    46, 280-281
North Korea, as sponsor of terrorism, 48, 301
North Valley Jewish Community Center, 255
Northern Ireland
    creation of, 209, 210
    Good Friday peace agreement, 207-208, 210
    political parties, 207, 208, 209
    religion and ethnic identity, 106, 209
    Unionists, 208
    See also Belfast; Irish Republican Army;
        Omagh bombing; Sinn Fein
Noyes, Alfred, 241
Nuclear reactors, 251-252
Nuclear weapons
    access to material, 62, 251, 252, 253
    countries possessing, 229
    effects, 252
    Hiroshima and Nagasaki bombings, 229, 250
    production, 253
    proliferation, 251, 253
    threat of terrorist use, 250-253
    See also Weapons of mass destruction
Nuremberg Files Web site, 262

OAS. *See* Organization of American States
Obscenity, 266
Ocalan, Abdullah, 47, 222
Odinism, 98, 99, 108
Offensive speech, 265-266
Office of Homeland Security, 277, 304
Official IRA, 209, 211
    See also Irish Republican Army (IRA)
Ohio, Criminal Syndicalism Act, 268
Oil, 82
Oklahoma City, bombing of Murrah Federal
    Building
    as independent operation, 116, 196
    defenders, 116
    failure as terrorist act, 133
    link to right-wing extremism, 99, 261
    media coverage, 124
    public reaction, 117, 282
Okudaira, Tsoyoshi, 176
Oliver, Revilo P., 256
Olson, Sara Jane, 88
Olympic Games
    bombing in Atlanta, 134
    Israeli athletes killed in Munich, 51, 131-132
Omagh bombing
    aims, 213, 214

casualties, 207, 215, 216
conspiracy suspicions, 217-218
description, 215-216
mistakes made, 216
reactions to, 207, 208, 216, 218
target selection, 213-215
Omagh (Northern Ireland)
as county town, 213-214
religious groups, 214-215
Republican supporters, 208, 214
Omnibus Crime Control and Safe Streets Act
of 1968, 272
OPEC (Organization of Petroleum Exporting
Countries), 51, 175
Operation Rescue, 113, 115, 116, 122
Order of the Illuminati, 100-101
Order, The, 102, 119, 256, 259, 260, 269
Organization of American States (OAS), 148
Organization of Petroleum Exporting Countries.
See OPEC
Organization on Security and Cooperation in
Europe (OSCE), 148
Orwell, George, 310, 311
OSCE. *See* Organization on Security and
Cooperation in Europe
Other Terrorist Groups (OTGs), 46, 344-359
Otis, Harrison, 42

Pakistan
Islamic extremists, 279
participation in U.S. war on terrorism, 281
suicide terrorism, 221
terrorists in, 194
See also Kashmir
Palestine Liberation Front (PLF), 199, 336-337
Palestine Liberation Organization (PLO), 47, 153
Palestinian Authority, 80, 222
Palestinian Islamic Jihad (PIJ), 145, 220, 222, 336
Palestinian terrorist groups, 47
education of children, 193
fund raising, 145, 270
hijackings, 51, 172, 176, 199
Iranian support, 48
links to other terrorist groups, 175, 176
media portrayals, 121
suicide bombers, 158, 220, 221, 222
women in, 158, 172, 176-177
See also Hamas; Popular Front for the
Liberation of Palestine
Palestinians
nationalism, 79, 80
peace negotiations, 197
Palladin Press, 272
Palmer, A. Mitchell, 288
Palmer raids, 288

Pan Am Flight 103, 48, 54-55
Panopticon, 307
Parsons, Tim, 305-306
Party of God. *See* Hizbullah
Pasechnik, Viktor, 249
Patriot movement, 99, 108, 116
Patterns of Global Terrorism, 147, 148, 321
Patterson, Wayne, 114
Paul, Apostle, 105
Pearse, Patrick, 209
Pennsylvania, Molly Maguires, 41-42
Pensacola (Florida), attacks on abortion
clinics, 113, 123
Pentagon. *See* September 11, 2001, terrorist
attacks; U.S. Defense Department
Perez Vega, Reynaldo, 173
Perón, Juan, 50
Peru
capture of Guzman, 135, 137
counterterrorism, 136
hostages at Japanese ambassador's
residence, 200
judicial system, 130
media coverage of terrorism, 136
Tupac Amaru Revolutionary Movement, 47,
200, 352
See also Shining Path
PFLP. *See* Popular Front for the Liberation
of Palestine
Philadelphia and Reading Coal and Iron
Company, 41
Philadelphia and Reading Railroad, 41
Philippines
nuclear reactors, 252
terrorists in, 49, 192, 200, 252
Phineas, 25-26
Phinehas Priesthood, 108
Pierce, William, 91, 101, 103, 116, 195, 196,
258, 260-261, 273
PIJ. *See* Palestinian Islamic Jihad
Pinkerton, Alan, 41
Pinkerton detective agency, 41
Pinochet, Augusto, 49, 174
PIRA. *See* Provisional IRA
Pirates, Barbary, 38-40
Pisacane, Carlo, 6-7
PKK. *See* Kurdistan Worker's Party
*Planned Parenthood v. American Coalition of Life
Activists*, 271-272
PLF. *See* Palestine Liberation Front
PLO. *See* Palestine Liberation Organization
Poison gas. *See* Chemical weapons
Political terrorism
history, 6-7
justifications, 42

Political violence in United States, 85, 92, 112
  See also Antiabortion violence; Leftist groups;
      Rightist groups in United States
Popular Front for the Liberation of Palestine
    (PFLP), 51, 52, 175, 176, 177, 337
Posse Comitatus, 98, 100, 102
Powell, Colin, 247
Premadasa, Ranasinghe, 221, 225
Press, freedom of. *See* Freedom of speech
Preston, Richard, 241
Prisons, 307
Product tampering, 198
Pro-Life Action League, 113
Prolife groups, 115, 125
  See also Antiabortion violence
Propaganda by deed, 6-7
Prostitutes, 309
Protestants
  anti-immigrant views, 99
  Church of England, 3
  conservatives, 100
  extremists, 103
  in Northern Ireland, 106, 212, 214-215
  links to anti-abortion groups, 115
  settlement of America, 99
  tension between universal love and
      ethnocentrism, 105-106
  See also Christianity
Provisional IRA (PIRA), 350-351
  British measures against, 224
  formation, 208-209, 211
  Good Friday peace agreement, 208
  involvement in peace process, 209, 210
  link to Sinn Fein, 208
  prisoners in Britain, 211
  reaction to Omagh bombing, 208, 216-217, 218
  splinter groups, 208, 209, 211, 213, 216-218
  supporters, 214
  See also Irish Republican Army
Public diplomacy, 301
Public health, 228, 231, 295
Puerto Rican Nationalists (FALN), 87, 198
Punjab, 222

Al-Qaddafi, Muammar, 51, 54, 55, 246
Qaeda, Al, 47, 338-339
  activities in Kashmir, 222
  attacks on U.S. facilities, 52, 53-54, 222
  background, 74
  capabilities, 220
  decision to target United States, 52-53, 81
  embassy bombings, 53-54, 194-195, 221, 225
  links to other terrorist groups, 78, 222
  organization, 52, 53
  prisoners at Guantanamo Bay, 287

religious motives, 75, 76, 222
  revolutionary goals, 77-78, 79, 80
  structure, 221-222
  Taliban support, 280
  U.S. counterterrorism efforts, 222, 297
  use of Internet, 262-263, 273
  view of Islam, 76
  See also Bin Laden, Osama; September 11,
      2001, terrorist attacks
Quon, Kingman, 271
Qutb, Sayyid, 77

Rabin, Yitzhak, 197-198
Racial profiling, 286, 309
Racial supremacy
  black separatist groups, 88, 90, 261
  cyberthreats, 270-271
  See also White supremacists
Racism
  free speech and, 266
  of rightist groups, 103, 106, 107
Racist skinheads, 91, 258, 261
Racketeer Influenced and Criminal Organization
    law. *See* RICO
Radiological weapons, 251
  See also Weapons of mass destruction
RAF. *See* Red Army Faction
Rahman, Omar Abdel, 77
Rajneesh, Bhagwan Shree, 175, 249-250
Ramirez Sanchez, Ilich. *See* Carlos the Jackal
Reagan National Airport, 303
Reagan, Ronald, 102, 118-119, 122, 152, 290
Real IRA, 339
  American supporters, 212
  asset seizures, 281
  formation, 208, 209, 217
  future of, 218
  goals and strategy, 209
  leader, 212, 217
  political wing, 211
  relations with Provisional IRA, 216-218
  terrorist operations, 211-213
  See also Omagh bombing
Reconstruction era, 89
Red Army Faction (RAF)
  biological weapons, 249
  bombings, 161
  links to other terrorist groups, 174, 175
  similarities to Shining Path, 163
  terrorist manual, 9
  use of violence, 163
  women in, 161, 162, 175, 185
  See also Baader-Meinhoff group
Red Brigades (Brigate Rosse)
  comparison to Mafia, 182

cooperation with Mafia groups, 68-69
goals, 31
kidnappings, 68, 185
links to other terrorist groups, 175
origins, 182, 184
terrorist manual, 9
use of violence, 182, 184
women in, 173-174, 182, 183, 184,
185, 188
Red Help, 175
Red Scare, 288
Reed, Ralph, 123
Religious extremists
Christian, 99-101, 123
global similarities, 104-105
history, 99-101
in United States, 91-92, 98-101
millenarian beliefs, 91-92
similarities across religions, 16-17
social structures, 103-104
tension between universal love and
ethnocentrism, 105-106
use of Bible, 108
use of violence, 106-107
See also Antiabortion violence
Religious terrorism
audience, 17
distinction from modern terrorism, 28, 30
future of, 104, 109
goals, 30
growth, 91, 98
Gunpowder Plot, 2-4
increase in, 49
justifications, 104, 278-279
misconceptions about, 28
motives, 104, 106-107
suicide bombings, 222
unconventional tactics, 227-228
See also Antiabortion violence; Assassins;
Islamic terrorists; Rightist groups in
United States; Thugs; Zealots
Removal Act of 1830, 86
*Reno et al. v. American Civil Liberties Union
et al.*, 264
Reno, Janet, 124
Reporters. *See* Media
Rescue America, 115
Resistance, 91
Retail terrorism, 87
Revolutionary Armed Forces of Colombia
(FARC), 340
activities, 47, 66
drug trafficking, 59, 65, 67
goals, 65
Rhodesia, 231

RICO (Racketeer Influenced and Criminal
Organization) law, 115, 119
Ridge, Tom, 277
Rightist groups
Italian, 173, 184
Japanese, 176
Rightist groups in United States
civil lawsuits against, 258, 259
common theological elements, 103-104
conspiracy theories, 90, 91-92, 100-101,
109, 116
effectiveness, 102
ethnocentrism, 106
federal law enforcement and, 119
links to anti-abortion groups, 116-117
neo-Nazis, 91, 118, 195, 258, 260, 261, 271
racism, 103, 106, 107
racist skinheads, 91, 258, 261
reactions to Ruby Ridge and Waco, 117, 124
recent history, 101-103
unconventional tactics, 227-228
use of violence, 259
view of U.S. government, 105
Web sites, 254
women in, 164
See also Antiabortion violence; Militia
movement; Religious extremists;
White supremacists
Right-to-life organizations, 115, 125
See also Antiabortion violence
Riina, Totò, 187
Robespierre, Maximilien, 4, 5-6
Rockwell, George Lincoln, 260
Roe v. Wade, 113
Roman Catholic Church
conservatives, 100
in England, 3
in Italy, 183, 187
in Northern Ireland, 106, 207, 209, 214-215
Mafia members and, 187
Masons and, 116
opposition to in U.S., 99
See also Christianity
Roman Empire, rule of Judea, 2, 24, 25, 26-28
Ronconi, Susanna, 183, 184, 185, 186, 188
Roosevelt, Franklin D., 289, 290
Roosevelt, Theodore, 40
Rouillan, Jean-Marc, 174
Ruby Ridge (Idaho), 102, 117
Rudolph, Eric, 116
Russia
assassinations, 7-8, 159
Aum Shinrikyo followers, 233
biological weapons research, 249
Chechen rebellion, 69, 70, 231, 252

civil war, 229
female revolutionaries, 157, 168, 170
Narodnaya Volya, 7-8, 31
Revolution, 157
smuggling of nuclear materials, 62
World War I, 242
See also Moscow; Soviet Union
Russian Mafia, 60, 62
See also Chechen Mafia; Mafia

Sabena Airlines, 172
Sadat, Anwar al-, 75, 78
Safir, Howard, 304
Safire, William, 287
Sagartians, 18
Said, Edward W., 279
St. Paul (Minnesota), attack on abortion
   clinic, 113
Saladin, 80
Salafiyya, 74-75, 76-77, 78, 79-81
Salvi, John, 114, 116
Sandinistas, 173
Sands, Bobby, 211
Sands-McKevitt, Bernadette, 211
Santamaria, Haydee, 173
Sarin, 232, 234-235, 242, 244, 247
Sartre, Jean-Paul, 50
Saudi Arabia
   bin Laden's view of, 73, 74, 78-79
   Khobar Towers bombing, xiii, 53, 296
   Medina, 23, 74
   participation in U.S. war on terrorism, 281
   U.S. bases in, 52, 74, 76, 78, 80
   U.S. support of regime, 82
   Wahhabism, 75
Savané, Marie Angélique, 177
Scheidler, Joseph, 113
Science fiction, 239-240, 241, 247
Scotland
   closed-circuit television cameras, 309
   Pan Am 103 crash, 48, 54-55
Sedition Act of 1798, 129
Sedition Act of 1918, 288
Seljuk Empire, 20
Sendero Luminoso. *See* Shining Path
Sentry Alarms Ltd., 309
September 11, 2001, terrorist attacks, xi-xii
   battle prayers of terrorists, 75
   business opportunities following, 303
   casualties, xi
   civil liberties restrictions, 130
   documents related to, 197
   goals, 73, 78, 79
   Muslim reactions, 76, 81-82
   preparations, 262

responses to, 46, 73-74, 130, 277, 280-281
Serbia, 69
Shan United Army, 67
Shannon, Rachelle "Shelley," 114, 124
Shari'a. See Law, Islamic
Al-Sharif, Khalid, 76
Shia Muslims
   Amal militia, 152
   in Lebanon, 150
   martyrs, 24
   millenarian beliefs, 21
Shigenobu, Fusako, 47, 176
Shining Path (Sendero Luminoso), 47, 342-343
   drug trafficking by, 64
   formation, 163
   government response, 130, 135-137
   leaders, 9, 135-138
   relations with media, 135, 136-137
   similarities to Red Army Faction, 163
   use of violence, 47, 163
   women in, 161, 162-163
Shinrito ("Supreme Truth") party, 233-234
Shute, Nevil, 251
Sicarii, 25
   See also Zealots
Sicily
   drug trafficking, 188
   See also Cosa Nostra
Sieff, Edward, 52
Sierra Leone, child soldiers, 193
Sikh groups, 222, 278
Silverman, Sheela P., 175-176
Simmons, William J., 255
Simon Wiesenthal Center, 255
Sinn Fein
   involvement in peace process, 209, 216, 217
   leaders, 144-145, 212
   Omagh mayor, 208, 214
   violence and, 208
   See also Irish Republican Army (IRA)
Skinheads, 91, 258, 261
Skirball Cultural Center, 255
SL (Sendero Luminoso). *See* Shining Path
SLA. *See* Symbionese Liberation Army
Smallpox, 245, 248
Snell, Richard Wayne, 259
Socialists, 171
Soliah, Kathleen, 88
Somalia, U.S. troops in, xiii
South Africa
   African National Congress, 118, 252
   biological weapons used, 231
   nuclear reactors, 252
South America. *See* Latin America
Southern Poverty Law Center, 254, 256, 259, 261

Soviet Union
    biological weapons, 246
    chemical weapons, 231, 242
    Chernobyl accident, 251
    collapse, 278
    invasion of Afghanistan, 52
    KGB assassinations, 246
    nuclear materials, 227, 253
    prisoners of war, 242
    revolutionaries trained in, 51
    See also Russia
Spain
    Communist Party, 177
    drug trafficking by terrorist groups, 59
    nuclear reactors, 251-252
    See also Basque Fatherland and Liberty
Speech, freedom of. *See* Freedom of speech
Spies
    German, 287
    women, 159
SPK (German Socialist Patients' Collective), 174
Sri Lanka
    assassinations, 221, 225
    counterterrorism, 224-225
    drug trafficking by terrorist groups, 59
    relations with Israel, 224
    See also Liberation Tigers of Tamil Eelam
State Department. *See* U.S. State Department
State-sponsored terrorism
    advantages to state, 48
    Barbary Pirates, 38-40
    citizen lawsuits, 283
    forms, 48
    French Revolution, 4-6
    in United States, 86-87
    media coverage, 134
    responses to, 280, 300-301
    sanctions against, 48, 54, 300
    U.S. State Department list, 48-49
Steganography, 196, 263
Stethem, Robert, 152
Stimson Center, 231
Stockholm syndrome, 20
Stoddard, Theodore, 100
Stormfront.org, 254, 260
Students for a Democratic Society, 87
Sturm, Beate, 175
Sudan
    as sponsor of terrorism, 48
    bin Laden in, 52
    extremist Islamic rule, 79
    U.S. cruise missile attack, 281
Suicide bombers
    attack on USS *Cole*, 53, 201, 278
    improvised explosive devices (IEDs), 223, 224

LTTE, 158, 201
    Palestinian, 158, 220, 221, 222
    training, 222, 225
    U.S. embassies in Africa, 53-54, 194-195,
        201, 216, 221, 225, 281
    women, 158, 223, 225
    See also September 11, 2001,
        terrorist attacks
Suicide terrorism
    battlefield operations, 221
    characteristics, 221-222
    conference on, 220
    defense against, 223, 224-225
    definition, 220
    future of, 225
    groups using, 220
    locations, 225
    modus operandi, 223-224
    motives, 222-223
    off-the-battlefield operations, 221
    spread of, 220
    state responses, 224-225
    targets, 221
Sunni Islam, 78
Super Bowl, 306
Supreme Court, U.S.
    abortion decisions, 113
    free speech decisions, 263-264,
        265-267, 268-269
    immigrant deportation decisions, 285-286
    Internet regulation decisions, 264, 265
Survivalism, 101, 102, 103
Sverdlovsk (Soviet Union), 246
Sweden, terrorists in, 174-175
Swift, Wesley, 100, 103
Symbionese Liberation Army (SLA),
    88, 159, 169
Syria
    as sponsor of terrorism, 48
    biological weapons, 246
    history, 77
    Islamic extremists, 79
    terrorist groups, 220-221
Syrian Nationalist Party, 221

Tactics. *See* Conventional terrorist tactics;
    Unconventional terrorist tactics
Taliban
    control of Afghanistan, 52, 79
    drug trafficking revenues, 65
    fall of, 196
    prisoners at Guantanamo Bay, 287
    support of terrorists, 52, 277, 280
    U.S. war against, 277, 279
Tania, Camarada, 159

Tanzania, bombing of U.S. embassy,
    53-54, 194-195, 201, 216, 221, 281
Tate, David, 259
TCOs. *See* Transnational criminal
    organizations
Technology
    bombing, 43
    changes, 28
    Luddite protests, 89
    use by terrorists, 16
    See also Biometrics; Computers; Internet
Technology Institute (Holon, Israel), 147
TER. *See* Texas Emergency Reserve
La Terraza, 68
Terror, xiii
Terrorism
    anonymous, 146
    causes, 295
    definitions, xiii-xiv, 60, 117-118
    goals, 73, 191
    media portrayals, 121
    modern, 28, 31
    motivations, 10, 60
    prevention, 87
    religious. *See* Religious terrorism
    use of term, 4
Terrorism (journal), 120-121
Terrorism Research Center, 46
Terrorist groups
    barriers to cooperation with criminal groups,
        61-62, 63, 68-69
    cell structure, 89
    distinction from criminal groups, 60-61
    links among, 174, 175, 176
    longevity, 191-192
    transformation into criminal organizations, 59,
        60, 63-64, 66-67, 70
    U.S. State Department list, 46-48, 49,
        282-283, 300, 321-359
    use of violence, 61, 92, 147
    See also Leftist groups; Religious
        terrorism; Rightist groups
        in United States
Terrorist studies, 15-16
Texas Emergency Reserve (TER), 256
Texas v. Johnson, 266-267
Thatcher, Margaret, 144
Thugs, 17-20
    comparison to Assassins and Zealots, 11,
        16, 29-30
    end of, 19, 29
    history, 17-18
    methods, 18, 19, 30
    Molly Maguires compared to, 41
    murders by, 18-19, 20

number of victims, 18
    rules, 19, 30
    sanctuaries, 19, 22, 29
    weapons, 17
Tolstoi, Aleksei, 241
Trail of Tears, 86
Transnational criminal organizations (TCOs)
    barriers to cooperation with terrorists,
        61-62, 63, 68-69
    distinction from terrorist groups, 60-61
    goals, 60
    relations with terrorist groups, 59-60, 61, 65,
        67-68, 69, 70
    strategic alliances, 68
    use of violence, 61, 65-66
    See also Mafia
Trepov, Dmitri, 170
Tripoli, 38, 40, 55
    See also Pirates, Barbary
Trochmann, John, 102
Truman, Harry S., 198
Tucker, Mindy, 285
Tunis, 38
    See also Pirates, Barbary
Tupac Amaru Revolutionary Movement
    (MRTA), 47, 200, 352
Turkey
    drug trafficking by terrorist groups, 59, 65
    Kurds in, 47, 222
    suicide terrorism, 223
    See also Kurdistan Worker's Party (PKK)
The Turner Diaries (Pierce), 91, 101, 116, 196,
    258, 260, 261
TWA
    crash of Flight 800, 134
    hijackings, 146, 152, 176
Tyrannicides, 1-2

UCI. *See* University of California, Irvine
Unabomber, 88, 132, 196
Unconventional terrorist tactics
    consequences, 228
    threat of, 227-228, 230-231
    See also Cyberterrorism; Weapons of mass
        destruction
Uniform Crime Report, 85
Unions. *See* Labor movement
United Kingdom. *See* Britain
United Klans of America, 259
United Nations
    Charter, 280
    conspiracy theories involving, 90
    mission, 280
    sanctions on state sponsors of terrorism, 54
    weapons inspections in Iraq, 246

United States
    African National Congress supporters, 118
    Barbary Pirates and, 38-40
    bases in Saudi Arabia, 52, 74, 76, 78, 80
    Constitution, 90, 129
    defense against bioterrorism, 228
    embassies bombed in Africa, 53-54, 194-195,
        201, 216, 221, 225, 281
    foreign policy and counterterrorism, 277-282,
        296-297
    immigration, 99, 284, 285-286
    IRA supporters, 64, 118, 212, 224
    Middle East policies, 76, 81, 82
    political assassinations, 2, 40, 198
    reasons for terrorist attacks on, 278, 281-282
    responses to Islamic extremists, 82-83
    Revolution, 196, 287-288
    seen as sponsor of terrorism, 49
    war on terrorism, 73, 131, 277, 280, 281
    See also Homegrown terrorism in United States
United States Industrial Commission, 43
United States Special Field Forces Militia, 105
United Wa State Army, 65
U.S. Army, biological weapons research, 249
U.S. Congress
    government-media relations, 147-148
    House Judiciary Committee, 123
    House Un-American Activities Committee, 290
    Internet regulations, 264-265
    Office of Technology Assessment, 248
    response to Barbary Pirates, 39
    Senate Judiciary Committee, 284
    See also Legislation
U.S. Court of Appeals, Ninth District, 271-272
U.S. Court of Appeals, Third District, 265
U.S. Defense Department, 250, 281, 305
    See also September 11, 2001, terrorist attacks
U.S. Department of Housing and Urban
    Development, 271
U.S. Justice Department, 117, 124, 285, 286, 288
U.S. Marine Corps, bombing of barracks in
    Lebanon, 222
U.S. Navy
    attack on USS *Cole*, 53, 201, 278
    Barbary Pirates and, 38
    history, 38, 39, 40
U.S. Secret Service, 225
U.S. State Department, 278
    counterterrorism coordinator, 297
    definition of terrorism, 118
    list of Foreign Terrorist Organizations, 46-48,
        49, 282-283, 300, 321-344
    Patterns of Global Terrorism, 147, 148, 321
    reports of biological weapons use, 246
    state sponsors of terrorism identified by, 48-49

U.S. Steel, 43
U.S. Treasury Department, 281, 284
University of California, Irvine (UCI), 270
University of Judaism, 255
UNSCOM, 246
Urban terrorism, 9-10, 50, 195
USA PATRIOT Act, 130, 272, 284-285
Uxbridge (England), 310
Uzbekistan, 49, 281

Vanbiber, Todd, 261
Velastin, Sergio, 307-308
Venezuelan Communist Youth, 51
Verne, Jules, 239, 241
Videos, 361-362
Vietnam War, 83, 87, 269
Vietnam, women activists, 173
Violence Against Women Act, 124
Visionics, 303, 304, 307

Waagner, Clayton, 262
Waco (Texas), Branch Davidian compound, 102,
    117, 123, 124
Wahhabism, 75
WAR. *See* White Aryan Resistance
War of the Worlds (Wells), 240, 241
Washington, George, 39
Washington Post, 132
Watts v. United States, 269
WCOTC. *See* World Church of the Creator
Weapons
    of Assassins, 21, 31
    of Thugs, 17
    of women terrorists, 186
    See also Guns
Weapons of mass destruction (WMD)
    availability to terrorists, 62, 227, 244,
        247-248, 249
    counterterrorism efforts, 228, 231
    criminal use, 231, 249
    disadvantages to terrorists, 250
    incident database, 231
    increased use, 231
    lack of preparation for, 231
    U.N. inspections in Iraq, 246
    use by states, 229, 231
    See also Biological weapons; Chemical
        weapons; Nuclear weapons;
        Radiological weapons
Weather Underground, 87, 88, 160-161,
    169, 174, 249
Weaver, Randy, 102
Web sites. *See* Internet
Weishaupt, Adam, 100-101
Wells, H. G., 239, 240, 241

White Aryan Resistance (WAR), 256,
    257-258, 259
White supremacists
    black groups formed in reaction to, 88
    computer bulletin boards, 256-257, 258
    conspiracy theories, 90, 91-92
    criminal activities, 269-270
    history, 89, 101
    leaderless resistance, 116-117, 258
    murders by, 260
    music, 91, 258
    terrorism, 116
    view of U.S. government, 90-91
    Web sites, 254, 260, 261, 271
    See also Ku Klux Klan; Rightist groups in
        United States
Wichita (Kansas), antiabortion protests, 122
Wickstrom, James, 101
Williams, Matthew, 259
Williamson, Jack, 241
Wilson, Ryan, 271
Wilson, Woodrow, 288
Wiretapping, 272, 284
WMD. See Weapons of mass destruction
Women
    analogy to colonized peoples, 177-178
    criminals, 168-169, 184-185
    involvement in revolutionary movements,
        157, 158, 168, 170-171, 173, 178-179
    lack of political power, 125
    roles in Mafia, 182, 186-188
    suffrage, 171
    sympathizers and camp followers, 158-159
    traditional roles, 159, 164, 170, 186-187
    treatment in legal systems, 172
    See also Antiabortion violence; Feminism
Women terrorists
    advantages, 223
    distinction from uprising participants, 168
    feminism, 168, 169, 183, 184, 186, 188
    gender equality, 185
    goals, 160, 163
    ideologies, 163
    Italian, 173-174, 183, 184, 185, 186
    leaders, 159-161
    numbers, 157
    Palestinian, 158, 172
    roles, 157, 158-161, 163-164

romantic and family ties, 172-175, 185
    Russian, 7-8
    suicide bombers, 158, 223, 225
    traditional roles, 159, 164, 170
    use of violence, 7-8, 168, 169, 184, 185, 188
    weapons used, 186
Workers Party (Northern Ireland), 209
World and Islamic Studies Enterprise, 145
World Church of the Creator (WCOTC), 99, 106,
    108, 258, 259
World Trade Center
    1993 bombing, xiii, 53, 77, 78, 123,
        146, 194, 282
    See also September 11, 2001, terrorist attacks
World War I
    biological weapons, 245, 246
    chemical weapons, 229, 241, 242
World War II
    biological weapons, 229
    chemical weapons not used, 242
    Hiroshima and Nagasaki bombings, 229, 250
    Japanese internment in United States, 289-290
    military tribunals, 287

Yahoo!, 268
Yemen
    attack on USS Cole, 53, 201, 278
    Egyptian military expedition, 243
    kidnappings, 201
Yenikomechian, Alexander, 174
Yousef, Ramsi, 194

Zapatista National Liberation Army (EZLN),
    60, 62-63, 158
Zasulich, Vera, 7, 170
Al-Zawahiri, Ayman, 75, 222
Zawodny, J. K., 168
Zealots, 24-28
    activities, 26
    comparison to Thugs and Assassins, 11,
        16, 24, 26
    goals, 26, 28
    impact, 24-25
    rebellion against Romans, 2, 24, 26-28, 29
    tactics, 26
    weapons, 24, 25
Zetkin, Clara, 170, 171
Zionism, 80

ABOUT THE AUTHORS

Pamala L. Griset is Associate Professor in the Department of Criminal Justice and Legal Studies at the University of Central Florida. She received a PhD in criminal justice from the State University of New York at Albany. She was formerly employed as a deputy commissioner at the New York State Division of Criminal Justice Services and as an assistant to the New York State director of criminal justice. Before turning to the study of terrorism, she authored a book and several articles on determinate sentencing policy, monographs on juvenile detention, and book chapters on various aspects of the administration of justice.

Sue Mahan is Associate Professor in the Criminal Justice Program at the University of Central Florida–Daytona Beach Campus. She received a PhD in sociology from the University of Missouri–Columbia and was awarded a Kellogg Fellowship in International Development and a Fulbright Distinguished Lectureship to Peru. She is the author of several other books, including *Unfit Mothers*; *Women, Crime and Criminal Justice* (with Ralph Weisheit); *Crack, Cocaine, Crime and Women*; and *Beyond the Mafia*, as well as journal articles and book chapters about crime and justice.

ABOUT THE CONTRIBUTORS

Terry Anderson wrote a volume of poetry called *Den of Lions* during the 7 years he was held hostage in Lebanon. His positions with the Associated Press included state editor, foreign desk editor, and chief Middle East correspondent. He received the Free Spirit Award from the Freedom Forum along with numerous awards for journalism and community service. He currently is a Scripps Visiting Professional at the E. W. Scripps School of Journalism at Ohio University.

James Dingley is a sociologist at the University of Ulster, where he lectures and does research on terrorism and political violence. Apart from his specific interest in Northern Ireland, where he has extensive contacts with all parties involved in the conflict, his main interests have been in ethnic-nationalist and religious conflicts, profiling terrorists, and the application of social theory to an understanding of contemporary political conflicts. He has written extensively in academic journals and has been a frequent commentator in *Time*, *The Guardian*, the BBC, and other local, national, and international media.

Chris Dishman was a research associate at the Center for Defense Information. He now serves with the U.S. Commission on National Security in Arlington, Virginia.

Michael Scott Doran is Professor of Near-Eastern Studies at Princeton University. He is the author of *Pan-Arabism Before Nasser: Egyptian Power Politics and the Palestine Question* and a contributor to *How Did This Happen? Terrorism and the New War* (Gideon Rose and James F. Hoge, Jr., Eds.).

Rohan Gunaratna is a research fellow at the Centre for the Study of Terrorism and Political Violence at the University of St. Andrews, Scotland. He is also an honorary fellow at the International Policy Institute for Counter-Terrorism in Israel. He has served as principal investigator of terrorism prevention for the United Nations and as a consultant on terrorism to both governments and corporations. He is the author of several books on armed conflict, including *Inside Al Qaeda: Global Network of Terror* and *Sri Lanka, a Lost Revolution? The Inside Story of the JVP*.

Alison Jamieson has published widely in English and Italian on issues of political violence, organized crime, and drugs. From 1992 to 1997, she was a regular guest lecturer at the NATO Defense College in Rome. She is the author of several books, including *The Antimafia: Italy's Fight Against Organized Crime* and *Terrorism and Drug Trafficking in the 1990s*.

Philip Jenkins is Distinguished Professor of History and Religious Studies at Pennsylvania State University. His publications include *Pedophiles and Priests:*

Anatomy of a Social Crisis, Hoods and Shirts: The Extreme Right in Pennsylvania, The Cold War at Home: The Red Scare in Pennsylvania, and *Moral Panic: Changing Concepts of the Child Molester in Modern America.*

Walter Laqueur was a Jewish refugee from Nazi Germany during his youth. He now chairs the Research Council of the Center for Strategic and International Studies in Washington, D.C. His numerous books include *The Age of Terrorism, The New Terrorism: Fanaticism and the Arms of Mass Destruction, Fascism: Past, Present, and Future*, and *The Israel-Arab Reader: A Documentary History of the Middle East Conflict.* He is the editor in chief of Yale University Press's *Encyclopedia of the Holocaust.*

Brian Levin is director of the Center on Hate and Extremism at California State University, San Bernardino. He is a graduate of Stanford Law School and former associate director of the Southern Poverty Law Center's Klanwatch Militia Task Force. He is the author of books, articles, and Supreme Court briefs on hate crime and terrorism.

Robin Morgan describes herself as a poet, a writer, a political creature, and a feminist. She writes from experience because she once participated in "terrorist activities" and barely extricated herself in time to avoid the fates of her colleagues: living as a fugitive, time in prison, or death. She is the former editor in chief of *Ms.* magazine and author of several books, including *Going Too Far: The Personal Chronicle of a Feminist, The Word of a Woman: Feminist Dispatches 1968-1992*, and *The Anatomy of Freedom: Feminism in Four Dimensions.*

Raphael F. Perl is a graduate of Georgetown University's Foreign Service and Law Schools and the author of numerous congressional and academic publications. A retired Army Reserve Lieutenant Colonel, he is a member of the National Academy of Science Committee on Confronting Terrorism in Russia and a fellow at the National Academy of Engineering, where he is involved in projects to bring science and technology to counterterrorism.

Paul R. Pillar is a retired Army officer and career officer in the Central Intelligence Agency, where he served in a variety of analytical and managerial positions, including Executive Assistant to the CIA's Deputy Director for Intelligence and Executive Assistant to Director of Central Intelligence William Webster. He received a PhD from Princeton University and is the author of numerous articles and books, including *Negotiating Peace: War Termination as a Bargaining Process.* He presently serves as National Intelligence Officer for the Near East and Southeast Asia.

David C. Rapoport is known as a historian of terrorism. He is Professor Emeritus of Political Science at UCLA and editor of the journal *Terrorism and Political Violence.* He is the author and editor of numerous books about assassination and terrorism, including *The Democratic Experience and Political Violence, Inside Terrorist Organizations*, and *Morality of Terrorism: Religious Origins and Ethnic Implications.*

Jeffrey Rosen is Associate Professor at the George Washington University Law School. He is a graduate of Harvard College; Balliol College, Oxford, where he was a Marshall Scholar; and Yale Law School. He is the legal affairs editor of *The New Republic* and author of *The Unwanted Gaze: The Destruction of Privacy in America*, which *The New York Times* called "the definitive text to privacy perils in the digital age." He is also a frequent contributor to *The New Yorker* and National Public Radio.

Jeffrey D. Simon formerly with the RAND Corporation, is a Senior Fellow at the National Defense University's Institute for National Strategic Studies and head of

Political Risk Assessment Company. He is a highly regarded expert consultant on terrorism and political violence, specializing in national military strategy and threat analysis, with focus on European institutions, Central and Eastern Europe, and the former Soviet Union. His recent books include *NATO Enlargement*, *NATO: The Challenge of Change*, and *European Security Policy After the Revolutions of 1989*. His work often appears in the *New York Times* and the *Los Angeles Times*.

Jonathan R. White works in the state and local antiterrorism training program at the Bureau of Justice Assistance, U.S. Department of Justice. Previously, he was Dean of Social Sciences and Professor of Criminal Justice at Grand Valley State University. A former police administrator, he has worked with law enforcement and military agencies in the field of counterterrorism and has written several articles and books on terrorism, including *Terrorism: An Introduction*.